Energy economics

growth, resources and policies

Energy economics

growth, resources and policies

Richard Eden, Michael Posner,
Richard Bending, Edmund Crouch, Joe Stanislaw

Cambridge University Press

Cambridge
London   New York   New Rochelle
Melbourne   Sydney

Published by the Press Syndicate of the University of Cambridge
The Pitt Building, Trumpington Street, Cambridge CB2 1RP
32 East 57th Street, New York, NY 10022, USA
296 Beaconsfield Parade, Middle Park, Melbourne 3206, Australia

First published 1981
First paperback edition 1982

Printed in the United States of America

British Library Cataloguing in Publication Data

Energy economics.
1. Power resources
1. Eden, Richard
   333.7   HD9502.A2   80.40858
ISBN 0-521-23685-1 hard covers
ISBN 0-521-28160-1 paperback

Contents

Contents

x   **Contents**

Preface

This book is intended as a contribution to energy studies. In many universities such studies form part of programmes in economics and social science, in engineering, or in management science, or they may be a central feature in courses on energy and the environment. Now and during the next few decades at least, energy problems, and recurrent crises in the way the world economy deals with these problems, must be expected to be an important factor in economic growth and technical change. An understanding of energy problems will therefore become essential for policy makers and for managers and advisers in both industry and government. In this book, the separate components of the energy system are described from a variety of viewpoints – economic, technical, social and environmental – but their inter-dependence is an essential feature.

We have written the book in a form which is accessible to the non-specialist. It is not an attempt to explain energy economics to trained engineers, or engineering science to those with degrees in economics. But it is not a 'chatty book', and we have tried to include all the hard facts and main steps in the analyses and arguments necessary to bring students, and an informed public outside the universities, towards the frontiers of knowledge in a complex of inter-related disciplines.

The book is structured in five parts, beginning with a discussion of the economics and technology of energy demand, and continuing in part two with a description of the main supply factors for hydro-carbons, nuclear energy and renewable energy resources. Part three is concerned with the market for energy, the structure of costs and prices, and the way in which the market is brought into balance. Part four considers the world energy outlook, taking account of the essential uncertainties of energy forecasting, and discusses energy prospects for different world regions. In the concluding chapters, energy policy issues are examined to illustrate the objectives, problems and constraints that arise, both within countries and between countries, in tackling the problems of obtaining and distributing energy resources.

Energy problems have a physical basis in the changing availability of energy resources – particularly oil – but they are magnified by anticipation or delay and changed by economic, social and political responses so that they become much more serious than would have been expected from the underlying resource situation alone. This makes the magnitude of future energy crises as uncertain as their timing or frequency, but it underlines the important role that could by played by successful energy policies. The conflict of policies is well illustrated by the dramatic changes in world oil prices in recent years and the attempts by governments in some consumer countries to shield their voters from the impact of these changes. On world oil prices we have taken a deliberately undogmatic position. There are those – possibly more in North America than elsewhere – who regard the dizzy rise in the oil price in the last seven years as evidence of only one event – the cartelization of the world oil market by the OPEC powers, possibly assisted to some extent by some of the larger oil companies. Other observers, including both Europeans and many in the Middle East, see the rise in the oil price as the inevitable consequence of shortages foreseen in the closing years of this century and the opening decades of next, possibly assisted by poorly timed purchases to increase oil stocks in consumer countries. It would be pleasant for the authors if they could claim to have reconciled the two approaches or viewpoints, but that is never completely possible. We certainly see technical forces influencing the oil price – changes in the pattern of supply and demand – that are separate from and additional to changing trends in market dominance. However, perceptions and attitudes, as well as the distribution of resources and institutional structures, are an important component of energy policies. We hope that this book will help towards an understanding of the problems and difficulties that policies seek to resolve.

In writing a book like this the authors must draw freely on the work of others. Where the source of the information is in written form, we hope that we have always made proper acknowledgement in the text; where our ideas and inspiration have been borrowed in the normal course of informal discussion, academic contact or joint endeavour, public or private, acknowledgement is more difficult. There is now an international community of energy experts, who meet together fruitfully and frequently, and we gratefully acknowledge meetings and discussions arranged by the World Energy Conference, the Workshop on Alternative Energy Strategies, the Organisation of Arab Petroleum Exporting Countries, the Organisation of Latin American Departments of Energy, the International Energy Agency, the International Association of Energy Economists, the UK Science Research Council and the Social Science Research Council, the Oxford Energy Seminar and numerous energy meetings in Cambridge.

We are indebted to many individuals both through personal discussions and through colleagues in their organisations, though we hasten to add that in energy matters there is rarely any consensus and they are by no means responsible for our views and conclusions expressed in this book. We wish to express our thanks to: Sir

William Hawthorne of Cambridge University, former Chairman of the UK Advisory Council on Energy Conservation, Norman Kendall, David Newbery, William Peterson, Brian Reddaway, Kenneth Riley and K. Velupillai of Cambridge University; Debi Sen Gupta of the Indian Institute of Science in Bangalore, David Henderson of London University, Gerald Leach of the International Institute for Environment Development, London, Robert Mabro of St Antony's College, Oxford University, Kenichi Matsui of the Institute of Energy Economics in Japan, David Pearce of Aberdeen University, Edward Rubin of Carnegie Mellon University, Pittsburgh, Robert Socolow of Princeton University, Richard Wilson of Harvard University, Ali Attiga, Secretary General of the Organisation of Arab Petroleum Exporting Countries, Lord Hinton, adviser to the Conservation Commission and honorary Chairman of the World Energy Conference, William Humphrey, World Bank, Washington, Frank Hutber, Philip Jones and Tom Kennedy of the UK Department of Energy, Carroll Wilson of Massachusetts Institute of Technology and Director of the WAES and WOCOL international energy studies, Robert Belgrave and John Mitchell of British Petroleum, Michael Parker of the UK National Coal Board, John Licence of British Gas, John Rhys of the UK Electricity Council and Hans Du Moulin and Gareth Price of Shell International.

We also wish to thank our colleagues in the Energy Research Group in the Cavendish Laboratory, particularly: David Bowers and David Pullin for their work on computing systems and energy modelling, Lynda Holian, Jan Jenkins and Sally Meadows for typing various versions of the book, and Victoria Rostow, Anne Swinney and Cynthia Wilcockson for help in correcting the final typescript, preparing the index and proof-reading.

Cambridge, August 1980

Richard Eden
Michael Posner
Richard Bending
Edmund Crouch
Joe Stanislaw

Introduction

1.1 Economics of energy

The economics of energy are concerned with the availability of energy resources and their relation to economic activity. The industrialised world is now in the early and uncertain stages of a lengthy period of transition from low cost oil and natural gas to higher cost alternatives. The developing world will provide an increasingly important fraction of world energy demand and its economic growth will be influenced and complicated by increasing competition for world energy resources. A smooth transition by the industrialised world and equitable growth in the developing world will be disturbed or frustrated by energy shortages, and these, through the coupling of the energy system, will affect almost every aspect of economic activity.

Energy is not a single commodity; there is scope for substituting one form of energy for another provided the costs can be met. Such substitution involves the cost of diversion of other resources, manpower and skills, and also requires time to achieve. The lead times for a transition to new energy sources or carriers vary widely and are generally much larger for higher cost than for lower cost supplies. Though cheap natural gas and low priced oil could in the past rapidly penetrate the market for fuel and displace coal, the transition back to coal will not come so easily or quickly. This is partly due to the change in scale, since the world energy demand is now two or three times its level when coal was the dominant fuel, and partly due to handling problems in the mining, transportation and utilisation of coal. However, the main problems of transition arise from the changed character of the demand for different forms of energy associated with changing life styles and rising standards of living.

The personal mobility provided by automobiles has become an entrenched characteristic of society in developed countries, and the rapid growth in automobile ownership in developing countries reinforces the view that world energy demand for transport will continue to rise. The average yearly finding rate for world oil reserves has been less than total consumption for some years, and if this continues it is inevitable on resource grounds alone that production from conventional sources of oil will eventually decline. However, oil conservation policies in producer countries are likely to be more severe than technical limitations to supply. Thus on average there may be very little increase above current world oil production, and there is the ever present spectre of sudden shortages due to disturbances or political change in major producing areas. Automobiles cannot conveniently be powered by coal; the alternatives of providing synthetic gasoline or diesel oil from coal are expensive and it would take a long time for the production of quantities that could take a large share of the market. These facts and the high priority attached by most societies to road and air transport suggests that their share of world oil supply is likely to rise significantly.

The petrochemicals industry of North America is already in transition from the use of natural gas or natural gas liquids (light hydrocarbons produced with natural gas but liquid at normal temperature and pressure) to the wider use of oil. Oil is likely to remain its preferred fuel until the price rises to the level of synthetic oil from coal, at which point petrochemicals could be produced in conjunction with synthetic gasoline or diesel oil for road transport. In the Middle East, however, the large quantities of gas associated with oil production and the large reserves of natural gas, together with the high cost of transporting it, will lead to the development and continued expansion of a petrochemicals industry based on natural gas, though the mix of products from that industry will be influenced by the relatively high cost of transporting them to the major markets. These products may include substantial quantities of methanol or gasoline to supplement road transport fuel derived from oil. Over 50 per cent of world oil production and most of the gas production is used to provide heat for industry and in buildings or dwellings. Much of this is low grade heat (i.e. less than 100°C), but it is mainly used in households or commerce where convenience is a dominant consideration. If oil and natural gas supplies to developed countries decline, an increased demand would be expected for synthetic gas or electricity, except in sectors or markets where bulk steam raising is required and coal is readily available, or in specialist markets such as blast furnaces for the reduction of iron ore.

Estimates of future world demand for different forms of energy (coal or oil products, natural or synthetic gas, and electricity) depend strongly on assumptions about future economic growth. However, even with relatively low world growth, and with plausible assumptions about energy conservation or improved efficiencies in its use, it is difficult to see how there can be a balance between projections of energy demand and energy supply, unless the supply of fossil fuels follows a path that most observers would regard as optimistic and unless also there was a substantial component of supply from nuclear power (WAES, 1977a and World Energy Conference, 1978b). The relationship between energy demand and economic growth, and the impact on economic activity of a potential or actual scarcity of energy, is one of the important subjects considered in this book.

The relation between the economics and technology of energy provides the central theme of the book. The separate components of the energy system are described from a variety of viewpoints – economic, technical, social and environmental – but the interdependence of these components is an essential feature of the energy system. The resulting energy problems and opportunities vary widely between different world regions and between countries. Although energy policies, like economic policies, are determined on a national basis, few countries can insulate themselves from a crisis in the world energy system. Investment and trade in energy supplies form so key a component of economic activity that no satisfactory economic policy can ignore the requirements of energy policies nor the potential political or social consequences of a scarcity of energy.

The time scales that need to be considered in formulating energy policies are an order of magnitude longer than those commonly considered for economic policies, being measured in decades rather than years. The reader may reasonably take the view that no-one can foresee the future energy situation for decades into the future. It is precisely this recognition of uncertainty that should play a major role in energy planning. Policies and strategies need to be designed to remain robust under a variety of alternative futures. The assessment of alternative energy strategies in terms of costs and risk avoidance is an essential part of planning under uncertainty. Some features of possible futures may seem more probable than others, but an unlikely future that involves severe penalties may demand planning to reduce the risk of it occurring or to reduce those penalties provided the cost of insurance is not too high. The assessment of costs and penalties as well as potential risks is likely to be more an art than a science in all but the simplest cases, but this does not absolve planners from the duty of careful analysis, including the assessment of environmental and general social costs and risks. The indirect penalties of lower economic growth may well outweigh the direct costs of an energy scarcity, and it may also be important to examine different effects on economic growth and employment in different parts of the world and in different sections of society. It is hoped that this book will help reveal some of the problems that may arise, and assist in providing methods for approaching their solution.

1.2 Analytical framework

The intention of this book is to provide an integrated account and analysis of the economics of energy. It is integrated in several senses: firstly, through a combined and coordinated account of both the economics and the technology of energy; secondly, through discussion of the demand and supply balances for various forms of energy; thirdly, through the global character of energy problems – no country is an island unto itself; and fourthly, through the impact of energy on global and national economic activity. Energy problems taken alone may appear to yield to simple analysis but, when considered in relation to the constraints and influences of the economic, social and political system, they assume a different and more complex character.

It is against this background of the complex relations between energy and other factors that energy problems should ultimately be analysed. However, in developing this analysis it is often convenient to present simple pictures and use idealised models. Such pictures or models are valuable both as a means of instruction and to clarify part of a problem. It may be splendid to consider energy problems in all their complexity and confusion, but the only model that would wholly satisfy this objective is the real world. The purpose of analysis is to provide a framework within which some of the more complex problems of energy strategy may be discussed.

The book is planned in five parts. First, we consider *energy demand*, examining the extent to which it may be possible to forsee changes in the long standing relation between gross domestic product (GDP) and the use of energy. If, in fact, this relationship is enduring, energy demand is bound to go on increasing over several more decades if economic growth is maintained in that period. The technological structure of energy demand in relation to economic activity is central to this question and forms an important chapter in this part of the book.

In the second part we go on to the *supply factors* for hydrocarbons, for nuclear energy, and for renewable energy resources. One of the critical factors in many of the problems foreseen is the future supply of oil. Ultimately this depends on the geological structure of world reserves and resources, but its potential depends strongly on social, economic and political factors affecting exploration and development of oil reserves. These wider factors also play an important role in their influence on interfuel substitution and the acceptability of alternatives to oil. This part of the book therefore includes a chapter on 'externalities', the social, technical and environmental costs of different forms of energy supply which are often considered in isolation. This chapter seeks to find an appropriate perspective from which to view these costs so that one can more readily perceive the choices that may need to be made.

Next, in part three of the book, we turn to the *market* for energy, examine the ways in which supply and demand balance, and consider the extraordinarily complex structure of costs and prices. This structure is of great importance in contributing to the inelasticity of demand for some forms of energy. The investment and lead time requirements for the production, transport and conversion of energy strongly affect costs and prices, and the need for long-term planning. High investment costs and long lead times may inhibit risk-taking for the development of new sources of energy or conversion facilities; they also characterize the technology for energy conservation, where investment is often required to achieve greater efficiencies.

In the international market, the availability of low cost oil reduced the importance of indigenous energy supplies, particularly during the period 1950–73. However, the increased price for oil in the post-1973 period has led at least to a theoretical awareness of the importance of indigenous supplies, both for security and for reducing balance of payments problems. Trade in alternatives to oil, such as liquefied natural gas (LNG), coal and uranium, poses different problems – environmental, social and economic in character. For some of these problems the

world is like a village with common social responses and environmental preferences, but for others – particularly when economic growth is in question – there
may be a divergence of views between rich and poor, developed countries and
developing countries.

Part four of the book is concerned with energy prospects. The future is uncertain
and long lead times (i.e. long times between inception and completion of energy
projects) require decisions that affect long-term prospects. Long lead times may be
anathema to politicians for whom theoretical benefits to future generations may
seem unrelated to the realities of power or the present needs of their electors.
However, for energy planners or forecasters, these long lead times have a major
influence in reducing uncertainty. All forecasts are conditional – conditional on the
assumptions from which they are derived. They are dependent on assumptions
about future economic growth, but once these economic assumptions are made, the
lead times for change in the supply, conversion, or substitution of different fuels
have the effect of reducing the range of uncertainty in projections of possible
futures (the development of scenarios). Interfuel substitution or conservation is
affected by relative prices, government policies and social preferences. Scenarios
are presented that illustrate some of the problems that may arise and the
alternative energy strategies that could be adopted by different nations or groups of
nations to reduce the difficulties that they may perceive.

The final part of the book takes the discussion of energy strategies into the wider
context of *energy policies* and economic objectives. National decisions on energy
supply are influenced by indigenous energy resources. Greater adoption of resource
conservation policies may become important in a period of rising energy prices,
while uncertainties due to national expectations for producer incomes or tax
revenues may inhibit development of new resources. In particular, national views
on resource conservation or environmental protection may restrict exports of coal
and hence limit its international trade. National policies on energy prices and taxes
lead to wide variations in prices to the consumer, they affect the elasticity of
response to a changed world energy picture and they affect the technical efficiencies with which energy is used. Instruments for government intervention in energy
demand, other than through the price mechanism, vary widely between different
countries and cultures, and their adoption may be delayed through institutional
difficulties or simply because governments have more urgent priorities.

The importance of a margin of potential supply of energy over actual demand
was illustrated by the Suez crisis in 1957 and the Arab oil embargo in 1973. Oil
imports will not be available for all countries to balance their expected projections
of demand and supply to the year 2000 unless world oil discoveries are far greater
than can reasonably be expected. National planning for economic growth and
energy demand requires an awareness of the global constraints and the related
uncertainties. Energy policies in the developed regions may be influenced by the
common objective of further economic growth, or by common constraints due to

changed views on social and environmental questions. The future economic growth of developing regions of the world may be dependent on their energy policies, for it may be inhibited by a scramble for scarce world energy resources in which economically robust and richer nations provide formidable competition. Continued world economic growth that permits the developing nations to achieve their plans will require a new appreciation of the world energy picture, and the interdependence of nations seeking potentially scarce energy resources will require a level of international cooperation that goes beyond present practices. The alternative solution to energy scarcity would be a rate of economic growth in the world as a whole markedly lower than that experienced in recent decades.

1.3   Historical background

The use of energy by mankind has been a key factor in the supply of food, in physical comfort and in the development of organised society. For most of the four million years or so of human existence, man's need for energy and materials was small and was limited to the energy from his food consumption together with the small comfort provided by his environment. The adoption of each new technological innovation that improved his chances of survival, or increased his power to control his environment, increased his needs for energy and materials. The controlled use of fire provided both protection and warmth, and also increased the variety of food that could be eaten. This created a need for firewood and provided an opportunity for innovation to improve the quality of tools that could be used for hunting or protection.

The classification of cultural development in terms of a few periods of rapid change or 'revolutions' is obviously an over-simplification. Some of the major changes took place over millennia and appear to have proceeded in parallel and at different stages of development in different parts of the world. However, the advantages of some innovations led to their relatively swift adoption within those communities that had communication with one another. The 'neolithic revolution' in which man changed from dependence on hunting to the development of primitive agriculture was just such a change. It involved interrelated developments such as cultivation of plants, domestication of animals, settlement of villages, the making of pottery and a series of improvements in tool-making. Communities began to change their environment by removing vegetation, planting crops, and by the use and increasing fabrication of materials.

The development of mechanical equipment based on water and wind power led to a substantial increase in the power that could be harnessed. The horizontally powered water-wheel (i.e. powered by water flowing horizontally) was used by the Babylonians for irrigation and typically would have had power output of about half a horsepower. The vertical water-wheel had been developed by the fourth century AD to give around three horsepower or two kilowatts (one horsepower is equivalent to 746 watts*). Water-wheels were used initially for irrigation and for grinding cereals, but by Roman times their use had been extended to other mechanical tasks such as driving saw mills or hammer mills. In mediaeval times they were used for lifting materials and pumping water from mines, while by the sixteenth century they had been developed to a stage that they provided the foundation for the early industrialisation of Western Europe. The Versailles waterworks at Marley-la-Machine in the seventeenth century is thought to have had a power output equivalent to 56 kilowatts. $= 75$ hp.

The Chinese were probably the first to use windmills, and these came into use in Western Europe in the twelfth century. Their power capacity ranged from two or three kilowatts to as much as 12 kilowatts, and they were used for grinding cereals, hoisting materials from mines and pumping water, though their value was limited by their intermittent operation. 16 hp.

During antiquity and until the Middle Ages, with a relatively small human population and a modest per capita consumption of heat and power, it was possible to maintain a fair balance between renewable energy sources and energy demand. The renewable sources tapped were wood used as a fuel, and wind and water to provide power, supplementing human and animal labour based on energy from food and agriculture. However, even in early times the balance between local production of wood and its consumption as a fuel was not maintained everywhere. Certain areas were devastated for wood fuel, notably parts of North Africa, the Cedar woods of Lebanon, and later the mountain ranges of the East coast of the Adriatic.

Until the development of metal technology there were no industrial requirements for energy that were 'energy intensive' in the sense of a high energy requirement relative to the output of the product. The consumption of wood fuel could, therefore, remain in balance with its production with the exception of those regions where extensive and prosperous agriculture permitted the growth of large urban settlements having a correspondingly large requirement of fuel for the preparation of food or for comfort. Copper was the first metal to come into widespread use, though not on a substantial scale. Although it is not very abundant, its reduction temperature is fairly low and the metal can be won fairly easily from its ore. High grade ores were scarce and limited the volume of production. As the local deposits near the centres of urban civilisation were used up, in Egypt for example, a complex network of trade routes for copper were developed that led as far afield as the British Isles and Scandinavia. These trade routes provided the means by which technological improvements in smelting and metal working could spread across Europe.

Iron is considerably more abundant than copper, but it is much more difficult to win from the ore due to the much higher reduction temperature that is required.

---

* Energy units and conversion factors are discussed in the fifth part of chapter 1 on page 20, and are tabulated on page 21.

coke is to coal what charcoal is to wood

Furnaces based on charcoal as a fuel that could be used to smelt iron were not developed until about 1100 BC. The new high-temperature technology first appeared in the Middle East and quickly spread westward across Europe. The widespread availability of iron ore and of forests to provide charcoal made it possible for the use of the metal to develop on an unprecedented scale. New tools made of iron helped to transform Europe from dense forest to fertile cropland.

The abundant resources of iron ore in England and its dense forests that provided charcoal for iron-smelting enabled the region to develop into a major supplier of iron and iron products for the rest of Europe. In the early Middle Ages as iron production expanded, the forests of England became depleted and the iron industry declined for a period. The shortage of wood fuel led to the use of coal as a fuel ('sea-coal' because it was initially a fuel derived from coal outcrops on the coast of England). However, although coal was suitable as a fuel for domestic uses and for some industrial purposes, it could not satisfactorily be used for the reduction of iron ore due to impurities in the coal that led to an inferior product. The same impurities led to pollution in dwellings and in their environment, so wood remained the preferred fuel but its price increased so that it was increasingly displaced by coal for domestic use, particularly in London and other towns that had previously depended on wood and peat fuel.

As the demand for coal increased, coal mines were developed using mining technology that had been required for metal ores, notably in the tin mines of Cornwall. It has been estimated by Nef (1932) that 210,000 tons of coal were mined annually in the British Isles in 1551 to 1560 and this increased more than tenfold to 3 million tons annually during 1681 to 1690, and to 10 million tons by 1800. Most of this coal was consumed in households, including household industries. Its use for reducing iron ore was delayed until the early eighteenth century, following the discovery by the Darby family iron industry that volatile impurities in coal could be driven off by heating it under suitable conditions to yield coke. Coke then provided a fuel that could produce iron of satisfactory quality.

By 1800, between half and two thirds of all coal produced in the British Isles was still used in households. The iron industry, already the largest industrial consumer, only took 10 to 15 per cent of the output. Other industrial users included brickmakers, brewers, distillers, bakeries, potteries, copper and tin smelters. Two per cent of coal output was exported.

The early mining of coal was based on outcrops above the water table, but as demand increased deeper mines were required; these were liable to flooding and required continuous pumping to lift and remove the water. In places where water power was available the pumps could be driven by water-wheels, but in many cases no usable water power was available and there was an urgent need for a new form of mechanical power. A coal fired steam engine was invented in 1692 by Savery. It was designed to pump water, but since its operation depended on the difference between atmospheric pressure and that in a vacuum, it was effective only for lifting water through a height of 10 metres. The idea of using a piston, originally introduced by the French inventor Papin, was applied in 1705 by Newcomen and his assistant Cawley to Savery's steam pump. The use of pistons permitted an increase in the heights through which water could be lifted.

Newcomen's steam engine was used for over half a century for pumping water from many British coal mines before major improvements were introduced by Watt between 1763 and 1782. Watt's first major improvement was the introduction of a separate condenser so that the same cylinder was no longer alternately heated and cooled as in Newcomen's engine. This gave greater efficiencies, permitted an increase in speed of the operating cycle, and reduced the fuel requirements for the equivalent power output. In his second patent (1781) Watt introduced a mechanism for turning the reciprocating action of the piston into the revolving motion of a shaft using a fly-wheel. In this way the use of the engine, originally restricted to pumping, could be extended to all kinds of driving mechanisms.

Further improvements by Watt, by Trevithick, and others led to improved efficiencies, which were sufficiently high to extend the use of the steam engine to more applications and finally to transport. The efficiencies of the earliest steam engines were such that less than one per cent of the energy in the fuel was transformed to work; the improvements by Watt raised efficiencies to around four per cent; by the mid nineteenth century engines with better than ten per cent efficiency were available, and modern steam turbines can achieve about forty per cent efficiency. (The definitions of these efficiencies and their limitations will be discussed in the next part of this chapter).

In parallel with these improvements in the efficiencies of steam engines, and the subsequent development soon after 1900 of the steam turbine, there were dramatic increases in the available power output from a single machine. This is illustrated on a logarithmic scale in figure 1.1, which also shows the maximum power output of the internal combustion engine whose development began in the second half of the nineteenth century. The total improvement in the maximum power output from a single machine increased by more than one million times from less than one kilowatt in 1700 to more than a million kilowatts in 1970. All are exceeded by the power of the largest liquid fuel rockets which develop a power of 16 million kilowatts for short periods.

The discovery of a coal-based technology for smelting iron and the invention of the steam engine provided the basis for the industrial revolution in Britain during the nineteenth century. The increasing power output of individual machines led to an increasing demand for coal as fuel that was only partly moderated by improvements in the efficiencies of energy conversion from heat to power. Following the scarcity of firewood beginning in the mid sixteenth century and the consequent increase in its price relative to coal and relative to the general price index, by the end of the sixteenth century most (perhaps 80 per cent) of Britain's

16,000,000,000 or 16 billion watts = 16 million Kw = 21,447,721 horsepower!

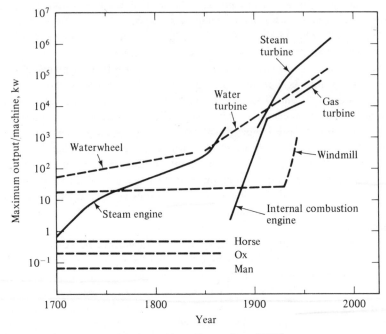

Figure 1.1   Power output of basic machines. *Source:* Starr (1971).

fuel was provided by coal, though most industrial power came from wind and water mills. In 1700 coal demand was 3 million tons for a population of 9 million; by 1800 demand had risen to 10 million tons but the population had increased to 16 million so the per capita coal consumption had increased by less than a factor of two (Nef, 1932). With accelerating industrialisation in the nineteenth century energy demand soared and UK coal consumption increased by a factor of 18 in the 100 years to 1900, compared with a population growth by a factor of less than 3. Thus by 1900 the annual per capita energy consumption in Britain had risen to 4 tons. The relation between this growth in energy demand and the growth in economic output will be described and discussed in chapter 2.

In the United States the prime sources of power for agricultural production were horses and mules until towards the end of the nineteenth century. There was one horse or mule for every four people and, had this ratio been maintained into the twentieth century, there would have been a formidable requirement for animal feedstock that would have inhibited urban and population growth. In 1875, however, steam power began to appear on farms and spread rapidly. But the era of the steam combine was short, and early in the twentieth century the use of the internal combustion engine (gasoline and diesel) on farms displaced steam engines and rapidly reduced the use of horses and mules.

The speed of change is an important factor in the assessment of possible future energy problems so it is instructive to note some dramatic changes that have taken place in the past. The substitution of coal for wood between 1550 and 1650 in Britain was stimulated by a relative price advantage that increased more than two-fold in the period. The operational advantages of steam-powered iron ships over wooden sailing ships were so great that Britain's merchant fleet was transformed in only 30 years between 1870 and 1900 from 90 per cent wooden sailing ships to 90 per cent steam powered iron ships. The major railroad networks in both Britain and the United States were built in periods of about 30 years duration during the nineteenth century under very different conditions of development.

The time scale of 30 years has been apparent in periods of major interfuel substitution in recent times. In the United States between 1870 and 1900 wood fuel lost half the share of the fuel market to coal. Similarly coal lost half its share to oil and gas during the period 1920 to 1960. The rapidly changing market shares of major fuels in the United States since 1860 are illustrated in figure 1.2(b). It should be noted that these changes took place during a period of rapid growth in the total energy demand, illustrated in figure 1.2(a). It is likely that the rate of growth of total market demand influences the rate of market penetration since new-energy-using equipment would be purchased at a high rate and is likely to be related mainly to the newly preferred fuel.

In the first years of the twentieth century in the United States nearly all inter-city passenger traffic was carried by railroads. By 1910 the private car was providing serious competition, and by 1920 the automobile accounted for more passenger miles between cities than did railroads. In the years following the second world war, the combined impact of the automobile and the aeroplane has so eroded demand for railroad passenger traffic that it has seriously impaired the profitability of the railroads.

The development of the automobile and other road transport in the United States was associated with the growth of the petroleum industry. Currently more than half of US demand for oil comes from the transport sector including rail and air transport. Similar rapid growth in automobile road transport took place in Western Europe at a much later date than in the US (after 1950), but with more compactly developed countries the railroads continue to play an important part. One of the first responses of developing countries to increasing prosperity is the rapid growth of demand for automobile transport.

In the next chapter the historical relations between total energy demand and economic growth will be described and discussed. In chapter 3 we will consider further the technological character of energy consumption by economic sector and industrial classification. First, however, we discuss some of the economic concepts that are used in the book and then we outline the scientific principles that underlie any discussion of energy conversion and utilisation.

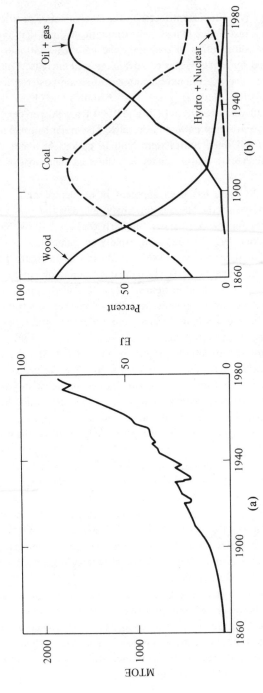

Figure 1.2 Demand for fuels in the United States 1860–1978. (a) Total demand for energy. (b) Market shares. *Sources*: Schurr and Netschert (1975), Hottel and Howard (1971) and OECD (1978).

1.4   Economic concepts

It is not the aim of this book to provide a guide to basic economic analysis. We have tried to write in a way that makes the argument accessible to the non-economist, not seeking to prove simple theorems but merely to say enough to make the results plausible. References to the literature are intended for those who seek further rigour of analysis. Trained economists will no doubt find some points at which to disagree, but we intend there to be sufficient analysis in the text to make the grounds for any disagreement transparent. Detailed points may be pursued further in Varian (1978) or Henderson and Quandt (1958).

Nevertheless, we assemble in this section some of the key concepts, with an indication of the points in the book where these concepts are used, explained, or developed. Some readers may find it useful to read through this passage before going on to the rest of the book; others may prefer to glance back to it from time to time, to see how particular concepts fit together.

a. Framework of choice – consumers and producers

At any point of time a consumer attempts to distribute his spending between the goods available to him at the prices imposed by the market so as to gain maximum satisfaction. Marginal satisfactions from one dollar's worth of different goods are, in equilibrium, equal; although when products are jointly consumed (e.g. household heating fuel and the accompanying boiler system) this 'equimarginal principle' becomes less clear. The consumer is constrained in his purchases by the money he has available. This is his 'budget constraint' – sometimes interpreted in ordinary discourse as 'consumer income', but better seen as a somewhat more sophisticated concept.

At any point of time, a consumer has an initial stock of wealth and an expected future income for the rest of his expected life; and possibly a target capital sum to leave to his children. He distributes the resulting spending power over his expected life time, and it is this calculation which imposes a constraint on his spending in any one year. This process of intertemporal distribution requires a market in which the consumer can trade money from one year to the next – a market in which to borrow or lend. The price at which transactions are conducted in this market is the rate of interest, or the rate of time discount, or the marginal productivity of capital investment: the price which the consumer pays for anticipating future income or receives for delaying consumption.

In a perfect capital market, where an individual can borrow or lend at one and the same interest rate, economic agents will trade off the present against the future according to their own tastes and the opportunities for real capital formation – 'investment' – that face them in their own enterprises. The play of the market (borrowing and lending operations) will, in principle, therefore lead to the establishment of a single 'price of capital' which embodies both the 'average rate of time preference' and the rate of return on new investment – the 'opportunity cost of capital'.

But in the real world, capital markets are imperfect and the lowest expected rate of profit at which many businesses are prepared to invest is well above the rate which an individual can earn on his savings. Indeed, realised rates of interest earned by individuals, after taking account of inflation and tax, have been in many OECD countries negative in more than one of the post war decades. There is no law of economics that time preference *should* be positive, but there are theories why it may be (for example see Hershleifer, 1970 or Dewey, 1965); intertemporal preferences for the present over the future by an individual may be rational if he values his grandchildren's happiness less than his own, or if he has systematic myopia (after all, death or the end of the world may supervene before tomorrow is reached), or because he expects to be richer tomorrow than he was today. This last belief is the basis normally used for justifying a positive rate of time discounting, but what that rate should be is not a matter of agreed dogma.

The divergence between social time preference rate, which some economists would put (on the basis both of theoretical considerations and of observed behaviour) as low as one or two per cent, and the observed opportunity cost of capital, which in many cases seems to be ten per cent or higher, poses severe problems for energy analysis, and for Government policy (on which see below in this section). A crucial concept is that the owner of a resource – public or private – will be the more conservationist the lower is his rate of time preference. For many purposes it turns out that the large range of possible values for the discount rate leaves basic decisions indeterminate – alternative A looks better at a two per cent rate, alternative B is better at ten per cent. For other purposes, fortunately, the choice is less critical. The reader is referred to Arrow and Kurz (1970), Arrow and Lind (1970), for a recent discussion of this important question, and is advised to view with suspicion policy recommendations that depend crucially on a particular discount rate assumption.

Reverting to the simplest point-of-time analysis, the consumer adjusts the quantities of the n commodities available to him at their several prices so as to achieve equimarginal satisfaction: this is the maximisation rule. Quantities of energy directly purchased by households thus depend on the prices at which they are offered; they depend on the incomes and wealth of consumers; and they depend also on the form of the objective or utility functions which describe household preference patterns – what are loosely called 'consumer tastes'. (See Phlips, 1974.)

Indirect use of fuels (through energy embodied in, or required for the production of, all other commodities) is governed directly by decisions of manufacturers but indirectly by final consumer demand. This indirect use can be analysed in economics by means of input–output techniques (see Chenery and Clark, 1959, and section 2.5).

A manager of an enterprise, with knowledge and skill to sell, is to some extent the opposite side of the coin to the consumer just described. He too, maximises something – say profit. Just as the consumer takes prices as given, so the producer takes all other prices except those for his own products as given, and fits into the economic space left to him: 'which of the products whose technology I understand,' he asks, 'can I most profitably turn my attention towards, given what I think I know about consumer tastes and the likely actions of my competitors?'

For the producer, this process is complicated by joint products (naphtha and diesel oil come from the same barrel); by the necessity to peer into the future; and by the actions of competitors with special market power. These problems all raise points of interest, and are explored immediately below.

b. Pricing complexities

When two products (naphtha and diesel oil) are jointly produced, there is no 'right' way of attributing the fixed costs of refining (or indeed of paying for the crude oil input to the refining process) to one rather than the other. A producer will charge what the market will bear – the more intense the demand for product A (the more inelastic it is to price changes: see below section e) the more of the overheads will be recovered from A rather than B.

Similar considerations apply to goods or services which are produced and sold at different points of time. The trajectory through time of a price need not be flat or even monotonic; in some markets a producer will launch his commodity at a low price, exploit his strength by raising the price when the product is at its peak, and drop the price later. In other markets, constant or even monotonically rising prices may be appropriate. An Electric Utility, planning an investment in a long lived power plant, will wish to recover a stream of revenue whose present value (PV) satisfies some minimum requirement; the shape of that stream through time is not of essential concern, provided the Utility can borrow or lend fairly freely on the money or capital markets at a rate of interest which would then be used as the discount factor for present value calculations (see section c below, and Arrow and Kurz, 1970).

But the future is uncertain. The problems introduced by timing considerations cannot be set aside merely by assuming that the discount rate will take account of everything: a whole new dimension of choice is in fact introduced into the analysis by acknowledgement of ignorance and uncertainty. Because the future is uncertain, simple maximising rules are inadequate to capture the nature of the choice open to individuals. The chance of greater benefit or advantage from a gamble has to be offset against the chance of a loss. Some individuals or communities might be more prone to take such bets than are others – this will depend on individual taste – but in addition economic and technical circumstance, the 'importance' of the gamble to the individual's life style, the nature of the possible losses – all these will sway the decision.

In chapter 18 various strategies in the face of risk and uncertainty are discussed. Two simple possibilities are to maximise the minimum win in the hope that all will go well (maximin); or minimising the maximum loss if all goes badly (minimax). It may not be otiose to offer a simple example. The weather is uncertain; by carrying an umbrella, I minimise the degree to which I get wet if it rains; by leaving the umbrella at home I maximise my pleasure if the sun shines – I shall be able to stroll along, unburdened. (A more Gallic version of the same simple choice can be based on the dilemma of the husband who is uncertain whether today is his wife's birthday; should he bring home flowers, risking suspicion if the birthday is next week; or should he bring nothing, risking misery if today is the right one?)

In choosing whether to equip ourselves with umbrellas (expensive energy savers) for the possibly rainy (energy scarce) future, this sort of gamble must be encountered. But its resolution may involve far more complex strategies than these simple examples suggest. Countries may be conceived of as having 'strategies for risk bearing', or indeed 'preference patterns for risk taking' akin to the 'tastes' for differing baskets of final goods, already discussed.

Finally, the relation between producer and consumer may not be one of free choice and equal power: the consumer's opportunity for shopping around, so as to achieve desired satisfactions from particular product groups at lower cost, may be limited by collusion between producers. In general, such 'imperfection' in the market results in lower volume of trade or production, and a shift in the distribution of benefits from consumer to producer. The producer in a protected or cartelised market enjoys a 'rent' from his property or from his membership of a cartel; and the consumer loses an amount which may be said to be greater than the gain to the producer.

Equally, a producer planning long lived expensive investment must be concerned about the actions of his competitors. If they are many, non-collusive, independent, he may well feel that his guess about the future, although necessarily uncertain, is as good as theirs: but if they seem to have market power, if they are at present rigging prices, or are likely to do so in the future – then an additional dimension of uncertainty is introduced. An owner of coal, or a potential developer of shale oil, or of a windmill system, is deterred from investment if he does not know the future expected price of conventional oil (see chapter 16). If all imperfections are known and stable, they merely introduce changes in the price set facing all economic agents. But if the imperfections are subject to change, they introduce frictions, which delay adjustment and raise costs.

c. Natural resource depletion

One important use of discounting techniques is to help the owner of a resource decide how quickly it should be depleted or used up. The detailed argument is deployed in section 16.2, and derives from Hotelling (1931). A peasant who finds a gold mine in his back garden, and believes firmly that the purchasing power of gold in terms of land or agricultural produce will never change, can exploit the resource until the marginal cost of getting (extracting, refining, marketing) the last ounce of gold will equal the price at which all gold is traded: the seam of gold bearing ore that he leaves unmined will be that whose cost of production is just in excess of the price. But if the peasant believes that the purchasing power of gold will change, he is in a different position: he has to compare the benefit he will get today, from selling gold at above its (average) cost of production, with the benefit he will obtain from waiting until the price of gold rises. Money obtained today from producing an extra unit of a raw material today can be 'invested' (placed in an interest bearing security) until tomorrow: the rate of interest on the security can then be compared with the rate of appreciation (price increase) of the raw material if left in the ground. The comparison of these two rates of return will then determine the pace of extraction.

Section 16.2 examines this relationship in more detail. Here we should note, first, that the 'rate of interest' is, for the individual business, the opportunity cost of capital; for the individual 'peasant' of this parable, it is the rate of time preference; and for the Government considering the question, it is the *social* rate of time preference. Under certain somewhat restrictive assumptions about the market, it can be shown that all these rates can be made identical – for instance, on the assumption of perfect capital markets, and shared perceptions of the future. But as suggested earlier, in real life these rates all differ, one from the other. And, secondly, a monopolist can choose not only the level of prices, but its trajectory through time. He will of course always reduce sales by restricting output, whether at a point of time or continuously: but it may be of benefit to him to do so. The market price for energy may be rising through time, *both* as a result of monopolistic restriction *and* as a result of a confident expectation that the future will be a time of energy shortage (see section 16.2).

d. The Government

Consumers and producers may be described as economic agents, maximising utility or profits. It is possible, but not very useful for present purposes, to see Government in a similar role, maximising the interests of the bureaucracy. However, in this book, Government seeks only to help the maximisation processes of others: spreading knowledge, reducing imperfections, establishing conditions under which rationality can rule, removing frictions (including the frictions introduced by previous Governments). In traditional conservative European circles (though not amongst radicals of left or right, and in very few parts of the United States at all), the Government is the collective expression of the general will on such key subjects as the rate of time preference: it is Government which speaks for the future.

But that is a point of controversy. Less controversial tasks include the imposition of safety codes, the enforcement of environmental standards, the countervailing of monopoly power, the provision of a tax structure which eliminates monopoly profits to the extent thought politically appropriate. The proper taking into account of effects which are external to the profit and loss accounts of the individual enterprise (see chapter 9) is especially a Governmental role. Non-economists, of all political persuasions, are apt (at least in European countries) to attribute more tasks and responsibilities to Government than do their professional economist colleagues. 'The Government should do such-and-such' is often usefully translated as 'market forces are distorted by *this* element of monopoly, or *that* piece of ignorance, or *this* type of myopia, or *that* type of externality, *and therefore* the Government can usefully act.'

e. Econometric methods

To complete these introductory remarks, a brief comment on econometric methods is appropriate (for a description of basic econometric methods see Theil, 1971; Maddala, 1977). Econometrics is a class of techniques in economic statistics concerned with the application of statistical methods to economic problems and to theoretical models of economic reality. Econometric studies begin by formulating a mathematical model – which necessarily leaves out many of the realistic details, but attempts to bond the main structural elements or variables of the model by mathematical relations. Then, making use of the 'best available' historical data (for example on energy demand, income or industrial production, or energy prices) statistical methods are used to obtain estimates of the parameters in the model. Economists debate sharply the 'correct' model specification – differing specifications lead to differing results. Econometric studies of energy use are concerned with developing and testing models that assist in the understanding and prediction of likely changes in the use of fuels by households directly and as inputs to firms' manufacturing processes. They are usually based on regression analysis of historic data in the form of both time-series and cross-section data. (The latter are statistical data relating to the same time period e.g. covering family expenditure on energy through the analysis of budgets of families at different income levels.)

Under suitable assumptions or simplifications the goods and services purchased by an 'average' consumer may be represented as variables in a demand function, which the consumer seeks to optimise, subject to the constraint that his total expenditure on all goods and services is less than or equal to his total income (which is known as his budget constraint). If there is an increase in the price of one of his purchases, namely energy (representing all fuels and electricity), the consumer will in general adjust his pattern of purchasing (re-optimise his demand function) so that he buys less energy than before. If the fractional change in his energy demand $\Delta Q/Q$ is small compared with the fractional change in its price $\Delta P/P$, then the consumer's demand for energy is said to be inelastic. More generally, provided these fractional changes are both small, the energy price elasticity β can be defined by the familiar formula:

$$\beta = \frac{\Delta Q}{Q} \left/ \frac{\Delta P}{P} \right. = \frac{\text{per cent change in } Q}{\text{per cent change in } P}.$$

If the fractional changes are not small it is often convenient to assume that the quantity Q and price P of energy purchased are related by the formula,

$$Q = KP^{\beta},$$

where the 'constant' K will, of course, depend on variables other than price. There is no a priori reason to suppose that the elasticity β will be constant over time, or for very different values of P, though for limited periods this may be a reasonable approximation. In practice, it may be difficult to separate price effects from time trends in other variables, and from the viewpoint of economic theory it may be more convenient to work with the demand function itself rather than with one of the derived equations involving only a single elasticity.

In energy analysis one is often concerned with the effects on purchases of one fuel of changes in the price of other fuels. These effects can be described by means of cross-elasticities, which are illustrated in chapter 2 (section 2.2), and may be used to provide an econometric interpretation of interfuel substitution. However, although there have been widespread and detailed studies of energy price elasticities, there is no general agreement on their values (UK Department of Energy 1977a). Their estimation, for example, is complicated by technological change and by the recent sharp discontinuity in energy prices, through the indirect effect of energy prices on the costs and prices of other goods and services, and more generally through their influence on economic growth and inflation.

The relation between energy used Q and income Y may also be expressed in terms of an elasticity – the energy income elasticity α – or derived by optimising a demand function under the constraint that total consumer purchases of goods and services plus savings equals income. Thus one can write,

$$Q = CY^{\alpha}.$$

We shall discuss energy income elasticities further in chapter 2, in relation to national energy consumption and economic growth, and to family expenditure.

One type of approach to energy use in industry is provided by standard production function analysis, where the volume of output depends on the quantities of factor inputs. For example, the Cobb–Douglas production function (see Varian, 1978) has a simple multiplicative form that can be used to relate output to energy consumed, labour employed, capital stock and raw materials, and which involves parameters that may be interpreted as elasticities (see sections 2.2 and 2.5). It is then possible to use appropriate econometric methods to estimate these elasticities provided adequate data are available. The latter may take the form of cross sections and time series, or pooled cross-section *and* time series. In this book, econometric methods are used or displayed only in their simplest form. The interested reader may refer for further information on econometric theory to Theil or Maddala (*op. cit.*), or, for applications of econometric techniques in the energy area, to Pindyck (1979a, b).

1.5   Scientific background

This book is not intended as an introduction to thermodynamics, nor is it an introduction to elementary science. It will therefore be assumed that the reader is familiar with the basic concepts of power, energy, and heat, but brief definitions will be given here in order to avoid ambiguity. The reader will be less familiar with the wide variety of units in which energy and power are measured; in this section some of the common scientific units (joules, kilowatt hours, etc.) will be introduced, and also commercial or field units (tonnes of oil or oil equivalent, etc.); these will be given in more detail in chapter 3 and appendix A (units and conversion factors). Thirdly, in this section, we will briefly state the first and second laws of thermodynamics and will indicate some of their consequences, particularly for energy efficiencies. These laws and their consequences for heat engines will be discussed in more detail in appendix B. Further concepts in science will be introduced when required in later chapters, for example aspects of energy conversion in chapters 3 and 12, basic ideas in nuclear physics in chapter 6, and aspects of energy relating to the environment in chapter 9.

The words 'power', 'energy', and 'work' will be used frequently throughout the book. In the context of physics and engineering:

Power is energy per unit of time;

Energy is the physical ability to do work;

Work is done when a body is moved by a force.

In the standard international system of units (SI units) the units for mass, length and time are the kilogram, the metre, and the second. The unit of force is called a 'newton' and is defined as the force that will accelerate 1 kilogram by 1 metre per second every second. Thus the gravitational force on a weight of one kilogram is about 9.81 newton.

The SI unit of energy is the *joule* defined as the work done when a force of 1 newton moves through 1 metre. The SI unit of power is the *watt* defined as 1 joule per second. The relation between these SI units and other units in common use is given in appendix A, and is illustrated for a selection of units in tables 1.1 and 1.2. The standard notations for decimal multiples are shown in table 1.3.

Mechanical energy exists in two different forms – as *potential energy* (due to gravity) and *kinetic energy* (energy of motion). Heavy bodies at a higher level can do work by descending to a lower level and hoisting a load by means of, for example, a rope and pulley. In this case the potential energy of the body is converted into potential energy of the load, the magnitude of the change in potential energy of each being expressed by:

$$E = mgh,$$

where m is the mass of the body in kilograms (kg), g the gravitational constant equal to 9.81 in newtons per kilogram, and h the height difference in metres, thus giving the energy change E in joules. Kinetic energy is gained by a body when it is set in motion and a mass m (kg) moving with velocity v (metres per second) has kinetic energy,

$$E = \tfrac{1}{2}mv^2.$$

If water descends from a reservoir through a hydroelectric power plant its potential energy is converted into mechanical work by driving the blades of the turbines, which in turn drive the rotors of the generators to produce electrical energy. For

Table 1.1. *Energy conversion factors.*

From	To Joules	Kilowatt hours	British Thermal Units
1 J =	1	2.78×10^{-7}	9.48×10^{-4}
1 kWh =	3.6×10^{6}	1	3412
1 Btu =	1055	2.93×10^{-4}	1

Table 1.2. *Power conversion factors.*

From	To Watts	Horse Power	Btu per hour
1 W =	1	1.34×10^{-3}	3.41
1 hp =	746	1	2.55×10^{3}
1 Btu/hr =	0.293	3.93×10^{-4}	1

Table 1.3. *Decimal multiples.*

kilo	k	10^{3}
Mega	M	10^{6}
Giga	G	10^{9}
Tera	T	10^{12}
Peta	P	10^{15}
Exa	E	10^{18}

example, water flow of 10 cubic metres per second falling through 300 metres and converted at 90 per cent efficiency to electrical energy would produce a power output of 26.5 MW.

Dissipation of energy

If water falls from a height into a large pool of water its potential energy is first converted into kinetic energy, then transformed (degraded) into less organised kinetic energy in the pool and finally dissipated into molecular motion of the water in the pool. Thus the ordered, directed motion of the falling water is converted into disordered motion of the molecules. The energy in disordered molecular or atomic motion of a body is its heat content, or energy in the form of heat. The equivalence of mechanical energy and heat energy is stated formally by the first law of thermodynamics:

First Law of Thermodynamics
'The total sum of all kinds of energy in a closed system is a constant.'
The total energy in a system is called its *internal energy*. This includes mechanical

and electrical energy as well as heat energy. Thus the first law states that energy is not lost when a change takes place but it may be converted from one form into another as when the kinetic energy of water falling into a pool is converted into heat energy in the pool. Alternatively a water wheel or a turbine might be placed in the path of the falling water so that some of the kinetic energy is converted to mechanical energy of rotation, or to electrical energy if the turbine was attached to an electric generator (see chapter 7).

An alternative form of the *First Law* which is convenient for discussing the flow of energy into a system is given by:

'The change in the internal energy of a system is equal to the net energy flow across the boundaries of the system.'

For precision and emphasis we state this also as an equation. Let U denote the internal energy of a system. Then the First Law states that

$$U_2 - U_1 = W + Q$$

where

$U_2 - U_1$ is the change in the internal energy,

W is the sum of the mechanical and electrical work done
   on the system

Q is the heat energy added to the system.

The internal energy U for a gas can be expressed in terms of 'state variables' such as temperature and volume, or temperature and pressure. Thus

$$U = U(T, V), \tag{1.2}$$

and

$$U_2 - U_1 = U(T_2, V_2) - U(T_1, V_1). \tag{1.3}$$

We have indicated above that the ordered kinetic energy of falling water can be wholly converted into the disordered heat energy of the pool into which it falls. The degree of disorder in a system can be expressed in terms of a quantity called the *entropy* of a system. It is found experimentally that the energy of a closed system tends to become increasingly degraded or disordered. Thus it is said that entropy tends to increase. This has the consequence that heat energy cannot, within a closed system, be converted entirely to mechanical energy. This experimental result is known as the second law of thermodynamics, and can be expressed in a variety of equivalent ways:

Second Law of Thermodynamics
'No self-acting and cyclic device (unaided by any external agency) can make heat pass from one body to another at a higher temperature.'

The second law has important consequences for the efficiencies of energy conversion, in particular for heat engines: A *heat engine* is any device that can absorb heat, convert some of it into useful work, and repeat this performance cycle indefinitely. Heat engines require a reservoir (heat source) to provide the heat input, and a lower temperature reservoir (heat sink) to absorb the heat rejected during the operation. For example in a steam engine the hot reservoir is the steam boiler (whose temperature is maintained by the heat from the fuel) and the fuel, and the cold reservoir is the cooling water and ultimately the environment. A second form of the Second Law of Thermodynamics states that, *'Unless both a heat source and a heat sink exist, any reversible cycle will be such that no net work can be done by the system'* (a reversible cycle is a cycle, in a heat engine, in which no frictional losses occur).

These formulations of the Second Law in terms of heat engines are related to our earlier statements about entropy and disorder and the fact that the energy in a closed system tends to become increasingly degraded or disordered. Thus, for a heat engine the closed system will involve both the engine and the hot and cold reservoirs. The energy for the hot reservoir of a steam engine is initially stored in a concentrated form as chemical energy in the fuel, but after burning this becomes more dispersed (or degraded) as heat energy in the steam contained in the almost random (disordered) motion of the water molecules in the steam. For steam at high temperatures the average speed of the molecules is greater than for low temperatures. Thus high temperatures involve more concentrated (less degraded) energy than low temperatures for a given volume. In a steam engine some of the disordered energy of these molecules represented by the heat energy in the hot reservoir is converted to mechanical energy or work. Mechanical energy involves all molecules (in a piston or a wheel, for example) moving in a coordinated or organised manner; it is 'ordered' in comparison with the disordered motion of molecules in hot gas or steam and its entropy is low. The second law of thermodynamics tells us that there is a penalty to pay when part of the disordered heat energy from a hot reservoir is converted into ordered mechanical energy or work. The penalty is that another part of the original heat energy must become even more disordered or degraded; this takes place through it becoming more widely dispersed as it is shared amongst the molecules of the cool reservoir of the heat engine. The resulting dispersed energy in the cool reservoir is less capable of doing work than the same quantity of energy in the hot reservoir, it has been 'degraded' and its entropy has increased. This lower grade energy (when arising from electricity production) is often in the form of warm water, slightly warmer than the environment, that could in principle be used to provide warmth, but in practice it is usually wasted or dispersed into the environment since few economically viable uses can be found (see 'combined heat and power' (CHP) in chapter 7).

The thermal efficiency η of a heat engine is defined as the ratio of the mechanical energy or useful work produced by the engine divided by the heat energy *input* required to produce this work:

$$\eta = \left[\frac{\text{net output of useful work}}{\text{heat input}} \right] = \frac{W}{Q_1}, \tag{1.4}$$

where W is the work output of the engine and Q_1 is the energy in the form of heat drawn from the hot reservoir in order to produce work W. In addition, as noted above, a part Q_2 of the heat input Q_1 is rejected or dispersed into the cool reservoir.

The First Law tells us that the total energy is conserved, so that, if there are just two reservoirs in the closed system containing the heat engine,

$$W = Q_1 - Q_2. \tag{1.5}$$

Hence, the efficiency η (sometimes called the 'First Law Efficiency') is given by

$$\eta = \frac{W}{Q_1} = \frac{Q_1 - Q_2}{Q_1} = 1 - \frac{Q_2}{Q_1}. \tag{1.6}$$

The Second Law of Thermodynamics, not only tells us that some waste heat Q_2 must be rejected when heat energy is converted to mechanical energy or work, but also establishes that there is a minimum value of Q_2 relative to Q_1. This means that there is a maximum value for the efficiency η for conversion of heat to work using just two heat reservoirs, one at a temperature T_1 and one at a lower temperature T_2. This can be made precise in the form of the *Carnot Principle* which is directly equivalent to the Second Law and states that:

> *'Given a reversible engine operating between two fixed temperatures, then no other heat engine operating between these same two temperatures can have an efficiency greater than that of the reversible engine.'*

Such a reversible engine is called an idealised Carnot engine. Its efficiency can be calculated using the laws of behaviour of an ideal gas in terms of its internal energy, temperature, pressure and volume (see appendix B). These show that the ratio of the heat rejected Q_2 to the heat input Q_1, for the Carnot engine, is equal to the ratio of the temperature T_2 of the cool reservoir to the temperature T_1 of the hot reservoir, provided these temperatures are measured on the Kelvin scale in which (absolute) zero corresponds approximately to minus 273°C. Using the definition [Eq. (1.6)] of the efficiency η and the result from appendix B,

$$\frac{Q_2}{Q_1} = \frac{T_2}{T_1}, \tag{1.7}$$

we obtain the efficiency η of a Carnot engine:

$$\text{Efficiency } \eta = 1 - \frac{T_2}{T_1} \tag{1.8}$$

where the temperature T is measured on the Kelvin scale (0° C = 273 K).

Carnot's Principle states that the efficiency η given by the equation (1.8) is the greatest that can be achieved from any heat engine using two reservoirs or sources. The efficiency η is sometimes called the 'first law efficiency', to distinguish it from the 'second law efficiency' which has a more sophisticated definition. The latter is related to the ratio of the least 'available work' that could be used to perform a given task (using any device) divided by the actual available work that is used (American Institute of Physics, 1975). In this book the terms 'efficiency' or 'thermal efficiency' refer to the first law efficiency defined above for heat engines by equation (1.6) and for the Carnot engine by equation (1.8).

The implications of the formula giving the efficiency η for the Carnot engine can readily be evaluated. Typically one might have $T_1 = 480°$ C (753 K) and, $T_2 =$

30° C (303 K) giving,

$$\eta = 1 - \frac{303}{753} = 0.60.$$

Thus an idealised heat engine operating between these temperatures would have a maximum efficiency of 60 per cent in converting heat into work. For a realistic engine the corresponding efficiency would be about 40 per cent.

The efficiency of a heat engine operating between two reservoirs at temperatures T_1 and T_2 is sometimes called the thermal efficiency since it refers to the conversion of heat to work. More generally, conversion devices may involve work in and work out, or may involve heat reservoirs at T_1 and T_2 and also the ambient temperature of the environment. A more general definition of the *first law efficiency* η, is given by

$$\eta = \frac{\text{(energy transfer of desired kind achieved by a device or system)}}{\text{(energy input to the device or system)}} \qquad (1.9)$$

For a heat engine η will always be less than unity, but for other devices, such as a heat pump, η may exceed unity. This does not violate the first law of thermodynamics, since a heat pump uses a high temperature T_1 to drive heat from the environment at T_0 to a warm temperature T_2. The maximum value η of the first law efficiency may be calculated and results are given in table 1.4. When the first law efficiency exceeds unity it is usually called the 'coefficient of performance'.

Conversion factors

Energy is often expressed in physical units such as tons of coal or oil, or tonnes (metric tons) of coal or oil equivalent. It is useful to have simple conventions giving the approximate or average conversion factors, even though there are considerable variations in the actual thermal content of a tonne of coal or oil. We will use conventions that correspond to the thermal content of a fuel at its 'higher calorific value'. This corresponds to including the heat obtained by condensing the water vapour or steam that is produced in the combustion of a hydrocarbon. Table 1.5 lists the approximate conversion factors that are adopted as a convention in this book. There are no standard conventions and the reader should not assume that a tonne of coal or oil equivalent means the same in different statistical sources or energy reports.

1.6   Chapter summary

The first part of this chapter is an introduction to some problems that concern the economics of energy. Economic growth and industrialisation during a major part of the twentieth century has been stimulated by the availability of plentiful supplies of cheap oil, readily transportable and convenient to use. The next 50 years will be a period of change for the industrialised parts of the world as oil supplies become increasingly scarce and need to be replaced by high cost alternatives. It will also be

Table 1.4. *First law efficiencies.*

Type of device or system[a]	Numerator in ratio defining η	Denominator in ratio defining η	η_{max}	Standard nomenclature
Electric motor (W/W)	Mechanical work output	Electric work input	1	Efficiency
Heat pump, electric (Q/W)	Heat Q_2 added to warm reservoir at T_2	Electric work input	$\dfrac{1}{1-(T_0/T_2)} > 1$	Coefficient of performance (COP)
Air conditioner or refrigerator, electric (Q/W)	Heat Q_3 removed from cool reservoir at T_3	Electric work input	$\dfrac{1}{(T_0/T_3)-1}$ (not restricted in value)	COP
Heat engine (W/Q)	Mechanical or electric work output	Heat Q_1 from hot reservoir at T_1	$1-\dfrac{T_0}{T_1} < 1$	Efficiency (thermal efficiency)
Heat-powered heating device[b] (Q/Q)	Heat Q_2 added to warm reservoir at T_2	Heat Q_1 from hot reservoir at T_1	$\dfrac{1-(T_0/T_1)}{1-(T_0/T_2)} > 1$	COP or efficiency
Absorption refrigerator[c] (Q/Q)	Heat Q_3 removed from cool reservoir at T_3	Heat Q_1 from hot reservoir at T_1	$\dfrac{1-(T_0/T_1)}{(T_0/T_3)-1}$ (not restricted in value)	COP

Notes: T_1 (hot) > T_2 (warm) > T_0 (ambient) > T_3 (cool).
[a]The symbols W and Q refer to work and heat, respectively.
[b]A furnace is a special case: for it, $\eta_{max} = 1$. More generally, the device could include a heat engine and heat pump; then $\eta_{max} > 1$.
[c]Absorption refrigerator means any heat-powered device for cooling.
Source: American Institute of Physics (1975).

a period when plans for growth in the developing regions of the world enhanced by increasing population should lead to their need both for an increasing share of available world oil supplies and to a need for widespread growth in the use of alternative forms of energy. The economics of energy is concerned with examining the problems of energy supply and demand and placing them in the context of the more general problems to which they contribute a substantial component.

The analytical framework of the book is outlined in the second part of the chapter. The book is structured in five parts, beginning with the main demand relationships; in particular the long standing relation between gross domestic product and the use of energy is discussed from the complementary viewpoints of economics and technology. The second part of the book describes the supply factors for hydrocarbons, for nuclear energy and for renewable resources. Next, in part

Table 1.5. *Approximate thermal equivalents (higher calorific values).*

Coal	1 tonne coal	= 28.8 GJ
Oil	1 tonne crude oil	= 44 GJ = 7.3 barrels oil
	1 barrel of oil	= 6 GJ
Natural gas	1 thousand cubic metres	= 38.2 GJ
Exajoules per year		
1 EJ per year = 10^{18} J/yr		= 32 GW
		= 35 million tonnes coal per year
		= 23 million tonnes oil per year
		= 0.45 million barrels oil per day

World energy consumption in 1978 was approximately 300 EJ, or 6.8 thousand million tonnes of oil equivalent.

three, the market for energy is examined with particular attention to the complex structure of costs and prices and the means whereby the market is brought into balance. Part four of the book is concerned with energy prospects and the problems of preparing scenarios that reflect the uncertainties of energy forecasting over long periods of time, and are a necessary requirement for planning with the long lead times that are associated with many energy projects. Finally, in part five of the book a number of policy issues are discussed that illustrate the objectives, problems and constraints that arise nationally and internationally from the need for energy, and the associated technological and economic factors.

The third section of this introductory chapter outlines the historical background of the growth of energy demand, from the primitive use of fire, through early industrialisation in England that caused a shortage of firewood and led to the introduction of coal as a major fuel, to modern industrialisation and its massive dependence on oil and world trade in oil. The historical growth in energy demand accompanied advances in the technology of its utilisation, which were often stimulated by economic need, as with the development of coal-fired steam engines for pumping water from mines. The growth in steam-powered machines continued through to steam turbines, and was later paralleled by the development of engines based on petroleum products. Improved efficiencies played a major role in allowing a massive increase in the use of powered machines without incurring a correspondingly large increase in the need for fuel, although world energy demand increased at an average rate above 3 per cent per annum through the major periods of industrialisation.

The fourth section of the chapter describes some of the key concepts in economics that are relevant to later discussions in the book, and references are given to basic economics reading on these concepts. This section begins with a brief discussion of the economic framework of choice by consumers or producers including, for example, some aspects of point-of-time analysis and questions on time preference rates. This leads into consideration of pricing complexities and the relation between producer and consumer, and to the economics of natural resource depletion. After some comments on the role of governments as viewed in this book, this section on economic concepts concludes with a brief guide to some of the simpler aspects of econometric methods.

The fifth and final section of the chapter briefly outlines the basic concepts of the thermodynamics of energy conversion that are essential to an understanding of the economics of energy and its close relation to technological change. Simple statements are given of the first and second laws of thermodynamics and their implication for the efficiencies of heat engines for converting heat into work. These are illustrated by results for the Carnot engine which gives the maximum efficiency for any reversible heat engine operating between two heat reservoirs. These results play a major role in their influence on the past and future demand for energy and the associated economics and policy options. The section concludes with notes on energy units and conversion factors.

Chapter 1   Further reading

American Institute of Physics (1975) *Efficient use of energy*, Conference Proceedings No. 25, American Institute of Physics, New York.

Arrow, K. J. and Kurz, M. (1970) *Public Investment, the rate of return and optimal fiscal policy*, Johns Hopkins University Press, Baltimore and London.

Chenery, H. B. and Clark, P. G. (1959) *Interindustry economics*, Wiley, New York and London.

Dewey, D. (1965) *Modern Capital Theory*, Columbia University Press, New York.

Hirshleifer, J. (1970) *Investment, interest and capital*, Prentice-Hall, London.

Lapedes, D. N. (ed). (1976) *Encyclopedia of energy*, McGraw-Hill, New York and London.

Lee, J. F. and Sears, F. W. (1962) *Thermodynamics* (2nd edition 1969), Addison-Wesley, Reading, Mass.

McMullan, J. T., Morgan, R. and Murray, R. B. (1976) *Energy resources and supply*, Wiley, New York and London.

Maddala, G. S. (1977) *Econometrics*, McGraw-Hill, New York and London.

Phlips, L. (1974) *Applied consumption analysis*, North-Holland, Amsterdam.

Ray, G. F. (1979) 'Energy economics – a random walk in history' *Energy Economics*, vol. 1, no. 3 July 1979, IPC Science and Technology Press, Guildford, UK, and New York.

Schurr, S. H. and Netschert, B. C. (1975) *Energy in the American economy 1850–1975*, Johns Hopkins University Press, Baltimore and London.

Scientific American (1971) *Energy and power*, Freeman, San Francisco, Calif.

Theil, J. (1971) *Principles of econometrics*, North-Holland, Amsterdam.

WAES (1977a) *Energy: global prospects 1985–2000*, McGraw-Hill, New York and London.

WEC (1978b) *World energy resources 1985–2020*, IPC Science and Technology Press, Guildford, UK, and New York.

CHAPTER 2

Economic Growth and Energy Demand

2.1   Questions on growth

The relation between energy demand and economic growth has become an emotive
issue. If economic activity is taken to be a measure of welfare and continued growth
is an objective, then the implications for future energy demand become central to
the debate about energy policies. Historical evidence shows that world energy
demand has on average increased at almost the same rate as gross world product
(GWP) over the past fifty years. For many individual countries the long-term
trends show a similar relation, but there are significant variations between average
rates of growth in different periods of time for energy consumption and gross
domestic product (GDP). These variations are reflected also in cross-section data
that compare energy consumption and national income per capita in different
countries. But the cross-section data also support the historical evidence – there is
indeed a close relation between energy consumption and GDP, or at least there has
been such a relation in the past. The economics of energy is concerned with the way
in which this relation changes through time and varies between countries, and the
way in which it may be affected by changes in energy costs and by changes in the
availability of other factors of production.

Higher energy prices, that followed from the quadrupling of world oil prices in
1973–74, have contributed to reduced economic growth in many countries and
have served to emphasise the dangers of dependence on exhaustible resources.
There is little doubt that past and future increases in energy prices will reduce
energy demand for a given level of economic activity, though the extent of the
likely reduction remains a matter for dispute. The implications of energy scarcity
and higher energy prices for future economic growth raise wider issues, since much
of the argument for 'time discounting' depends crucially on the proposition that the
future will be more prosperous than the present. The response to higher energy
prices through conservation, through changes in technology and in lifestyles,
particularly in the richer industrialised countries, will affect not only the future
standard of living in those countries but will also influence the extent and nature of
economic growth in developing countries.

In order to examine the potential response to variations in fuel prices or
availability, it is necessary to study energy consumption in individual economic
sectors, for example in households, transport, and industry. This disaggregation is

29

especially important in assessing the time that changes will take, which depend on the rate of equipment replacement in each sector, and more broadly with the general rate of investment. A similar approach is required for the analysis of energy demand in relation to economic growth, for example, in a developing country during industrialisation, or in a developed country where energy demand for some activities can be expected to reach saturation. The penalty for using a disaggregated approach to energy demand is that disaggregated relationships between energy use and economic activity are less stable, and frequently the data are less reliable. A variety of different approaches are therefore required for the analysis of energy demand. Some will be illustrated in this chapter, and others, particularly those emphasising the technology of energy demand, will be considered elsewhere, for example in chapters 3 and 12. Questions about energy costs and prices will also be considered further in chapter 10.

First, some definitions. In a sense most energy consumption is a derived demand, in that its use derives from a demand for goods and services. However, it is convenient to distinguish *direct* consumption, where energy in the form of fuels or electricity is purchased directly by the consumer, and *indirect* consumption which arises from energy required to produce goods and services used by the consumer:

$$Q(\text{total}) = q_1(\text{direct}) + q_2(\text{indirect}). \qquad (2.1)$$

Thus for a private household q_1 refers to energy used for cooking, heating, lighting, transport, etc. Similarly for an industrial company q_1 refers to final energy demand including all direct purchases of fuel and electricity. An industrial company will also purchase intermediate products that require energy for their manufacture and give rise to an indirect demand for energy: this indirect demand may be important if the intermediate product is energy intensive. Its significance for a particular industry can be obtained by the use of input–output tables for industrial production. The distinction between direct and indirect energy consumption is not in practice precise–for instance, gasoline can be treated as final demand or as an intermediate good for the production of a service, e.g. bus transport. In the remainder of this chapter the terms 'energy demand' and 'energy consumption' will refer to directly purchased energy q_1; except where otherwise stated we essentially forget q_2, and define $Q = q_1$.

2.2   Income and price elasticities

In this section we define energy elasticities (already briefly mentioned in chapter 1, p 18) with respect to income and price and indicate how they may be used to give simple models of energy demand. For a more comprehensive review of energy elasticities the reader is referred to UK Department of Energy (1977c).

Assuming that all other factors remain unchanged, the demand for energy Q can be expressed as a function of the income Y of a consumer. It is often convenient to express this dependence in the form

$$Q = K_1 Y^\alpha \qquad (2.2)$$

where K_1 is a constant and α denotes the *income-elasticity* of energy demand. There is no reason to suppose that α is a constant, and it is plausible that α will tend to zero if the income of the consumer becomes sufficiently large and we consider only the q_1 component of Q, that is, further increases in income will not increase direct energy demand at all. However, if Y refers to national income (GDP) and Q to national energy demand, which means that q_2 is introduced into the story, the income elasticity appears to change only slowly when averaged over a number of years, though with strong year to year variations. For small changes ΔY in income, α is approximately given by the familiar formula

$$\alpha = \frac{\Delta Q}{Q} \bigg/ \frac{\Delta Y}{Y} = \frac{\text{per cent change in } Q}{\text{per cent change in } Y}. \tag{2.3}$$

The *price elasticity* β of energy demand is defined similarly in relation to the (average) price P paid by a consumer for purchased energy. Thus the dependence of energy consumption Q on the price P is given by

$$Q = K'P^\beta \tag{2.4}$$

and for small changes ΔP in the price P,

$$\beta = \frac{\Delta Q}{Q} \bigg/ \frac{\Delta P}{P} = \frac{\text{per cent change in } Q}{\text{per cent change in } P}.$$

Usually, as the price increases consumption decreases, so that the price-elasticity of consumption is negative. By convention, if the elasticity becomes more negative it is said to 'increase'. In a competitive market, where substitutes are available, the price elasticity of a commodity will tend to be high, but conversely where there is little scope for substitution elasticities are usually low and demand is said to be 'inelastic' against changes in price.

If Q_1 refers to demand for a particular fuel used for a purpose for which other fuels are available, consumption will depend not only on its own price P_1 and its own price elasticity β, but also on the prices of other fuels, P_2, P_3. This gives a generalisation of equation (2.4)

$$Q_1 = K(P_1^{\beta1} P_2^{\beta2} P_3^{\beta3}). \tag{2.5}$$

Where β_2 and β_3 are called the cross elasticities of demand, so β_2 determines the response of demand Q_1 for fuel 1 to a change in price P_2 of fuel 2. In practice the response to a change in price is often not immediate, but may be lagged, following a complex path over a number of years to a new equilibrium. In this event one needs to define a long run elasticity which can be used to calculate the new consumption level when behavioural and technical changes have fully adjusted to the new price level, and ideally a series that shows how the adjustment takes place. A simple assumption for demand $Q(t)$ at time t can be represented by

$$Q(t) = KP^\beta[Q(t-1)]^\lambda \tag{2.6}$$

where $Q(t-1)$ is the consumption in the previous time period and λ is less than one. To make demand today dependent upon quantities bought yesterday is, at one level, largely an econometric convenience. But it can be simply interpreted for our purposes: the quantity of a fuel bought by a consumer this year will be strongly related to what he bought last year; his household circumstances, his fuel or energy conversion equipment and his habits are all strongly related to what has been true in the past (see Johnston, 1972). Simple algebra* shows that the immediate or short-run response to a price change is given by the elasticity β, and the long-run change is given by $\beta/(1 - \lambda)$. Thus (since $\lambda < 1$) the long-run elasticity is greater than the short-run elasticity.

Since energy prices changed only slowly during the two decades before 1973, it is sometimes instructive to examine time series for average growth in national energy demand in terms of the equation,

$$Q = KY^{\alpha}. \qquad (2.7)$$

Using this formula, the income elasticity α becomes equal to the 'energy coefficient', which, however, suffers from the grave disadvantage that it takes no account of price effects or time trends. However, if it is evaluated from data in successive decades, or comparisons made between different countries, variations in the energy coefficient do give some initial insight into the effect of the development process on the relation between energy demand and economic growth.

2.3   Energy and economic growth

Long-run trends

The close relationship between energy consumption and economic activity, defined by income or output, is illustrated in figure 2.1 for the UK since 1800 and the US since 1880. This figure illustrates how energy intensity, or energy per unit of output, has changed during periods of industrialisation and interfuel substitution. Long-run series for energy and output should be treated with caution, but some characteristics of the development process do appear. More detailed discussions have been given by Humphrey and Stanislaw (1979) for the UK, and by Schurr and Netschert (1960) for the US.

By 1800, in the United Kingdom, the dominant fuel was already coal, which accounted for more than 90 per cent of the fuel consumed. About half to two thirds of this fuel was used by households (including household industries). Between 1800 and 1830, energy consumption grew at the same rate as output or GDP; the share of agriculture in total output fell from a third to a quarter, while the share of manufacturing, mining and construction rose from 23 to 30 per cent. Energy associated with animal and human labour is not included in the total, and energy from water power is also excluded. Water power in fact provided the motive power for textile mills during the early stages of the industrial revolution, but by 1839, although water power provided 20 thousand horse power, this represented only one

---

* For example consider a single price change at $t = 1$ and choose units so that at $t = 0$, $P(0) = 1$, $Q(0) = 1$, and $K = 1$. Then $Q(1) = P^{\beta}$, $Q(2) = P^{\beta}[Q(1)]^{\lambda} = P^{\beta+\beta\lambda}$, $Q(3) = P^{\beta}[Q(2)]^{\lambda} = P^{\beta+\beta\lambda+\beta\lambda\cdot\lambda}$, etc.

After further iteration it follows that at $t = \infty$, $Q(\infty) = P^{\beta/(1-\lambda)}$ giving a long-run price elasticity of $\beta/(1-\lambda)$.

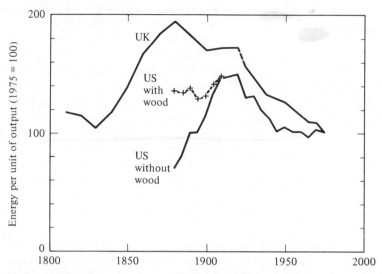

Figure 2.1   Energy per unit of output: United Kingdom and United States. *Sources:* Humphrey and Stanislaw (1979); Schurr and Netschert (1960).

quarter of the total power used in the textile industry. Steam power was not widely used until the 1830s, so the path for the energy–output ratio shown in figure 2.1 for the period 1800–30 is not surprising. However, 1830 marks a turning point. There was a marked shift towards investments for railways and construction, and later for shipping, which led to a rapid growth in energy intensive iron and steel production. The share of the iron and steel industry as a fraction of national output trebled from 3.6 per cent in 1831 to 11.6 per cent in 1871, and in the latter year the industry used one third of the coal consumed in the United Kingdom. Other energy intensive industries that developed rapidly during this period were mining, steam powered railway transport, gas and electricity, cement production and brick manufacture. At the same time there was an increased use of coal in households.

The decline of the energy–output ratio in the UK after 1880 can be attributed in part to a gradual shift in industrial production away from energy intensive industries, but it was mainly due to improvements in the efficiency with which fuels were used. For example between 1900 and 1960 there was a five-fold increase in the efficiency of electric power production from coal, and similar improvements have taken place in power production in industry and transport. (This type of analysis is considered further in section 2.5 where we discuss sectoral energy demand.) Coal continued as the major fuel until after 1960 when there was a rapid increase in the use of oil and natural gas.

Figure 2.1 shows the historical path of two measures of energy per unit of output for the United States since 1880, one of which includes the estimated consumption of wood fuel. Wood and farm waste used as fuel are often described as 'non-commercial' energy; although they may sometimes be collected free and sometimes traded, their use is rarely recorded in commercial statistics. The replacement of non-commerical energy by fossil fuel or other forms of commercial energy (such as electricity) during industrialisation is a common feature of the development process. It leads to an accelerated growth in the energy–output ratio for commercial energy, which in part merely reflects this substitution but is also in part caused by the faster growth of energy intensive industries during the early stages of industrialisation. After 1920, wood-fuel ceased to be significant in the US, and output from light industry and service industries increased relative to heavy industry; from that point on, continuing improvements in the efficiencies with which energy is used dominate the statistics and cause the energy–output ratio to decline.

Medium-run trends

Changes in world population, energy consumption and total world output (GWP) during the fifty years after 1925 are shown in table 2.1. In 1925 coal provided 80 per cent of the total world commercial energy consumption of 43 EJ, but its share had fallen to 26 per cent by 1975, although the total quantity of coal used had increased (from 35 EJ to 65 EJ). Meanwhile the share taken by oil had increased from 14 to 48 per cent, and natural gas from 3 to 19 per cent. We estimate that the total world use of non-commercial energy (wood fuel, farm waste, etc.) remained approximately constant in the region of 20 to 30 EJ during the period 1925–75.

The percentage shares of world energy, economic output, and population, for the three major world groups are shown in table 2.2. Between the years 1925 and 1975 the shares of world energy taken by both the centrally planned and the developing groups increased faster than their share of GWP. It is instructive to use a modified form of figure 2.1 to compare the behaviour of the energy-output ratio for world regions at different stages of development. This is done in figure 2.2, which shows changes in the energy–output ratio as a function of income per capita for each of the three world groups, and for the world average. If there was a single development path followed by all world regions, for the period 1925–75, each would span a different segment of a single curve in figure 2.2. Variations in climate between the group of developing countries and the communist countries probably account for part of the difference between these groups in 1925, but the different relative shares of non-commercial and commercial fuel would also have a significant effect (proportionally more commercial fuel in communist countries).

The characteristic growth in the energy–output ratio during industrialisation, which was noted for the UK and US in figure 2.1, is also apparent for the world groups illustrated in figure 2.2. This suggests that the energy coefficient (equal to the energy growth rate divided by the economic growth rate) is greater than unity during the early stages of industrialisation but less than unity during the later

Table 2.1. *World commercial energy economic growth and population 1925–76.*

World	1925	1975
Commercial energy (Exajoules)[a]	43	250
Gross world product		
10^9 (1972 US dollars)	770	4880
Population (thousand million)	1.9	4.0

	Average annual percentage growth rates	
World	1925–50	1950–75
Energy growth rate	2.4	4.8
Economic (GWP) growth rate	2.6	4.6
Population growth rate	1.1	1.9

[a]1 exajoule (EJ) = 10^{18}J is approximately 23 million tonnes of oil equivalent; 1 EJ per year = 0.45 million barrels per day of oil equivalent.
Sources: Darmstadter *et al.* (1971); World Bank (1974, 1975); United Nations (1975, 1976, 1977, 1978); League of Nations (1927, 1931, 1941).

Table 2.2. *Commercial energy, GWP and population in world groups.*

	OECD		Centrally planned[a]		Developing regions	
	1925	1975	1925	1975	1925	1975
Percentage of world energy	86	59	9	29	5	12
Percentage of GWP	74	64	13	22	13	14
Percentage of world population	23	18	39	33	38	49

[a]Including China.
Sources: See table 2.1.

stages of development, the transition taking place at around $1000 (1972 US dollars) per capita average income. Future changes in the world price of oil may significantly alter this simple picture, but it is useful to proceed further along these lines by comparing energy coefficients in recent years for different world groups.

Growth rates for output and energy and the corresponding energy coefficients are given in table 2.3 for three world groups for the period 1960–72. The developing group is further subdivided into high, middle and low income countries. The average GNP per capita for OECD countries was over $2,000 in 1960 and

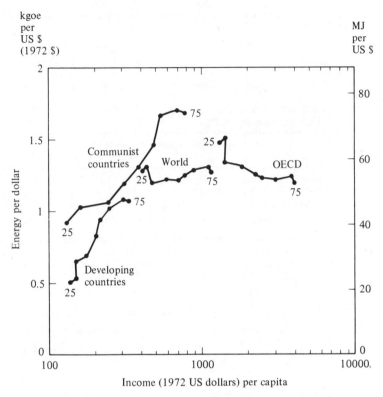

Figure 2.2   Energy per unit of GNP versus GNP per capita 1925–75. *Source:* See table 2.1.

over $3,000 in 1972, both being measured in 1972 US dollars. The major part of OECD was already fully industrialised by 1960 and there were only relatively small structural changes between 1960 and 1972 in the economy of the group as a whole. The energy coefficient was 1.0, but this reflects a balance between a relative fast growth in energy demand for sectors such as transport and a relatively slow growth in energy for industry, where efficiency improvements continued to reduce the energy–output ratio.

The USSR and East Europe region has a faster rate of growth for energy consumption than for GNP through most of the period 1925 to 1975. In the early part of this period this can be plausibly attributed to the relative decline in the use of wood fuel and to structural changes in the economy from agriculture, having low energy use per unit of output, to heavy industry having a high energy intensity. However, for the period 1960–72 there were only minor changes in the industrial structure, and it is surprising that the energy coefficient remained as high as 1.2, which is similar to its long-run average value from 1925–75.

Table 2.3. *Economic growth and energy demand 1960–72.*

	1960–72 Growth rates and energy coefficients		
Region[a]	Economic growth	Energy demand growth	Energy coefficient[b]
OECD	5.0	5.0	1.00
USSR/	4.5	5.4	1.21
East Europe			
Developing[c]			
High	6.4	6.9	1.08
Middle	5.5	8.9	1.63
Low	3.8	5.2	1.37
All developing	5.6	6.8	1.21

[a] Excludes China and centrally planned South East Asia.
[b] Energy coefficient equals energy growth rate divided by economic growth rate.
[c] High income greater than $400 per capita (1975 US dollars) Middle income from $200 to $400. Low income less than $200.
Sources: United Nations (1975, 1977); World Bank (1974).

The growth rates for developing countries given in table 2.3 support the general thesis that industrialisation, the decline in relative importance of agriculture, and substitution of commercial for non-commercial fuels, lead to an increasing energy coefficient; but after a period, when structural changes become slower and commercial fuel provides the major part of energy consumption, the energy coefficient declines towards unity, and at a later stage becomes less than one.

2.4   Inter-country comparisons

In the previous section we have emphasised the similarities in underlying trends for energy and economic growth in world regions, as reflected by the historical behaviour of energy–output ratios and energy coefficients. The similarities are remarkable, but the variations and diversity amongst countries, to which we now turn, are of equal or greater importance in our understanding of the relationship between energy and economic growth. Both the average trends and the diversity amongst different countries are illustrated in figure 2.3, which gives a cross-section of energy consumption per capita and income per capita for a number of countries.

The variations between countries are somewhat masked by the logarithmic scale used in figure 2.3. They are more clearly illustrated by the energy–output ratios for five countries shown in figure 2.4, which indicates that there is no common trend. From our earlier discussion it could be argued that each of these countries is in a post-industrial stage of development so that their energy–output ratios should have declined. It is clearly necessary to examine special features such as the influence of the rapid increase in oil refining and in the use of cheap natural gas in the

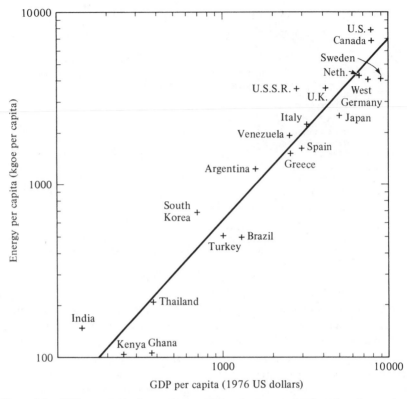

Figure 2.3   GDP per capita versus energy consumption per capita for selected countries 1976. *Sources:* World Bank (1978; 1979).

Netherlands during the 1960s, and the structural differences between the economies of these countries.

There are a number of obstacles and pitfalls in the path towards detailed inter-country comparisons of energy and output. Energy consumption needs to be measured in a common unit, for example the thermal content of the fuels used with a suitable convention for the primary energy equivalent of hydroelectricity. But this does not take account of the differences in the convenience of different forms of fuel, so the 'useful energy' may depend significantly on the mix between different fuels. The problem of 'non-commercial' energy has been noted earlier. Some energy statistics use standard conventions for converting different fuels to a common unit, others use the estimated or actual thermal content of each fuel, some use higher calorific values (see chapter 3), others use lower calorific values, the differences being about 10 per cent for gas and 5 per cent for oil.

There are similar or greater difficulties in comparing sectoral activity or output

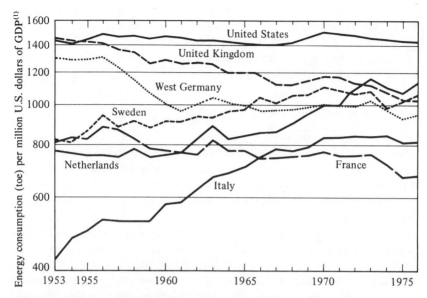

Figure 2.4   Energy consumption per unit of output 1953–76. *Source:* Dunkerley, J. *et al.* (1979). *Note:* GDP is expressed in constant 1972 US dollars converted at 1972 purchasing-power-parity exchange rates.

between different countries. If the output is measured in financial terms, the comparison between countries requires an assumption about conversion rates between different currencies. Market exchange rates, even when averaged over several years, tend to be dominated by trade and money flows which may be small compared to GNP. Comparison based on the purchasing power of people in different countries may prove more helpful and the resulting 'purchasing power parities' have been used both by Darmstadter *et al.* (1977) and by Pindyck (1979c).

In some sectors, such as transport or households, it may be more informative to compare energy use between countries in terms of physical activity such as average energy consumption per vehicle or vehicle mile, or consumption per household. This type of approach was used extensively by WAES (1977a) in their study of the world energy outlook. It needs to be supplemented by whatever economic informa-tion may be available, for example on energy prices and direct energy consumption in households and for personal transport as a function of family income. Physical activities may also provide a measure of output in some industries, for example tons of iron or steel produced, but for industries with mixed or complex products it is necessary to use a financial measure for the output. The term 'energy intensity' for an industrial sector is commonly used for the ratio of the direct expenditure on purchases of energy to the output of the sector; it varies from about 1 per cent for the electronics industry to 20 per cent for the steel industry and 30 per cent for the cement industry. (The same term 'energy intensity' may also be used for the energy-output ratio for the sector, where the energy is measured in physical units and the output in financial units.)

2.5   Sectoral energy demand

Cross section analysis

The percentage shares of energy demand in major economic sectors are shown for 9 industrial countries in table 2.4. The definitions of these sectors are liable to vary between countries and sources so care must be taken in making comparisons. Transport includes private, commercial and public transport but it is sometimes difficult to separate out energy that is used for bunkers (fuels supplied to ships and aircraft in international transport) from inland or coastal consumption. Industry in table 2.4 includes the energy content of chemical feedstocks (oil and gas), lubricants and bitumen for roads, collectively called 'non-energy uses'. It may also include the energy industries' own use (refinery and electricity distribution losses, etc.) as opposed to conversion losses in the electricity industry (see chapters 3 and 7), though it is more logical to include all of these in the energy supply sector, called 'conversion losses' in table 2.4. The industry figures also include some of the energy used for agriculture, though part of this would be included under transport, and energy for mining (though energy for coal mining could alternatively be included in the energy supply sector). Conversion losses should include refinery conversion (5 to 10 per cent of output) as well as conversion losses for electricity generation (65 to 75 per cent of fuel input, or 2 to 3 times the electricity output). For inter-country comparisons it is convenient to introduce notional conversion losses for the production of hydroelectricity that are similar to those for electricity generated by fossil fuel, although the actual losses may be less than 20 per cent of the potential energy of the water used.

An analysis of energy demand by sector was carried out by the Workshop on Alternative Energy Strategies (WAES, 1977a) for 13 countries (including those in table 2.4) for 1972 with illustrative projections or scenarios for 1985 and 2000. The WAES reports provide additional information on energy demand in further subsectors. A comparative analysis of the variations in the energy-output ratios for the 9 countries listed in table 2.4 has been carried out by Darmstadter *et al.* (1977). This study sought to understand or explain the different contributions to the energy-output ratio shown in table 2.5 for each of the major sectors. (The numbers in table 2.5 can be derived from those in table 2.4 by scaling each row in proportion to the national energy-output ratios, with US equal to 100.)

Darmstadter et al concluded that differences in the transport sector account for the largest part (40 per cent) of the difference between the energy output ratios

Table 2.4. *Sectoral energy demand: percentage shares for nine industrial countries in 1972.*

Country	Transport	Industry[a]	Household & commercial	Conversion losses	Total
US	22	36	25	17	100
Canada	17	33	27	23	100
France	15	39	28	18	100
W. Germany	13	42	29	16	100
Italy	15	46	24	15	100
Netherlands	10	44	32	13	100
UK	13	40	24	23	100
Sweden	11	31	33	25	100
Japan	12	51	19	17	100

[a] Industry includes non-energy uses (e.g. chemical feedstocks).
Source: Darmstadter *et al.* (1977).

Table 2.5. *Energy-output ratios by country and sector for nine industrial countries in 1972.*

Country	Transport	Industry[a]	Household & commercial	Conversion losses	Total[b,c]
US	22	36	25	17	100
Canada	21	40	32	27	120
France	8	22	15	9	54
W. Germany	9	29	20	11	70
Italy	9	28	15	9	62
Netherlands	9	38	28	11	86
UK	10	31	18	17	76
Sweden	8	22	24	18	72
Japan	7	30	11	10	57

[a] Industry includes non-energy uses (e.g. chemical feedstocks)
[b] Normalised with US equals 100. The actual US ratio was 1.5 kgoe per dollar (1972) or 66 MJ/$.
[c] The conversion between GDP in different currencies has been carried out using purchasing power parities.
Source: Darmstadter *et al.* (1977).

(table 2.5) of the US and Canada, and the other 7 countries. The higher energy used for transport is partly due to the greater distances travelled by passengers or goods relative to GDP, partly due to the greater use of private cars rather than public transport, and partly due to the fact that, on average, more energy is used per vehicle-mile. Differences in other sectors are more complex. Darmstadter et al found that energy intensities for some subsectors of industry tend to be higher in the US and Canada than in other countries but warned against reliance on disaggregation by industry since the definitions of subsectors are rarely uniform between countries. However, if the energy industries are excluded from the industrial sector, there is less variation between the industrial contributions to the national energy output ratios. For example, the large refinery industry in the Netherlands explains the relatively high figure of 38 for that country in table 2.5.

The variations in the household and commercial contributions are largely explained by differences in climate and in the characteristics of dwellings and other buildings, though the unusually low figure in Japan may also be due partly to differences in lifestyle. The physical reason for the differences in the conversion losses column of table 2.5 is that some countries use more electricity than others in relation to GDP. Greater electricity use is partly explained by the lower costs of electricity from hydroelectric power, particularly for Canada and Sweden, but this does not account for the high use of electricity in the UK and the US, nor its low use in France where hydroelectricity provided about half of the electricity used in 1972.

Time series studies

A number of other studies have been carried out to examine the relationship between energy use and economic output and other factors, by analysing both the changes over time of certain variables, such as fuel inputs, labour inputs etc., and the variations between countries at similar income levels. One such study by Bossanyi et al. (1980) is an econometric analysis of differences in energy use in the UK, West Germany and Italy. In this study industry is disaggregated into seven manufacturing sectors plus mining and quarrying. Energy use and energy intensity in the three countries are analysed taking account also of the other factor inputs, whose costs are, of course, in total normally far larger than energy costs.

The movements in energy intensity for each sector are illustrated for two benchmark years in Table 2.6. For the UK and West Germany there was a decline in the energy intensity in almost all industrial sectors in the period 1953–74, and these improved 'efficiencies' are the principal reason for the decline in the average energy intensity for industry as a whole. Bossanyi et al. show that although the effects of changes in the sectoral mix on industrial energy use were not insignificant, their total effect on the industrial energy intensity was not large. The increase in the average industrial energy intensity in Italy, shown in Table 2.6, is believed to be due largely to changed technologies associated with industrialisation, including for example the production of higher quality steels and chemicals, and increased mechanisation of industry as a whole.

Having identified improved efficiencies in each industrial sector as a major contributor to the reduced energy intensity for industry in the UK and West Germany, Bossanyi et al. examined the influence of interfuel substitution on these changes. For the sectors, food and engineering in the UK, and paper in West

Table 2.6. *Sectoral industrial energy intensities for UK, West Germany and Italy (megajoules per 1970 US dollar).*

| | Energy consumption/value added | | | | | |
| | United Kingdom | | West Germany | | Italy | |
	1954	1974	1954	1973	1955	1973
Food	50	48	19	19	31	23
Iron & steel	371	231	176	107	126	152
Engineering	20	20	13	6	15	15
Chemicals	121	112	91	53	78	132
Textiles	47	29	19	13	19	16
Bricks	241	126	154	72	165	183
Paper	48	31	28	16	17	24
Mining	85	49	179	88	41	53
Total industry	70	49	56	29	45	50

Source: Bossanyi *et al.* (1980).

Germany, the time series data are consistent with the hypothesis that substitution from coal to oil and gas was responsible for the changes in energy per unit of value added. In almost all other cases, however, (the major exception being UK chemicals and West German mining) the results indicate that improved energy efficiencies are not closely correlated with interfuel substitution. It seems likely that the improvements were mainly due to technological improvements as old equipment was replaced and new factories were established, though this hypothesis is hard to test without more detailed information about capital stock than is generally available.

Bossanyi et al examined also the influence of labour costs and relative prices on energy consumption and interfuel substitution. The results of the study are consistent with the hypothesis that the price of labour has influenced substitution of oil for coal (a higher labour price favouring oil) and that it has influenced mechanisation (higher wages leading to more electricity consumption). These results can be explained: the use of oil instead of coal, and more mechanisation using electric power can often reduce labour costs; thus energy is substituted for labour and labour productivity rises.

Input–output analysis

One of the drawbacks of the sectoral analyses presented earlier in this section is that the energy used in each sector has been represented only by the direct purchases of fuels and electricity by that sector and does not include the indirect energy embodied in the other goods and services used by the sector. Thus some of the differences between the apparent energy intensities of different industrial sectors may be explained by differences in the energy content of materials or components 'bought-in' from other sectors. For example, if an aluminium industry makes extensive use of imported aluminium billets or ingots its apparent energy intensity would be much less than if the energy used in smelting aluminium were included. Again, in some countries the automobile sub-sector of the engineering industry includes the manufacture of iron and steel, but in others iron and steel intermediate products are bought-in by the car industry. These variations can have a large effect on inter-country comparisons for individual sectors if these are based only on the *direct* use of energy. The *indirect* use of energy can sometimes be assessed by physical observations (for example, see Berry and Fels, 1973), but in an industry with complex products or inputs it is necessary to use formal input–output techniques.

An input–output table (a matrix of inter-industry transactions) provides detailed data on what each industry buys from every other industry and what it sells to each industry or to final consumers. The matrix cells are usually in money units, and each cell shows purchases by industry *i* from industry *j*. But Bullard and Herendeen (1975) and Herendeen (1974) have developed, through the use of input–output tables and energy balance tables, input–output matrices in physical terms for several countries. These matrices provide estimates for the total direct and indirect energy requirements for each industrial sector per unit of final output.

Input–output tables can be used to quantify and confirm the expectation that in some countries, such as the UK and France, the fabricated metals sector has high indirect energy consumption, whereas primary production sectors such as iron and steel, glass, bricks and cement have high direct energy but relatively low indirect energy consumption per unit of output. Such results are particularly important when assessing the consequences of changed energy prices on the costs of different industries (NEDO, 1974). These methods may also be useful when estimating the potential change in energy demand that would result from a change in product design, for example a change from using steel to aluminium, or from glass to plastic; though the final outcome will also be affected by how the product is used and whether it may be recycled.

The study of Darmstadter *et al.* (1977), noted earlier, used input–output analysis to estimate the extent to which the differences in the US energy/GDP ratio relative to other countries were due to differences in the mix of final demand. The estimates of energy consumption include both direct and indirect energy used in producing, transporting and delivering each type of energy to the consumer. Thus they will be far higher than the conventional 'heat supplied basis' that is normally used to measure direct purchases of energy; for example, electricity purchased will be given in primary energy terms and will include the energy that is lost in generating the electricity.

The Darmstadter study shows that the indexes for the direct purchases of fuel and power by households are substantially lower in other countries than in the

United States: while other consumers spend between 1.0 and 3.3 per cent of their income on direct energy purchases, in the USA consumers spend 5.4 per cent of their (higher) income. However, in other countries only 10 to 39 per cent of these purchases are for gasoline, whereas in the US about 50 per cent are for gasoline. Since the energy content per dollar is lower for gasoline than for the rest of fuel and power, the higher proportion of gasoline purchases in the US means that, for direct energy purchases as a whole, the energy content per dollar spent is slightly higher in most other countries than in the US. Nevertheless, after taking account also of the indirect energy component of all other consumer purchases, it follows that the overall energy use per dollar expenditure in the US is substantially larger than in other countries. (This result is, of course, in agreement with the results on the energy–output ratios that were discussed earlier and are listed in table 2.5.)

Family expenditure

The difference between countries in the percentages of consumer income that goes on direct (or on indirect) energy purchases raises important questions about relative energy prices and energy price elasticities and about relative incomes and energy income elasticities. We will turn to price elasticities in the next section, and continue here with another approach to consumer expenditure.

Herendeen and Tanaka (1976), O'Neill (1975) and others have made studies of family expenditure on direct and indirect energy purchases. The former authors obtained the direct and indirect energy expenditure using input–output analysis and the energy intensities of consumer goods. They further examined the effects of income, household size and place of residence on the household expenditure pattern. Their findings for per capita purchases of energy by representative 'poor', 'average' and 'rich' four-person households are summarised in table 2.7.

Table 2.7 shows that, as a family becomes richer, both its direct and its indirect purchases of energy increase, but the ratio of direct to indirect purchases falls. Thus, going from poor to rich, the direct energy component falls from 65 per cent of total energy purchased to 35 per cent. If the direct, indirect and total purchases of energy in table 2.7 are related to per capita expenditures by a simple formula using income elasticity α(direct), α(indirect) or α(total), namely

$$(E/E_0) = (Y/Y_0)^\alpha, \tag{2.9}$$

it is found that, approximately,

$$\alpha(\text{direct}) = 0.5, \quad \alpha(\text{indirect}) = 1.1, \quad \alpha(\text{total}) = 0.8.$$

These results suggest some degree of saturation in direct use of energy as income increases, but the picture is considerably altered when indirect energy is also taken into account. It is interesting to note that a time series with rising national income would bring more families into the 'average' and 'rich' (1961) categories so the indirect energy purchases could become relatively more important, though the individual energy intensities (energy consumption per capita per dollar of income) in each category of expenditure may decline as energy efficiencies improve. Finally, from table 2.7 we see that the energy used per dollar of income for the poor

Table 2.7. *Per capita energy use by category of expenditure, for a poor, average, and rich household of four members in the United States in 1961.*

Category of expenditure	Consumption in GJ/person/year		
	Poor	Average	Rich
Direct			
Residential direct	43	58	131
Auto fuel	15	31	38
Subtotal direct	58	89	169
Indirect			
Food	11	21	44
Housing	6	26	70
Clothing	4	6	23
Medical, personal care	4	6	15
Auto purchase and maintenance	3	10	19
Savings, investment, insurance	2	5	98
Education	1	1	9
Recreation	1	2	7
Transportation besides auto	–	4	29
Subtotal indirect	32	81	316
Total	90	170	485
Per capita expenditures (1961 $)	$655	$1467	$5724
Energy intensity (MJ/1961 $)	137 MJ/$	116 MJ/$	85 MJ/$

Source: Socolow (1977).

is higher than for the average and markedly higher than for the rich, and, thus, higher energy prices or taxes would be regressive (their impact would be relatively more severe on the poor than on the rich, and they would tend to move more families back towards the (1961) 'poor' category).

Price elasticities

Energy costs and prices will be discussed extensively elsewhere in the book, particularly in chapters 11 and 16, but it is useful to note here some general points about the influence of energy prices on energy consumption. If q denotes an energy consumption index (Q/Q_0) and p denotes an energy price index (P/P_0), as described earlier in this chapter, they may be related by means of a formula based on a short-run price elasticity β,

$$q = p^{\beta},$$

or by a short-run elasticity β and long-run elasticity $\beta(1 - \lambda)$ using,

$$q(t) = p^{\beta}[q(t - 1)]^{\lambda}.$$

In a detailed econometric study of world energy demand, Pindyck (1979c), has applied generalised versions of these formulae to obtain estimates for short-run and long-run elasticities. His study uses both time series analysis for major economic sectors and cross-section analysis for a number of consuming countries. The latter procedure overcomes some of the difficulties inherent in seeking to isolate price effects in long-run time series of sectoral energy demand where there is continuing technological change, income growth and other time trended changes. And it is true that in using cross-section analysis there is always uncertainty about the lead times one should allow before assuming that the long-run elasticity has been fully effective. Pindyck's estimate for the own-price long-run elasticity of residential energy demand (averaged over nine countries) is $-(1.1)$, with slightly smaller elasticities in the region of $-(1.0)$ for individual fuels. Other studies noted by Pindyck give estimates for these long-run elasticities in the range $-(0.28)$ to $-(1.70)$, though only one other study (Nordhaus, 1976) gives a value greater than one. For industrial energy demand, Pindyck obtains an own-price long-run elasticity of about $-(0.8)$, again larger than other estimates, which are generally in the range $-(0.3)$ to $-(0.6)$. He notes that other estimates are usually based on time series so their evaluation may be over-influenced by short-run price effects, but there is uncertainty about how long is 'long run'.

It is important to recall that the relevant prices in these elasticity formulae are the real (deflated) prices paid by final consumers – householders, industrialists, or motorists. Only part of these prices is proportional to the world price of crude oil; other parts include taxation, transport and handling charges, and conversion costs, and final demand also includes energy from fuels other than oil. Thus, for example, although the world price of oil quadrupled in 1973–4, the real price of heavy fuel oil to industry in the UK only doubled by 1978, and the average real price paid by industry for all fuels increased by only 50 per cent. More generally, the authors take the view that although final energy prices may have doubled by 1990, giving eventually 30 per cent or more reduction in energy demand, this response will not be swift enough to avoid economic disturbance and loss of growth each time there is a substantial increase in the price of oil – more about this in chapters 11, 14 and 16.

Estimates for energy elasticities have been made by numerous authors, many of whom are listed by Pindyck (1979c), and in the review of work on energy elasticities prepared by the UK Department of Energy (1977c).

2.6   Exhaustible resources and economic growth

The resource base and potential supply for each major source of energy will be discussed in later chapters. None of the major fuels is likely to be exhausted on a global scale during the next century but some will become more costly. For example the world supply of oil in 100 years time is expected to be similar in magnitude to current production, probably more than half and less than twice today's level. But those supplies will involve more costly forms of secondary recovery from conventional sources of oil and expensive production from unconventional sources, such as tar sands, shale oil, and heavy oil deposits. At the higher prices that would be needed to bring oil supply and demand into balance, a number of alternatives will become competitive with oil in the world energy market, including natural gas shipped as LNG (liquefied natural gas), coal used directly and also coal products after conversion to synthetic gas or synthetic oil. In developing countries, or in some areas of developed countries, wood fuel harvested as an agricultural product could assume major significance. For the production of electricity, further hydroelectric power will be developed, and nuclear power could become a major source if it is not found to be socially unacceptable.

Social attitudes to energy supply systems are already an important feature of industrial planning and energy strategies. Local or general opposition to the production of coal or the use of nuclear energy may prevent or delay the growth of these main alternatives to oil in some regions. Such delays are bound to increase the costs of energy supplies, and, coupled with a fairly inelastic world supply of oil, this could lead to higher energy prices at levels that would be likely to have an adverse effect on economic growth, at least in some regions of the world and probably world-wide. Thus a discussion of oil as an exhaustible resource cannot be treated in isolation from the impact of price changes on world economic growth.

The expectation of higher prices for oil (in real terms) will influence the attitudes of producers, particularly in countries such as Saudi Arabia and other Gulf States, whose own immediate needs for income from oil are relatively low. It is in these countries that the possible long-term consequences of exhaustion of oil, their major indigenous asset, may have the greatest influence on their energy policies and their wider plans for economic development. The idea of exhaustible resources is easy for the public to grasp and is of evident importance politically and socially; the question of the best response in national or regional terms is both complex and uncertain. It raises issues that will arise frequently throughout this book, though we do not plan to provide the reader with any simple or single solution. Each option has advantages and disadvantages, costs and penalties – nobody gets a free lunch.

2.7   Chapter Summary

World energy demand has increased at almost the same rate as gross world product, averaging about 3.5 per cent growth per annum over the past 50 years. This apparently close relation between energy and output is supported also by historical data on individual countries and by cross-section data on a number of countries having different levels of energy and income per capita in a given year. It is argued in this chapter that two important factors are changing and these may lead to different relations with energy demand increasing more slowly than output or GDP. The first of these arises from higher world oil prices and increasing costs for most forms of energy, and the second is a result of saturation of energy demand in some major sectors of many developed countries. However, three quarters of the world's population live in less developed countries, and if these follow development paths through industrialisation there will be continued growth in world energy demand.

Historical evidence presented in this chapter suggests that the energy coefficient (defined as the average rate of growth in energy demand divided by the average growth of GDP) for developing countries has been larger than unity due partly to industrialisation and partly to the substitution of commercial energy (fossil fuels and electricity) for non-commercial energy (wood fuel and farm waste). The coefficient then stabilises near to unity for a period and then becomes less than unity in a mature industrial country. Thus the energy–output ratio, on average, generally increased during industrialisation as energy intensive industries were more rapidly developed than other parts of the economy, but later declined as the industrial mix became more stable and there were continuing improvements in the efficiency of the use of energy. These historical features relate to a period when energy costs were fairly constant or falling, and with higher energy prices and an expectation of increasing costs for future energy supplies it is expected that in future the energy–output ratio will decline more quickly in OECD countries and increase more slowly in developing countries.

The differences between energy–output ratios for different countries are examined in this chapter using a number of alternative approaches based on sectoral energy demand. These include: cross-section analysis comparing sectoral demand for several countries; time series analysis examining the effects of a changing industrial mix, a changing fuel mix and improved sectoral efficiencies; input–output analysis to identify indirect energy demand arising from the energy used to manufacture and supply goods and services; variations with income in family demand for both direct and indirect energy; analysis of price elasticities of energy demand using both time-series and cross-section data for sectoral energy demand in a number of countries. The chapter concludes with a short discussion of exhaustible resources in relation to the supply of different forms of energy and the possible influence of higher energy costs and prices on economic growth.

Chapter 2   Further reading

Allen, R. G. D. (1968) *Macro-economic theory*. Macmillan, New York.
Conservation Commission of the World Energy Conference (1978). *World energy: looking ahead to 2020*, IPC Science and Technology Press, Guildford, UK, and New York.
Darmstadter, J., Dunkerley, J. and Alterman, J. (1977). *How industrial societies use energy*, Johns Hopkins University Press, Baltimore and London.
Darmstadter, J., Teitelbaum, P. D. and Polach, J. G. (1971) *Energy in the world economy*, Johns Hopkins University Press, Baltimore and London.
Dunkerley, J. (ed.) (1978) *International comparisons of energy use*, Proceedings of the

workshop on international comparisons of energy use, sponsored by Resources for the Future and the Electric Power Research Institute, Washington DC.
International Energy Agency (IEA) (1977a) *Energy Conservation in the International Energy Agency*, OECD, Paris.
Macrakis, M. S. (ed.) (1974) *Energy: demand, conservation and institutional problems*, MIT Press, Cambridge, Mass.
NEDO (1974) *Energy conservation in the United Kingdom* report prepared by Dr. R. J. Eden for the National Economic Development Office, HMSO, London.
Pindyck, R. S. (1979c) *The structure of world energy demand*, MIT Press, Cambridge, Mass.
Schurr, S. H. and Netschert, R. (1960) *Energy in the American economy*, Johns Hopkins University Press, Baltimore and London.
Socolow, R. H. (1977) 'The coming age of conservation' *Annual Review of Energy*, vol. 2, pp. 239–89.
WAES (1977a) *Energy: global prospects 1985–2000*, McGraw-Hill, London and New York.

Statistical references

IEA (1979b) *IEA workshop on energy data of developing countries*, IEA/OECD, Paris.
OECD (annual) *Statistics of energy*, OECD, Paris.
OECD (1976) *Energy balances of OECD countries 1960/74*, OECD, Paris.
OECD (1978) *Energy balances of OECD countries 1974/76*, IEA, Paris.
United Nations (1975) *Single-year population estimates and projections for major areas, regions and countries of the world 1950–2000*, prepared by the Population Division, Department of Economic and Social Affairs, United Nations, New York.
United Nations (annual) *Statistical Yearbook*, United Nations, New York.
United Nations (1976, 1977, 1978) *World energy supplies*, Statistical papers series J, United Nations, New York.
United Nations (annual) *Yearbook of international trade statistics*, United Nations, New York.
United Nations (annual) *Yearbook of national accounts statistics*, United Nations, New York.
World Bank (1979) *World development report, 1979*, World Bank, Washington, DC.

Technological structure of energy demand

A modern industrial society can be viewed as a complex machine for degrading high quality energy into waste heat while extracting the energy needed for creating an enormous catalogue of goods and services [Summers, 1971].

3.1   The use of energy

Energy is used for heating, cooking, lighting, and for other facilities. It is used for transporting people and goods, and it is used for manufacturing consumer goods and capital equipment. These varied demands for energy are met by different forms of secondary energy or 'energy carriers'. For particular uses some of these carriers are readily interchangeable, for others they are not. Natural gas can readily substitute for oil for many heating purposes with relatively low costs for the modification of equipment, and oil can be used to replace gas provided it has a moderate cost advantage. However, for the provision of motive power in fixed machinery, electricity will often have an advantage over fossil fuels in spite of its higher cost per unit of energy supplied. This advantage arises partly from the greater conversion efficiency of electrical energy to work, compared to fossil fuel, and partly from economic factors such as convenience or a reduced need for labour or capital.

Consumer preferences for particular forms of fuel or energy carriers have both arisen from and been stimulated by technological advance, for example in the invention of the steam engine to convert the energy in fuel to mechanical power, the invention of mechanically generated electricity, and the development of equipment powered by electricity. These preferences have been met through expansion and increasing sophistication in the energy industries and an increasing requirement for energy conversion. Energy is used for the production and conversion of primary fuels into the forms of secondary energy desired by the final consumer. The economic advantage derived by consumers in using their preferred energy carriers is offset, to some extent, by the inevitable energy losses in converting primary fuels to those preferred carriers. Although there may be a reduction through time of energy intensity when that is measured in terms of delivered (secondary) energy divided by value added in an activity, this reduction will often be less significant, and may change to an increase, if energy intensity is instead expressed in terms of primary energy including an appropriate share of losses in energy supply and conversion.

In 1975 the energy used by the energy supply and conversion industries in the United States was about 23 per cent of the total primary input. This is illustrated in figure 3.1.

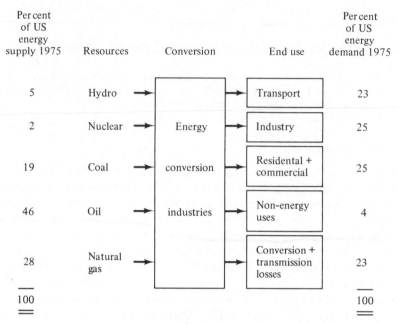

Per cent of US energy supply 1975	Resources	Conversion	End use	Per cent of US energy demand 1975
5	Hydro		Transport	23
2	Nuclear	Energy	Industry	25
19	Coal	conversion	Residental + commercial	25
46	Oil	industries	Non-energy uses	4
28	Natural gas		Conversion + transmission losses	23
100				100

Figure 3.1 Primary energy input proceeding to final (secondary) energy demand in the United States 1975. *Source:* US Department of the Interior (1976).

3.2   Energy conversion

The energy conversion provided by the energy industries themselves is only the first stage of its preparation to perform any one of a multitude of end uses. Each stage involves conversion, some at high efficiencies, such as the 99 per cent efficiency for converting rotating mechanical energy into electric power, and some at low efficiencies such as the 5 per cent efficiency for converting electrical energy into light in an incandescent electric light bulb.

The efficiencies of major conversion devices, such as heat engines for producing mechanical energy and hence electrical energy, have improved dramatically since they began to be used. The early steam engines had efficiencies less than 1 per cent, and those of early generators for electric power were less than 5 per cent. Today the average efficiency for converting the energy in fossil fuel to electric power is about 33 per cent in the US. The latest units take steam superheated to 810 K (or 537°C), with a cooling reservoir at 310 K (or 37°C): this would give a maximum Carnot efficiency of 1 - (T_1/T_2) equal to 0.62 or 62 per cent. The properties of steam make it impractical to use a Carnot cycle, however, and with practical cycles the maximum theoretical efficiency is more like 53 per cent. In practice modern steam turbines achieve nearly 90 per cent of this theoretical value and can have efficiencies of up to 47 per cent. To obtain the overall efficiency of a steam power plant this value must be multiplied by the efficiencies of other energy converters in the chain from fuel to electricity. The conversion from fossil fuel to steam in the boiler can be as high as 88 per cent, and mechanical to electrical energy 99 per cent, giving overall $(0.88) \times (0.47) \times (0.99) = 0.41$, or 41 per cent.

The overall system efficiency in electricity production requires an average over the power stations in the system weighted by their annual load factors. It should also include an allowance for distribution losses and own use by the electrical industry operating the system. These losses may amount to 15 per cent of the output. Thus, if the average efficiency of generation is 33 per cent, the system efficiency would be 33×0.85 or 28 per cent. An additional allowance for the energy required to manufacture the materials in the generating system may reduce this figure to about 27 per cent.

Examples of the efficiency of energy conversion devices are given in figure 3.2, which is taken with minor changes from a diagram by Summers (1971). It should be recalled that these devices are themselves often only part of a chain of conversion devices. In some cases where efficiencies are necessarily low, such as for steam locomotives due to their mode of operation and to the laws of thermodynamics, radical improvements in efficiencies can be obtained only by radical changes in the system. For the railroads this was achieved by changing to diesel and diesel-electric units. The conversion of chemical energy to electrical energy via a fuel cell provides much greater energy efficiency than via a thermal mechanical route, but the technology has not yet advanced sufficiently for this route to be economic. The incandescent lamp provides 95 per cent heat and only 5 per cent light from its electrical energy input, but for aesthetic reasons it is often preferred to the more efficient fluorescent lamp. (Its heat energy is not wasted when heating is required, but it is counter-productive when cooling or air-conditioning is necessary.) The diesel engine is more efficient than the petrol or gasoline internal combustion engine, but it has proved less popular for automobiles in the past, partly because inadequate technological effort has been made to provide a diesel that operates as smoothly and responsively as a gasoline engine. An electric vehicle driven by a storage battery would have advantages in saving fossil fuel, particularly if electricity is increasingly generated by nuclear power, but the widespread use of electric cars is dependent on the development of improved and lighter storage batteries. We will return to the discussion of special cases of energy conversion by category of use later in this chapter and also in chapter 12 in a discussion of interfuel substitution and energy conservation.

3.3 Energy balance tables and conversion conventions

One of the necessities for economic analysis of the energy industries and their relationship to each other and to the rest of the economy is to trace for any fuel or energy carrier the components that make up its supply, such as imports or

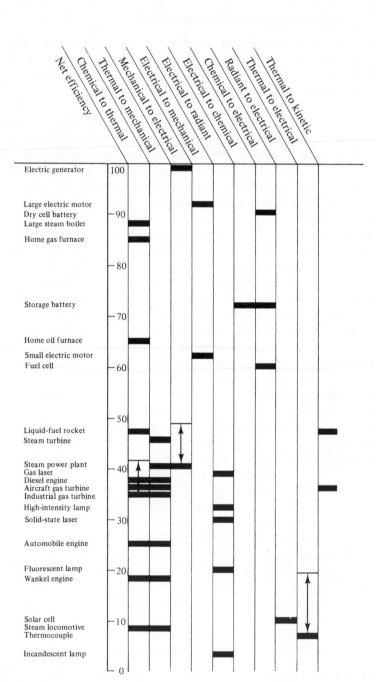

Figure 3.2 Efficiencies of energy converters. *Source:* Summers (1971), with minor changes by authors.

indigenous production, the uses for energy conversion for each fuel in each of the energy industries, and the distribution amongst final consumers. An energy balance table in which all forms and uses of fuel are recorded in a common accounting unit provides the framework for analyses of this kind. At the same time such an accounting framework provides a means for testing the internal consistency of the basic energy data relating to supply, conversion and demand. Finally, an energy balance table provides a basis from which to construct 'forecasting models' that produce internally consistent pictures or scenarios for possible future national energy demand.

There are a variety of alternative forms of energy balance table in use, each having its own format and its own conventions. The basic features of these tables will be described and a simple example will be given. For further information the reader may refer to statistical publications by individual agencies or to an excellent review by the UK Department of Energy (1977b).

The original units in which fuels are measured vary widely, tons (short and long) or tonnes for coal or oil, or barrels for oil, kilowatt hours or some multiple of them for electricity, Btu, ft^3 or cubic metres for gas. In order to combine these usefully into a single table, conversion factors are required from the original units to a common accounting unit. This raises the associated problems of choosing an accounting unit and defining the routes by which the conversion factors may be derived. Possible candidates for the accounting unit include money values of the fuels, and these are in fact used when constructing the energy rows or columns of the input–output matrices used in other areas of economic analysis. However, prices of fuels are unstable and provide a poor quantitative measure of the amounts of energy used. The thermal content or the heat of combustion of each fuel provides a more stable convention. It can be measured for samples of a fuel using a bomb calorimeter, giving either the higher calorific value which includes the energy associated with condensing the water vapour formed when a hydrocarbon is burnt, or the lower calorific value which excludes this part of the heat combustion. These calorific values differ by about 10 per cent for natural gas, 5 per cent for oil, and 2 per cent for coal. Statistical information on energy is usually based on the average thermal content, some countries using the higher and some the lower calorific value. When this information is not available various conventions are used for converting field units or natural units (tons of coal, etc.) into thermal units (Btu, calories, kilowatt-hours or joules), or into a conventional unit such as toe (tonnes of oil equivalent). Agencies sometimes convert to conventional units such as toe without defining their choice of thermal content which may vary from less than 40 GJ to more than 45 GJ for different reports. It is sometimes desirable to use conventional units such as toe, but their meaning should always be explicitly stated in terms of Standard International Units (SIU).

In these units, energy is measured in multiples of the joule (GJ = 10^9 J, EJ = 10^{18} J, etc. as noted in table 1.3) and power is measured in multiples of the

Table 3.1. *Approximate thermal equivalents for various fuels* (higher calorific values–see text).

Coal
  1 tonne coal = 28.8 GJ = 28.8×10^9 J
  1 tonne lignite = 16 GJ
Oil
  1 tonne crude oil = 44 GJ = 1 toe
                  = 7.3 barrels (bbl) crude oil
  1 barrel (bbl) of oil = 6 GJ
  1 million barrels of oil per day = 50 million toe per year
Natural gas
  1 thousand cubic metres = 38.2 GJ
  1 thousand cubic feet   = 1.08 GJ
Electricity
  1 kilowatt hour (kWh) = 3.6 MJ = 3.6×10^6 J
Exajoules per year
  1 EJ per year = 10^{18} J/yr = 32 GW
                        = 35 million tonnes coal per year
                        = 23 million toe per year
                        = 0.45 million barrels oil per day

watt (equal to one joule per second). It is not possible to recommend any particular convention for converting field units to joules, but a typical set of conversion factors is summarized in table 3.1 and a more detailed list of conversion factors is given in appendix A.

After converting energy consumed for activities in different economic sectors it is possible to draw up an energy balance table. The simplest format for national accounting could consist of a balance table of three lines only giving primary energy consumption, production, and imports or exports. A more detailed energy balance table showing energy consumption by type of fuel and major economic sector is illustrated for world energy in table 3.2. In this table lines 1 to 4 show the energy used in final demand sectors measured on a heat supplied basis, the total final demand being given in line 5. Line 6 shows the thermal content of fuels used for electricity production and (with a negative sign) electricity output also measured by its thermal energy content. The inputs from nuclear and hydro are based on a convention that their thermal heat content is equal to three times the energy in the electricity generated from these sources. This means that nuclear and hydro energy input has a relation to electricity output that is similar to that for fossil fuels. Synthetic gas production in line 7 shows the coal and oil input and gas output (with a minus sign). Energy sectors own-use in line 9 does *not* include conversion losses for electricity generation which are already allowed for in line 6. It does include: energy for mining coal and coal lost during transport; energy for pumping oil and energy used in oil refineries; energy for pumping gas and losses in distribution. It also includes transmission losses in the distribution of electricity

Table 3.2. *World energy balance table 1972* (exajoules (= 10^{18} J)).

	Coal	Oil	Gas	Elec.	Heat[b]	Wood	Sol.	Nucl.	Hydr.	Total
Transport	1.9	41	0	0.5	0	—	—	—	—	43.4
Industry	22.3	21.7	18.9	9	3.5	5.2	—	—	—	80.6
Domestic	8.1	17.9	12.7	7.6	1.3	20.9	—	—	—	68.5
Feedstocks	0.1	9.7	0.7	—	—	—	—	—	—	10.5
Total final consumption	32.4	90.3	32.3	17.1	4.8	26.1	—	—	—	203
Electricity generation	27.4	15.1	9.1	−20.3	−5.8	—	—	1.6	13.8	40.9
Synthetic gas	2.7	1.9	−3.8	—	—	—	—	—	—	0.8
Synthetic oil	0	−0	—	—	—	—	—	—	—	0
Energy sector own-use	3.1	6.8	8.4	3.2	1	—	—	—	—	22.6
Primary energy input	65.6	114.1	46	—	—	26.1	—	1.6	13.8	267.2
Indigenous supply	65.8	115.2	46	—	—	26.1	—	1.6	13.8	268.5
Net imports[a]	−0.2	−1.1	0	—	—	—	—	—	—	−1.3

[a]And items unaccounted.
[b]'Heat' cogenerated with electricity.
Source: Eden *et al.* (1978)

(and heat if co-generated) and electricity used by the energy production industries.

There are a wide variety of formats and conventions for energy balance tables. Some of those used internationally are described and reviewed in a report by the UK Department of Energy (1977b).

The percentage shares of world energy used in each major sector of demand are shown for different world regions in the year 1972 in table 3.3. About 27 per cent of the primary energy is taken by energy conversion and distribution losses and the energy supply industries for their own uses. The remaining 73 per cent is used by the major sectors discussed in this chapter, namely, transport, industry and the household and commercial sector.

3.4   Transport

Energy demand for transport is about 20 per cent of the world demand for primary fuels if one includes the associated refinery energy consumption with the direct use

Table 3.3. *Percentage shares of energy demand taken by major economic sectors in major world regions (1972).*

Year 1972	North America	Western Europe	Japan Aust. + NZ	USSR + E. Europe	Developing Countries[a]	World
Transport	23	14	18	9	24	18
Industry and agriculture	22	26	32	45	38	31
Residential and commercial	21	27	17	15	17	20
Non-energy uses	6	6	9	1	3	4
Energy conversion and losses	28	27	24	30	18	27
Primary energy	100	100	100	100	100	100
Imports %	10	60	68	−(4)	−(127)	0
Total energy EJ	83	50	16	53[b]	39[b]	241
Energy/capita GJ (in 1972)	360	148	133	141	16[b]	65

[a]Includes China and centrally planned Asia.
[b]Excludes wood fuel and farm waste.
Source: WAES (1976, 1977b, 1977c), Eden *et al.* (1978).

by the transport sector. This energy, equivalent to over 1000 million tonnes of oil each year, is used to transport passengers and goods by land, sea and air. The major part, about 56 per cent, goes to road transport, about three quarters being for passengers and about one quarter for freight. Railroads and water transport each take about 18 per cent, whilst air transport takes an increasing share, currently about 8 per cent.

Railroads provided much of the growth in transport during the early stages of industrialisation, but this growth has been moderated through competition from road transport, particularly since 1950. The use of fuel for railroad transport has declined in many countries through the introduction of diesel or diesel-electric engines to replace steam engines, giving as much as a five-fold improvement in the efficiency of using energy. Growth in tonne-kilometres of freight transport has however continued in many regions, notably in the USSR, Asia and Africa, and more slowly in North and South America and in Western Europe. The world total nearly trebled between 1950 and 1975 reaching nearly 6 million million tonne-kilometres, of which about half is in the USSR and one quarter in North America. In the same period the tonnage loaded for movement by international shipping has increased more than five-fold to more than 3000 million tonnes, of which more than half is petroleum.

Energy demand for world air transport increased at more than 7 per cent per annum between 1960 and 1972, compared with about 4.4 per cent for all transport energy. It may be expected that demand for air transport will continue to increase, though the increase in energy requirements will be moderated by improved efficiencies of the new generation of aircraft now planned or coming into widespread use.

The largest component of energy demand for transport comes from road passengers in automobiles, primarily in North America and Western Europe, but forming an increasing and important component of energy demand in all world regions. The share of total world transportation energy taken by North America and Western Europe is about 60 per cent, whilst developing countries (including China), which account for over 70 per cent of the world's population, use about 16 per cent of the total and provide an additional 4 per cent for international shipping bunkers.

In this section we illustrate the growth in transport energy demand and its increasing dependence on gasoline for automobile transport by examples from the US and UK. We then go on to outline the technology of the gasoline engine, the diesel engine and the gas turbine which account for most of the use of energy for transportation, and are the primary cause of the strong preference for the use of petroleum products as the principal fuels for transportation.

In the United States, energy used for transport increased by an average annual rate of 2.7 per cent from 1947 to 1977. This increase was dominated by the growth in the use of automobiles and the resulting demand for gasoline, whose average increase was 4.1 per cent annually in the same period. In 1947, US consumption of gasoline in energy terms was less than 50 per cent of the total energy used for transport, but by 1977 this had increased to 70 per cent. Not all gasoline is used by automobiles but the growth in demand is closely related to the growth in automobile use. Growth in car ownership is compared for the US and the UK in figure 3.3. There is no clear evidence for saturation levels, though it may be expected that there would be some reduction in average use per car when the number of cars exceeds 0.5 per capita.

The gasoline engine, diesel and gas turbine

Gasoline is liquid at ordinary temperatures but evaporates rapidly to form an explosive mixture in air. It usually consists mainly of hexane (C_6H_{14}), heptane (C_7H_{16}) and octane (C_8H_{18}). These hydrocarbons occur in different isomers (different molecular patterns), the relative abundances of which affect the characteristics of the fuel when it is used in an internal combustion engine. A gasoline internal combustion engine derives its power from explosions of a gasoline–air mixture in a closed cylinder containing a reciprocating piston linked by means of a crank to a rotating shaft. A fuel air mixture is admitted to the cylinder on a piston down stroke and compressed on the subsequent up stroke. Close to maximum compression the mixture is ignited by an electric spark, and the high pressure from the resulting explosion drives the piston down, rotating the main shaft via the

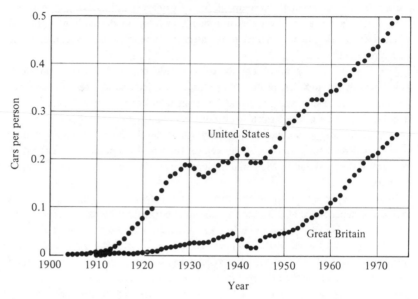

Figure 3.3   Trends in car ownership 1900 to 1975 in the US and UK. *Source:* Tanner (1977).

crank. Cam driven valves control the times of admission of the mixture, and also the subsequent exhaust of combustion products to the atmosphere. Energy storage in a flywheel attached to the shaft, and/or the use of multiple cylinders, smooths the power output and provides the driving force for the compression (and exhaust) stroke.

The efficient operation of the gasoline engine depends firstly on the choice of parameters relating to the piston and cylinder to determine the compression ratio during its cycle of operation and secondly on the characteristics of the fuel. The theoretical efficiency of the corresponding idealised thermodynamic cycle is given by:

$$\eta = 1 - \left[\frac{v_1}{v_2}\right]^{1-\gamma}$$

where v_1 and v_2 denote the effective volumes of the cylinder before and after compression; and γ is the ratio of the specific heats (of air) at constant pressure and at constant volume, being equal to 1.4, so $(1 - \gamma) = -0.4$. In order to avoid pre-ignition the compression ratio (v_1/v_2) is usually kept below a maximum of 10, for which the idealised cycle would correspond to an efficiency of 0.60. In practice the efficiencies for engines with a compression ratio of 10 are found to be in the region of 25 to 30 per cent.

Inefficiencies arise if the fuel is not correctly evaporated in the carburettor before being drawn into the cylinder since droplets of fuel would lead to incomplete combustion. This is not a problem when the engine is hot, but it means that for cold starting the fuel must be readily volatile, hence gasoline is made from the lighter and more volatile fractions of petroleum. However, there is also a tendency for the vapour–air mixture to pre-ignite since it becomes hot under compression. Pre-ignition is more likely in engines with a high compression ratio, and is called knocking or pinking. In order to avoid inefficiencies and engine damage the nature of the fuel has to be carefully chosen to meet the characteristics of the engine. The anti-knock properties of gasoline can be measured by comparing them with those of a mixture of pure n-heptane and pure iso-octane. The percentage of iso-octane in this comparison mixture determines the octane rating of the gasoline.

The octane rating of gasoline can be enhanced by the addition of anti-knock agents such as tetra-ethyl lead. However, with growing concern about lead pollution the percentage of lead is currently being reduced by regulation in many countries. This leads to more complex and more energy intensive requirements for processing and refining petroleum so as to maintain a high octane rating. Reduction in environmental pollution requires a reduction in certain exhaust emissions consisting of products from incomplete combustion such as carbon monoxide and hydrocarbons together with oxides of nitrogen (the 'normal' combustion products include carbon dioxide, water vapour, and nitrogen from the air). The combination of environmental needs and the prospect of scarcity of world oil have encouraged improved design of automobile engines. With the added stimulus of government intervention on fuel economy and higher gasoline prices it is thought that the average efficiency of new automobiles in the US could improve from its value of 15 miles per US gallon (5.4 MJ per km) in 1973 to 27 mpg (3.0 MJ per km) by the late 1980s.

Diesel engines for vehicles use gas oil or diesel oil that boils in the range 250° to 350°C. The cycle of operation differs from that of the gasoline engine. Air, rather than a fuel–air mixture, is initially drawn into the cylinder. The air is then compressed, thus raising it to a high temperature, at which stage fuel in the form of a fine spray is injected and ignites spontaneously. Fuel injection continues during the subsequent stroke so as to maintain its power. The different characteristics of the diesel engine compared with the gasoline engine lead to different requirements for the most suitable fuel; volatility is not necessary but spontaneous ignition is essential. Thermodynamic analysis shows that the theoretical efficiency of the diesel engine, like the gasoline engine, depends on the compression ratio. However, since there is no problem of pre-ignition this ratio can be as high as 20 to 1. Large diesel engines can achieve efficiencies in practice that are above 40 per cent, and smaller engines suitable for cars and small vans should reach near to 40 per cent efficiency. They also have an advantage that, when properly adjusted, they have lower emissions of hydrocarbons and carbon monoxide than conventional gasoline engines. Their main disadvantages are their greater weight to power ratio, and hence their higher cost, and their greater noise and vibration compared to the gasoline engine.

The internal combustion gasoline engine and the diesel engine provide the power units for most road transport. In all but the smallest aircraft the piston engine has been replaced by the gas turbine engine using kerosene as a fuel. This engine draws air into a multistage axial fan compressor, finally achieving high compression and high temperature in a combustion chamber. Fuel is then sprayed in and ignites thus further raising the temperature and pressure of the air. The air and combustion products pass through the turbine blades, but give up only enough power to drive the compressor, and leave as high speed exhaust gases through the exhaust nozzle. This provides the basis for the pure jet engine, suitable for high speed aircraft. For slower aircraft the gas turbine is modified to drive a propeller, forming a turboprop engine.

approx .82 toc is required to produce a ton of steel!

3.5   Industry

On a heat supplied basis the industrial use of energy is about 30 per cent of total world demand, but if the associated losses arising from energy conversion and the energy content of chemical feedstocks are included, industrial energy needs amount to about 50 per cent of the total. The variations between different world regions are substantial. The corresponding figures for North America are 22 per cent (see table 3.3) and about 42 per cent.

The demand for industrial energy arises from the demand for manufactured goods and the associated needs for services, agriculture, mining, construction, etc. World annual demand for steel products requires the production of some 600 million tonnes of steel. About 36 GJ, or 0.82 toe, are required on average to produce one tonne of steel, so the energy demand arising from the production of 600 million tonnes of steel amounts to about 22 EJ, or 500 mtoe, representing 9 per cent of the world total demand for energy. World demand for steel increased at an average of 5 per cent annually during the period 1960 to 1972, almost the same as the rate of growth of the gross world product in the same period. There are similar large and readily identifiable energy requirements for the production of other relatively homogeneous commodities, such as more than 600 million tonnes of cement, over 10 million tonnes of aluminium (1972, but increasing at 8 per cent per annum) and over 8 million tonnes of copper.

The net energy (on a heat supplied basis) used by industry in the United States during the period 1947 to 1978 is illustrated in figure 3.4. There have been significant changes in the percentage shares taken by different fuels; coal provided 55 per cent of the total net energy in 1947 but its share had declined to less than 20 per cent by 1978. Natural gas increased its share from 23 per cent in 1947 to 47 per cent in 1971 but since then its share has declined. Electricity used has increased from 4 per cent to 14 per cent on a heat supplied basis – on a useful energy basis the

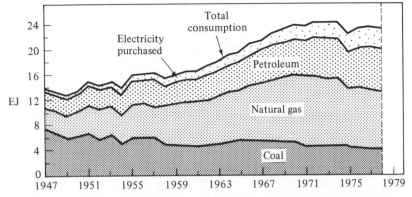

Figure 3.4 Energy consumption by US industry 1947–78. *Source:* US Department of the Interior (1976), US Department of Energy (1979). *Note:* From 1947 to 1978, total energy consumption by the industrial sector increased at an annual rate of 1.6 per cent. While total energy consumption by the industrial sector for coal declined at an annual rate of 2.1 per cent, consumption of natural gas and petroleum increased at annual rate of 3.4 and 3.2 per cent during the 1947–78 period.

corresponding shares were perhaps in the region of 8 per cent to 20 per cent respectively. The growth in energy demand by the industrial sector averaged 1.8 per cent annually for the period 1947 to 1975, compared with 3.5 per cent for the value added in manufacturing measured in constant dollars. Thus there was an annual decrease of 1.6 per cent in the energy requirements per dollar of value added. If both non-energy uses of fuels for chemical feedstock, and the requirements for energy conversion (particularly for electricity for industry) are included, the annual growth in US industrial energy demand was 2.3 per cent, so the annual efficiency improvement in the energy intensity (energy per dollar of value added) was 1.2 per cent.

The shares of total net industrial energy demand coming from major sectors of industry for the US and the UK in 1972 are shown in table 3.4, which also includes figures for the energy intensities of each sector expressed as energy per dollar of value added. The energy consumed by the major industries can often be regarded as a derived energy demand arising from products supplied to other industrial sectors. For example, the iron and steel industry rarely supplies products directly to the final consumer. The largest customers of this industry include the transport equipment sector, the engineering sector, miscellaneous manufacturing and the construction industry. However, as can be seen from the energy intensities given in table 3.4, these subsequent uses of iron and steel do not themselves involve such a large amount of energy per unit of value added as does the production of iron and steel.

Average figures for the energy used in the main stages of steel-making given in

Table 3.4. *Percentage shares and energy per value added for US and UK industry.*

1972 Net industrial energy demand sector	Percentage shares (energy)		Energy/value added[a]	
			US	UK
	US %	UK %	MJ/$	MJ/$
Iron and steel	20	24	243	354
Non-ferrous metals	5	2	118	82
Chemicals and allied	16	14	98	128
Paper and allied	8	5	125	44
Food and related	6	7	30	45
Transport equipment	2	4	11	29
Cement	b	5	—	80
Mineral products	8	5	114	338
Engineering	b	8	—	20
Misc. manufacturing	13	11	13	35
Non-energy uses	22	15	c	c
Total	100	100	53[d]	71[d]

[a]1972 US Dollars ($2.40 = £1).
[b]Included elsewhere.
[c]Not applicable.
[d]Includes non-energy uses of fuels.
Source: WAES (1976).

table 3.5 show how the energy requirements are dominated by the blast furnace operation in which iron ore, sinter and coke are converted to pig iron. Different routes for steel-making use widely differing proportions of pig iron and scrap iron ranging up to 100 per cent of scrap in some electric arc furnaces. The main sequence of operations in the manufacture of steel is:

1. Mining and transport of iron ore, fuel and other materials, the conversion of coal to coke and coke oven gas, the preparation of sinter for use in blast furnaces and the smelting of iron ore with limestone and coke in blast furnaces to produce molten pig iron.

2. Steel-making furnaces which remove unwanted impurities from the iron and may involve the addition of other metals to form steel alloys. There are three main types of steel-making furnace: open hearth (now largely phased out); basic oxygen in which the oxygen burns with residual carbon in the pig iron; electric arc furnaces.

3. Finishing stages from crude steel to finished or semi-finished products, including soaking pits and rolling mills or forges, or continuous casting processes.

There are wide variations in energy demand per tonne of final steel product, depending on the nature of the product, wastage or recycling of material, and the alloy type. Efficiency improvements often require substantial investment in new *ton of aluminium ≈ 6.7 TOE to produce*

Table 3.5. *Approximate average energy used in the main stages of steel-making in the UK in 1972.*

	Percentage share	Energy, GJ/tonne of finished steel
Coke oven plant	8	3.1
Ore and sinter preparation	5	1.9
Blast furnace plant	35	13.6
Steel-making furnaces	9	3.5
Rolling and finishing	28	10.8
Miscellaneous	15	5.8
Total	100	38.7[a]

[a]Electricity supplied has been converted to primary energy assuming 28 per cent efficiency.
Source: Eden (1974). *about 1½ TOE to produce 1 ton of aluminium*

capital equipment, but in view of the high cost of fuel to the iron and steel industry (in the range of 20 to 25 per cent of total costs), improvements in energy efficiencies have always had a high priority. In the UK, the energy requirements per tonne of product improved at an average rate of about 1.6 per cent per annum in the period 1955 to 1972.

Energy consumption in the non-ferrous metals industry is dominated by the energy used for the production of aluminium. About 4 tonnes of bauxite are required to produce 2 tonnes of alumina (aluminium oxide), which is then dissolved in molten cryolite (aluminium fluoride and sodium fluoride), and reduced by electrolysis to yield 1 tonne of aluminium metal. The energy requirements are dominated by the electricity used in electrolysis, which uses about 65 GJ of electrical energy per tonne of aluminium product. If this electricity was obtained from fossil fuel at 35 per cent conversion efficiency, the primary energy equivalent would be 186 GJ. Combining this with 18 GJ of energy in the carbon anodes used in the electrolysis, 50 GJ for mining and preparation of alumina, and an average of 40 GJ per tonne in the finishing plant (fabricating by rolling, or extrusion) leads to a total primary energy requirement in the region of 294 GJ (6.7 toe) per tonne of aluminium product. However, a substantial fraction of the world aluminium production is obtained from hydropower, often in under-developed regions where the local infrastructure does not provide any alternative major use for electricity. Therefore, the world demand for more than 10 million tonnes of aluminium places a smaller requirement on fossil fuel than is indicated by the above calculation.

The chemicals and petrochemicals industries in both the US and UK use about 15 per cent of the total industrial energy, and an additional 15 per cent if the energy content of petrochemical feedstock is included. Inorganic chemicals production in the UK accounts for about 13 per cent of the total used in the chemicals industry, of which about half goes for the production of chlorine and caustic soda (sodium hydroxide), which are jointly produced by electrolysis of brine and require about 25 GJ of primary energy per tonne of the joint products. Chlorine is used for the manufacture of vinyl chloride, a basic material for plastics production, and for household and industrial bleach. Caustic soda is used in the manufacture of wood pulp and paper, glass and rayon and in the home as an oven cleaner. Another major inorganic chemical is ammonia, which may be manufactured from natural gas (methane), and requires 35 to 40 GJ per tonne including the energy content of the raw material. Ammonia is used extensively in the manufacture of fertilisers.

The major part of the organic chemicals industry is based on derivatives of petroleum and natural gas. It is concerned mainly with the production of intermediate chemical compounds including ethylene, propylene, butadiene, benzene and other hydrocarbons that lead ultimately to plastics, synthetic fibres, synthetic rubber, etc. The energy required for production of these intermediate hydrocarbons ranges from 9 GJ per tonne for ethylene to 31 per tonne for butadiene, to which must be added the energy in the feedstock amounting to about 40 GJ per tonne.

Plastics or synthetic resins are formed by polymerisation. Polymers formed by addition reactions consist of monomer units identical in composition to those from which they are formed. Polymers formed by condensation reactions have structural units from which certain atoms of the original monomers have been removed. Products based on addition reactions include polyethylene, polypropylene and other polyolefins, vinyl resins, styrene resins, and acrylic resins. Those based on condensation reactions include polyester resins and phenolic resins. The energy required for the production of plastics or synthetic resins increases with the complexity of the product measured by the number of reaction stages required for their manufacture. Thus, including direct and indirect energy costs through all stages, the production of polythene requires 84 GJ per tonne, whereas polyester fibres require 203 GJ per tonne, both figures including 40 GJ of feedstock energy. It is important to note, however, that the value added in general increases with the complexity of the product (or number of stages) substantially more than the energy requirements for the product.

Some further aspects of the energy requirements for producing manufactured products will be discussed in relation to interfuel substitution and energy conservation in chapter 12. We turn next to energy consumption in households and in buildings.

3.6   Household and commercial

The share of world commercial energy consumption that is used in households and commercial and government buildings given in table 3.3 amounts to about 20 per cent on a heat supplied basis. If the appropriate fraction of energy used by the energy supply and conversion industries is included, this becomes 31 per cent, and if wood fuel and other non-commercial energy is included it becomes about 36 per cent. In a pre-industrialisation period, most of the energy consumed would be used in dwellings for cooking, heating and lighting and for cottage industries. This share rapidly declines during industrialisation, and, for example, if non-commercial fuel is included, it is believed that about half the energy used in India or China is used in households and other non-industrial buildings. In the UK the corresponding share, 30 per cent on a heat supplied basis in 1950, continued to decline and amounted to only 27 per cent by 1975. In the US, already down to 22 per cent in 1947, the share increased slightly to 24 per cent by 1975. In Japan this share was only 14 per cent in 1972 but is expected to increase as the growth of industrial production slows down.

In the US the use of energy in commercial and public buildings totals about one third of that in households, and in the UK it is about one quarter. The major part of this energy goes to space heating, though air-conditioning of commercial and public buildings in the US provides a substantial part (10 per cent) of electricity demand for the sector. The total energy consumption of the combined household and domestic sector in the US for the period 1947 to 1978 is shown in figure 3.5. The share of this energy from coal declined from 47 per cent in 1947 to only 1.5 per cent in 1975, whilst natural gas increased from 16 to 39 per cent and electricity from 5 to 22 per cent measured on a heat supplied basis. Similar changes in the fuel mix were experienced elsewhere, for example in the UK the share of coal declined from over 80 per cent to about 20 per cent in the same period.

In the UK, total energy demand in the household sector measured on a heat supplied basis remained nearly constant during the period 1950 to 1975 although the number of households increased by nearly 50 per cent in the period, the number of appliances increased and the level of heating increased substantially in much of the housing stock. This implies a major improvement in the efficiency with which energy is used. The main reasons for the improved efficiencies are:
1. Improvements in the efficiency of all types of heating installation.
2. Improved insulation and draught proofing in new dwellings compared with those they replace.
3. Many dwellings have lower ceiling heights than those they replace, thus reducing the volume relative to floor space.
4. Replacement in many dwellings of space heating from low efficiency open fires using solid fuel, by gas fire or electric fires, or by central heating using various fuels or electricity.

It is important to take account of historical improvements in efficiencies, such as those noted above, when making estimates of the potential for energy conservation. Historical trends already contain substantial effects due to interfuel substitution and increasing efficiencies.

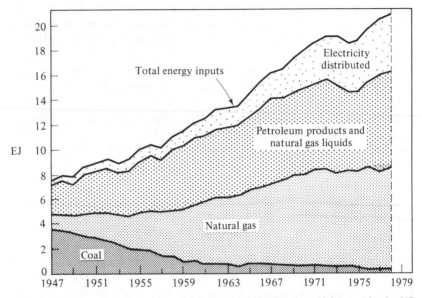

Figure 3.5   Energy demand by fuel in the household and commercial sector in the US 1947–78. *Source:* US Department of the Interior (1976), US Department of Energy (1979). *Note:* During the 1974–78 period, total energy inputs to the household and commercial sectors increased at an annual rate of 3.3 per cent. Total electrical energy consumption to these sectors increased at an annual rate of 8.1 per cent, natural gas consumption at an annual rate of 6.4 per cent, and petroleum products and natural gas liquids increased at an annual rate of 3.9 per cent. Consumption of coal to these sectors declined at an annual rate of 7.7 per cent. In 1978, natural gas consumption constituted 39 per cent of total energy consumed in the household and commercial sector.

The household use of energy by the 19 million households in the UK in 1972 was 1.518 EJ, averaging 80 GJ per household on a heat supplied basis. The manner in which this consumption arose is shown in table 3.6. This shows that 85 per cent of the energy was used for space heating and water heating and it suggests that better insulation could, therefore, lead to further substantial energy conservation in this sector. The use of electricity for 'other' purposes is significant and has increased at a rate averaging more than 5 per cent annually since 1950. It can be seen from table 3.6 that nearly 60 per cent of total electricity in households went to space and water heating, compared with 11 per cent for cooking. More detailed tables show that lighting took about 8 per cent and appliances (TV, refrigerators, kettles, washing machines, irons, freezers, etc.) took the remainder.

In the US there was a total of 67 million occupied dwellings in 1972 which used a total of 12 EJ, or an average of about 180 GJ per dwelling (double the UK average). As in the UK, most of this energy (85 per cent) was consumed for space heating and water heating.

Table 3.6. *Total household energy consumption in the UK by function and fuel type in 1972 (for 19 million households).*

	Space heating	Water heating	Cooking	Other	Total
Solid fuel	568		2	0	570
Oil	159		1	0	160
Gas	376		96	4	476
Electricity	109	74	33	96	312
Total	1286		131	100	1517

Source: Pullin (1977).

Table 3.7. *Energy consumption by fuel in regions of the developing world (OPEC taken separately).*

Energy in exajoules (10^{18} J) 1972	Total primary energy consumption (exajoules (10^{18} J)) 1972					EJ total	Gigajoules per capita
	Coal	Oil	Gas	Wood	Hydro		
OPEC	0.1	3.2	1.6	1.6	0.2	6.7	25
Latin America	0.4	6.7	1.1	1.7	0.9	10.8	38
Middle East and North Africa	0.2	1.8	0	0.5	0.1	2.6	22
Africa south of the Sahara	1.8	1.3	0	4.3	0.2	7.6	32
East Asia	0.5	2.6	0.1	0.9	0.1	4.2	29
South Asia	2.2	1.4	0.2	5.6	0.4	9.8	13
China and centrally planned Asia	8.7	2.2	1.0	9.8	0.4	22.1	25
Total developing	13.9	19.2	4.0	24.4	2.3	63.8	24

Source: Eden *et al.* (1978).

3.7   Developing countries

Throughout the rural areas of the developing world, the primary sources of energy other than food and sunlight are provided by human and animal labour, and by wood fuel and farm waste. These sources barely meet the minimum energy that is required for the necessities of food, warmth and light for those (more than half the world's population) who live in the villages and small towns of Asia, Africa and Latin America. The average per capita use of wood fuel and farm waste is about 10 GJ, or one third of a tonne of coal equivalent for these 'non-commercial' forms of energy (so called because they are not recorded in commercial or governmental statistics, though they are often traded). For 2500 millions, the total use is about 25 EJ, equivalent to nearly 1000 million tonnes of coal or about 8 per cent of the world consumption of all forms of energy. One of the critical questions for the developing world is the manner in which energy demand will change and increase as the population grows to exceed 5000 million soon after the end of the century and as the standard of living improves. In many regions the natural fuels are limited by the need for agricultural land or by depletion of forest areas for wood fuel. The increase in population alone is therefore likely to lead to an increased demand for commercially traded energy to meet the necessities of life. If this is accompanied by industrialisation, and this is certainly widely planned as a basis for improved living standards, it will change the character of energy demand and increase the potential for its growth and dependence on fossil fuels.

There are wide variations in the annual per capita use of energy between different regions of the developing world. Although these variations are illustrated in table 3.7, this understates the extremes which may be as low as 3GJ per capita in rural areas of Africa where wood fuel is scarce and used only for cooking, but could, in the cities of more prosperous regions of the developing world, even be comparable with the annual average of 350 GJ used in the US. Industrialisation and the corresponding growth in the use of energy tends to be associated with urban development, but the growth of commerce and internal trade also leads to an increase in the demand for energy for transportation. In some regions scarcity of wood fuel may lead to an increased demand for fossil fuel, in others the increased use of fossil fuel may be associated with improved standards of living and the greater convenience of its use.

In the poorer rural areas of the Third World energy is mainly used for cooking and heating. In India wood burning stoves are estimated to use 5 to 7 GJ per capita annually, perhaps as much as 80 or 90 per cent for cooking, in areas such as the plain of the Ganges where wood is scarce. This is a larger per capita consumption for cooking than in many industrialised countries where the type of fuel and the cooking equipment give much greater efficiencies. In India it is estimated that when liquefied petroleum gases (LPG) are used for cooking in cities the annual energy consumption drops to one or two giga joules per capita. Industrial equipment is likely to be replaced more slowly in poorer countries and therefore will usually be older and have lower energy efficiencies than similar equipment in more prosperous countries. On the other hand a rapidly developing country would have more modern equipment than in some of the older established industrialised countries.

Energy consumption and the energy outlook in developing countries are discussed further in chapters 14 and 15.

3.8   Chapter summary

Primary energy in the form of fossil fuel, nuclear or hydropower is transported and converted by the energy industries into the forms of secondary energy required by the consumer. It is then used in households for heating, cooking, lighting, etc., for transporting people and goods, and by manufacturing and other industries. A substantial share of the primary energy, 23 per cent in the United States, is used by the conversion industries, the largest part of this being due to losses in electricity generation. A few per cent is used for non-energy purposes – chemical feedstock, road oil and bitumen, and lubricants.

The efficiencies of energy conversion from heat to work and hence to electric power have improved from less than 5 per cent at the start of the century to about 40 per cent in a modern power station. The overall system efficiency is much lower due to the use of older equipment and losses in electrical transmission, being in the region of 28 per cent in the United States. Conversion efficiencies for a variety of devices are illustrated, and range from a few per cent for light from electricity in an incandescent lamp to 99 per cent for conversion of mechanical energy into electricity.

It is important to have an energy accounting system that can conveniently summarise the flow of energy through a national economy from primary fuels through the energy conversion industries to the final consuming sectors. These systems are illustrated by energy balance tables and simple examples are given involving an accounting unit of heat or thermal content in multiples of the standard international unit of energy–the joule. Final sectors of demand are aggregated into: transport, household and commercial, industrial, and non-energy uses, with appropriate allocations to the energy supply and conversion industries.

Energy demand for transportation is dominated by its 56 per cent use for road transport, of which the major part goes to automobiles. Road freight, railroads, and water transport (mainly international) take approximately equal shares of energy used by the sector, and the fastest growing share goes to air transport, now at 8 per cent. North America, Western Europe and the USSR account for over 80 per cent of the energy used for transport, whilst developing countries with over 70 per cent of the world's population use less than 20 per cent of the transportation energy. The use of automobiles is illustrated by the growth of ownership in the US and the UK, neither of which seem to have reached saturation level. The characteristics and the energy efficiencies are briefly described for the main types of engine used in transportation–gasoline, diesel and gas turbine.

The demand for energy by industry arises from the demand for manufactured products, the construction industry, and the service industries. The largest shares are used by the basic industries–iron and steel, and chemicals including petrochemicals, whose products go principally to other industries for further processing before distribution to the final consumer. Energy requirements for these primary products can readily be identified, 36 GJ on average for one tonne of steel, nearly 300 GJ of primary energy for one tonne of aluminium, 25 GJ per tonne for joint production of chlorine and caustic soda, 31 GJ per tonne for butadiene (but 71 GJ if the energy content of the petrochemical feedstock used to manufacture the product is included).

Energy consumption in households is dominated by its use for cooking and heating, for which the main supplies come from oil and gas, though electricity has a significant share of the market in some countries. Other uses for electricity are still growing through increasing ownership of appliances such as colour televisions, refrigerators, freezers and washing machines.

For more than half of the world's population, living in rural areas of Asia, Africa and Latin America, the only available fuel comes from wood and farm waste, and its consumption is limited to essential needs of cooking and heating. The total use of wood fuel and farm waste amounts to about 8 per cent of the total world consumption of primary energy. This fuel is used mainly in slow-burning wood stoves but their energy efficiencies are low compared with the facilities available for cooking in developed regions. In some areas where wood fuel is scarce, the per capita use of fuel may be as low as 3 GJ per year compared with the world average per capita consumption of 75 GJ.

Chapter 3   Further reading

Darmstadter, J., Dunkerley, J. and Alterman, J. (1977) *How industrial societies use energy*, Johns Hopkins University Press, Baltimore and London.

Eden, R. J. *et al.* (1978) 'World energy demand to 2020' in *World energy resources 1985-2020*, World Energy Conference report, IPC Science and Technology Press, Guildford, UK, and New York.

McMullan, J. T., Morgan, R. and Murray, R. B. (1976) *Energy resources and supply*, Wiley, New York and London.

Makhijani, A. and Poole, A. (1975) *Energy and agriculture in the third world*, Ballinger, Cambridge, Mass.

NEDO (1974) *Energy conservation in the United Kingdom*, report prepared by Dr. R. J. Eden for the National Economic Development Office, HMSO, London.

Rose, J. W. and Cooper, J. R. (1977) *Technical data on fuel*, World Energy Conference, and Scottish Academic Press, Edinburgh.

UK Department of Energy (1977b) *Energy balances–some further problems and recent developments, Energy paper no. 19*, HMSO, London.

WAES (1976) *Energy demand studies: major consuming countries*, MIT Press, Cambridge, Mass.

Oil and gas

4.1 Historical background

Oil

Throughout most of its history the oil industry has been strongly influenced by an inherent surplus in production, with more available than is wanted at the current price. In contrast, significant changes have sometimes developed through local, company, or national, fears of scarcity of oil supplies or desire to conserve oil resources, that may be seen as precursors to the world oil crisis that is with us now and is likely to remain a major world problem for many decades.

Oil was discovered in Pennsylvania in 1859 and within a few years it was in widespread use throughout the United States. The producers, weakened by overproduction, were gradually taken over by the refining and distribution companies led by Rockefeller's Standard Oil Trust. Standard Oil dominated the oil industry in the US until, under anti-trust legislation, it was ordered in 1911 to divest itself of all its subsidiaries. Of the 38 companies in the group, three, in particular, developed to take a major part in the world oil market. These are Exxon (formerly Standard Oil of New Jersey, or Esso), Mobil (developed from Standard Oil of New York), and Socal (Standard Oil of California). Together with four other companies, two American (Gulf and Texaco) and two European (Shell and BP), these dominated the world oil scene throughout the first half of this century, and they continue to form a substantial part of the industry. In 1950 they were responsible for over 80 per cent (165 million tonnes) of the oil production in the non-communist areas of the world outside the United States, and as late as 1969 they still retained over 70 per cent (900 million tonnes) of this production (Adelman 1972).

The influence of these seven major oil companies (the 'seven sisters') on the world oil scene has been widely discussed (Adelman 1972, Frankel 1946, Hartshorn 1967, Penrose 1968, Sampson 1975). During the 1920s and 1930s there was a period of intense competition, with the threat of overproduction aggravated by new discoveries and by a fall in demand during the economic depression. In the United States the discovery of the East Texas oilfield at the start of the depression produced a new glut of oil unwelcome to the big companies and to the many small producers. Prices fell in a chaotic market, until the State intervened with the establishment of the Texas Railroad Commission, which introduced a system of 'prorationing', whereby demand in any one month was shared amongst producers using a quota based on a number of days' production.

On the international scene, the discovery and development of oil in Mexico, Venezuela, Sumatra, and Iran (Persia), together with supplies from the US and the USSR, led to the threat of overproduction. The major international oil companies led by Exxon, Shell and BP developed in 1928 a secret agreement (not fully revealed until 1952) to accept their current volumes of business, to decide jointly the shares in future increases in production, and to restrict competition in the provision of new oil supply facilities (Sampson, 1975). The resulting cartel continued until it was terminated by anti-trust action in the 1940s in the United States, but cooperation between oil companies remained an important factor in international trade in oil.

Throughout this period the prices paid for crude oil were determined by negotiation between oil companies and governments in producing countries. This procedure continued into the 1960s, but by that time the continuing discovery and development of large low cost oil supplies in the Middle East had led to a post-war decline in the price paid to producing countries. In an attempt to halt this decline a group of producing countries, whose GNP was substantially dependent on oil income, formed OPEC, the Organisation of Petroleum Exporting Countries. The foundation of OPEC in 1960 was seen as a defensive measure by the producers following a unilateral reduction by Exxon of the posted price they would pay for their supplies of Middle East crude oil, which was followed (reluctantly by some) by other major oil companies. The five founder members of OPEC (see table 4.1) were at that time responsible for 80 per cent of internationally traded crude oil.

After the foundation of OPEC, the oil companies continued to negotiate prices directly with each producer country. However, in 1964, OPEC was able to negotiate an additional royalty payment (of 4 cents a barrel) to each producer country. Meanwhile new fields were discovered and developed in the Middle East, and the diversification of sources of supply, as production increased in new oil countries, meant a slower increase and possible cut-back in oil from existing producers.

Intervention by governments in the activities of oil companies in their countries had begun dramatically in Mexico in 1938, when all operating companies in that country were nationalised, following their refusal to accept instructions to provide improved conditions for workers in the oilfields. The new national oil company PEMEX was boycotted by major consumer countries and eventually paid the expropriated companies substantial compensation. Much earlier, in 1913, the British government had taken control of BP (then Anglo Persian) by providing additional finance in exchange for 51 per cent of the shares, but this was an action by Churchill to ensure oil supplies for the UK navy, and it has rarely involved any intervention in the company's commercial management. In 1938, under threat of nationalisation, Venezuela, then a major exporter, obliged the major companies

Table 4.1   *Members of OPEC (1979) (*founders in 1960).*

Algeria	Libya
Ecuador	Nigeria
Gabon	Qatar
Indonesia	*Saudi Arabia
*Iran	United Arab Emirates
*Iraq	*Venezuela
*Kuwait	

(Exxon, Shell, Gulf) to increase their royalty payments, and ten years later in 1948 it successfully implemented a law giving the Venezuelan government a 50 per cent share in all profits. This profit-sharing arrangement was soon demanded elsewhere and in the 1950s and 1960s it was adopted in most oil producing countries. The financial arrangements were somewhat complicated as profits were calculated from a (nominal) 'posted price' for oil that was agreed by companies and governments. The payments to host governments out of company profits were tax deductible in the company's country of origin, and the actual price paid for oil was often below the posted price.

The weakening relations between the major oil companies and the host governments of the countries where they operated assisted the entry of new companies into oil production and international marketing. These included the French company CFP, the Italian State Oil Company, and companies from Japan, Belgium, and elsewhere. As total world oil production grew at a rate of 7 per cent per annum throughout the 1950s and 1960s, new firms could enter the market without any absolute reduction in the oil lifted by the majors although their percentage shares declined.

In 1973 the world oil outlook changed dramatically, following an embargo imposed by the Arab members of OPEC on countries that they believed were providing assistance to Israel at the time of the (1973) October war between Israel and her neighbours. By coincidence, when the war began, representatives of the oil companies, led by Piercy of Exxon, were meeting representatives of OPEC, led by Sheik Yamani of Saudi Arabia, to negotiate an increase in the posted price of oil. They failed to reach agreement, and, later in October, OPEC ministers meeting in Kuwait decided to raise the price of oil unilaterally from $3.00 to $5.12. This price refers to the so-called 'marker crude', which is Saudi Arabia light oil f.o.b. from Ras Tanura in the Persian Gulf; the prices of other oils from other sources are adjusted in relation to the price of 'marker crude', with some degree of variation that depends on market conditions.

The day following this OPEC price rise in October 1973, the Arab members (OAPEC) agreed an immediate 5 per cent reduction in oil production and agreed further reductions and selective cuts in supplies unless there was an Israeli withdrawal. The latter objective was not achieved but due to the reduction in supplies coupled with frictional problems in the market, which failed to adjust rapidly enough to local scarcities, the price of oil rose rapidly on the spot oil market in Rotterdam to more than $20 a barrel, and Iran obtained bids up to $17 in an oil auction in December 1973. Shortly after this OPEC increased the oil price to $11.65 per barrel, giving a five-fold increase over the price two years earlier. After that the price declined gradually in real terms, due to inflation and the fall in the US dollar relative to other currencies, until late in 1978, when once again the spot market rose, this time in response to local scarcities consequent on the interruption of Iran's oil production. Following the lead from the spot market, OPEC began to move posted prices upwards again. Further sudden adjustments can be expected: the demand for oil is inelastic in the short term, and substitutes for conventional oil involve long lead times. The critical issues which we shall discuss later in this chapter and in other chapters, include the possible extent and circumstances of future increases in the price of oil, and the impact that they may have on world economic growth.

During the period from 1859 to 1890, United States oil production increased from zero to more than 3 million tonnes per annum (mt p.a.), and by 1920 it was nearly 60 mt p.a. Peak production came in 1970 at 475 mt p.a., but US consumption continued to increase so that US oil imports are now a major factor in the world oil market. World oil production now amounts to about 2,500 mt p.a. in the WOCA (world outside communist areas), and about 650 mt p.a. in communist areas. The world oil production pattern since 1940 is summarised in table 4.2.

Natural gas

Natural gas was discovered in the United States about the same time as oil and by the year 1900 nearly 6 mtoe (million tonnes of oil equivalent) was being produced annually. Production increased at an average rate of about 7 per cent per annum until, by 1970, 564 mtoe was being produced (1 mtoe is approximately equivalent to 1.2×10^9 m^3 natural gas). Worldwide the development of natural gas was restricted to local or regional requirements, limited by the accessibility by pipeline until the development of trade using LNG (liquefied natural gas) tankers in the 1960s. The cost of such shipments is high and this has restricted the growth in LNG trade. World consumption (approximately equal to production) of natural gas is summarised in table 4.3. There is considerable potential for future trade in natural gas, particularly by drawing from the large reserves known to exist in the Middle East.

The next sections of this chapter are concerned with the main features of the technology of oil and gas production, and estimation of reserves and resources. The chapter concludes with a discussion of prospects for oil and gas and some comments relating to the oil and gas market.

Table 4.2 *World oil production by region 1940–75.*

	1940		1960		1975	
World region	mt	(%)	mt	(%)	mt	(%)
North America	184	(73)	374	(43)	483	(24)
West Europe	1	(0)	14	(2)	26	(1)
Middle East	14	(6)	262	(30)	965	(47)
Africa	1	(0)	14	(2)	244	(12)
Asia (Pacific)	11	(4)	27	(3)	109	(5)
Latin America	42	(17)	184	(21)	211	(10)
Total WOCA	253	(100)	875	(100)	2038	(100)
Communist areas	40[a]	–	161	–	583	–
World total	293[a]	–	1036	–	2621	–

[a] Author's estimate.
Source: Petroleum Publishing Company (1976).

Table 4.3 *World natural gas consumption by region 1960, 1978.*

World region	1960 mtoe	1978 mtoe
North America	332	552
Western Europe	10	179
Rest WOCA	21	123
WOCA total	363	854
Communist areas	50	387
World total	413	1241

Source: British Petroleum (1978b).

4.2 Origins of oil and gas

Oil and gas are names given to a wide variety of hydrocarbons found in sedimentary basins on or under the earth's surface. Gas is generally a mixture of the lighter hydrocarbons with methane (CH_4) predominating, often with varying fractions of nitrogen and impurities such as hydrogen sulphide. Oil or petroleum is a complex mixture of the heavier (non-gaseous) hydrocarbons, averaging about two atoms of hydrogen to each carbon atom (compared to nearly four for gas). Oil found in different reservoirs differs in composition, and may even vary within a single reservoir. Its properties vary from a light fluid to viscous heavy oil, grading to asphalt.

The process of oil formation started with the mixing of marine organisms with sand and silt to form sedimentary deposits, in periods ranging from tens of millions to hundreds of millions of years ago. Continued deposits of material led to burial, with a concomitant rise in pressure and temperature, resulting in compaction of the sediment into sedimentary rock, called the 'source rock', and conversion of the organic material into hydrocarbons (oil) embedded in the source rock. Increasing pressure from continued burial, together with the movement of water, with which rock below the water table is saturated, resulted in movement of the small oil globules into the more porous and permeable environment of reservoir rocks. In some situations the oil became trapped in the reservoir rocks by a neighbouring layer of impermeable rock, and these oil-bearing reservoir rocks are the sources from which oil is now obtained.

On the microscopic scale, a reservoir rock consists of a collection of similar sized grains, often embedded in a matrix of smaller grains and cemented together by a deposit of clay. The pores between the grains contain (usually salty) water, which wets the surface of all the grains. In an oil pool some of the pore space is occupied by oil, gas or a gas/oil solution, but some water (with which they are immiscible) is always present as a film on the rock grains (see fig. 4.1).

Many types of geological structure can give rise to possible traps for oil, and three types are illustrated in figure 4.2. The first, called an anticline trap, is in the form of a dome, in which gas, oil and water are held within the reservoir rock overlain by a layer of impermeable rock that prevents the oil and gas, more buoyant than the underlying water, from escaping to the surface. The second type, figure 4.2(b) is called a fault trap, and may occur where impermeable rock at a fault in the strata of reservoir rocks prevents upward movement of oil. In the third type shown in figure 4.2(c) the reservoir rock changes in permeability so that further movement of oil through the pores of the reservoir rock becomes impossible.

To summarise: hydrocarbons are generated in source rocks from the remains of marine organisms deposited and buried in the rocks. They are transported by surface tension, gravitational and pressure forces into reservoir rocks, where, if there are suitable traps, they accumulate in the pores of the rock and form the reservoirs of oil and gas found today. For oil to be formed within the source rocks, they must have been buried for a million years or more at depths over 1 km, to get the pressure and temperature high enough, but rarely more than about 4 km, or the higher temperature at those depths would usually decompose the oil, leaving methane gas and petroleum coke.

4.3   Exploration and production

The first oil wells were only a few tens to hundreds of metres deep, but exploration drilling has steadily gone deeper. Most accumulations lie in the depth range 500 to 3000 metres, but the deepest producing wells are at 6500 m for oil and 7500 for gas. Similarly, variations in pressure from atmospheric to about 1000 atmospheres

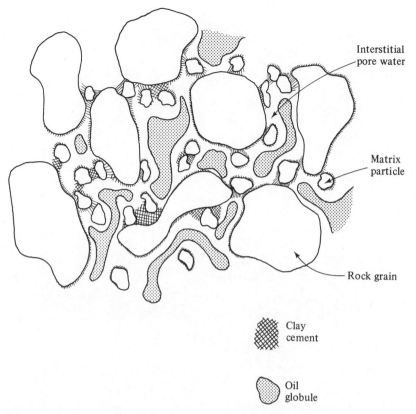

Interstitial pore water

Matrix particle

Rock grain

Clay cement

Oil globule

Figure 4.1   Schematic diagram of reservoir rock containing oil

have been found, although the pressure usually increases by 100 to 150 atmospheres per km in depth corresponding to the weight of the overlying column of rock pore water. Temperature also increases with depth at a rate given by the geothermal gradient, generally in the range 15 to 40° C per km in oil producing areas, though temperatures in oil reservoirs (i.e. in reservoir rocks) are usually below 110° C.

The production of conventional oil depends on the reservoir fluids flowing under pressure out of the reservoir rock into the borehole. The character of this flow is influenced by the nature of the reservoir rock (its grain size, porosity, etc.) by the viscosity of the fluids, and by the pressure in the reservoir. The viscosity of oil is reduced by increases in the pressure, temperature, and the amount of gas dissolved in the oil. Light oils can have very low viscosity (even lower than water), and the viscosity increases with the density of the oil up to the heavy bituminous oils which are solid at ambient surface temperatures. The relative flow rates of oil and water

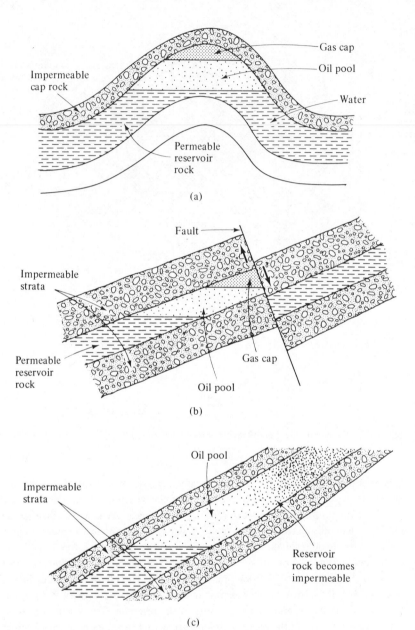

Figure 4.2 Examples of types of oil trap: (a) Anticline. (b) Fault (c) Variable permeability.

in the reservoir rock depend on their relative densities in the mixture, on their viscosities, and on the amount of dissolved gas. It is quite possible for the water flow rate to exceed the oil flow rate even though water constitutes less than 30–50 per cent of the fluid present in the rock. In practice, oil–water mixtures are a common feature of oil production. One of the important constraints on the rate at which oil is allowed to flow in a well is provided by the need to prevent increasing quantities of gas and water moving into the reservoir rock near the well thus displacing the oil. Another requirement is the maintenance of the pressure in the reservoir rock near the borehole, and this will drop if the flow rate is too fast, and again this may increase the possibility of gas or water displacing oil.

Early exploration for oil was concentrated in the neighbourhood of oil seepages that showed on the surface. Subsequently, it moved on to a search for geological structures, in potential oil areas, that might give rise to traps. Initially this was done by geological surveys, measuring the angles of tilt of the rock strata that emerged at the surface, and correlating with the results of drilling where these were available, to attempt to delineate the layout of the rock strata underground. These techniques have now been augmented by the introduction of seismic surveying. The basic method involves the generation of an acoustic signal on the earth's surface, for example by a small explosion, and measurement of the pattern of reflections from successively deeper layers of rock as the reflected sound arrives at a number of detectors on the surface. From this pattern, using a series of observations, it is possible to obtain quite detailed information about the overall contours of the rock layers or strata, and identify faults in them or other possible oil traps. Seismic surveying on land can be slow, since the shots have to be fired in shallow boreholes, but at sea they can be done rapidly from the surface, and detected by stringing out a series of microphones behind a moving ship. Although seismic surveys are the mainstay of exploration efforts, other methods are also used, including: geomagnetic and gravitational surveys, geochemical tests for the hydrocarbon content of rocks, geothermal, radiation and electrical conductivity surveys.

These exploration methods allow the identification of structure that may be traps but they can only rarely establish the presence of oil and gas. In order to determine whether possible traps actually contain hydrocarbons, and to find the properties and extent of any oil in them, it is necessary to drill into the structure to allow measurements at depth, and to take samples. Standard well logs now include physical (temperature and pressure) measurements, together with electrical (conductivity) and nuclear (neutron reflection) measurements, even if the wells turn out to be 'dry' (containing no oil or gas). In addition, a continuous log is kept of rock chipping produced, and, in especially interesting regions, core samples may be taken.

The basic method of drilling is standard, though there are wide variations of detail. A tower structure is required so that the lengths of drill pipe may be handled vertically. The drill pipe (called the 'string') itself is a hollow steel tube, screwed together in lengths, with a drilling bit at the bottom. It is generally rotated from the surface, and pressure applied to the drilling bit by allowing it to bear all or part of the weight of the drilling 'string'. A fluid called drilling mud is pumped down the middle of the drill pipe, and returns up the borehole. It acts as a lubricant and coolant for the bit, and carries away the rock chippings generated by the drilling. It also provides a sealant for the borehole (it forms a cake on the walls of the hole and prevents the loss of the rest of the mud into permeable strata), and as a pressure maintenance device (by adjusting its density), so as to prevent a blow-out if oil or water under high pressure is discovered. In addition the mud is designed so that it gels when the drilling is stopped, thus preventing the rock chippings from collecting at the bottom of the borehole.

The assessment of an oil or gas accumulation develops through a series of stages, beginning from the seismic survey that indicates a trap, and the extent of the volume of the rock structures beneath the trap that might contain hydrocarbons. In practice most possible structures will extend through several strata. A single successful exploration well will locate the depth and thickness of the reservoir (at one location), and details of the saturation of the reservoir rock with oil and gas, some details of its chemical composition, and reservoir conditions such as porosity, temperature and pressure.

This information can be extended and confirmed by allowing oil to flow for a period from the well, though this leaves considerable uncertainty and additional wells are usually required to determine the probable extent of the oil reservoir. After a well is brought into production, further measurements over a period of time will increase the accuracy with which the 'recovery factor' can be estimated. This is defined as the ratio of the amount of oil expected to be recovered, to the total amount of 'oil in place' in the reservoir rocks. Initial production from a well is normally nearly constant for a period ranging from a few days to years. Thereafter the production rate declines as the pressure drops and the oil has to move further through the reservoir rocks to reach the borehole.

Reserves to production ratio (R/P)

Oil is driven from the reservoir rocks into the borehole by the difference in pressure. This pressure difference can be controlled by 'choking' the flow of oil from the borehole, and is usually limited in order to improve the recovery factor. If the pressure in the borehole is too low compared with that in the reservoir rock, there is a risk that gas dissolved in the oil will start to come out of solution and flow from the well at a faster rate. This would reduce the amount of gas dissolved in the oil and hence increase its viscosity, thus making it more difficult to extract and decreasing the recovery factor. Adverse effects from too rapid depletion can also arise from lack of uniformity in the reservoir rocks that may leave pockets of oil that are bypassed by gas or water flows.

The rate of production from any well is therefore limited. The production rate from a reservoir can be increased by drilling a number of production wells, but their number is limited by their cost compared with the extra rate of flow of oil. In a similar way, production from an oil field is limited (a field is a group of reservoirs in the same area). As production wells are drilled, the production from a field will rise to a maximum rate, perhaps in three years or so, and remain at this rate (with further wells being drilled) for a period that may last from 5 to about 20 years. After this the rate of production of oil begins to fall as the amount of oil remaining in the field declines.

A measure of the rate of production from a reservoir (or set of reservoirs) is the *reserves to production ratio* (R/P) measured in years, which is defined as the ratio of total remaining reserves divided by the yearly production (reserves are discussed in the next section). Generally the R/P ratio starts high early in the life of a reservoir, and as the reservoir is depleted the R/P ratio decreases, production being held at its maximum value. At a later stage production starts to decline and R/P tends to become constant in the range from 5 to about 15 years.

4.4   Oil reserves and resources

Recovery factor

An assessment of the amount of oil that may be recovered from a reservoir requires information on the amount of *oil in place* and an estimate of the *recovery factor*. The amount that can be extracted is related to the conditions in the reservoir, the composition of the oil, and the method by which it is extracted (the type of 'drive mechanism' that is used).

The types of recovery include gas or water drive and various enhanced recovery methods. In gas drive, as the oil flows into and up the borehole the pressure in the reservoir begins to drop and gas starts to come out of solution in the oil. The gas may flow out of the well with the oil ('associated production'), or it may remain in the reservoir and form a gas cap above the oil. In the latter case this gas cap helps to maintain the pressure that drives oil from the well, the technique known as 'gas drive'. When water can flow (from below) into the reservoir, it will replace the oil as it flows into the borehole, and also helps to maintain the pressure; this is known as 'water drive'. In practice, gas drive alone may recover only 5 to 15 or 20 per cent of the oil in place. More commonly, a combination of gas and water drive will contribute, and the recovery factor may range from 5 per cent with heavy oil up to 80 per cent from light oil in a reservoir with rocks that have high permeability.

Recovery is often assisted by pumping water into the reservoir below the oil in order to help maintain the pressure that provides the drive. Another method of 'secondary' or 'enhanced' recovery in common use reinjects gas that is extracted with the oil. Other enhanced recovery methods that are more expensive to operate, but may become more widely used as the real price of oil increases, include: hot water injection, solvent injection, and steam injection.

Reserves and resources

At present the world average for the recovery factor is estimated to be between 25 or 30 per cent, so less than one third of the oil in place in existing oil fields is available for use. In any reservoir, the *proven reserves* are defined as the quantity of oil that can be commercially produced with existing technology. Thus the proven reserves are equal to the quantity of oil in place multiplied by the recovery factor. At present the total world proved reserves (including the USSR and China) amount to about 600×10^9 barrels (bbl) (8.5×10^9 toe). It is often suggested (but by no means established) that the use of more expensive enhanced recovery methods could raise the average recovery factor from its present value of less than 30 per cent to 40 per cent by the year 2000. This would increase the amount of oil that could be obtained from existing fields to more than 800×10^9 bbl.

Estimates of possible world oil resources include: existing proven reserves, extensions to existing oil fields, increases due to enhanced recovery, and estimates of the possible recoverable oil in undiscovered fields that may eventually be discovered (or found by some stated date). Most of the sedimentary basins where oil may be found have been identified, and many of them have been partially explored. An estimate of possible world oil resources can be made by assigning a probability distribution of reservoir sizes in each sedimentary basin, taking into account any information about each basin that is known, and relating the basin by analogy to well-explored basins.

An example of the distribution of reservoir or field sizes, which corresponds approximately to oil fields in the US (a well-explored region) is given by the formula.

$$S_N = S_1 N^{-3/4}$$

where

S_N = size of the field of rank N

S_1 = size of the largest field (about 7×10^9 bbl in the US)

N = rank of field, when the fields are numbered in order of size (largest equals 1, next largest equals 2, etc.)

The total reserves C_N available in the largest N fields are then

$$C_N = \sum_{n=1}^{N} S_1 n^{-3/4} \simeq S_1(4N^{1/4} - 3.4) \quad \text{(for } N \gtrsim 5\text{)}.$$

However,

$$N = (S_1/S_N)^{4/3}, \quad \text{so}$$
$$C_N \simeq S_1[4(S_1/S_N)^{1/3} - 3.4]$$
$$= 4S_1^{4/3} S_N^{-1/3} - 3.4 S_1.$$

This formula should *not* be extrapolated to very large values of N, since the size S_N of the smallest field (and hence N) is determined by economic and geological conditions. With this proviso, the total reserves estimated for a basin is insensitive to the size chosen for S_N. For example if the size S_N of the smallest viable field is halved the estimate of total reserves increases only by 26 per cent.

Estimates of remaining reserves in a well explored region like the US can also be made by extrapolating the past history of finding rates, or alternatively of drilling success rates. The finding rate extrapolation may be done in two ways. The first is to plot year by year the change in proved reserves plus total oil produced. The resulting curve is extremely peaky, but fitting it by a smooth function suggests that the finding rate for the US (excluding Alaska) reaches a peak in about 1957 and decreases thereafter. This method has the disadvantage that in the past, fields were rarely fully explored before production commenced, so the reserves at the time of discovery were considerably underestimated (the estimation of proven reserves also depends on legal requirements which vary from country to country). The second discovery rate method overcomes this difficulty (and possibly overcompensates) by crediting back to the year of discovery of a field all the reserves subsequently proved. When this is done, the resultant discovery curve for the coterminous US is seen to have peaked in the period 1935–40.

Estimates for ultimately recoverable world oil resources have recently been assessed through a Delphi poll carried out for the World Energy Conference by Desprairies (1977). The questionnaire was based on oil recovery technologies that would be available if the oil price rose to $20 (1976 US dollars) by the year 2000. The results (excluding 3.30×10^9 bbl already produced by 1977) for total remaining recoverable resources average 1900×10^9 bbl, with a probable range between 1280×10^9 and 2560×10^9 bbl. These figures include existing proved reserves at 600×10^9 bbl, further increases in reserves figures for existing fields due to improved information about them and due to improved recovery factors, and estimated future new discoveries of conventional oil reserves. The average figure of 1900×10^9 bbl was estimated to be distributed amongst world regions as in table 4.4.

WAES (1977a) lists 19 estimates for ultimate resources made between 1942 and 1975, which are reproduced in table 4.5. The 11 most recent (made between 1958 and 1975) lie within the range 1280 to 2560 billion barrels given by Desprairies. The consistency of these estimates suggests that it is most unlikely the oil crisis will go away due to unexpected large new discoveries. This view is reinforced by historical evidence on additions to proven reserves, and it is important to emphasise that, from the viewpoint of actual or potential production, it is additions to *proven* reserves that are most important. In section 4.6 we will therefore consider the question of expected annual addition to proven reserves and their relation to annual consumption.

4.5 Unconventional oil

First, however, it should be observed that the figures in table 4.4 refer to conventional oil resources, and do not include unconventional oil such as heavy oil deposits, tar sands and shale oil. The extent of these potential resources is thought

Table 4.4 *Mean values of estimates for ultimately recoverable world resources of oil, based on Delphi poll.*

	Percentage of world	10^9 bbl	10^9 tonnes
North America	11	210	29
Western Europe	4.5	85	12
Middle East and North Africa	42	800	107
Africa south of the Sahara	4.5	85	12
Latin America	9	170	24
South and East Asia	6	115	18
Communist areas (USSR, China, etc.)	23	435	59
World total	100	1900	260

Source: Desprairies (1977).

Table 4.5 *Estimates of ultimate world resources of conventional oil.*

Year of estimate	Source	In 10^9 barrels
1942	Pratt, Weeks and Stebinger	600
1946	Duce	400
1946	Pogue	555
1948	Weeks	610
1949	Levorsen	1500
1949	Weeks	1010
1953	MacNaughton	1000
1956	Hubbert	1250
1958	Weeks	1500
1959	Weeks	2000
1965	Hendricks (USGS)	2480
1967	Ryman (ESSO)	2090
1968	Shell	1800
1968	Weeks	2200
1969	Hubbert	1350–2100
1970	Moody (MOBIL)	1800
1971	Warman (BP)	1200–2000
1972	Weeks	2290
1975	Moody and Geiger	2000
1977	Desprairies (WEC Delphi)	1280–2560

to be very large and illustrative estimates are given in tables 4.6 and 4.7. It seems likely that during the next century unconventional oil resources will yield quantities of oil comparable with those from conventional oil this century. The average costs of production would, however, be considerably higher, probably near or somewhat

Table 4.6   *Tar sands and heavy oil resources in place.*

Tar sands and heavy oil resources in place	10^9 bbl
Venezuela	
(Orinoco)	700
Canada	
(Athabasca)	600
(Other)	320
USSR	
(Olenek)	600
USA	27
Total probable resources in place	2247

Note: Recovery factor is estimated to be in the range 10–50 per cent.
Source: Sande, in an appendix to Desprairies (1977).

Table 4.7   *Reported recoverable oil from oil shale.*

Reported recoverable oil from oil shale	10^9 bbl
USA	1100
China	160
USSR	26
Europe	22
Rest of world	18
Total probable resource	1326

Note: In addition to these reported resources, speculative resource estimates for shale oil in the USA suggest figures up to $20,000 \times 10^9$ bbl.
Source: Roberts, in an appendix to Desprairies (1977).

above the upper limit of $20 (1976 prices) used by Desprairies in the WEC Delphi poll on conventional oil resources. If we take the median figure of 1900 billion barrels for conventional oil and assume that a similar quantity of unconventional oil could be obtained over the next 120 years, the total of 3800 billion barrels shows that oil supplies could be available at current production levels (22 billion annually) for more than 150 years. The oil crisis has arisen and will continue because oil production cannot readily increase very far beyond present levels; the basis for this will be described in the next section. This means that future growth must be based on higher cost energy to supplement continuing but more expensive oil supplies.

The worldwide inventory for unconventional oil resources is not well known, because many of the deposits are not economic at today's prices and with known technologies. The figures in tables 4.6 and 4.7 should therefore be treated with caution, particularly in relation to estimates for recovery factors which will depend on technologies not yet developed.

Tar sands and heavy oil

Tar sands and heavy oils range from bitumens that cannot flow at normal ambient temperatures to heavy oils that can. In both cases the petroleum is of low quality in that the lighter hydrocarbons are missing. Bitumens usually have specific gravity heavier than water, or less than 10° on the API scale.* Heavy oils are mostly in the range 10° to 20° API.

The bitumen content of tar sand suitable for production normally lies between 10 and 20 per cent by weight, the balance consisting of about 5 per cent water and 75 to 85 per cent sand and clay. The mineable area in the Athabasca tar sands deposits in Canada has an overburden 20 ft to 120 ft in thickness – mainly glacial drift, consisting of water saturated sands and clays supporting swampy scrubland called muskeg. Two methods for removing the overburden and mining are currently in use, one using draglines carrying very large buckets with a capacity of 80 cubic yards; the other using bulldozers and trucks for overburden removal and bucket wheel excavators for mining the tar sands. During winter months mining must proceed faster than frost penetration since frozen tar sands have the consistency of concrete and would require blasting before excavation. The oil is extracted by a process using hot water and is upgraded by coking and hydrogenation to give a high quality synthetic crude oil. About 15 tons of tar sands are required to produce 1.2 tons of heavy oil, which after processing yields 1 ton of high quality (35° API) crude oil together with sand, gas, coke and sulphur. Thus the production of 125,000 barrels a day requires the processing of about one quarter of a million tons of tar sand each day, or 92 million tons a year. Investment costs amount to about $20,000 for one barrel a day (1976 dollars), or about twice those for North Sea oil. Extensive work is in progress for developing underground mining for oil from the Canadian tar sands. This would not only considerably increase the resource base but it may eventually lead to oil at a lower cost than from surface mining.

The Orinoco heavy oil deposits in Venezuela have not yet been developed on a commercial scale. It is believed that considerable quantities could be extracted by drilling a large number of conventional wells, possibly using steam to assist recovery. The resulting heavy oil does not flow at ambient temperatures and contains a high fraction of heavy metal impurities. It would require upgrading and processing and the overall costs are likely to be high compared with production costs for conventional oil in Venezuela, though possibly lower than those for oil from Canadian tar sands.

---

* The API scale is a measure that roughly indicates the quality of petroleum in which lighter fractions rate more highly than heavy fractions. 10° API corresponds to a specific gravity of 1.00, equal to that of water at 60° F, 25.7° API corresponds to 0.90 specific gravity, 45.4° API to 0.80, 70.6° API to 0.70, and 104.3° API to 0.60.

Shale oil

Estimates for shale oil resources are illustrated in table 4.7. An absolute limit on feasible extraction is set by the energy required to remove the oil from the shale and upgrade it – this gives a minimum richness of about 4 per cent by weight which compares with about 10 per cent for deposits currently under study for possible commercial extraction.

Oil shales consist of highly compressed clays that split readily into planes, containing organic minerals of high molecular weight and variable composition generally known as kerogen. Some also contain extensive impurities such as the heavy metals in black shale. Kerogen is not soluble in organic solvents but can be extracted from the shale by heating. The conventional exploitation of shale involves four phases: extraction from a mine, crushing the ore, heating in a retort to extract oil from the ore and to recover the gas produced, and upgrading the resulting oil by distillation and hydrogenation. Finally, the retorted shale must be disposed of, its quantity being more than 10 times (by weight) the amount of oil produced and somewhat larger in volume than the amount of ore extracted.

The principal obstacles to conventional surface retorting of shale are its high cost, the energy consumed, the consumption of water (in regions with water scarcity, as for the US deposits), and the disposal of the waste products. In-situ combustion would reduce the problems of water and waste disposal, but this has not yet been developed sufficiently for commercial operation.

4.6   Prospects for oil

World proven reserves of oil are currently about 600×10^9 bbl compared with annual production of about 22×10^9 bbl. Thus the world R/P ratio is 27 years. Since annual additions to proven reserves are on average less than annual consumption, and oil consumption is still increasing, the R/P ratio is falling. In a single oil reservoir, in order to maintain the pressure in the producing wells, it is necessary to limit the flow, so that yearly production rarely exceeds about 10 per cent of remaining proven reserves. This sets a lower limit of 10 (years) for the R/P ratio, but world wide there are many fields that are in earlier stages of development and have much higher R/P ratios, and on average it can be expected that technical considerations would limit the world R/P ratio to be greater than 15. This consideration was used by WAES (1977a) to estimate the potential (technical) maximum world production profile for oil, using a method which we will briefly outline.

It is assumed that the maximum production is set by an R/P ratio of 15. As long as oil demand is below this limit, actual production will equal demand, but when this limit is reached potential production, equal to $(1/15)$ times reserves, will determine the maximum consumption. Thus it is possible to project a maximum world oil supply profile based on the following factors:

1. Proven reserves $R(O)$ at the end of a base year.

2. An estimate $A(n)$ of future gross annual additions to reserves in the year n.

3. An assumption of a limiting R/P ratio, which we take to be 15 years.

4. An estimate of future oil demand $D(n)$ in year n from the base year.

At the end of year N, the proven reserves $R(N)$ will be given by

$$R(N) = R(O) + \sum_{n=1}^{N} A(n) - \sum_{n=1}^{N} D(n) \qquad (4.1)$$

and we require R/P to exceed 15, hence in year N

$$D(N + 1) = P(N + 1) \le R(N)/15. \qquad (4.2)$$

Initially $D(n)$ may be assumed to increase exponentially, and for illustration we choose an average annual growth 3 per cent (compared with 7 per cent before 1973), so

$$D(n) = D(O) (1 + 0.03)^n. \qquad (4.3)$$

The average annual additions to proved reserves of oil in WOCA, using a five-year average (with supplemental discoveries backdated to the year of a field discovery) varied between 15 and 23 $\times$ 10^9 bbl in the period 1945–75. We will assume a constant figure of 18 $\times$ 10^9 bbl, representing both new discoveries and re-evaluations of oil fields (including enhanced recovery). Taking 1977 as the base year ($N = 0$), when proved reserves of oil in the WOCA were 500 $\times$ 10^9 bbl, and the total demand for oil $D(O)$ was 18 $\times$ 10^9 bbl, we obtain the maximum potential oil production profile shown in figure 4.3. With these assumptions the production of oil could increase exponentially following demand only until the year 1992, when demand would be 28 $\times$ 10^9 bbl (or 78 million barrels a day - mbd). Thereafter demand would be constrained to equal production, which would be $(1/15)$ times the declining reserves $R(n)$.

The idealised WOCA oil production profile shown in figure 4.3 does not take into account the policy constraints that may be applied by major oil producers, or political crises such as that in Iran in 1979, but it illustrates an important feature that will be taken into account as these policies are formulated and revised, namely that within a decade or two world oil production would be constrained to decline on technical grounds alone. In practice, it is to be expected that the potential scarcity of oil, implied by the peak in 1992 of the production profile in figure 4.3, will be anticipated, for example, by increases in the price of oil, so that the growth in oil demand slows down at an earlier date. The future decline in potential oil production also emphasises to the main producing countries the fragility and impermanence of their dependence on oil exports for their economic growth, and is leading to a re-assessment of their production and development policies.

The currently proven reserves and the R/P ratios are shown in table 4.8 for major world regions or groups of countries. More than one third of the world proven oil reserves, or 50 per cent of WOCA reserves, have been found in the Arabian peninsula in countries such as Saudi Arabia, Kuwait and the United Arab Emirates, where populations are small compared to oil production, and development plans require less income than is obtained from their current production. At

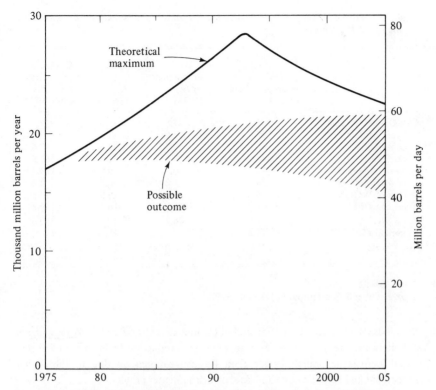

Figure 4.3   WOCA maximum potential oil production (see text for assumptions).

the same time governments in these countries are becoming increasingly aware of
the need to conserve their oil resources and income for future generations. If
countries in the Arabian peninsula or elsewhere were to limit their production more
severely than is implied by results from our model in figure 4.3 the production
profile (for conventional oil) could be near that shown by the shaded area in figure
4.3. The adjustment of oil demand to meet this lower production profile would take
place through a response to higher oil prices leading to conservation, interfuel
substitution away from oil, and possibly to lower economic growth. As the price of
oil rises on the world market, more costly fields can be developed, and more
unconventional oil deposits will become economic. The recent discoveries of new
conventional oil resources in Mexico will help to maintain the production of
conventional oil. Heavy oil deposits in Venezuela are comparable in magnitude
with the oil reserves in Saudi Arabia, and could be commercially produced at
current oil prices. Tar sands in Canada are already producing oil, and shale oil
deposits in the US contain large reserves which could be produced at little more

Table 4.8   *Proven oil reserves, production and R/P ratios, and cumulative production for major world groups.*

	Remaining proven reserves 10⁹ bbl (Jan. 1978)	Production (mbd) (1978)	R/P (years)	Cumulative production (10⁹ bbl) (July 1978)
OPEC Saudi Arabia	165.7	7.8	58.2	32.1
Other Middle East	192.6	12.0	44.1	72.1
Other OPEC	86.6	9.7	24.5	65.6
Total OPEC	444.9	29.5	41.3	169.8
North America	34.5	10.0	9.5	123.2
Western Europe	24.0	1.8	36.8	3.8
Rest of WOCA	44.2	5.0	24.3	22.8
Total non-OPEC	102.7	16.8	16.7	149.8
Total WOCA	547.6	46.2	32.5	319.6
Communist areas	94.0	13.8	18.7	N/A
Total world	641.6	60.0	29.3	

Note: 7.3 bbl = 1 toe.
Source: Oil and Gas Journal (1978 and 1979).

than today's oil price if environmental difficulties could be overcome. An important consideration though is that the lead times for production from these unconventional sources are much longer than for conventional oil due to the higher investment and running costs and due to environmental problems.

If we include oil from both conventional and unconventional sources it is expected that total oil production in the non-communist world (WOCA) will level out between 45 and 65 mbd (16 to 24 × 10⁹ bbl per annum). At the turn of the century the upper figure could be reached if OPEC was to maintain production at 30 mbd, while oil from other low-cost (but high price) sources provided 15 mbd, with another 20 mbd from high-cost areas such as Alaska or the North Sea and high-cost sources such as heavy oil, tar sands, and shale oil. If OPEC and the other low-cost sources were to produce a total of only 25 mbd (instead of 45), there would be a greater incentive to develop high-cost conventional and unconventional oil and in the longer term these might be expected to produce more than 20 mbd, giving a total of more than the lower end of our suggested range for WOCA oil production. However, in the short to medium term, the long lead times for developing high-cost oil resources would prevent them from replacing any serious loss of OPEC oil production, caused either by policy constraints or by political changes or conflicts in the Middle East, so we certainly cannot exclude the possibility of a shortfall of world (WOCA) oil production below 45 mbd. The factors that may cause the greatest concern are that any disturbances or political changes in oil-producing countries would be likely to lead to lower levels of production, and the lead times for developing alternative sources of oil are too long for them to be relevant in a crisis. In the longer term, however, it could be possible to maintain WOCA oil production within or near to the range 45 to 65 mbd until the middle of the next century. In addition there could be substantial additional supplies of products currently derived from oil but obtained in the future from coal or natural gas. The problem of achieving an overall world energy balance, taking account of conversion and interfuel substitution, will be considered from a modelling viewpoint in chapter 13. There will be many difficulties, but oil is expected to continue to make an important contribution to world energy supplies through most of the next century, though its percentage share of the energy market is likely to decline considerably.

4.7   Prospects for gas

Natural gas currently provides nearly 20 per cent of the total world supply of energy. Increases in natural gas supplies during this century have been almost as dramatic as those of oil. However, the development of the natural gas industry has generally been limited to markets that could be economically connected by pipeline to natural gas reserves. The expense of constructing costly pipeline networks could only be justified where there are both large reserves and an assured demand. Thus there are wide variations in natural gas consumption ranging from 2 per cent of total energy used in Japan to about 25 per cent in the US and the USSR. The future role of natural gas will be largely determined by transport costs, as those gas resources most convenient for existing markets become depleted, and the world depends increasingly on large gas reserves and resources in areas further from major markets.

World proven reserves of natural gas are shown in table 4.9, which also gives annual and cumulative production, and estimates for undiscovered resources in different world regions (McCormick et al., 1978). It is evident that much will depend on when, and how much of, the estimated undiscovered resources in North America and Western Europe are found and developed. However, the longer-term prospects are dominated by the potential use of the large proven gas reserves in OPEC, particularly in Iran and Saudi Arabia, which account for more than half of OPEC gas reserves.

An alternative to gas pipelines is provided by transport by tankers carrying liquefied natural gas (LNG). The technology has been available on a commercial scale only since the 1960s and the costs are high ($6 to $12 per barrel of oil equivalent (boe)). The gas must first be liquefied by cooling to minus 161° C, then carried in specially designed refrigerated tankers, and re-gasified at receiving terminals. Approximately 25 per cent of the energy is lost in processing the LNG, and allowing also for transport, only about two thirds of the original supply of gas is delivered to the consumer. In addition there is concern that an LNG tanker accident might lead to serious loss of life and damage to property (see chapter 9).

Table 4.9 *World gas production, reserves and resources.*

Region	(1976) Production 10^9 boe p.a.	(1975) Proved reserves 10^9 boe	Estimated undiscovered resources 10^9 boe	(1976) Cumulative production 10^9 boe
North America	3.8	52	273	106
West Europe	1.1	25	53	7
Japan, Australia, New Zealand	0.05	7	39	0.3
OPEC	0.6	156	453	14
Latin America	0.3	7	67	2
Middle East & North Africa	0.05	4	10	0.3
Africa south of Sahara	0.02	1	2	0.2
East Asia	0.02	4	20	0.2
South Asia	0.05	3	7	0.3
USSR, East Europe	2.1	133	370	23
China, centrally planned Asia	0.2	4	63	0.3
World total	8.4	394	1358	155

Note: 1 boe (barrel of oil equivalent) $\simeq$ 6 GJ.
Source: McCormick *et al.* (1978).

An LNG processing and transport system requires high capital expenditure, and this will limit the rate of growth of international trade in LNG.

Natural gas provides a clean and convenient fuel and an important chemical feedstock, and major consuming countries have substantial investments in the infrastructure of national and local distribution of gas. The choice for consuming countries, as their indigenous gas supplies decline, will depend on the relative economics of higher cost pipelines, LNG imports, conversion from coal to synthetic gas, and conversion from gas to the use of alternative fuels based on coal or nuclear energy. In addition demand may be reduced through energy conservation measures and increasing use of solar energy.

Producing countries with large reserves of natural gas but not large existing local demand, have a variety of options: Export by pipeline may be feasible, as with Iran to the USSR and hence to Eastern or Western Europe, or Mexico to the US. LNG trade could be developed, though payments to producers are severely reduced from the delivered price of gas by the high transport costs. A local consumer network could be built up, though in a developing country with large reserves it is unlikely that this could take a major share of the potential supply. The gas could be used to develop a local chemicals and petrochemicals industry, for export of fertilisers and 'intermediates' for further use in petrochemicals. This would depend on whether the cost advantage on feedstocks would be sufficient for a newly developed industry to compete with the highly efficient petrochemicals companies in developed countries. The cost disadvantage in transporting gas means that natural gas in a producing country provides the cheapest fuel for electricity generation. If a gas field is remote from possible consumers it may be desirable to use the gas to generate electricity where the gas is co-produced with oil and would otherwise be flared. A major possibility in the medium- to long-term future is the conversion to methanol for shipping to consumer countries for use in transport, either mixing it with gasoline, or by using catalytic conversion to produce high quality gasoline from methanol. If this route to fuel for transport becomes economic, it is possible that natural gas could meet a substantial part of the energy required for transport by the early part of the next century. For example, if world production of natural gas were to increase from its present value, equivalent to 24 mbd (8.7×19^9 bbl oil equivalent per annum), to 30 or 50 mbd, this level of production might continue well into the next century. It is possible that half of this, say 15 to 20 mbd could be converted to a liquid hydrocarbon for use in transport or for petrochemical feedstock.

4.8   Chapter summary

World proved oil reserves amount to 600×10^9 bbl, but if the average recovery factor could be increased from its present value of 25–30 per cent to about 40 per cent, this figure could increase to 800 to 900×10^9 bbl. Estimates for additional undiscovered oil resources increase the possible total to 1900×10^9 bbl that could be recovered with today's best technology at prices up to $20 a barrel (1976 US dollars). This figure may be compared with current annual world oil consumption, which is 60 mbd or 22×10^9 bbl per annum. Thus the probable oil resource base does not itself present a serious limit on the possible growth in production. The more serious limits arise firstly from the fact that oil production potential depends on actual proved reserves, so the annual gross additions to proved reserves are important, and these are estimated to be (on average) below current consumption. Secondly, the world oil reserves to production ratio is unlikely to fall below 15 years due to technical constraints on rates of production from oil fields. Thirdly, the proved and possible reserves are very unevenly distributed, with about half the proved reserves in the non-communist world found in the Arabian Peninsula. It is likely that some of the major producing countries with large oil reserves will limit their production to levels that yield an income appropriate to their own long term development needs, giving oil production well below the technical potential. Taking all of these factors into account it is expected that world oil production of conventional oil resources will remain well below 80 mbd and possibly not very different from present levels. The pressure of demand in a situation where supply is constrained will lead to increased oil prices, conservation, interfuel substitution, and the development of higher cost sources of oil.

There are very large 'unconventional' oil resources, in the form of heavy oil deposits (in Venezuela, for example), tar sands (in Canada) and shale oil deposits (in the US). At costs in the range $10 to $30 (1979 US dollars) per barrel, the development of substantial parts of these resources could be economic, and it would be reasonable to estimate that the total oil likely to be available is comparable with that for conventional oil. The capital costs for development will be high and the rate of growth of oil supplies from unconventional sources will therefore be relatively slow, possibly reaching 10 per cent of conventional oil production near the end of the century.

Natural gas production and its future prospects are dominated by the problem of transporting and distributing gas from the well to the consumer. Almost all of the present world production of natural gas is transported by pipeline to the distribution network in major consuming areas. The main direct alternative to pipeline transport involves the high cost of liquefaction and shipment in LNG tankers. When production begins to decline in the older gas fields near major markets in North America and Europe, there will be an increasing need for long range pipelines from Iran to the USSR and Europe, and across the USSR from Siberian gas fields, and to the US from Mexico, Northern Canada or Alaska. However, most of the world's gas reserves outside the communist areas are found in the Persian Gulf area. The major possibilities for their future use include LNG shipments, local industrial use, and conversion via methanol to gasoline for use in transport.

World natural gas production may level off in the range 30 to 35 mbd of oil equivalent, with an increasing fraction converted for use as a liquid hydrocarbon for transport or for feedstock. This could then supplement the increasing production of oil from unconventional sources, so that taken together they could make up for gradually declining supplies of conventional oil during the first half of the next century. On this basis the production of liquid hydrocarbons from oil and gas (but not including synthetic oil from coal) could be maintained near to current levels until past the middle of the next century.

The development of the world oil market was briefly outlined at the beginning of this chapter, and the oil and gas markets will be considered further in chapters 10 and 16.

Chapter 4   Further reading

Adelman, M. A. (1972) *The world petroleum market,* Johns Hopkins University Press, Baltimore and London.
American Petroleum Institute (1975) *Basic petroleum data book,* American Petroleum Institute, Washington, DC.

Craft, B. C. and Hawkins, M. F. (1959) *Applied petroleum reservoir engineering,* Prentice-Hall, Englewood Cliffs, New Jersey.

Hobson, G. D. and Tiratsoo, E. N. (1975) *Introduction to petroleum geology,* Scientific Press, Beaconsfield, UK.

Sampson, A. (1975) *The seven sisters – the great oil companies and the world they made,* Hodder and Stoughton, London.

WAES (1977a) *Energy: global prospects 1985–2000,* McGraw Hill, New York and London.

World Energy Conference (WEC) (1978b) *World energy resources 1985–2020,* IPC Science and Technology Press, Guildford, UK, and New York.

Coal

5.1   Growth of coal demand

Coal has probably been used as a fuel in small and localized areas for several millennia. The Chengi mines in China were worked many hundreds of years BC, and much later Marco Polo (1280 AD) refers to the use of a 'black inflammable earth' that he observed during his visit to China. In Europe, coal was known to the Greeks and called 'anthrax' from which the name anthracite is derived, and the Romans observed its excavation and use near St. Etienne when they invaded Gaul. Its use remained very limited until the firewood crisis in England in the sixteenth century led to the widespread adoption of coal as a domestic fuel. However, as early as the year 1307 the industrial use of coal for lime manufacture had created such atmospheric pollution in Southwark as to cause Edward II to issue a proclamation forbidding the lime-burners to burn coal (Nef, 1932, vol. 1, p. 157). In the north of England the blacksmiths of Wearmouth and Sheffield used coal in the twelfth century, but its use for metallurgical purposes grew slowly until the eighteenth century, when Darby developed the use of coke for reducing iron ore. Until then the preferred fuel for ironmaking was charcoal and it was partly the extensive demand for wood to make charcoal that led to the shortage of firewood in England beginning in the middle of the sixteenth century.

It has been estimated by Nef (1932) that annual coal production in the UK was about 210,000 tons in the period 1551–60, but had increased to nearly 3 million tons by 1681–90. Thus by the end of the seventeenth century most households in the UK were burning coal, and wood probably accounted for less than 20 per cent of total energy consumption. By 1800 coal production had increased to about 11 million tons (Deane and Cole, 1969) but between one half and two thirds of this was still consumed by households. The rapid industrialisation of the UK in the mid nineteenth century led to increased coal production and a substantial coal export trade. UK coal production and export figures are shown in table 5.1, and the distribution of consumption is shown in table 5.2. It should be noted that there are no reliable mineral statistics for the UK prior to the 1850s, and the figures given for earlier years are based on incomplete statistics and estimation or extrapolation.

The changing rates of growth of the UK coal industry during the nineteenth century can be partly explained by the changing character of the market, illustrated in table 5.2. After 1800, coal became increasingly used for power

98

Table 5.1. *UK coal production and exports 1700–1977.*

	1700	1800	1840	1869	1887	1913	1929	1955	1977
Production	3	11	34	110	165	287	262	236	120
Consumption	3	11	32	97	132	193	201	224	121
Exports	0	0.2	2	13	33	94	61	12	−1
Consumption per capita (tons per year)	0.3	0.7	1.2	3.1	3.6	4.2	4.5	4.4	2.2
Coal as percentage of total energy consumed	80	80	95	99	99	99	95	86	36

Notes: (1) Units for production, consumption and exports are millions of tons per year. (2) Eire is excluded for 1929 and later.
Sources: Deane and Cole (1969); UK Department of Energy (1978a); Humphrey and Stanislaw (1979).

Table 5.2. *UK coal consumption by sector 1840–1977.*

Year	1840	1869	1887	1913	1929	1955	1977
Sector				Percentages			
Iron industry	25	30	17	11	10	12	9
Mines	3	7	7	6	5	4	1
Transport	1½	5	12	6	6	5	0
Gas & electricity	1½	6	6	8	11	30	65
Other industry	32	26	26	22	23	23	16
Domestic	32	17	17	14	15	18	9
Exports	5	9	15	33	30	6	0

Source: Deane and Cole (1969) and UK Department of Energy (1978a).

production, to pump water from mines and to supplement water power in the textiles industry, and for expanding production of iron and other metals. However, the rate of growth averaged a modest 2.4 per cent annually from 1800 to 1830, when the development of the railways began and not only directly increased the demand for coal but also permitted it to be transported much more cheaply, both to domestic markets and to new industrial centres. Coal production increased at an average annual rate of 3.0 per cent for the period 1840 to 1913, though the growth in UK consumption averaged only 2.4 per cent. The high percentage of coal exports and the potential for improved efficiencies in its use during the nineteenth century meant that the market was unstable both through fluctuations in world trade and through fluctuations in the rate of technological change towards energy conservation. Thus prices varied widely although there was continuing growth in demand throughout the century, and the contribution of coal output to GNP varied from about 5 per cent in 1881 to about 3 per cent in 1886, and over 6 per cent in 1900 to about 4 per cent in 1905 (Deane and Cole, 1969).

In 1840, the UK coal production of 34 million tons probably represented about two thirds of the total output of the Western world, and even as late as 1913 the 94 million tons exported from the UK met about 10 per cent of total world consumption. In 1850, coal consumption in the United States was only about 8 million tons but, under the combined impact of industrialization and population growth, it increased at an average annual rate of more than 6 per cent to about 440 million tons in 1910. Thereafter, the coal market in the USA was disturbed by the rapid growth of oil production and soon afterwards by the growth of natural gas production. Wood fuel dominated the energy market in 1850 and fell to about 10 per cent by 1913. The demand for coal in the United States is compared with the consumption of other fuels in figure 5.1 for the period 1850–1980.

Interfuel substitution of the type illustrated for the United States by figure 5.1, from wood to coal followed by displacement of coal by oil and gas, took place in all world regions where coal was available and where industrialization developed in the late nineteenth or early twentieth centuries. The timing of the transition from coal towards oil and gas also depended on the availability of indigenous supplies, and for this reason Western Europe lagged behind North America. The percentage shares of total energy consumption provided by coal are illustrated for different world regions in table 5.3. The fall in the energy market share provided by coal was common to all world regions although (as shown in the last line of table 5.3), the total world coal consumption rose in each 25 year period. This growth was due mainly to the increase in demand for coal in the centrally planned economies, although there was also some increase in the OECD due to the use of coal for generating electricity and for the iron and steel industries, which more than compensated for its decline in other sectors. We will return to questions on the markets for coal later in the chapter when we examine also the possible future markets. Before this we will outline the characteristics of coal reserves and coal production potential.

5.2   Coal production

Formation

Coal is composed mainly of carbon though it also contains hydrogen and oxygen and varying small amounts of nitrogen, sulphur and other elements. It was formed by the decomposition of the remains of vegetation growing in swamps or in large river deltas undergoing intermittent subsidence. The decomposed material from plants and trees was transformed first by bacterial action into peat which became

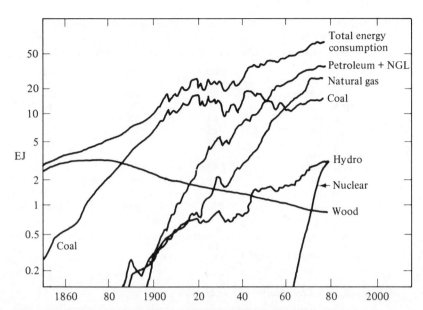

Figure 5.1 Consumption of fuels in the United States 1850–1978. *Source:* Hottel and Howard (1971); OECD (1978); *Nuclear Engineering International* (1979). *Note:* Primary energy equivalent has been used for hydro and nuclear.

buried by later sedimentary deposits. Later, under movements of the earth's crust the layers of peat became more deeply buried, and under the influence of heat and biochemical reactions they were transformed into various types of coal or lignite. During this coalification process the carbon content increased as oxygen and hydrogen were released. Methane (CH_4) was formed and either escaped into the atmosphere or migrated until it was captured in a geological trap so that it formed a natural gas reservoir contained by an impervious layer similar to those that contain petroleum.

Properties

Coals are ranked according to their carbon content. Under mild conditions of heat and pressure the lowest rank coals were formed, consisting of brown coal and lignite. At higher temperatures and pressures sub-bituminous and bituminous coals were formed, and under very high pressures the highest rank coals, called anthracites, were formed. The anthracites contain more than 92 per cent carbon with 2 or 3 per cent hydrogen together with oxygen, volatile matter and impurities. Bituminous coals contain about 5 per cent hydrogen and have a carbon content ranging from about 70 to 80 per cent. The lowest ranks of lignite and brown coal may have less than 50 per cent carbon content. The ranking is summarised in table 5.4.

Table 5.3.   *Coal shares in total primary energy for world regions 1925–75 (percentage shares).*

	1925	1950	1975
N. America	72	40	17
W. Europe	94	79	16
Japan	87	69	19
USSR	65	76	31
Other	94	93	63
Developing countries	62	40	18
World	81	57	26
World total coal (m. tonnes)	794	1015	1467

Source: Darmstadter *et al.* (1971).

Table 5.4.   *Classification of coal by rank.*

Class	Group	Carbon content
Anthracite	Meta-anthracite	98% or more
	Anthracite	92 to 98%
	Semi-anthracite	86 to 92%
Bituminous	Low volatile	78 to 86%
	Medium volatile	69 to 78%
	High volatile	less than 69%[a]
Sub-bituminous	A, B, C	[a]
Lignite	Lignite	[a]
	Brown coal	[a]

[a] Classified by heat content (see text). For further details see: Gordon (1971), and Van Krevelen (1961).

The rank by carbon content approximates to a ranking by heat content though with some overlap between classes. Lignite and brown coal, and sub-bituminous coal have thermal yields in the range 9 to 14 GJ per tonne. Bituminous coals may be expected to lie in the range 20 to 30 GJ per tonne, and anthracites between 30 and 34 GJ per tonne. Other classifications of importance include the coking qualities for metallurgical coal, which relate to the mechanical strength of the coke, the ash content, and the volatile matter content. Sulphur is an important impurity as it appears in combustion products as oxides of sulphur. Some countries, notably the USA, have statutory limits on the emission of these oxides, and owing to the cost of their removal this sets a premium on coal with a low sulphur content.

Mining

Most hard coal (bituminous and anthracite) is obtained by deep mines, though modern technology has led to the increasing use of open-cast methods. The latter may use large excavators capable of shifting hundreds of tons per hour and the mines may reach depths of several hundred feet in steps of about 100 feet. Surface, strip, or open-cast mining is feasible in the Western coal areas of the United States though subsequent reclamation of the land may be handicapped by the relatively low rainfall. Even with allowance for such environmental costs, surface mining is not only likely to be cheaper than deep mining, but it is also capable of more rapid expansion provided this is not inhibited by limited facilities for moving the coal to major users.

Deep coal mines range in depth from a few hundred feet to several thousand feet. Several shafts may be required (at least two) and in the UK a new mine can be expected to take 10 years to bring into operation at a cost of £40 to £50 per annual tonne. Thus a new mine producing 5 million tonnes a year would cost more than £200 million (at 1977 prices). The mine shafts play a critical role in providing ventilation to the mine, which is required both to remove methane associated with the coal and to reduce heat and humidity. In some cases the initial methane concentrations are so high that pipes are driven ahead of the mining operation to draw off methane in a useable form.

Two principal methods of deep mining are in use: (i) Longwall, (ii) Bord and Pillar or Room and Pillar. In the Longwall method the coal is extracted in one operation from a face that may be 600 ft in length. In the older Bord and Pillar method the area to be mined is divided into rectangles by driving a series of roadways at right-angles to each other and then mining from each of these rectangles or pillars. In modern mines over 90 per cent of the coal is mined, loaded and transported mechanically. Transport underground is mainly by means of conveyor belts (replacing earlier tubs) which bring the coal to the main shaft for raising to the surface. At the mine head the coal is cleaned, sorted or screened, and blended.

Resources and reserves

Geological *resources* include all coal that may become economic at some time in the future. *Reserves* include all coal that is known to be technically and economically recoverable under today's conditions. Global surveys of resources and reserves carried out by the World Energy Conference (WEC, 1978b) distinguish between hard coal (including anthracite and bituminous coal) and brown coal (sub-bituminous and lignite), divided at an energy content of 23.8 GJ per tonne (on an ash-free basis). The depth limits set on hard coal are 1,500 m, and on brown coal are 600 m, and the minimum seam thicknesses are 0.6 metres for hard coal, and 2 metres for brown coal. The estimated world coal resources and reserves are summarised in table 5.5. Although these are the best estimates publicly available,

Table 5.5   *World coal reserves for selected areas (10⁹ tonnes).*

	Resources		Reserves	
	Hard coal	Brown coal	Hard coal	Brown coal
Africa	173	n.a.	34	n.a.
Latin America	22	9	5	6
Australia	214	49	18	9
Canada	96	19	9	1
USA	1190	1380	113	64
China	1425	13	99	n.a.
USSR	3993	867	83	27
Western Europe	536	54	95	34
Other	76	7	37	3
World total	7725	2399	493	144

Source: WEC (1978b).

it is known that international oil companies have further information through their drilling records, and it is believed that coal resources and reserves may be substantially larger in some regions than is indicated in the table. In particular, Africa may have very much larger resources, perhaps by an order of magnitude, and both Asia and Latin America may have substantially larger resources.

Potential production

Potential production of coal depends not only on the availability of reserves but also on their technical characteristics, the existence and potential for development of an infrastructure for coal production, local coal demand and willingness to export. The conditions prevailing in the deposit include the thickness of seams, the coal quality, the depth of the seams for deep mining and the nature of the local geological structure, and the depth and type of overburden for seams that could be mined by surface excavation. Key features for the required infrastructure include environmental problems and the availability of water supplies required not only for cleaning and processing coal but also for land restoration in some countries and possibly for moving the coal in slurry pipelines. If pipelines cannot be economically used, a railway system is required and associated port facilities if water transport is to be used. Skilled manpower is required and the necessary capital for development. Investment will depend on estimates of assured coal demand, and investment may be available only if potential customers are prepared to sign long-term contracts with potential suppliers. In many countries the most reliable future demand may be from domestic needs, particularly electric utilities based on coal fired power stations, but potential competition from nuclear power production sets a limit on the economic cost of coal for production of electricity.

The WEC study of potential coal production (WEC, 1978b) gives the figures summarised in table 5.6 for major coal producing countries to the year 2020. It must be noted however, that production will be driven by demand, and if coal demand grows only slowly in the next decade the potential production at a later date may be correspondingly reduced. The figures in table 5.6 correspond to an initial average annual growth for world coal production of 4.1 per cent from 1975 to 1985, then 2.7 per cent to the year 2000, and 2.1 per cent from 2000 to 2020.

Although coal reserves are widely distributed geographically, the most extensive are in China, the USSR and the USA. These three countries together account for nearly 90 per cent of the total world resources and about 60 per cent of the world reserves (see table 5.5). The corresponding figures for estimated potential production given in table 5.6 add up to nearly 70 per cent of the world total for the year 2020. It has already been remarked that the resources and reserves in new coal areas may be considerably larger than those given by current official estimates, and there may be greater potential for expansion of production of 'other countries' than is indicated in table 5.6. Since many of these new coal areas are in countries with low domestic demand for energy they may have a major impact on potential world trade in coal. Countries not listed explicitly in table 5.6 that may develop substantial coal exports include Botswana (with coal resources estimated at 100 thousand million tonnes (WEC, 1978b), Zimbabwe, Swaziland, Colombia and Indonesia.

The WEC coal study (WEC, 1978b) included estimates of possible world trade in coal but these were derived mainly from the expectations of existing major coal producing countries and may underestimate future potential, both through conservatism in estimates from producing countries and through uncertainty about potential new areas. The WEC estimates that world coal trade, currently 7.7 per cent of total production, may rise to 10.1 per cent in the year 2000 and become 8.9 per cent in 2020. Thus coal trade, now at 200 million tonnes a year, is estimated to rise to about 800 million tonnes a year by the year 2030. If the potential of new coal production areas is both required and realised it seems possible that world coal trade could be considerably larger than these WEC estimates.

Amongst the major coal producers, there is considerable export potential from the United States but this may be limited by environmental concern. The USSR has ample reserves but may have some difficulty in developing the railroads and other infrastructure required for moving coal for domestic production and this may severely limit possible exports. Similar difficulties over investment and infrastructure may limit coal production in China, but it is possible that coal exports may receive high priority due to the need for foreign currency to finance imports required for industrial expansion. Coal production in India, currently 73 million tonnes a year, is estimated to expand to 500 million tonnes by 2020 and here also

Table 5.6. *Potential world coal production 1975–2020.*

Country	Coal production in million tce			
	1975	1985	2000	2020
Australia	69	150	300	400
Canada	23	35	115	200
China	349	725	1200	1800
German F.R.	126	129	145	155
India	73	135	235	500
Japan	19	20	20	20
Poland	181	258	300	320
Rep. S. Africa	69	119	233	300
UK	129	137	173	200
USA	581	842	1340	2400
USSR	614	851	1100	1800
Other countries	360	483	619	751
World total	2593	3884	5780	8846

Sources: WEC, 1978b; Peters and Schilling, 1978.

there may be a high priority for exports. South Africa, Australia and Canada are expected to expand production considerably and to maintain a large percentage of production for exports. In Europe, Poland may continue to export at around the current level of 40 million tonnes a year but this potential depends on how Poland's domestic demand grows in relation to production. The UK plans to expand coal production but it seems unlikely that much UK coal could be exported at competitive prices in the world market and in the long term the UK coal production may fall below national demand.

Transportation costs are an important component of the delivered price of coal. Land transport by rail from mine mouth or port will vary widely between individual countries but may average about $5 per tonne using railways over a distance of 200 km (IEA, 1978b), or inland waterways over 400 km. Alternatively, the same figure would cover the cost of local seaborne transport from a major ocean coal terminal to a consumer at a coastal site. A major terminal of this type is projected in Japan and may also be desirable in Europe in order to localise and reduce environmental problems and to gain the advantage from economies of scale in long distance ocean transport of coal. The OECD report on steam coal (IEA, 1978b) estimates that transport costs of coal over a 26,000 nautical miles round trip (e.g. between Australia and Western Europe) would be about $30 per tonne in a vessel of 25,000 ton (dwt) but fall to below $15 per tonne for a vessel of 200,000 ton (dwt). These transport costs may be compared with production costs for coal as low as $12 per tonne (1976 dollars) for Western mined US coal, or about $20 for deep mined US coal and possibly twice this for high cost coal in Western Europe; this will be discussed further in section 5.4.

5.3   The market for coal

The major changes in coal consumption in the different sectors and regions of the OECD between 1960 and 1976 are summarised in table 5.7. Coal consumption in the OECD total domestic/commercial sector fell between these years by 120 million tonnes from 194 mt to 74 mt. There were also similar declines in coal for industry excluding iron and steel-making (71 mt), transportation (39 mt) and gas manufacture (23 mt). On the other hand there was a substantial increase of 296 mt from 342 mt to 638 mt in coal used for electricity generation.

In the domestic and commercial sector the past decline in the direct use of coal has been associated with market penetration of oil, gas and electricity. The domestic (household) sector is likely to remain a priority area for the supply of natural gas and its supplies may be protected by government controls in some countries. However, as local or pipeline natural gas supplies decline they would need to be replaced by higher cost supplies imported as LNG (liquefied natural gas) or by synthetic gas manufactured from coal. The resulting higher prices may lead to some potential for the growth of electricity for heating and possibly to the direct use of coal in particularly favourable circumstances for commercial use or in district heating for houses or apartments. Thus coal will be used indirectly in the domestic/commercial sector to provide synthetic gas and to provide a proportion of the electricity consumed. It seems unlikely that the direct use of coal by households will increase because it is generally regarded as less convenient than oil or gas, and it may cause more environmental pollution than gas or electricity. However, it is possible that in some areas the cost advantage of coal over synthetic gas or electricity may lead to an increased domestic use either of coal or of manufactured (smokeless) solid fuel. Such increased potential demand would depend on improved designs for solid fuel stoves or boilers.

Industrial energy consumption accounts for 30 to 40 per cent of the OECD's primary energy requirements, and two thirds of this demand is currently met by oil and gas, compared with less than one third in 1960. The main industrial coal market is for metallurgical coal (coal used in iron and steel-making). It is likely that iron and steel production in the OECD will increase more slowly than other industrial production and service industries, since increased world demand is more likely to be met by expansion in developing countries. Fuel consumption in the 'other industry' sector in the OECD, excluding public electricity and feedstocks, is split fairly equally between steam generation and direct heat for large kilns, heaters, ovens and dryers. In principle, many of the steam or heat requirements for major establishments in the more energy intensive industries such as chemicals,

Table 5.7.   *Consumption of coal by sector in OECD regions (mtce).*

	North America		OECD Europe		Japan	
	1960	1976	1960	1976	1960	1976
Transport	3	0	29	1	6	0
Domestic/commercial	41	10	144	57	7	5
Iron and steel	63	50	85	68	10	49
Other industry	57	61	89	30	21	4
Energy sector use	24	23	60	26	2	13
Electricity generation	177	403	133	195	21	13
Total coal	365	547	540	377	67	84

Source: OECD (1976), IEA (1978a).

petroleum refining, paper manufacture, building materials and food processing could be provided by the direct use of coal in the long run. However, in practice many of these possible candidates for coal utilisation would be poorly located in relation to centres of coal production, or they may be in areas where indigenous coal is expensive, or they may be limited by the lack of storage space for coal or inhibited by problems of handling coal. Thus the future substitution of coal for oil and gas in 'other industry' is likely to be highly selective, being confined at first to major establishments requiring coal for bulk steam raising and located at a coastal site or near to a coal mine.

The major problems in non-boiler uses of coal appear to be (i) product contamination by coal, ash, dust, sulphur and trace materials, (ii) the breakdown of refractory surfaces, (iii) the difficulty of precise temperature control due to the variability of coal supplies and coal combustion, and (iv) corrosion that reduces the efficiency of heat exchangers. It is possible to avoid most of these difficulties on a large industrial complex by using coal at only one location on the site to produce low Btu gas which is then distributed throughout the complex. A small establishment would normally choose to purchase synthetic gas provided by a gas utility.

The wider direct use of coal will depend on the development of improved coal handling and combustion equipment. The successful commercial development of fluidised bed combustion could enhance the prospects for coal, and, together with improved cleaning, blending, distribution, and handling systems, it could help to overcome some of the current environmental constraints, space limitation and personnel problems associated with the industrial use of coal.

There may be significant economic gains if the problems of using more coal can be overcome. A large part of the coal would come from indigenous production in countries having the greatest degree of industrialisation and would ease the balance of payments problems that might otherwise arise. Potential importing countries could obtain coal more cheaply on world markets than oil or natural gas as these become less readily available. Potential coal exporters include a number of developing countries for whom the enhanced foreign trade would usefully assist their economic growth. The increased use of coal in the OECD will reduce the pressure on world supplies of oil and gas but will also lead to technological developments in coal utilisation that would benefit developing countries having indigenous coal production potential or convenient access to world traded coal.

5.4   Coal and electricity generation

Sixty per cent of the coal used in the OECD is consumed for the generation of electricity (see table 5.7). In different regions the percentage varies, from 70 per cent in North America, to 50 per cent in Western Europe and only 15 per cent in Japan. The comparative costs of electricity generation from nuclear energy, fuel oil, or steam coal, have been estimated in the OECD report on steam coal (IEA, 1978b) under the assumption that the real price of oil rises by $2\frac{1}{2}$ per cent per annum after 1985 whilst the real price of coal rises by 1 per cent per annum. A discount rate of 10 per cent is assumed in computing capital charges.

The comparative costs depend on whether the fuel oil or the steam coal has low sulphur or high sulphur content and on the environmental limits that have to be met. Flue gas desulphurisation (FGD) increases the cost of oil-based electricity by between 5 and 8 per cent depending on the load factor (ranging from 80 per cent to 34 per cent). With bituminous coal requiring desulphurisation, 100 per cent FGD may increase electricity costs by about 27 per cent. Illustrative costs of electricity produced by nuclear, fuel oil or coal are given in table 5.8. The ranges of costs for oil and coal correspond to exclusion or inclusion of FGD to meet environmental constraints. At the upper end of the range of costs coal would not be competitive even with nuclear power at 3000 h/a (hours/annum, equivalent to a 34 per cent load factor). Using low sulphur coal without FGD, the production of electricity from coal would be slightly cheaper than from nuclear power even at 7000 h/a (80 per cent load factor), assuming conversion efficiencies of 36 per cent from coal to electricity. The coal price assumed for this low sulphur coal is $31 per tonne (assuming 29 GJ/tonne coal). The breakeven price of low sulphur coal would be $32 per tonne at 7000 h/a load and $48 at 3000 h/a. However, for high sulphur coal with FGD the breakeven price of coal would be $17 per tonne at 7000 h/a and $24 per tonne at 3000 h/a. At prices of coal above these breakeven values, nuclear electricity would be cheaper than coal-based electricity for the same load factor or hours per annum of operation.

It is clear that the potential use of coal for electricity production depends crucially on the price of coal delivered to an electric utility. In the United States, the national average (in 1976 dollars) is around $25 per tce (ton of coal equivalent, here taken as 29GJ) with a regional high of $36 per tce in New England and a low

Table 5.8. *Cost estimates for electricity generation in new nuclear, oil and coal-fired power stations.*

Cost in mills per kWh over first 20 years	Nuclear 2 × 1.1 GW	Fuel oil 2 × 0.6 GW	Bituminous coal 2 × 0.6 GW
Capital cost	14.9	7.5–9.6	9.6–12.4
Operation and maintenance	2.4	2.0–4.2	2.2–5.1
Fuel cost	6.5	31.0–29.0	10.8–11.3
Total cost per kWh at 5500 h/a	23.8	40.5–42.8	22.6–28.8
Total cost per kWh			
at 7000 h/a	20.7	38.9–40.8	20.6–26.1
at 5000 h/a	25.3	41.2–43.8	23.6–30.0
at 3000 h/a	36.3	46.7–50.8	30.6–39.1

Notes: Nuclear power station is assumed to be a pressurized water reactor (PWR)

	Nuclear	Oil	Coal
Construction costs $/kW	$700	$350–$450	$450–$580
Average fuel costs for period 1986–2006 $ per GJ	$0.62	$3.16–$2.82	$1.07

Source: IEA (1978b).

of $12 per tce in the Western mining areas. These prices are decisively below those for fuel oil which range from $50 per tce to $83 per tce. However, at the load factors shown in table 5.8, the cost of nuclear electricity lies within the range of coal-based electricity costs. The costs of transporting coal and the costs of meeting environmental constraints appear to bring the costs of coal-based electricity in New England above the cost of nuclear electricity. In parts of the United States near to cheap sources of coal it is likely that coal based electricity will be cheaper than nuclear electricity, though many of the lowest cost coal areas are remote from major centres of electricity demand.

In Western Europe all imported coal and much of the indigenous coal is competitive with oil at today's prices. It is possible that in the future coal could be imported into Western Europe at $34 to $42 per tce. This is unlikely to be competitive with nuclear power for base load (80 per cent load factor) operation, but at load factors below 40 or 50 per cent imported coal used at coastal power stations may be competitive with nuclear power, provided the imported coal has a low sulphur content and environmental regulations do not require FGD. The chances of indigenous coal in Western Europe being produced at price levels that permit it to compete with nuclear power depend critically on the development of new and more efficient mines. Productivity per miner at large new mines in the UK may be as much as 4 times the current national average and if coal from these mines is costed separately it may be competitive with nuclear power unless FGD is required in order to satisfy environmental requirements.

5.5 Social and environmental costs

Expansion of coal production and use could lead to great social and environmental stress. The development of new mining areas and the associated closing of older less economic coal-mines could involve social and environmental disturbance in the new areas and social deprivation in the old areas. The social and environmental impacts may be divided into hazards of health and safety, deterioration of water quality, material damage and contamination, visibility reduction and other visual losses, weather modification and possible climatic changes, damage to the agricultural and plant ecosystem, and changes in landscape and land use. To these should be added the special problems of older and declining mining areas, where there may be few alternative opportunities for employment, and where the settled character of the mining communities and the specialised skills of the miners may both discourage emigration from these areas and inhibit the development of alternative industries (Posner 1973).

The mining of coal presents the main health and safety hazards to the workforce. The main dangers to the workforce in coal-mining have been recognised for many years within the industry and there has generally been a continuing improvement in working conditions and safety precautions. However, there are wide variations in safety standards between different countries, and even in those countries with the highest standards coal-mining remains one of the most dangerous of industrial occupations (see chapter 9).

The combustion of coal leads to the main health risks to the general public, in the form of air pollution and by toxic trace elements released into the air, the water supply, or the food chain. Increasing awareness of these environmental and health problems has led many countries to introduce legislation for pollution control.

Other environmental problems include land reclamation after mining and the strain on water resources in some areas. The greatest potential risk from increased combustion of coal and other fossil fuels comes from possible climate modification resulting from the increased emission of carbon dioxide (CO_2) into the atmosphere. Unfortunately, it is extremely difficult both to assess the risk of CO_2 affecting the climate and to assess possible damage that could result.

Coal mining
Risks in coal mining arise from explosion or fire due to the methane and coal dust that are always associated with deep mining. They also include the danger of collapse or flooding, and dangers arising from working with machinery under

difficult conditions. Longer-term risks include miners' black lung disease and other health hazards arising from working in wet or dusty conditions. It is estimated that the safety requirements of the Mining Enforcement and Safety Administration in the United States have increased underground mining costs by $4 per tonne whilst considerably improving occupational safety conditions in coal mining. Protection and insurance measures in the United States specifically related to black lung have been estimated to cost $2 per tonne. Hazard statistics for deep-mined coal in the EEC for the period 1970 to 1974 are summarised in table 5.9.

Some of the safety problems in deep mines do not arise in surface mines, others are reduced. However, environmental disturbance may arise from both. In deep mines the principal problems are mining subsidence, which affects the surface, and acid mine drainage, which also occurs in surface mines. Subsidence can be reduced by leaving more coal in place using, for example, the room and pillar method, thus increasing the costs of each tonne mined. Water pollution arises most seriously from oxidation of pyritic matter (iron sulphide) in wet conditions leading to sulphate. The risk of water pollution can be reduced by drainage control to reduce water in mines, by careful disposal of sulphur-bearing materials to avoid their contact with water, by sealing old mines, and possibly by chemical treatment of mine drainage. The cost of water control in mines can range from a few cents to 40 cents per tonne of coal mined.

The reclamation of land where surface or strip mining has taken place is of particular importance, since without adequate land treatment environmental legislation may prevent the development of large coal reserves, notably in the United States, Australia, Canada and West Germany. Reclamation involves both recovery of the land itself and associated plants or trees, and the avoidance of water pollution or the disturbance of underground aquifers that may affect water at a considerable distance from the mine. Reclamation is easiest in flat areas, harder in contour mined mountain areas, and it may be difficult in arid areas where little water is available. Costs in the United States may range from $3000 to $8000 per acre, or $0.16 to $2.91 per tonne (1977 US·dollars).

Other environmental problems from coal mining, cleaning and transportation include coal dust in the atmosphere, arising from a mine, transport or storage system, acid water from transport or storage, and both water and waste material from coal cleaning and washing. A more detailed discussion of environmental issues related to coal is given in section 9.3.

Coal utilisation

The main environmental problems from coal combustion arise from the ash waste and the emission of air pollutants. The pollutants emitted include oxides of sulphur and nitrogen and particulates and can cause adverse effects on the public, on agricultural producers, and on buildings. They may also lead to acid rainfall at

Table 5.9. *Hazard statistics for producing one million tonnes of deep-mined coal in the EEC during 1970–74.*

	Total per million tonnes
Injuries	
Rehabilitation in less than 20 days	197
Rehabilitation in more than 20 days	146
Deaths	0.8
Occupational illness	
Some disablement	21
Total disablement	0.8
Deaths	1

Source: IEA (1978b).

considerable distances from the place of emission. Thermal discharge from electric power stations may modify aquatic life or cause localised climatic effects. Waste ash disposal may require about 150 acres for a 1 GW electric power plant using coal over a 30-year period.

Most industrialised countries have emission control regulations that limit SO_2 and particulate emissions and some countries also limit emissions of nitrogen oxides and hydrocarbons. Particulates can be removed from the stack gas in coal fired power plants by means of electrostatic precipitators or by venturi scrubbers, at costs of $1 to $2 per tonne of coal burned. Emissions of oxides of sulphur may be uncontrolled but instead dispersed by the use of high chimney stacks. Where sulphur oxides control is required they may be removed from stack gases by using limestone scrubbers, though this leads to a waste disposal problem for the resulting lime sludge. Costs range from $7 to $12 per tonne of coal burned.

Environmental regulations on emissions from coal burning appliances may inhibit the increased use of coal except in major plants where the required technological skills are available to maintain the antipollution systems. Alternatives to the direct use of coal include the use of steam provided from a central service plant, electricity based on coal-fired power stations, or synthetic fuels. Amongst the latter, high Btu gas (methane) has all the advantages of natural gas. Low Btu gas (mainly carbon monoxide) may be used within an industrial complex but its wider use is likely to be limited since carbon monoxide is harmful and the gas also initially contains contaminants (hydrogen sulphide, ammonia, cyanide) whose removal is likely to be expensive. Similarly, the combustion of solvent-refined coal would retain some of the disadvantages of coal combustion. It is evident that stringent environmental standards on coal combustion may inhibit its widespread use if these standards are imposed before there is time to complete research and development on lower cost methods of pollution control.

5.6   Coal in world regions

North America

The large proven coal reserves and the associated very large resource base provide the United States and Canada with a wide range of options for their future production and use of coal. In the United States 555 million tons of coal were produced in 1976, of which 500 million tons were consumed and 54 million tons exported. The major part (370 mt) was burnt by utilities for electric power production, with the remainder shared between metallurgical uses (77 mt) and other (54 mt), the latter being dominated by industrial use largely localised in the main north-central industrial regions near to existing coalfields. Most projections of future energy demand in the US include a proportionately greater increase in coal demand. The OECD study of steam coal (IEA, 1978b) suggests a median projection of production rising to 1181 mt by the year 2000 with utility coal more than doubling to 800 mt, 'other uses' more than trebling to 161 mt, with metallurgical coal increasing slightly to 92 mt, and exports at 129 mt (with exports of steam coal rising to 59 mt from the 1976 value of 10 mt).

There can be no doubt about the technical ability for coal production in the US to expand at these rates and to continue further expansion well into the next century. The base of reserves and resources is ample (economically recoverable reserves 235 billion tonnes) and industrial capacity is available for developing the required infrastructure. The demonstrated (proven & indicated) reserve base for US coal is summarised in table 5.10, showing sulphur content and type of mining. This table illustrates some of the important problems that are liable to be concealed by aggregated figures, particularly in a country as large as the US. The major part of the low sulphur coal is located west of the Mississippi river, and for surface coal the low sulphur reserves east of the Mississippi are relatively small. Thus the major areas of electricity consumption in the eastern United States will have to meet high transportation costs if they wish to use low sulphur coal from western surface mines. Their alternative would be to use higher cost deep mined coal from the east-central mining areas, or to use coal with a higher sulphur content and incur greater costs for desulphurisation. The problem of long-term coal forecasts is increased by the uncertainty that surrounds the environmental constraints on western surface coal that there may be in areas of low rainfall, thus making reclamation difficult, and the uncertainty of public opinion of nuclear power. It is therefore not at all evident that coal demand will be determined by the lowest cost solutions. If environmental controls in the US require that all new coal-fired power stations install equipment for removal of sulphur, regardless of the percentage sulphur content of the coal to be used, this will favour the use of eastern coal, since once the cleaning equipment is installed the savings on transport costs compared with western coal outweigh the additional costs associated with burning high sulphur coal.

Table 5.10. *Demonstrated US coal reserves by sulphur content and location.*

Thousand million tonnes of demonstrated coal reserves	Sulphur range				
	Below 1%	1–3%	Above 3%	Unknown	Total
Deep mined					
East of Mississippi	24	44	60	24	152
West of Mississippi	90	10	7	12	119
Surface					
East of Mississippi	5	6	13	5	29
West of Mississippi	62	24	4	5	95
Total	181	84	84	46	395

Note: The economically recoverable reserves are estimated by the same source to be 235 billion tonnes.
Source: IEA (1978b).

Community resistance to environmental disturbance from production of western surface coal may be even more severe for export contracts than for consumption in east and east-central parts of the US. Export coal could be moved from the coal areas of Wyoming by rail or by slurry pipeline to Texas or Arkansas at about $11 or $7 respectively for transport costs. These costs may limit the initial growth of US coal exports from western mines because they could be more expensive delivered in Europe or Japan than coal from Australia or South Africa.

The economically recoverable reserves of coal in Canada are much smaller than those in the US, totalling 5 billion tons, but the estimated resource base is large at 165 thousand million tons. Most of the proved and probable coal is located in western Canada (British Columbia, Alberta and Saskatchewan). Canadian coal production in 1976 was only 26 million tons. Transport costs are high, but rail and sea transport could take coal from eastern parts of British Columbia to Japan at costs around $40 per ton (similar to coal from the US), which would be not very much higher than the costs of Australian coal.

Western Europe
The production of coal in Western Europe is primarily in the United Kingdom and West Germany, each of whom produces between 120 and 130 million tons a year. Consumption approximately matches demand in these two countries, and the rest of Europe consumes about the same amount (125 mt) but meets only half of this demand by indigenous production. The United States and Poland provide most of the European coal imports, the former mainly metallurgical coal and the latter

steam coal, but coal imports from South Africa are currently increasing in volume.

The United Kingdom, with 6 billion tons of economically recoverable reserves (45 billion tons technically recoverable), has experienced a decline in coal demand from over 200 million tons a year to less than 130 million tons in the past 20 years, initially due to increased use of imported oil but more recently due to increased production and use of natural gas. The current plans for coal call for the production of 135 mt by 1985 and 170 mt by 2000. There are adequate reserves for these production figures to be met and maintained, but the rate of development may be constrained by three factors: environmental difficulties and community resistance to the opening of mines in new areas, limitations due to shortage of skilled manpower in the regions where expansion is planned, and the possible slow build-up of coal demand which could inhibit the necessary investment required to meet long-term production targets. The possibility of an initially slow growth in coal demand arises partly from the high cost of much of the UK coal, which makes it less competitive with fuel oil for electricity production (or other uses) and partly because the continuing increase in supplies of natural gas will reduce the growth in electricity demand. Beyond the year 2000 it is reasonable to assume that increased production of UK coal could make an important contribution to the UK energy balance at a time when North Sea oil and natural gas production are both expected to decline. It is unlikely that substantial quantities of UK coal could be exported in the face of competition from internationally traded coal from other sources. However, it is possible that some of the newly planned mines will produce coal at costs considerably below current average costs so the 'new coal' should be highly competitive with other energy sources for inland consumption.

West German technically recoverable coal reserves are put at 24 thousand million tons for hard coal and 10 billion for sub-bituminous coal, but reserves that could be mined at current international coal prices are probably considered smaller. Further, most of the lignite is located in the built-up region between Cologne, Dusseldorf and Aachen, and since it would require open cast mining the costs would be high because of the need to relocate homes and other activities. Projections therefore indicate only small increases in lignite production, for example from 34 mt in 1975 to 38 mt in 2000. German hard coal is very costly and average costs per ton are estimated to be about $70, which may be compared with delivered prices of imported steam coal at $33 to $36 per ton or metallurgical coal $50 to $60. It is unlikely that German hard coal will become cheaper in the future since continuing high economic growth means that miners' wages are likely to increase at 4 per cent per annum. Projections based on current plans suggest that production will be maintained, partly through subsidies, at about 125 mt annually, and imported coal is expected to increase from 3 mt in 1976 to between 20 mt and 65 mt in the year 2000.

In the countries of Western Europe other than the UK and West Germany, current annual production is 55 mt and demand is 125 mt. In the period to the end of this century there is expected to be some increase in production, notably in Greece and Spain, but some other producers may find it difficult to maintain existing production levels in the face of increased labour costs. Plans exist for a considerable expansion of coal imports rising perhaps to more than 200 million tons a year compared with 66 mt in 1976, the largest expansion being in coal for power stations. As in the UK and West Germany, this need for coal depends on the relative emphasis between coal and nuclear energy in new electric power stations. If steam coal imports to Europe are to increase so substantially there will be a need for new port handling facilities capable of taking coal carriers of 200,000 tons dwt. Expansion is planned to take the coal throughput in Rotterdam from 4 mt to 20 mt annually. Stignaes and Aaberaa in Denmark are being expanded as possible coal centres in Scandinavia, and there will be a need for several other ports to act as major European coal distribution centres.

Japan
Indigenous coal production in Japan has declined since 1965 from 50 million tons to 20 mt but it is expected now to remain at the latter level for the rest of the century. Meanwhile, consumption of steam coal has fallen, but the use of metallurgical coal has increased from 24 to 68 mt with expansion of the iron and steel industry. Further expansion is expected in the use of metallurgical coal but at a slower rate than in the past, whilst a major expansion is planned for coal-fired power stations. By the year 2000 the demand for coal may have increased to nearly 200 million tons compared with 83 mt in 1976.

The Japanese government is taking an active part in promoting the development of coal utilisation to moderate the dependence on imported oil. This includes the provision of subsidies or preferential loans for coal-fired power plants including aid for stack-gas desulphurisation, and guarantees or other financial support for overseas coal development and trade. The feasibility of a large coal port to act as a 'coal centre' for ocean trade using very large coal carriers is being studied. The coal centre would be planned to handle an initial volume of 7 to 15 million tons annually. If the longer-term plans for coal are developed it is likely that more than one such centre would be required. The main uncertainties in these plans arise from environmental protection requirements relating to the use of coal that do not yet have adequate technological solutions, and policies for the rate of development of nuclear power.

Coal exporters and developing countries
It has already been noted that there is considerable potential for the expansion of world trade in coal. Australia and South Africa are capable of major expansion in low cost coal production that would be competitive in world markets. A number of developing countries have large reserves although their full extent is not yet known. These include Indonesia, Swaziland, Zimbabwe, Botswana, Colombia. India is expected to expand coal production for inland use and may also develop an export

trade. There may be large additional resources in other developing countries, particularly in Southern Africa and Latin America, where coal production could play an important role in permitting high economic growth without encountering an impossible requirement for oil imports. There will be formidable problems in developing the infrastructure required for coal production and export, and these may cause delays until the need for coal is sufficiently near and obvious that potential consumers are prepared to enter commitments for long-term contracts.

Centrally planned economies

Coal production in the USSR in 1976 was 495 mt of hard coal and 210 mt of brown coal, lignite and peat. A substantial part (about 30 per cent) of this coal is produced from surface mining. The total coal resources and reserves are very large, with estimated resources exceeding 4 million million tons and reserves exceeding 100 thousand million tons. However, 95 per cent of the resources are located east of the Ural mountains with perhaps 70 per cent of these in Northern Siberia. Similarly, about 80 per cent of the currently recoverable coal is east of the Urals. The three main coal deposits in the European part of the USSR are the Moscow, Donetsk and Pechora Basins, but the first two of these have limited life. The Kuznetsk Basin east of the Urals already provides some 20 per cent of USSR coal production, and development is expected for the Kansk–Achinsk Basin in Siberia which has the largest known coal deposits in the world.

The Soviet Union faces formidable transportation problems with coal. Already the average haulage distance for coal exceeds 700 km, and haulage over 5000 or more km from Eastern Siberia to the western USSR would considerably increase the costs of coal. Studies are under way for moving coal by slurry pipeline over 4000 km from the Kansk–Achinsk deposits to the Ukraine. Alternative possibilities include electricity production and transmission by very high voltage lines up to 2.5 million volts. The existing railway systems from Siberia to the USSR are not adequate to move the quantities of coal that may be required and one solution would be to increase the railroad capacity.

Total production of coal in the USSR, now at about 600 million tons a year, is expected to reach more than 1000 mt by the year 2000 and could be double this amount by 2020. At present there is a net export, mainly to Eastern Europe, of about 20 mt each year, but the growth of exports is likely to be limited by the same infrastructure problems as were noted previously in relation to the USSR's own consumption.

Poland has large coal deposits but few other energy resources. It receives most of its oil and gas from the Soviet Union. Almost 85 per cent of its energy needs are met by coal and this emphasis is expected to be continued. This will require major expansion in coal production to meet a planned 4 per cent annual increase in total energy demand. About 24 million tons of coal are currently exported, mainly to western Europe, and it is expected that opportunities for coal exports will increase, provided production can be expanded sufficiently. Reserves amount to 57 thousand million tons of hard coal and 13 thousand million tons of brown coal, so future production will be constrained mainly by the rate of investment and the availability of labour. Current plans call for a doubling of production by the year 2000 to nearly 500 million tons of hard coal and lignite.

China is the third largest coal producer in the world (after the USSR and the US), and it has the third largest coal reserves and resources (reserves are about 100 thousand million tons and resources 10 times larger). Coal production in 1976 is estimated at about 470 million tons. It is believed that coal output has been growing at about 6 per cent annually, but expansion may have been slower in recent years due to increased availability of indigenous oil, and in 1977 the coal industry received a serious setback due to a severe earthquake in the Peking region. In the north and west of China there are large coal deposits at shallow depths suitable for surface mining. Many of these are not fully explored and the railway systems will need to be extended to exploit them adequately. With increased mechanisation it is possible that China could increase coal production sufficiently to provide substantial exports.

5.7   Chapter summary

The use of coal as a fuel has been known since ancient times, but its widespread use first developed in England in the sixteenth century when wood became scarce and increased in price. Its use as an industrial fuel probably commenced with lime burning and early metal smelting, but even as late as 1800 it is likely that about two thirds of the coal in the UK was used for domestic purposes. However, industrial consumption was then increasing rapidly, and for example the iron industry was using 25 per cent of all UK coal by 1840.

The UK continued to dominate world coal production and consumption until the second half of the nineteenth century and even as late as 1913 the 94 million tons of coal exported from the UK met 10 per cent of the total world coal demand. Coal consumption in the United States was only 8 million tons in 1850 but as a result of rapid industrialisation, population growth and conversion from wood fuel, it increased to 440 millions tons in 1910. After this the energy market share taken by coal in the US declined until in 1975 it met only 17 per cent of the total demand. Elsewhere the pattern was similar though with different timing. Coal met 81 per cent of the world energy needs in 1925, but although it increased from 794 million tons in that year to 1467 million tons by 1974 its market share had dropped to only 26 per cent.

The second part of the chapter is concerned with the production of coal and briefly outlines the following topics: coal formation, its classification, mining methods, resources and reserves. The largest reserves are located in the USSR, the US and China, but there are substantial reserves and resources in most world regions. This section includes estimates for potential future production in the principal coal producing countries. It is likely that Japan and Western Europe will become major coal importers as world oil production levels off and this will lead to export possibilities for a number of developing countries.

The market for coal has undergone a rapid change in most world regions since 1960. Its share of the transport and domestic sectors' fuel supply has declined dramatically, and the main uses of coal are now in the iron and steel industry and for electricity generation. One of the key questions in coal development is the time and nature of a revival in the use of coal by industry when heating oil becomes scarce.

In the OECD, 60 per cent of coal consumption is used for electricity generation. The comparative costs of nuclear energy, fuel oil, and steam coal are discussed. It appears that the relative costs of nuclear and coal depend critically on the transport costs for coal and the availability of cheap (possibly surface-mined) coal with a low sulphur content. With the exception of coal used at the mine mouth, transport costs may range from 15 per cent to more than 60 per cent of the delivered costs of coal; emission control costs may amount to 20 or 30 per cent of the delivered costs. This is likely to lead to widely different patterns of fuel use for future electricity generation in different parts of the world. The chapter concludes with a brief discussion of special features of coal production, use and future potential in different world regions.

Chapter 5   Further reading

Berkovitch, I. (1977) *Coal on the switchback*, Allen and Unwin, London.
Ezra, D. (1978) *Coal and energy*, Ernest Benn, London.
Gordon, R. L. (1978) *Coal in the US energy market*, Heath, Lexington, USA.
Gordon, R. R. (1971) 'Solid mineral fuels' in *Materials and technology*, vol. II, ed. van Thoor, T. J. W., Longman, London.
IEA (1978b) *Steam coal – prospects to 2000*, OECD, Paris.
McMullan, J. T., Morgan, R. and Murray, R. B. (1975) *Energy resources and supply*, Wiley, New York and London.
Nef, J. U. (1932), *The rise of the British coal industry* (2 vols.), Routledge, London.
Van Krevelen, D. W. (1961), *Coal: typology, chemistry, physics, constitution*, Elsevier, Amsterdam.
Wilson, C. L. (ed.) (1980) *Coal – bridge to the future*, Report of the World Coal Study (WOCOL), Ballinger, Cambridge, Mass.
World Energy Conference (WEC) (1978b) *World energy resources 1985–2020*, IPC Science and Technology Press, Guildford, UK, and NewYork.

CHAPTER 6

Nuclear power

6.1 Concepts in nuclear power production

Nuclear power production is based on the energy released when an atomic nucleus such as uranium undergoes fission (breaks into several parts) following the absorption of a neutron. The production of electricity through the controlled use of nuclear fission now accounts for more than 10 per cent of world electricity supplies and by 1990 this share is likely to be approaching 20 per cent. The technical potential for nuclear power and social attitudes to its development are major factors in national energy planning and world energy prospects. In this chapter the physics of nuclear energy will be briefly outlined before describing the main features of nuclear power reactors and the nuclear fuel cycle. This is followed by a discussion of the costs of nuclear power and its potential and prospects as a major source of energy in the future.

Fission is a process in which a neutron strikes a heavy nucleus and is absorbed to form a compound nucleus. This compound nucleus is unstable and may break into two or more smaller atomic nuclei with the simultaneous emission of several neutrons. These neutrons may themselves be absorbed by other nuclei, and if enough of these are uranium nuclei it is possible for a chain reaction to develop. Chain reactions form the basis of the operation of a nuclear reactor and they will be described in more detail in the next section.

Fission of a single atom of uranium yields 200 MeV (million electron volts; 200 MeV equals 3.2×10^{-11} J), whereas the oxidation of one carbon atom releases only 4 eV (6.4×10^{-19} J). On an equal weight basis, this 50 million ratio becomes about 2.5 million; the total energy from nuclear fission of 1 ton of uranium is approximately as great as that from 2.5 million tons of coal. The intensity with which nuclear energy is released both requires and permits the use of sophisticated, capital-intensive, equipment for its controlled conversion to heat and electric power.

Natural uranium consists of 99.3 per cent ^{238}U and only 0.7 per cent of the lighter isotope ^{235}U, but it is the latter that provides the most readily available fission energy in nuclear reactors. (The superscript indicates the weight of the atomic nucleus; different isotopes of an element have the same chemical properties but different weights – these terms will be discussed more fully later.) When a reactor has been in continuous operation for some time the percentage of ^{235}U may have fallen significantly, and there is also contamination of the fuel elements by fission products, so that the chain reaction cannot be sustained. Then the old fuel elements must be replaced by new ones with a higher concentration of ^{235}U. The old fuel elements still contain useful quantities of ^{235}U, and they contain large quantities of ^{238}U and small amounts of plutonium, each of which could be used in other types of nuclear reactor. They also contain radioactive fission products, some of which may be useful though they are normally described as radioactive waste. The mining of uranium ore and its conversion to a form suitable for use in nuclear reactor fuel elements form the initial stages of the nuclear fuel cycle, whilst the processing of the used fuel elements, and possible recycling or storage of the products, form the later stages of the nuclear fuel cycle. This is discussed in more detail in a later section of this chapter. Environmental and social aspects of nuclear power are mentioned in this chapter in connection with nuclear costs; they are also taken into account in indicating prospects for future growth in nuclear power, but their detailed consideration is postponed to chapter 9.

5.2 Physics of nuclear energy

An atom consists of a heavy nucleus surrounded by electrons. The nucleus is composed of N neutrons and Z positively charged protons (collectively called nucleons) densely packed in the central region of the atom. It is surrounded by a cloud of Z negatively charged electrons moving in orbits round the nucleus and bound to it through the Coulomb force that attracts bodies with opposite electric charge. The size of the atom is determined by the size of the electron cloud and is typically about 10,000 times the size of the nucleus at its centre. However, each neutron and proton has about 2000 times the mass of an electron and so about 99.98 per cent of the mass of an atom is concentrated in its nucleus. The electric forces between the electrons and the nucleus mean that energy is required to separate an electron from an atom. This energy, amounting to a few eV for removal of the most loosely bound electrons, is the origin of the chemical energy locked up in chemical compounds and released, for example, in combustion, so that the energies arising from such reactions are of the order of a few eV per atom.

The number N of neutrons in a stable nucleus exceeds the number Z of protons for all except a few light nuclei. The mass number $A = N + Z$ is used to label nuclei. Thus ^{238}U denotes uranium in which the nucleus contains 146 neutrons and 92 protons, whereas ^{235}U contains 143 neutrons and 92 protons. The chemical properties of these two isotopes of uranium are the same, but their atomic weights are slightly different, and the response of their nuclei to the absorption of neutrons is different. The neutrons and protons in a nucleus are held together by strong short-range nuclear forces, whose strength is much greater than that of the electrostatic forces that bind electrons in an atom. It would take several MeV (10^6eV) to separate a neutron from a stable nucleus, and this value is known as the binding energy. Because of the equivalence of mass and energy (explained in Einstein's (special) theory of relativity), the mass of a nucleus is less than the sum of its component parts. The mass deficit (Δm) is given by Einstein's well known formula $E_b = \Delta m c^2$ where E_b is the binding energy and c is the velocity of light, and the mass deficit may be found from

$$\Delta m = N m_n + Z m_p - {}^A_Z m$$

where

$A = N + Z$ is the mass number

Z is the number of protons (the atomic number)

N is the number of neutrons

m_n is the mass of a (free) neutron

m_p is the mass of a (free) proton

${}^A_Z m$ is the mass of the 'nuclide' (nucleus) with mass number A

and proton number Z.

One can display the binding energies for each element, but a more convenient measure of nuclear stability is the binding energy per nucleon $\Delta m c^2 / A$. This is illustrated by the curve shown in figure 6.1, drawn through a discrete set of points corresponding to 'nuclides' (atomic nuclei) of mass number A. It can be seen that the binding energy per nucleon starts low at low mass number, increases to a maximum around mass number 130 and then decreases again. This immediately suggests two possible ways of obtaining nuclear energy. Firstly, if two nuclides of low mass number could be fused together, the average binding energy per nucleon would increase, and the difference between the initial and final binding energies would be released in some way. Secondly, energy could also be released if a nuclide of high mass number could be induced to break up into smaller nuclides. The first approach, known simply as *fusion,* is the source of energy of the sun and in thermonuclear bombs, the second, called *fission,* is the source of energy (in a controlled form) for nuclear reactors and (in a relatively uncontrolled form) for fission bombs. It is the controlled release of energy by nuclear fission with which most of this chapter is concerned.

It has been observed that certain heavy nuclides ($A > 230$) occasionally undergo spontaneous fission. In this process the whole nucleus breaks up into two or more smaller parts, each part carrying off some of the excess energy liberated (because the smaller parts have higher binding energy per nucleon). It is usual in such a process for there to be two major fragments, called fission products, of nearly equal mass (around 120 mass units) together with one, two or more neutrons:

$${}^A_Z X \rightarrow \text{fission products} + \text{neutrons.}$$

The reason there are neutrons emitted is that the ratio N/Z of neutrons to protons in a stable nuclide increases with atomic number Z (and mass number $A = N + Z$). Thus the fission products from the break-up of a heavy nuclide will have an excess of neutrons compared with stable nuclides having the same atomic number. Before considering nuclear fission further we will outline the other main radioactive processes.

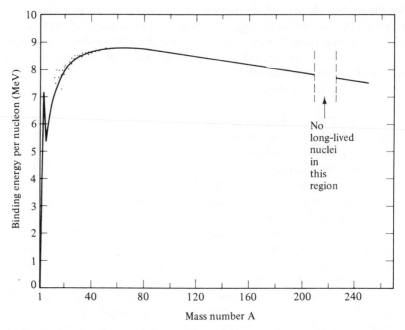

Figure 6.1   The binding energy per nucleon for stable atomic nuclei. *Note:* The curve is a smooth approximation to the discrete points representing stable nuclei (half life $> 10^{10}$ years) for A $\leq$ 209 and quasi-stable nuclei (half-life > 1600 years) for A $\geq$ 226.

Isotopes, radioactivity, half-life

Each chemical element corresponds to a fixed number Z of protons in its nucleus, but it generally has several isotopes. Thus there are several nuclides with the same proton number Z but differing mass numbers A due to differing numbers of neutrons N. These nuclides are distinguished by labelling the chemical element with the mass number, thus carbon-twelve is denoted $^{12}_{6}C$. In general $^{A}_{Z}X$ denotes the element whose name is abbreviated to X and has atomic number Z with mass number A (and neutron number $N = A - Z$). The two isotopes of uranium, $^{235}_{92}U$ and $^{238}_{92}U$ are of great importance to nuclear power production, natural uranium containing 0.7 per cent of the former isotope and 99.3 per cent of the latter.

Most elements have naturally occurring stable isotopes, but all elements have unstable isotopes that contain either too few or too many neutrons for them to be stable. In such cases the 'parent nuclide' may undergo radioactive decay by emitting one or more particles leaving a 'daughter nuclide'. The decay process may be repeated, thus releasing energy and changing the number of neutrons until the end product is a stable nuclide. Types of radioactive decay include:

(a) Beta decay, in which a neutron converts into a proton with the emission of an electron and an antineutrino (or a proton converts to a neutron, positron and neutrino).

(b) Alpha emission, in which two neutrons and two protons forming an alpha particle (the helium nucleus) are emitted.

(c) Gamma emission, in which a high energy photon or gamma ray (very high frequency electromagnetic radiation) carries off excess energy from the nucleus.

(d) Spontaneous fission, in which the parent nucleus breaks into two approximately equal parts (fission products) which almost instantaneously emit some of their excess neutrons.

A common feature of all of these types of decay is their statistical nature. The probability per unit time of the decay occurring in a particular atom is independent of what happens in other atoms, and is found to be a constant. Thus, if at time t we have $n(t)$ atoms of material undergoing some kind of radioactive decay, then during time dt, some fraction λdt of them will decay, so that

$$n(t + dt) = n(t) - \lambda dt\, n(t), \text{ or } \frac{dn}{dt} = -\lambda n$$

hence $n(t) = n(0)\exp(-\lambda t) = n(0)2^{-(t/T_{1/2})}$. The parameter $T_{1/2}$ is known as the *half-life* – in each half-life, half of the initial number of atomic nuclei decay, so that, after k half-lives, a fraction 2^{-k} of the original nuclei remains. The half life for radioactive decay varies from nuclide to nuclide over a range from a very small fraction of a second to 10^{10} years (for comparison, the age of the earth is about 4 × 10^9 years).

Neutron reactions

The observation of spontaneous fission in heavy elements prompts the question of what would happen if such elements were made even more unstable by the addition of another neutron. Since the operation of a nuclear fission reactor depends on the action of neutrons on heavy elements we will briefly describe the reactions between neutrons and atomic nuclei.

When a neutron hits a nucleus, there are essentially three possibilities for subsequent events. Firstly, it can simply bounce off the nucleus, like a marble off a billiard ball, leaving both neutrons and nucleus unchanged except that they would normally rebound in different directions from their original motion. Secondly the neutron may be absorbed by the nucleus to produce a slightly heavier nucleus, which will be in an excited state (a state with some excess energy) since the binding energy of the neutron is released and shared amongst the rest of the nucleus when the neutron is absorbed, and also the new nucleus has absorbed most of the kinetic energy of the neutron. This excess energy is usually emitted rapidly as a gamma ray, though other radiation processes may be involved.

The third possible outcome, and the most important for this discussion, is that the neutron may be absorbed by the nucleus, producing a new excited nucleus as above, but this excited nucleus may be so unstable that it almost instantaneously (in less than 10^{-15} seconds) disintegrates by fissioning into lighter nuclei and neutrons. Most of the difference in binding energies between the original nucleus

Table 6.1. *Average distribution of energy in fission.*

	MeV
Kinetic energy of fission fragments	168 ± 5
Instantaneous gamma ray energy	5 ± 1
Kinetic energy of fission neutrons	5 ± 0.5
Beta particles (electrons) from fission products	7 ± 1
Gamma ray from fission products	6 ± 1
Neutrinos	10 approx.
Total fission energy	201 ± 6

Notes: These values apply to ^{233}U, ^{235}U, ^{239}Pu.

and the fission products appears as kinetic energy – the fission products and neutrons moving rapidly away from the site of the collision – although some is bound up in the fission products which decay later by beta and gamma emission, or by further (delayed) neutron emission, to stable nuclides. The quantities of energy involved are illustrated by table 6.1, which shows its magnitude and distribution among products from the fission of $^{235}_{92}$U and $^{239}_{94}$Pu (plutonium) following absorption of a slow neutron. The nature of the fission products and the number of neutrons emitted (see table 6.2) varies, though the probabilities of particular outcomes are well defined, so that mean values can be obtained for all parameters that describe the process.

Cross sections
In order to discuss the relative importance and absolute magnitude of the effects of neutrons described above, it is convenient to define a parameter, called a *cross section,* which measures the apparent size of the nucleus as 'seen' by the incident neutron. The total cross section is the effective area within which the incident neutron may be expected to interact with the 'target' nucleus, and it can be accurately measured by counting the rates of various reactions with a thin target containing atoms of a particular nuclide. Cross sections (partial cross sections) can also be defined for particular reactions rather than for the total of all possible interactions with the target nuclide. Of these, the most important for our discussion are the absorption cross section σ_c (c for capture) and the fission cross section σ_f.

Each of these cross sections varies between different nuclides, and they also vary with the energy of the incident neutron. The way in which σ_f varies for both ^{235}U and ^{238}U is shown in figure 6.2, in which σ_f is shown on a logarithmic scale in 'barns' (1 barn is 10^{-28} m^2) and plotted against the neutron energy in MeV, also on a logarithmic scale. The fission cross section σ_f is one measure of the probability of nuclear fission taking place, and figure 6.2 shows that for ^{235}U it increases by a

Table 6.2. *Average number of neutrons emitted per fission.*

Isotope	Incident neutron energy	Average number of neutrons emitted per fission
^{235}U	0.025 eV	2.44
	1 MeV	2.50
^{239}Pu	0.025 eV	2.87
	1 MeV	3.02
^{238}U	1.1 MeV	2.46

factor of 10 or more at low neutron energies, but for ^{238}U it is smaller by several orders of magnitude and only becomes significant at fairly high neutron energies.

6.3 Chain reactions, moderators and nuclear fuels

We have described how a neutron may be absorbed by a heavy nuclide, such as ^{235}U, leading to nuclear fission in which several further neutrons may be emitted (table 6.2), together with the release of a considerable amount of energy (table 6.1). If it could be arranged that one of these neutrons causes fission in a nearby nucleus, it would be possible to sustain a *chain reaction,* with equal numbers of nuclei being fissioned per unit time. If, respectively, fewer or more than one neutron continued on to produce further fissions, the chain reaction would either die out or continuously increase in intensity. The maintenance of a chain reaction, with exactly one neutron (on average) eventually causing another fission, is the design objective of any nuclear reactor.

Each of the neutrons emitted in fission of a nuclide (for example, ^{235}U or ^{238}U) carries a fraction of the fission energy, the fraction varying from collision to collision, so that these neutrons are emitted with a continuous spectrum of energies, as shown in figure 6.3. If enough of these emitted neutrons are slowed down to very low energy without being absorbed there will be a high probability that one of them will cause fission in another ^{235}U nuclide since the fission process then has a large cross section (figure 6.2). There would be a correspondingly much smaller chance of producing a fission of ^{238}U, and in fact it is not possible to develop a chain reaction in pure ^{238}U because its effective absorption cross section for neutrons is so large compared with its fission cross section. However, for the lighter uranium isotope ^{235}U the fission cross sections are sufficiently large that nuclear reactors can be designed to produce stable chain reactions.

If the ratio of ^{235}U to ^{238}U in a mixture of the two is low, it is necessary to arrange that the neutrons be slowed down by a *moderator* (a light material mixed, usually inhomogeneously, with the fuel) in order to take advantage of the increase in fission cross section for low energy neutrons (figure 6.2). If the concentration of ^{235}U

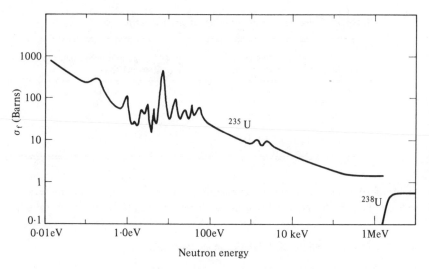

Figure 6.2   The fission cross-sections for uranium-235 and uranium-238.

compared to ^{238}U is higher, it is possible to design reactors that are based on fission caused by fast (higher energy) neutrons. Slow neutrons are sometimes called thermal neutrons (since their energies are comparable to those of particles in thermal motion), and reactors based on them are often called *thermal reactors,* in contrast to *fast reactors* whose design makes use of fission caused by fast neutrons.

Natural uranium contains only 0.7 per cent of ^{235}U, and at this level it is essential to base reactor designs on slow neutrons. By *enriching* the fuel up to above 3 per cent ^{235}U (<97 per cent ^{238}U) it is possible to gain more flexibility of design, but slow neutrons remain essential. A moderator material is included amongst the fuel elements in order to slow down the fission neutrons from their fairly high average energy in the region of 1 MeV (figure 6.3) to values less than 1 eV. The moderator is required to have good ability to slow down neutrons; from Newton's laws of conservation of energy and momentum in a collision, this means that the atoms of the moderator should be as light as possible. But a good moderator must also have a low absorption cross section for neutrons. A 'figure of merit' (called the moderating ratio) may be devised, which takes account of slowing down power per collision, the absorption cross section and also the number of moderating nuclei per unit volume. The fission process and the slowing down process from fast neutrons (fn) to slow neutrons (sn) is illustrated in figure 6.4 where the moderator is taken to be hydrogen having a nucleus composed of one proton. The average number of collisions required to achieve the desired slowing down of neutrons is given for different types of moderator in table 6.3.

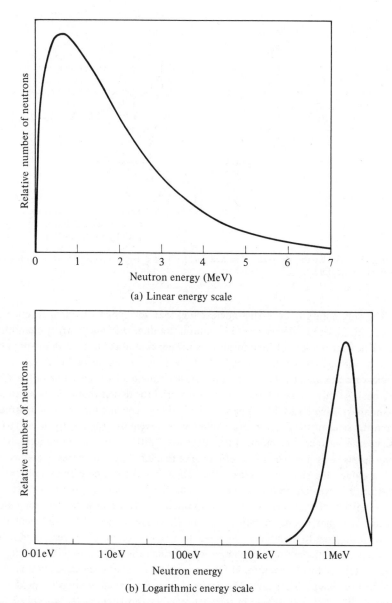

(a) Linear energy scale

(b) Logarithmic energy scale

Figure 6.3   The fission neutron energy spectrum for uranium-235. (a) Linear energy scale. (b) Logarithmic energy scale. *Note:* In both cases the area under the curve between two energies is proportional to the number of neutrons emitted in that energy range.

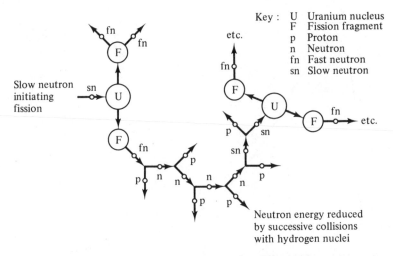

Figure 6.4 Schematic diagram of a neutron path in a chain reaction with a hydrogen (water) moderator.

The only naturally occurring nuclear fuel that will support a chain reaction is $^{235}_{92}U$. This isotope is always mixed in natural uranium with much larger quantities of the heavier isotope $^{238}_{92}U$ and forms only 0.7 per cent of the total uranium present (except for one known deposit at Oklo, Gabon, where the operation of a natural nuclear reactor about 1.95 billion years ago has caused a local depletion of the $^{235}_{92}U$ present). At this low percentage of fissile material the fission chain reaction can be maintained using a suitable moderator, but only by reducing the losses of neutrons from the sides of the reactor to a minimum. This requires the reactor to be large (since the surface to volume ratio decreases with size) and in practice the dimensions using a carbon moderator involve reactors 10 to 30 metres in diameter.

To reduce the size and increase the options for the choice of materials for a reactor, it is possible to *enrich* the uranium, that is to enhance the fissile $^{235}_{92}U$ in some portion of the available natural uranium at the expense of the remainder (which then has a smaller percentage of $^{235}_{92}U$). The higher the enrichment the easier it becomes to maintain a chain reaction, so the volume of the reactor may be reduced, and a moderator with a lower moderating ratio may be used. For example, light water reactors (moderator H_2O) use uranium that has been enriched from 0.7 per cent to about 3.0 per cent. The depleted uranium, called 'tailings', is predominantly $^{238}_{92}U$. It is not useable in thermal reactors and is currently stockpiled for possible future use in 'breeder' reactors, in which it can be exposed to high energy neutrons that convert it to fissionable isotopes such as $^{239}_{94}Pu$ (and other isotopes of plutonium). These artificially produced isotopes may themselves be used as the basic fissionable material in suitably designed reactors.

Table 6.3. *Moderators used for slowing down neutrons.*

Moderator	Average number of collisions required	Moderating ratio
Water (H_2O)	18	70
Heavy water (D_2O)	25	21,000
Helium (as 15°C gas at		
1 atmosphere pressure)	43	83
Beryllium	86	150
Carbon	114	170

Notes: A high moderating ratio implies that the moderator is more effective, i.e. less absorption relative to the number of neutron collisions required.

Fissile isotopes are produced also in the normal operation of thermal reactors through absorption of neutrons by $^{238}_{92}U$ to form $^{239}_{92}U$, which decays (with half-life 23 minutes) by electron emission to $^{239}_{93}Np$, which then itself decays (half-life 2.3 days) by electron emission to plutonium $^{239}_{94}Pu$. Similarly the fissile isotope $^{233}_{92}U$ may be produced from thorium. In thermal reactors the production of fissile isotopes is lower than the burn-up of the fissile component of uranium $^{235}_{92}U$ in the fuel. Thus the 'conversion gain' is less than one and their continued operation is dependent on continuing supplies of the 0.7 per cent of the fissile isotope in natural uranium. However, in a *fast reactor,* using high energy (fast) neutrons, the number of neutrons produced per fission is higher than in a thermal reactor, and some fission of $^{238}_{92}U$ also occurs (see table 6.2), so that there are more 'spare' neutrons available for absorption by the common uranium isotope $^{238}_{92}U$, giving a higher rate of conversion to fissile decay products. By suitable design the conversion gain can be chosen so that more fissile material is produced than is consumed. Reactors of this type are called 'breeders' or *fast breeder reactors.* Reactors not designed to breed but nevertheless containing 'fertile' material (natural uranium or thorium), may be called 'converter' reactors, and there is of course a continuum of possibilities for the amount of conversion obtained, the upper ranges being breeders.

It is necessary to have some form of control in a reactor that allows a chain reaction to develop, then continue at a steady level, and be shut down when desired. Such control is possible by changing the total loss rate of neutrons, either by altering the absorption or the escape rate of neutrons from the reactor core, so that the average number of the neutrons emitted in a fission event which subsequently causes another fission event varies in the neighbourhood of one. It is therefore important to know the average time interval ℓ from one generation of neutrons to the next since this determines the rate of growth of the fission rate $n(t)$ (the number of fissions per unit time). If conditions are such that $(1 + k_{ex})$ neutrons of one generation produce fission, (k_{ex} is the number of excess neutrons), then

$$\frac{dn}{dt} = (n/\ell)k_{ex}, \quad \text{giving } n = n_0\exp[(k_{ex}/\ell)t].$$

When a neutron hits a nucleus and causes fission, most of the next generation are produced promptly in less than 10^{-15} seconds. For thermal reactors they are then slowed down and diffused until they meet a fuel nucleus, which takes 10^{-4} to 10^{-3} seconds; thus this is the generation time for prompt neutrons. However, a small fraction of the total number of neutrons are not emitted promptly in fission but are emitted through decay of the various fission products with effective half lives ranging from 0.4 sec upwards. In total the delayed neutrons form a fraction of all fission neutrons equal to 0.0027 for $^{233}_{92}U$, 0.0065 for $^{235}_{92}U$, and 0.0021 for $^{239}_{94}Pu$. The weighted average of the generation time for all neutrons from fission of $^{235}_{92}U$ is about 0.1 sec. Then for $^{235}_{92}U$, provided $k_{ex} < 0.0065$ (the fraction of delayed neutrons), for example $k_{ex} < 0.003$, the output power will increase more slowly than

$$\exp[(0.003/0.1)t] \approx \exp(0.03t).$$

A 3 per cent change in neutron intensity in each second is acceptable for the design of reactor control systems, for example through the movement of control rods composed of material that absorbs neutrons.

It is useful to note that if k_{ex} is greater than 0.0065 (for $^{235}_{92}U$) there will be exponential growth for a short time, but then parts of the reactor would heat up and vaporise, moving apart at speeds greater than the neutrons in a thermal reactor, so there would not be a nuclear explosion. The situation is similar for a failure in a fast reactor, where localised heating would produce a thermal explosion, thus reducing the core density and stopping the chain reaction. The potential danger from a thermal explosion is that it might disrupt the pressure vessel, and possibly also the outer containment shell, so radioactive material or gases might escape into the environment. Considerable precautions must therefore be taken in the design of the reactor and its containment system to prevent this from happening.

6.4   Nuclear power reactors

The essential components for the two principal types of power reactor, *thermal* and *fast,* can be summarised as follows:

Thermal reactors
(a) A fissionable fuel in which the fission chain reaction is to be maintained;
(b) a moderator, to slow the fission neutrons down to thermal energies;
(c) a coolant, to be circulated through the fuel to remove the heat liberated in fission;
(d) control devices, for example neutron absorbers, to reduce the number of neutrons.

In addition there are:

(e) a diluent for the fissionable fuel, usually $^{238}_{92}U$;

(f) structural materials for support and to keep various of the above components physically separate.

Some of the functions mentioned above may be performed by the same materials, in particular, in many thermal reactors the coolant is also the moderator.

Fast reactors

(a) A fissionable fuel (usually $^{235}_{92}U$ but $^{239}_{94}Pu$ can be used);

(b) a coolant;

(c) control devices, the usual method being the movement of neutron absorbers and/or 'reflectors' (which change the rate of escape of neutrons from the reactor core).

In addition there are:

(d) a diluent for the fuel (usually $^{238}_{92}U$);

(e) structural materials for support and to keep the above components physically separate.

In addition, if the fast reactor is a breeder (the usual reason for using a fast reactor)

(f) fertile material around and within the fuel, suitable for conversion (usually $^{238}_{92}U$ for conversion to $^{239}_{94}Pu$ in current practice).

Practically all power reactors currently in operation use uranium-235 ($^{235}_{92}U$) as a fuel, and this is diluted by the more common isotope uranium-238 ($^{238}_{92}U$). The main types currently in operation are described in the remainder of this section. The choice of the type of reactor and its design has generally been made on economic grounds, but taking into account national experience, so there have often been different choices in different countries.

The following notes on the main types of reactor contain a short description of the PWR, for illustration, and brief mention of the main characteristics of other types.

Light water reactors (LWR)

There are two main types of LWR in use, the Pressurised Water Reactor (PWR) and the Boiling Water Reactor (BWR). Together, they account for most of the current world power reactors.

Pressurised water reactors (PWR)

The fissionable fuel is $^{235}_{92}U$, fresh fuel being uranium enriched to about 3.3 per cent $^{235}_{92}U$ (the balance being $^{238}_{92}U$), in the form of uranium dioxide (UO_2), a highly refractory ceramic. Ordinary (light) water is used as both moderator and coolant in this type of reactor, so it is one of those referred to as a 'light water reactor' (light in this context refers to the common or light isotope of hydrogen ^1_1H in water H_2O,

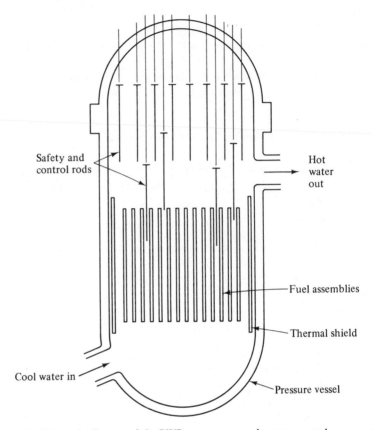

Figure 6.5   Schematic diagram of the PWR reactor core and pressure vessel.

compared with heavy water which contains the heavy hydrogen isotope $^2_1$H known as deuterium). Structural materials are mainly stainless steel, while control is effected by neutron absorption in movable control rods containing boron (boron has a high absorption cross section for thermal neutrons).

The basic constituents of the PWR are illustrated schematically in figure 6.5 and figure 6.6. The fuel consists of uranium dioxide pellets, which are inserted into zircalloy tubes to form the fuel rods, about 1 cm diameter and 4 metres long. The fuel rods are contained in assemblies of about 200 rods, interspersed with control channels in which the control rods move, which are assembled together to form the core of the reactor (figure 6.5). The core is contained in a stainless steel pressure vessel with walls more than 20cm thick. Water under high pressure is forced through the spaces between the fuel rods, thus cooling them and also acting as a moderator to slow down the fission neutrons. This water is heated by the reactor

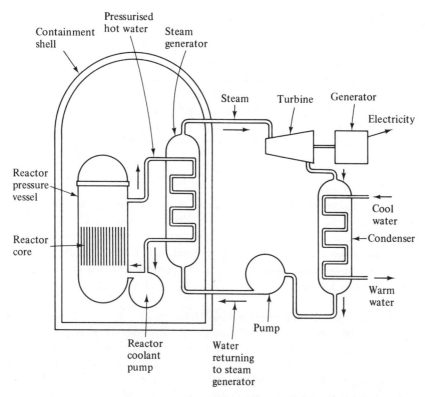

Figure 6.6   Schematic diagram of the PWR reactor and electricity generating system.

core and then passes through a steam generator (figure 6.6) where it heats a secondary circuit of water. The latter provides the steam which passes through a steam turbine to generate electricity (figure 6.6). The pressure vessel containing the reactor is itself contained (with the steam generator) inside a containment shell of reinforced concrete, which simultaneously acts as a biological shield against radiation and a containment vessel in the event of leakage from the radioactive part of the system. The water in the secondary circuit is essentially free from radioactivity.

   In addition to the boron-containing control rods there are various emergency methods of shutting off the fission chain reaction, the usual one being injection of a solution of boron salt into the primary coolant. If the primary coolant water were to escape, the chain reaction would automatically end, since without the water moderator fewer thermal neutrons would be produced and the core would become sub-critical. However, after operation for a period of time the core contains radioactive fission products, which must be cooled following a loss of coolant even though the chain reaction has stopped, so additional emergency core cooling systems are also provided.

The total weight of uranium metal in a PWR of 1 GW(e) (one gigawatt electrical output) is about 90 tonnes (i.e. about 102 tonnes of uranium dioxide). Its composition changes as the uranium-235 is used and fission products are formed. Refuelling is achieved by shutting down the reactor, depressurising the pressure vessel, removing its top, then replacing assemblies of fuel rods one at a time. In a commissioned power reactor this operation is generally planned to occur once a year, and about one third of the core is replaced at each fuelling (see *fuel cycle* below).

Boiling water reactor (BWR)

This is the second major type of light water reactor. The basic ideas differ little from those in the PWR, and fuels, coolant and moderator are all similar. The major difference in the BWR is that the primary coolant water is allowed to boil and produce steam from the reactor core. This steam is used directly to drive a steam turbine to generate electricity, instead of transferring heat to a secondary circuit as in the PWR.

Heavy water reactors (CANDU, SGHWR)

The moderator (and in CANDU the coolant) in these reactors is heavy water (the oxide of $^2_1$H, or D, deuterium, often written D_2O). Because the moderating ratio for heavy water is very high (table 6.3), it is very effective in converting fast neutrons to slow neutrons. This permits the use of natural uranium, of which the basic fuel $^{235}_{92}$U only forms 0.7 per cent, in the reactor core.

Gas – graphite reactors (including Magnox)

In this type of reactor, the fuel is also natural uranium, in metallic form. The moderator used is carbon and the coolant is carbon dioxide gas under pressure. Control is again by neutron absorbing rods. Such reactors have very large cores compared with the PWR and BWR, because the critical size for a chain reaction is very large using natural uranium with a carbon moderator.

Advanced gas reactor (AGR)

This is a development of the Magnox reactor, and uses enriched uranium as fuel in oxide form, but retains the use of carbon as moderator and carbon dioxide as coolant.

Fast breeder reactors (FBR)

Several experimental and pre-prototype fast breeders have operated or are operating. The principal design uses liquid sodium metal as coolant (LMFBR – liquid metal FBR). The fissionable fuel is currently $^{239}_{94}$Pu or a mixture of plutonium isotopes and/or $^{235}_{92}$U, and this is diluted with $^{238}_{92}$U. No moderator is required since this reactor type is operated by the fast neutrons produced in fission. To maintain such a chain reaction it is necessary to have a high concentration of fissionable fuel in the core (more than 20 per cent). The liquid sodium coolant has the advantageous properties of high heat transfer capability, high temperature operation at low pressure, low absorption of fast neutrons, and low moderating effects. Control of the chain reaction is achieved by movement of control rods. The core is surrounded by a blanket of $^{238}_{92}$U to utilise excess neutrons. Since uranium-238 absorbs fast neutrons in both the core itself and the blanket, the FBR acts as an efficient converter of $^{238}_{92}$U to fissile products such as $^{239}_{92}$Pu. The reactor can be designed to *breed*, or produce more fissile material than is consumed. This would permit the use of a much higher percentage of natural uranium than is possible with thermal reactors, increasing the potential utilisation from 1 or 2 per cent to 60 per cent or more. This type of reactor may therefore be of considerable importance in the future in view of the possible limitations on the resources of good grades of uranium ore. A concept of particular importance in a practical breeder reactor is the *doubling time*, defined as the number of years it takes to double the amount of fissionable material associated with the reactor. Thus after this period the reactor will still contain an amount equal to that in the original core and will have converted uranium-238 in an equal amount to fissionable material.

In operation the LMFBR has a primary circuit of molten sodium (which becomes radioactive) to cool the core. This provides heat to a secondary circuit of molten sodium (non-radioactive) which in turn heats a circuit containing water in which steam is generated to drive a turbine and generate electricity.

Other reactors

Other reactors that we have not discussed include the high temperature gas cooled reactor (HTGCR) that may be of importance in industrial processes due to its higher operating temperature, and the gas cooled fast breeder reactor (GCFBR) that may be developed as an alternative or a supplement to the LMFBR.

Most commercial nuclear reactors have been designed and developed to raise steam from which one can generate electricity, and it is likely that this will remain their dominant use over the next 25 years. In the longer term it is possible that some designs of reactors could be used to generate direct high temperature heat for use in industrial processes.

Fuel requirements

Given the power output of any reactor, it is straightforward to compute the rate at which atomic nuclei must be fissioning and hence the rate of consumption of the fuel. Each fission of a heavy nucleus releases an energy of about 200 MeV (see table 6.1) but about 10 MeV per fission is lost, because it is carried away by neutrinos which have so little interaction with matter that almost all of them escape from the earth (in travelling through the earth fewer than 1 in 10^{15} would be stopped). Thus each fission provides about 190MeV of usable energy (as kinetic energy of the fission products and neutrons) which is converted to heat in the reactor core.

One gram of $^{235}_{92}$U contains about 2.6×10^{21} atoms, so its complete fission would provide energy equal to

$$2.6 \times 10^{21} \times 190 \text{ MeV} = 2.6 \times 10^{21} \times 190 \times 1.6 \times 10^{-13} \text{ J}$$
$$\approx 78 \text{ GJ} \approx 0.9 \text{ MW days.}$$

Using this result the energy produced from the complete fission of uranium may be compared with that obtained by burning conventional fuels. The amount of each fuel required to produce thermal energy of 1MW day is shown in table 6.4. If this thermal energy is used to generate electricity, about two thirds will normally be lost as waste heat, so only about 0.3 MW day(e) of electrical energy will be generated.

Since it has become usual practice to refer all quantities to a 'standard' size of 1 GW(e) (1000 MW(e) $\approx$ 3300 MW thermal), we can compute the annual fuel requirements if we assume some load factor (actual output divided by potential output with full time use). For a load factor of 0.7 the quantity of uranium fuel actually fissioned from a standard 1 GW(e) power plant in one year would be

$$3300 \times 0.7 \times 365 \times 1.1 = 927 \times 10^3 \text{g} = 0.927 \text{ tonnes}$$

If the fuel were pure $^{235}_{92}$U, this would be the annual fuel requirement, but matters are complicated by three features – the fact that the uranium only contains a small percentage of $^{235}_{92}$U, the presence of $^{238}_{92}$U (some of which is converted and fissioned), and the production of fission products.

Fresh fuel in a typical PWR (pressurised water reactor) is enriched uranium (oxide) containing approximately 3.3 per cent $^{235}_{92}$U, the remainder being $^{238}_{92}$U. The main nuclear processes in the reactor are the fission of $^{235}_{92}$U and the conversion of $^{238}_{92}$U by neutron absorption to $^{239}_{94}$Pu (plutonium). The latter process takes place at about half the rate of the former, thus the amount of plutonium generated (and the amount that subsequently undergoes fission in the reactor) depends on how long the fuel is kept in the reactor. This duration is limited because the total quantity of fissionable material decreases with time (plutonium is created more slowly than uranium-235 is fissioned), and because some of the fission products act as neutron absorbers and hence reduce the reactivity of the fuel. In practice fuel is kept in a reactor until a significant fraction of it ceases to support the chain reaction.

The actual utilisation of fuel is measured by its *burn-up*, which is defined as the total amount of heat energy created from unit weight of the heavy metal (uranium) in the original fuel. For a typical LWR (with 3.3 per cent initial $^{235}_{92}$U), the standard aim is to achieve a burn-up of 33,000 MW days per tonne, corresponding to fission of $33,000 \times 1.1$ gram of uranium.

From the burn-up achieved, it is possible to estimate the fuel requirements for a reactor. For example, consider a 1 GW(e) = 1000 MW(e) LWR reactor requiring a thermal output of 3300 MW(t), operating at a load factor of 0.7, and with a fuel

Table 6.4. *Masses of different fuels required to produce 1 MW day (or 86.4 GJ) of thermal energy* (see also table 6.5).

Oil about 2 tonnes $= 2 \times 10^6$ g
Coal about 3 tonnes $= 3 \times 10^6$ g
Uranium (with complete fission) about 1.1 g

Table 6.5. *Annual fuel required for a 1 GW(e) power station at 30 per cent efficiency and 70 per cent load factor.*

	Annual fuel required
Oil	1.5 million tonnes
Coal	2.3 million tonnes
Uranium (enriched fuel in LWR)	26 tonnes
[Natural uranium required	150 tonnes][a]

[a]The 150 tonnes of natural uranium is required to produce 26 tonnes of enriched uranium fuel for an LWR.

burn-up of 33,000 MW days per tonne. Then the annual thermal energy needed is

$$3300 \times 0.7 \times 365 (\text{MW day}) = 8.4 \times 10^5 (\text{MW day})$$

This requires an annual use of uranium by the reactor equal to

$$(8.4 \times 10^5) / 33,000 = 25.6 \text{ tonnes uranium.}$$

The approximate requirements of alternative fuels to maintain a 'standard' 1 GW(e) electric power station at 70 per cent load factor for one year are shown for oil, coal, and uranium (for a PWR) in table 6.5.

The above calculations indicate the fuel needed to provide the energy output from the reactor, but they do not indicate the *fuel inventory* required by the reactor. This inventory is set by two main conditions. Firstly in the reactor core configuration used, it must be sufficient to achieve criticality (maintain a chain reaction), and secondly the power density (rate of heat production per unit mass of fuel) must be low enough for the circulating coolant to remove heat sufficiently quickly so that the fuel and its containers remain at a reliable operating temperature. The fuel inventories in the core of a 1 GW(e) power reactor range upwards from about 90 tonnes. In such a reactor, operating at around 0.7 (or 70 per cent) load factor, approximately one third of the fuel in the core has to be replaced with fresh fuel each year.

6.5   Nuclear fuel cycle

The nuclear fuel cycle is illustrated in figure 6.7, which shows the main stages of finding and processing uranium for use in a light water reactor, and the subsequent stages of processing, possible recycling, and waste disposal or storage. These stages will be briefly outlined in this section, firstly for the uranium cycle for LWRs, and then for the LMFBR (breeder) cycle. It is important to note that some stages of these fuel cycles are not yet operating on a commercial basis. For example, there is uncertainty about the best procedure for long-term disposal of some parts of the radioactive waste. Other problems are indicated in the following notes.

Mining and initial concentration

Economically viable concentrations of uranium range from about 3.0 per cent down to about 0.05 per cent, so that extraction of one tonne of natural uranium will involve the mining of between 30 and 2000 tonnes of ore. In addition it may be necessary to remove overburden (the layers of rock and soil above the ore) up to 20 times the weight of the ore, though this figure is usually much lower. It has been noted (table 6.5) that about 150 tonnes of natural uranium are required annually for a 1 GW(e) power station. With the above concentrations, this would require mining between 4500 and 300,000 tonnes of ore. This may be compared with the 2.3 million tonnes of coal needed for a similar coal fired station.

The mined ore is mechanically crushed, and the uranium (in the form of its oxide U_3O_8) is chemically extracted. Additional uranium may be obtained by 'heap leaching' in which piles of the ore are treated with aqueous solvents, and uranium extracted from the run-off from these piles. The uranium obtained is in the form of impure uranium oxide (U_3O_8) known as 'yellow cake'.

Conversion and enrichment

After further chemical purification, the pure uranium oxide is converted to the gaseous uranium hexafluoride (UF_6) to be used as a feedstock for the enrichment process. It was noted earlier that natural uranium contains only 0.7 per cent of uranium-235, with the balance as uranium-238, while most current reactors require fuel containing 2.7 to 3.3 per cent uranium-235. The enrichment is carried out by making use of the slight mass difference between ^{235}U and ^{238}U that is due to the different numbers of neutrons in their nuclei.

There are two methods of enrichment currently in use – gas diffusion and centrifuge. Gas diffusion utilises the slight difference in the rates of diffusion of the gaseous hexafluorides of uranium-235 and 238, the relative rates being approximately 1.0043. With such a small difference many stages of this process are required, and since at each stage the gas has to be pumped to high pressure, the power consumption is considerable. This process was developed during the 1939–45 war, and the same plants in the US are still in use today, providing enrichment capacity commercially.

In the gas centrifuge method, centrifugal force causes the heavier $^{238}UF_6$ to move preferentially towards the outer wall of the rotor of the centrifuge, leaving the gas

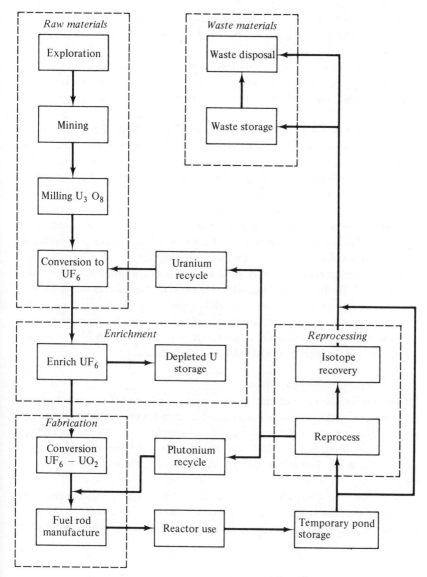

Figure 6.7 Nuclear fuel cycle for light water reactors (LWR).

in the centre slightly enriched. This enriched gas is extracted and separation is enhanced by making use of an axial temperature gradient imposed along the rotor. The high strength material requirements for the centrifuges prevented economic competition between the two techniques until the later 1970s. The centrifuge method has the advantage of lower power and energy consumption than the diffusion method.

A radically new and very promising method based on the use of lasers is currently being researched (in secrecy due to its potential use in nuclear weapons production) and may lead to nearly complete separation of the isotopes in one stage.

In current methods of enrichment of uranium, two outputs are produced – the desired enriched product and a 'tails' residue of uranium depleted in uranium-235. Typically each tonne of natural uranium leads to 170 kg of enriched fuel and 830 kg of depleted uranium. The 170 kg enriched component contains 3 per cent (5 kg) of ^{235}U, while the 830 kg depleted component contains 0.25 per cent or 2 kg of ^{235}U. The usual measure of the effectiveness of a uranium enrichment plant is the 'separation power', which is independent of the isotopic concentrations and is reported in kilograms of uranium per year, a unit called a 'separative work unit' (SWU). The amount of energy consumed by an enrichment plant is approximately proportional to the separative work performed. Gaseous diffusion plants use about 2500 kWh of electricity per SWU, while for gas centrifuge plants the corresponding figure is only about 100 kWh. This difference in power consumption, a major part of the cost of enrichment in diffusion plants, is offset by the higher cost of equipment in centrifuge plants, a major factor in the latter case being the periodic replacement of the highly stressed individual centrifuges.

Fuel element fabrication

Taking pressurised water reactors as an example, the enriched uranium hexafluoride from the enrichment plant is converted to uranium dioxide (UO_2), a ceramic material, formed into pellets, and inserted into stainless steel or zircalloy fuel pins (about 1 cm in diameter) which are welded closed and subjected to stringent testing. These are then fabricated into the fuel crates for insertion into reactor cores.

In the case of CANDU and MAGNOX reactor types, enrichment is not necessary (the penalty being a greatly increased uranium inventory) so the entire enrichment stage is omitted. These reactors use metallic uranium instead of its oxide.

Radioactive materials

All the operations thus far described for the fuel cycle involve natural or unirradiated enriched uranium. Although uranium is radioactive and hazardous on ingestion or inhalation, the radiation levels from it do not require extensive radiation shielding procedures. Thus the operations generally use standard industrial procedures, but carried out under clean-room conditions and with extensive quality control. Fresh fuel encased in its pins or cans emits virtually no radiation, so may be safely handled without shielding.

The next stage of the fuel cycle is the loading and use of the fuel in the reactor to produce heat and give power output. About one third of the core in an LWR in operation is replaced annually. On discharge from the reactor, the spent fuel is highly radioactive and always has to be handled by remote control, with heavy shielding for any people in the vicinity.

Used fuel handling and reprocessing

On discharge from a reactor, the spent fuel contains fission products together with plutonium, some remaining uranium-235, small but significant quantities of heavier elements (actinides), with the bulk composed of uranium-238. It is intensely radioactive from decay of the fission products, and needs to be cooled because of the heat generated in these decays. Initially it is stored in water filled 'cooling ponds' (metal lined concrete pools) on the reactor site, while the shorter lived fission products decay, partially reducing the cooling and radiation shielding requirements. Some of the options for subsequent handling of the fuel are illustrated in figure 6.7, and are briefly discussed below.

'Once through' cycle

One possible procedure is to discard the spent fuel rods entirely in some form of final repository. The disadvantages of this seemingly simple procedure are that fissile uranium-235 and plutonium would be wasted, and the uranium-238 would not be available for possible future use in a breeder reactor programme. A further disadvantage is that the 'once through' cycle would impose more stringent demands on the design of the final repository if the spent fuel was not reprocessed to separate out the fissile material.

Plutonium and/or uranium recycle

Any other option requires reprocessing of the spent fuel. This is first mechanically chopped up, and the uranium dioxide or metal is dissolved. The solution is chemically treated to separate out uranium and plutonium from fission products and higher actinides. The fission products and actinides are sent to temporary storage in heavily shielded, cooled steel tanks. The uranium, now free from fission products, and thus not very radioactive, may be recycled back into the enrichment plant (uranium recycle), or stored. The plutonium may be stored (for possible future use in breeder reactors), or converted to oxide form and used to enrich uranium to form a 'mixed oxide' fuel, the fissile component of which is a mixture of plutonium and uranium-235.

Waste disposal and storage

In addition to the output streams described above and illustrated in figure ·6.7, there are also streams containing waste of intermediate and low radioactivity. The intermediate-level solid wastes are (currently) usually encapsulated in concrete or bitumen, while intermediate-level liquid wastes are solidified in concrete. Those low-level streams which cannot be concentrated up to intermediate-levels are diluted and dispersed into the environment. Such dispersion has to be kept to a very low level and is rigorously monitored and regulated.

At present the high-level radioactive wastes are stored in liquid form in storage tanks, designed with extensive precautions to avoid leakage and local heating due to the high level of radioactivity. It is ultimately planned that these fission products be solidified before permanent storage, possibly by incorporation into borosilicate glass which would be formed into cylinders 0.3–1.0 m diameter and up to 2 m long. After a further cooling period, to reduce the heating due to radioactivity, the cylinders could be encapsulated in some further containment and placed in a final repository. The latter might be underground at a depth greater than 300 metres in some form of stable, low permeability, rock formation. Various possible sites are being studied in a number of countries, with a view to designing repositories with a negligible risk of the radioactive elements finding their way back into the biosphere. Since most of the highly radioactive wastes have half-lives of the order of decades, after a period of about 600 years most of the remaining radioactivity of the waste would arise from the long lived actinides, the total potential ingestion hazard being then about 100 times that of the original uranium that has been used. After $\sim 10^6$ years this potential hazard has dropped below that of the original uranium.

Breeder reactor fuel cycle

There is no further use for the depleted uranium that is formed during the enrichment process (see figure 6.7), unless breeder reactors are included in the nuclear power system. The depleted uranium consists mainly of uranium-238 which has a low probability of fission (see figure 6.2) or conversion by the slow neutrons that are predominant in thermal reactors. As noted in section 6.4 these reactors are dependent for their energy mainly on the fission of the uranium-235, which enriches the uranium in the core but is consumed during reactor operation – these are 'burner reactors'. However, (section 6.4), breeder reactors are based on fission using fast neutrons which not only sustain the chain reaction but also have a relatively high probability for absorption by uranium-238 to form uranium-239 which subsequently undergoes further transitions to form fissile products, particularly plutonium.

In order to maintain fast neutron reactions in breeders, natural or depleted uranium for the core is highly enriched by plutonium. The reactors can be designed so that the consumption of the fissile plutonium and uranium-235 in the chain reaction is matched – or more than matched – by the production of plutonium through conversion from uranium-238 in the core and in the depleted uranium blanket (see section 6.4). Through this conversion process it is possible eventually to utilise most of the fission energy in uranium-238, which forms 99.3 per cent of natural uranium. Allowing for the fact that there is some conversion also in burner reactors, this means that breeders can yield up to 60 times the energy output of thermal reactors (burner reactors) using the same amount of natural uranium.

The breeder reactor fuel cycle therefore differs from that shown in figure 6.7 in that the plutonium recycle is essential for its operation, and the depleted uranium would be taken from storage and – after enrichment – used in fuel fabrication for core or blanket. The potential for using the depleted uranium opens up a large reserve of energy that could not otherwise be utilised. The use of breeders also provides a method of consuming the plutonium that is produced in thermal reactors. Since a minimum initial stock of plutonium for enrichment is required for a breeder reactor, the plutonium currently produced by thermal reactors is usually stored – either before or after reprocessing – in order to maintain the option of a possible future breeder programme, though as noted above it could be recycled in thermal reactors.

The improvement in breeder reactors, by a factor of up to 60 in the efficiency with which uranium can be used, not only opens up the large reserves of energy in depleted uranium, which has obvious strategic implications for countries not having natural uranium resources, but also extends the uranium resource base. Very low grade uranium ore which would be uneconomic in thermal reactors can be economic in a system including breeders. The increased efficiency in the use of uranium by breeders and the resulting enlargement of the uranium resource base would extend the potential use of nuclear power on a large scale from several decades to several centuries or more. The opposing arguments that give rise to the greatest concern arise from the risks associated with the extensive use of plutonium. These questions are discussed further in chapter 9.

Current situation
The fuel cycles discussed above are idealised versions of those most likely to be adopted. In actual practice no final repository has yet been built, so no radioactive waste products have been irretrievably isolated. The current situation varies from country to country. In the US, where the large majority of reactors are PWRs or BWRs there are currently no commercial reprocessing facilities in operation, and a decision has been taken to defer reprocessing indefinitely, although this decision could, of course, be changed in the future. All spent fuel rods (except for a few used experimentally) are being stored at reactors in temporary storage ponds, or at one or two other licensed sites. A political decision has postponed the development of a prototype commercial fast breeder, though research continues at a high level. An

intermediate option of increasing the conversion efficiency of LWRs is also being examined. In Canada the reactors use natural uranium, and since Canada has large reserves of uranium there is little incentive to develop breeder reactors.

For Europe and Japan the situation is different since indigenous resources of uranium are small, so there is much greater incentive to proceed to breeders. Prototype commercial breeder reactors are therefore being developed or are in operation, and France, Germany and the UK all have thermal reactor fuel reprocessing facilities in commercial operation.

In many countries there have been delays in developing nuclear power due to increased requirements for safety and safeguards arising, in part, from opposition to nuclear power on environmental and social grounds. The environmental and social aspects of nuclear power, and also of other forms of energy, are considered in chapter 9. Energy costs for different types of energy production are discussed in chapter 11, and illustrative costs for electricity generation from new nuclear, oil and coal-fired power stations are given in chapter 5. In the next section we briefly discuss the derivation of the costs of electricity generation by nuclear power, and chapter 7 contains a general survey of electricity production in the context of energy demand and economic growth.

6.6   Costs of nuclear power

The high technology and safety requirements for nuclear power lead to a large component in the capital cost that increases only slowly with size. This creates large economies of scale, so that although the first power reactors had thermal power output of 200–600 MW(t), the modern trend is towards 3000–3600 MW(t), which yields an electrical output of 1000–1200 MW(e). Where cheap coal is available, this size is required to compete favourably with coal fired power stations. There are proposals to develop small reactors of about 200 MW(t) to produce steam for industrial use, but none has yet come to fruition. The principal use of nuclear power, at least for some decades, is likely to be for electricity production.

Burn-up of uranium fuel is (taking the PWR as an example) about 33,000 MW day (thermal) per tonne, so at 30 per cent efficiency 1 kWh(e) requires 4.2×10^{-6} kg of fuel, or about 2.5×10^{-5} kg of natural uranium, since each kg of enriched fuel requires (1/0.17) kg of natural uranium. The current cost of natural uranium is about $80 kilogram, giving a natural uranium cost of about 2 mills per kWh, which is increased to about 4 to 5 mills/kWh by the cost of enriching and fabricating the fuel (one mill is $0.001). Thus the major part of the costs of electricity from nuclear power arise from the capital costs, which are higher than those using fossil fuel, due to the higher technology and safety requirements of nuclear power.

Actual and estimated capital costs of nuclear power vary widely, since they are based on different size units, different sites in different areas, using costs evaluated in monetary units that change with inflation, and using different interest rates, accounting procedures and periods of construction, all of which affect capital costs. Figure 6.8 shows a series of capital cost estimates in the US for a single 1 GW(e) LWR under relatively similar accounting procedures, but reported in current US dollars at the start of each project over the period 1967 to 1976, during which the GNP price deflator increased by a factor of about 1.7. The apparent capital costs rise by a factor 5.5 over 9 years, and the costs at constant dollars increase by a factor 3.3. There are three main causes of this increase. Firstly, increased numbers and stringency of safety and environmental regulations that increase considerably the total quantities of materials required to construct the plant (for example, requirements for concrete, steel, pipes, cables almost doubled in the US). These increased quantities lead to corresponding increases in the costs of labour and management. Secondly, and in part due to the previously noted effects, the time from initial planning to complete construction in the US has doubled from about 6 years to nearly 12. This increases the relative importance of indirect costs and interest charges. Finally, the general increase in interest rates has also caused a marked rise in interest charges. If interest rates were to fall and construction times to shorten at some time in the future the real costs of nuclear power could decrease.

The numbers shown in figure 6.8 represent the estimated cost at the time of completion expressed in reference year dollars (at the start of the project). Assuming high and low capital costs in 1976 US dollars of $1000 and $700 per kW(e), high and low capital and interest charge of 20 per cent and 10 per cent (real), and 70 per cent load factor (see chapter 7), the equivalent capital charges per kWh would be 33 mills (high) and 11 mills (low). Any study of the costs of using alternative fuels for electricity generation (see chapters 5 and 7) would assume the same interest rates for each fuel, but major uncertainties in total capital costs would remain.

6.7   Historical growth and potential future growth of nuclear power

The first commercial nuclear power stations were completed in the 1950s in the UK at Calder Hall and in the US at Shippingport, Pa. Both countries maintained a steady development and construction programme during the 1960s so that, by 1970, there was nearly 6 GW(e) of nuclear capacity in the US and nearly 5 GW(e) in the UK, while other European countries together had 4 GW(e), Japan 1 GW(e), Canada 0.2 GW(e) and India 0.4 GW(e). The total nuclear capacity in the non-communist world increased from 16 GW(e) in 1970 to 86 GW(e) in 1977, and is expected to reach 130 GW(e) in 1980 and about 240 GW(e) in 1985.

The primary energy equivalent of electricity produced by nuclear power is conventionally put equal to the energy for an average fossil fuel station that produces the same electricity output. 1 GW(e) at 70 per cent load factor annually

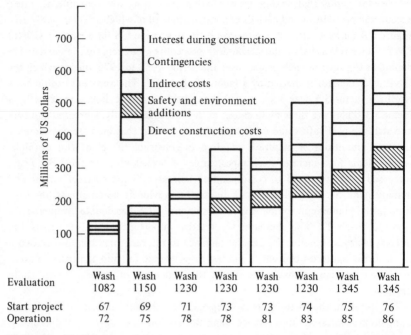

Figure 6.8 Nuclear plant (investment) capital cost estimates for a single 1000 MW(e) LWR plant, 1967–76 in current US dollars (see text for a note on inflation during the period).

produces 22 PJ of electrical energy and at 33 per cent efficiency would require a thermal input of 67 PJ, or 1.5 million tonnes of oil equivalent (mtoe). Thus the 1980 world nuclear capacity of 147 GW(e) corresponds to an annual primary energy equivalent of 220 mtoe.

Estimates of future nuclear energy have changed steadily downwards since 1975, as it became evident that lower economic growth, and reduced growth in electricity demands, were leading to excess capacity in many national electricity systems. At the same time, expectations of the costs of nuclear power were revised upwards, and expected future growth in electricity demand was revised downwards. Early estimates of nuclear power made in 1974 for the year 2000, presented by the IAEA (International Atomic Energy Agency) but based on national atomic agency estimates, ranged up to 2400 GW(e). Since it now takes 10 to 12 years in most countries to proceed from an initial decision to the completion and operation of a nuclear power station, the maximum figure of about 450 GW(e) for capacity in 1990 can already be confidently stated. However, programmes can be delayed and actual achievement may fall below this maximum. The author's estimates for possible future nuclear capacity are shown in table 6.6.

Table 6.6. *Nuclear generating capacity estimates for WOCA 1977–2000.*

Units GW(e)	1977	1980	1985	1990	2000
North America	48	60	90–110	150–180	200–300
Western Europe	29	55	80–90	125–150	210–300
Japan	8	12	18–22	32–42	60–90
Rest of WOCA*a*	1	3	9–15	15–30	30–60
Total nuclear	86	130	197–237	322–402	500–750
Total electric power	1400	1550	1700–1900	2000–2250	2800–3400

*a*WOCA denotes World Outside Communist Areas.

Uranium requirements and resources

The uranium demand corresponding to the world nuclear programme suggested in table 6.6 can be fairly readily estimated on the assumption that contributions from breeder reactors will be negligible up to the year 2000. The use of uranium is approximately 26 tonnes (at 3.3 per cent ^{235}U) for a 1 GW(e) reactor for one year, which corresponds to about 150 tonnes of natural uranium. From this, assuming the programme shown in table 6.6, the annual and cumulative use of natural uranium can be calculated on the basis of a 'once through cycle'. At any time the uranium requirement should also include the fuel inventory for the reactor core and enough fuel for (say) 7 years, or about 10 years supply in all; this should be added to the cumulative fuel used to give the total requirement.

The cumulative world (WOCA) requirements for uranium to the year 2000 are illustrated in figure 6.9 for nuclear programmes in the range illustrated in table 6.6. Figure 6.9 also shows estimates of proved and probable reserves of uranium that are likely to be available at prices up to US $130 per kilogram. The proved and probable uranium resources are shown in more detail in table 6.7.

Of the WOCA totals given in table 6.7, about 70 per cent (1453 thousand tonnes reasonably assured, 1546 thousand tonnes estimated additional) are expected to be recoverable at up to $78 per kilogram. At considerably higher costs (several hundred dollars per kg) uranium could be extracted from very low grade deposits such as Chattanooga shale (45 to 65 parts per million (ppm) or Conway granite (12 to 15 ppm) in the United States, and similar types of deposit elsewhere.

The information on uranium resources as a function of price is limited by the high cost of exploration which is expected to be several dollars for each kilogram of proven reserve. It is therefore unlikely that accurate information on reserves will be obtained very far ahead of a need for their production although such information would be important for decisions on breeder reactors.

From figure 6.9 it is apparent that continued growth in nuclear power beyond

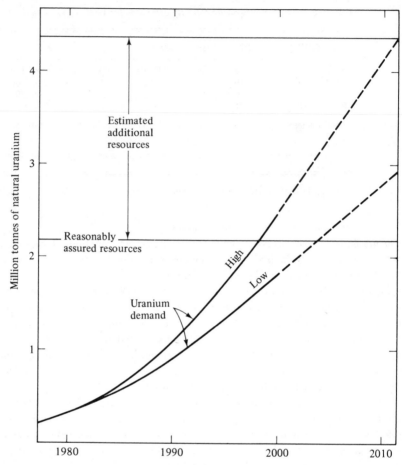

Figure 6.9   World (WOCA) cumulative requirements for uranium from 1977 to 2000, and estimated uranium resources at costs up to $130/kg. *Note:* The requirements include stocks equivalent to 10 years use.

the year 2000 cannot be long maintained on the basis of thermal reactors alone unless there are quite unexpected developments in the discovery of uranium resources. If breeder reactors come into general commercial use from the year 2000 onwards, this would both prolong the use of existing uranium reserves but it would also make the available resource base much larger since considerably higher costs for uranium would then be commercially viable. For illustration, a long-term projection of nuclear power production to the year 2050 is shown in figure 6.10. The corresponding requirements for natural uranium, analogous to those in figure

Table 6.7.   *Estimated world (WOCA) uranium resources available at up to $130/kg.*

	Thousand tonnes of uranium	
World region	Reasonably assured	Estimated additional
North America	825	1710
Western Europe	389	95
Australia, NZ		
Japan	303	49
Latin America	65	66
Middle East & North Africa	32	69
Africa south of the Sahara	544	163
East Asia	3	1
South Asia	30	24
WOCA total	2191	2177

Note: The USSR and China are expected to be self-sufficient in uranium supplies for their own nuclear programmes.
Source: Duret *et al.* (1978b).

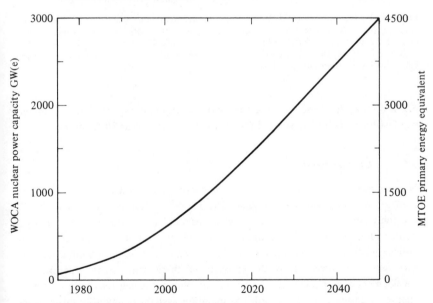

Figure 6.10   An illustrative long-term projection of world (WOCA) nuclear power capacity. The right hand scale shows the equivalent primary energy input in mtoe (million tonnes oil equivalent).

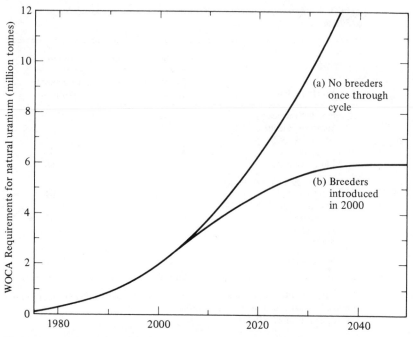

Figure 6.11   Cumulative world (WOCA) natural uranium requirements (a) with no breeder reactors, (b) with breeder reactors beginning in year 2000. *Notes:* (i) Curves include core inventory and seven years future fuel reserve. Reactor life 40 years. All reactors built after 2020 are breeders. (ii) Alternatives with recycle of uranium and/or plutonium would fall below (a) but substantially above (b).

6.9, are shown in figure 6.11, together with the uranium requirements if commercial fast breeders were developed fairly rapidly from the year 2000 onwards.

6.8   Chapter summary

Nuclear power production is based on the energy released when a heavy nucleus, such as uranium, undergoes fission. The fission process is stimulated when a neutron is absorbed by the atomic nucleus, particularly in uranium-235, the light isotope of uranium, which forms 0.7 per cent of natural uranium. It leads to radioactive fission products, nuclides of about half the mass of uranium, together with several neutrons. It is the emission of these neutrons that permits the development of a chain reaction, when one or more of the neutrons causes fission in another uranium nucleus. In order to maintain a chain reaction in low-enriched uranium, it is necessary to slow down the neutrons to 'thermal' energies so as to increase the probability of absorption by uranium-235 and subsequent (almost immediate) fission. Without this slowing down, too many neutrons would be absorbed by the heavy isotope uranium-238, which does not normally lead to fission, but instead becomes converted to other nuclei such as plutonium-239. The slowing down of neutrons is achieved by including a moderator, such as water or carbon, in the reactor core with the uranium. The probability of nuclear fission, and hence the flexibility of reactor design, is increased by increasing the concentration of uranium-235 giving enriched uranium fuel having about 3 per cent (in light water reactors) of uranium-235. Reactor control is achieved by means of neutron absorbing control rods in the reactor core.

The common types of nuclear reactors in commercial use for power production are briefly described, including the two main light water reactors (LWR), the pressurised water reactor (PWR) and the boiling water reactor (BWR). The fast breeder reactor (FBR) is also described, particularly noting its ability to convert the common uranium isotope, uranium-238, to the fissile product plutonium. If desired this conversion can produce fissile products faster than they are used in the reactor, possibly with a doubling time in the region of ten years.

The main features of the nuclear fuel cycle are described, and the chapter concludes with sections on the costs of nuclear power, and its potential future development, including the requirements for uranium. Social and environmental aspects of nuclear power have been taken into account in assessing its future potential, but the discussion of these aspects is postponed to chapter 9.

Chapter 6   Further reading

Connolly, T. J. (1978) *Foundations of nuclear engineering,* Wiley, New York.
Eden, R. J. *et al.* (1966) *The analytic S-matrix,* Cambridge University Press, Cambridge, UK.
Eden, R. J. (1967) *High energy collisions of elementary particles,* Cambridge University Press, Cambridge, UK.
Glasstone, S. (1967) *Sourcebook on atomic energy,* Van Nostrand Reinhold, New York and London.
Inglis, D. R. (1973) *Nuclear energy: its physics and social challenge,* Addison-Wesley, Reading, Mass.
National Petroleum Council (1973) *US energy outlook: nuclear energy availability,* US National Petroleum Council.
OECD Nuclear Energy Agency, International Atomic Energy Agency (1977) *Uranium: resources, production and demand,* OECD, Paris.
OECD Nuclear Energy Agency (1978) *Nuclear fuel cycle requirements,* OECD, Paris.
Rotblat, J. (1977) *Nuclear reactors – to breed or not to breed,* Taylor and Francis, London.
Semat, H. and Albright, J. R. (1972) *Introduction to atomic and nuclear physics* (5th edition), Chapman and Hall, London.
World Energy Conference (1978b) *World energy resources 1985–2020,* IPC Science and Technology Press, Guildford, UK and New York.

Other further reading relevant to this chapter is suggested at the end of chapter 9

Electric power

7.1 The development of electric power production

In 1976 the average production of electricity per head of population was 4956 kWh in the UK and 9844 kWh in the United States. So dependent have we become on an ample and reliable supply of electric energy that it is difficult to realise that the widespread use of electricity is a fairly recent development. For example, per capita electricity consumption in England and Wales increased by a factor of 30 in the half-century before 1975, and the first power stations to provide a public supply of electricity were commissioned less than a hundred years ago.

Static electricity and magnetism have been subjects for speculation for centuries, but serious scientific study was difficult until Volta's invention, in 1796, of a primitive chemical battery. In 1809, Humphry Davy demonstrated the principle of the electric arc light, though this invention could not be widely used without suitable generators. A member of the audience at this demonstration was Michael Faraday, who became interested in the relationship between magnetism and electricity. This interest bore fruit in 1831 when Faraday discovered the principle of electromagnetic induction – that an electric current flows in a conductor which is in motion relative to a magnetic field. This discovery opened the door to the conversion of mechanical energy into electricity, from which developed the generation and use of electricity on a large scale.

For about half a century development was slow, though there were several inventions concerned with electric motors and electric traction, and an experimental battery-powered railway locomotive was operated between Edinburgh and Glasgow in 1842. In 1858 an arc light powered by a steam engine driven dynamo was installed in a lighthouse, and became a model for subsequent installations.

The major impetus for the large-scale development of electric power came from the introduction of the vacuum filament lamp, developed by Edison in the US and Swan in the UK. In order to create a market for the lamps, Edison built the Pearl Street Power Station in New York in 1882. The first power stations for public supply in the UK, including those at Holborn Viaduct in London and in Brighton, were opened in the same year. Thus was created the pattern of central power stations, serving consumers through a distribution network, which has remained until the present day.

The first quarter of this century was marked by the debate – sometimes heated – between those favouring direct current (DC) systems and those who supported alternating current (AC) systems. This was resolved in favour of the AC system, mainly because of the ease with which voltage levels in an AC system can be changed using transformers.

The development of a country can to a great extent be judged by its electricity consumption, ranging from such countries as Burundi (6 kWh per person per year) to Canada (12,680 kWh per person per year). Figure 7.1 (Economist, 1978) shows the per capita GDP and the per capita electricity consumption in 1976 for most OECD countries and for a selection of developing countries – the association between these two parameters is clear. It is also true that electricity consumption tends to rise faster than GDP; in the OECD countries as a whole, electricity consumption grew about 1½ times as rapidly as GDP in the period from 1960 to 1976 (IEA, 1978c) though this ratio is expected to fall in the future. The determinants of electricity consumption are, of course, very complex, and any attempt to forecast future electricity requirements by means of a simple relationship with GDP would be foolish.

A key characteristic of electrical energy is its versatility. It is useful for light, motive power and communications, and may be a source of high or low grade heat (though in the latter role it has many competitors). This is in contrast to most alternative energy sources, which, apart from petroleum for transport, are used almost solely as sources of heat.

Electricity is also versatile in the choice of fuels from which it can be generated. Though coal and oil are the most widely-used fuels, electricity may be made from peat, wood, industrial waste or domestic refuse. Electricity may also be made from nuclear energy (see chapter 6) and from a range of renewable energy sources including hydro-electric schemes, wave power generators, tidal barrages, windmills and geothermal energy schemes. These will be further discussed in chapter 8.

7.2 Characteristics of electricity supply and demand

It is not practicable, at least with present technology, to store electricity on a large scale. The amount of power generated by a supply system must, therefore, match the instantaneous demand. Demand varies greatly with the time of day and with the season, as illustrated by the typical daily patterns shown in figure 7.2. The forecasting of short term variations in demand, and the scheduling of power stations to meet those variations, are important aspects of the operation of an electricity supply system.

The total installed capacity of the generators, i.e. the maximum power that can be produced, must at least be equal to the expected peak demand if supply is to be maintained. In practice, the installed capacity usually exceeds the expected peak demand by a margin, typically 10–20 per cent, for four main reasons:

(a) to cover unforeseen plant breakdowns, including water shortages for hydro-electric plant;

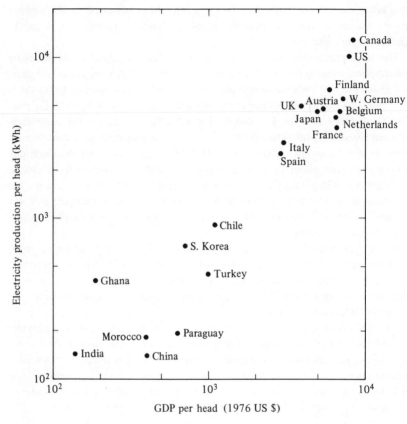

Figure 7.1 Economic growth and electricity consumption 1976. *Source:* Economist (1978).

(b) to allow for errors in forecasting the peak demand – since the decisions which control installed capacity have to be made some years in advance, allowance is made for the possibility that demand will grow faster than expected;

(c) to cover variations in peak demand due, for example, to unusually severe weather;

(d) to allow for planned maintenance of plant – this will be relevant only if maintenance cannot be scheduled outside the season in which peak demand occurs.

The factors which cause variations in peak demand and in the capacity of plant available for use are statistical in nature, and it is not possible to guarantee that demand can be met in full. The assessment of the required margin of capacity over demand is often based on a statistical argument, using the probability of failure to meet the full demand, or the likely extent of any such failure, as a criterion.

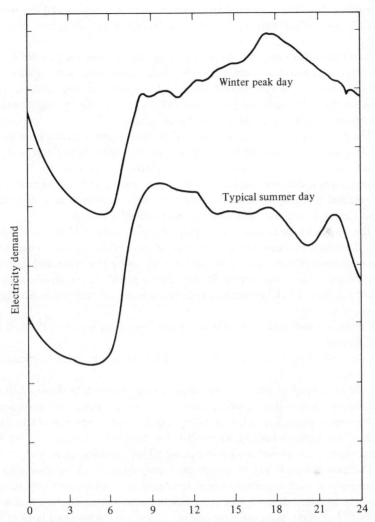

Figure 7.2 Typical daily variation of electricity demand. *Source:* Central Electricity Generating Board (1974).

The provision of a margin of generating capacity is usually expensive, and one of the ways of reducing the margin without increasing the risk of power cuts is for neighbouring supply systems to combine. In the combined system, uncertainties both in demand and in the capacity of available plant are likely to be smaller in proportion to total demand than in either system in isolation. In addition, for stable operation of power supply systems, it is necessary to be able at any time to bring rapidly into use enough generating capacity to replace the loss of the largest generating unit (this capacity is known as the spinning reserve), and this requirement is much less expensive, in relative terms, in a large system than in a small one.

A further advantage of a large system is that it makes it possible to take advantage of economies of scale in large power stations. In a small system, such advantages would be substantially offset by the operational and reliability problems involved. The scheduling of power stations to meet the varying demand at minimum cost is also more effective in a large system.

The practicality of combining local supply systems into a network spanning a whole country or continent is largely due to the relatively low cost and high reliability of overhead transmission lines. The total network may take the form of an integrated system with unified control, as in England and Wales, or control may be retained by local utilities who trade with their neighbours on a commercial basis – this is common in the US and on the mainland of Europe.

The way in which an electricity supply system is operated to minimise costs is best illustrated by means of the load duration curve. This is a curve which shows the proportion of time that the demand exceeds any given value, and it may be constructed for an entire year or for any shorter period. An example is shown in figure 7.3, from which two features (which apply in most real situations) may be noted:

(a) there is a minimum below which demand never falls, known as the base load demand;

(b) demands close to the peak are exceeded for only a very small fraction of the time.

The characteristics of different types of generating plant will be discussed later in this chapter. At this stage it will be sufficient to note that some, such as nuclear or hydro-electric plant, have a low operating cost and high capital cost, while others, such as gas turbines running on distillate oil, have a low capital cost but high operating cost. Large coal or oil fired stations lie between these extremes.

The most economic way to operate the supply system is to use plant with low operating cost, such as nuclear stations, running as near continuously as possible, to meet the base load demand. The next block of demand above the base load is met by fossil fuel plant, using the most efficient (usually the newest and largest) first, followed by older and less efficient plant. This plant, which is meeting demands which are exceeded for only a small proportion of the time, is likely to be brought into use for frequent short periods, and needs to be flexible – a requirement which older, small generating units are usually able to meet. Demands very close to the peak are met by the plant, such as gas turbines, which combines the lowest capital cost with the greatest flexibility; its high operating cost is only a minor penalty in view of its low load factor.

The above outline is applicable to systems which comprise mainly thermal plant.

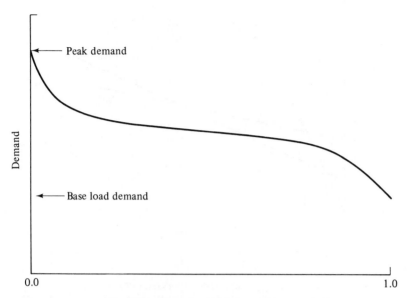

Figure 7.3   Example of load duration curve.

In systems with a high proportion of hydro-electric plant, the situation is more complex. Hydro-electric plant combines very low operating costs with great flexibility, and the use of such plant will also depend on the availability of water over the period as a whole. Detailed discussion of the role of hydro-electric plant is beyond the scope of this book.

It is the responsibility of those in control of system operation to make into a reality the description given above. This task (which will usually be assisted by computing facilities) requires a knowledge of the operating costs and status of all plant – whether it is undergoing maintenance, usable but cold, ready to supply power, or on load. It is also necessary to estimate the short-term variations in demand, using past experience, weather forecasts and knowledge of any special circumstances. A spinning reserve must also be retained sufficient to cover the loss of (at least) the largest generator. In the unlikely event of supply falling short of demand (due perhaps to several plant or transmission failures in a short period), the generators will begin to slow down, causing the alternation frequency of the electricity to fall. In most systems, the fall in frequency will be detected automatically and some consumers will be disconnected until a balance can be restored. Operator action bringing new generators into operation will then allow consumers to be reconnected.

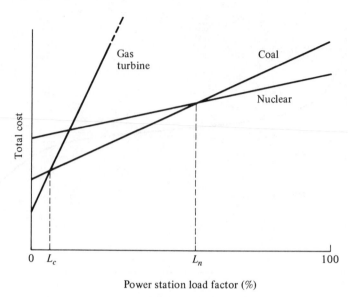

Figure 7.4   Choice of plant mix for minimum cost.

Decisions on the type of new plant to be installed reflect the way in which the system is operated. Economic assessment of different types of plant is a complex process involving the minimisation of total costs over a long period. The process may be illustrated by considering the 'best' plant mix for a fixed set of fuel prices. Figure 7.4 shows the total cost of running three types of power station, as a function of their individual load factors (the load factor is here defined as the ratio of the average plant output in a given period to the total which the plant could produce if operated continuously). Nuclear plant is installed until the load factor of the last unit installed falls to L_n (the implied capacity depends, of course, on the shape of the load duration curve), followed by coal plant until its marginal load factor falls to L_c, with gas turbines providing the remainder.

7.3   Electric power generation

All large scale generation of electric power depends on the principle of electro-magnetic induction. A voltage is induced in a coil by placing it in a changing magnetic field. If the coil is connected to an external load, a current will flow and electrical energy will be dissipated. At the same time forces will be generated which oppose the changing magnetic field. Thus the mechanical work which is being used to change the magnetic field (by turning the rotor in a generator) is converted into electrical energy.

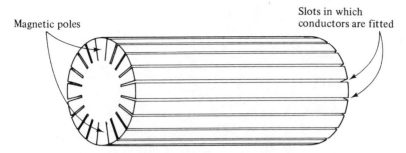

Figure 7.5 Generator rotor – schematic.

In most modern generators, the rotor consists of a solid steel core, with slots which accommodate the field windings (figure 7.5). The rotor usually has two or four magnetic poles spaced around its circumference, and is energised with a direct current. Power is generated in coils located in slots in the laminated iron stator surrounding the rotor. A typical generated voltage is 22 kV. The rotor speed for generation at 50 Hz is 3000 or 1500 revs/min for a two or four pole rotor; for generation at 60 Hz the corresponding speeds are 3600 or 1800 revs/min.

Different types of generating station use different sources of mechanical energy to drive the generating units. In the remainder of this section the following types of power station will be discussed.
– Hydro-electric stations
– Conventional (i.e. fossil fuel fired) steam power stations
– Nuclear power stations
– Gas turbine stations
– Combined heat and power schemes

Hydro-electric stations

In a hydro–electric plant, the mechanical energy comes from the potential energy of water. In one sense hydro-electric power is derived from solar energy, since the water cycle which is being tapped is powered by the sun. The energy available from stored water is proportional to the mass of water and the height through which it moves, and the conversion efficiency of the generating plant is high – over 85 per cent. To give some idea of the quantities involved, a 200 MW (electrical) plant with a head of 40m requires a flow rate of about 600 m³/sec.

The type of water turbine used in a hydro-electric plant depends on the head of water. For heads greater than around 150 m, an impulse turbine, of which the commonest type is the Pelton wheel, is used (figure 7.6). A jet of water impinges on cups on the turbine wheel, imparting almost all its kinetic energy to the turbine. For lower heads, a reaction turbine is used. There are several types, including a Francis turbine (in which the water flows through a spiral casing inwards to

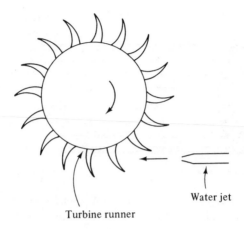

Water jet

Turbine runner

Figure 7.6   Pelton wheel impulse turbine.

impinge on a set of blades around the hub, figure 7.7) and a propeller turbine in which the rotating element resembles a ship's propeller.

Though it is possible to use flowing water directly, it is usual to modify the natural flow by means of a dam. This provides storage, reducing the vulnerability of the station to variations in rainfall and allowing output to be controlled without loss of water. The head created by a dam also allows a high ratio of peak to average power, which may be valuable for the electricity supply system as a whole.

The lake area required for a hydro-electric scheme may be very large. Consider the previous example of a 200 MW(e) scheme with a 40 m head, operating at base load, and suppose that, in order to even out rainfall variations, three months' storage is required. If the peak fluctuation of the water level is 5 m, the required surface area of the lake is 950 km^2 (about 20 miles square).

The capital cost of a hydro-electric scheme is very dependent on the geographical situation. Since the water is usually treated as free, the running costs are very low, and if sufficient water is available such a scheme may be used for base load generation. Hydro-electric plants are also very flexible and can be brought to power in a very short time (a few minutes), making them suitable for meeting peak demands. Environmental and social effects (which are discussed more fully in chapter 9) are largely confined to the neighbourhood of the scheme, and may include loss of productive land and habitations, geological disturbance, and a small risk of dam failure.

It is appropriate to include pumped storage schemes at this point. These are hydro-electric schemes with upper and lower reservoirs and (usually) reversible pump-turbines. Water is pumped from the lower to the upper reservoir at times of low demand, using cheap power from, for example, nuclear plant, and the water is

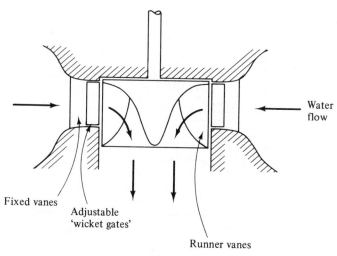

Figure 7.7   Francis turbine.

used to meet peak demands at low cost. The combined efficiency of the pumping and turbine stages may exceed 70 per cent.

Conventional steam stations

In conventional (i.e. fossil-fuel fired) steam plant, mechanical energy is obtained by burning fuel to raise steam, which is then passed through a turbine. The fuel is either coal (which is usually ground to form pulverised fuel), or heavy fuel oil. Steam is produced in large water tube boilers (in which water passes through tubes surrounded by the hot combustion gases, as opposed to fire tube boilers in which the combustion gases pass through tubes within a water-filled shell).

The thermal energy of the steam is converted to mechanical energy in a steam turbine. As discussed in chapter 1, the efficiency of such a conversion is limited by the Second Law of Thermodynamics. The usual process, shown schematically in figure 7.8, is outlined below.

Steam emerges from the boiler at typical temperature and pressure, for a large modern station, of 566° C and 159 atmospheres, and enters the high pressure cylinder of the turbine. After leaving the high pressure cylinder, it is returned to the reheater section of the boiler where its temperature is raised again before it is passed through the intermediate and low pressure cylinders of the turbine.

Steam exhausted from the turbine is condensed to water in the condenser, and the water is reheated in feed heaters and then passed through the economiser – a bank of tubes within the flue gas stream – before entering the main boiler tubes.

The overall thermal efficiency of a large conventional steam power station

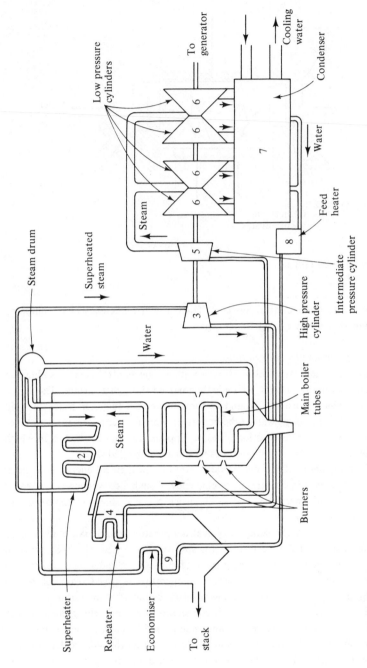

Figure 7.8 Schematic diagram of boiler and steam turbine. *Notes*: (a) This diagram is not to scale. (b) Combustion air route, fuel preparation and flue gas route not shown. (c) Numbers 1–9 indicate steam cycle.

Table 7.1. *Typical losses in a conventional steam generating station.*

Plant	Losses
Condenser	51
Stack and other losses	14
Total	65

Source: Central Electricity Generating Board (1975).

operating at high load factor is about 35 per cent. The breakdown of losses depends on the detailed design and operating regime of the station, but is typically shown in table 7.1, from which the dominance of condenser losses is clear.

As noted above, the capital cost of conventional steam stations is between that of nuclear power stations and gas turbines. Running costs are dominated by the cost of fuel, and the difficulty of predicting fuel price variations in the present energy situation creates problems for the economic assessment of this type of plant.

Operational flexibility depends on the mechanical and thermal inertia of the plant and on its tolerance of temperature changes. In general, smaller and older plants are more flexible than the largest modern ones.

The principal environmental issues raised by conventional steam power stations are those of particulate and gaseous (particularly sulphur dioxide) emissions, and the ecological effects of the cooling water. Environmental and social problems remote from the power station itself, such as those arising from the mining and transport of coal, may also be relevant.

Nuclear power stations
Nuclear power stations will be discussed only briefly in this chapter, as a fuller outline of the principles of nuclear energy has been given in chapter 6. Essentially, the process is the same as that used in fossil fuel fired stations, except that the boiler is replaced by a nuclear reactor. Reactors in which the core is cooled by water (PWR, BWR) are characterised by steam temperatures around 300° C – substantially lower than conventional stations, with a consequent low thermal efficiency. This drawback is largely overcome in most gas cooled or liquid metal cooled reactors.

Most types of reactor use separate primary and secondary coolant cycles, heat from the reactor coolant being used to generate steam, in a heat exchanger, for use in the turbine. Exceptions include the BWR and SGHWR (steam-generating heavy water reactor) in which the reactor coolant flows directly through the turbine.

Nuclear power stations are characterised by high capital cost and fairly low running cost. Though the price of uranium may be difficult to predict over the next

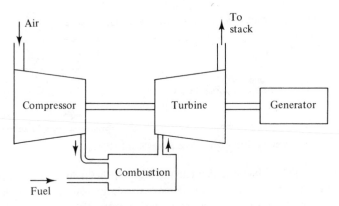

Figure 7.9   Schematic diagram of gas turbine.

few decades, this represents a fairly small fraction of fuel costs, which are dominated by the costs of enrichment, fabrication and reprocessing.

Gas turbines

Gas turbine power stations use premium fuels (natural gas or distillate oil), and the hot combustion gases – mainly steam, carbon dioxide, nitrogen and excess oxygen – are passed directly through a turbine resembling that used in an aircraft engine (figure 7.9). They are capable of very rapid start-up and load variation, and may be remotely controlled.

Taken together with their low capital cost and high fuel cost, this makes them ideal for peak-load operation. With this operating regime, typical thermal efficiencies are 20–25 per cent. Because no cooling water is required (the exhaust gases are released directly to the atmosphere) gas turbine stations may be sited in urban areas, and the high exhaust gas temperature allows adequate plume dispersion with a low stack height. There are few environmental problems.

Combined heat and power schemes

An unavoidable consequence of the Second Law of Thermodynamics is that a large proportion of the heat input to power stations is rejected at a low temperature, usually in cooling water. Possible uses for this low grade heat are clearly of interest. Such combined heat and power (CHP) schemes may be divided into three classes:
(a) applications requiring a low temperature rise, such as horticulture or fish farming;
(b) applications in which domestic or commercial space heating is provided from power station reject heat;
(c) industrial applications where process heat and electricity are produced by the

same plant; in such cases it may be appropriate to regard the electricity as a by-product of the industrial boiler plant rather than the other way round.

There are several types of plant suitable for use in CHP schemes. In a pass-out turbine (figure 7.10), some steam is removed at an intermediate pressure and condensed in a heat exchanger through which passes the water used to carry the heat to its point of application. In a back-pressure turbine (figure 7.11), all the steam is condensed at a higher temperature and pressure than in a normal turbine, again transferring heat to water for use outside the plant. Pass-out turbines are generally more flexible than back-pressure turbines, allowing the ratio of electricity to heat to be varied to match different load conditions. On the other hand back-pressure turbines are usually cheaper owing to the saving in cooling water plant. It is also possible to base a CHP scheme on a gas turbine plant, passing the exhaust gases through a waste heat boiler. However, the demands made on a gas turbine for electricity generation within a larger system are unlikely to be consistent with the demands for heat.

The economics of CHP schemes depend very much on the situations in which they are applied. No generalisations can be made on industrial systems, though it is worth noting that for industrial users in Great Britain the ratio of electricity generated on-site to that obtained from public supply has fallen from 0.33 in 1955 to 0.23 in 1977. For both physical and economic reasons, heat transmission over very large distances is impracticable, and district heating schemes appear most promising in local areas where the density of use is fairly high. This may conflict with economies of scale, which favour large power stations, usually remote from load concentrations. The capital cost of the heat distribution system needs to be taken into account when assessing the role of CHP.

The heat obtained from a CHP plant is not, of course, free – the modification of the steam cycle will reduce the amount of electricity produced. The ratio of electricity lost to heat produced is likely to be between 0.1 and 0.2, (UK Department of Energy, 1977d), rising with the temperature of the water produced. In most circumstances, however, there is a net saving in fuel when compared with a system in which electricity and heat demands are met separately, as the following example shows.

Suppose that we need to meet a heat load of 100 units, using one of two options:
(a) a CHP scheme using a back pressure turbine in which 3.6 units of heat are produced for every unit of electricity;
(b) a heat-only boiler.

If the boiler efficiency is assumed to be 86 per cent in each case, then the CHP scheme will produce 28 units of electricity and 100 units of heat, and will consume 149 units of fuel; the overall efficiency for option (a) is 86 per cent. The heat-only boiler will consume 116 units of fuel, and the electricity which in the first option is produced by the back pressure turbine will be generated with an efficiency of, say,

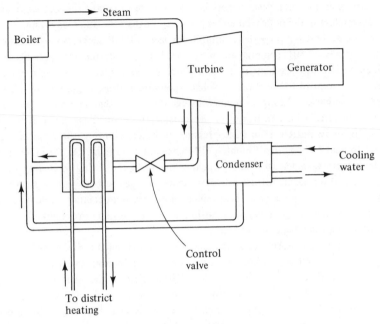

Figure 7.10   Schematic diagram of pass-out turbine.

35 per cent. This will require a further 80 units of fuel, making a total for option (b) of 196 units, or an overall efficiency of 65 per cent. Thus the use of the CHP scheme results in a saving of 47 units of fuel for every 100 units of heat produced. The 149 units of fuel used in the CHP scheme could have been used in a central power station to produce 52 units of electricity, so the ratio of electricity lost to heat produced is $(52-28)/100 = 0.24$.

For the CHP option to be viable, the fuel savings which it generates must be sufficient to pay off the additional capital costs incurred. Two factors which are not evident in the above example make economic evaluation more complex than it seems at first sight:

(a) The demand for heat, and therefore the load factor at which the plant will operate, varies widely during the year. The capital cost is related to the peak load rather than the average load, and it may prove economic to install a smaller CHP scheme with an additional heat-only boiler to meet peak demands;

(b) The plant may need to be operated to provide heat at a time when electricity generating plant using cheaper fuel is standing idle; in these circumstances the plant burns expensive fuel in order to save a larger quantity of cheaper fuel, which may not be economic.

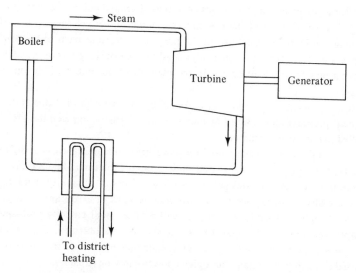

Figure 7.11 Schematic diagram of back-pressure turbine.

The design of a CHP scheme must take these factors into account, and also recognise that the local heat load may take many years to develop.

7.4   Distribution of electricity

Except in very remote areas where a power station may be connected only to a local load, electricity reaches the consumer through an integrated transmission and distribution network. This network has a number of functions in addition to its main one of transferring electrical energy from the power station to the consumer. It reduces the margin of generating capacity over peak demand required to provide a reliable supply, it enables power stations to be scheduled to meet demand in the most economic way irrespective of location of power stations and loads, and it helps to maintain the stability of the system as a whole, so that for example voltage and frequency remain very nearly constant.

The choice of transmission voltage is a compromise. A higher voltage creates a requirement for higher transmission towers (to increase ground clearance) and longer insulators. To transmit the same power at a lower voltage would necessitate larger and heavier conductors, requiring stronger supports. The cost of energy lost in transmission also needs to be considered. Other things being equal, the energy lost as heat in the conductors is proportional to the square of the current, so that an increase in voltage will reduce this type of loss.

The net result of these considerations is seen in the trend, in most countries, towards the use of very high voltages. Voltages of around 400 kV are common (this voltage is used for most of the UK supergrid) and higher voltages up to 1000 kV are being considered or used for special purposes in various parts of the world. In general, a need for transmission at high load factor over long distances, such as to connect a remote base load hydro-electric plant to a load centre, will favour higher voltages.

Within the local distribution networks fed by the main transmission system, the voltage is progressively reduced by means of transformers, to reach the 110–240 V supplied to domestic consumers.

Overhead lines are normally used for power transmission. In areas of high visual amenity, these may be obtrusive and underground cables may be used instead, at substantially higher cost and possibly with some loss of reliability. Underground cables are also necessary for the distribution network in urban areas. In general, the use of higher transmission voltages will reduce visual amenity problems. For example, though an individual 400 kV tower is more obtrusive than a 132 kV tower, this is more than outweighed by the smaller number of transmission lines required at the higher voltage for a given power-carrying capacity.

Loss mechanisms in transmission lines include heat loss, proportional to the square of the current and to the conductor resistance, and corona discharge, which is a loss to the atmosphere, particularly in damp conditions and at high voltages, which is reduced by using a cluster of conductors in place of a single conductor. Further losses are introduced by transformers. Total losses in the transmission and distribution systems in the UK amount to about 7 per cent of the electricity generated.

7.5   Uses of electricity

Electricity is a clean fuel, versatile, and easy to control. In most applications it has a high end-use efficiency. As a secondary fuel produced mainly from fossil fuels at around 30 per cent efficiency, it is inevitably expensive. In practice, therefore, electricity tends to be used where it has no convenient substitute, or where special circumstances offset its cost disadvantage.

Lighting, the first large scale use of electricity, remains an important application. The efficiency depends on the type of lamp, and is summarised in table 7.2. Most of the remainder of the energy is lost as heat, and this may contribute to space heating requirements.

Another important application is the production of mechanical power using electric motors. A full discussion of the many types of motor is beyond the scope of this text – the choice of motor for a given application will depend on the power required, the extent of load variation, and any requirements for constant speed or high starting torque. Broadly speaking, alternating current motors fall into three types: synchronous, induction and commutator motors. A synchronous motor

Table 7.2. *Efficiency and characteristics of electric lighting.*

Type of lamp	Efficiency (%)	Characteristics
Incandescent filament	5	Good light colour, cheap
Fluorescent	Up to 22	Good light colour with suitable fluorescent layer
Sodium (low pressure)	27	Strong red colour, suitable for street lighting
Sodium (high pressure)	29	Orange/white colour
Mercury	15	Blue/white colour

Source: NATO (1973).

resembles a generator operating in reverse. The alternating current in the stator windings creates a rotating field which interacts with the magnetic field of the rotor, causing the latter to rotate at a speed determined by the supply frequency and the motor geometry. In an induction motor, the rotor windings (which may resemble conventional windings or may consist of conductor bars embedded directly in the rotor) are short-circuited. The stator field causes the rotor to rotate at below synchronous speed, with a torque which increases as the degree of slip (i.e. the difference from synchronous speed) increases. Thus the speed of the motor falls with increasing load. An AC commutator motor differs from an induction motor in that the supply current is also fed to the rotor winding through a commutator; such motors can be designed for a wide speed range and for various speed/load characteristics.

The efficiency of a large electric motor may be as high as 95 per cent, falling to 60 per cent for small motors.

A third application in which there are no major substitutes for electricity is in electronics, control and automation – this is an area which has experienced great development in recent decades, and this development is likely to continue. The electrical energy required to perform a given function is, however, falling with time, especially in electronics (compare the desk calculator of the late 1960s with its modern counterpart) so that the consumption of electricity for this type of application may not grow.

The applications of electricity in which it is in direct competition with other fuels mainly involve the supply of heat. Electric space heating using simple resistance heaters (such as a domestic radiant electric fire) is usually economic only where a very small load is required or where the load factor is low, so that the low capital cost of the appliance is dominant. Electric storage heaters make use of electricity generated in efficient, low cost plant at times when other demands are low, releasing heat to the environment several hours later.

A heating device which allows the efficiency of electricity use to be increased by a factor of two to three is the heat pump, more familiar in its reverse role as an air conditioner. This is a heat engine which uses mechanical energy to increase the temperature difference between a cold reservoir (usually the outside air) and a warm reservoir such as air inside a house. The ratio between the total energy transferred to the warm reservoir and the electrical energy input is known as the coefficient of performance. The high efficiency of a heat pump is offset by high capital cost, and in some devices by problems of noise and ice formation. These problems are by no means insoluble, however, and heat pumps seem likely to find a growing market as the prices of all fuels increase.

Heat pumps are also applicable in many industrial situations where low temperature process heat is required. They are particularly valuable for drying applications, where the energy released when water vapour is condensed enhances the coefficient of performance of the device.

In situations where there is a need for heating and cooling at different seasons, a reversible heat pump can be used with only a small loss of performance when compared with a one-way pump.

It should be noted that heat pumps may also be driven by engines using gas or oil products, the reject heat from the engine providing an additional source of low grade heat. The emergence of a strong market for heat pumps may not therefore solely benefit the electricity industry.

Electricity finds uses in industrial heating where its cleanliness, ease of control and lack of environmental problems gives it an advantage. Uses include the melting of metals or glass, heat treatment or drying of metals, timber or food products, paint stoving and plastic curing, the heating of baths or vats for chemical processing, and welding. Techniques include resistance heating, infra-red heating, induction heating and radio frequency or microwave heating. Electricity is also used in electrochemical applications, for example in the production of aluminium and phosphorus from their ores.

7.6   Electricity and the fuel market

It has already been noted that electricity may be manufactured from many fuels. The mix of fuels used in a particular country will be influenced by their relative prices and availabilities, the capital costs of different types of plant, and by the historical factors which have determined the mix of older generating units. Table 7.3 shows the mix of fossil fuels, nuclear energy and hydro-electric energy (in terms of the percentage of electricity produced) for three groups of countries within OECD.

A similar picture emerges for each of the areas, with fossil fuels accounting for about 70% of production. The percentage share of nuclear energy is expected to increase rapidly – the planned nuclear production in the third area (OECD-

Table 7.3. *Percentage of electricity produced from different fuels, 1976.*

Area	Fossil fuel	Nuclear	Hydro-electric
USA, Canada	2.2	8.4	19.4
Australia, New Zealand, Japan	74.7	5.6	19.7
W. Germany, Austria, Belgium, Denmark, Spain, Finland, France, Greece, Ireland, Iceland, Italy, Norway, Netherlands, Portugal, United Kingdom, Sweden, Switzerland, Turkey	69.0	8.2	22.8

Source: IEA (1978c).

Europe) in 1985 is higher than the 1976 figure by a factor of more than five, leading to a share of 27.9 per cent.

Table 7.4 shows the breakdown of fossil fuel use for electricity generation for six individual countries.The great differences in fuel mix reflect the location of natural resources or (for example the low use of gas in the UK) specific energy policies. Several features of the different fuel breakdowns may be noted:

(a) the dominance of coal in the UK and, to a lesser extent, in the US;
(b) the substantial use of lignite in W. Germany, leading to a 65 per cent share for coal and lignite combined;
(c) the dependence on oil in Italy and Japan and to a lesser extent in France; this is a cause for concern in these countries in view of the uncertainty of future oil prices.

In many countries, electricity generation absorbs a substantial proportion of all primary fuel use. Table 7.5 shows the percentage of each fossil fuel which is used for electricity generation for the six countries previously discussed.

It may be seen from table 7.5 that the electricity industry is the major consumer of coal in the UK, the US and W. Germany, and that the proportion of oil used for electricity generation is highest in Italy and Japan, which have limited coal supplies. The proportion of all fossil fuels used for electricity is highest in the UK and lowest in Italy, and is correlated with the extent of electricity's dependence on solid fuels. The results for primary energy as a whole are consistently higher than those for fossil fuels because the non-fossil energy sources (mainly nuclear and hydro power) are wholly used for electricity generation. The figures show the same general pattern as those for fossil fuel, with ¼ to ⅓ of all primary energy going to electricity generation.

The way in which electricity use is split between different sectors in different countries is shown in table 7.6. If the US and UK are omitted, a broadly consistent

Table 7.4.   *Electricity generated from fossil fuels – percentage for each fuel, 1976.*

Country	Coal	Lignite	Liquid fuels	Natural gas	Manufactured gas	Other
France	35.3	0.7	51.5	7.5	4.6	0.5
Italy	3.1	1.1	79.9	12.0	2.8	1.1
Japan	5.2	0.0	83.2	7.4	4.2	0.0
United Kingdom	75.9	0.0	20.5	3.1	0.4	0.0
United States	58.8	1.8	20.5	18.9	0.0	0.0
W. Germany	32.8	32.2	11.3	18.7	3.8	1.1

Source: IEA (1978c).

Table 7.5.   *Percentage of various fuels used for electricity generation 1974.*

Country	Solid fuels	Liquid fuels	Gas	All fossil fuels	All primary energy
France	32.9	12.4	15.3	16.6	24.4
Italy	15.1	19.7	7.1	17.7	23.6
Japan	13.6	22.2	45.6	21.0	27.1
United Kingdom	55.0	18.1	8.3	29.2	32.6
United States	70.8	10.7	17.8	25.2	29.8
W. Germany	56.8	5.5	35.9	26.6	28.6

Note: The value for the total of each fuel available is indigenous production + imports − exports + stock adjustment.
Source: OECD (1976).

pattern emerges, with $\frac{1}{2}$ to $\frac{2}{3}$ of consumption in industry, $\frac{1}{5}$ to $\frac{1}{4}$ in households, and most of the remainder in commerce, services and agriculture. The US and UK depart from this pattern, with a lower proportion in industry and higher in households and in commerce, services and agriculture.

The proportion of energy delivered to final consumers in the form of electricity is also of interest, and is shown in table 7.7. Japan emerges as the leader both in terms of electricity share in industrial energy use, in which it is followed by the US, and in energy use as a whole. France and Italy are noteworthy for the low share of electricity in 'other sectors', which includes households. The UK is also unusual in that it combines the lowest share in industry with the highest share in 'other sectors'.

A comparison between tables 7.5 and 7.7 shows that electricity's share of delivered energy is only about half its share of primary energy, as a result of the low efficiency of electricity generation.

Table 7.6. *Division of electricity sales between sectors, 1976 (%).*

Country	Industry	Transport	Households	Other
France	53.4	3.5	23.6	19.4
Italy	63.8	3.6	21.2	11.4
Japan	66.5	3.2	21.3	9.0
United Kingdom	42.3	1.2	35.9	20.6
United States	37.3	0.2	31.1	31.5
W. Germany	54.1	3.1	24.3	18.6

Source: IEA (1978c).

Table 7.7. *Electricity use as a percentage of total delivered energy, 1974.*

Country	Industry	Transport	Other sectors	All sectors
France	15.4	2.1	12.0	11.2
Italy	15.6	1.8	12.0	11.7
Japan	19.7	2.9	17.3	16.0
United Kingdom	14.0	0.8	22.1	14.3
United States	16.9	0.1	20.3	12.6
W. Germany	15.5	2.5	15.7	13.2

Note: Non-energy uses of fuels are excluded.
Source: OECD (1976).

It was noted in section 7.5 that electricity uses fall into two categories:
(a) those uses for which there are no effective substitutes – lighting, motive power other than transport, and communications;
(b) those uses for which there is direct competition from other fuels – mainly involving the supply of heat.

These two classes are often referred to as premium and non-premium uses respectively, and it is sometimes suggested that at a time of fuel scarcity the use of electricity (at around 30% generation efficiency) for non-premium uses should be discouraged. Table 7.8, which is based on unpublished data assembled by the Energy Technology Support Unit, Harwell, UK, shows how electricity and other fuels were used in UK industry in 1976. It is clear that electricity is indeed used almost wholly as a premium fuel, with direct process heating (i.e. heat used in the course of the manufacturing process, without the use of steam or water as intermediate heat carriers) the only area which is shared to a significant extent with other fuels.

Forecasting the future role of electricity in the fuel market in quantitative terms

Table 7.8.   *Uses of electricity and other fuels in UK industry, 1976 (%).*

	Process heat using steam	Direct process heating	Space and water heating	Motive power	Other
Electricity	0.0	20.7	2.5	66.5	10.3
Other energy sources	41.5	28.2	24.7	4.7	0.9

Note: The iron and steel sector is excluded.

is a hazardous exercise, as is clear from a comparison of today's forecasts with those made a decade or so ago. On a world scale, an expanding market seems likely, for two main reasons:
(a) Historically, electricity consumption in most countries has risen faster than national product. The rate of increase is expected to move more into line with economic growth in the developed nations, but it is difficult to envisage any satisfactory development patterns for the less-developed countries which would not involve a very substantial increase in electricity consumption.
(b) Satisfactory solutions to the world's current energy problems depend on a transition away from dependence on short-lived resources such as oil and gas, towards long-lived or inexhaustible resources. Nuclear energy can only be made available on a large scale through electricity. Though coal can be used directly for final consumption, the use of this fuel for electricity generation is for many final consumers a more convenient route. Many renewable sources – tidal, wave and wind power, for example, – can only be tapped on a large scale for electricity generation.

7.7   Electricity costs and prices

We may consider the cost of a unit of electricity from a particular power station to be the sum of three components:
– capital cost
– operating and maintenance cost
– fuel cost
The operation, maintenance and fuel costs may for practical purposes be treated as a true marginal cost, independent of the number of units generated. The capital cost is more complicated. The primary quantity is, of course, the cost of building the station and any equipment associated with it, together with any interest paid on borrowed capital during the construction period (the latter item may be significant, particularly for long lead time projects such as nuclear stations). How this is apportioned to the electricity generated depends on three parameters:

Table 7.9.   *Capital cost component of nuclear electricity cost (mills/kWh).*

	Load factor %	Discount rate, %		
		5	8	10
20 year life	40	16.0	20.3	23.4
	60	10.6	13.5	15.6
	80	8.0	10.1	11.7
	100	6.4	8.1	9.4
30 year life	40	13.0	17.7	21.1
	60	8.6	11.8	14.1
	80	6.5	8.8	10.6
	100	5.2	7.1	8.4

– the expected life of the station
– the station's expected load factor
– the discount rate used.

For example, consider a nuclear power station whose initial cost (including any interest charges accrued during construction) is \$700/kW. If the station life is denoted by n, and the discount rate (analogous to the interest rate on a householders' mortgage) by r, then the fraction of the initial investment which must be paid off in each year in order to clear all debts by the end of the year n is:

$$\frac{r(1 + r)^n}{(1 + r)^n - 1}$$

With $n = 20$ years and a 5 per cent discount rate ($r = 0.05$), this fraction is 0.0802, or \$56.17 per kW of capacity. This figure must be set against the electricity produced annually by that unit of capacity, which at an 80 per cent load factor would be $24 \times 365 \times 0.8 = 7008$ kWh. Thus the capital cost component of electricity costs is $(56.17/7008) \times 1000 = 8.0$ mills/kWh (1000 mills = \$1).

The relative importance of these factors is shown by table 7.9, which gives the capital cost component in mills/kWh of the cost of electricity from a nuclear power station whose initial cost is \$700/kW. It is clear from the table that the load factor is of fundamental importance, that the capital cost component rises with increasing discount rate and decreasing station life, and that station life becomes less important for higher discount rates.

A comparison between the overall costs of nuclear, oil and coal-fired generation is given in IEA (1978b). Some of the IEA results, together with further calculations designed to exhibit the effects of two alternative discount rates, are shown in table 7.10.

The importance of the discount rate can be seen from a comparison between coal and nuclear power. With the cost estimates used, coal is preferred to nuclear power

Table 7.10.   *Comparative costs of electricity generation (mills/kWh).*

	Nuclear		Oil		Coal	
Operation and maintenance	2.4		2.0		2.2	
Fuel	6.5		31.0		10.8	
Discount rate	10%	5%	10%	5%	10%	5%
Capital at 100% load	9.4	6.4	4.7	3.2	6.0	4.1
factor, 20 year life						
Total electricity cost:						
40% load factor	32.3	24.9	44.8	41.0	28.1	23.3
60% load factor	24.5	19.5	40.8	38.4	23.0	19.9
80% load factor	20.6	16.9	38.9	37.0	20.5	18.1
100% load factor	18.3	15.3	37.7	36.2	19.0	17.1

Notes: All costs are in 1976 $. Nuclear station is 2 × 1100 MW PWR: cost $700/kW. Oil station is 2 × 600 MW burning low sulphur heavy fuel oil and has no flue gas desulphurisation: cost $350/kW. Coal station is 2 × 600 MW with no flue gas desulphurisation: cost $450/kW.
Source: IEA (1978b) with additions by the author.

at any load factor below 81 per cent if a 10 per cent discount rate is used. With a 5 per cent discount rate, coal is preferred only if the load factor is below 55 per cent. It should be noted that the use of flue gas desulphurisation substantially changes the economics of coal and nuclear energy.

For a privately owned utility, the chosen discount rate will be related to the return on capital obtainable from other investments, and to the real rate of interest on borrowed capital. (For the proper treatment of inflation, see section 11.3.) A higher discount rate may be used for projects which are considered risky owing to possible technical problems, plant life uncertainty, liability to be replaced by improved plant, or possible environmental or social problems. For a public utility, the discount rate may be set by the government, whose choice may be influenced by a desire to reflect social time preference (that is, the balance of interests between current and future generations), or, more mundanely, by general policies on the level of public expenditure. It is difficult to establish a consistent approach to the choice of discount rate, particularly in periods of general inflation when real interest rates are very low and very variable (see section 1.4).

The foregoing discussion has dealt only with the components of electricity cost from a single station. When a new power station is installed, it changes the load factor of other stations (because stations are brought into use in order of marginal cost to meet instantaneous demand). This change should be reflected in the economic assessment. For example, using the estimates of table 7.10, if a nuclear power station were installed in an all-coal system at a time of static demand, then every unit generated by the nuclear station would save one unit from a coal station. The *net* cost of a unit from the nuclear station (at say 80 per cent load factor and 10 per cent discount rate) would be lower than the total cost by the marginal cost of a unit from a coal station, i.e. 20.6 − 13.0 = 7.6 mills/kWh.

In a utility's published accounts, capital costs appear in the form of depreciation and interest on loans. It is common practice to depreciate in historic cost terms (for example to write off 5 per cent of the plant's original cost in each year of its life). In periods of high inflation this is misleading, and despite the fact that many utilities are moving towards some form of inflation accounting (usually based on the continuous revaluation of assets in current terms) the confusion remains (see section 11.4).

A general discussion of electricity costs from an economist's viewpoint is given in Turvey and Anderson (1977). Essentially, there are two differing concepts of costs. From the point of view of an existing utility company, an accountant can calculate the price at which he would need, on average, to sell all units generated in order to cover his costs, interest charges and a target profit (the latter may be subject to government regulation). Similarly, a planner in a forward-looking utility can ask at what price he would need to be able to sell all units, on average, to make it worthwhile to build a new plant. Neither of these two approaches yields an unambiguous concept of electricity costs, because the price at which individual units will be saleable, or will be willingly offered, has little to do with overall *average* costs of production.

It was noted in section 7.5 that electricity was likely to be more expensive than other fuels because of its low production efficiency. Historical changes in fuel prices are illustrated in figure 7.12, which gives real prices to UK industrial consumers since 1954 (UK Department of Energy (1978a) – the index of wholesale prices for manufacturing industry – Central Statistical Office (1977) – is used as a deflator). Several observations may be made from this figure:

(a) in terms of cost per delivered unit of energy, electricity is, as expected, substantially more expensive than other fuels;
(b) electricity price shows less short-term variation than the other prices – this is because of the component for capital costs in electricity prices, and the fact that electricity uses a mix of different fuels, chosen according to economic criteria, and will therefore tend to average out fuel price variations;
(c) apart from gas (where there is a transition from manufactured gas to natural gas) only electricity shows a fall in real price over the period – this is mainly due to improvements in generation efficiency. The dip in 1974 in all fuels except oil is the result of the high inflation in the immediate aftermath of the oil crisis.

Systematic price differences occur between different classes of electricity consumer, reflecting the higher distribution costs for small consumers in comparison with larger consumers. In the US in 1975, for example, the price to industrial consumers was 28 per cent below the average, and that to domestic consumers was 18 per cent above the average (Electrical World, 1976); the corresponding figures

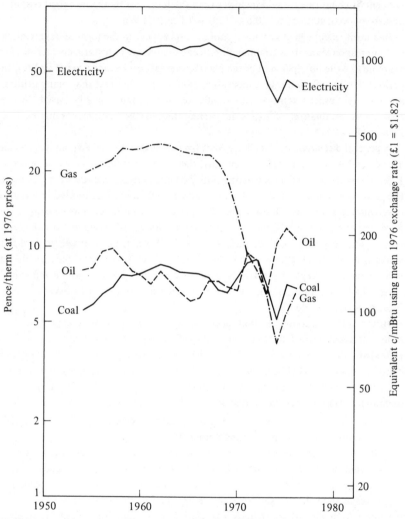

Figure 7.12   Real prices of fuels to industry in the UK 1954–76. *Source:* UK Department of Energy (1978a); UK Central Statistical Office (1977).

for England and Wales (Electricity Council, 1976) were 17 per cent and 11 per cent respectively.

A wide variety of electricity tariff structures is found in practice. In some instances a fixed charge is made (perhaps to cover the cost of connecting the consumer and invoicing), plus a constant price per unit used. Alternatively, the first few units may be priced at a high level (a two-part tariff) to achieve the same result. With both these structures, the cost of an additional unit tends to decrease as more units are used. This approach is sometimes criticised on the ground that it encourages wasteful use of a scarce resource, and inverted tariffs are proposed as an alternative. With such tariffs the first units are charged at a low price, with subsequent blocks charged at higher rates. This, it is claimed, discourages the wasteful use of electricity, while providing protection for those who depend on electricity for basic needs. On the other hand, most economists would argue that a well-designed two-part tariff gives a proper indication of the fixed capital cost of supply and the variable cost of the primary fuel input.

A type of tariff which is often used for industrial consumers is the maximum demand tariff, in which a penalty is imposed if instantaneous demand exceeds an agreed level. This encourages consumers to spread electricity use evenly through the day, which benefits the electricity industry by reducing the ratio of peak to average demand and so reducing the capacity of plant needed to meet a given total energy requirement. The penalty can be set to reflect the incremental cost of generating plant installed to meet peak demands.

Mention should also be made of 'time-of-day' tariffs, in which the price varies according to the time of day. These are used to encourage the consumption of electricity at times when demand is low and additional units can be generated in low cost, efficient plants (especially nuclear plant), and to discourage peak period use which requires additional generating capacity. Storage heaters and large domestic hot water tanks, which can be operated through a time switch, provide suitable loads for such tariffs. Time-of-day tariffs were introduced in England and Wales in the late 1950s, and units sold at low price during periods of low demand reached a peak of nearly 12 per cent of all sales in 1973/74.

The economist's approach to pricing is to treat prices as a set of signals designed to reflect the underlying cost structures of the electricity supply industry and the preference structure of the consumers. In particular, if the allocation of resources is to be optimised the price structure should reflect the marginal (incremental) cost which the consumer imposes on the supply system by taking an additional unit at a particular time of day: the price paid by the consumer for a marginal unit should be equal to the marginal cost of producing that unit (cf Drèze (1964), in particular pp. 8–34; but cf also Baumol and Bradford (1970)).

Realisation of this ideal is made difficult by the long lead times and high capital costs involved and uncertainty over future prices, both for the utility and the consumer. In a capital intensive industry, a large proportion of costs have to be incurred long in advance of consumers switching on the marginal electric light bulb. The suppliers incur costs as a result of their expectation of what demand will be. On the other hand, the consumer, making decisions about his choice of fuel, heating equipment or home insulation, needs to know today what relative costs and tariff structures will be in the future if he is to make an optimal decision. All these considerations are of course subject to uncertainty, and will also be affected by differences of view between supplier and consumers on the relative priorities of current and future expenditure – see section 1.4.

Many forms of metering and pricing may be used to convey the appropriate cost messages, and the problem of future uncertainty may to some extent be offset by warning the consumer of likely future developments. For example, it may be possible in the future to use advanced electronic meters which charge the consumer according to how near the system peak his demand appears. This could be combined with multi-part tariffs so that infra-marginal use could be charged so as to recover capital costs. The problem of future uncertainty is much more complicated. In particular, in the aftermath of the oil crisis, the prediction of fuel prices in absolute or relative terms is liable to error, although the use of subsidies and taxes may make it possible to reduce some of the uncertainty in relative prices. The risk to the consumer of undertaking capital investments when the level and structure of future energy prices are unknown may, for example, be offset by subsidies such as home insulation grants.

In present practice, tariffs have to be very simple, except for very large consumers and for intermediate suppliers (such as the area boards in the United Kingdom, or small city distributors in the United States). In view of the necessary complexity of 'optimal' tariffs, and the variety of simplifications in current use, however, it may be misleading to compare 'the price of electricity' between countries, or even between years in a single country.

For further discussion of electricity pricing structures, see Posner (1973) and Turvey (1974).

7.8   Chapter summary

Electricity on a commercial scale is about a century old. The principle of electromagnetic induction, on which electricity generation is based, was discovered in 1831, but development was slow until the invention of the vacuum filament lamp created an expanding market. Electricity consumption is a good measure of a nation's development, tending to increase more rapidly than the domestic product. Electricity is versatile, both in its uses and in the choice of fuels for generation.

Because electricity cannot be stored on a large scale, supply and demand must match continuously, and the capacity of a supply system will be related to maximum rather than average demand (with a margin to cover supply and demand uncertainties). Economic considerations favour large systems, using a transmission network to pool resources. As demand varies, power stations are brought into use in order of operating cost – nuclear plant being followed by large fossil-fired plant, with gas turbines used only when demand is very high.

In a generator, a magnetic field in the rotor interacts with coils in the stator (the fixed electromagnet surrounding the rotor), and the mechanical energy used to turn the rotor is converted to electrical energy in any load connected to the stator coils. Hydro-electric schemes convert the potential energy of water behind a dam to kinetic energy using an impulse or reaction turbine. In stations fired by coal or heavy fuel oil, mechanical power is generated by passing steam from a water-tube boiler through a steam turbine. Nuclear power stations also use steam as an energy carrier, but the heat is generated in the nuclear reactor core, and in most systems the reactor coolant is kept separate from the steam used in the turbines. Gas turbines use natural gas or distillate oil, and generate mechanical energy by passing the combustion gases directly through a turbine. Combined heat and power schemes (CHP) make use of the reject heat from electricity generation for district or industrial heating; pass-out turbines, back-pressure turbines or waste heat boilers attached to gas turbines may be used.

Electricity is distributed to consumers through a transmission and distribution network in which the voltage is successively reduced using transformers. There is a trend towards higher transmission voltages as supply systems become larger.

The main uses of electricity are for lighting, motive power, electronics and specialist heating applications. Heat pumps are very efficient where low grade heat is required.

In most countries, fossil fuels provide the main source of electricity, though hydro-electric power is important where it is available, and nuclear energy is making an increasing contribution. The choice of fossil fuels varies widely between different countries due to variations in fuel availability. In developed countries, electricity generation accounts for $\frac{1}{4}$ to $\frac{1}{3}$ of primary fuel use. Industry is often the leading electricity-consuming sector, followed by households. Electricity's share of delivered energy is only about half its share of primary energy. The future of electricity on a world scale seems assured in view of its growing importance in developing countries and its role in making use of nuclear energy and renewable resources.

Electricity costs are the sum of capital and running (i.e. fuel, operation and maintenance) costs. The capital cost component depends on plant life, plant load factor and discount rate; the choice of the latter may influence the decision between nuclear and coal-fired plant. Economic evaluation also needs to include the effects of a new power station on the operation of existing stations. Electricity is usually more expensive to the consumer than other fuels, but shows less variation with time; industrial consumers usually pay less than households. A wide range of tariff structures may be found.

Chapter 7   Further reading

Central Electricity Generation board (1971) *Modern power station practice* (8 vols.), Pergamon Press, Oxford.
Connolly, T. J. (1978) *Foundations of nuclear engineering,* Wiley, New York.

International Energy Agency (IEA) (1978b) *Steam coal – prospects to 2000*, OECD, Paris.
Porter, A. *et al.* (1978) *Our energy options – seven important aspects of electric power planning examined by well-known authorities*, Government of Ontario.
Turvey, R. and Anderson, D. (1977) *Electricity economics – essays and case studies*, Johns Hopkins University Press, Baltimore and London.
UK Department of Energy (1979a) *Combined heat and electrical power generation in the United Kingdom, Energy paper no. 35*, HMSO, London.
Wright, J. P. (1974) *The vital spark*, Heinemann, London.

CHAPTER 8

Unconventional and renewable energy sources

8.1 Overview

In chapters 4 to 7, an outline has been given of the major sources of the world's energy now and for at least the next few decades. Other possible sources of energy exist, which make only a small (or zero) contribution at present, but which may emerge as of great importance during the next century. In this chapter it will be possible to give only a brief review of these sources.

Many of these additional energy sources may be classified as renewable, in the sense that they are powered by natural forces which on any relevant time scale are unchanging and inexhaustible. Into this category come solar energy, tidal, wave and wind power, various sources based on non-fossil biological material, sources using ocean thermal gradients, and geothermal energy. To these may be added new sources of fossil fuels (such as tar sands), the combustible waste products of human activity, and fusion power; the latter is, for all practical purposes, an inexhaustible source, but has yet to be proven technologically. Other options affecting energy supply in the long term include advanced thermodynamic cycles, fuel cells and the use of hydrogen as an energy carrier.

From the perspective of history, it is fossil fuels, not renewable sources, that are a new development. For almost all of his history, man, like the rest of the biosphere, has depended on the natural system of energy flows powered by the sun. Early technological and industrial developments continued this dependence, as demonstrated in sailing ships, wind and water mills, and of course, in the use of wood fuel. It was the expansion of industry beyond the limits of these natural energy sources (for example the deforestation to provide charcoal for iron smelting) which prompted the use of coal and introduced the fossil fuel era. Our present understanding of the world's reserves of fuel and its probable energy requirements suggests that this era will be a temporary one, and that within a century or so we shall be mainly dependent on non-fossil sources, including nuclear fission, renewable sources and, perhaps, nuclear fusion.

Attitudes to unconventional energy sources vary widely. Most commentators view them as an insurance against the failure of the major sources to meet expanding requirements. Others, starting from a position of basic dissatisfaction with one or more major sources, regard renewable resources in particular as potential major energy suppliers deserving vigorous research and development.

185

Some renewable resources are also promoted as part of an argument in favour of small scale, simple technology and diversification. It is also sometimes suggested that these sources are a wise choice for some developing countries which lack the technological infrastructure required for, say, a coal or nuclear power industry.

Many of the renewable sources, and also fusion power, make energy available in the form of electricity. The effective exploitation of these sources is therefore dependent on a viable electricity industry and on the efficient use of electricity by consumers.

8.2   Unconventional sources of fossil fuels

Mention has been made of unconventional fossil fuel sources in the relevant chapters. The aim of this section is to summarise possible developments so that they may be seen alongside other unconventional energy sources.

Substantial quantities of oil could, in principle, be obtained from tar sands and oil shale, though at present this is not economic (Penner and Icerman, 1975). Open-cast mining is the approach usually considered, though this is only feasible where the overburden is fairly thin. Recovery of bitumen from tar sands is fairly straightforward. Oil in oil shale is held in the form of the hydrocarbon wax kerogen, and oil recovery is more difficult. A limiting factor in shale oil recovery may be the large quantities of water required. In situ recovery of oil from tar sands (by water or solvent injection) and from oil shale (by underground heating) is being considered. It has been estimated (see chapter 4) that the recoverable reserves of unconventional oil are comparable with those of conventional oil. Cost estimates are difficult to obtain, and are tending to rise rapidly, partly due to the expenses associated with environmental control.

The production of synthetic gas or oil from coal does not represent a new energy source; indeed the conversion process represents an overall loss of energy, which may in part be offset by efficient use of the products. However, coal conversion is based on a fuel whose resource life is very great, and the products are substitutes for fuels on which the world has become very dependent, and whose resource life is relatively short.

Many processes for coal gasification exist, of which the simplest, pyrolysis (heating in the absence of air) to obtain a mixture of methane, hydrogen and carbon monoxide, is familiar. More modern processes aim for higher efficiency and a higher grade product. The essentials of most processes are as follows (Hottel and Howard, 1971; Penner and Icerman, 1975):

Coal and steam are fed into a heated vessel in which the coal breaks down, mainly into methane, carbon and hydrogen, and at a higher temperature carbon and hydrogen combine to form further methane. At the same time, carbon and steam react to yield carbon monoxide and hydrogen, and some of the former is oxidised to carbon dioxide by further steam. The resulting mixture of methane, hydrogen, steam, carbon monoxide and carbon dioxide then undergoes a catalytic reaction, either the oxidation of carbon monoxide by steam to increase the hydrogen content, or the reduction of carbon monoxide by hydrogen to increase the methane content. After purification, the gas is ready for use.

Example of coal-to-gas processes are the Lurgi process (well-established), the Hygas Electrothermal system, the IGT Hygas Oxygen system, the IGT Hygas Iron system, the Texaco Partial Oxidation gasifier, the Consolidated Coal Co. CO_2-Acceptor process, the Kellog Molten Carbonate Reactor, the Bituminous Coal Research Institute Bigas system and the US Bureau of Mines Synthane process (Penner and Icerman, 1975; Lapedes, 1976).

The economics of substitute natural gas (SNG) are at present unclear, depending on future technological development, the price of coal and the price of natural gas; fossil fuel prices are, of course, to some extent determined by policy considerations.

Technological developments for the production of syncrude (a synthetic equivalent of crude oil) from coal are less advanced than for gas production. In some processes (e.g. the SASOL process – SASOL is an abbreviation for South African Coal, Oil and Gas Corporation) a mixture of hydrogen and carbon monoxide is converted to hydrocarbons by catalytic synthesis. Direct or catalytic hydrogenation of coal at high pressures may also be used to yield sulphur-free hydrocarbons with large molecular weight (the Pott-Broche or Bergius processes), and liquid hydrocarbons may also be produced in limited quantities by sequential pyrolysis. The most advanced processes are at present at pilot-plant stage.

Economic assessment suggests that the widespread use of syncrude would not be economic until some time after the introduction of SNG.

In-situ gasification of coal was proposed more than a century ago, and various methods have been tried. Major problems have included combustion control, roof stability, lack of permeability for the movement of gases, fracturing, leakage and ground-water. The product gas after removal of diluents, such as nitrogen and carbon dioxide, is mainly hydrogen and carbon monoxide and upgrading is required to produce a direct substitute for natural gas. Development work is continuing, for example at Hanna, Wyoming (Penner and Icerman, 1975), but considerable further experience will be needed before this technology can be exploited on a commercial scale.

8.3   MHD electricity generation

Magnetohydrodynamic (MHD) generators provide a method of enhancing the efficiency of electricity generation from fossil fuels (or from some types of nuclear reactor) by increasing the upper temperature used. The conversion of mechanical to electrical energy in a generator depends on Faraday's principle of electromagnetic induction (see chapter 7). MHD systems utilise this principle more directly.

A very hot, ionised (and therefore conducting) gas is passed along an expanding duct (figure 8.1) across which is placed a magnetic field. An electric field is generated at right angles to both the direction of flow and the magnetic field, and this can be connected to an external circuit. The expanded and somewhat cooled gas emerging from the duct can be used as the heat source for a conventional steam cycle. In this way, the drop in temperature which occurs in conventional plant between the combustion gases and steam is avoided, and an overall thermal efficiency of 50–60 per cent may be obtained. Angrist (1976) gives a more detailed description of the principles involved and of practical systems.

In open cycle systems, hot combustion gases are used directly, while closed cycle systems use a recycled inert gas in the MHD duct. In either case, it is usually necessary to promote ionisation by 'seeding' the gas, usually with an alkali metal; this must be recovered in open cycle systems. For large scale systems, a superconducting magnet would be likely to reduce running costs. MHD generators are usually direct current systems, though alternating current systems have been proposed.

Practical problems associated with MHD systems include corrosion by alkali metals, the selection of electrode and insulating materials to withstand temperatures of 2000–3000° C, losses by heat transfer to the duct walls (especially where these are cooled), magnet losses, and losses due to eddy currents at the ends of the duct.

Though the principles of MHD generation are well-established the technique has yet to be shown to be practical on a large scale, and no useful estimate of costs is available. The fuel savings resulting from the use of MHD generators could, however, be very great.

8.4   Fusion power

Nuclear fusion systems make use of the energy released when two light nuclei fuse to form a heavier nucleus (see chapter 6). This is the energy source used in the hydrogen bomb, and also that which powers the sun. The raw materials required for this reaction are abundant, and the energy released is very great. However, extremely high pressures and temperatures are required to initiate the reaction, and fusion power requires very advanced technology. An overview of the subject is given by Connolly (1978).

There are several possible nuclear reactions suitable for fusion systems. That between deuterium and tritium demands the least extreme physical conditions:

$$D + T \rightarrow He^4 + n + 17.6 \text{ MeV}$$

The tritium, however, is very rare in nature, and must be bred from an isotope of lithium by the reaction:

$$Li^6 + n \rightarrow T + He^4 + 4.8 \text{ MeV}$$

At the temperatures and pressures required, the reactants are in the form of an

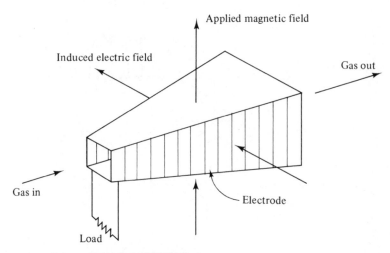

Applied magnetic field

Induced electric field

Gas out

Gas in

Electrode

Load

Figure 8.1   Schematic diagram of MHD duct.

ionised plasma. Fusion systems may be categorised by the way in which this plasma is confined, into magnetic confinement and inertial confinement systems, the principles of which are outlined below.

In the D−T reaction shown above, most of the energy released is carried by the neutron, which is very likely to escape from the plasma. Its energy is ultimately released as heat in the materials surrounding the plasma, and this is the major part of the heat used for electricity generation. Some of the generated power is required to operate the confinement and heating system. This defines a physical break-even point for the technology − the point where the energy produced, converted to electricity through a conventional thermal cycle, is just sufficient to maintain the system in operation. The economic break-even occurs when the revenue from excess electricity generation is sufficient to pay off the capital and operating costs of the reactor.

Magnetic confinement systems use magnetic fields to confine the plasma. Many geometries have been suggested, but most current effort is being directed towards toroidal geometries such as the Tokamak, shown schematically in figure 8.2. Such a geometry prevents leakage of the plasma, but introduces problems of adding fuel and removing waste products. The plasma is surrounded by a blanket of lithium and beryllium which both absorbs heat and breeds tritium. The lithium itself may be used as a coolant, or (to avoid the problems of pumping a conducting liquid in a magnetic field) helium may be used. The blanket is surrounded by shielding and by the coils maintaining the magnetic fields. The temperature range involved is very great − from over 50 million K in the plasma to some 900 K in the coolant and 4 K for the superconducting magnets. This imposes severe engineering problems.

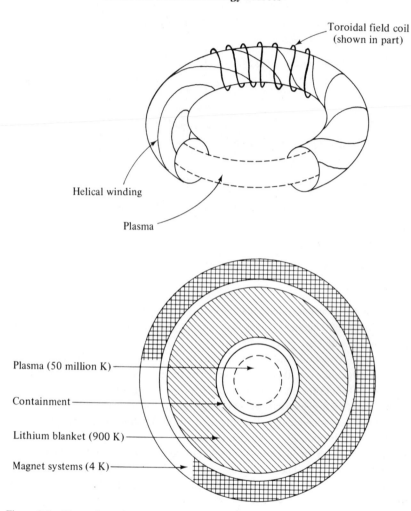

Figure 8.2   Magnetic confinement fusion reactor – schematic.

Materials have to be chosen to meet the appropriate temperature and strength requirements, to have acceptable neutronic properties, and to withstand the high levels of radiation without excessive loss of strength and without forming hazardous activation products.

Inertial confinement systems (figure 8.3) seek to achieve fusion by creating extremely high pressures for a short time, unlike magnetic confinement systems which are effectively continuous with more moderate pressures. A frozen pellet of

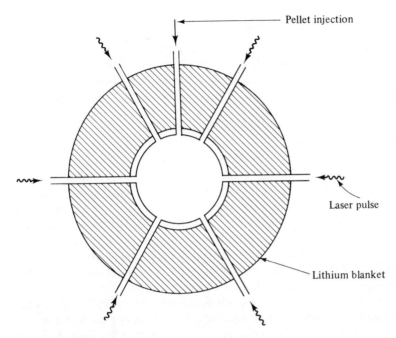

Figure 8.3   Inertial confinement fusion reactor – schematic.

mixed deuterium and tritium is dropped into the reactor cavity and imploded by high powered laser beams (electron or ion beams have also been suggested). The laser beams create a spherically symmetric shock wave which heats and compresses the inner region of the pellet to initiate the fusion reaction; in effect the pellet becomes a miniature hydrogen bomb. The blanket and shield surrounding the reactor cavity is similar to that used for magnetic confinement systems (except of course that no magnets are required). Lithium is used for breeding tritium and as a coolant. An inertial confinement reactor would probably be much smaller than a magnetic confinement reactor (around 200 MWe compared with 2000 MWe). The key technological requirement for the development of inertial confinement systems is for a high conversion efficiency laser capable of high pulse rates; two possible candidates are carbon dioxide and neodymium-glass lasers.

Fusion reactor systems have yet to show technological feasibility (let alone economic viability), but steady progress is being made, with inertial confinement some way behind magnetic confinement systems. If these systems prove feasible, they represent an unlimited and inexhaustible source of electrical energy. Their contribution is unlikely to be significant, however, until well into the next century.

8.5   Solar energy for low grade heat

The total amount of solar radiation reaching the earth is vast – some 4.14×10^{15} kWh per day. This is equivalent to $1.354 \, \text{kW}/\text{m}^2$ ($429.2 \, \text{Btu}/\text{hr}/\text{ft}^2$) on a surface normal to the direction of incidence (Cheremisinoff and Regino, 1978). The proportion of the direct radiation reaching the earth's surface depends on the effects of the ozone layer, dust and, of course, clouds and in the US is typically 40 to 75 per cent; for areas measured on the surface of the earth it is also necessary to introduce a latitude correction.

Demands for low grade heat are widely dispersed. Low grade heat is not readily transportable, so that to make use of conventional fuels it is necessary to employ a high grade energy vector such as electricity or a concentrated form of stored energy such as coal, oil or gas. Solar energy is also widely dispersed, and is readily convertible to low grade heat, and so appears to be well-suited to this application. Its major drawback, of course, is that the demand for heat and the supply of sunshine do not match, and that long-term (i.e. seasonal) storage of low grade heat is bulky and expensive. Short-term variations in sunlight are less important for this application, as short-term storage of low grade heat is not difficult.

The technology of solar low grade heat is straightforward. A typical collector (figure 8.4) consists of a black metal absorber containing pipes for water or air to remove the heat, placed under one or more layers of glass. The function of the glass is to transmit incident light while reflecting back the infra-red radiation from the absorber. Radiation from the absorber may also be reduced by the use of special multi-layer coatings which rely on interference effects. A flat panel constructed in this way absorbs diffuse (e.g. from clouds) as well as direct radiation, and can conveniently be mounted on a wall or roof. Various forms of concentrating collector have also been devised, some of which will be discussed below in the context of solar thermal electricity systems. The collector can readily be plumbed into the hot water system of the premises involved; a common approach is to use the solar panel to pre-heat cold water, relying on a conventional system to 'top-up' to the temperature required and to supply the bulk of the heat during the winter.

Alternatively, solar space heating can be provided passively through the architectural design of the premises. At its simplest, this involves only the orientation of the building and the siting and size of windows. More radical possibilities include the provision of an entire wall of double-glazed windows, a flat roof covered by a pond of water over which insulating screens can be drawn at night (this also provides summer cooling) or a heavy dark-coloured south-facing wall behind a layer of glass, with room air circulating by convection between the wall and the glass.

A further means of tapping solar energy discussed earlier in the context of electricity is the heat pump, which uses the outside air as its heat source. This

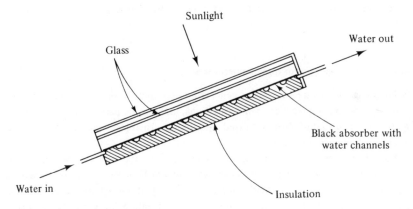

Figure 8.4   Simple solar water heater.

dependence on solar energy can be made more explicit by using a solar collector as the heat source (such collectors are more efficient at lower fluid temperature).

Solar energy may also be used directly for cooling buildings, through an absorption type of refrigeration system; this has the advantage that the incidence of sunshine matches the cooling load. The same collectors can, of course, contribute to heating during the winter.

Solar low grade heat also has industrial applications, particularly in drying. Crop drying, which requires air up to about 180° F, is a promising market, in which the seasonal nature of sunshine might not be a drawback. The higher temperatures required for other drying applications would be obtainable from simple types of concentrating collector.

The economics of using solar energy for low grade heat depend very much on the location, the pattern of heat demand, and the details of the system used. Systems in which the solar collector is built into the architecture of the premises are particularly difficult to assess in economic terms. One author (J. R. Williams, 1974), writing in a US context, suggests that solar heating costs compare favourably with electricity, but do not compete with oil or gas. Similar conclusions emerge from a UK study (International Solar Energy Society, 1976). It would be expected that the economic case for solar heating would be stronger in many other parts of the world.

In assessing the optimum role for solar heating in a national context, its impact on other fuels must be considered. If the supplementary fuel (mainly for winter use) is electricity, the load factor on the electricity supply system is likely to be lower than it would have been if the solar heating were not used, leading to higher electricity costs. If the supplementary fuel is oil or gas, the effect is to increase the difference between summer and winter rates of use, increasing storage requirements.

8.6   Solar energy for high temperatures

Solar furnaces provide a means of generating extremely high temperatures (up to around 3500° C) under very clean conditions, and can be used to melt refractory materials. The manufacture of fused aluminium crucibles is an example of the application of such a furnace.

Solar furnaces exist in France, Massachusetts, Japan and the Soviet Union (J. R. Williams, 1974). The best-known is at Odeillo-Font Romeu in the Pyrenees, which has a power of 1 MW. Sunlight is incident on 63 steerable mirrors (heliostats) spread over a hillside, and is reflected onto a large parabolic mirror which forms the side of a building. The furnace itself is at the focal point of this mirror; some 600 kW can be concentrated in an area one foot in diameter.

This type of furnace is likely to remain a specialist device, with no significant impact on the fuel market as a whole. A development of the same principles could, however, provide central electricity generation, and this will be discussed in the next section.

8.7   Solar electricity – thermal

Solar energy may be used to heat a fluid, which then generates electricity through a conventional heat engine. To obtain an adequate working temperature, some form of concentration is required, so that for most designs there is little contribution from diffuse sunlight. The systems which have been considered fall into two categories:

(a) systems in which individual mirrors track the sun continuously;
(b) systems in which the mirrors are fixed or can be adjusted from day to day, but
     do not track continuously.

Continuous tracking systems use a large number of plane or curved mirrors (heliostats), each steered to reflect sunlight onto a single tower mounted boiler. This gives a high temperature and high efficiency but requires complex, rugged and accurate mechanisms for the heliostats.

The most common forms of non-tracking system consist of assemblies of trough-shaped collectors (cylindrical or parabolic), usually aligned east to west. The absorber takes the form of a tube above each collector through which a heat transfer fluid passes. A wide range of possible mirror and absorber geometries is described in Meinel and Meinel (1976). In some instances the absorber is moved continuously as the focal line of the reflectors changes. One unusual design uses a fixed hemispherical bowl reflector with a linear absorber through its centre of curvature, continuously aligned parallel to the incident sunlight. Non-tracking systems have the advantage of comparative simplicity, but may introduce problems from thermal and pumping losses in the heat transfer fluid, and will probably have a lower thermal efficiency than tracking systems.

Economic assessment of solar thermal generating systems is difficult, as few designs have progressed beyond the conceptual and preliminary testing phases. It has been suggested, however, (J. R. Williams, 1974) that in suitable areas, such as southern California, these systems are close to economic viability. In an electricity system whose peak demand occurred during the summer (e.g. for air conditioning), such systems would contribute to the peak demand as well as to total energy requirements. In a system whose peak demand occurred during the winter, the solar station would not contribute to the peak, and its total cost would need to be justified by the fuel savings which it produced.

8.8   Solar electricity – photovoltaic

Photovoltaic electricity generation involves no moving parts, no fluids and no heat engine, and must therefore be an attractive option if it is technically and economically viable.

Photovoltaic cells make use of the properties of semiconducting materials such as silicon. In their pure crystalline form, the electrons in such materials are tightly bound and the materials are poor conductors of electricity. The introduction of small quantities of impurities, however, often increases conductivity considerably. An impurity such as phosphorus, when introduced into the silicon crystal lattice, leaves one electron loosely bound, and these 'free' electrons permit the conduction of electricity. Silicon doped in this way is known as n-type silicon because conduction results from the negatively charged electrons. Conversely, an impurity atom such as boron leaves unfilled one space in the crystal lattice which would normally be occupied by an electron. This space, known as a 'hole', can migrate through the crystal lattice and permits the passage of an electric current in much the same way as a free electron. Silicon doped in this way is known as p-type silicon because the 'holes' are positively charged.

At its simplest, a silicon photovoltaic cell (figure 8.5) consists of a single crystal of p-type silicon with a surface layer of n-type silicon. When light falls onto such a p–n junction, electrons and holes move in opposite directions across the junction, and if an external circuit is connected across the junction, an electric current will flow. The theoretical maximum efficiency is 22 per cent, but the practical range is 10–16 per cent (Cheremisinoff and Regino, 1978). By assembling a large number of cells in an array and providing protective encapsulation an electricity generating system can be constructed.

The drawback of this seemingly simple approach is the high cost of preparing crystals of pure silicon and processing them to form arrays of solar cells. With

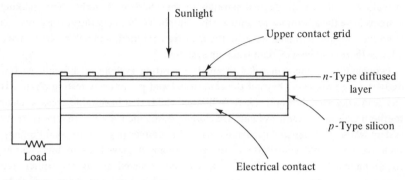

Figure 8.5   Solar photovoltaic cell.

present technology, the cost per peak kW is around $20,000 (Cheremisinoff and Regino, 1978), ruling out the use of this technology except for space craft and very specialised terrestrial applications. Developments which may lead to a reduction in cost include the use of mono-crystalline silicon ribbon, a polycrystalline silicon film, amorphous silicon, cadmium sulphide and gallium arsenide.

Solar cells may be combined with concentrators, increasing their efficiency and reducing the amount of cell material needed for a given collector area. Against these gains must be set the extra complexity of the concentrator system, the loss of input from diffuse radiation, and the requirement for cooling (cell efficiency and life reduces as the temperature rises). The system used to cool the solar cells may, of course, provide a source of low grade heat.

The use of concentrators also makes it possible to consider thermoelectric or thermionic systems. The former depend on the voltage generated when a junction of dissimilar metals is heated; typical conversion efficiencies are up to 2.5 per cent, and this approach has attracted little interest. Thermionic systems depend on the movement of electrons in an evacuated envelope between a hot cathode and a cool anode; the temperature required is 1200° C to 2600° C, requiring very sophisticated concentrators. With a suitable choice of cathode materials the efficiency could be 10–15 per cent.

Several schemes have been suggested for mounting solar cells on satellites in a geosynchronous orbit. Insolation would be almost continuous, and there would be no atmospheric losses to reduce the power input. The electricity produced would be beamed to earth by a microwave system.

The economics of the direct conversion of sunlight to electricity are very difficult to predict. At present, solar cells are used only in specialist applications where cost is of minor importance, and very great reductions would be needed to make these techniques viable for large scale power generation. However, the technologies based on solid state physics have seen massive reductions in costs in recent years, and a breakthrough to economically viable solar cells cannot be ruled out. The impact of solar cells on the electricity supply system would be similar to that of solar thermal systems.

8.9   Solar chemical conversion

Two technologies exist which involve the use of solar energy through a cell resembling that used for electrolysis. Photoelectrolysis is the decomposition of water by the action of sunlight, to give hydrogen and oxygen. Hydrogen is of course, a versatile and storable fuel in its own right as well as a starting point for the synthesis of other fuels (see section 8.17 on the hydrogen economy). The electrodes are composed of a photo-active semiconductor material, and the cell may be regarded as a modified $p–n$ junction. However, the requirements for the semiconductor material are far less onerous than for conventional photovoltaic cells. One particular problem is electrode corrosion, but this has been inhibited in some experimental systems by suppressing the production of oxygen. In some systems, both hydrogen and electrical energy are produced.

The second technology, electrochemical photovoltaic cells, is intended solely for electricity production; the cells have one semiconductor electrode and one metal electrode.

These techniques, which are outlined in Cheremisinoff and Regino (1978), are far from being commercially viable, but they depend on recent discoveries, and substantial further progress may well be possible.

8.10   Tidal power

Tide mills were in use in Western Europe during the eleventh century, and it was only the advent of cheap fossil fuels during the nineteenth century that rendered such systems, temporarily at least, obsolete. As fossil fuel prices rise, large tidal power schemes are now being considered in many countries.

The origin of the tides is the gravitational interaction between the earth, moon and sun. The change in surface level due to the tides is small in mid-ocean, but becomes amplified near coasts. The extent of this amplification depends very much on the shape of the coastline. The maximum difference between high and low tides (the tidal range) occurs when the shape of a bay or estuary leads to resonance effects. This effect is sufficient to merit the consideration of a tidal power scheme in a limited number of sites; some of the possibilities (from Penner and Icerman, 1975) are:

North America:	Bay of Fundy
United Kingdom:	Severn Estuary, Carlingford Estuary, Strangford Estuary
France:	Lorient, Brest, Alber-Benoit, Alber-Vrach, Arguenon and Lancieux, La Fresnaye, Rance (where a 240 MWe scheme was commissioned in 1966), Chausey, Somme

USSR: Kislaya Bay (at which there is a 400 kWe experimental installation)

Argentina: Gulf of San Jose

Tidal power is tapped by placing a barrage across the bay or estuary concerned, and forcing the tidal flow to pass through turbines or sluiceways as required. The nature of tidal flows means that, in the simpler schemes, generation is intermittent; more complicated schemes seek to reduce this drawback so that the scheme may be treated as a source of firm capacity as well as energy.

Single-basin schemes (figure 8.6) have one barrage and one water storage basin. In one-way systems, the incoming tide is allowed to fill the basin through sluiceways (perhaps assisted by turbine-generators used as pumps) and the impounded water is used to produce electricity during the ebb tide. In a two-way system, power is generated both from the incoming and the outgoing tide, increasing the energy output and the degree of 'firmness', but reducing the average head and increasing costs.

A more complex barrage may be used to define two (or sometimes more) storage basins (figure 8.7). By placing turbines between each basin and the sea, continuous (though varying) output can be achieved. Various combinations of turbines or pump-turbines may be installed in different parts of the barrage; the optimum arrangement in a particular location will depend on all the relevant costs and on the system into which the scheme is to be integrated.

Tidal power schemes require low-head turbines, which are larger and more expensive than high-head turbines of similar power. A common type is the bulb turbine, in which the generator is enclosed in a bulb-shaped housing at the centre of the water channel, directly connected to the turbine runner; these can also be operated as pumps.

The most onerous problems in the use of tidal power are those of barrage construction (and particularly closure) in areas of high tidal flow, and corrosion of the barrage, sluiceways and turbines by salt water.

The economics of tidal energy schemes depends on the value to be placed on firm capacity, which in turn depends on the system into which the scheme is to be integrated. This makes assessment and comparison difficult. Most schemes appear to be some way from economic viability at present fuel prices, but this situation may be changed by rising fossil fuel costs, improvements in barrage construction techniques, and improved turbine designs.

Because tidal power schemes are feasible only at sites of unusually high tidal range, their maximum possible contribution to energy needs, though useful, is fairly small.

8.11   Wave power

The source of wave energy is the wind and so, ultimately, the sun. Unlike most other forms of solar energy, however, wave energy is most readily available during

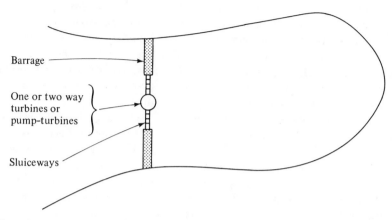

Figure 8.6   One-basin tidal power scheme.

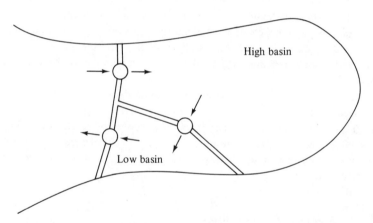

Figure 8.7   Two-basin tidal power scheme. *Note:* Various combinations of turbines, pump-turbines and sluiceways may be used, depending on economic considerations. The arrows indicate the normal direction of water flow.

the winter months, when in most countries electricity demand is at its highest. The amount of energy available is very large; the power theoretically obtainable from waves off the UK coast averages 80 kW/metre, amounting to a potential of 120 GW (around twice the present installed capacity of the electricity supply system in England and Wales) in UK territorial waters (Central Electricity Generating Board, 1976). Unlike tidal energy, which is very site-specific, some potential for the extraction of wave energy exists on almost any coastline.

Many devices have been proposed for the extraction of wave energy, and a review is given in National Engineering Laboratory (1976). Some, like the 'duck', the wave-contouring raft and the triplate converter (figure 8.8) float at the surface and convert the wave motion into relative motion of the components of the device. Others, much as the Masuda buoy (fig. 8.9), are rigid floating structures in which wave motion forces air through a turbine. Others are mounted on the sea bed and rely on changes in hydrostatic pressure. There are also several schemes suitable for shore location which allow waves to run up ramps or along converging channels (fig. 8.10) to fill a reservoir which is above the mean sea level.

Construction costs and efficiency will be the key parameters in determining which, if any, of these devices become commercially viable. Other important aspects will be the integrity of the device in the hostile marine environment, maintainability, and the cost and reliability of the transmission system used to bring the energy ashore (this is usually electrical but could involve hydraulic pumping or compressed air). These considerations favour simplicity and the absence of large moving parts exposed to sea water; they also favour sea-bed rather than surface systems, though cost factors may favour surface systems.

Development of wave power devices is, for those on which most work has been done, at the stage of small and medium-scale testing. Economic analysis of the most promising systems (National Engineering Laboratory, 1976) indicates that they could be close to economic feasibility in the UK, though in view of the development work remaining to be done such estimates must be regarded as tentative.

Within the electricity supply system, wave power devices could be regarded as a base load energy source. The variable nature of the output would limit the usefulness of the devices as sources of firm power, however, weakening the economic arguments in their favour. Consideration could be given to combining wave power systems with tidal barrage or pumped storage schemes to increase their firm power value.

8.12   Ocean thermal power plants

The surface layers of the ocean, particularly in tropical areas, are substantially warmer than deeper waters, and this temperature difference may be used to drive a heat engine. Ocean thermal energy conversion (OTEC) systems, most of which are at present only at a conceptual stage of development, seek to exploit this opportunity.

The low temperatures involved require the use of a low boiling point working fluid such as freon or ammonia, though open-cycle systems (operating by the flash evaporation of warm sea water under a partial vacuum) have been tested. Most systems being studied at present are, however, closed cycle systems, with the basic structure shown in figure 8.11. The working fluid is evaporated in a heat exchanger through which warm sea water flows, expanded through a turbine to generate electricity and condensed using cold sea water before being pumped to the

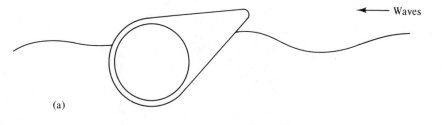

(a)

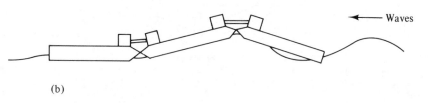

(b)

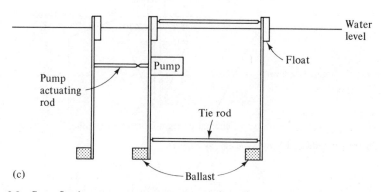

(c)

Figure 8.8   Some floating wave-energy converters – schematic.

evaporator. The temperature difference is low (around 25–40° F), imposing a low thermal efficiency, and this requires large heat transfer areas and high flows (with high pumping requirements) per unit of electrical output. Nevertheless, some of the designs so far produced show promise of becoming economic. An outline of some of the many systems proposed is given in Cheremisinoff and Regino (1978).

Where the output of the OTEC systems is electric power, the device must be

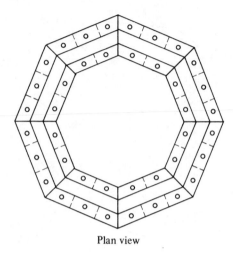

Plan view

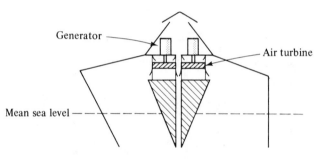

Schematic diagram of single chamber

Figure 8.9   Masuda buoy wave energy converter.

situated sufficiently close to the shore to permit the use of submarine cables for power transmission. It might also be possible to use the systems for on-site manufacture of energy-intensive products (e.g. ammonia or aluminium), in which case the restriction on siting would not apply. An unexpected bonus of OTEC systems might be the enrichment of fishing grounds due to the transfer of nutrients from the unproductive deep waters to the warmer surface water.

Unlike other sources of solar electricity, the output of an OTEC system would show very little daily or seasonal variation, and would be very easy to integrate into a wider electricity supply system as a source of base load power.

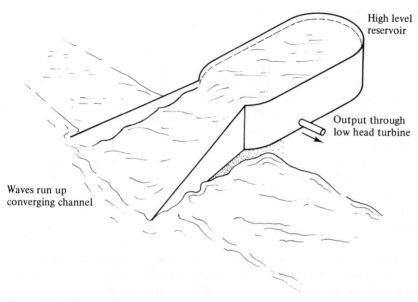

Figure 8.10   Shore-based wave energy converter.

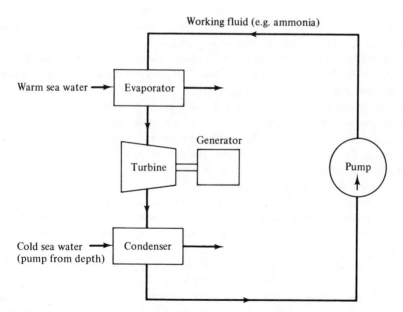

Figure 8.11   Ocean thermal energy converter (OTEC) – schematic.

8.13   Wind power

Wind power is as old as the first sailing ship, and windmills for grinding corn or pumping water are a familiar part of the scenery in many countries. The use of windmills for electricity generation on a small scale is not new, and was particularly popular in rural areas in the first half of this century, before rural electrification became widespread (Cherimisinoff and Regino, 1978). One of the first large aerogenerators was the Smith-Putnam wind turbine in Vermont, rated at 1.25 MW. This was commissioned in 1941, but was abandoned after a catastrophic blade failure in 1945.

Wind turbines may be divided into two types – those having a horizontal axis (conventional windmills) and those having a vertical axis.

Many designs of horizontal axis turbine have been suggested. These turbines have to be steered into the wind, which is automatic if the rotor is located downwind of the support tower, but requires a tail fin if the rotor is in front of the tower. Other things being equal, the output of a wind turbine is proportional to the square of the radius and the cube of the wind speed. The latter dependence makes output very variable, and many designs incorporate automatic adjustment of the blades to compensate partially for this effect. Such adjustment also protects the turbine from damage in very high winds. In some designs, this adjustment is made automatic by the use of flexible blade materials. Most designs use two or three blades, but at least one (developed by Chalk) is multi-bladed and bears a superficial resemblance to a bicycle wheel. One unusual design by Salter uses three rotors in a triangular configuration on a single tower.

A key advantage of vertical axis wind turbines is that they respond equally and instantaneously to winds in any direction. There are two main types, the Savonius rotor and the Darrieus rotor (figure 8.12). The Savonius rotor is very easy to fabricate (though rather heavy) and will start at very low wind speeds. The aerodynamics of the Darrieus rotor are not well understood; the starting torque required is high, and the relationship between wind speed and rotor speed is obscure. Once the dynamics of this type of rotor are better understood, it is expected that the capital costs may be quite low and that the device may be suitable for large and small scale applications.

An unusual wind power device which is at present only at a conceptual stage is the 'tornado turbine' proposed by Yen. In this system, air passing into and over a vented cylindrical tower creates a vortex and draws air at high speed past a fairly small rotor at the base of the tower.

The use of wind power for electricity generation on a small scale is already economic in remote locations. At present it does not appear to be economic for large scale generation, but in view of the number of different concepts being considered, substantial cost reductions are possible. Integration within an existing power supply system presents some problems due to the intermittent nature of wind generation. These problems may be solved by providing electricity storage at the

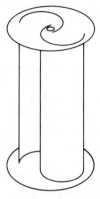

(a) Savonius rotor

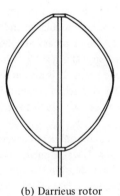

(b) Darrieus rotor

Figure 8.12   Vertical axis wind turbines. (a) Savonius rotor. (b) Darrieus rotor.

wind turbine (which is expensive), by using the wind energy to pump water in a local pumped-storage scheme, by treating wind power as complementary to existing hydro-electric schemes or flexible fossil-fired stations, or by compensating for variations in wind power by automatic load control. The economic assessment of this energy source will depend on which of these options is used as well as on the device itself. The extent of wind power developments may be limited by the availability of suitable sites, though this limitation could be reduced by the use of offshore siting.

Wind power may well also find a significant market as a source of mechanical power, for example for pumping water or operating simple machinery. This is particularly relevant to developing countries where electricity supply may be absent or of limited capacity, and where internal combustion engines may be expensive and difficult to maintain. Little technological development is necessary for such small-scale applications.

8.14   Biomass

Plants capture solar energy by photosynthesis, incorporating carbon from the carbon dioxide of the air into their tissues. All living things depend on this process for food, and man has also for most of his history depended on plants for energy. In terms of the total mass of plant material produced, photosynthesis is a rather inefficient process (typically 1 per cent and rarely above 5 per cent). Nevertheless the amount of energy which could be made available in this way is very large.

Land plants considered for energy production include sugar cane, sugar beet, sorghum, corn, wheat, grasses, kenaf, eucalyptus, short rotation hardwoods, sunflowers and comfrey (Cheremisinoff and Regino, 1978). These plants vary in their total biomass yield, their ability to grow on poor soils or in areas of poor climate, and the suitability of the end product for different uses. There is competition between biomass energy production and food production, which means that the most promising options for biomass are those where an existing agricultural waste product (e.g. wheat straw) is used, or where energy crops can be grown in situations unsuitable for food crops. It is also necessary to take into account the need to preserve soil structure and nutrient content. There is considerable scope for plant breeding to enhance the biomass yield or to optimise the combined usefulness of the plant for food energy.

Some water plants are particulary efficient converters of solar energy, including the water-hyacinth (which also aids water purification), some species of algae, and giant kelp. These are harvested with a high water content, and are generally best suited to different forms of processing from those which suit land-based plants.

Experiments have also been carried out to persuade simple plants (by environmental control and breeding) to modify the photosynthesis process to produce hydrogen directly. As yet the efficiencies obtained have been very low.

The simplest way of using biomass energy sources is to allow them to dry out in the sun (not required for wood), and burn them. Though appropriate for static applications such as domestic heating or power generation, this does not provide substitutes for oil or gas. One alternative is anaerobic digestion to yield methane, which is also a suitable treatment for animal manure. This approach is particularly applicable to water-based plants, avoiding any requirement for drying, and the residue may be used as a fertiliser.

Another processing route, applicable to sugar or glucose from starchy grains, is fermentation; the ethanol produced is a potential substitute for gasoline as well as having a wide range of industrial uses.

Pyrolysis may also be used, particularly for wood, yielding methanol and hydrocarbons among other products. Methanol may be used as a gasoline additive, or modified chemically to provide a direct substitute for gasoline.

The use of wood fuel for heating is widespread in many parts of the world, and is economic in the US or UK where local conditions are favourable. The production of methane (particularly from human or animal wastes) is also becoming more widespread, and may have additional value in intensive agricultural systems as a method of avoiding pollution. Other biomass energy sources have yet to establish a significant economic role.

Within the energy supply system as a whole, biomass sources have the advantage over many other renewable sources that they provide a stored form of energy, in many cases in a form suitable for vehicle propulsion. Thus their function is complementary to that of the renewable sources used for electricity generation, and as pressure on oil supplies grows they will compete with synthetic liquid or gaseous fuels manufactured from coal.

8.15   Waste products as fuel

The use of biological waste products to produce energy has already been mentioned in section 8.14. This is already proving economic in a number of areas, including the use of methane from sewage to provide pumping power at sewage works, the use of bark and wood waste for process heat in the timber industry, and the use of waste straw in agriculture.

Such wastes are one part of the wider class of all domestic and industrial waste products, many of which have a value as energy sources. At present, most municipal and industrial waste is buried or burned without recovery of either valuable materials or energy. Commercial systems are becoming available which convert much of this waste into pelletised refuse-derived fuel (RDF) which can be used in coal-fired boilers (Cheremisinoff and Regino, 1978).

Conversion to liquid or gaseous fuel would allow waste materials to compete in a far larger market. This can be achieved by pyrolysis, though there are problems due to the variations in waste composition, and this process is not yet viable.

With present costs and technologies, the most common situations in which waste products are used for energy production are when the source is readily available (such as wood waste in the timber industry) or where disposal by other means would be expensive or prone to environmental problems.

8.16   Geothermal energy

Though the total quantity of heat stored in the earth is vast, geothermal energy can only be exploited in particular areas where geological formations lead to high temperature gradients. Potential areas are divided into hyper-thermal and semi-thermal areas according to the temperatures encountered; hyper-thermal areas are in practice confined to regions of seismic activity. For an area to be an exploitable field, it must contain permeable rocks so that a working fluid (usually water and often naturally present) can be used to remove the heat. Wet hyper-thermal fields produce water under pressure at over 100° C, while dry hyper-thermal fields produce dry steam under pressure. An introduction to geothermal energy is provided by Armstead (1978).

Hyper-thermal fields have been used for local heat supply throughout man's history, for example in the North Island of New Zealand. Electricity generation from such a field began in 1913 in Lardarello in Italy. Other places in which such fields occur are Iceland, Japan and the West Coast of the United States, and it is usually economic to exploit these fields for electricity generation or direct heat use.

Scope for major expansion of geothermal energy use lies in two developments. Firstly, semi-thermal fields, which are far more widespread than hyper-thermal fields and are not confined to seismic areas, can be used to produce water up to 100° C. Secondly, impermeable rock in hyper-thermal or semi-thermal areas can be fractured (by hydraulic pressure or, more exotically, by a small nuclear explosion) to allow adequate heat transfer to circulating water. Ultimately, the exploitation of non-thermal areas (in which temperatures of 100° C are located at a depth of 3–4 km) might be economic.

Though geothermal energy as a whole can be treated as an inexhaustible resource, a single bore will have a limited life (perhaps 10 years in economic terms). The life of a field is likely to be considerably more than this due to the drilling of new bores and the deepening of existing ones, but at economic rates of heat extraction an ultimate decline in output is inevitable.

Geothermal energy can be used as a direct heat source if appropriate loads can be found nearby. Possible loads include district heating, hot water supply, air conditioning, horticulture (grapes and bananas are grown in Iceland using geothermal energy), and industrial applications, especially evaporation of solutions and drying. The most important use of geothermal energy at present, however, is electricity generation, with world total installed capacity in 1976 of 1362 MW, and more than double this capacity planned (Armstead, 1978). A combined electricity/low grade heat load is ideal, owing to the inefficiency of electricity generation at the temperatures concerned. For wet fields, flash evaporation at low pressure may be used to extract additional work from hot water, and in principle systems using low boiling point working fluids (such as ammonia or freon) could be used.

No simple statement can be made about the economics of geothermal energy. Hyper-thermal fields are often economic at present. Semi-thermal fields may become economic as fossil fuel prices rise and techniques of exploration and drilling improve; economic assessment would be expected to differ markedly from field to field. Too little is known about the effectiveness of rock fracturing, or the costs of new very deep drilling techniques, to assess the economics of impermeable dry rocks or non-thermal areas. Within the electricity supply system, geothermal sources could provide steady base load power with very low variable costs.

8.17 The hydrogen economy

This title is given to the concept of a future energy supply system in which hydrogen plays a major role as an energy vector. The hydrogen is not, of course, a new primary fuel, but the use of hydrogen as a secondary fuel could have a number of benefits:

(a) as oil and gas supplies dwindle, the need for a new convenient and storable fuel will grow. Hydrogen and chemicals based on it are among the candidates for that role;

(b) many of the sources which may acquire an increasing role as fossil fuels decline – nuclear fission, fusion and renewable sources – can only be used for electricity production. Electricity is difficult to store and is not generally useful for transport. The manufacture of hydrogen from electricity is straightforward, and hydrogen is storable and suitable as a starting point for transport fuels;

(c) the technology exists (fuel cells, see section 8.18) for the efficient conversion of hydrogen into electrical energy;

(d) hydrogen would be a very useful chemical feedstock as oil and gas availability falls.

Hydrogen can be stored under pressure, by liquefaction at very low temperatures, or in an easily dissociated chemical compound. Liquefaction gives the highest energy density but is impracticable for most applications. Residence within metallic hydrides appears the best option; iron–titanium hydride and magnesium nickel hydride yield storage densities of 240 and 977 kWh/lb respectively, compared with 108.5 kWh/lb for pressurisation at 2000 psi (Cheremisinoff and Regino, 1978). An iron–titanium alloy will absorb hydrogen at room temperatures, requiring a temperature of about 200° F to release it. Pressurisation, probably using underground caverns, would remain appropriate for bulk storage.

The production of hydrogen by electrolysis is straightforward and efficient. An interesting, but more remote, possibility is the direct production of hydrogen by the photolytic decomposition of water, a direct application of solar energy (see section 8.9).

8.18 Fuel cells

The efficiency of electricity generation using a heat engine is limited by the Carnot cycle efficiency, and in practice rarely exceeds 35–45 per cent. Fuel cells provide a means for generating electricity which is not subject to this efficiency limitation; an efficiency of 100 per cent is theoretically possible, and values of around 60 per cent are achieved in practice.

The fuel cell process is, essentially, the reverse of electrolysis, and is shown schematically in figure 8.13. Hydrogen (or a similar gaseous fuel) and oxygen are introduced at the negative and positive electrodes respectively. Ionisation occurs, producing electrons which can do work in an external circuit, and the ions combine in the electrolyte to form water. The potential difference generated is usually about 1 volt, so that large numbers of cells need to be combined to form a complete system. Catalysts are usually required at the electrodes to promote the reaction, though the use of high temperatures (many cells are designed to operate at 650–1000° C) reduces the need for catalysts. The electrolytes used in cells currently being developed include molten alkali metal carbonates, solid ceramic oxide and phosphoric acid. In the molten carbonate cell, for example, the carbonate is held in a ceramic matrix and the electrodes are of nickel; the cell consists of a simple 'sandwich' of separators, current collectors, electrodes and electrolyte which can readily be combined into a larger system.

The most common fuel is gaseous hydrogen, though carbon, carbon monoxide and propane have been suggested. In order to obtain the fuel in the correct chemical form and with adequate purity, it is usually necessary to include a fuel processing stage, usually one in which a hydrocarbon feedstock is heated with steam to yield a hydrogen-rich gas; this reduces the efficiency of the system as a whole.

In 1972, fuel cell capital costs were twice those of fossil-fuelled power stations (Penner and Icerman, 1975). The differential in total costs is likely to narrow as development proceeds and as fuel prices rise (because the efficiency advantage of fuel cells will become more significant). Fuel cells are also attractive as peaking plant within the electricity supply systems because of their ease of operation and the fact that efficiency need not be impaired at low output. They are also, of course, readily compatible with the hydrogen economy concept discussed above.

8.19   The role of unconventional sources

It is difficult to predict the role of unconventional sources. Where substantial technological development is required (for example fusion power or solar photovoltaic electricity), little confidence can be placed in cost estimates. Some other sources, such as tidal power and solar low grade heat, require at most modest extensions of existing technology, and their role will be determined mainly by fossil fuel prices and the developments in competing technologies.

Economic assessment of unconventional sources usually treats them as small increments to the present energy supply system. This is the correct way to judge initial market penetration, but has the drawback that systematic relationships between different unconventional sources, which could greatly influence their

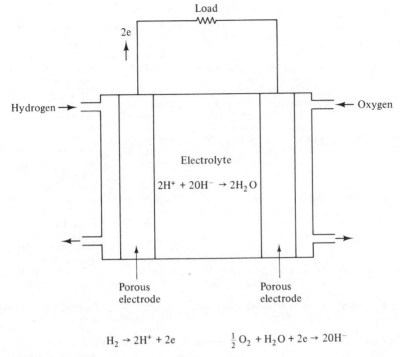

Figure 8.13 Schematic diagram of fuel cell.

long-term role, are not taken into account. Examples of such systematic relationships include:

(a) the complementarity between electricity sources and sources (mainly biomass) which are potential substitutes for hydrocarbon fuels;

(b) the seasonal complementarity between solar energy (with a summer peak) and wave and wind power (peaking during the winter);

(c) the compatibility of many unconventional sources with the use of hydrogen as an energy carrier, which would also ameliorate the problems of energy storage in a system dominated by electricity. The existence of adequate energy storage techniques has a substantial effect on the economics of non-continuous energy sources.

Tables 8.1 and 8.2 summarise the characteristics of the unconventional energy sources discussed in this chapter.

Tentative estimates of the long-term contribution of various unconventional sources are given in table 8.3, based on WEC (1978b). The values are derived from literature surveys and questionnaires. For comparison, current world annual

Table 8.1.   *Unconventional sources for electricity generation.*

Technology	Status	Potential	Remarks
Geothermal energy	Economic now in some areas; room for further technological development	Ultimately large	Also a useful source of low grade heat
Tidal power	Feasible now but room for further development; marginally economic	Limited to favourable sites	Could become economic in medium term
Wave power	Principles demonstrated but many practical problems remain; may be marginally economic	Fairly large in favourable areas	Could become economic in medium term if large scale feasibility demonstrated
Wind power	Feasible now but room for further development; economic only for remote applications	Limited by site availability	Likely market for small turbines (electrical or mechanical); role in large scale power generation not clear
Solar electricity – thermal	Close to feasibility; may be marginally economic in some areas	Large in favourable areas	Useful only in areas of high direct sunlight
Ocean thermal power	Close to feasibility; economics uncertain	Large in favourable areas	Most useful in tropical areas
Solar electricity – photovoltaic	Basic technology well-known, but major cost reduction needed	Very large	Far from economic but major breakthrough is possible
Fusion power	Feasibility not yet shown, but steady progress being made	Effectively unlimited	Could lead to electricity/hydrogen based system

energy consumption is around 300 EJ, and may be 800 to 1000 EJ by 2020. The estimates can only be regarded as a general indication of the scale of the contribution of unconventional sources; in the event the size of this contribution will depend on technological developments, conventional fuel prices and market penetration rates, all of which are highly uncertain.

The estimates suggest that the listed sources will provide at most 10 per cent of world energy requirements by 2020 and that as much as two thirds of that contribution might be from solar heating and cooling. Biomass sources are not included above. It has been estimated that these sources provide some 30 EJ at present. Though the current level of use places some strain on natural resources, particularly forests, there can be little doubt that with good management and some technological development this contribution could be substantially increased.

It would be unwise either to hail unconventional sources as the answer to mankind's energy problems, or to dismiss them as irrelevant. Their ultimate contribution could be very large indeed, and some sources are economic at present

Table 8.2. *Unconventional sources – non-electric.*

Technology	Status	Potential	Remarks
Solar low grade heat	Feasible now but room for further development. Economic now in some areas	Very large	Market penetration could be rapid with favourable prices
Biomass and waste products	Economic in some forms (e.g. wood fuel) now; scope for considerable development	Very large	May be limited by land use competition. Very useful in that solid, liquid or gaseous fuel produced can be stored and may be usable for transport
Solar high temperatures	Feasible and economic for specialist applications	Limited	Special uses only
Solar chemical conversion	Embryonic	Possibly large	May also be used for electricity generation

for some purposes and in some parts of the world. Continuing development of these sources will help to create options for energy supply in the next century.

8.20   Chapter summary

Unconventional sources of energy include new hydrocarbon resources, nuclear fusion and a wide range of renewable sources. Unconventional conversion technologies promise to increase fuel use efficiency or reduce dependence on short-lived fuels. New energy sources are regarded by some as 'insurance' technologies, and by others as potential major suppliers.

Substantial quantities of oil could be recovered from tar sands and oil shale, by mining and processing or, more speculatively, by in-situ extraction. Oil shales have the greater potential, but also pose greater problems of processing and environmental impact. Oil and gas substitutes may also be made from coal; the key value of such a process is that it reduces dependence on short-lived fuel resources. Magnetohydrodynamic (MHD) generation is an option for increasing electricity generation efficiency; many practical problems need to be overcome to establish commercial viability.

Nuclear fusion, whose potential is almost unlimited, depends on the fusion of light nuclei under extreme temperatures and pressures. The reacting plasma may be confined magnetically (usually using toroidal geometry) or by inertia – the latter system depends on the implosion of small fuel pellets using powerful lasers. The reaction between deuterium and tritium is used, with tritium being bred in a lithium blanket which also absorbs heat. Steady progress towards energy break-even is being made, though engineering problems are likely to be considerable.

By contrast, solar low grade heat requires simple technology and is economic

Table 8.3. *Estimated world contribution from unconventional sources in 2020.*

Source	Annual contribution (EJ)	Remarks
Geothermal electricity	10	Author's estimate; quoted source suggests 2.4–3.2 in 2000; calculated potential in 2020 is 32 EJ
Geothermal (heat)	6.6	Calculated potential is very much larger
Tidal power	Up to 0.3	
Wave power	Up to 0.3	
Wind power	Up to 6.6	Mainly mechanical work
Solar electricity	3.2 – 9.5	
Fusion	Up to 1.6	
Solar heating and cooling	16-63	
Total	Up to 98	

now in many areas; despite seasonal variability, its potential contribution is very large. A solar panel may be used to heat air or water, or roof or wall architecture may be modified to capture solar energy. Solar low grade heat may also be used for industrial tasks such as crop drying.

Solar energy may also be concentrated, using steerable mirrors, to give very high temperatures for specialist industrial applications. A similar approach may be used to heat a fluid for electricity generation; such systems may be close to economic viability in suitable areas.

Photovoltaic electricity generation, though well-established in principle, is far from large scale commercial viability. New cell materials and fabrication methods may lead to major cost reductions. Satellite-mounted solar power stations, using microwave power transmission, have also been proposed. More remote still is the photolytic production of hydrogen or electricity – a young technology in which major advance is possible.

Tidal power, though limited to favourable sites, requires no major new technology. Optimum design is very dependent on the location and on the electricity system into which the scheme is to be integrated. Many devices have been proposed for the extraction of energy from sea waves, some floating, some on the sea bed and some shore-based. The principles are well established, but engineering problems are substantial. Ocean thermal energy converters (OTEC) exploit vertical temperature gradients in tropical waters to generate electricity; their economic role is not yet clear.

Small wind turbines may be used for mechanical power (e.g. to pump water) or for electricity generation; the former may well represent a significant market in developing countries. Large turbines might also be useful for large scale power generation. Various designs of horizontal and vertical axis turbines are being considered. The variability of the wind makes integration into a larger supply system difficult.

Biological materials, including waste products from human activities, are a traditional fuel source with future potential. In addition to direct combustion, fermentation or pyrolysis may be used to produce substitutes for oil or gas. There is considerable scope for the optimisation of combined biomass and food production and for technological developments in processing and plant breeding.

Geothermal energy is a potentially very large resource, suitable both for electricity generation and low grade heat. Feasible and economic in some areas now, it has scope for technological development to extend the range of fields which can be tapped.

It has been suggested that hydrogen might emerge as an important energy vector, taking over the storable fuel role at present occupied by oil and gas. It is readily produced from electricity by electrolysis, and convertible to electricity at fairly high efficiency in fuel cells; it can also be converted into oil and gas substitutes.

Though it is generally expected that unconventional sources will play only a minor role over the next few decades, development work creates options for energy supply in the long term.

Chapter 8   Further reading

Angrist, S. W. (1976) *Direct energy conversion,* Allyn and Bacon, Boston, Mass.

Armstead, H. C. H. (1978) *Geothermal energy,* Wiley, New York.

Cheremisinoff, P. N. and Regino, T. C. (1978) *Principles and applications of solar energy,* Ann Arbor Science Publishers, Ann Arbor, Mich.

Connolly, T. J. (1978) *Foundations of nuclear engineering,* Wiley, New York.

Hottel, H. C. and Howard, J. B. (1971) *New energy technology – some facts and assessments,* MIT press, Cambridge, Mass.

National Engineering Laboratory (1976) *The development of wave power – a techno-economic study,* NEL, Glasgow, UK.

Penner, S. S. and Icerman, L. (1975) *Energy, volume II: non-nuclear energy technologies,* Addison-Wesley, Reading, Mass.

Williams, J. R. (1974) *Solar energy – technology and applications,* Ann Arbor Science Publishers, Ann Arbor, Mich.

World Energy Conference (WEC) (1978b) *World energy resources 1985–2020,* IPC Science and Technology Press, Guildford, UK, and New York.

Environmental and social costs of energy

9.1   Fundamental concepts

Within the framework of economic theory, firms or consumers are assumed to make decisions between different courses of action on the basis of the costs and benefits associated with each action. While it is generally accepted that money is an imperfect measure of utility, monetary valuation is usually used to enable costs and benefits for different actions to be compared quantitatively.

To the decision-maker, the relevant costs and benefits are those which are applicable to him directly. However, not all costs or benefits are felt by the decision-maker. The firm whose factories pollute the atmosphere will not bear the cost of cleaning the cars or buildings in its neighbourhood, nor will it meet the extra health care expenses incurred by those who breath polluted air. Conversely, the man who fills his garden with flowers feels adequately recompensed by the pleasure which they give him; the extra benefits enjoyed by his neighbours do not influence his decisions.

Costs or benefits which do not contribute to the individual firm's or consumer's decisions are known as externalities. They may be divided into three groups:

(a) Costs or benefits which have economic significance, but not to those making the relevant decisions. The cost of purifying water from a polluted river, for example, is likely to be met, but by those using the water rather than by those responsible for the pollution.

(b) Costs or benefits which, though quantifiable, cannot be assigned a price through conventional market mechanisms. Examples include such things as clean air, which are sometimes paid for, and enjoyed by, the community as a whole, but whose monetary value must be assessed through a political rather than an economic process, because society often chooses to tolerate pollution rather than to pay for its removal.

(c) Costs or benefits which are not quantifiable, such as the loss of visual amenity resulting from the construction of an oil refinery or power station, the social impact of short-lived capital intensive construction projects, or the risk of nuclear weapon proliferation resulting from increased use of nuclear energy.

The picture of firms and consumers making decisions according to strict economic criteria is, of course, a caricature. In the real world, externalities will feature, at least to some extent, in the decision-making process. Firms will find that some attempt to limit pollution, to make their factories pleasant to look at or work in, and to be aware of their social impact, will earn the approval of workers, customers and shareholders alike. To the extent that concern for the environment is becoming widespread, that concern is likely to be shared by those who make decisions.

It would, however, be naive to suppose that personal concern and the value of good public relations are sufficient to ensure an adequate regard for externalities, and for this reason it is usually considered to be necessary to limit pollution and other diseconomies by some form of external regulation. Forms which such regulation might take will be discussed later in this chapter.

Some externalities have a direct physical effect on people, such as air or water pollution, contamination by toxic or radioactive chemicals, or accidents. In such cases it may be important to distinguish between hazards to those employed in the energy industries and hazards to the public at large. Others offer a less tangible but none-the-less real effect, such as the disruption of local communities caused by major construction work (and the often worse disruption when such works ceases), or the risks of terrorism, nuclear weapon proliferation and the erosion of personal liberty possibly associated with nuclear energy.

Other externalities have little direct effect on man, but affect biological systems. In this category we may include the ecological effects of power station cooling water, oil spills and tidal barrage schemes. It is also appropriate to include in this category global issues such as possible changes in the weather due to the release of carbon dioxide from burning fuel. Finally, externalities may be concerned only with amenity. Visual amenity is the most common issue: the criticism on such grounds may be levelled at power stations, oil refineries, coal mines, electricity transmission towers or windmills. Other amenity problems may arise from noise or from radio interference.

Some problems arise in the normal course of events, while others arise only rarely, for example: mining accidents, serious releases of radioactive material from nuclear power stations, and dam failures. The consideration of unlikely events whose consequences may be substantial introduces some problems of methodology. For example, how should different events be compared? Is an accident which is likely to occur once in 1000 years and to lead to 100 deaths more or less important than an accident leading to one death every ten years? How much higher can we allow risks to be for those working in an industry than for those outside it?

Energy is often singled out when environmental issues are being discussed. This need not imply that the diseconomies associated with energy are greater than those associated with other activities. The period since the mid 1950s has seen a growing awareness of the need to protect the environment, and a realisation that man is a part of the natural world rather than its master. The biosphere (the totality of all living things) has a great capacity to withstand abuse, but this capacity is not unlimited, and the fear is now being voiced that the biosphere's very tolerance has given us a false sense of security and brought us close to causing serious and irreversible damage. Energy is prominent in the environmental debate partly because some forms of pollution (air pollution, carbon dioxide levels in the atmosphere, and thermal pollution of water) are particularly associated with energy supply and use, and partly because energy provides the clearest test of our attitude to the loss of non-renewable resources.

There are two methodological issues which need to be borne in mind if a discussion of externalities is to be useful. Firstly, it is essential to specify the boundaries of the system being considered. In comparing two energy sources, do we include the externalities associated with the materials used for construction or transport? Do we include the risks or diseconomies associated with final use? Secondly, it is necessary to ensure equity between different fuels when making comparisons. The environmental debate is too often marked by trenchant criticism of one fuel without a serious examination of the environmental impact of alternatives.

It is not the purpose of this chapter to put forward any one view of the respective merits of different energy sources. Instead a brief review is given of the externalities associated with each energy source, and some quantitative assessments, drawn from the literature, are presented. A discussion is included of the options available to ensure that externalities are reflected in energy policy decisions.

9.2   Oil and gas

The externalities associated with oil and gas fall under five heads – exploration and extraction, transportation, refining, storage and use.

As less accessible fields are exploited, particularly those under deep water, the technology of oil and gas extraction is becoming more demanding, with a corresponding increase in risks and environmental impact. Accident risks to personnel need not be greater than in any heavy industry, but are likely to be enhanced in remote or inhospitable areas, and especially in offshore developments. In the North Sea, for example, the number of fatal accidents per 1000 offshore employee-years in the period 1972–1976 was 1.9 (UK Department of Energy 1977a), compared with 0.24 for coal mining in Great Britain in the same period, and 0.07 for British industry as a whole (Central Statistical Office, 1977).

The major ecological hazards of oil and gas extraction probably arise from oil spillages, which range from the very small losses during normal operations to the major but infrequent losses incurred in an oil well blowout. Such large losses bring risks of fire and explosion as well as air, ground or water pollution. The ecological impact of an offshore blowout is discussed below in the context of transport. Disruption of a fragile ecosystem is also a hazard where extraction takes place in remote areas such as the Alaskan North Slope.

The social and economic impact of oil and gas extraction may be considerable. Particularly in remote areas, the activities associated with extraction may create a short-lived economic boom, drawing personnel into the area, raising property prices, forcing wage rates in other local industries to rise, and straining the local infrastructure. Once oil or gas production nears its peak, economic activity is likely to fall sharply, so that the longterm effect on the area is adverse.

The transport of oil by tanker is a significant source of hazard. Though it is major accidents, such as the loss of 50,000 tons of oil from the Torrey Canyon in 1967, which make the headlines, most marine oil pollution arises from far smaller spills, including the illegal discharge of polluted ballast water, and some is also caused by breakage of underwater pipelines. The effects of an oil spill vary widely according to the location and the weather conditions. An oil slick will in time be broken up and degraded by wind, waves and biological processes. Major hazards arise if the slick reaches the coast, when it may affect birds and fish (and their breeding grounds) and the shore or estuary ecosystems as a whole. Economic effects may also be felt by the tourist and fishing industries. The effects may be reduced (at a cost) by using booms to contain the slick, and chemical agents to disperse it and to clean beaches; the long-term ecological effects of the latter are uncertain. Regrettably, the deployment of such measures is sometimes delayed by the difficulty of establishing responsibility for the incident concerned.

Tankers carrying LNG also represent a hazard, though in this case the main concern is fire, with consequent air pollution and risk to personnel, the tanker itself and shore installations.

Hazards from onshore oil and gas transport arise mainly from pipeline breakages and road or rail accidents. In any such incident there are serious risks of fire, explosion and pollution of water, ground and air.

Refineries present similar hazards, though they differ from transport in that the main risk of physical injury is to workers rather than to the general public. Refineries may also give rise to air pollution, including sulphur dioxide, hydrogen sulphide, oxides of nitrogen, carbon monoxide and hydrocarbons, in the course of normal operation. The visual impact of refineries may also be considered to be a significant diseconomy.

The high energy density of oil and gas, and the ease with which it may be stored, are some of the reasons for the usefulness of these fuels; they are also sources of hazard. Any fire or explosion in storage facilities will cause air pollution and possibly ground and water pollution. The risk of death or injury depends upon the location of the storage tanks. A particular source of concern is the siting of large LNG tanks near centres of population. In 1944, for example, LNG tanks in Cleveland, Ohio ruptured, and LNG entered sewers, causing fires which killed 133 people (Wilson and Jones, 1974).

The hazards arising from the use of oil and gas are mainly fire and explosion, the latter being especially relevant for gas. Town gas, manufactured from coal, contained carbon monoxide and was poisonous. This is not true of natural gas, though the gas diffuses slowly and asphyxiation is possible. In addition, the normal use of these fuels will lead to air pollution, which is separately discussed in section 9.7.

To the externalities already outlined must be added the impact of oil and gas developments on the economy of the country concerned and on world trade; this impact is not always anticipated when the decision is made to exploit reserves. In a country such as the UK, which depends in the long term on the export of manufactured goods, a rapid change from dependence on imported oil to self-sufficiency may so strengthen the currency that exports are hindered and long-term economic prospects damaged. When the export of oil creates revenues which cannot immediately be spent, as in the OPEC countries following the 1973 crisis, the resulting world recession affects the oil-exporting countries themselves, as well as other developing countries.

9.3   Coal

Coal has diverse social and environmental costs which, owing to its familiarity, are not always appreciated. The discussion below is divided into extraction, transport, storage and use.

The externalities associated with underground mining are different from those involved in strip mining, and the two methods of extraction will be considered separately.

The physical hazards of underground mining include roof falls, flooding, fire and explosion in addition to the normal industrial hazards from using heavy machinery in enclosed spaces. The risks have fallen steadily as mining practice has improved, as shown in figure 9.1 for Great Britain (Central Statistical Office, 1977). Increasing productivity has led to a steeper decline in risk per unit output than in risk per employee.

To these accident risks must be added the occupational diseases suffered by underground coal miners, mainly caused by the inhalation of dust. Pneumoconiosis is the most widespread of these, but the incidence of the disease is falling as dust control measures improve. For a sample of 57 collieries in Great Britain, the proportion of miners suffering from the disease (even at a sub-clinical level) has fallen from 10.2% in 1961–62 to 6.5% in 1976 (NCB Medical Service, 1977). Of those suffering in 1976, three quarters showed the condition at a sub-clinical level, while only one tenth showed the more serious condition of progressive massive fibrosis. The improvement is more marked for younger miners; the proportion of those under 35 suffering from the disease fell from 0.8% in 1961–62 to 0.1% in 1976. The situation in the US is broadly similar, with risk very much lower than historical levels in mining activity which meets the conditions of the 1969 Coal Mine Health and Safety Act.

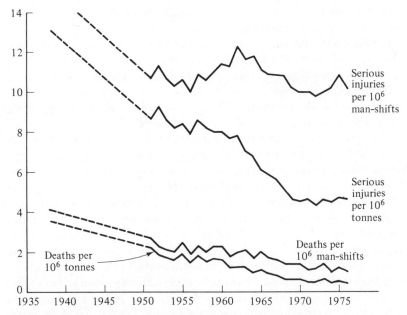

Figure 9.1   Deaths and injuries from coal mining in Great Britain.

Hazards to the public from coal extraction are mainly due to subsidence. This is a particular risk in old workings where wooden roof supports may rot and collapse without warning. Subsidence is a hazard when it occurs suddenly and varies over a small area; gradual subsidence over a large area may cause few problems, and modern mining techniques have reduced this type of hazard. A further risk to the public arises from spoil heaps, and was demonstrated by the Aberfan disaster in Wales in 1966, when a spoil heap slid into a school and caused 144 deaths. Such risks can be greatly reduced by the siting of spoil heaps, control of their shape and drainage, and by reclamation or underground disposal.

Social and economic effects of underground coal extraction include the loss of land due to spoil heaps, which can be minimised by prompt reclamation, and the less tangible hazards of local dominance by a single industry. Because mining is labour-intensive (though becoming less so), the social consequences when mines are worked out or become uneconomic may be very serious.

Spoil heaps are the principle source of ecological hazards from underground coal mining, causing acid drainage and altering water flows to cause soil erosion or flooding. Reclamation or underground disposal to reduce these problems is not difficult in principle, and current risks mainly arise from developments at a time when such hazards were less appreciated.

Finally, coal mines themselves and the spoil heaps which they produce may be considered to have an adverse effect on the landscape as a whole.

The situation for strip mining is less complex than that for underground mining. Risks from fire are much reduced, though there are risks associated with blasting, and there is little physical hazard to the general public. The economic impact due to the temporary or permanent loss of land use may be substantial, depending on the type of use to which the land would otherwise be put. Local water supplies may also be affected by strip-mining, since coal is an aquifer.

The principal area of environmental concern associated with strip mining is the fate of land which is left unreclaimed or where reclamation is delayed. Under these circumstances, soil erosion may be rapid, making deliberate or natural revegetation more difficult. The extent of the problems involved depends on the rainfall and the steepness of slopes, and varies from area to area. Of necessity, strip mining has a major visual impact on the landscape, and may also give rise to problems of noise.

Coal is transported by sea, rail and locally by road. Though international coal trade is small in comparison with that of oil, it is likely to become more important as oil provides a smaller fraction of world energy needs. The hazards of marine coal transport are similar to those for any other cargo with some additional risk of fire; there is no ecological hazard comparable with that arising from marine oil pollution. Rail transport introduces accident hazards, and may introduce amenity problems as the scale of coal use increases. Some furthur accident hazard is introduced by local road transport.

Storage of coal is generally without hazard unless the volume stored in one place is very large (for use in a power station, for example). In these circumstances the spontaneous oxidation which always occurs at a slow rate may cause a large enough temperature rise to ignite the coal, with resulting fire risk, economic loss and air pollution. In order to avoid this, the depth to which coal is stored must be limited, and this controls the amount of land needed for coal storage. Coal storage areas represent a loss of land to other possible uses, and a loss of visual amenity.

As for other combustible fuels, the use of coal brings a risk of fire, though there is no risk of explosion comparable with that for gas. In other respects coal use is fairly safe. Combustion will, of course, cause air pollution, including the release of radioactive elements from the coal, and this is discussed in section 9.7. Ash disposal may present problems, but pulverised fuel ash is a useful cement additive and is a valuable by-product when produced in bulk.

9.4   Nuclear energy

Radioactivity

Nuclear energy is often criticised on the grounds that its environmental and social impacts are unacceptable. Because there is no single agreed measure of environmental or social impact, experts may agree to differ on the truth of this assertion. Before itemising the hazards associated with nuclear energy, it may he helpful to be reminded of the nature and effects of radioactivity.

Radioactive elements have unstable atomic nuclei which decay, sometimes in several stages, to stable forms. This decay is a random process, and is characterised by a half-life, i.e. the time taken for half the nuclei in any given mass of the element to decay. Decay is accompanied by the emission of one or more particles, which may be of three types:

(a) Alpha-particles, which comprise two neutrons and two protons and are identical to helium nuclei.

(b) Beta-particles, which are free electrons.

(c) Gamma-rays, which are high energy photons.

Radiation damages living material by causing ionisation. Within an individual cell, the damage may well be lethal; this type of damage is generally not serious for the organism as a whole if only a small proportion of cells are affected. Where the radiation dose is large enough to cause lethal damage to a significant proportion of cells, radiation sickness results. As far as low radiation doses are concerned, the main problem arises when genetic material within the cell is modified, but not to an extent sufficient to kill the cell. Subsequent divisions of such cells may lead to cancer, or, in the case of sex cells, to mutations in later generations.

The unit of radiation dose is the rem, which is a measure of the ionisation caused by radiation, modified to take into account the fact that intense local ionisation (caused for example by alpha-particles) is more damaging than diffuse ionisation. For most practical purposes, the unit used is the milli-rem (mrem).

In considering risks from radioactive material, it is important to distinguish between radiation from outside the body and radiation from inhaled or ingested material (contamination). The latter may be of much greater importance, for two reasons:

(a) Active materials may come into close contact with vulnerable organs, for example radioactive iodine becomes concentrated in the thyroid, or strontium in bone tissue. By contrast, alpha particles from external sources are always stopped by the skin, and beta particles penetrate to a depth of only one to two centimetres.

(b) The active material will continue to cause damage until it decays to a negligible level or is excreted from the body. In some cases (for example inhaled plutonium particles) this may be a very long period.

Radiation is a part of the natural environment, arising, for example, from natural radioactive minerals and cosmic rays. Exposure to radiation also arises from medical procedures, fallout from atomic weapons tests, and other minor sources. Table 9.1 shows the dose rates to the bone marrow for an average person in the UK from a range of sources (Pochin 1976, quoted in Flowers 1976). It is clear that the present contribution from nuclear power is very small, much smaller than other man-made sources or natural sources.

Statistics on the health risks caused by radiation are difficult to obtain, and, because they are based largely on industrial accidents or on studies of people in the vicinity of the Hiroshima and Nagasaki explosions, relate mainly to doses much higher than those arising from normal operation of the nuclear energy system. A key question is whether there is a dose threshold below which damage may be regarded as negligible, or whether any dose, however small, must be considered to have some harmful effects. In the absence of either a full understanding of how the body reacts to radiation damage, or a clear indication from statistical data, it is prudent to assume that even small doses carry some risk.

Standards limiting the levels of radiation to which workers or members of the public may be exposed are laid down by an independent body, the International Commission on Radiological Protection, and are adhered to (or bettered) by all major countries. The maximum annual whole-body dose for radiation workers was specified as 5 rem/yr in 1966, with a corresponding limit of 0.5 rem/yr for members of the public. It has been estimated that the latter dose would give rise to a fatal cancer with a probability of 1 in 20,000 for each year of exposure; for comparison the dose required to cause death from acute radiation sickness in 50% of those exposed is about 500 rem.

Uranium mining, transport and fuel fabrication

Uranium miners face significant risks of accidents, which, as in any mining activity, are greater for underground mining than for open-pit mining; the death rate for underground mining has been estimated as 0.2 deaths per reactor year (based on a 1000 MWe power plant with a 70% load factor, and an ore concentration of 0.1% U_3O_8, Nuclear Energy Policy Study Group (NEPSG) 1977). In addition, miners are exposed to external radiation and to the inhalation of gas and contaminated dust. The resulting risk of deaths from cancer has been estimated by the source quoted above as 0.06 fatalities per reactor year. Risk to the general public may arise from the radon released by the mining operations; the main mechanism here appears to be the ingestion with food of the radon decay products polonium-210 and lead-210 (Nuclear Regulatory Commission, 1976).

Associated with uranium extraction is the ore milling operation and the large volume of radioactive tailings which it produces. The risk to workers has been estimated as 0.03 cancer deaths per reactor year (NEPSG, 1977); the risk to the public may be significant owing to the long half-lives of many of the isotopes concerned, but could be greatly reduced by reburial or other stabilisation of the tailings.

It should be noted that the hazards of uranium mining are very dependent on safety precautions and good practice, and vary with time and from country to

Table 9.1.   *Dose rates in the UK from ionising radiation (to bone marrow)*
(mrem/yr).

Natural:	
Cosmic rays	33
Soil and airborne	44
Within the body (mainly potassium-40)	24
Man-made:	
Diagnostic X-rays	32
Radiotherapy	12
Medical use of radioisotopes	2
Fallout from weapons tests	6
Nuclear power industry	0.25
Other (mainly occupational doses)	0.7
Total	154

country. This makes the extraction risks for a future nuclear power programme difficult to assess.

The environmental and social costs of the transport and enrichment of uranium, and the fabrication of reactor fuel, are low. The volumes of material involved are small, and it is not highly radioactive.

Reactor operation and accidents
The hazards from reactor operation fall into two categories – those associated with normal operation and those resulting from accidents. The former are in general small and can be reduced by suitable technology if necessary.

The range of conceivable accidents in different types of reactor is very large, from a leak in a single fuel pin to the meltdown of the entire core. For any potential accident, it is necessary to ask three questions:

(a) What is the probability that the event will occur?
(b) How will the reactor safety systems respond and what is the probability that the reactor containment will be breached?
(c) If a breach of the containment is credible, how much activity would be released, and in what form and by what processes could it reach workers or the public?

Accidents might be caused by outside agencies (aircraft impact, earthquake, etc.) or by internal failure such as the blockage of a coolant channel leading to progressive overheating and the melting of the fuel. Reactor systems are designed to provide a high margin of safety against such incidents.

It is sometimes suggested that a serious reactor accident could lead to a nuclear explosion. However, even if a critical mass of material could be assembled, the fission heating would cause rapid disassembly, with only a very small fraction of the fuel undergoing fission. In all types of reactor, an increase in temperature increases the rate at which neutrons are absorbed, and in thermal reactors it also decreases the fission rate. In a thermal reactor, a fuel meltdown is likely to be associated with the loss of the moderator (through loss of coolant in a light water reactor or by fuel melting out of the graphite in a carbon-moderated reactor) which would make criticality very unlikely. This extra assurance is not applicable to fast reactors. In summary, the worst credible accident would be a modest thermal explosion, some of the energy of which might (particularly in a fast reactor) come from the fission of a small quantity of fuel.

Despite these assurances, a thermal explosion which released a substantial proportion of the fission products and heavy radioactive elements to the environment would be very serious indeed, and the reactor must be designed so that such an incident is exceedingly improbable. It has been estimated (NEPSG, 1977) that the typical consequences of an 'extremely serious' accident would include 3300 prompt fatalities, 45,000 cancer fatalities over a thirty year period, and 30,000 genetic defects over 150 years. An area of 3200 square miles would be contaminated. These extreme consequences would occur only if the major radioactivity release coincided with unfavourable weather and a large exposed population; the overall probability of such an event for an LWR has been suggested, somewhat tentatively, to be 5×10^{-9} per reactor year.

In the US, attention has focussed on the 'Loss-of-Coolant Accident' (LOCA), which is of particular relevance to light water reactors. Loss of coolant is one of several possible initiating events which could, in principle, lead to core meltdown, which might in turn lead to rupture of the primary containment. Emergency core cooling systems (ECCS) are installed to reduce the probability of such an accident, and there has been much debate on the reliability of such sytems and their efficiency in the uncertain environment inside the reactor following the loss of coolant.

A much-publicised accident was that at the Three Mile Island PWR station on 28 March 1979. A complex accident sequence occurred, including equipment malfunction and operator error. Some radioactive coolant was released to the environment, but the public hazard which this release represents is very small. Overheating of the fuel led to some melting and the production of hydrogen from a reaction between steam and the zircalloy fuel cladding. Though superficially alarming, this situation was brought under control and the reactor shut down safely. It may be suggested that the very occurrence of such an accident demonstrates the inherent risks of nuclear power. Conversely, the successful containment of the accident may be regarded as a vindication of the 'safety-in-depth' philosophy of the nuclear industry. It is certain that any such incident provides lessons which should help to make future accidents less likely.

A key study of reactor safety is the Rasmussen Report (Nuclear Regulatory Commission, 1975), which predicts a probability of core meltdown with breach of containment of 5×10^{-5} per reactor year, though this figure is very uncertain. The effects of a breach of containment range from a minor release of activity, resulting in few deaths, to the far less likely extremely serious accident described above. Reactor operation may also bring risks of sabotage or terrorism. The most likely threat would be to damage the plant, or to interfere with control and safety systems, to such an extent that there was a substantial release of radioactive material. The design of the plant and the external security arrangements make such action very difficult, but it is not easy to ensure that a serious incident is impossible. To the risk of sabotage must be added the possibility of human error which escapes the automatic safeguards; it has been suggested that this may become more likely as nuclear capacity grows and, perhaps, power station staff become less vigilant.

Theft of active material from a thermal reactor is not a major problem unless plutonium-bearing fuel is used. Unirradiated uranium fuel is not very hazardous and cannot be used for bomb-making without furthur enrichment. Irradiated fuel, though very hazardous as a source of contamination, is for that reason very difficult for would-be terrorists to handle. Unirradiated fast reactor fuel could more readily be used for bomb manufacture.

A further area of concern associated with reactor operation is that the security which might be required (for example checks on employees' backgrounds and political affiliations) would represent an unacceptable loss of civil liberties. This fear is usually voiced in connection with the widespread use of plutonium in fast reactors.

Irradiated fuel, reprocessing, plutonium recycle and waste disposal
Because irradiated fuel is highly contaminated with fission products and active heavy isotopes, transport for reprocessing or disposal is a potential source of hazard. Transport may be by sea, road or rail, using massive containers which are subjected to stringent tests to ensure that their contents will not be released in an accident. Despite these precautions, there is a small risk of accidental release, to which must be added the small risk of terrorist diversion of the material in transit.

The reprocessing or disposal of irradiated fuel has been the subject of major debates in recent years. Options include the following:
(a) Reprocess the fuel, separating out plutonium and uranium for re-use, and disposing of other products.
(b) Reprocess the fuel, separating uranium for re-use but leaving plutonium in the waste stream.
(c) Dispose of the fuel in its entirety without reprocessing.

If reprocessing is carried out, there is a further choice of whether to reprocess as soon as possible and store the uranium (and plutonium if appropriate), or whether to store the irradiated fuel elements and reprocess only when the products are required.

Reprocessing itself brings some contamination hazard to personnel, a small release of active material to the environment, and a risk of accidents. Much of the hazard from normal operation arises from nuclides such as krypton-85, carbon-14, iodine-131 and caesium-137 which are released to a smaller extent in reactor operation. Accidents have occured in reprocessing, such as the contamination of 35 workers with ruthenium-106 at Windscale, UK, in 1973. Reprocessing in which plutonium is separated from the waste streams is also criticised on the grounds that it makes this element more readily available for theft or for the manufacture of bombs by the government concerned. In favour of reprocessing, it should be noted that such action reduces waste disposal problems by reducing the long-lived uranium and plutonium content of the waste and by reducing wastes to a fairly manageable form, and also that reprocessing reduces the need for uranium mining which is itself a source of occupational and public hazard.

It is appropriate at this point to mention the special problems of plutonium. Plutonium is manufactured in any reactor by the absorption of neutrons by uranium-238. It is a fissile material suitable for use as fuel. Fast reactors in particular are designed to have a higher output of plutonium than their input of uranium-235, thus increasing by a large factor the energy obtainable from the world's uranium, which is mainly uranium-238 (see chapter 6). The problems associated with plutonium are:

(a) It has a very long half-life (24,000 years for Pu-239, 86 years for Pu-238; the latter is the greater source of hazard over the time-scale usually considered relevant owing to its higher radioactivity).

(b) It is very dangerous if inhaled: small particles lodged deep in the lungs are insoluble and are removed only very slowly: they remain strong emitters of highly damaging alpha particles.

(c) It is suitable for direct fabrication into bombs which, though somewhat unreliable, would be extremely dangerous; only a few kg of plutonium are required for criticality.

Storage of the useful products of reprocessing is hazardous only in the case of plutonium. This introduces a risk of theft, and of pollution in the event of, say, a serious fire. Stored plutonium also becomes contaminated with the decay product americium-241, which is highly radioactive and a source of risk when handling the plutonium.

Other products of reprocessing, which may be highly radioactive, require permanent disposal. Low-activity wastes are usually buried with only simple containment, or discharged into the sea; this is a source of concern since the volume of such wastes (and therefore the total activity involved) may become large, and because contamination may include highly dangerous nuclides. High-activity wastes are at present stored as liquids, in storage tanks which require continuous monitoring. Clearly this is not a satisfactory policy for long-term storage (serious leaks have occurred), and ultimate disposal in a solid form, either by calcining or vitrification, is likely. The solid waste, suitably contained, may be placed in stable geological formations or the sea bed. The risks from waste disposal are difficult to assess, as they require estimates of the long-term reliability of the containment.

If the useful products of reprocessing are recycled for use in reactors, opportunities for theft may arise from the transport of plutonium. This is particularly so if the plutonium is for use in fast reactors, when it is likely to be transported in a form readily adaptable for bomb manufacture. For use in thermal reactors, plutonium and uranium oxides may be mixed to provide a material suitable for fuel but not for bomb-making. In either case, the risk of theft may be reduced by irradiating the material so that it is dangerous for terrorists to handle, or by siting reactors and reprocessing plant in a single complex.

The alternative to reprocessing is disposal of the complete fuel, perhaps after a long period of storage. Though this obviates most of the risks of diversion of active material by terrorists or by government, it still poses severe environmental problems:

(a) because the volume of solid waste to be disposed of would be very large,
(b) the form of the solid waste might make reliable containment difficult,
(c) large quantities of plutonium would be at risk of reaching the biosphere, whereas plutonium re-used in reactors is mainly converted to less harmful fission products.

Nuclear weapon proliferation

The foregoing discussion has dealt with hazards from the nuclear power system in normal operation, from accidents, and from terrorism or sabotage. To this must be added the risk that possession of nuclear power technology may enable more nations to acquire nuclear weapons, with a destabilising effect on world politics. Any nation with uranium enrichment facilities, or with nuclear reactors and a reprocessing capability, is able in principle to prepare weapon material. Several international treaties aim to limit the proliferation of nuclear weapons while encouraging the peaceful use of nuclear energy, including the 1956 International Atomic Energy Agency Statute, the 1957 Treaty Establishing the European Atomic Energy Community, and the 1970 Treaty on the Non-Proliferation of Nuclear Weapons. To these treaties may be added the US policy, initiated by President Ford in 1976 and developed by President Carter in 1977, to discourage the acquisition of enrichment or reprocessing capabilities by nations which do not at present have such capabilities, and to defer indefinitely the commercial recycling of plutonium in the US.

9.5   Electricity

Environmental and social costs which are specific to particular primary fuels are discussed elsewhere in this chapter, as is the air pollution resulting from fuel combustion. In this section we outline the externalities specifically associated with electricity generation, transmission and use.

Power station construction is itself a source of risk, which has been estimated as 0.07 to 0.2 deaths per station-year for a 1000 MWe nuclear station (NEPSG,

1977), with rather lower figures for fossil fuel stations. Power station construction and operation may also have a substantial social and economic impact, particularly in remote areas; this may include long-term benefits as well as costs.

Almost all primary energy consumed is ultimately released to the environmental as heat. The overall effect on climate is likely to be small (Study of Critical Environmental Problems (SCEP) 1970), but local effects may be substantial. Because of their low efficiency, power stations reject very large quantities of heat to the environment, which may give rise to problems of thermal pollution. This problem is more serious for nuclear reactors (especially water-cooled reactors), which because of their low efficiency reject some 30% more heat per unit of electricity produced than fossil fuel plants.

The effects of power station cooling on the environment are diverse and not fully understood. They include the following (Wilson and Jones, 1974):

(a) Change of fish species as a result of higher temperatures (especially in river or estuary systems).

(b) Fish kills due to sudden temperature changes, resulting from variations in river flows or power station use.

(c) Fish kills due to chlorine used to clean condenser tubes.

(d) Disturbance of fish breeding patterns.

(e) Destruction of small organisms and young fish not caught by water inlet screens, with consequent disturbance to food chains.

(f) Changes in vertical temperature profile and water mixing, especially in lakes, which may have complex ecological consequences.

These effects are reduced when cooling towers or ponds are used, when most of the heat is released to the atmosphere with only a small requirement for river water. The penalties, in addition to the expense involved, are the addition to local cloud formation, the visual impact of the cooling towers, and the land required for cooling ponds.

Hydro-electric schemes may have significant environmental and social costs. A small risk to the public arises from dam failure, caused, for example, by earthquakes or landslides. The seepage of water from the lake into underlying rocks may lubricate geological faults and trigger local seismic disturbances. Economic and social costs include the loss of habitation and land use, though this may be offset by the improvement in irrigation systems and reduction of flooding made possible by the scheme, as well as increased recreation potential. The life of a hydro-electric scheme may be limited by the deposition of silt in the lake; this may also have economic and ecological consequences if the silt which would otherwise be carried in the river flow is rich in plant nutrients.

The transmission and distribution of electricity carries some risk of injury to workers and the public, and may lead to radio interference. It is also often considered that transmission towers have a substantial visual amenity impact which reduces landscape value. Electricity use introduces risks of fire and electric shock.

9.6 Renewable and unconventional sources

It is often thought that renewable energy sources are environmentally benign, but this need not be the case. It is only possible in this section to give a brief outline of the environmental and social costs of these and other unconventional sources.

Solar energy has relatively little environmental impact; it produces no overall thermal pollution, though if used for centralised power generation it would contribute to local thermal pollution. Some accident risk arises from the installation and maintenance of solar collectors. In addition, because solar energy has a low spatial density, the material requirements for solar energy collectors are large, and the social and environmental costs which these represent may exceed the corresponding costs for other sources.

The main diseconomies for tidal power lie in its effects on the estuarine or marine ecosystem, which may be substantial, though not necessarily harmful. Tidal power schemes may also exacerbate the effects of other sources of pollution (thermal, industrial or domestic) within their vicinity. A significant accident risk during construction is also likely. The amenity impact of barrage schemes would be substantial, but might be beneficial on balance if the schemes were designed to enhance opportunities for recreation or to improve communications.

The ecological effects of wave-power devices, through their interference with normal wave action on the shore line, is difficult to predict, and in some circumstances a measure of protection from waves might be economically beneficial. Significant risks would probably arise in the construction, installation and maintenance of the devices and the cable connections to the shore, and there might also be risks to shipping. Amenity impact would probably be small unless the devices were situated much closer to the shore than is at present anticipated.

Wind-power devices would have a considerable visual impact if designed for large-scale power generation, and it also seems likely that there would be problems of radio and television interference. Installation and maintenance of the devices would carry some risks, and there would be a small risk to the public from accidents.

Biological energy sources are too diverse to permit a simple description of the diseconomies involved. Taking wood fuel as an example, the felling of timber carries a significant occupational risk, and there are additional risks from transport and use. Similar hazards may be suggested for other biomass sources, and for the use of combustible waste materials.

Ocean thermal power plants are too speculative for much to be said about their social and environmental costs. Some ecological impact might result from the disturbance of the natural temperature profile of the ocean.

Geothermal energy appears to have little environmental impact, though when used for power production it produces local thermal pollution, and requires cooling towers or other heat dissipation systems which have an impact on amenity. Fusion power is sometimes hailed as a 'clean' successor to nuclear fission. While radioactive heavy metals, one of the greatest hazards from fission power, are not present, this energy source is not free of environmental problems:

(a) The most likely reaction involves the production, separation and use of large quantities of tritium, which is a radiobiological hazard because of the difficulties of containment and its rapid absorption into living systems.

(b) The reaction produces high levels of radiation, which will lead to the accumulation of activation products.

(c) Many designs envisage a lithium blanket used both as a tritium breeder and a coolant; under accident conditions a highly dangerous lithium – water reaction might take place.

(d) For a magnetic confinement reactor of the envisaged size, the sudden release of the energy stored in the superconducting magnets would do substantial damage.

9.7   Air pollution and climatic effects

Combustion leads to gaseous and sometimes particulate products which enter the atmosphere. These may affect living organisms, and they may also have local or global climatic effects. In this section each major pollutant will be discussed in turn.

Carbon dioxide is a natural constituent of the air and is not a hazard to life in the concentrations normally encountered. The burning of fossil fuels may have a significant effect on the global average concentration of the gas, and this is a matter of concern because of its possible effects on climate (SCEP, 1970). The main mechanism by which carbon dioxide affects climate is the 'greenhouse effect' (the tendency of carbon dioxide to transmit incident sunlight while reflecting back the infra-red radiation emitted from the earth's surface, so increasing the global temperature). It is suggested in the source quoted above that carbon dioxide level might rise 18% by 2000 as a result of burning fossil fuels, leading to 0.5° C temperature rise. Insufficient is known about the natural mechanisms controlling carbon dioxide, or about the effects on climate of a small temperature rise; it is becoming clear, however, that the factors determining climate are complex and finely balanced, and that relatively small disturbances could lead to significant change, with unknown economic and ecological effects.

Sulphur dioxide is a serious pollutant, arising from the combustion of coal or oil containing sulphur. It has an easily identified smell, and causes bronchial irritation at concentrations of 1–5 ppm. With water, it oxidises to form a highly irritating mist of sulphuric acid; this reaction is promoted by the presence of particulates or nitric oxide. Studies have shown a clear correlation between deaths from bronchitis and sulphur dioxide level (see for example Wilson and Jones, 1974); to these must be added the cost of damage to buildings by the sulphuric acid washed out in rain.

Sulphur dioxide pollution is a particular health hazard in urban areas, where it is introduced into the atmosphere at a low level from industrial premises, houses and vehicles (diesel engines are a more serious source than petrol engines, because of the higher sulphur content of the fuel). Pollution in urban areas is worsened by a temperature inversion, in which warm air containing the pollutant is trapped beneath a layer of cold air. Sulphur dioxide was an important contribution to the smogs in London and elsewhere during the 1950s, the worst of which, in 1952, led to nearly 4000 excess deaths. Pollution control measures and changing patterns of fuel use have largely eliminated these extreme conditions.

At the other extreme, there has been controversy over the possibility that sulphur dioxide, mainly from coal-burning power stations, may move across national boundaries, leading to pollution at great distances from the source. In particular, UK and European power stations have been blamed for increased sulphur pollution in Scandinavia.

Sulphur dioxide emission can be controlled by fuel desulphurisation, coal liquefaction, fluidised bed combustion with added limestone, or flue gas de-sulphurisation. All of these options have an economic penalty, with the possible exception of fluidised bed combustion, where the economics of the basic process are not yet fully established (Chem Systems International Ltd, 1976). They are also likely to reduce the overall efficiency of fuel use.

Fuel combustion also leads to the emission of oxides of nitrogen (the nitrogen coming from the air). Natural sources, mainly biological decay, account for most atmospheric nitrogen oxides, and the main problem from man–made sources is in cities. The contributions from transport and stationary fuel combustion are of similar magnitude. The initial combustion product is nitric oxide (NO), but this is readily oxidised in the presence of sunlight to the opaque orange gas nitrogen dioxide (NO_2) which, as well as being toxic and irritating, is a major constituent of photochemical smog.

There is no wholly adequate technology for the control of nitrogen oxides emission, though much can be done by engine or furnace designs, by the control of combustion conditions or, in the case of automobiles, by catalytic decomposition.

Unburnt hydrocarbons are a further significant source of pollution, arising mainly from motor vehicles, and including crankcase emissions and evaporation losses. Diesel engines are usually preferable to petrol engines, though a badly adjusted diesel engine may yield substantial hydrocarbon pollution. Aldehydes contained in engine exhaust gases lead to irritation of the nose and respiratory system, and some aromatic compounds are known to be carcinogenic (though road vehicles are a minor source of such compounds). Under certain climatic conditions, hydrocarbons combine with oxides of nitrogen to form a photochemical smog.

Carbon monoxide is a product of combustion which is poisonous at quite low concentrations. The main source is from petrol-engined vehicles (diesel engines being preferable in this respect); there has been a steady decrease in the emission rate as engine designs have improved, offset by the increased number of vehicles. Significant risk to the public is confined to urban areas.

Control of hydrocarbons and carbon monoxide, both of which arise from incomplete combustion, can be achieved by operation with a high air/fuel ratio or by optimisation of carburation and timing; these measures are likely to improve fuel use efficiency. Alternatively (or in addition), hydrocarbons and carbon monoxide may be removed from exhaust gases by catalytic or thermal reactors; the latter have a lower capital cost but incur a fuel economy penalty.

Particulate emissions arise from both stationary combustion and vehicles. Fly-ash from coal is a well-known example, but oil may also produce smoke due to incomplete combustion. As well as being an amenity problem, particulates contribute to the formation of smog and provide sites for the absorption of other pollutants, facilitating their passage into the lungs. Several techniques are available for removing particulate matter such as fly ash. These include inertial collectors, electrostatic precipitators, wet scrubbers and fabric filters. Smoke from mobile sources, mainly diesel engines, can be controlled by adequate engine tuning and maintenance.

Other forms of pollution arising from fuel use include lead (from petrol additives), mercury, vanadium, beryllium, nickel and radioactive nuclides such as radium and thorium (from coal). Of these, lead has received the most attention. Lead emissions may be controlled by reducing the lead content of petrol (or, more expensively, removing it altogether), or by removing lead from exhaust gases.

9.8   The comparison of externalities

Some environmental or social costs may be expressed directly in economic terms. In other instances the appropriate measure is in terms of human disease or death, or the impact on an ecosystem as a whole. In some cases the measure is a political or ethical one (for example the destabilisation resulting from the proliferation of nuclear weapons), while in others the issues relate to amenity and aesthetic value.

The wide range of measures makes the comparison of externalities very difficult. Some of the non-economic measures may be assigned an economic equivalent (for example by costing deaths, years of active life lost, health care requirements) but this is not wholly satisfactory, and is not applicable at all to political or amenity effects, or to unquantifiable hazards such as climatic change.

Table 9.2 gives a qualitative indication of the types of hazard arising from the four main primary fuels due to normal operation. Hazards arising from accidents may also include injury to members of the public and economic loss. To emphasise the judgemental nature of the table, hazards have been ranked as low, medium or high (L, M or H) rather than given quantified values.

The perception of risk, on which depends the response which ultimately determines policy decisions, varies from one situation to another in ways which are

Table 9.2.   *Types of hazard arising from normal operation.*

	Oil	Gas	Coal	Nuclear energy
Injury to workers	M	M	M	L
Health risk – workers	L	L	H^b	M
– public[a]	M	L	H	L
Ecological impact	M	L	M	L
Climatic change	M	M	M	L
Amenity impact	L	L	M	L

[a]Mainly due to air pollution
[b]Substantial improvement is likely

not wholly reflected in any quantitative assessment. Several factors influencing risk perception may be suggested:

(a) The scale of the event; major catastrophes elicit more concern than everyday hazards, despite the fact in most situations a large fraction of total risk arises from small, fairly frequent incidents.

(b) Whether the risk is incurred voluntarily; risks arising from the working situation, or particularly those incurred in sporting activity, are of less concern than those involving the public at large.

(c) Whether the risk can be managed actively; a risk which can be minimised by the skill of the person concerned is less onerous than one which must be borne passively.

(d) Other hazards to which the subject is exposed; a man who is ill-fed and lacks medical care will be indifferent to some of the risks which concern more affluent subjects.

(e) The source of the risk estimate; the attitude to risks estimated for a new technology may differ from that adopted towards risks based on historical experience. In particular a theoretical assessment of risk may elicit suspicion when those responsible for estimating the risk have an interest in showing it to be low or high.

A thorough comparison of the risk associated with conventional and non-conventional sources has been published by Inhaber (1978). Though not immune from criticism, the comparisons provided are clearly of considerable qualitative value. The analysis includes the occupational and public health hazards associated with the procurement of structural materials as well as those arising in fuel extraction, transport, conversion and use. The measure of hazard used is man-days lost per MW yr of energy output, with a death equated to 6000 man-days lost. Accidents are included, but not risks associated with sabotage, terrorism or nuclear weapon proliferation. In summary, the conclusions are:

(a) Coal, closely followed by oil, carries the highest total risk (nearly 3000 man-days lost per MW yr for coal), which is dominated by risk from air pollution.

(b) The lowest-risk fuel is natural gas, with about 6 man-days lost per MW yr.

(c) Nuclear energy (non-breeding thermal systems) ranks second to gas in safety, with just over 10 man-days lost per MW yr.

(d) The renewable sources considered – wind power, solar space heating, solar thermal electricity generation, solar photovoltaic electricity generation and ocean thermal electricity generation – carry risks intermediate between gas and nuclear energy at one extreme and coal and oil at the other. The hazard range for these sources is 30–1000 man-days lost per MW yr. Materials used for construction, and the hazards from back-up energy supplies or storage required to compensate for the intermittent nature of these sources, make a substantial contribution (the assumed back-up source is coal; use of nuclear energy as a back-up would reduce the top-of-range risk from 1000 to about 200 man-days lost per MW yr).

(e) Risk to the general public is dominated by air-pollution from burning coal or oil, and these fuels carry the highest risk (around 2000 man-days lost per MW yr). Renewable energy sources carry a high risk, also from air pollution, due to the use of coal both as a back-up supply and in the manufacture of construction materials.

A broadly similar picture emerges from a UK report (Health and Safety Commission, 1978). Dealing only with deaths caused by accidents, and excluding public health effects, the report suggests 1.8 deaths/GW yr for coal, 0.3 for oil and gas, and 0.25 for nuclear energy. No allowance is made for construction materials, and non-fatal accidents are excluded. A report by Hamilton and Manne (1978) compares the health and economic costs of different energy sources, with particular emphasis on hazards from air pollution, basing the analysis on possible scenarios for energy use in the long term.

An alternative way of presenting risk estimates is to compare the risks arising from different energy sources with risks arising in everyday life. Such a comparison, using order of magnitude estimates, is given in table 9.3. The figures are based on Flowers (1976) and NEPSG (1977); a similar approach is used in Rothschild (1978). Many of the figures are necessarily very uncertain, but the overall ranking which the table shows is likely to be fairly realistic. The estimates suggest that the risks to the public associated with energy supply are very low in comparison with other risks which are, in practice, taken for granted. The risk from coal (mainly from air pollution) considerably exceeds that from nuclear energy.

9.9   Externalities and the decision-making process

How can we ensure that environmental and social costs are given their proper weight in the decision-making process? One approach is to internalise these costs

Table 9.3.   *Probability of death for an individual per year of exposure.*

Hazard	Risk
Smoke 10 cigarettes a day	1 in 400
All types of accident	1 in 2000
Road accidents	1 in 8000
Work in industry	1 in 30,000
Cancer caused by natural background radiation	1 in 100,000
Accidental poisoning	1 in 100,000
100 GWe base load coal-fired power stations,	1 in 80,000 to
meeting current emission standards,	1 in 5,000,000
in a nation of 200 million people (public risk only)	
100 GWe base load nuclear power stations, without	1 in 10,000,000
plutonium recycle, in a nation of 200 million	
people (public risk only, excluding accidents)	
Lightning	1 in 2,000,000

by applying them to the organisation involved – the 'pollutor-pays' principle. This could be done by a simple tax on pollution, set at a level related to the cost of dealing with the pollutant and its consequences. If removal of the pollutant at source were then found to be cheaper than dealing with it in the environment, the organisation would have an economic incentive to prevent the pollution. Though useful in some circumstances, this approach has problems:

(a) It requires adequate (preferably continuous) monitoring of the pollution, which is likely to be expensive.

(b) It requires the costs of pollution to be quantified, which may be difficult even when the pollutant itself is easily measured.

(c) It would be effective only if the tax levied were used to deal with the pollutant and its consequences.

(d) It is inapplicable to a wide range of externalities which are not quantifiable.

An alternative version of the 'pollutor-pays' principle is to offer licences. An assessment would be made of the total level of a particular pollutant which could be tolerated, and organisations would be invited to bid for permits to release specified quantities of the pollutant. The price arrived at by this process would be expected to be close to the cost of dealing with the pollutant at source.The advantages of this approach over the 'pollution tax' method are that continuous monitoring would be necessary only for successful bidders (any release would be illegal for others) and the costs of pollution would not need to be quantified. On the other hand, the decision on the maximum acceptable level of the pollutant concerned might be artificial. If the revenue from the licences were used to deal with the pollutant in the environment, and if the acceptable level of pollution were adjusted in response to the availability of funds to deal with it, then this approach, like a simple pollution tax, would promote the efficient use of resources to prevent or deal with pollution. Like the pollution tax, it is suitable only for quantifiable externalities.

In most instances, current practice is not to internalise environmental and social costs into the decision-making process, but to force recognition of those costs by a system of regulations. These regulations control the short-term and long-term concentration of pollutants, the installation of pollution control equipment, the provision of facilities for dealing with the results of accidents, health care provisions for workers, and so on. The fundamental advantage of this method is its simplicity. It is, however, an inefficient approach to pollution abatement, because society will not in general obtain maximum value for money. The cheapest way to constrain the total quantity of a pollutant released by a number of factories, for example, is to concentrate effort where the pay-off – cleanliness achieved per dollar spent – is greatest, not by imposing an arbitrary rule which may at one or two points be vastly expensive to observe.

Where unquantifiable externalities are involved, especially social, ecological and amenity impacts, planning consent systems are used. The proponents of a particular project, and those who have objections to it, state their arguments in a public debate which, in the case of major projects, may last for several months. The final decision is made at local or national government level in the light of the discussions. This approach is best regarded as a way of making the arguments available to public scrutiny, and mobilising consent, rather than as a means of reaching an 'optimum' solution. Its effectiveness depends on the responsiveness of local or national government to the issues raised. An example of the working of such a system in a controversial area is the UK Report on the Windscale Inquiry (Parker, 1978).

The methods used in current practice to take externalities into account are clearly imperfect, prone to unfairness and bureaucracy. From an economist's point of view, they are very untidy. Nevertheless, they extend environmental issues from the technical into the political area, which, in view of the many interests involved and the absence of a common measure, may well be the right place for them.

The environmental debate is often pictured as a simple confrontation between cash-motivated decision makers and environmentalists. It is to be hoped that this is not the case, and that, as all parties to the debate become better informed, the decisions which emerge will properly reflect the many issues and objectives involved.

9.10   Chapter summary

The extraction, transport and use of fuels have many effects which may not be fully reflected in economic decisions. These include injury or health risks to workers or the public, impacts on the local or global environment, economic and social effects, and amenity impacts. Some of these externalities arise in the normal course of events; others are very unlikely, but might have very serious implications if they occurred.

Extraction of oil and gas carries a risk of injury to workers, particularly in offshore fields, it may have a substantial (and not necessarily positive) social and economic impact, and it may disrupt the local ecosystem. Extraction and marine transport bring hazards from oil spillage, with both ecological and economic implications. Onshore storage of oil and gas is also a source of fire and pollution risk. The refining of oil and the use of oil and gas contribute to air pollution.

Undergound coal-mining (and to a lesser extent strip mining) carries significant risk of injury or ill health to workers, though these risks are falling. Risk to the public arises from subsidence or the movement of spoil heaps, and the latter may also have significant ecological effects. Economic and social impact arises mainly from the loss of land use (especially for strip mining) and the loss of employment when mines are exhausted. The use of coal contributes to air pollution.

The principle hazards of nuclear energy arise from radioactivity, though the present contribution of nuclear power to average radiation dose is small in relation to the natural background level or other man-made sources.

Uranium mining brings conventional injury risks as well as risks from radioactivity; tailings (the waste from ore milling) are a particular source of hazard which may affect the public. Risks from normal reactor operation are small, but the impact of a conceivable (but highly unlikely) accident could be very great. Fuel reprocessing reduces waste disposal problems but introduces some risk to workers and to the public. The separation of plutonium (a necessary corollary to the widespread use of fast breeder reactors) is a matter of concern because of its high activity, its persistence in some parts of the body, and its suitability for bomb manufacture. Plutonium theft can however be made very difficult or hazardous. Several international treaties exist to prevent the use of nuclear power technology to develop nuclear weapons, but the risk of proliferation remains significant.

Externalities specifically associated with electricity include the physical risks of power station construction, thermal pollution of rivers, estuaries or lakes, and the visual impact of power stations, cooling towers and transmission lines. Hydro-electric schemes carry risks of dam failure as well as economic impact through loss of land use.

Renewable and other unconventional energy sources have a wide variety of environmental and social effects. Tidal barrage schemes, for example, may affect the estuarine or marine ecosystem, while wave power devices are likely to bring risks in construction, installation and maintenance.Wind power devices are likely to be visually intrusive and may cause radio interference. Fusion power, though eliminating some of the possible hazards of nuclear fission, introduces several radiological or conventional problems of its own.

All combustion leads to air pollution. Carbon dioxide is a matter of concern because the increases in atmospheric concentration may lead to climatic changes with unknown consequences. Sulphur dioxide, from sulphur-bearing coal or oil, is a serious pollutant with well-established health hazards. Other sources of pollution include oxides of nitrogen, carbon monoxide, unburnt hydrocarbons, particulates, and specific poisons such as lead and mercury. In most cases control is possible, at a cost, with existing or developing technology.

The comparison of externalities is made difficult by the absence of a common measure of impact and the lack of adequate data. The way in which risks are perceived depends on many non-quantitative factors. A major published study suggests that gas and nuclear power are the safest sources, coal and oil the most dangerous, with most renewable sources falling between these extremes. The risks associated with energy supply appear small in relation to other everyday hazards such as road accidents.

Externalities may be incorporated in the decision-making process by adopting the 'pollutor-pays' principle, either through a pollution tax or pollution licences. Many types of externality fall outside the scope of this approach, and current practice is to control all externalities by means of regulations and planning consent systems. This approach is probably wise in view of the many issues involved.

Chapter 9   Furthur reading

Beckmann, P. (1976) *The health hazards of not going nuclear*, Golem Press, Boulder, Colorado

Chem Systems International Ltd (1976) *Reducing pollution from selected energy transformation sources*, Graham and Trotman, London.

Flowers, Sir B. (1976) *Royal Commission on Environmental Pollution – sixth report: Nuclear power and the environment*, HMSO, London

Inhaber, H. (1978) *Risk of energy production*, Report AECB 1119, Atomic Energy Control Board, Canada.

Nuclear Energy Policy Study Group (NEPSG) (1977) *Nuclear power issues and choices*, Ballinger, Cambridge, Mass.

Parker, the Hon. Mr Justice (1978) *The Windscale Inquiry*, vol. 1, HMSO, London.

Patterson, W. C. (1976) *Nuclear power*, Penguin, Harmondsworth, Middx, and New York.

Study of Critical Environmental Problems (1970) *Man's impact on the global environment – assessment and recommendations for action*, MIT, Cambridge, Mass.

Wilson, R. and Jones, W. J. (1974) *Energy, ecology and the environment*, Academic Press, New York and London.

The world energy market

10.1 Overview

In the post-war period up to 1973 the world energy market was dominated by the availability of plentiful supplies of cheap oil regulated by the major oil companies in their traditional role as market regulators. There was stability in energy trade flows and prices, and there was an established pattern of conduct in the energy market. Fuel generally, in particular the petroleum component, was traded in a buyer's market throughout the 1960s and the early 1970s. During this period, because of the growth of income and industry, transactions in internationally traded oil grew rapidly, aided by new oil discoveries, the declining relative price of oil, and the growth of new low-cost transport for oil. The relative importance of coal declined, and in the period between 1960 and 1973 oil increased its share of the world energy market from 34 to 46 per cent. By 1973 imported oil represented nearly 60 per cent of energy consumption in Western Europe and 70 per cent in Japan. Even in the United States, the original home of the modern oil industry, in 1973 oil imports accounted for one quarter of the oil used, and by 1978 these imports had increased their share to nearly one half and were taking nearly one third of all internationally traded oil. And developing countries, who use about 15 per cent of total world energy, rely upon oil for about half of their commercial energy, though only about one third if wood fuel and farm waste used as fuel are included.

The foundation of OPEC in 1960 (see chapter 4) can be seen as a defensive measure by the producing countries to protect themselves against the international oil companies in a weak oil market. In 1964 OPEC, negotiating with the major oil companies, was able to arrange an additional royalty payment (of 4 cents a barrel) to each producer country. However it was not until the early 1970s that OPEC became the major force in determining world oil prices. Until 1973, OPEC negotiated the price of oil with the major oil companies, but in that year the world oil market changed decisively following a short-term reduction in output imposed by the Arab members of OPEC in connection with the Arab–Israel conflict. Competition amongst consumers of oil led to panic buying and very high prices on the very small spot market for oil, and this in turn encouraged OPEC to impose a fourfold increase in the price paid for the oil produced in its member countries.

Subsequently OPEC has continued to set the price of oil through negotiations amongst its members without reference to either the oil companies or the governments in consumer countries.

In the five years following 1973 the world demand for oil was relatively weak, partly due to conservation following the price increase and partly due to the economic recession of 1973–75, and in real terms the price set by OPEC declined. By 1978, however, the demand for Saudi Arabian oil had risen near to that country's preferred limits, and light oil in particular was becoming scarce. The situation was complicated by the fact that oil companies had found themselves with excessive stocks in the spring of 1978, and during the year they had begun to run down these stocks. In the autumn, at a time when the companies would have been renewing their stocks for the coming winter, the Islamic revolution in Iran caused production there to fall from a high of 6 mbd to a low of about 1.5 mbd, and for a period no Iranian oil was being exported at all. This disturbance underlined the political vulnerability of the world energy market, and major imbalances between the supply and demand of oil were avoided only because countries like Saudi Arabia raised their production to make up part of the shortfall, and oil companies in major consuming countries used their stocks of oil to make up the remainder. Even so there were local shortages, due to the inability of the oil market to adjust its pattern of distribution, which resulted in high prices in the oil spot market during the winter and spring of 1978/79. This led OPEC to increase the price of marker crude to about $18 a barrel in June 1979, but the oil market continued to remain very strained even though Iranian production had risen again to nearly 4 mbd, and some oil exporting countries were able to sell their oil at prices well above $20 a barrel. Thus the limits on production set by individual members of OPEC, and also by other oil producing countries, led to an upward movement in prices – which was subsequently followed by an upwards adjustment in the price administered by OPEC.

Limits on production that are below their technical potential have become general amongst oil producing countries including countries outside OPEC, for example Norway; and, through limits on foreign participation, Mexico; and, through limits on exploration and profits, even the United States and the United Kingdom. These limits are being set as much from concern about the longer term scarcity of oil and the economic needs of the producing countries, as for the purpose of controlling the market. It is doubtful whether there is a uniform wish amongst members of OPEC to use the organisation as a traditional cartel to push oil prices upwards by inducing scarcity, but there is no doubt that some members would take this view and all would argue for the need to restrain oil depletion to meet longer-term needs. It is possible that OPEC are doing no more than following (approximately) the long-term trend that is appropriate for a commodity that has a limited resource base and high cost substitutes.

The availability of oil and the operation of the world energy market will depend not only on decisions about oil prices and production in OPEC countries. Availability will also depend on factors such as discoveries outside OPEC, new sources of energy supply, energy conservation, and economic growth; that is, those factors influencing the production and consumption of all forms of energy everywhere in the world. This is because, in the medium to long term, the various primary sources of energy are substitutes for each other, and the market for oil, just as the market for gas, coal or nuclear power, is part of the world energy market. This view is important for an understanding of how the balance of power, and the enormous uncertainties facing the traders in the energy market, might change in the future, and how the direction of change and the uncertainties might be influenced by policy measures in different countries. The world energy market in the 1970s and beyond is neither purely economic nor purely political in its arrangement. It is the result both of historical patterns and of continuous processes of change in power hierarchies and institutions.

10.2   General concepts of a world energy market

Within the framework of standard economic theory, a market can be defined as consisting of those buyers and sellers of a homogeneous product who are in sufficiently close contact for a single price to be established for transactions. While this is theoretically straightforward, in practice there are relatively few areas of production and consumption where it is meaningful to refer to a single homogeneous product within a market.

In the case of the energy market, energy is used in households, for transportation, and for manufacture of goods and services, these varied demands being met by different forms of energy or, more properly, energy carriers. Energy is not a single homogeneous product, but is embodied in a number of differentiated energy carriers, some of which are more readily interchangeable than others. Nevertheless, the elasticities of substitution between energy carriers and the cross-elasticities of demand among buyers are sufficiently great to ensure that a decision by the supplier of one energy carrier will depend upon the actions of the others.

To add precision to the discussion of markets, economists distinguish 'market structures', which are sets of selected organisational characteristics that establish the relationships between buyers and sellers. It is useful to identify the four main characteristics used to distinguish market structure:

(a) Seller concentration. This is the structure of *supply*, that is the number and size distribution of sellers of a particular product or more generally the extent to which overall control of the product is held by a few sellers.

(b) Buyer concentration. This is the structure of *demand* and refers to the number and size distribution of buyers of a product. The Galbraithian notion of countervailing power and the model of bilateral monopoly have been developed to show that a high degree of buyer concentration may be conducive to improved market performance. However, as we have seen in 1974 and 1979, both with the formation and the operation of the International Energy Agency (IEA) by the main oil consuming countries, there is no a priori reason to expect the producers (OPEC) to lower or limit prices when faced by a group of consumers (IEA).

(c) Product differentiation. This occurs whenever the products of the sellers within the market are not regarded by the buyers as close or perfect substitutes. Whatever the reason, the buyers are willing to pay more for the preferred variety of the product than for another and do not easily change from the preferred choice. Markets with a high degree of product differentiation are often characterised by producers with a high degree of control over prices.

(d) Entry conditions. These refer to the ease with which new producers may establish themselves in the market. Entry barriers are usually classified into three categories: cost advantages, product barriers and scale economy barriers. In the extreme cases of market types, entry conditions are straightforward: with perfect competition they are easy, with pure monopoly they are not possible; while it is in oligopolistic markets that the degree of freedom of entry becomes more important.

It would be foolish to suppose that a single theoretical definition of a market or of market structure can describe the world energy market: it is far too complex for simple straightforward classification, but several characteristics discussed above can be identified. For example, there is a high degree of product differentiation. Buyers still prefer and are willing to pay more for oil rather than bear the costs of switching to other energy carriers. As a result, the oil producers acting via OPEC have a high degree of control over crude oil prices and market shares are slow to change. However, a greater degree of competition exists in the distribution of refined oil products in consuming countries, just as a greater degree of competition exists in the sale of coal, uranium, and solar equipment.

Numerous energy carriers with different structures of supply designed to perform a number of activities – production, transportation, conversion, distribution, etc. – make up the world energy market and are all competing in the long run to supply the various structures of final demand. The market has a number of traders in the roles of suppliers, intermediaries and consumers faced with uncertain positions. These involve the major producing countries, and oil companies, energy companies and customers in both consuming and producing countries.

Standard economic theory presumes links among market structure, market conduct, and market performance and behaviour – normally assuming a one way flow from structures to performance. However, this directional flow has come under question, and a number of feedbacks have been suggested between behaviour, performance and structure, and between performance and conduct (Phillips, 1970). This, in effect, implies that market structure is not an exogenous determinant of market behaviour but a variable in a process by which sellers and buyers achieve a new market equilibrium.

The energy market, in particular the oil component of it, is an example where the traditional linkages between structure and performance and behaviour discussed in economic theory may come under suspicion. Up to the early seventies, the major oil companies exemplified the Galbraithian rule of vertical integration, dominating every step of the oil industry from exploring for crude oil to the delivery of home heating oil. They reaped high profits and increased their assets but were also able to maintain flexibility in their manoeuvres in the world market. However, as OPEC began to realise its power and control, the Majors lost the control and ownership of oil reserves and the power to set prices and volume. The effect of this structural change in the market has left the Majors responsible for only part of the world's oil and responsible only for passing on prices, not setting them, and they have thus lost control of oil operations. Market structure is not a constant, it varies in response to economic and political changes.

The question that remains to be answered is whether the Majors' withdrawal from the producing countries will mean a significant shift of emphasis in their operations to other kinds of energy. The characteristic stance of the Majors towards market circumstances beyond their control was, in the sixties, to shift the incidence of costs in their integrated structure between branches and between parent and subsidiary. Thus in the eighties, if they wish to regain their previous level of control of upstream activities, the Majors may initiate a new series of mergers and acquisitions into coal operations and solar or nuclear technology: changed performance leads to changed market structure. The economic and organisational reasons for this product diversification and horizontal integration are clear. Product diversification may enable them to be less prone to fluctuations in the demand for any one form of energy, to obtain short-run advantages by offsetting one loss against another gain, and to broaden the base for the long-run existence and security of their organisational structures and expertise. Some economists have suggested another possible reason – the Majors are diversifying into new energy sources so as to control the output and the prices of these new sources in the interest of maintaining the prices and market share of petroleum. However, although the Majors have been involved to varying degrees in coal activities, solar research and nuclear development for some time, there is as yet little substantive evidence they are using these activities for restrictive purposes – 'not proven' is the most severe verdict possible in face of this accusation.

10.3   Petroleum

Petroleum transactions in the world energy market were and are the result of decisions taken by three main participants in the market: the international oil companies operating in both oil importing and oil exporting countries, the governments of the oil exporting countries (OPEC: Saudi Arabia, Kuwait, Libya, Algeria, United Arab Emirates, Qatar, Indonesia, Nigeria, Iran, Venezuela, Iraq, Ecuador and Gabon) and the consuming countries. The price and production of petroleum have always been regulated and, until the early 1970s, the major international oil companies (Majors: Exxon, Standard Oil of California, Mobil, Gulf Oil, Texas Company, The Royal Dutch Shell Group, British Petroleum and Compagnie Française des Petroles) behaved as the market regulator or administrator. During the fifties and the sixties, the Majors operated as intermediaries between the oil producing countries and the oil consuming countries. They dominated every step of the oil process from obtaining and operating concessions in oil rich areas, finding and extracting oil, and selling in markets which they had allocated among themselves. As the Majors extended their operations throughout the oil producing areas, horizontal integration became characteristic of the industry. However, over the years a number of smaller less integrated companies have managed to enter the market, to grow and to flourish (for example: Atlantic Richfield, Occidental, Ente Nazionale Idrocarbuti (Italy) and other national oil companies).

The vertical and horizontal integrated structures of the Majors established them as the regulators of petroleum transactions in the world energy market in the period between 1920 and 1939 (Penrose, 1968). They were capable of regulating and planning market conquest and control, since pricing policy could be used to match supply to market clearing demand so as to provide a steady flow of oil. Their success permitted them to supply a cheap source of energy to consumers in the developed and developing world, to bring increased revenue and an economic stimulus to oil producing countries, and to maintain high profits for themselves. This structure of petroleum transactions enhanced the economic and political interests of all the participants – regardless of the uneven distribution of benefits favouring the Majors and consumer countries. It was successful as long as the oil producing countries remained politically heterogeneous lands, the principal consuming countries (OECD) were committed to a solid political front on the Middle East, the capacity existed for the Majors to increase production outside the main oil producing areas and the Majors continued to dominate the market (Mendershausen, 1976).

However, even as early as the 1950s the concentrated, tightly integrated structures of the oil industry had begun to loosen. Market enlargement, unification of Western European economies, changing market centres, and expectations of high profits – all began to attract both business and governments as competitors in the petroleum industry. Firstly, the Independents – oil companies mostly American in origin – began to grow in the anti-trust environment of the US market and began to seek out oil possibilities in areas not firmly controlled by the Majors. Secondly, the governments in Europe, Japan and some developing countries began to form state or national oil companies and subsidised their activities to secure independent sources of oil for their domestic markets. Government involvement is not new: the British government acquired majority ownership of BP before the First World War, and Italy established a national oil company in the 1950s. More recently

Japan, West Germany, Norway, India, Pakistan and others formed national oil companies but were too late to obtain major concessions. In 1964, the Majors controlled about 82% of crude production, 65% of refinery activities, and 60% of final product sales (Posner, 1973) whereas in 1973 they controlled 73% of crude, 50% of refinery activities and 50% of final products. The Independents and National Oil Companies were a threat to the Majors not only because they took some of the market but also because their entry changed buyer concentration and weakened the unified resistance to the producing countries.

In the sixties, as the oil industry became more diverse, the capacity of the Majors to increase production significantly outside the main producing countries declined. In the market of the fifties and early and mid sixties, when available supplies of oil could exceed demand, they expected that competition amongst the producing countries for *market* shares would keep any demand for higher shares of the economic *rent* in check. If a producer country became restless, the Majors would use their control over reserve productive capacity in the US or elsewhere to shift supply centres and the reshuffling of oil flows would bring the producer into line. But the reserve capacity in the US disappeared in the late sixties and early seventies and oil companies were becoming deeply committed to assets in the Middle East and South America. For example, by 1973 about four fifths of the production activities of the Majors occurred outside the US (Mendershausen, 1976).

Concomitantly, over the post-war period, the main petroleum producing countries were evolving into an effective economic and political force. Throughout the period, the major oil companies and the consuming countries underestimated continually the power and influence of the producers. One political factor began more and more to bind the producer countries – an anti-imperialistic attitude directed against both the international oil companies and the consuming countries. In addition, producer countries began to seek two economic objectives: to raise their share of the economic rent and to break the West's hold on oil. The post Second World War period up to 1971 was characterised by a steady reluctant erosion of the original terms obtained by the oil companies from the producing countries.

Most of the original concessions were granted to the Majors at various times between 1900 and the Second World War. The agreements usually granted the companies control over large geographic areas for extensive periods (60-99 years) and complete control over production and prices and exemption from taxes and duties. The companies agreed to pay the host governments a fixed royalty of 20¢–25¢ a barrel of oil produced (Sampson, 1975). This arrangement, possibly economically justified in the pre Second World War period when reserves were unknown and increasing, prices were falling and large investments were necessary, came under increasing pressure after the Second World War.

The first sign of discontent in the oil world occurred in Mexico in 1938 when

Mexico nationalised all oil operations. This was followed by concern over royalty payments in Venezuela in 1943 which resulted in the imposition of taxes that provided the government with 50% of the net income earned by the oil company operators in Venezuela. Similar 50–50 agreements were made in other producing countries. As a result receipts per barrel for the producing countries rose to about 60 cents and government revenues increased (Sampson, 1975). This was a turning point, not in terms of exercise of power, but in a change in perception on the part of producing countries – price, not just production volume, was the main variable in determining net profits and revenues.

In the 1950s it was the major oil companies who were responsible for successfully maintaining a relatively stable system of oil prices. However, in the late 1950s, increased activity by the Independents, increasing Soviet exports and the emergence of Libyan oil began to exert pressure on their control of oil activities and the existing stable price regime. In the new more competitive environment the Majors responded by lowering posted prices and thus lowered the base on which host countries were paid royalties and taxes. This battle for market control provoked the leading oil producing and exporting countries to come together in 1960 to form OPEC in an attempt to restore the posted prices. OPEC started cautiously but successfully in preventing further price reductions. During the period of excess supply in the early sixties, OPEC tried to implement a pro-rationing scheme to limit production and influence price, but failed because Iran refused to cooperate.

The 1960s were relatively quiet in the international oil industry. The 1967 June Israeli–Arab War shattered this uneasy calm with the closure of the Suez Canal and an embargo on petroleum exports from Arab producers to Great Britain and the US – neither of whom took much oil from Saudi Arabia, the main producer. It was the availability and control by the oil companies of the huge tankers that carried oil around the Cape of Good Hope and the willingness of Iran, Venezuela and North African producers to push up exports that enabled Europe and the US to avoid oil shortages following these events. The embargo was short-lived; nevertheless the June war underlined the consumer countries' vulnerability to political events in the Middle East.

The events of 1967 increased major consuming countries' dependence on North Africa, and in particular Libya, for oil. The continued closure of the Suez Canal combined with a rapid rise in oil demand, decreased supplies from Nigeria (due to Civil War) and from Saudi Arabia (due to Syrian interference in the Arabian pipeline) – all led the oil companies to increase output from Libya from 1.5 mbd in 1966 to over 3.1 mbd in 1969, further increasing European dependence on Libyan oil to the point where it provided nearly 30% of its requirements (Yager and Steinberg, 1974).

Again, political events disrupted the relative calm – a left wing government took over in Libya in 1970 and quickly used consumer dependence on Libyan oil to its advantage. Striking quickly, the new government in Libya cut back production, negotiated an increase of 30¢ in posted prices to $1.80 a barrel and an increase in the tax rate (Shell International, 1978). These price and tax increases in Libya were quickly followed by similar demands by other oil producing countries. Thus a new situation had developed: the OPEC countries fully realised for the first time the power they could exert to raise prices, but the consuming countries and oil companies failed to recognise the new and growing power of OPEC and its individual constituents.

In 1971 OPEC successfully negotiated price and tax increases in the Tehran agreement and the Tripoli agreement. These included increases in the posted price by 35¢ per barrel and the producing country share of profits to 55%, further provided Libya with a 76¢ increase on low sulphur Libyan oil and made provision for annual increases in the posted price (Sampson, 1975). Then followed a wave of confiscations and nationalisations of oil operations in a number of OPEC countries (Algeria, Libya, Iraq, Venezuela). Those countries that had not nationalised the assets of foreign oil companies began to press for further control over their oil resources through negotiated participation agreements whereby over a period of years the producer country would acquire majority control of the oil company assets. The oil companies would continue as producer and marketer. Thus participation provided a mechanism by which the producer countries could assume a dominant position in the world market while retaining the services and skills of the oil companies.

Then, in 1973/74 the world perception of the energy market changed decisively. The economic objective of OPEC to increase its share of the economic rent and the political objective of the Organisation of Arab Petroleum Exporting Countries (OAPEC) were mutually supportive. This coincidence of objectives resulted in an embargo and a large price increase ($2.898 to $11.651 a barrel) (Shell International, 1978). Suddenly, OPEC supply management became feasible – implementation was possible at little or no cost (as oil can be retained in the ground), employment impact was negligible, and the expansion of other energy sources was limited, OPEC – or the dominant producers of OPEC – became the regulator of the market.

When control and regulation shifted from the companies to OPEC, another perceptual change struck the world – because of the sovereignty of nations and their increased sensitivity to control of their own resources, the role of oil companies chasing around the world in search of more hospitable oil became more limited; national boundaries provided political barriers; hence a new kind of geographical constraint emerged. The Majors went through a period of accommodation, withdrawal and adjustment. The decline in their importance is likely to continue, but the pace will be moderated by the fact that they possess a substantial advantage over the Independents and the National Oil Companies, through their experience, personnel and financial resources, and integrated structure.

During the 1975 to 1977 period of excess supply, the Majors were needed by OPEC to assist in shoring up a soft market and were enticed to participate through access to oil at preferred prices to keep their refineries operating at full capacity. But by 1978/79 when oil became (temporarily) scarce, the influence of the Majors again declined, and their role was primarily one of responding to market circumstances beyond their control, and assisting towards an equitable distribution of scarce oil supplies to the world market.

The National Oil Companies in Japan, West Germany and Italy have had little success in acquiring secure sources of oil. They have sought to operate through joint ventures with the newly formed national oil companies in OPEC, but results are still unimpressive. The National Oil Companies in the UK, Mexico and Norway have been more successful due to oil rich areas within their boundaries. In the UK and Norway, oil has been developed jointly with the private oil companies but primarily with the Majors. In a number of developing countries national oil companies have been formed to explore and develop indigenous oil resources and to control the importation of foreign oil. These national oil companies often operate jointly with the World Bank and an international oil company. This type of involvement exists in India, Thailand, Turkey, Zaïre, Pakistan, Egypt and others.

The price of oil is influenced on the one hand by the costs of oil production and the costs of substitutes, and on the other hand by the international financial implications of price, that is the ability of importers to pay and the income requirements of exporters. It is also influenced by political factors depending, for example, upon the cohesion of OPEC regarding the long-term political interests and foreign policies of its members. Since 1973 the general level of prices for internationally traded oil has been set through negotiation amongst members of OPEC at periodic meetings to determine the price of 'marker crude' – namely, the price for a barrel of light Arabian crude oil f.o.b. Ras Tanura in the Persian Gulf. During the period to 1978 Saudi Arabia had enough spare capacity to control the marginal supply and so regulate the market on behalf of OPEC. The prices paid for other types of oil, or to other oil producers, were determined in relation to marker crude largely by their quality (specific gravity, sulphur content, etc.) and their physical location in the world market. Members of OPEC were left free to determine their own levels of production – there was no formal 'pro-rationing' scheme of the type introduced for United States producers in the 1930s although some implicit understandings may have been arrived at.

Between 1974 and 1978 the real price of oil fell by 25 per cent. This took the form of an erosion in the nominal price through inflation and the unwillingness of OPEC to raise prices. It was due mainly to slack demand and was mirrored in the spot market by prices lower than the OPEC price. In fact, with the nationalisation of oil in OPEC countries, the previously dominant characteristic of vertical integration had been partially eliminated and the spot market and other short-term transactions became potentially more important. The spot market is a market that deals in relatively small supplies of crude and products and in the past has reflected supply and demand conditions for the market generally only in an erratic and patchy way, though its influence has been substantial in recent years and it could be more important in the future. The violent upward surge in spot market prices in the spring of 1979 ($20–$30 a barrel when the reference price was $14.50) highlighted the tightness in supply and demand and the competitive conditions for buyers in the market, and to some extent influenced the OPEC decision in June 1979 to raise the reference price to $18 a barrel. However, this did not stabilise the market and further increases brought the average OPEC price to over $30 a barrel by mid 1980. The changes in average current prices and average real prices from 1972 to 1980 are illustrated in figure 10.1.

OPEC is a cartel in the sense that its members determine prices through their control of most of the internationally traded oil and 60 per cent of all the oil produced outside the Communist bloc. In order to control prices, there must also be some control over production; this is mainly exercised by Saudi Arabia (the biggest and most flexible producer) but other members also set limits on their output. The large jumps in the price of oil in 1973/74 and in 1979 were almost accidental (though reflecting an underlying shortage) in that they followed from a temporary scarcity of oil and a loss of confidence by consumers that was only partially related to the actions of OPEC acting as a cartel. The 1973/74 crisis and price increases were nearly unavoidable once the Arab members of OPEC had decided to limit their production – for political reasons and not as part of the cartel's policy. However, the shortfall in supply and price increases in 1978/79 due to the loss of Iranian production could have been avoided if Saudi Arabia and other members of OPEC had increased their production more decisively for a period. They did not do so, at least in part, because collectively the members of OPEC considered the 1978 price of oil to be too low and those of its members with spare production capacity did not wish to step too far out of line. This view remains. Members of OPEC are constrained also by public opinion in their own countries to limit production and to seek a steady increase in the real price of oil.

Many economists (particularly in North America) were inclined to believe, in the aftermath of the sharp price increases of 1973/74, that the 'OPEC cartel' were solely to blame for the oil shortage: a rigged market, with collusive restriction of output, deliberately to force up prices. And this analysis led them to believe that the OPEC cartel would eventually go the way of all other restrictive price rings – some eager sellers would break the implicit 'pro-rationing' rules, and this extra output would lead to a price break. Only political or religious fervour would hold the price ring together.

The fashion had changed by the end of the 1970s. Little evidence had appeared of any deliberate international controls by OPEC of national output levels; and even the alternative version of the cartel doctrine, according to which the Saudi Arabian authorities acted as price leaders and quantity regulators (because of the great weight and flexibility of Saudi output, and their financial strength), was hard to fit to the facts. Economists, in response to recognition of the facts, began to

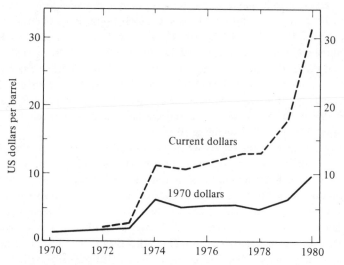

Figure 10.1   Petroleum prices 1972–80 (US $ per barrel). *Source:* World Bank (1979) and authors' estimates. *Notes:* Prices are averaged over OPEC exports weighted by volume, and are shown in current dollars and in constant 1970 dollars. The latter are obtained using a deflator based on the prices of manufactured goods exported by industrialised countries.

argue that:

> One important implication of this analysis is that OPEC is *not* acting as a cartel in the technical sense of the word. Cartel action is the collusion of a group of producers to restrict supply and raise prices even though each individual producer would wish to produce more at the higher price. In this instance, the oil exporters are contemplating reducing production in their own individual self-interest, not in response to collusive pressure. This has important policy implications for consuming nations. It suggests that attempts to lower prices by organising collusive oil-buying to break cartel discipline will fail because it is not cartel discipline but individual producer's interests which are restricting production.

Our view, however, remains that OPEC *as an organisation* retains some cohesion and some powers independent of, and tending to reinforce, the national tendencies to modesty in output targets. The political dimension must not be neglected, and national sentiments on oil conservation are in part the reflection of the views and analysis of 'OPEC' as such.

10.4   Natural gas

Natural gas is found either independently or in association with crude oil and it is not surprising to find that countries with large oil reserves generally have significant natural gas resources. Substantial natural gas resources are located in the United States, Canada, Mexico, the USSR, the Middle East, North Africa, the United Kingdom and the Netherlands.

However, the structure of the gas industry differs markedly from that of oil. The international gas industry is dominated by state owned companies in the gas rich countries. These natural gas companies are responsible both for the production and for the sale of gas. Often, gas importing countries have founded state-owned gas companies or government departments charged with the administration and control of gas imports and their distribution. The United States is the exception – there the gas industry is made up of a number of privately owned companies that can be responsible for one or all of the activities of the industry from production to sale. Even though private enterprise dominates the US gas industry, until 1978 the price for domestic gas was determined by government regulations rather than by market forces.

Unlike crude oil, the long distance transportation of natural gas from producing to consuming areas is expensive and requires large investments in pipelines suitable only for natural gas or in conversion and transportation facilities suitable only for liquefied natural gas (LNG). So the control of gas resources does not offer large economic rents from consumers as in the case of oil. Rather than a seller's market as is oil, the gas industry is a buyers' market. Thus, the governments controlling gas resources seek to enter into bilateral agreements with importing countries that are in a position to contribute to the large investments required for the development of gas. Typically, gas agreements are arranged on an intergovernmental basis, and prices for gas exports and investment contributions in gas networks are established through bilateral negotiations between governments and state-owned companies.

There is some scope for further increases in international trade in natural gas by pipeline. For example, extensions of existing gas networks or new networks could be developed in any of the following: from the Soviet Union to Western Europe, from Canada to the United States, from Mexico to the United States, from Iran and the Middle East to the Soviet Union or Europe or the Far East, and by underwater pipeline from North Africa to Western Europe.

If pipeline transport is not possible, natural gas can be converted into LNG (liquefied natural gas) for transport by ship and then reconversion to gas upon delivery – a method pioneered by the British purchases from Algeria in 1958. This involves the transportation aboard ships of containers with liquid at minus 162°C which involves high cost construction and control and some accident risks. To date, Japan with its limited domestic energy resources has been the most ambitious in arranging a number of long-term LNG contracts and from present activity seems likely to increase LNG imports in the future. Even with large indigenous gas resources the United States has concluded a long-term contract to import LNG from Algeria and may enter into a similar arrangement with Nigeria. Some authorities suggest that Mexico might consider securing long-term contracts to supply Western Europe with LNG in exchange for investment funds, although this seems unlikely as Mexico has a potential market in the US nearby that it can supply with the existing or an upgraded pipeline network. In the near future Western Europe may not import much LNG, as gas resources in the North Sea are significant, and, if imported gas is required, it might be acquired by pipeline from the USSR, the Middle East or North Africa. However, LNG trade to Western Europe may increase towards the turn of the century, making use of the large resources of natural gas in Nigeria and the Middle East. Recently, a Western European consortium has been negotiating a long-term contract to import LNG from Nigeria.

10.5   Coal

World coal production is currently running at about 3 billion tonnes a year, but less than 10 per cent of this total is traded on the world market. According to recent figures, world coal trade was up 5 per cent in 1977 over 1976 from 191 to 201 million tonnes. However, due to a four-month coal miners strike in the US in 1978, US coal exports fell by about 2 million tonnes. This contributed to a slight fall in world coal trade to 199 million tonnes in 1978 (Markon, 1979).

The rising trend in the coal trade figures is attributed to a slight increase in demand for power station (steam) coal, a relative stability in demand for coking coal from the steel industry, coupled with the coming onstream of new mine capacity. The major exporting countries are – the United States, Poland, Australia, the USSR, West Germany, Canada and South Africa. Of the importers Japan is the leader with around 52mt imported in 1978, followed by France and Italy, importing 23.6mt and 11.8mt respectively (Markon, 1979).

Even though much of any future increase in coal consumption will probably take place in those countries where it is produced, there may be a significant increase in the medium and long-term in internationally traded coal and the share of traded coal in the world market. One reason for the increase would be the predicted change in the distribution of steel produced in the world. The location of steel production is moving from traditional centres such as the US, UK, and West Germany which are major coal producers to new centres such as Japan, Brazil, Korea, India, Venezuela and Spain, which (except for India and Korea) are not major coal producers and will need to increase imports of coking coal.

A second reason would be the expansion of open cast coal mining with its lower costs in developed countries (US, Canada, Australia and USSR) and the development of low cost coal operations in general in certain developing countries (India, South Africa, Colombia, Indonesia). A third reason is the possible continued horizontal integration of the international oil companies into the coal industry. With their expertise in finance, personnel, transportation and marketing applied to coal the matching of centres of demand for coal with supply could be enhanced.

The new low cost coals as estimated in table 10.1 will lead to increased

Table 10.1. *Estimated costs of steam coal (1976 US $ per tce).*

	Estimated average cost per tce	
Supply region	Western Europe	Japan
US		
East	40–53	50–63
West	40–50	34–40
Canada		
East	43	
West	48	44
South Africa	38	38
Australia	45	40
Poland	38	
USSR		37
China		38
Indonesia		42
Colombia		38
Mozambique		40

Source: IEA (1978b).

international competition in coal pricing. In particular, this could have long-term implications for the coal industries of the UK, West Germany, Belgium and France, where coal production is by deep-mining and is often much higher in cost. Western Europe could become a large market in the 1990s for imported foreign coal, especially if hints that the West German government may not extend regulations to keep cheap imported coal off the domestic market when they expire in 1981 materialise, and if UK government disapproval of coal imports is withdrawn.

Coal production in the United States is a competitive industry with a substantial number of independent private firms. Coal operations by coal firms controlled or owned by other energy companies form about 20% of the total. Ownership of coal reserves is widely distributed; about one half of the US coal reserves are located in public domain lands, and Federal laws and regulations seem likely to prevent any one firm or group of firms gaining a dominant position (US National Coal Association, 1977). In Western Europe the coal industries are nationalised. In the USSR and in China, coal production is under state control. In most other coal producing countries, state owned companies or government departments control production and sales. Thus, most international trade in coal is arranged on a bilateral basis involving governments and private firms. Furthermore, even with the possible entrance of the international oil companies into coal activities, the diversity of political, social and economic interests of the major coal exporters makes the emergence of an international coal cartel seem improbable.

Coal trade is expected to increase substantially in Asia, especially if Japan, presently the world's largest importer, decides to increase coal imports (subject to meeting environmental standards) to reduce dependence on imported oil. Japan's sources of supply could be Australia, Indonesia, the USSR, China and possibly the US. Due to stringent environmental restrictions on coal production in the US, the future levels of coal exports are very uncertain but it is possible that the US would be a major source of coal for Japan or other countries. The other potential sources seem more likely, considering the willingness on the part of Japan to enter into bilateral deals to finance production and transportation of coal in exchange for a secure source. The developing countries may also seek to increase coal imports if coal costs and prices compare favourably with the cost of oil. If Japan provides capital to develop sources of coal supply in the Far East as suggested, coal trade with the developing countries of Asia might also increase.

10.6   Nuclear power

At the moment nuclear power is much more advanced than other potential alternative sources to the fossil fuels. This is partly due to the fact that governments of several major countries developed nuclear power for military purposes which provided the basis (large R & D efforts, a scientific community, specialist industries, and relevant government bodies) for the development of commercial nuclear power. Subsequent development in the United States, Western Europe, Japan, China, India and Brazil, was made partly because nuclear power was seen as the cheapest way to generate electricity and partly as a contribution to longer-term security in energy supply.

Uranium mining operations, the first step of the nuclear fuel cycle, are concentrated in those countries, listed in table 10.2, which possess the majority of the world's known uranim resources. Except for the United States, they are not major consumers of uranium. Most uranium mines supply several customers. Uranium mining operations are undertaken by numerous domestic private firms under government licence in the United States, Canada, Australia and South Africa, by foreign firms under licence in some developing countries, and by state-owned companies in other developing countries, e.g. Venezuela, Mexico, India.

The uranium market today is influenced, like other markets, by the world energy picture – but there are special features. Firstly, the number of large uranium producing countries is small and they are geographically and politically diverse. Secondly, with the growth of nuclear power slower than initially expected, uranium should be in adequate supply up to the later 1990s though the longer-term outlook is doubtful. Prior to 1973 the world uranium price had been steadily falling for ten years, which led to responses by individual countries – in 1966 the US put an embargo on imported uranium to maintain a floor price, the Canadian government established minimum prices by buying up excess Canadian produced supplies,

Table 10.2. *Uranium production capabilities (in order of resource potential).*

Major resources	Minor resources
US	Finland
South Africa	Germany
Canada	Italy
Australia	Portugal
Algeria	Spain
India	Sweden
Gabon	Yugoslavia
Niger	Japan
France	Mexico
Argentina	Turkey
Brazil	Central African Empire
	Zaire
	Korea
	UK
	Venezuela

Source: Duret, M. F. *et al.* (1978a)

Australia ceased production in 1970, and South Africa has been stockpiling uranium (Yager and Steinberg, 1978). Whether the uranium producers exercise monopoly power in determining the price and production of uranium is uncertain and uranium could become in short supply around the year 2000 – not initially because of physical shortage, rather due to long lead times and high costs of industry development. However, to secure against such an eventuality several countries in Western Europe and Japan, which have no major uranium resources have entered into joint-venture arrangements or made direct investments in uranium operations in some producing countries.

The nuclear power programme requires the development of a whole new series of industries – uranium mining, uranium enrichment, fuel manufacture, reactor construction, fuel storage, transportation and reprocessing. To a large extent, the economic and technical aspects of nuclear power have predetermined the institutional structure of the nuclear industry. Military security combined with complex new technology, high costs and long lead times required that governments should (initially) be the developers of nuclear energy. The United States became the leader in the development of nuclear power because of its large commitment to the weapons programme, and its ability to channel large investment funds into the nuclear programme.

Until recently the private manufacturers in the United States dominated the production of nuclear reactors in the world market, and the United States had a near monopoly over the provision of enrichment facilities. Uranium enrichment facilities in the United States are the only phase of the nuclear fuel cycle still operated entirely by the government. The US is the only country in the world in which reactor construction is entirely privately undertaken. In Western Europe reactors are built and operated with government funds, and even the costs are kept down to some extent by buying licences from the United States. Companies (state owned or private firms with state assistance) in West Germany, France, the United Kingdom and Japan are steadily competing more successfully with US manufacturers in supplying reactors to the world market. At one time the international oil companies began to enter the nuclear power industry, but have since reduced their commitment.

At present the principal reactors in use or under construction are PWRs and BWRs (see chapter 6), based on the light water reactor concept (LWR) originally developed in the United States. These require uranium fuel that must undergo a complex enrichment process before it can be used and thus countries with these reactors are largely dependent upon the United States for enriched fuel. To break this dependence several countries in Western Europe are undertaking a joint effort to develop an enrichment capability using the gas centrifuge technology. There is also the option of adopting heavy water reactors (HWR), as already installed in Canada and India, which use natural uranium, thus avoiding the enrichment process and therefore also avoiding dependence on the United States. Other aspects of reactor development, e.g. the breeder reactor and high temperature gas reactors, together with import barriers to US power equipment and the expiration of licencing agreements by US firms, are certain to diminish the dominance of the United States and to bring about further changes in the pattern of reactor sales.

Physical, technical, economic, and social factors dictate the extent to which aspects of the nuclear fuel cycle will be under the control of private firms or governments, and which countries will be involved. Table 10.3 illustrates the relative influence of these different factors on the control of fuel cycle operations. For example, if an operation involves high degrees of technical control and high capital costs, it is unlikely that a small developing country will undertake involvement in that operation on its own, either through a state owned company or private firm.

Because of the high capital costs, large minimum economic size of plant, high degree of technical control, and high technology required for enrichment, fuel storage and reprocessing, few individual countries can undertake these activities alone and several joint efforts are being developed. In addition to the joint European effort to develop enrichment facilities, the Japanese have negotiated with the French and the British the joint development of storage and reprocessing facilities in the UK and France. The size of the effort required for enrichment, storage and reprocessing reduces the appeal of nuclear power to those developing countries who seek energy independence. Furthermore, the tight control on nuclear technology by developed countries at all phases of the fuel cycle and the specialised manpower requirements constitute what appears to many developing countries as a

Table 10.3. *Factors affecting national or private involvement in nuclear fuel cycle operations.*

Fuel cycle operation	Life of plant (yrs)	Representative size of plant	Capital stock in plant (million US $ (1978))	Need for technical control	Potential profitability	Relevance to nuclear weapon proliferation	Scope for international cooperation
Mining	10–25*	2000 te/yr* U_3O_8	100–200 (M)	L	H	L	L
Uranium enrichment	30	1000 te/yr	500 (H)	VH	M	H	H
Fuel manufacture	50	500 te/yr	30 (L)	M	M	L	L
Reactor	30	1300 MWe	1000 (H)	H	L	L	M
Fuel storage	50	1000 te	400 (H)	H	L	M	H
Fuel reprocessing	30	1200 te/yr	1300 (H)	H	M	H	H
Fuel transport		10 te	0.6 (L)	L	L	L	L

Notes: VH Very high, H High, M Medium, L Low.
*Variable depending on geological factors.
Source: Authors' estimates.

rich country cartel. However, the threat of such a cartel does not seem serious, especially with the intense competition amongst the several nuclear power industries to increase their export performance to developing countries, and the significant barrier of capital availability to these countries.

10.7   Summary and market outlook

The problem about oil is that its supply has quite suddenly lost the flexibility that in the past has enabled production to increase as required to meet the needs of consumers. This loss of flexibility has brought with it a new risk of unreliability since supply that is interrupted by events such as those in Iran in 1978/79 cannot so readily be replaced from other sources. The changed outlook for oil, of which the first clear warning was given by the 1973 oil crisis, has come partly from physical and economic causes and partly from political and social responses or perceptions. The main physical basis for the problem is that oil is being used faster than it is being found, and since 1968 world proven reserves of oil have been declining. Over 80 per cent of these proven reserves in the non-communist world are found in countries that are members of OPEC. Important producers in OPEC have set limits on their production levels that are below the technical potential, and it is to be expected that future production will be increasingly planned on the basis of the revenue needed for long-term development. Moreover, it is hard to see any conceivable changes in the political views of OPEC countries that would induce higher production levels.

Limits on world oil production are likely to cause a long-term increase in the real price of oil, but they will also cause short-term fluctuations, so for periods the price may exceed the long-term trend. Sharp upward movements in the price provide a strong stimulus to national producers to take control not only of production but also of the first stages in marketing their oil. The oil companies, like the importing countries, are searching for security of supplies. Their difficulties in an unstable world oil market include the fact that contracts are liable to last only until the world oil price, or the price on the spot market, changes, or until the producer country adopts a new policy on production limits, or in some instances until a political incident arises which causes a change in sales policy by the producing country. The individual actions by producer countries in OPEC during the strong market of 1979 are not unlike the behaviour of members of a cartel in that total production was effectively limited. If unstable market conditions continue, then world oil prices will fall as well as rise, and it will be interesting to see how well OPEC can manage either to stabilise the market towards its long-term trend or to limit the effect on its members of an intermittently weak oil market.

During the 1970s the major oil companies were endeavouring to adjust to their new role of service contractors to the OPEC countries and their increasing role as international buyers of oil rather than producers. In order to broaden the base for their long-term operation and security they acquired rights to coal resources in a number of countries and engaged in active research on coal technology, oil shale and tar sands, and some aspects of solar and nuclear technology. In the future the major oil companies may play an important part in developing international trade in LNG and in coal, both of which could increase substantially over the next few decades, due to new sources of gas distant from major markets, new lower cost coal coming on stream, and changing centres for demand and supply. In view of the high capital cost for transport facilities, natural gas trade and some coal transactions in the world energy market seem likely to develop on a bilateral basis with producers and consumers sharing the costs of development.

The position and pattern of nuclear power in the world energy market is clouded by uncertainties about the growth in electricity demand, problems of power plant siting, licencing delays, technical problems on the power plants and the nuclear fuel cycle, and public and political attitudes to nuclear power. With a downward revision of nuclear forecasts the uranium market has become somewhat easier, and it now appears as though uranium supplies will be able to hold up better for the next decade or two than had been expected in the early 1970s. The United States is losing its dominant position in supplying nuclear reactors, and with increased specialisation the nuclear industry is becoming more worldwide, with important contributions from Western Europe and Japan.

The energy market does of course depend ultimately on the behaviour of the final consumer under the impact of changing prices and changing availability of different types of fuel. Illustrative projections showing the pattern of demand for different fuels are presented and discussed in chapters 13 and 14. Expectations of the type illustrated by these projections are taken into account by the participants in the world energy market, whether they be governments in producing countries, international energy companies, governments in consuming countries, or final consumers. Each of these parties is subject to different constraints and perceptions. Some of them try to influence the energy market to their own advantage, whether to secure supplies, high prices and revenues, or high profits, although most of them may be simply trying to get through to next week or next year without causing themselves more problems than those they are already having to face. The energy world is experiencing substantial changes in the relative importance of each energy carrier and each participant in the market. The participants operate within a changing framework of mutual dependence, based upon energy trade and trade outside energy, together with technical, financial, political and social constraints.

However, interdependence does not mean that the participants in the market have common objectives. Members of OPEC are increasingly concerned with the long-term future, and if they are producing oil at a faster rate than would be justified by their own development plans they would seek some kind of 'store of value' that would safeguard for the future the value of oil revenues. In principle, they may favour a stable price regime which would bring the price to a level reflecting its expected long-term scarcity, but avoid sudden increases and minimise the disruptive effects on the world economy. However, it is doubtful whether OPEC can control the oil market in such a way as to avoid short-term crises. Members of OPEC may also turn out to have little control over the price of oil in the long-term future, since the high technology and alternative energy sources that are available in the industrialised countries will give the latter control over their long-term energy future if they follow sufficiently robust policies. Even for oil in the industrialised countries the long-term future holds the prospect of developing their extensive but high cost resources in tar sands and oil shale, and conversion of coal to oil. Once the capital has been invested in these resources, their marginal *cost* will be far less than the *price* of OPEC oil, so it would be prudent for OPEC *not* to stimulate such development at too fast a rate in their own long-term interest. The OPEC countries will be aided in this effort by the fact that the industrialised countries are subject to social and environmental constraints, and are not entirely free to develop their energy resources in a way that might be appropriate in response to the signal from the international market alone.

Stability will not return quickly to the world energy market – there are too many constraints, too many uncertainties, and too many participants with conflicting objectives. However this instability is itself part of the adjustment process, each new oil crisis and each new increase in the price of oil clarifies the perception of consumers and other decision makers that there is a need for change. Once the need for change becomes widely recognised, it becomes also of political importance and the environment for investment in new energy sources, particularly coal and nuclear power, and in energy conservation, will improve. It would be naive to suppose that wise and effective policies by governments could resolve the problems by themselves, nor should one suppose that these policies would arise without the stimulus of higher energy prices, energy crises, and inconvenience to the public through periodic scarcity of energy.

Chapter 10   Further reading

Adelman, M. A. (1972) *The world petroleum market,* Johns Hopkins University Press, Baltimore and London.
Ezzatti, A. (1978) *World energy markets and OPEC stability,* Lexington Books, Lexington, Mass.
Frankel, P. H. (1946) *Essentials of petroleum: a key to oil economics,* Chapman and Hall, London.
Gordon, R. L. (1978) *Coal in the US energy market,* Heath, Lexington, Mass.
Hartshorn, J. E. (1967) *Oil companies and governments,* Faber and Faber, London.
International Energy Agency (IEA) (1978b) *Steam coal – prospects to 2000,* OECD, Paris.
Mabro, R. (ed.) (1980) *World energy: policies and issues,* Oxford University Press, London.
Mendershausen, H. (1976) *Coping with the oil crisis,* Johns Hopkins University Press, Baltimore and London.
Noreng, O. (1978) *Oil politics in the 1980s,* McGraw-Hill, New York.

Penrose, E. (1968) *The large international firm in developing countries: the international petroleum industry,* Allen and Unwin, London.

Pindyck, R. S. (ed.) (1979a) *The structure of energy markets,* vol. 1 of 'Advances in the economics of energy and resources' JAI Press, Greenwich, Connecticut.

Rosenbaum, W. (1978) *Coal and crisis: the political dilemmas of energy management,* Praeger, New York.

Sampson, A. (1975) *The seven sisters – the great oil companies and the world they made,* Hodder and Stoughton, London.

Willrich, M. *et al.* (1975) *Energy and world politics,* The Free Press, New York.

Wilson, C. L. (ed.)(1980)*Coal - bridge to the future,* Report of the World Coal Study (WOCOL), Ballinger, Cambridge, Mass.

World Energy Conference (WEC) (1978b) *World energy resources 1985–2020,* IPC Science and Technology Press, Guildford, UK.

Wyant, F. R. (1977) 'The role of multinational oil companies in world energy trade' in *Annual Review of Energy,* vol. 2, pp. 125–51.

Yager, A. and Steinberg, E. B. (eds.) (1974) *Energy and US Foreign Policy,* Ballinger, Cambridge, Mass.

The cost of fuels

11.1 Introduction

Perhaps the most difficult, yet the most critical, economic question about energy is – what, in the long term, will be the cost of a unit of fuel? The costs, and in part the prices, of energy depend on the economics of the entire fuel cycle – production, conversion, transportation, distribution and disposal. All costs must be included – capital costs, direct costs (labour and related items), costs of energy used up in the cycle itself, and so on. On the one hand, consider an individual in the private sector who is trying to decide whether to invest in a solar heating system: the time at which such an investment becomes economically attractive depends not only on the costs of solar technology today, and on the expected time path of improvements, but also on the availability of fossil fuels and electricity and on the price which will prevail for those fuels. On the other hand, Government must consider whether to offer incentives to encourage the development of solar technology, or to subsidise users of this technology. Decisions will depend in part on the domestic availability of fossil fuels as well as on the state of the world fuel market and developments in other energy technologies.

The important factors that must be considered are those that will affect the marginal producer of a fuel in the future. These include factor prices, the consequences of environmental standards, the dynamics of technological change, the availability of capital and the effects on unit costs of scale.

Between 'costs' and 'prices' lies that uneasy and important term in the economics of natural resources – 'rent', or profit. Non-economists often approach this area of analysis by seeking to discuss simultaneously *costs* and *availability* of supplies – price will rise if costs increase, but will rise also if availability decreases. Economists prefer to consider the marginal – least profitable, highest cost – unit of output, which, by definition earns no rent or monopoly profit. For that unit of output, in equilibrium, cost can sensibly be defined as identical with price; but it is then necessary to ask – how far up the curve of increasing cost will the output of particular fuels be pressed? And 'availability' pops straight back into the argument as common sense requires: the two modes of analysis deploy the same facts and assumptions, but arrange them in different ways.

To discuss costs of energy, we need to examine both fixed and variable costs and the movement of both average and marginal costs over time. Unfortunately, such highly detailed cost figures are not widely available. The cost information that does exist is known with certainty only for those sources of supply which are currently commercially producible and, even for those, data are imperfect. The costs of new energy sources and new equipment are even more uncertain.

The discussion in this chapter will focus on the current best opinion (guesses) both about costs in the past and the costs of future additions to levels of output. It is not the purpose of this discussion to put forward a definitive view on the exact movement of future energy costs, but instead to provide an account of those elements that have influenced and may influence future costs. The discussion includes an account of the importance of different ground rules – for example environmental rules – on the different costs of energy sources.

11.2   Fundamentals of rising costs

Historically, the fuel production industries and the electric power industries around the world have experienced decreasing costs – average costs have declined as total output increased: economies of scale have been achieved. Moreover, technical progress has been rapid, and the unit costs of adding to plant and capacity have been less than the historical average costs of existing plant. During most of the post Second World War era up to the early seventies, the economies of scale and improving technology were sufficient to outpace the relatively low rates of inflation and to allow falling average prices for energy.

However, the picture began to change in the early seventies. For example, in the United States, electric industry construction costs and the domestic oil price began to rise more quickly than the corresponding rate of increase of the wholesale price index, as shown in figure 11.1. These trends provide a convenient illustration for a general discussion of many fundamental factors that have combined and interacted to force up the average price of energy since the early seventies. The most important of them may be grouped into three categories:

(a) Inflation and adverse changes in real relative costs through time. The important distinction is between rising absolute factor prices and changing relative prices, for example through slower improvements in technology in the energy trades than was happening elsewhere.

(b) Environmental and social costs. These include increases in the relative importance of environmental, health, and safety regulations and measures on the cost of energy, when compared with costs of other things.

(c) Geographic distribution of energy sources, availability of capital, economies of scale, and variations in the degree of monopoly.

11.3   Inflation and changes in real relative costs

It is necessary to distinguish between rising absolute costs which arise through inflation and changes in real relative costs which tend to occur because of technical

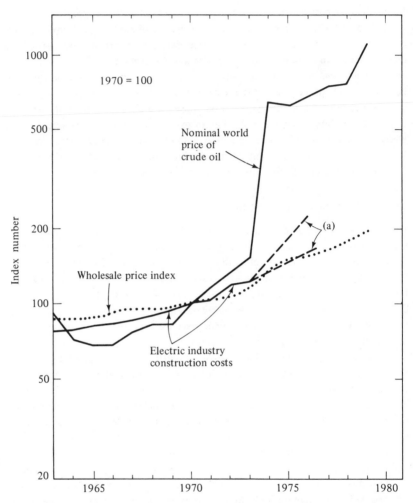

Figure 11.1   US historical trends (current year dollars indexed 1970 = 100). *Sources:* Berlin *et al.* (1974); World Bank (1979); Adelman (1972). *Notes:* (a) After 1973 construction costs were strongly affected by delays due in part to sharply lower· growth in demand and in part to changes in regulations – the broken lines indicate the uncertainties and do not necessarily reflect long-term trends.

changes and changing conditions of supply. Theoretically, what is of interest is resource allocation and in this context it is changes in relative costs, not rising absolute costs, that are important. However, whilst the distinction between rising absolute and changing relative costs is useful at the conceptual level, it is of more limited help at the practical level. As the impact of inflation differs from one energy industry to another so do the effects of technical change and the impacts of changing conditions of supply: hence the practical difficulties in separating these two effects. The important methodological point to keep in mind is that an attempt to exclude inflationary effects should be made before judging the changes in real costs that have taken place.

For example, during the early and mid seventies several factors have combined to raise the costs of factor inputs and to force up the price of electricity, and, to a lesser extent, have significantly affected the price of other fuels. The primary problems are: (a) inflation allowances in conventional accounting practice were too low; (b) stretching out of construction schedules from low cost years to the higher cost future; (c) higher interest rates; (d) greater complexity of work than anticipated; (e) apparent declines in the productivity of labour; (f) increased quality and safety standards; (g) introduction of new standards after construction began; and (h) increases in labour fringe benefits (Berlin et al., 1974).

Inflation affects the costs of electricity and other fuels in two ways: firstly, directly through the increased costs of labour, materials and components for new facilities, and, secondly, by raising the cost of borrowing money – nominal interest rates tend to be linked to inflation rates. Inflation also causes problems if conventional accounting methods induce insufficient sinking funds for replacement of depreciating assets.

These effects are more significant for the energy industries, especially the electricity industry, than for most borrowers because they are in most cases expanding rapidly and involve high risk and capital-intensive ventures: increases in interest rates will have a greater impact on more capital-intensive industries. In real terms, interest rates may be no higher during inflation; but to borrow long-term funds for investment at historically high interest rates is a dangerous game, and is often perceived as an increased cost.

Technical changes which have had a significant beneficial effect on the costs of fuels and electricity include higher transmission and distribution voltages, the reductions in electric plant thermal losses, improvements in transport of fuels (such as block tankers, unit trains and improved large diameter pipes), and advances in open cast coal mining. Recent developments include improved and developed technologies in nuclear generation, solar energy technologies, new techniques for deep sea petroleum and natural gas production, underground electricity transmission and distribution systems, and techniques for enhanced recovery of petroleum. However, in the early stages technical advances may fail to lower costs and may even increase them. Problems and difficulties arise, and require solution; learning by doing is a significant development cost. This has been the case with nuclear plants, solar systems and high voltage underground transmission systems.

In general technical progress is uncertain and is not a continuous process. When comparing costs for different technologies, it is hard to be 'fair' in the assumptions to be made about the pace of technical progress along different paths; e.g. will deep sea drilling technology improve faster than the design of pumps for LWR cooling, or than the development of low cost photovoltaic solar cells?

In summary, the way an economist would wish this batch of problems to be handled is as follows. All cost figures should be prepared on common assumptions about the general rate of increase in prices over the life-time of the project, and on common assumptions about rates of interest: there are formal reasons for preferring all calculations to be presented in 'real terms', but it is often difficult to make correct and uniform corrections from money terms to real terms, and economists willingly accept calculations using nominal interest rates and expected inflation rates, provided only that the required assumptions are common to all costs that are being estimated.

No such common basis can be expected for assumptions about technical progress. Necessarily, rates of technical progress vary from sector to sector, and from technology to technology. Moreover – and this is more important – views about the likely pace of technical change in any particular sector differ from observer to observer, and the element of controversy thus introduced is the very stuff of energy economics.

But there are certain guidelines which the informed commentator will strive to observe. In comparison between any two modes of investment or techniques of fuel transformation, he will try to be equally 'optimistic' about relative rates of technical progress. In interpreting past events, he will strive to separate the effects of general inflation from the effects of changes in relative real prices. He will attempt to ensure that the same 'ground rules' (about load factors, rates of physical depreciation, time periods for construction, scale of operation, etc.) are made for the various techniques being compared.

Despite all this striving, the experienced economist will expect to find a systematic difficulty in separating out technical progress from changes in the general level of prices, and in standardising the degree of pessimism or optimism embodied in sets of technical cost forecasts.

11.4   Non-monetary costs

The development and production of fuels and the generation and distribution of electric power impose a wide variety of environmental and social costs on society. These include the deterioration of air and water quality, the emission of low level radiation, scarred and unproductive land, risk of fire, subsidence, accidental risks and aesthetic costs of the loss of unmarred scenery. Their effects are variable and, as discussed in chapter 9, their measurement is difficult. But we need to attempt their assessment so that our estimates of energy costs may reflect not only private costs but also social and environmental costs.

Some of these social costs are already reflected in private costs; because of governmental regulations imposing air and water quality standards; through safety and health measures, land reclamation standards, plant siting restrictions and other measures designed to reduce the environmental and social impacts of energy industries, private costs have been increased. Such regulations result in additional costs for the installation and maintenance of cooling towers, for reduction of stack gas emissions, and the use of higher cost fuels (low sulphur coal, low sulphur oil) to contain pollution. Increased safety standards in construction of nuclear plants are a notable cause for increased private costs.

In this way, environmental and social costs are to some extent gradually incorporated directly into the perceived private costs of producing energy. However, there are limits to the way our system can convert these non-monetary costs into dollars. The incorporation of these costs into profit and loss accounts by only one industry (e.g. the nuclear industry) may distort the process of efficient resource allocation. What would be best is that *all* industries published cost estimates which would include all the costs of all safety or environmental aspects that we, the public, wished to improve. But this is not yet the case.

Further, the uncertain and inadequate knowledge of environmental and social impacts has led to prolonged licensing proceedings. Often, even after plans are agreed upon, they may have to be altered to take new and revised requirements into account. These changes in licensing procedures have increased needs for skilled personnel, and have introduced delays in scheduling which ultimately have led to higher total unit costs. New environmental standards can only push up the financial costs of the energy industries and this effect is increased by uncertainty about the effects of environmental protection measures; this again tends to slow the development of new energy supplies.

11.5 Rent, availability of capital, economies of scale

The availability and the cost of different energy sources will depend on the geographical distribution of resources – the physical accessibility and the country in which resources are located. As exploration and development move into the less accessible regions the costs of development and operation increase. However, the ability to increase production depends on the willingness within the individual country to open new facilities, the lead times in different countries associated with new facilities, the manpower and planning required to train workers, the installation of infrastructure in sparsely populated areas, the extension of transport facilities and the willingness of the different countries to allow the immigration of higher cost labour.

As demand for a fuel increases and supply begins to tighten, the markets move further from the sources of supply, and the costs of transport and storage increase.

The geographical inequalities in the distribution of oil deposits, and possibly also of uranium and coal deposits, raise problems of political economy. The rise in oil prices after 1973 could be said to result from two interrelated phenomena. Firstly there was a conscious attempt by sellers to extract economic rent: any finite resource in inelastic supply and without close short-run substitutes can command economic rent in the market. Secondly, there was an element of monopolistic rent, caused by the restriction of market forces by OPEC. The producing countries became aware of their seller's position in the market and hence combined to extract a *monopolistic*, as well as an *economic*, rent on oil.

In the next few decades the energy industries will require larger shares of the supply of available investment funds. Demand pressures for available capital may be expected from competing financial requirements. In the energy industries, funds will be required for environmental protection, the development of petroleum and coal-associated technologies such as gasification and liquefaction, and recovery of oil from shale and tar sands. In industry as a whole, there will be pressure for the recovery of leaner grades of metallic ores, investment in more energy-efficient and resource-efficient plant and equipment, and investment in increased productive capacity. Social pressures may be expected towards new or improved transport networks, new housing and higher social welfare expenditure.

During the period 1966 to 1970, 15 per cent of gross domestic product in the US was used for capital projects, and of that about one fifth was used for capital purchases of energy systems. Thus energy system capital formation represented 3 per cent of gross domestic product per year, which is about average for most developed countries. It has been estimated that energy system capital formation in the US might rise to about 5 per cent of gross domestic product in 1990 – not a very substantial increase over historical levels (Pelley, Constable and Krupp, 1976).

But this does mean that energy industries will have greatly to increase their call on the capital markets for their investment funds. In the US, the energy industries may require nearly 30 per cent of their capital needs from external sources, somewhat higher than the historical average of 20 per cent (Pelley, Constable and Krupp, 1976). The inability to generate the required new capital funds internally will put additional pressure on the capital markets and may tend to increase the costs of finance. The ability of the energy industries to command their share of the capital market depends on whether the industries are attractive to investors and on the extent to which the rates of return on energy investments are competitive with other investments.

In developing countries, many new energy systems will require large initial investments both for actual construction and for the related infrastructures. Given that the average capital formation rates range from 5 to 15 per cent of GDP in the poorest countries, and 15 to 30 per cent for the more advanced developing countries (Chenery and Syrquin, 1975), most developing countries will be under some pressure to find energy investment, and will need to sacrifice the demands for 'lower priority' capital. It seems likely that energy investment will markedly increase the call on foreign borrowing. Developing countries which rely on a flow of capital from rich countries often find that this flow is not evenly distributed and not smooth. This suggests that financial requirements will be a major constraint on energy investment in developing countries.

During the last few decades economies of scale have helped the energy industries to achieve lower average real costs as total output increased. Economies of scale are conventionally distinguished both from short-run decreasing costs (costs per unit are lower when a plant is used at full capacity than when it is working at under full capacity) and from cost reductions due to technical change (costs are lower from a new plant than from an old one even though both are on the same scale and used to full capacity). Scale economies are measured by comparing the total costs of production from plants of differing capacities but designed by engineers with a shared common stock of technical knowledge.

For example, figure 11.2 illustrates the declining cost curve associated with the choice of larger nuclear power plant; larger units have lower costs per unit of installed capacity than smaller units. In general in the nuclear electricity industry the rule of thumb has been that units of about 1000 MWe were the optimally sized plants and that the effect on costs of increasing size above 1000 MWe was uncertain; whereas in conventional fossil fuel thermal plants the optimal size was at about 600 MWe. Scale economies are realised largely through improved heat transfer rates which enhance efficiency of operation. However, it is debatable whether improvements in heat transfer rates for thermal plants beyond present size are likely without sacrificing reliability. Furthermore, due to the combined effects of the larger size of plant on system reserve requirements and more complex maintenance requirements there may be a limit beyond which economies of scale are not obtainable.

For some fuels the transportation phases of the fuel cycle also exhibit economies of scale. For example, the costs for long distance tanker transport of crude oil indicate that significant economies are achieved as tanker size increases. The cost of transport for crude in 1973/74 from the Middle East to the eastern US falls by more than half for a tanker up to 500,000 tons ($1.50/barrel 1979 prices) as compared to one of 50,000 tons ($3.53/barrel 1979 prices) (Anderson and De Haven, 1975). Thus economies of scale accrue to tankers up to a size of 500,000 tons. However, large deep water ports are required to support the larger size tankers, and the economies of scale in tanker transport cannot be realised without adequate port facilities.

The shift to large size block tankers, whole unit trains, large diameter pipelines, larger size generating capacity, and larger size refinery capacity tended to result in the downward trend in unit costs of energy through most of the 1960s. Whether limits to the achievement of economies of scale in the various phases of the fuel cycle have been reached is uncertain.

11.6   Coal

Since 1950, world coal consumption has increased by 1.5 per cent per year, considerably less than the 4.8 per cent per year increase in the demand for energy,

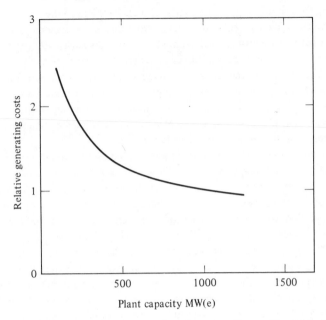

Figure 11.2   Relative generating costs vs. size of reactor. *Source:* Unpublished industry estimate in 1979.

thus indicating the declining popularity of coal relative to that of oil and gas. But this trend is likely to be reversed as the amounts of oil and gas diminish towards the end of this century. The speed with which the reversal takes place will depend in part on the costs of coal relative to other fuels. In its simplest form the cost of coal can be broken down into the costs of mining, preparation, transporting and marketing.

The costs of mining depend on mining recovery factors, which include such factors as mine size, seam thickness, geological setting of the mine, depth of mine (surface or underground), proportion of workers in underground production, ownership patterns restricting access to reserves, and type of mining technique. For surface mines, recovery factors range between 50 and 90 per cent and for underground mines the factors range between 25 and 60 per cent. Other factors affect coal costs: technical ones such as roof conditions, gas emissions, seam gradients and water, and less quantifiable ones such as skill and experience of the labour force. Thus wide bands of costs are evident for coal and can range from double to one half best practice mines (Stanford Research Institute, 1977).

One major development in the coal industry has been the progressive increase of surface mining. In 1973, surface mining in the US was 50 per cent of the national total, whereas surface reserves were only 32 per cent of the US reserves (Gordon,

1975). This increased mining of surface coal is a general trend observed also in the USSR and other countries and is due to the progress of mechanical handling equipment and the increasing reluctance of the labour force to work underground. Surface mining is one of the fastest ways to ease the transition back to coal, but due to technical limits to the depth of operation and land availability we must in the future again rely on underground mining, whether by solid continuous handling or possibly by in-situ gasification.

Illustrative costs of mining coal in the US in both surface and underground mines are given in table 11.1. For both surface and underground mines the general rule applies that the larger the size of the mine, the lower are the unit capital costs and operating costs; and, for underground mines, the thicker seam mines have lower costs per ton of production (Gordon, 1975). Underground mining is more labour intensive than surface mining; labour costs (including welfare funds) typically amount to 50 and 24 per cent of total costs respectively. As most coal resources are deep underground, this suggests that the cost of coal will increase, unless labour productivity in coal mining increases as fast as it does in the economy as whole. The total cost of the average underground mine is about equally divided between the cost of inputs that do not vary and those that do vary with labour productivity. Labour productivity itself is influenced by such factors as seam thickness, gassiness of mines, absolute depth of mine, slope of mine shafts and level of mine output. Of the costs listed, a number will be subject to variability in the future. The bulk of cost variation will be due to changes in wages relative to changes in productivity.

Coal occurs under a wide range of technical, political and geological conditions; in particular, geological conditions, and consequently coal mining costs, vary widely. A number of factors have combined to force up the cost of coal in many developed countries since the early seventies; in addition to labour costs, the main causes are increased costs introduced by new health and safety legislation and pollution regulations. Most observers believe that these factors will lead to increasing real costs in the future.

Coal preparation processes are widely used to reduce sulphur and other impurities, to increase heat content and to produce coal with special chemical and physical properties for specialised markets. The processes include crushing, screening, air cleaning, mechanical dewatering and thermal drying. Just as for coal mining, preparation costs vary widely depending upon location, preparation objectives, degree of upgrading, raw coal quality, water availability, water disposal regulations, and air and water pollution regulations. It is estimated that, on average, coal preparation added about $2 in 1979 dollars to the cost of a ton of coal in the US. About 55 per cent of total US bituminous coal and lignite received some form of cleaning. Furthermore, a higher proportion of underground coal receives some degrees of upgrading than does surface mined coal (Stanford Research Institute, 1977).

Table 11.1.   *Estimated production cost of US western surface mine and deep mined coal (1979 US dollars per ton).*

| | 1974 | | 1978 | | 1982 | |
	Surface	Deep	Surface	Deep	Surface	Deep
Capital	1.20	3.74	1.39	4.40	1.57	5.07
Labour	0.63	5.80	0.84	7.57	0.94	8.48
Union welfare	0.29	1.14	0.57	1.86	0.86	2.14
Supplies	1.01	3.57	1.01	3.57	1.01	3.57
Taxes	0.50	0.21	0.57	0.21	0.64	0.21
Rent and royalty	0.14	0	0.17	0	0.20	0
Total $/ton	3.77	14.46	4.55	17.61	5.22	19.47

Source: Gordon (1975) (updated to 1979 US dollars).

Marketing costs of coal are small as the residential market for coal is likely to decrease and most other coal is sold directly to the major consumers, primarily electric power generation. Transport costs are dependent upon the tariffs of common carriers and the distance to be carried and thus depend upon the distribution of the coal reserves and the markets for coal. Delivered costs rise steadily as coal is moved farther from the supply point. Some estimates in the US indicate that, depending upon the type of coal carried, transport costs per ton increase by 15 to 25 per cent as the distance carried increases from 800 to 1600 miles (Gordon, 1975). Transport costs will further depend upon size of containers, number of destination points, number of source points, efficiency of system, and load factors, and will thus also be subject to a wide band of variability. The use of unit trains, improved loading and unloading schedules, and minimum weight contracts have tended to minimise transport costs. Nevertheless, the markets for coal have tended to be near the mines and, in fact, there is a trend to locate coal-fired electric generating plants near the mine mouth which may reduce the impact of coal transport costs, though this must be balanced against the cost of transporting electricity.

The availability of coal on a global basis will depend on the geographical and national location of individual coal deposits. Most of the factors mentioned above will affect the cost of coal to varying degrees in each potential coal producing country. However, the ability to increase coal production will depend on political and economic decisions regarding the opening up of new deposits and the installation of new mines. Including the time for exploration and exposure of new coal deposits, the lead time for developing surface mines is 3 to 5 years and for underground mines is 10 to 15 years, depending on depth and on the extent of infrastructure already in existence. Any increase in coal production requires the training of mine workers and personnel, the installation of mining infrastructure in sparsely populated areas, the consideration of social and environmental impacts of coal mining and use, the existence of transport facilities from the mine to the inland consumer, and the necessary importing and exporting facilities to accommodate the world trade in coal. All of these underlying problems affect the availability and cost of coal, and are themselves affected by the cost of capital.

In summary, there are upward tendencies in the cost of coal, in real terms; but these are limited by the geographical and geological spread of coal deposits.

11.7   Petroleum and natural gas

There is no single universally accepted forecast of the amount of oil left in the ground. Speculation about the crude oil resource base has become a popular exercise and depends on assumptions about discovery rates, production per exploratory well, efficiency of recovery, accessibility of resources and the technical difficulties associated with the less accessible regions. The extent of recovery depends on pressure in the reservoir, the viscosity of the oil, the nature of the sedimentary rock, and other factors, and thus varies from location to location, well to well. Uncertainties in estimating the world resources and thus the production of petroleum and natural gas are augmented by uncertainties in the costs of discovery, development and production, refining, and transport of petroleum and natural gas.

Exploration for petroleum must go increasingly into more difficult and costly geological areas, although the random nature of the exploration process means that some low-cost wells are found quite late in the life of a petroleum province. Exploration and discovery are necessary in order to prevent long-run operating costs from rising unduly; new deposits, even if they are not initially less expensive to develop and operate than existing deposits, enable operators to avoid a falling reserves to production ratio, which would be likely eventually to increase costs, and save the high costs of further improving recovery factors in old fields. Development costs include the costs of finding the physical potential and the limits of a reservoir, but they are usually dominated by the costs of drilling and equipping production wells. Costs increase as the further development of old fields continues, and, coupled with the declining productivity from installed equipment, the cost per barrel increases.

Until the early 1970s, most investment costs for developing petroleum production showed a downward trend. For example, in the Middle East (in current year dollars) they declined from about $500 per daily barrel in 1960 to about $300 in 1969 (a period when the general price level rose by 12 per cent) (Adelman, 1972). This downward trend in the Persian Gulf, and a similar trend in investment costs per well in the US during this period, was partly due to technological improvements in exploration and drilling techniques, but the downward movement did not occur for all countries and regions. More recently, when development of oil resources began in the less accessible and less traditional regions, such as the Alaskan North

Slope, the North Sea, offshore Venezuela, and offshore in the Atlantic and Pacific United States, both costs for exploration and investment costs for development have been at a very much higher level. In 1979 US dollars, the investment costs in these more difficult areas range from $4,000 to $12,000 per daily barrel in the Alaskan region, and from $2,000 to $9,000 in offshore Venezuela, Atlantic and Pacific United States and in the North Sea.

The real posted price of oil fell between 1960 and 1969, as was discussed in chapter 10, because of the combined effects of improved technology and the nominally-constant tax on Middle East oil – whose real value was eroded by inflation. After 1973 everything changed. The rapid growth in world oil demand had created the conditions for sharp increases in price, while in the US domestic oil prices rose both in response to the higher world oil prices and because of increased reliance on higher cost domestic sources – for example, Alaskan oil. However, rising oil prices and technological improvements have an effect on the recovery factor with which conventional oil resources can be exploited. At present the world average recovery factor for petroleum (the ratio of total oil recovered to total oil in place in proven fields) is estimated to be between 25 and 30 per cent of the total oil in place for all wells in current production; thus more than 70 per cent is left in the ground because its recovery would be too difficult and costly. With technical improvements in advanced recovery methods, coupled with rising oil prices that permit higher cost techniques to be exploited, the world average recovery factor could rise to 40 or 45 per cent. The possible extent of such an improvement is of great importance since it has a major effect on the size of the world's 'ultimately recoverable' oil resources, but it is not known at all well and any more precise estimate could only be made through a major study, requiring extensive international collaboration.

There is no universal method for improving recovery factors – the technique chosen will depend on the nature of the oil reservoir and the quality of the oil, which may be as thin as water or as thick as glue. Possible techniques include steam injection, in-situ fires, and chemical flooding, and their use can add anything from $2 to $20 (in 1979 dollars) to the cost per barrel. Thus the minimum price of oil required to justify these techniques could range from $11 to $16 per barrel for steam drive, and up to $20 to $32 for chemical flooding, if associated with medium to high cost wells.

The price of oil and improvements in technology also have an important bearing on the timing and the rate of development of non-conventional oil resources, namely oil shale, tar sands and heavy oil deposits. Venezuela has very large resources of tar sands and heavy oil, Canada has both tar sands and oil shale, and the US has tar sands and heavy oil together with very large resources of oil shale, and each of these countries is beginning to accelerate their development. Preliminary studies in Venezuela suggest that the development costs per daily barrel from their heavy oil deposits could lie between $5,000 and $10,000 (1979 dollars), with refinery costs per daily barrel in the same range; work in Venezuela is already beginning to move towards the pilot plant stage. In Canada production from tar sands has been under way for some years and production could reach a million barrels per day by the early 1990s; similarly, in the US, development is likely to be rapid over the next two decades. Even though existing processess for recovering non-conventional oil are already economic in some areas, there are very large requirements for investment capital, production units must be large to be economic – perhaps costing $1,000 million to produce 100,000 barrels a day – and lead times are likely to be long. In addition some of the deposits, such as the US oil shale, are located in semi-arid areas, and water resources may prove to be a major constraint using present technology. It should also be recalled that both the costs of improved recovery techniques and of non-conventional oil are 'current' estimates, and historically as the price of oil has risen so have the estimated costs of producing oil by these methods.

Natural gas, like oil, has exhibited an upward movement in price since the early 1970s. This reflects an increase in the economic rent, but it is also associated with increased costs which arise partly because an appreciable fraction of gas is produced in association with oil so its cost is a function of the same factors that have led to increased oil costs. In future, more natural gas is likely to be transported in the form of LNG and incur the associated high transport costs.

The cost of refining crude oil depends on the mix of product produced. Table 11.2 illustrates the importance of refining costs in relation to the other costs that are included by the time the final consumer buys gasoline. The cost of refining is much less than both the cost of distribution and the dealer margin, and it is considerably less than the price of crude. The important point is that the cost of buying crude and the uncertainty about it is much more important than refining costs in the consumer prices of petroleum products.

During the sixties the consumer benefited also from economies of scale in the transport of petroleum, natural gas and LNG. It was during these years that transport shifted to block tankers, whole trains and larger diameter pipelines. As mentioned in section 11.5, freight rates per barrel of crude from the Persian Gulf to the US east coast fall progressively as tanker size increases from 50,000 to 500,000 tons. However, in the early 1970s the growth of oil demand outstripped the availability of efficient large tankers and transport costs increased. Lower growth in oil demand in the late 1970s led to a surplus of oil tankers but the higher cost of their fuel limited the consequent reduction in oil transport costs.

Even though the consumer may potentially benefit from reduced costs due to economies of scale in tankers and in pipeline construction and size, higher unit delivery costs of petroleum or natural gas can still occur as a result of under-utilisation of pipeline and transport facilities. Furthermore, the costs of new pipeline construction need to be included since gathering facilities, as well as offshore pipelines and storage, are continually increasing.

Table 11.2.   *Representative cost breakdown of gasoline in the US in 1976* (expressed in 1979 US dollars).

Cost component	Cost per gallon (cents)
Crude oil	37
Refining	6
Distribution and dealer margin	19
Taxes	19
Total cost to consumer	81

Source: Stanford Research Institute (1977) (updated to 1979 US dollars).

In summary, the costs of producing oil are rising in real terms, but not as fast as the real price has risen since 1973. However, as secondary extraction practices spread, and more difficult sources of oil are tapped, so the costs of extraction rise to meet the price. The owners of 'old' oil sources can grow fat, while newcomers strive competitively at the technological frontiers. But because there is an 'intensive margin' as well as an 'extensive margin' – recovery factors can increase if more money is spent – perceived costs will rise in old fields as well as in new ones. Figure 11.3 illustrates the trends.

11.8   Nuclear

The cost of nuclear energy is determined by the series of activities in which uranium is mined, milled, processed, enriched, fabricated, used in reactors, reprocessed to recover fuel and dispose of wastes – that is the entire nuclear fuel cycle. The dominant component in the cost structure of nuclear energy (shown in the illustrative example in table 11.3) comes from the capital charges, which are due mainly to the cost of the reactor and generating plant. The other important cost factors are the price of uranium, the cost of enrichment, disposal costs, and the cost of reprocessing the spent fuel.

The capital costs reflect the costs of plant construction. As has been discussed in section 11.3, the cost of constructing power plants has greatly surpassed the original estimates. In the US, the cost per kilowatt for a nuclear plant which became operational in 1976 was nearly double that for a plant which became operational in 1970 (Keeny *et al.*, 1977).

Future construction costs will be affected by a number of factors which are subject to considerable variation and uncertainty. One is the problem of scaling from average sized units of 400–800 MWe to 800–1300 MWe, which will ultimately lead to scale economies but initially may suffer teething problems. However, if a number of plants are located at the same site, savings can be realised if the additional plants are of the same type and construction and are built

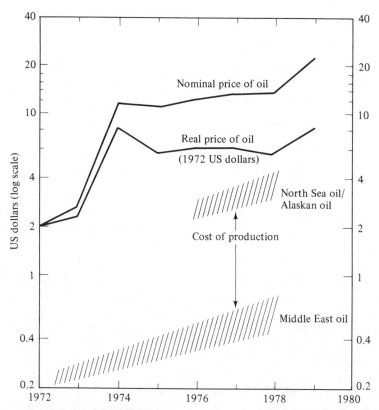

Figure 11.3 The price and cost of crude oil 1972. US dollars per barrel (except for top curve) using an inflation index related to OECD exports (World Bank 1979). *Sources:* World Bank (1979) and authors' estimates.

relatively soon after the first. Changes in the scope of work will significantly affect the reactor costs. In the past these changes were usually the result of design changes due to more stringent safety and environmental standards and were often introduced after construction was begun, thus incurring heavy costs. Such changes result in additional inspection and documentation, increases in engineering manpower, increases in materials such as steel, concrete, and wire; all of which contribute to the increase in labour costs and material costs. As a result of events like the Three Mile Island accident, further changes will no doubt be introduced in existing and planned plants. If construction periods continue to increase above the present 8–10 years, interest charges will become an even larger fraction of plant cost, just as they have in recent years in the US where interest charges have risen from 8 per cent of capital costs for plants becoming operational in 1972 to nearly

Table 11.3. *Projected costs of nuclear generated electricity in the US in 1985* (mills/kWh in 1979 US dollars).

Component	Cost (mills/kWh)
Capital charges	20.5
Operation and maintenance	2.5
U_3O_8	3.1
Conversion to UF_6	0.1
Enrichment	2.5
Fabrication	0.5
Spent fuel storage and disposal	0.5
Total without reprocessing	29.7
Reprocessing	0.3–0.5
Total with reprocessing	30.0–30.2

Source: Authors' estimates based on Barrager *et al.*, (1976), Miller (1976), Anderson and De Haven (1975), Keeny *et al.* (1977).

20 per cent for those scheduled for operation in 1983. Economists will note, however, that increasing rates of inflation, with constant real interest rates, and constant construction periods, will give extra but misleading rises in the relative weight of interest costs (Keeny et al., 1977). Nuclear plant costs will also be subject to variation because of site-specific design differences such as cooling towers instead of offshore diffusers, or seismic design in earthquake zones.

The capacity at which the reactor operates will affect capital charges. The capacity factor or load factor is the ratio of electricity produced during a time period to the amount which would be produced if it operated at full capacity during the whole fixed time period. The higher the capacity factor, the lower the capital charges per kilowatt produced.

The key factor in nuclear *fuel* costs is the cost of uranium. Uranium costs vary with the deposit size, location and technique of production. During the 1950s the capital costs associated with the development of the Canadian uranium industry were estimated at between $34,800 and $36,800 per annual tonne of uranium, exclusive of the cost of related infrastructures. The comparable figure for 1976 at the 1950s price level is about $100,000 per annual tonne of uranium. However, this estimate does not include the costs of the new more stringent environmental, health and safety provisions. According to both Canadian and US experience these may raise the estimate by between 25 and 50 per cent, to nearly $150,000 per annual tonne. Furthermore, over this period non-nuclear fuel and electricity costs nearly tripled, chemical costs doubled, and taxes and royalties increased. Similar increases occurred in the US, and increases of 25 per cent per year have been estimated in South Africa (Foster *et al.*, 1978).

The world price of uranium has responded to these cost movements by rising from $19 per lb of U_3O_8 in 1974 to $25 in 1975, to nearly $50 per lb U_3O_8 in 1976 (each in 1979 dollars; $1 per lb of U_3O_8 = $2.6 per kg U). Note, however, that due to existing long-term contracts the average price for 1976 deliveries in the US was $13.25 per lb U_3O_8 and the range was $12 to $25 per lb U_3O_8. A study by the Dept. of Energy, Mines and Resources in Canada suggests prices could move from 1976 levels to $55 per lb U_3O_8 in 1980, $61 in 1990, $68 in 2000 and $80 in 2020 (each in 1979 dollars) (Foster et al., 1978). These projected increases in cost would increase the cost of nuclear power, but the uranium costs are such a small element of the cost of nuclear based electricity that uncertainty about them should not significantly affect the cost of nuclear power before the year 2000.

The estimate of the enrichment costs in table 11.3 is based on the use of expensive and energy-intensive gaseous diffusion techniques. Considerable progress has been reported on the gas centrifuge technique and the laser enrichment method. If progress continues on these two, the cost and energy requirements of enrichment could fall significantly in the eighties.

In summary, nuclear costs are rising somewhat in real terms, but not as fast as the price of oil.

11.9   Renewables

The 1976 World Energy Conference survey of hydro-electric energy resources indicated that there is a potential of 2.2 TW of installable generating capacity with a possible annual production of 35 EJ (9.7 PWh) of electrical energy. Present installed capacity is about 372 GW producing 5.7 EJ of electrical energy annually, representing about 16% of the world hydro-electric potential. The extent to which this potential is already realised varies from country to country but the largest remaining potential exists in the developing countries (Armstrong, 1978).

Comparative costs of hydro facilities are difficult to generalise because the costs of hydro are highly dependent upon the size of plant and the particular topography of each site. A Bechtel Corporation estimate for the capital cost of a US 200 MW utility in 1974 was $550/kW or $785/kW in 1979 dollars (Bechtel, 1976). A 1977 estimate suggests that the capital cost for new hydro plant is in the range of $800–1500/kW or $1000–2000/kW in 1979 dollars (Armstrong, 1978).

Hydro plant is capital intensive but incurs virtually no fuel costs. After construction the only recurring costs are the indirect and direct operating and maintenance costs, which represent only about 10 per cent of the total cost per kWh. A hydro plant operating at a load factor of 90% and with capital costs of $750/kW and a 7% cost of capital would yield unit output costs of 7.0 mills/kWh; while a plant with capital costs of $1125/kW and a 7% cost of capital would give 9.98 mills/kWh. The most important factors affecting the development of hydro resources in developing countries are the availability of capital coupled with the institutional problems in establishing the international cooperation and agreements needed to develop multi-national water resources. Further, a hydro project involves not only energy supply, but the full range of water resource considerations, such as flood control, navigation, land use, irrigation, wildlife and recreation. Other important factors that can affect the cost of hydro resources are the development of the understanding of hydrology and topography and the development and use of appropriate hydro technology. Since much of the potential hydro resources will require an increase in the use of small generating units, cost-saving improvements in design for small scale local production and use are likely. Further, large hydro projects distant from demand centres are becoming more economic as high voltage transmission of electricity improves.

The status of the technology for a number of the other unconventional or renewable energy sources is summarised in table 11.4. As most of them, even those already in actual use, have scope for substantial technological development, little confidence can be placed on cost estimates. Thus, instead of a detailed economic assessment of each of these unconventional sources, a brief overview is presented by the developments that might influence their long-run costs, and in some cases recent quantitative assessments are given for illustrative purposes. More detailed discussion of the unconventional sources has been presented in chapter 8.

Solar energy is an important primary energy source that is fairly evenly distributed globally and non-depletable, yet the technology to use it widely in a developed country is not yet competitive economically or reliable. To date the systems using solar energy are expensive and capital intensive. Solar energy is well suited to conversion to low temperature heat, but two major problems exist, the mismatch between demand for heat and sunshine and the storage problems. Flat plate solar collectors can be used to provide low temperature heat for water heating, space heating, and even air conditioning; the latter application has the advantage that the demand matches the incidence of sunshine. Other applications include crop-drying, which by its seasonal nature coincides with the incidence of sunshine.

The economics of solar low temperature applications depend upon the location, pattern of demand and the actual system used. Estimates of the cost of an uninstalled flat plate collector for water-heating range from $100/m^2$ to $250/m^2$ (in 1979 dollars), while for solar space heating systems the costs for installed systems range from $250/m^2$ to $600/m^2$ (in 1979 dollars) (Auer et al., 1978). Two studies cited in chapter 8 suggest that in certain contexts solar heating costs compare favourably with electricity but not oil or gas. However, the case for these applications would vary in strength from region to region and country to country. For example, cost reductions might occur in developing countries, where local factor prices are lower, and solar technology might be developed to use the appropriate low-cost local materials and factor inputs.

Another use of solar energy is to generate high temperature heat for electric conversion. Complete solar power systems involve some form of optical concentration, an absorber, a heat transfer system and generator. The economics are uncertain, but in some areas such as southern California the systems may be close to economic feasibility.

Table 11.4. *Status of technology of new energy sources.*

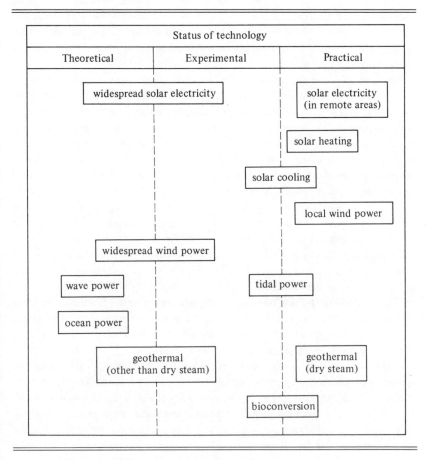

Source: Authors' estimates.

Photovoltaic electricity generation converts sunshine directly into electricity. Photovoltaic cells are made through the same process used by the semi-conductor industry to make transistors and integrated circuits. The main cost uncertainty surrounds the cost of preparing and processing the silicon required for the solar cells. The average commercial price in 1979 was between $15,000 and $25,000 per peak kilowatt, but some recent estimates suggest new installation costs in the range of $3000 to $5000 per peak kilowatt (Maidique, 1979). But, to penetrate the broad consumer market, not just specialised markets, cost reductions by a factor of ten or more are required to make the photovoltaic technique competitive. If continued advances occur in solid state technology, such cost breakthroughs are not impossible. However, the cost to the user of low and high temperature applications of solar energy is only part of the economic calculation. The intermittent nature of solar radiation usually necessitates the installation of a conventional back-up. Thus, the conventional utility would be required to install facilities to accommodate both regular customers and the intermittent demand of those normally satisfied by energy from solar systems.

The cost of wind-generated energy depends upon many factors, the most important being the mean wind-speed. Others include daily and yearly wind-speed variations; accessibility of sites to transmission systems; daily and yearly load demands; the scale of wind generating unit production and the pace of technological development. The use of wind-power for electricity generation appears economic when produced in small units and used in remote locations. This is important in developing countries or isolated farms in developed countries where conventional electric supply is costly and where oil powered machinery is expensive. Wind-power could also increase its contribution as a source of mechanical power for raising water or grinding. However, it does not yet appear economic for large scale generation. Estimates of the cost of aero-generators are scarce and inconsistent in their methods of costing and in distinguishing between costs of development and costs of producing prototypes. For illustration, recent estimates of windmill generator cost run between $285 and $1700 per kilowatt (1979 prices). (UK Dept of Energy, 1977e). To this the costs of storage and integration into the existing power system must be added. The overall economic assessment of wind-power systems will then depend on the type of wind generator selected, the sites available, the costs of supply integration and of any storage system.

One possible energy storage system is provided by living plants, and the organic matter from plants and animals, or biomass, constitutes a source of solar energy. Biomass in its broadest definiton includes agricultural industry wastes, wood, forestry wastes, crop residues, dairy and feedlot manures, crops grown specifically as energy feedstocks and municipal solid wastes. The most ambitious biomass programme exists in Brazil where sugar cane is grown for conversion into alcohol which is then either combined as a 80% petrol/20% alcohol mixture for use as motor fuel in ordinary vehicles, or used as an exclusive fuel in converted or newly designed vehicles. It is estimated that a litre of cane alcohol will cost about 26 US cents in the mid-eighties (or 98 US cents per US gallon). Similar experiments are being attempted in the US with wheat crop residues.

Wood for heating is widespread and is economic in the US, Western Europe and other areas where conditions are favourable. Even wood for electricity generation is becoming economic in those areas where wood and forestry wastes are abundant. For example, a utility in Burlington, Vermont in the US generates one third of its electricity with pelletised wood in wood burners (Maidique, 1979). Similarly, other crop wastes are used to raise steam for electricity generation: in Hawaii sugar cane residues provide about 20 per cent of the utility power on the island (Maidique,

1979). Another possibility is the anaerobic production of methane from manure, which is economic in many developing countries, though often limited by the availability of capital.

Geothermal energy can be used for electric power generation from geothermal steam or water and, where site-specific conditions allow, for space heating or process heat. Other forms such as geopressurised areas and hot rock areas (without associated water or steam) are more speculative in their potential. Little can be said about the economics of geothermal energy. Some sites are economic at present and others may become so as fossil fuel prices rise. Little is known of the effectiveness of techniques to capture the hot rock or geopressurised resources. Costs are expected to decline as techniques improve, but will differ substantially from site to site.

11.10   Electricity

The cost of electricity to the final consumer is a function of many variables. The most commonly used division of costs is three-fold: (1) maximum demand or capacity costs that vary with the quantity of plant and equipment for generation, transmission and distribution and the associated investment that consists primarily of capital costs (return on investment, taxes and depreciation); (2) energy or output costs that vary with the quantity of kilowatt hours produced, and are made up of fuel and labour costs; and (3) customer costs that vary with the number of customers served and include the metering, billing, distribution, collection and accounting costs.

This three-fold division of costs applies to the activities in the electricity generation cycle, which include generation, transmission, distribution, administration and environmental protection. Table 11.5 analyses the long-run marginal costs of electricity by component activity and compares them with historical average costs for the US. The estimated future cost increases are a function of increasing fuel costs, construction costs and interest charges.

Generation costs account for nearly half of the average total cost of electricity supply and depend on the type of equipment used. They can be divided into four categories: (1) capital costs; (2) indirect operating costs (rent, rates, overheads); (3) direct operating costs (wages, repairs, maintenance); (4) fuel costs. Capital and indirect costs depend on maximum demand, whereas the direct operating and fuel costs depend on total electricity used. The costs for different forms of electricity generation are compared in table 11.6. The capital component depends on initial construction costs, plant capacity factor and the required rate of return. Fuel costs are a relatively minor element for hydro and nuclear plants, but they are a major item for coal, oil, and gas fired plants. Future generation costs will therefore depend on movements in construction and fuel costs, and interest charges, and on changes in the mix of generating plants in the system.

Table 11.5   *The costs of electricity service in the US* (mills/kW in 1979 US dollars).

Function	Future long-run marginal cost	Average historical cost
Generation	12.9–30.3	11.3–11.7
Transmission	2.4–7.0	2.6
Distribution	8.6–17.1	5.7
Other	2.9	2.4
Environment	5.7–12.1	included in generation
Total	32.5–69.4	22.0–22.4

Source: Anderson and De Haven (1975) (updated to 1979 US dollars).

Since about three quarters of the cost of electricity generated from nuclear power arises from capital charges, a 10 per cent increase in the latter would raise the cost of the electricity by about 8 per cent. However, only about half of the costs of coal-based power are due to capital costs, so a 10 per cent increase in these would raise the cost of coal-based electricity by only 5 per cent. Increases or decreases in the capacity factor (or load factor) produce changes in the cost of electricity similar to those due to movements in capital costs. Thus the fuel cost advantage of nuclear power over coal, illustrated in table 11.6, would be reduced if a lower load factor had been assumed for the nuclear plant (this question is discussed further in chapters 5 and 7; see especially tables 7.9 and 7.10).

The transmission and distribution costs shown in table 11.5 both contain maximum demand, energy, and customer-related cost elements. Over the past twenty-five years, transmission capacity in the US has grown in line with generating capacity and average circuit size has nearly quadrupled. This reflects considerable economies of scale due to the use of higher transmission voltages, the concentration of power demands at load centres, and the growth in the average size of generating plants. The movement in future transmission costs will depend on increases from greater transmission distances, partly compensated for by decreases due to the use of higher voltages, and on the extent to which underground transmission replaces overhead lines, thereby increasing costs. However, transmission requirements represent only a relatively small share of total electricity costs. Distribution costs are more important. Investment in distribution is similar in quantity, and historically in the US has followed closely, investment in generating capacity. As more metering is introduced to the consumer, and as underground systems replace overhead ones, the investment costs for distribution will increase. Thus, capital charges, load densities, capacities, and technology, will all influence the future movements in distribution costs and are likely to have a significant effect on the total cost of electricity. The other major cost component shown in table 11.5 comes from systems required for meeting environmental regulations, for example

Table 11.6. *Comparison of costs of electricity generation in the US and UK in 1974 (expressed in 1979 US dollars).*

	Capital		Indirect costs		Direct costs		Fuel	Total
	$/kW	mills/kWh	$/kW/yr	mills/kWh	$/kW/yr	mills/kWh	mills/kWh	mills/kWh
Hydro	1000–1850	14–26	0.40	0.13	2.3–5.4	0.3–0.8	—	14.4–26.9
Nuclear	500–835	7–12.1	13.3–18.4	1.9–2.6	13.3–20.0	1.8–2.9	5.0–6.7	15.8–24.3
Coal	340–500	7.6–11.4	3.5–3.7	0.7–0.9	6.7–10.0	1.6–2.3	10.7	20.6–25.3
Oil	300–400	6.9–9.1	3.3–3.7	0.7–0.9	5.0–10.0	1.1–2.3	20.4	29.7–32.7
Gas	200–300	7.6–11.4	3.3–3.7	0.7–0.9	5.0–6.7	1.9–2.6	5.0–26.7	15.2–41.6

Notes: (1) Capital depreciated at 10 per cent per annum. (2) Nuclear and hydro load factors at 80 per cent. (3) Coal and oil load factors at 50 per cent. (4) Gas turbine load factors at 30 per cent.
Sources: Bechtel (1976) (updated to 1979 US dollars); author's estimates.

to control emissions of sulphur dioxide and oxides of nitrogen, which are likely to lead to future increases in costs of electricity.

11.11   Chapter summary

The final consumer is primarily concerned with the quality and cost of a delivered unit of energy, and this depends on the associated capital and operating costs over the entire cycle arising for each fuel or energy carrier – mining, processing and/or conversion, transport, storage, distribution, and disposal. The costs of any one source or form of energy depend on the technology, scale factors, density of demand, etc. The costs of energy are imperfectly known, even for energy technologies that are in current use, and there is uncertainty about how they will change in the future.

During the 1950s and 1960s the energy industries operated under conditions where there were decreasing costs. Economies of scale and improvements in technology outpaced the relatively low inflation during the period. However the picture changed in the 1970s and some energy costs increased rapidly. Apart from inflation, the rising *real* costs were due to sharp increases in the economic rent for petroleum, which forced up prices and stimulated production from high cost sources, and, to a lesser extent, to increased requirements for environmental protection, and to a higher cost of capital. Coal costs have increased in the 1970s in the US as a result of new safety regulations, environmental controls, and higher labour costs. The upward trend may continue until the lower costs of surface mining and improved technologies make an impact, though this could be reduced through higher economic rent taken in the form of taxes in producing areas.

The upward trend in petroleum costs is expected to continue, as the high prices due to OPEC controls and to scarcity encourage the increased use of advanced recovery methods, the development of more difficult areas, and the exploitation of unconventional resources, such as tar sands, heavy oil, and shale oil deposits. The cost of associated gas production is influenced by the same factors as petroleum, and gas transport costs are expected to rise due to its movement to major markets from increasingly remote areas.

The costs of nuclear power are dominated by the capital costs of the reactor and generating plant. Other important cost factors are the price of uranium, the cost of enrichment, and the costs of disposal and reprocessing of spent fuel. Nuclear power has been affected by severe capital cost escalation due in part to delays in construction schedules and to changing safety and environmental regulations. These may moderate in the future but the uncertainties about them remain large.

Hydro-electric power has been developed on a large scale in both developed and developing countries, though the latter retain great potential for further expansion. Its cost depends on location, size of plant, topography of the site and area, interest rates, etc. Most other renewable energy sources, with the exception of non-

Table 11.7.   *Estimated energy production costs (1979 US dollars)* (excludes taxation, refining, storage, transmission and distribution costs).

Source	1979 US dollars per barrel of oil equivalent
Indigenous coal (US)	3–5
Imported coal (NW Europe)	8–14
Indigenous coal (NW Europe)	10–15
Middle East oil	0.25–1.00
North Sea oil and Alaskan oil	7–12
Other United States oil	3–7
Nuclear input break-even value[a]	7–11
Low BTU gas from indigenous coal (US)	19–25
LNG imports	10–23
Synthetic natural gas from indigenous coal (US)	23–35
Liquids from coal (US)	30–37
Liquids from imported coal (NW Europe)	30–44
Liquids from oil sands	15–25
Liquids from shale	15–35
Biomass (crops for fuel) as liquid	30–60
Solar hot water (35 degree latitude)	50–130

[a]The fuel input cost required for fossil-fueled plants to produce electricity at the same cost as nuclear plant.
Source: Authors' estimates.

commercial energy (wood-fuel and farm waste) used in developing countries, are still in early stages of development. Their costs are uncertain even for those already in (small scale) use, though, where local conditions are favourable, some solar low-temperature systems, small scale wind-power, and certain biomass applications, appear to have costs comparable with those for conventional fuels.

The future cost of electricity will be influenced by increasing fuel costs, higher construction costs, arising partly from higher safety and environmental standards, and possibly by slower improvements in technology, but the character and extent of any increase in future generation costs will depend on the mix of generating plant that is installed. A comparison of estimated costs of energy from a variety of different sources or conversion routes is shown in table 11.7. Further increases in the price of oil, and improvements in technology, should cause changes so that more of the higher-cost sources move towards the margin of choice.

Chapter 11   Further reading

Adelman, M. A. (1972) *The world petroleum market,* Johns Hopkins University Press, Baltimore and London.
Anderson, K. P. and De Haven, J. C. (1975) *The long run marginal costs of energy, Report to the US National Science Foundation, Rand, Santa Monica, California.*

Armstrong, E. L. (1978) 'Hydraulic resources' in *Renewable energy resources*, Full report to the Conservation Commission of the World Energy Conference, IPC Science and Technology Press, Guildford, UK.

Auer, P. *et al.* (1978) 'Unconventional energy resources' in *Renewable energy resources*, Full report to the Conservation Commission of the World Energy Conference, IPC Science and Technology Press, Guildford, UK.

Foster, J. *et al.* (1978) *Nuclear resources*, Full report to the conservation Commission of the World Energy Conference, IPC Science and Technology Press, Guildford, UK.

Gordon, R. L. (1978) *Coal in the US energy market*, Heath, Lexington, Mass.

International Energy Agency (IEA) (1978b) *Steam coal – prospects to 2000*, OECD, Paris

Keeny, S. M. *et al.* (1977) *Nuclear power: issues and choices*, Ballinger, Cambridge, Mass.

Miller, S. (1976) *The economics of nuclear and coal power*, Praeger, New York.

UK Department of Energy (1976) *North Sea costs escalation study, Energy Paper no. 7*, HMSO, London.

Energy conservation

12.1 Conservation and energy efficiencies

Energy conservation involves the following interrelated sets of problems:

1. The optimal choice of primary energy sources and assessment of their rates of depletion so as to conserve those resources whose scarcity could lead to adverse social or economic effects.
2. The avoidance of unnecessary waste of energy.
3. Technological or managerial changes leading to improvements in the efficiency with which energy is used.
4. Changes towards alternative products or alternative patterns of demand that reduce the rate of energy consumption.

Discussions on energy conservation are often concerned primarily with the second and third of these aspects of energy conservation, though the more efficient use of energy cannot be fully discussed without some consideration of energy supply and demand for manufactured products. Questions about energy supply are considered in other chapters, but the impact on energy efficiencies of interfuel substitution is an important facet of energy conservation and will be considered in this chapter. The demand for manufactured products and the changing pattern of demand forms part of the wider question of changing lifestyles. This is clearly of great importance in the long term, but it seems that lifestyles in relation to energy demand change only slowly except under conditions of extreme stress or scarcity. Historical studies discussed in chapter 2 suggest that the relation between energy demand and economic activity changes only slowly compared with alterations in the pattern of fuel consumption or the pattern of demand for goods. However, although it would be difficult to establish on a quantitative basis, one cannot rule out the possibility suggested by advocates of a change in lifestyle that rapid changes may be possible and/or necessary as a result of the coincidence of many factors of which energy is one.

Fuel scarcity leads to higher prices or rationing of the scarce fuel. It is often convenient to distinguish three aspects of the social response:

1. Doing without, in the sense of lowering standards of comfort or convenience.
2. Using energy more efficiently so as to achieve higher standards for a given consumption of energy.
3. Interfuel substitution to permit an alternative fuel to replace the scarce fuel,

with or without a loss of amenity or a gain in efficiency. Thus the substitution of coal for wood in UK households in the seventeenth century involved a loss of amenity, though similar substitution in industry at a later stage led to greater efficiencies.

Energy conservation represents only one aspect of the optimal allocation and use of resources, and it can rarely be considered in isolation from other resource problems. In general, measures for energy conservation involve costs as well as benefits, which may sometimes be economic and sometimes social. A significant part of the problem of energy conservation is the assessment of these costs and benefits. The difficulty of the task is compounded by the fact that decisions relating to energy may determine lifestyles and the pattern of energy use far into the future. In order to move towards a better understanding of the future and the potential for energy conservation one must begin by seeking to understand the past.

Energy conservation is largely concerned with more efficient and more careful use of energy. This is not necessarily limited to seeking methods for using less energy though this could be regarded as the first of several objectives, provided the methods are adequately assessed in terms of costs and benefits or other value judgments. Other objectives may include wider questions concerning the efficient use of energy, in which it may be found that in some circumstances a higher rate for using energy may be beneficial. Thus it might be desirable to save energy in one area but use more in another if such a re-allocation brought sufficient benefits.

Although the overall efficiency of energy utilisation should be kept in mind it will be necessary to take a less global view in practice, if only because the decision makers who may cause changes have responsibility only in limited areas, whether it be in households, in industry, or in government. A useful starting point for energy conservation could be the technical efficiency of fuel utilisation, but here there is also a wide choice of definitions and the choice appropriate to a decision maker must be selected. There are technical ambiguities in defining the heating value in fuel, but these are less important than wider questions concerned with definition of the system in which the energy is used. For example:

> Energy efficiency may refer to the energy input and output of equipment such as a coal fire for space heating, a boiler for central heating, an electric water heater, or an internal combustion engine. This definition may be appropriate for comparing equipment having the same type of energy input (coal or electricity, etc.) and a similiar function, but it is necessary also to consider the cost of the energy if one heater has a coal input and another an electrical input.

> In physical terms, energy efficiency may refer to equipment in a larger system. Thus a coal-fired central heating boiler may be regarded as a subsystem in which a more significant measure of efficiency is given by the energy to heat the building, and the options of changing other aspects of the building design should then also be considered. The efficiency of an electric water heater should be considered in a wider

context that includes conversion and distribution losses for the supply of electricity, and also includes the benefits of convenience and flexibility if these can be quantified. For the motor car, the system efficiency includes the effects of energy losses in the tyres as well as those in the engine, and wind conditions as well as consequences of the weight and power of the car and the number of passengers.

When equipment does not have energy conversion as its dominant function energy efficiency must be considered in relation to the overall use of resources associated with the equipment. This is obviously necessary also when an energy conversion device is considered in a wider context, for example, in relation to industrial output, or in relation to modal changes in transport, or in relation to heating and thermal insulation of buildings. The amount of energy used is one of the parameters whose variation may provide an option for improving the system. The more efficient use of energy is rarely the most important option available, but its achievement can often yield important benefits.

Decisions on the use of energy often involve long lead times before they take effect. This means that efficiency in energy utilisation should refer not only to the present but also to future consumption and future costs and benefits. For example, the regulations concerning thermal insulation for new houses should take into consideration the future possibility (appropriately discounted) that electricity for space heating may be in common use towards the end of the century although at the present time cheaper methods for space heating are available.

12.2   Assessing energy inputs

One of the objectives of a study of energy conservation is to find out whether energy can be saved by doing things differently. This requires assessment of the energy inputs associated with each option. The term 'energy inputs' (sometimes confusingly called 'energy costs') refers to the amount of energy used in a particular process, or in the manufacture of a certain product, or for some other specified purposes (Slesser, 1974). By 'energy accounting' one can seek to establish the energy inputs for the manufacture of one tonne of aluminium ingot, or the energy inputs for making an automobile, or the comparative energy inputs for manufacturing aluminium cans or plastic containers.

A knowledge of energy inputs for a wide range of products and a wide variety of processes is useful in comparing efficiencies in the use of energy and indicates options for saving energy. It can also help in assessing the economic impact on processes or products of a change in energy supply or in fuel prices, thus permitting better economic optimisation in the use of energy. It may also assist in forecasting changes in energy demand that would be consequent on changes in the pattern of production or of consumer demand.

Energy inputs are not fully defined either for a product or a process unless all the contributing processes that are to be included are specified. The best choice of the contributing processes (or the boundaries of the systems to be analysed) depends on the purposes for which knowledge of the energy inputs is required.

Other points that need to be made clear include: the choice of the calorific values for fuels used (which may be actual values or average or conventional values), the assumptions about the conversion efficiencies of the supply industries in converting from primary fuels to secondary forms of energy, the conventions that are used for partitioning energy inputs between different products of the same-energy-using process or plant, and the full specification of the product.

Methods for assessing energy inputs include statistical analysis, input–output methods and process analysis.

Statistical analysis

This can be used to give an idea of energy inputs only in particular circumstances, for example, in an industry where the product is reasonably homogeneous and where the main energy consuming processes are covered by the aggregated statistical data. Thus energy inputs for automobile production cannot be obtained from data on the automobile industry alone but must also take account of the energy inputs for steel and other raw materials purchased by the industry. However, the cement industry normally processes its own raw materials and has a fairly homogeneous product. In the UK in 1973, the cement industry used a net energy (heat supplied) total of 134 million GJ to produce 20 million tonnes of cement, and neglecting minor products or activities by the industry one can deduce an approximate figure of 6.7 GJ/tonne as the energy input for cement production. However, this figure is based on net energy input for which electricity is treated on a heat supplied basis. If this input is replaced by the primary energy for producing the electricity used, the figure becomes 7.7 GJ/tonne. Industrial sources quote an average figure of 5.65 GJ/tonne of cement in 1973 of which 0.4 GJ was electrical energy. Using primary energy inputs leads to a total of 6.7 GJ per tonne which is in reasonable agreement with the figure obtained from statistical data. The difference is probably due to 'overheads' such as heating of office buildings and energy for ancillary activities by the industry that are included in the statistics but are not directly related to the manufacture of cement.

Input–output analysis

Input–output tables give the values of the goods provided to each industrial sector by other industrial sectors. Thus they can be used, for example, to give the total directly purchased energy used in a given year by the iron and steel industry and obtained from each of the energy supply industries – coal, oil, gas and electricity. The average quantity of each fuel that is used per tonne of iron and steel produced can then be calculated from the value of the energy purchased, the average price of each fuel, and the total quantity of iron and steel produced. Using standard techniques the input–output table can also be used to obtain the direct plus the indirect purchases of energy, and hence the direct plus indirect energy required per unit of output. For example, the energy used for manufacturing a motor car would be dominated by the indirect use of energy that is required for producing the iron and steel that are used in making motor cars.

The method has several limitations however. A high level of aggregation is used in input–output tables so the industrial output usually involves a multitude of different products – such as motor cars and trucks with other engineering products. Also, the tables refer to financial costs of energy which cannot always be readily converted to physical quantities of energy since the prices of energy to each industrial consumer may not be known very accurately. Further, the tables relate to the last census of production which may be some years ago, so they do not provide up-to-date information, particularly where there has been significant interfuel substitution, for example to natural gas in the UK.

Process analysis

Process analysis involves detailed 'in factory' studies of the energy used at each stage of manufacturing a product. For example, in the production of aluminium ingots it could involve evaluating the energy used for mining bauxite, for conversion of the bauxite to alumina, and for smelting to give the ingots. Alternatively the quantity of relevant interest to the manufacturer might exclude that used for mining if his own material input is bauxite, or exclude the energy used to convert the bauxite to alumina if his own raw material is alumina. On the other hand the energy analyst might wish to enlarge the system considered so as to include the energy lost when producing the electricity that is used in very large quantities for smelting aluminium. The chain of direct and indirect processes relating to a product needs to be specified and the energy inputs identified and apportioned between multiple products. The disadvantages of assessing energy inputs by process analysis arise from the amount of detail required, which may involve wide variations between different equipment or alternative means of production, and from the fact that detailed information of the type required is often not available in a suitable form – for example, because of inadequate metering of the flows of energy. An advantage of this detailed approach is that the study of a factory will itself bring to light inefficient practices in the use of energy and indicate opportunities for saving energy – often by changes that involve very little investment cost in relation to the energy savings that could be achieved.

Some illustrative examples of energy inputs required for various manufactured products are given in table 12.1. These figures relate to production and they do not necessarily reflect the overall energy efficiency including the end-use of the material. For example, a lighter material (aluminium instead of steel) used in a transport vehicle may save more energy ultimately than a heavier material that

Table 12.1.   *Estimated energy inputs for the production of certain materials.*

Material	GJ/tonne	tonne oil equivalent per tonne
Magnesium[a]	300–360	7–8
Aluminium[a]	240–320	5–7.5
Recycled aluminium	20–45	0.5–1.0
Steel (bulk)	25–35	0.5–0.8
Copper[a b]	50–100	1–2
Recycled copper	(approx.) 10	(approx.) 0.2
Glass	25–50	0.5–1.0
Paper	10–20	0.2–0.4
Plastics:[c]		
polythene	90	2
polyester fibre	220	5

[a]These figures are particularly sensitive to assumptions about electricity conversion efficiencies.
[b]Energy for copper depends strongly on the percentage of copper in the ore.
[c]'Plastics' energies include approximately 1 kg oil equivalent per kg for the energy content of the petrochemical feedstock.
Source: Eden (1974).

required less energy for its production. Similarly a plastic bottle may be only one fifth of the weight of a glass bottle of similar capacity, so the manufacture of the former may require less energy than the latter. The importance of recycling is illustrated for copper and aluminium in table 12.1. These recycled metals require less than 20 per cent of the energy required for virgin metals. Figures for recycled metal often include scrap that is created by the industry during the manufacture of products and which may itself represent an energy-wasteful practice. Therefore caution needs to be exercised by distinguishing between energy saved through recycling finished products that have been fully utilised and recyling internally produced scrap metal. The financial costs of recycling end products need to be carefully assessed in relation to energy savings – if they are high there may be more effective ways of using other resources with a view to saving energy.

12.3   Energy efficiencies

In this section we shall discuss energy conversion efficiencies in different economic sectors with a primary emphasis on thermodynamic efficiencies rather than economic efficiencies. The former may be used to find out whether energy can be saved and, if so, how much, whereas the latter will indicate whether and how much of this potential energy saving is worth carrying out in relation to the costs in terms of other resources. The simplest use of thermodynamic efficiency relates to a single device such as the heat engine discussed in chapter 1. In that case the efficiency was defined as the ratio of the energy of the work output divided by the energy of the heat input. There are two qualitatively different ways in which this definition may be generalised, namely by extending the system boundary or by changing the definition of efficiency.

The boundary of the system being considered may be extended whilst retaining the energy/energy definition of efficiency. Thus instead of considering the efficiency of the single device (car engine or domestic boiler, for example), one could extend the system boundary 'upstream' to include the conversion from primary energy to the specific fuel used by the device. Additionally one could extend the boundary 'downstream' to include other loss mechanisms (this has pitfalls: in most instances all energy is ultimately lost to the environment and 'efficiency' dwindles to an unhelpful zero if the system boundary is unduly wide).

Alternatively the definition of energy efficiency may be changed to the 'energy required to fulfil a purpose'. The latter may not be quantitative. For example, with the same physical system transport efficiency could be discussed in terms of energy per passenger mile, or this could be compared for different systems such as transport by road, rail or air.

The thermodynamic efficiency of a gasoline engine may be in the range 15 to 25 per cent, but if by widening the system boundary the 80–90 per cent efficiency for converting crude oil to gasoline is also included the overall efficiency would be about 13 to 22 per cent. Similarly an electric vehicle with rechargeable batteries may convert electricity to work at 65 per cent efficiency but if the electricity is derived from fossil fuel at 30 per cent conversion the overall efficiency would drop to 20 per cent. A saving of fossil fuel could, of course, be achieved by the use of electric cars if the major part of the electricity was generated by hydro or nuclear power.

Using a more general interpretation of efficiency in transport, energy could be saved by increasing the load factor (average occupancy) in a car, for example by using car pools, though this may involve some loss of personal freedom. Similarly an increased load factor for a truck or lorry may save energy, but this needs to be balanced against other costs such as extra time delays in the transport of goods. The costs and benefits of energy that could be saved through modal changes, such as from road to rail or road to bicycle, are more complex. For passenger traffic this may involve lifestyle changes where costs and benefits are hard to compare. For freight the choice is usually between road and road–rail–road transport, and the road systems near rail terminals may be an important factor in making the choice.

The development of diesel powered locomotives to replace coal-fired steam engines brought dramatic improvements in the efficiency of rail transport, partly from better engine efficiencies but also very significantly from their greater operational flexibility. This improvement is illustrated for the UK in table 12.2.

In the household and commercial sector, the efficiencies of heating equipment may range from about 30 per cent for an open coal fire to about 70 per cent for a

Table 12.2.   *Rail transport energy and activity in the UK 1960–75.*

	1960	1965	1975
Rail energy consumption (PJ)[a]	335	165	84
Passenger km (10^9)	31	30	30
Ton km (10^9)	30	25	24

[a]Primary energy equivalent (includes conversion losses).
Source: UK Department of Energy (1972, 1976); UK Department of the Environment (1961; 1966; 1976).

coal, oil or gas fired boiler, or up to nearly 100 per cent for a radiant electric fire. The overall efficiency falls if primary energy conversion is included, and for electric heating it could be 30 per cent or less. In practice, fossil fuel heating systems rarely operate at optimum conditions since their load factor varies with temperature and climate. Losses due to intermittent operation may reduce efficiencies on central heating systems to 50 per cent or less during parts of the year.

Improvements in the operation of domestic heating and other equipment are of obvious importance, but it is often suggested that even greater gains could come from improved thermal insulation of buildings and draught proofing or more carefully controlled ventilation. Widening the system boundary further there is the possibility of using the combined generation of heat and power, though (as discussed in chapter 7) this will save energy only when there is a consistently satisfactory balance over the day and the year between demand for heat and demand for electricity.

The energy supplied to households in the UK during 1960–75 provides an interesting case of energy conservation where the benefit from improved efficiencies was taken in the form of improved standards of comfort rather than through a reduction in the energy consumed. The number of households increased by over 20 per cent but there was almost no change in the energy used on a heat supplied basis, though primary energy requirements increased by 23 per cent, the difference being due mainly to a rapid increase in electrical heating and the consequent additional conversion losses. As can be seen from table 12.3, this was a period of rapid interfuel substitution, and an associated rapid turnover in household equipment, particularly in the replacement of open coal fires by more efficient heaters and/or central heating systems. Additional energy savings resulted from improvements in the insulation and draught-proofing of new dwellings compared with those that they replaced.

Historical improvements in the efficiencies with which energy is used in industry may be assessed either in physical terms such as the energy requirements to produce a tonne of steel, or in financial terms such as industrial energy used per dollar of value added. The former is illustrated in table 12.4 with data from the UK

Table 12.3. *Energy used by UK households* (petajoules (PJ)).

Fuel	1960(PJ)	1975(PJ)	Average annual percentage growth 1960–75
Solid fuel	1192	459	−(6.2)
Town gas	137	52 ⎱	10.6
Natural gas	—	569 ⎰	
Oil	71	151	5.2
Electricity	121	321	6.7
Net energy total	1520	1552	0.1
Electricity conversion losses	327^a	714^b	5.3
Primary energy total	1847	2266	1.4
Million households	16.0	19.1	0.4

^{a}Assuming 27 per cent conversion efficiency.
^{b}Assuming 31 per cent conversion efficiency.
Source: UK Department of Energy (1972, 1976); UK Central Statistical Office (1961, 1976).

steel industry, which maintained an average annual improvement of 1.5 per cent in the energy used per tonne of crude steel in the period 1960–72. The improved efficiency in the use of energy for steelmaking in the UK was due to technological improvements at all stages, largely resulting from new equipment, and to the use of an increasing fraction of high grade imported iron ore instead of the lower grade indigenous one.

Overall improvement in industrial energy use in relation to value added is shown for the US in table 12.5. This table also gives the average cost of fossil fuel in the US, and it is apparent that in the period 1947–70, when the average real (deflated) price of energy fell by a total of 32 per cent, there was also a fall of 26 per cent in the energy used by industry for each dollar of value added. This suggests that following the more recent large increases in the real price of energy there may be considerable potential for further and more rapid improvements in energy efficiencies. However, it is in general easier to improve the technical efficiencies at relatively early stages in the development of new technologies, and in some areas current practices may be asymptotically approaching their best values. For example, the average system efficiency of electricity generation from fossil fuel in the UK more than doubled from below 10 per cent in 1920 to 20 per cent in 1938, but it took 36 years to achieve a further increase by a factor 1½ to 30 per cent in 1974. The corresponding efficiency for the US was 22 per cent in 1948 rising to 33 per cent by 1974. Substantial technical improvements of this type are implicit in historical data on energy and economic growth and, when assessing the potential

Table 12.4. *Trends in energy for steelmaking in the UK.*

	1960	1972
Crude steel production 10^6 tonnes	24.7	25.3
Net energy supplied PJ	768	623
Gross energy including electricity losses PJ	846	718
Specific net energy for crude steel GJ/tonne	31.1	24.6
Specific energy for crude steel including electricity losses GJ/tonne	34.2	28.4
Average ratio finished steel to crude steel	0.731	0.734
Specific energy for finished steel including electricity losses GJ/tonne	46.8	38.7

Source: Eden (1974).

Table 12.5. *Industrial energy–output ratio and average fossil fuel prices (USA).*

	1950	1960	1970	1974
Industrial energy use (EJ) (including chemical feedstock)	12.9	15.9	22.4	23.4
Value added in manufacturing 10^9 (1972)[a]	199	260	394	444
Energy–output ratio MJ per dollar (1972)	65	61	57	53
Average US price of fossil fuel: dollars per GJ				
Current dollars	0.25	0.28	0.29	0.71
Deflated (1972)	0.46	0.41	0.32	0.66

[a]Value added in 1958 dollars converted to 1972 dollars by factor 1.51.
Source: US Dept. of Interior (1976).

for future energy conservation, it is useful to recall that continued gains in technical and economic efficiencies are required merely to maintain energy–output ratios on their trend lines or curves.

12.4   Decision making on energy conservation

It is convenient to consider two classes of measures in energy conservation:
1. Measures that are economic at present energy prices.
2. Measures that take account of potential problems of energy scarcity such as future price increases, or adverse economic or social consequences of such a scarcity.

The first class includes measures that are clearly in the interest of the decision maker using his own preferred discount rate. The obstacles are often lack of knowledge about these measures, coupled with the uncertainty about the likely benefits from them, but they are also commonly associated with inability or unwillingness to devote the management effort required for carrying through the necessary actions, whether these be improved insulation in a house, new heating systems for an apartment building, or heat recovery in a factory. In such situations, intervention by a third party may be beneficial. Government action through housing regulations could ensure at least that new dwellings are constructed to achieve a good level of cost effective energy conservation taking account of the discount rate that is appropriate to an average householder, and possibly with some allowance for future increases in the real price of energy. Similar results could be achieved in principle by taxing energy use. An oil company providing oil for heating to an apartment building could provide energy management services to give a better heat balance in the building at relatively little cost and share the resulting energy savings with the tenants or occupiers (such procedures are in use in France). In general the company's profit on the energy savings could significantly exceed their lost profit on lower sales, and both company and occupier would benefit. Such a system would be more difficult for individual dwellings due to management overheads and possible changes in consumer behaviour. For an industrial establishment the related 'easy' energy conservation could be achieved by appointing an energy manager full time or part time, or in the case of a large company an energy management team.

The dilemma in decision making is illustrated semi-quantitatively in table 12.6, which compares approximate payback periods for various conservation measures with the perceived time horizon and the equipment lifetime.

In addition to the problems of lack of knowledge and of management time, two further obstacles to energy conservation, justifiable with present practices and present prices, can be identified. These are, firstly, divided decision making, for example where the owner or manager of a building makes decisions about capital expenditure but the tenant meets the energy costs and would achieve the benefits from energy savings, and, secondly, the wide variation between discount rates that are in practice used in connection with energy conservation. A small industrial establishment for example, will commonly require a one year payback on investment for energy savings and will rarely accept more than a two year payback, unless energy costs are a substantial fraction of the firm's total costs; such a payback period is likely to be obtained only for very basic conservation measures. A major industrial firm, on the other hand, would expect between ten and twenty per cent real return on an investment, and provided it is moderately energy intensive it would normally apply the same discount rate to investment for energy conservation, allowing it to undertake more advanced conservation measures requiring higher capital investment. Householders can rarely obtain better than a ten per cent real rate of return on an investment, and if taxes on investment income and

Table 12.6. *Payback time, subjective time horizon and equipment lifetime for various conservation measures.*

Conservation measure	Pay-back time (years)	Subjective time horizon (years)	Equipment lifetime (years)
Industry			
Good housekeeping	1–3	1–2	n.a.
Heat recovery	2–10	2–4	15
Residential			
Improved gas appliances	1–3	2–4	12
Improved central heating	1–4	2–4	12
Insulation	3–10	2–4	25
Thermostats	3–10	2–4	25
Double glazing	10–20	2–4	25
Highly insulated new house	5–15	5–10	25
Private cars	3–5	1–3	8

Note: The 'subjective time horizon' is the period over which the user would like to recover this type of investment.
Source: Author's qualitative estimates based in part on a report on *Energy efficiency* by Shell International (1979).

inflation are both taken account of he will commonly get a zero rate of return, at least in the UK. Householders would therefore be expected to accept a long payback period, particularly if the investment made is fully reflected in the market value of the house, and thus investment in energy conservation should be attractive to the householder. The favourable position in the domestic sector is further strengthened by the possibility that the householder may do the necessary work himself, without counting the cost of his own time. The installing of some forms of insulation, for example, is straightforward and can often provide much better than a ten per cent real return. Governments have their own attitudes to discount rates – see section 1.4.

Governments may intervene to alleviate some of the problems and to assist energy conservation but it is far from clear where the optimal intervention lies. If judged purely from the best national return from a given investment, government money spent encouraging (by subsidy if necessary) industry to take action to implement measures having a quick payback would come high in the list. Politically this is difficult, since it appears to involve subsidies for actions that are already profitable (on subsidies in general, see section 17.4). If intervention was through regulations or inspection it could involve more bureaucracy and losses in management time that significantly reduce the benefits. On the other hand, government intervention in rented accommodation to ensure minimum standards of house insulation or heating improvement may be politically attractive even though it gives a lower rate of return.

In most countries energy prices are subject to government intervention to some degree, and this can have a major effect on energy conservation, encouraging it through taxation or discouraging it through price controls. Governments may take the view that a high level of oil imports presents a strategic risk or an economic risk, particularly if a world oil scarcity, temporary or long term, led to a sharp rise in world oil prices. Since the development of alternative energy sources and of energy conservation has long lead times, a sudden rise in world oil prices is unlikely to give a short-term fall in demand except through reduced economic growth. This may be induced at least in part by problems in re-cycling oil payments. It may seem preferable for individual governments to tax oil consumption, since this involves only an internal transfer of resources, rather than wait until the world oil price increases due to scarcity. This policy has been followed in most consuming countries through a tax on gasoline. However, it is equally important in many oil exporting countries to conserve energy through restraining internal consumption, either to increase export potential or to conserve their resources. Unfortunately, in oil exporting developing countries gasoline prices are preserved like sacred cows, just as in developed countries fuel prices to the household market are included amongst those sacred cows not to be disturbed by political action.

Thus in the short- to medium-term future energy prices, often linked to oil prices, are doubly uncertain through market forces responding to disturbance or to anticipated scarcity, and through the vagaries of political intervention. In the longer term, perhaps ten years or more from now, there seems very little doubt that energy prices will be higher in real terms, both through higher costs and higher taxes on primary energy and through an increasing need for converting from primary to more convenient forms of secondary energy such as electricity, synthetic gas from coal, and synthetic oil from coal. It may therefore be prudent to anticipate these changes and reduce their potential impact by taking action in advance. This applies at all levels, governmental, commercial and industrial, and individual.

What then can be done? Governments can provide information and advice on measures for energy conservation. They can initiate price trends for energy and taxation on energy that will in due course reflect long-term costs. Governments can set regulations and standards for buildings and energy-using equipment, particularly where the market may be unresponsive, as with automobiles. Equipment manufacturers should recognise the enhanced value of their product if it uses energy efficiently, and householders and builders should respond to the added value of dwellings having a reduced energy consumption obtained by a 'technical fix' rather than by deprivation of the occupants. Better insulation is an obvious measure that is relatively cheap if installed at construction stage, but with governmental assistance on a rolling programme, district by district, it would also be cost-effective on many other buildings. Improved controls are important both in dwellings and in equipment, and the advent of cheap microprocessors should make sophisticated control systems economically viable even with small energy-using systems.

12.5   Conservation and interfuel substitution

The higher per capita energy consumption in developed countries means that over the next few decades, as world population and energy demand increases, there will need to be major changes in the pattern of fuel consumption. An increasing fraction of the oil barrel will go to transport and petrochemicals, since for these uses the cost penalties of turning to fuels alternative to oil are high. The non-premium uses of oil, particularly bulk steam raising, will increasingly be met by coal. This can be expected to happen first where there is convenient access to cheap coal, as in the western coal areas of the United States, and in some parts of North America, Europe and Japan where cheap coal can be brought by sea direct to the industrial site or power station where it is to be used. The availability of coal at higher costs will be important in the longer term though there may be a significant period, perhaps as much as a decade or more, when the availability of cheap world traded coal from places such as Australia, Southern Africa, Indonesia and Colombia, and possibly some from the United States, will moderate any increase in the prices of heavy fuel oil so that it remains competitive with higher cost coal in Western Europe and in the eastern United States. Similarly, the high cost of shipping liquefied natural gas from areas where it is plentiful such as the Middle East may mean that for a time some oil may be converted to synthetic gas to supplement dwindling supplies of natural gas, before the period when it becomes clearly economic to make gas from coal.

In addition to these constraints on the rate of market penetration of coal that arise from differential costs of coal for steam raising, the rate of penetration will be limited by equipment replacement. It will rarely be economic for oil-fired boilers to be replaced by coal-fired boilers except near the end of the efficient life-time of the former. Replacement of equipment tends to be faster during periods of high economic growth; thus under high growth conditions we may expect more rapid interfuel substitution which may partly compensate for the additional pressures on oil supplies that would arise from the faster growth in energy demand associated with higher economic growth.

At the other end of the market, premium fuels such as light oil or natural gas may also be expected to increase in price. In the medium to long term the real price of electricity should be stabilised in regions that have access to cheap coal either locally or on the world market, and in regions where a substantial fraction of electricity is generated by hydro or by nuclear power. This suggests that electricity will increasingly penetrate the quality end of the heating market though in some areas it will be in competition with LNG and SNG, though these will be priced at levels considerably above the traditional prices for natural gas.

In the transport market, owing to the high component of tax in the price of fuel, future prices depend more on national taxation policies than on the world price of oil. However, balance of payments problems will become more serious if the world price of oil rises relative to prices of other traded goods. This will encourage many governments to increase the taxation on gasoline and diesel oil. In anticipation of such developments automobile and truck manufacturers may be expected to continue the current trend towards more efficient vehicles. In some countries, as in the United States, mandatory targets may be set for efficiencies of vehicle fleets. From these influences the average efficiencies of automobiles in the year 2000 may be double those in 1973 in North America, and they may increase by 50 per cent elsewhere. At these efficiencies there should be sufficient supplies of oil available on the world market for most transport to continue to be based on petroleum products for many decades into the future. The main period of transition to electric vehicles will depend on a breakthrough in battery technology. Electric vehicles based on re-chargeable batteries can scarcely take a significant share of the market until the year 2000, and they may be further delayed by a breakthrough in the use of fuel cells to convert petroleum products directly to electric power for vehicles, which could substantially improve efficiencies and further extend the use of petroleum products for transport.

12.6   Potential for energy conservation

The potential for energy conservation can be estimated in a variety of ways by econometric analysis, activity analysis or through a mixture of these approaches. The meaning of various estimates can be defined only in relation to the methods used, but their general objective is to assess how much future energy demand may (or could) fall below some trend curve. The trend curve for energy demand would normally be calculated from assumptions about future economic growth, assuming also that energy–income relations in the future are the same as those in the past. Typically, it is thought that the energy conservation response in the five years following the 1973 oil crisis may have been between 6 and 12 per cent of total energy demand for a developed country. Thus demand is 88 to 94 per cent of what it would have been on a trend curve that already includes the effects of lower economic growth. Similarly, estimates may suggest energy savings of 15 to 30 per cent by the year 2000. In this section we will outline the main techniques used for such estimates and note some of the ambiguities and uncertainties that should be associated with their conclusions. For an outline of the basic economic principles involved, and examples of the use of the techniques suggested, see sections 1.4 and 2.5.

Econometric analysis that makes use of historical data on energy demand, income or industrial production, and energy prices, will in principle give a precise estimate of the energy conservation that will result from higher energy prices. The trend curve can be defined in terms of a future in which real prices of energy remain constant, say at 1972 levels. Then projected demand curves can be calculated using the same assumptions about future economic growth but with actual price increases plus assumed future price changes. In this context energy conservation would mean simply the changes in energy demand expected from higher prices. Then if real prices of energy doubled by the year 2000 compared with 1972 and if the price elasticity was 0.4, the actual demand would be $(2)^{-(0.4)}$ times the demand given by the trend, which is 76 per cent of the trend. In practice, there is considerable doubt about both future energy prices and price elasticities, and there would be delayed responses since some types of energy-using equipment may not be modified or replaced for many years. Price changes, price elasticities (short run or long run) and lead times will be different in different economic sectors and countries. In addition, rates of replacement of equipment depend on economic growth, so it is not correct to assume that price responses are independent of assumptions about economic growth. Thus instead of a precise calculation such as that indicated above, it is more likely that econometric methods would suggest short-term price elasticities of between 0.1 and 0.3 and long-term price elasticities between 0.4 and 0.8. Then, depending on when the price changes took place, a doubling of average real prices of energy to consumers by the year 2000 (medium-term) might lead to savings of between 15 and 30 per cent in that year compared with the trend figure, and perhaps 20 to 40 per cent in the longer-term future.

These uncertainties using econometric methods may be reduced in particular cases where good historical information is available but there are also some more general doubts relating to saturation of demand, changing lifestyles and government intervention, each of which may lead to future changes in energy–income elasticities. Such changes are evident during the process of industrialisation and were discussed and illustrated in chapter 2. They may also be significant during a post-industrialisation period of adjustment, particularly if there is an increasing awareness of the need to husband the world's energy resources. Some of these problems may be clarified by estimating future energy demand using activity analysis.

The use of energy in transport can be related explicitly to activities. For example, the total annual use of energy by a fleet of automobiles is (their total number) × (the average distance (km) driven by one automobile in one year) × (the average energy used per kilometre). Estimates for future years can be made for the number of automobiles, allowing for saturation of ownership levels, and of mileage trends and fuel consumption efficiencies. These estimates may take account of changes in incomes and prices, and also of technical improvements in vehicles, possibly in response to government regulations rather than prices, and of changes in lifestyles that may affect the estimates. Similar estimates of future energy demand can be made for other activities, including energy use in the domestic sector. Thus the energy for heating dwellings might be estimated from a product of six factors, namely;

(number of dwellings) × (mean floor area per dwelling) × (heat loss per degree day per unit floor area) × (degree days to maintain comfort level) divided by (efficiency of household heating equipment) × (efficiency for conversion of primary energy to energy delivered to the dwelling). There are several possible sources of error in estimating energy demand through activity analysis. Firstly, since there are several factors multiplied together, it is not difficult to build in an exceptional level of conservation by estimating each factor optimistically. Although no single factor can be shown to be unreasonable the total effect may be unlikely. Secondly, detailed historical data on activity levels and their relation to energy demand may be inadequate for statistical analysis, thus leaving undue scope for judgmental errors. Thirdly, it is difficult to relate activities to overall economic growth in a consistent manner, particularly in the long term when changes in life styles may develop. Other difficulties arise from the uncertainties associated with the rates and extent of market penetration of energy conserving technologies and their relation to assumptions about future energy prices. Finally, in the industrial sector there is inadequate information for the direct use of physical activities, except in a few industries such as iron and steel. If econometric methods are used, based on energy per unit value of production, long-run trends are required and price elasticities are rarely known well. If specific energy conservation technologies are used to estimate potential energy savings, there are problems of market penetration in relation to energy prices and discount rates for capital investments, and there are problems of double counting since historically there have been major improvements in the technical efficiencies with which industry uses energy. Estimates of energy conservation made by activity analysis fall into the same range as those indicated above from econometric methods, namely between 15 and 30 per cent by the year 2000 if real energy prices double, and 20 to 40 per cent at a later stage.

The importance of energy conservation

The complexities of energy conservation and the uncertainties that surround any estimations of how much will be achieved should not be allowed to divert attention from its importance. Conservation can make valuable contributions to the standard of living, economic growth and the quality of life. In the home the efficient use of energy can help reduce fuel bills and improve the standards of heating, in transport it can reduce fuel consumption or give more mileage for the same cost, in industry it can make useful contributions to overall effectiveness in the use of resources. From a national viewpoint energy conservation can help the balance of payments through a reduction in energy imports, or through permitting extra exports, or it can allow the retention of reserves for use in the future. Conservation is important internationally because it will help reduce the need to use increasingly scarce or costly energy resources, and will help ameliorate energy and economic crises that may arise from time to time through periods of energy scarcity and sudden changes in the prices of internationally traded energy. From a global viewpoint, energy conservation is essential so that continued economic growth can give rising standards of life throughout the world and so that the period of dependence on irreplaceable energy resources can be extended to provide enough time for a satisfactory transition towards future dependence on renewable energy sources.

12.7   Chapter summary

Energy conservation represents only one aspect of the optimal allocation and use of resources and it can rarely be considered in isolation from other resource problems. It is therefore necessary to examine costs as well as benefits from saving energy, though this need not imply acceptance of conventional cost accounting. Social costs may not be so readily quantifiable but they form an essential part of the assessment of the benefits or the disbenefits from saving energy.

Energy scarcity or anticipation of scarcity may lead to higher energy prices, or changes in the differential between prices of fuels from different energy sources, and perhaps cause rationing of some fuels. It is often convenient to distinguish three types of energy conservation:

1. Using less energy by lowering standards;
2. Using less energy by increasing efficiencies;
3. Using less of a particular fuel by substituting one that costs more or is less convenient.

In practice all three responses play a role and much of the chapter is concerned with questions about their interpretation and implementation. The first section of the chapter concludes with a brief discussion of the problem of drawing boundaries to a system whose energy efficiency is to be considered.

The second section takes up this problem in more detail from the technical viewpoint of 'energy accounting', and considers how 'energy inputs' may be defined and used in discussing energy efficiencies. Methods include statistical analysis, input–output analysis, and process analysis, each of which may have special advantages or disadvantages that depend on the objective of the analysis. This section concludes with some examples of energy inputs for the production of certain materials.

The major part of the next section is concerned with the efficiency of energy use. Efficiencies are discussed and examples given for energy conversion in transport, in housing and commercial buildings, and in industry. These include engine efficiencies in transport vehicles, rolling efficiencies, load factors and modal efficiencies including the influence of changed electronic communication systems on transport energy demand. In buildings, energy efficiencies may include not only the efficiencies of appliances but the conversion efficiencies in power stations or refineries to provide the secondary energy used in such appliances. Building system efficiencies may be extended from questions of insulation and ventilation to questions of life-style and urban and regional patterns of development. Industrial energy conservation ranges from energy saving through good housekeeping measures and proper maintenance of equipment, to redesign of equipment and changes in the end products. No single measure can be adequate to measure energy efficiencies, and final choices will depend on an assessment of overall costs and benefits including, for example, both the use of energy in relation to value added and the quality of the environment in which the workforce operates.

The problems of decision making on measures for energy conservation are discussed in the next section, which distinguishes between measures that are clearly economic at the present time, and those that may be or may become economic if future scarcity of energy or particular fuels is fully taken into account. The widely varying criteria of different decision makers is noted, ranging from those for a landlord who may bear the capital cost of improved house insulation to those of a tenant who may be bearing the current cost of high fuel bills. The role of government is examined particularly in relation to energy pricing and the different criteria that may be important to a country or a community and those that would affect individual decisions on energy conservation. In the fifth section of the chapter these questions are extended to include interfuel substitution where governments may retard or accelerate market trends by price controls or by taxation. The long lead times for substantial changes in many aspects of national energy consumption provide both opportunities and risks through government involvement. The next section discusses the problem of estimating future energy conservation and illustrates the uncertainty of two methods, one based on econometric techniques and the second on analysis of the energy used for specific activities.

Chapter 12   Further Reading

American Institute of Physics (1975) *Efficient use of energy (a physics perspective)*, Conference Proceedings No. 25, American Institute of Physics, New York.

Blackmore, D. R. and Thomas A. (eds.) (1977) *Fuel economy of the gasoline engine*, Macmillan, London.

Dryden, I. G. C. (ed.) (1975)*The efficient use of energy*, IPC Science and Technology Press, Guildford, UK.

Energy and Buildings (Journal) (1978), vol. 1 no. 3, April 1978 (Princeton issue), Elsevier Sequoia, Lausanne, Switzerland.

Ford Foundation Energy Policy Project (1974) *A time to choose: America's energy future*, Ballinger, Cambridge, Mass.

Leach, G. *et al.* (1979) *A low energy strategy for the UK*, Science Reviews Ltd, London.

Lyle, O. (1947) *The efficient use of steam*, HMSO, London.

NEDO (1974) *Energy conservation in the United Kingdom*, report prepared by Dr. R. J. Eden for the National Economic Development Office, HMSO, London.

Newman, D. K. and Day, D. (1975) *The American energy consumer*, Ballinger, Cambridge, Mass.

Shell International (1979) *Energy efficiency* (report by A. Beijdorff), Group Planning, Shell International, London.

Socolow, R. H. (1977) 'The coming age of conservation' in *Annual Review of Energy*, vol. 2, pp. 239–89.

UK Building Research Establishment (1975) *Energy conservation: a study of energy consumption in buildings and possible means of energy saving in housing* (CP56/75), Building Research Establishment, Garston, Watford, UK

UK Department of Energy (1979b) *Energy technologies for the United Kingdom (vol. I and vol. II), Energy Paper no. 39*, HMSO, London.

UK Department of Energy (1979c) report by the Advisory Council on Energy Conservation *Energy Paper no. 40*, (this also lists earlier UK reports on energy conservation), HMSO, London.

UK Department of Industry (1977–79) *Energy Audit Series*, 1. Iron casting industry, 2. Building brick industry, 3. Dairy industry, 4. Bulk refractories industry, 5. glass industry, 6. Aluminium industry.

UK Department of Industry (1978–79) *Industrial Energy Thrift Series* (reports on energy use in industry), Department of Industry, London.

US National Academy of Engineering (1978) *US energy prospects (an engineering viewpoint)*, National Academy of Sciences, Washington, DC.

Watt Committee on Energy (1978) *The rational use of energy*, Watt Committee, 1 Birdcage Walk, London.

Williams, R. H., ed. (1975) *The energy conservation papers*, Ballinger, Cambridge, Mass.

Energy models and forecasts

13.1 Approaches to energy modelling

It is widely, but not universally, accepted that Governments have some responsibility to manage energy supply and demand in the long run. Their strategies may influence energy activities also in the short run, for example through regulations and prices, or through incentives for energy conservation. However, both the long-run and short-run development of energy demand will be strongly influenced by the level of economic activity and hence both by the world economic picture and by the economic policies of Governments. Conversely, if there is a major disturbance in energy supply leading to scarcity and higher prices, this could lead to a significant reduction in the levels of economic activity and economic growth. For example, the experience in the United States in 1973–74 has been analysed by the Brookings Institution (Fried and Schultz, 1975): oil supplies fell by just over a third for six months (about 15 per cent of total energy supplies) and the average price paid for energy increased by about 50 per cent (money terms). The effect over the following years depends on the assumptions used but was estimated to be a loss of between 1½ and 2 per cent of GDP and a decrease in employment of similar magnitude. In the world as a whole, it was three years before oil consumption regained its 1973 levels, though this effect was due not only to the rise in oil prices but also to the changed level of economic activity, which can be attributed partially to the problems arising from the new oil prices.

One of the key questions, with which we are concerned in this chapter and the next, is whether there may in the future be physical shortages of oil and possibly (because of long lead times) of other forms of energy, and whether these shortages could give rise to severe economic disruption on a global scale. It is certainly possible to develop a picture of future energy scarcity whose disruptive effects on the world economy could be more severe and long lived than those experienced in the period 1973–77. However, if the circumstances that may lead to such an energy crisis can be identified in advance, it is not only possible that governments can plan to avoid an energy shortage or at least reduce its impact, but it is also possible that the market would anticipate the problems through changes in prices based on expectations of future scarcity. The question that we ask is whether such expectations by the market and action by governments will take place in time so that there can be a smooth transition from economic growth based on cheap oil to growth based on other energy sources: more about this in chapter 16.

In this chapter we shall outline various types of model used for projecting energy demand, giving alternative scenarios for energy demand and supply based on different assumptions about economic growth and the levels of energy conservation that might be achieved. We define a *scenario* as any projection of energy demand and supply that is internally consistent within a stated set of assumptions. A scenario must correspond to a feasible development of the world energy picture but we emphasise that a scenario is not a forecast but is conditional on the assumptions from which it is derived. In chapter 14 we will discuss alternative energy prospects in the context of different scenarios, both from the global viewpoint and from national or regional viewpoints.

Energy models
There is no single or simple way to classify energy models but in order to illustrate their range and variety we will briefly discuss five different types of model:

(i) Energy/economic models which model the relationship between energy demand and the whole (national) economy.

(ii) Optimising models concerned with optimal allocation of fuels within a sector of the economy, or within the economy as a whole.

(iii) Industry models that are concerned with the supply and demand relationships for individual fuels or for electricity.

(iv) Sectoral demand models that analyse potential energy demand in particular economic sectors such as transport, housing and industry, or subsectors of these markets.

(v) Energy system models that provide an integrated picture of supply and demand for all energy sources.

Hoffman and Wood (1976) have provided a useful review of energy models in the above classes.

In each of the above groups, both activity or engineering process models and econometric models may be used. Thus an economic model or an econometric analysis could project the number of vehicles or vehicle miles corresponding to the scenario assumptions, and engineering analysis could be used to estimate future energy requirements per vehicle mile.

(i) *Energy/economic models* in their simplest form may represent total energy demand as a function of GNP and the price of energy. Individual countries often form economic units that are too small for energy–GNP relationships to remain stable even when averaged over a period of several years. Long-run averages, particularly for groups of countries, show more stable relations and it is found that energy growth and GNP growth are similar when averaged over long periods – we discussed some results in chapter 2, and return to the uncertainties of energy – price and energy – income elasticities in a later section of this chapter.

At a more detailed level most national economic models will contain explicit reference to economic activity in the energy sector and some may be designed to relate energy demand to other economic activities. For example, Hudson and Jorgenson (1974) have developed a macroeconomic growth model for the United States economy integrated with an interindustry energy model. The latter is based on a nine sector classification of US industrial activity – 5 energy producing sectors and 4 energy using sectors.

The sector output prices and the demand for consumption goods from the growth model are used as inputs to a model of consumer behaviour that determines the distribution of total consumer demand to the nine producing sectors. Given these final demands, the input – output coefficients may be used to determine the industry production levels required to support a given level and distribution of real demand. Thus the Hudson and Jorgenson model has been used to forecast long-term developments in energy markets within the framework of a consistent forecast of macroeconomic and interindustry activity.

(ii) *Optimising models* concerned with optimal allocation of particular fuels relate to part of energy supply and/or part of demand. For example, supply models based on the processes involved have been extensively developed for the analysis of oil refining and transportation operations. These methods are used extensively by oil companies, and have been generalised to give global allocation models. An example of such a global model is that developed by Deam and collaborators (1974). This model includes 25 geographical areas, 52 types of crude oil, 22 refining centres and 6 types of transporting tankers. The model determines the optimal allocation and routing of crude oil and products between sources, refineries and demand centres at a given future date. It also determines the requirements for new production facilities, tankers and refineries to meet the future demand. The model contains the costs for shipping and refining different crude oils, and can therefore also be used to analyse the relative prices of these crude oils either in a competitive market or in a controlled market. Other types of model for energy supply are reviewed in Pindyck (1979b). Optimising models can also be used to analyse the economy as a whole, such as the ETA model developed by Manne (1976).

(iii) *Industry models* are directed primarily towards planning industrial expansion or change and studying the effects of regulatory policy. Much of the modelling in this area involves a combination of process techniques on the supply side with econometric methods for assessing possible future demand. This is illustrated in a review by Anderson (1972) of models used in the electricity supply industry. In the electricity industry optimisation models, the demands for electricity and costs of fuels and facilities are usually exogenous inputs, and the models are used to select the least cost investment to satisfy increased demands. The output may include the specification of the type of plants to be built (nuclear, coal, oil, hydro, gas turbine, etc.), the location of plants and the timing of their replacement, or the optimal scheduling of plants on daily, weekly or seasonal basis. The input for such models requires an estimate of sectoral energy demand.

(iv) *Sectoral demand models* seek to project energy demand in particular economic sectors such as the transport, industry, domestic housing, etc. The projections may be based mainly on past econometric data, possibly including some allowance for saturation in the use of automobiles or appliances. In general they will also depend on exogenous assumptions about future economic growth and future prices and relative prices of fuels or energy carriers. Both future economic growth and future energy prices are uncertain, and the scenario method described later in this chapter is essential for obtaining alternative projections. Moreover, the relation between energy demand for a particular fuel, and income or GNP and prices requires explicitly or implicitly an estimation of the appropriate elasticities (see chapter 2 and UK Department of Energy 1977c). The recognition of the uncertainty of estimates of future demand is essential for the proper use of demand models. The merit of modelling is that it clarifies the process of decision making and helps to separate components of a problem that can be quantified and discussed analytically (possibly including estimates of the degree of uncertainty and the penalties of wrong decisions) from those parts of the problem that cannot be usefully quantified and require judgemental decisions. A more detailed account of the sectoral demand method is given in a report by the UK Department of Energy (1978b) and in Leach (1979).

(v) *Energy system models,* including supply and demand sectors as well as all fuels and energy carriers, were stimulated largely by the need to develop forecasts of total energy demand aggregated by fuel under conditions where the (indigenous) supply potential for individual fuels may lead to constraints on the pattern of demand. Thus in the United States the expectation and subsequent fact of the rapid increase in petroleum imports during the 1970s led to models giving US energy balances that could be used to study alternative energy policies (for example Dupree and West, 1972). The energy balance methodology is employed to develop scenarios (and sometimes forecasts) in the following way:

> Estimates of demand are made for each of the major end use sectors by relating demand to assumptions about aggregate economic activity (GNP) and trends in energy consumption, together with trends or preferences for the use of particular fuels or energy carriers in each sector. These estimates assume or imply a knowledge of energy prices and the various elasticities for energy demand. Independent estimates are made on similar price assumptions of (indigenous) supply potential for the various energy types and are compared with the demand estimates, after allowing for the energy consumption by the energy industries and in the conversion process from primary energy input to the secondary fuel or electricity that constitutes the final consumer demand. Differences are

resolved by assuming sufficient imports or exports to close the gap between supply and demand for primary fuels. Some adjustment of the demand or supply projections may be necessary since imports (for example of natural gas in liquid form) may be much more expensive than alternative indigenous or imported fuels; these adjustments are often carried out judgementally.

For a world model it is necessary for individual fuels to maintain a balance between total supply and total demand, and a series of adjustments may be necessary, such as those described later in this chapter for fuel substitution in a world energy model.

More detailed energy system models may evaluate the flows of energy along fuel conversion and utilisation process routes in more detail than is given by an energy balance table. This additional detail may permit costs of the energy systems to be estimated within the model and to compare costs associated with alternative energy technologies. The reference energy system approach is a model of this type and was developed for the United States by Hoffman and Palmedo (1972) and extended to give a linear programming optimising model by Hoffman and Cherniavsky (1974).

13.2   World energy studies

At the time of writing (1979) two of the more substantial studies of the world energy outlook are those by the Workshop on Alternative Energy Strategies (WAES, 1977a) and the World Energy Conference (WEC, 1978B), in both of which the authors of this book participated.

The WAES study is for the World Outside Comecon and China (WOCC) and is based on input from 14 national teams from countries that together consume about 80 per cent of the energy used in WOCC, or about 56 per cent of total world consumption. The supply studies were made by subgroups in the collaboration, and the World Bank assisted with projections of energy demand for developing countries not amongst the WAES group. The global (WOCC) picture obtained by addition of national energy supply and demand projections led to an 'energy balance table' which contained 'gaps' between projected demand and supply in the year 2000 for high economic growth. The 'gap' was particularly significant in the case of oil demand, where the sum of individual national estimates exceeded the estimates of potential supply by some 30 per cent by the year 2000, and in one case studied it was suggested that the oil shortfall could begin around 1980. Total energy demand also exceeded estimated supply but the difference, although indicative of possible difficulties, was not large enough to be so significant as that for oil demand and supply.

The World Energy Conference study (WEC, 1978b) was carried out by separate resources groups who prepared projections for the potential supply from different energy sources to the year 2020, and an energy demand group, who projected world energy demand for the same period and developed scenarios giving approximately consistent energy balance tables. The programme was coordinated by an international group, the Conservation Commission of the WEC, for whom one of the authors acted as Consultant and also led the demand study (Eden *et al.*, 1978), which was carried out by members of the Energy Research Group in the Cavendish Laboratory of the University of Cambridge.

The WEC study presented several scenarios corresponding to different assumptions about economic growth and levels of achievement in energy conservation. The general conclusion was that world energy demand in the year 2020 would be likely to increase to between 3 and 4 times the consumption in the mid 1970s if average economic growth is between 3.0 and 4.1 per cent per annum (compared with 3.6 per cent p.a. for 1925–75) and there are vigorous and successful measures for energy conservation. Even with vigorous conservation, there would be an increased demand for all forms of energy, including particularly large increases in coal and nuclear power. The supply situation now appears less favourable than in 1977 when the WEC report was prepared. In the OECD most nuclear power programmes have been substantially reduced, and coal production is receiving less stimulus from increased demand than is required for long-term requirements. In OPEC it seems likely that oil production will be more severely constrained by a desire to conserve resources for the future than had been anticipated by the WEC study.

With all these factors in mind we have chosen to illustrate the world energy outlook by means of variants around a 'median growth' scenario which is not very different from the low growth scenario that was used for our WEC projections of energy demand. The median projection is *not* a forecast since at best it described a smooth trend rather than fluctuating growth with peaks and troughs. It will, however, be used as a reference case, for which some of the basic problems can be illustrated, and from which various alternative scenarios can be derived and discussed so as to demonstrate the essential uncertainties. The next two sections will outline the projection methods firstly for demand and then for supply but emphasising their close dependence on each other. This is followed by illustrative projections of demand and supply in the median case and a discussion of the uncertainties.

13.3   Projecting energy demand

The model used to prepare projections of world energy demand for the World Energy Conference was developed to give a framework for discussing alternative supply – demand balances that is conceptually fairly simple and consistent with available data. It is essentially heuristic and does not assume or seek to derive detailed parameters such as relative energy prices or cross-elasticities – thus it necessarily lacks the formal elegance of some of the more academic models, and at many points relies on informed judgement.

The main steps or stages in preparing projections are:

1. Make scenario assumptions, including future economic growth in different world regions.
2. Derive activity levels in each major economic sector for the world regions, either using physical activities or economic output levels.
3. Prepare base year energy balance tables and relate each activity to energy consumption. Assume future changes or improvements in the energy-activity relations, thus deriving future sectoral energy demand.
4. Allocate energy demand in each sector amongst different fuels using an interfuel substitution model that takes account of expected rates of market penetration, relative prices, indigenous supplies and conversion potential in each region, and ability to import.
5. Calculate requirements for energy conversion in each region, and obtain total primary energy demand for each fuel or energy source.
6. Estimate ranges for potential indigenous supplies for each fuel in each world region, make an allocation for the region's own use, and derive a range for required imports or possible exports.
7. Obtain total world demand for each primary fuel by adding demand for the regions and compare with the ranges for total potential supply. If total demand exceeds the potential supply for any fuel, revise step (4) by changing the pattern of interfuel substitution (implicitly changing relative fuel prices), but keeping within reasonable rates of change. If the total primary energy demand exceeds the total potential supply, revise step (3) by reducing energy – activity ratios (implicitly increasing average energy prices), but keeping within reasonable rates of change.
8. If the revisions in step (7) do not yield a reasonable supply – demand balance for each fuel, revise step (1) by reducing the assumed rates for economic growth either globally or for those regions that appear to encounter the most severe energy import problems. This forms a new 'averaged' scenario. It is possible that the original scenario could remain realistic until near the period of fuel scarcity and that the adjustment could take place through an energy crisis and a recession, as during 1973–75. Indeed this may be the standard 'mechanism' of adjustment to different patterns of fuel demand. The averaged scenarios would then represent a 'trend line' drawn through a period of varying energy demand, consequential upon unsteady economic growth.

The projections are based on the eleven world regions listed in table 13.1, which are aggregated into three groups, OECD, centrally planned, developing, in order to give simple summaries of the main assumptions and results.

The median scenario is based on average world economic growth of 3.4 per cent per annum from 1975 to 2000 which may be compared with 2.6 per cent from 1925 to 50 and 4.6 per cent from 1950 to 75. Further details are given later in table 13.5.

Table 13.1. *WEC world regions and groups.*

Group	Region
OECD (1, 2, 3)	1. North America
	2. West Europe
	3. Japan, Australia, New Zealand
CP (4, 5)	4. USSR/East Europe
(Centrally planned)	5. China and centrally planned Asia
Developing (6 to 11)	6. OPEC
OPEC developing (6)	7. Latin America
Non-OPEC developing (7 to 11)	8. Middle East and North Africa
	9. Africa South of the Sahara
	10. East Asia
	11. South Asia

The demand for oil in the premium markets of transport and petrochemicals is expected to be less responsive to changes in the world price of oil than those non-premium markets where coal could be more readily used as a substitute. The percentage shares of oil used for transport, non-energy and fuel oil in 1972 are illustrated in table 13.2. Subsectors of these categories of use are listed in table 13.3. These may be related to possible future energy demand by means of a model based on activities. For example, the energy consumption for automobiles in one world region may be estimated by means of a formula of the form:

$$E(autos) = C_1 \times C_2 \times C_3 \times C_4 \times C_5$$

Where the factors are time dependent and are defined by

C_1 = automobiles per person

C_2 = populations in the region

C_3 = average kilometres driven per automobile per year

C_4 = average (base year) fuel consumption per automobile in megajoules per kilometre (MJ/km)

C_5 = factor giving improvements in fuel consumption

At a more sophisticated level, allowance could also be made for diesel driven automobiles and electric vehicles. These factors will depend on GNP per capita and generalised costs that include the effects of world prices for crude oil. There will be saturation effects, of particular importance for C_1, the number of automobiles per person; and many other problems of fact and interpretation in determining values for the coefficients. Calculations similar to those for automobiles may be applied to the other *transport* subsectors listed in table 13.3, giving projections for future energy demand. In 1972, over 90 per cent of the energy used for transport was derived from petroleum. In view of their convenience for transport, and lead times for change, petroleum products are likely to dominate this market for many decades. Some increase in electric vehicles can be expected and this growth may

Table 13.2. *World oil consumption percentage shares in 1972.*

	Percentage of oil for transport	Percentage of oil for non-energy uses	Percentage of fuel oil consumption	Percentage of total oil
OECD	70	74	67	68
Centrally Planned	12	9	21	17
Developing	18	17	12	15
World	100	100	100	100
Percentage of total world oil consumption	39	7	54	100

Table 13.3. *Subsectors for method 2; the oil demand model.*

Transport	Non-energy uses for oil	Fuel oil, etc.
Automobiles and gasoline demand	Road oil and bitumen	Includes all other uses of petroleum
Commercial vehicles and diesel oil demand	Lubricants	
Air transport	Petrochemicals	
Rail transport		
Water (inland and coastal)		
Pipelines		
Bunkers (international)		

accelerate near the turn of the century. However, it is likely that the dominant features of transport during the next few decades will be improved efficiencies and the saturation of demand for transport in most of the OECD group.

In those countries where adequate statistics are available, future energy demand in the *household* sector can also be projected using activity analysis with explicit allowance for improved efficiencies. This type of approach is described in detail by Leach *et al.* (1979) for the UK, and the WAES (1977) reports also used this method when detailed data was available (see also UK Department of Energy, 1977c).

In the *industrial* sector it is rarely possible to make energy projections based on physical activities, with the exception of iron and steel and aluminium production. In general, projections are based on assumptions about future energy per unit of value added in each major industrial sector, the value added being derived from the GNP assumptions via an economic model. When these projections of energy demand in each sector are allocated amongst fuels using an interfuel substitution model and integrated with the energy conversion and supply requirements, we obtain projections of energy balance tables for world regions in future years (see chapter 3 for a discussion of energy balance tables). The 'tuning' or revision of the projections requires a view on potential world energy supplies for each fuel, to which we now turn.

13.4   Energy supply potential

Developments in energy production are generated by the growth and the anticipated growth in energy demand, both directly through increased prices and also by the changing climate of opinion on long-term energy needs. Thus if high demand growth is sustained over the next 10 years the total potential supply in 20 years time will in general be greater than if there was low growth. However, the impact differs considerably between one fuel and another. Locally the production of oil in the long term could be increased if reserves are husbanded and short- to medium-term demand is kept low. Worldwide, a low or zero growth in oil demand would weaken the price of oil and discourage the development of higher cost resources. Thus although conventional oil would be depleted more slowly, the resource base would also widen more slowly. However, world production of oil is expected to be fairly inelastic to changes in price and is likely to change only slowly over the next few decades. Current production is just over 60 mbd and in the year 2000 production is expected to be between 55 mbd and 77 mbd. This expectation is summarised in table 13.4 for oil, and appropriate estimates are also made for other fuels. The ranges given do *not* represent lower and upper limits, but they should be interpreted as the upper and lower quartiles of a probability distribution to indicate the authors' level of confidence. The totals for several fuels or regions have a reduced spread in uncertainty, since the estimates for each fuel and each region are (at least partly) independent of each other.

The starting points for the supply estimates in table 13.4 are the WAES (1977b) and WEC (1978B) resource studies. The potential oil supply has been reduced to take account of preferences by producers for conserving their oil resources. The potential supply of natural gas depends largely on one's view about the rate of growth of demand for the large resources in the Middle East which will probably involve high transport costs as LNG or methanol. Thus the gas supply potential is influenced strongly by the demand model and preferences between fuels. There is a similar dependence of nuclear potential on the growth in the demand for electricity and the relative preferences between coal and nuclear for its generation. However, in the short and medium term, up to the year 2000, the potential for nuclear power is largely determined by existing programmes, which involve much less nuclear capacity than was planned in the early 1970s. Where there are large indigenous coal reserves it is possible to treat coal as the residual fuel, but it is not clear that world traded coal can freely increase so as to provide the residual fuel worldwide. The estimates for coal in table 13.4 therefore involve expected limits on exports

Table 13.4. *Guidelines for potential world energy supply.*

	Coal	Oil	Gas	Nuclear	Hydro	Wood + solar	Total
OECD							
1976	31	25	32	4	12	1	105
2000	50–70	30–42	20–32	30–40	14–20	4–8	150–200
2030	50–90	16–36	6–18	60–120	15–25	10–30	180–300
Centrally planned							
1976	42	23	14	1	3	8	91
2000	60–90	20–36	16–32	16–32	4–10	8–16	140–200
2030	70–140	15–40	15–40	50–100	8–16	10–30	200–340
Developing							
1976	8	74	4	—	3	15	104
2000	14–22	60–100	16–36	2–5	5–10	12–30	120–180
2030	20–40	40–80	20–40	10–20	7–14	15–45	130–215
World							
1976	81	122	50	5	18	24	300
2000	130–160	120–170	60–90	50–75	25–40	30–50	440–560
2030	160–260	80–145	50–90	120–240	35–50	50–100	530–840

Notes: For illustration the upper and lower ends of the ranges should be interpreted as the upper and lower quartiles of a probability distribution.
Source: Authors estimates, Units: 1 EJ = 10^{18} J = 23 million toe = 0.45 mbdoe.

from North America. They also assume relatively little trade in fuels between the centrally planned economies and the rest of the world.

The expected ranges for potential supply of fuels given in table 13.4 provide guidelines for adjusting fuel preferences when developing scenarios. Although the adjustments are carried out by a computer model they are essentially judgemental. The results are given in the next section.

13.5   Scenario definition and illustrative projection

The assumptions about economic growth for the illustrative median projection are summarised for the three major groups in table 13.5, and the corresponding shares of population and GWP are illustrated in figure 13.1.

We emphasise that these assumptions for the median projections do *not* represent an economic forecast. In the first period (1975–2000) they represent a median value between possible high or low assumptions taking account of historical growth rates. For the second period (2000–30) the growth rates were chosen to be low enough for the resulting energy demand not to unduly stretch the supply potential. This then leaves flexibility to discuss variations to higher or lower economic growth for different world regions (for example the developing regions)

Table 13.5. *Population and economic growth rates* (average annual percentage growth rates).

Period	Historical growth rates 1925–50	1950–75	Median growth rates 1975–2000	2000–30
Population				
OECD	0.9	1.0	0.5	0.2
Centrally planned	0.7	1.5	1.0	0.5
Developing	1.6	2.5	2.2	1.3
World	1.1	1.9	1.6	1.0
GNP (real)				
OECD	2.3	4.2	2.8	1.6
Centrally planned	4.0	5.5	3.8	2.0
Developing	2.6	5.0	4.6	2.7
World	2.6	4.6	3.4	1.9
GNP per capita				
OECD	1.4	3.2	2.3	1.1
Centrally planned	3.3	4.0	2.8	1.5
Developing	1.0	2.5	2.4	1.4
World	1.5	2.7	1.8	0.9

without encountering levels of energy demand that involve improbable growth rates for world energy production. It may be noted that the per capita economic growth rates in the period 2000–30 are in line with very long-run historical per capita growth and it is therefore not unreasonable to describe them as a median projection.

The projections of world energy demand are obtained from these economic assumptions using the methods outlined earlier, and assuming also that energy conservation effects correspond approximately to a doubling of real energy prices (i.e. average real prices paid by consumers) between 1975 and the early part of the next century. The resulting projections of energy demand are summarised in table 13.6. They correspond to the energy – output ratios shown in table 13.7, which illustrate that the detailed assumptions for the projections imply a transition in the mid 1970s, after which there is consistently more conservation than in the earlier period. If the worldwide reduction in the energy – output ratio from 56 in 1975 to 44 in 2030 was attributed entirely to a price elasticity effect, it would correspond approximately to a doubling in the average real price of energy to the final consumer and a price-elasticity of $-(0.35)$. However, this reduction arises in our model from continuing technological change, saturation effects and conservation in the OECD, combined with changing patterns of energy use and conservation in other world regions. It will be noted that in the OECD after the year 2000 the model implies that efficiency improvements and saturation of demand almost compensate for the increased wealth implied by the GNP growth, so there is very

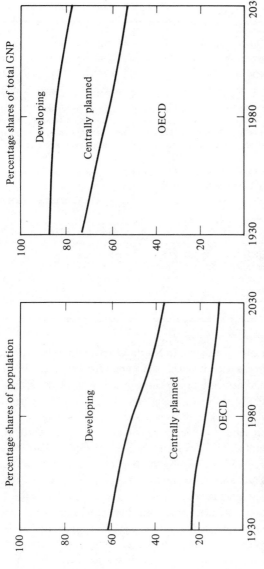

Figure 13.1 World shares of population and gross world product.

Table 13.6. *Median projection of world primary energy demand* (EJ per annum).

Energy in EJ	1925	1950	1975	2000	2030
OECD	37	58	154	254	292
Centrally planned	4	14	77	177	314
Developing	2	6	30	96	204
World	43	78	261	527	810

Notes: (1) 1 EJ p.a. = 23 mtoe p.a. = 0.45 mbbl per day. (2) Wood fuel has been excluded for 1975 and earlier years. Incremental use of wood fuel is included for future years. The total wood fuel in 1975 is estimated to be equivalent to 24 EJ. (3) The uncertainties associated with these projections are discussed in section 13.6.

Table 13.7. *Energy–output ratios for the median projection* (energy per (1972) US dollars (MJ/dollar)).

Energy/GNP MJ per dollar	1925	1950	1975	2000	2030
OECD	65	58	53	45	32
Centrally planned	41	52	77	69	67
Developing	22	29	47	48	46
World	56	52	57	51	44

little growth in energy demand. In North America, saturation of vehicle ownership has already almost been reached, and improved vehicle efficiencies are likely to lead to a gradual decrease in the energy used for road transport – which, in the past, has generally increased faster than GNP. The same result is likely for Western Europe a decade or two later. In the housing sector, also, there is considerable potential for energy conservation both in North America and in Europe, and with slower growth in the number of dwellings there may be little growth in energy demand beyond the turn of the century. In the industrial and commercial sectors, the mature industrial countries in the OECD can be expected to continue their gradual decline in average energy intensities that have been observed in recent decades. In our median projection these contributions to a reduction in the energy – output ratio are partly compensated for by an increase in the energy used in converting primary fuels to the energy carriers required by the consumer, but our assumptions do imply a substantial overall reduction in the energy – output ratio for the OECD (table 13.7), though the average rate of decrease is only one per cent per annum. The distribution amongst different fuels of the median projection of world energy demand is shown graphically in figure 13.2

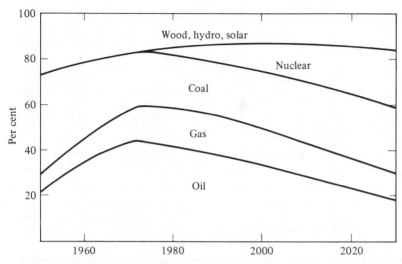

Figure 13.2   World energy shares by fuel 1950–2030.

and is compared with the estimated potential supply in table 13.8. The distribution of total world demand amongst different economic sectors is illustrated in figure 13.3. Further details of possible future energy demand and supply for different world regions will be presented in chapter 14. First, however, we discuss the uncertainty associated with projections of energy demand.

13.6   Uncertainty

The energy demand forecasting model described in the two previous sections is controlled partly by the assumptions about supply availability and partly by economic growth. There is an interaction between the two because some aspects of supply are driven by demand, which depends on economic growth. This applies in particular to electricity demand and hence nuclear power, but it will also affect those fossil fuel supplies that are not resource limited or policy limited, for example coal in some regions such as the USSR and China, and international trade in natural gas will also depend on economic growth. More generally, fuel production from indigenous sources and required for local use is likely to depend on local demand and hence on economic growth, but production for export may be limited by policy decisions even when considerable reserves are available.

The uncertainties about potential fuel supplies therefore arise from several sources: some are mutually dependent on economic growth, others are independent. Thus the potential for the indigenous production and use of oil in some countries

326   Energy models and forecasts

Table 13.8.   *Median world demand projection by fuel showing expected range for potential supply* (EJ).

Year	1976 D	2000 D(S–R)	2030 D(S–R)
Coal	81	149 (130–160)	257 (160–260)
Oil	122	173 (120–170)	141 (80–145)
Gas	50	84 (60–90)	87 (50–90)
Nuclear	5	64 (53–79)	211 (120–240)
Hydro	18	36 (25–40)	49 (35–50)
Solar + wood	24	45 (30–50)	89 (50–100)
Total	300	551 (440–560)	834 (530–840)

Notes: (1) D = demand; (S–R) = supply range (see table 13.4). (2) If oil demand was constrained, for example to 144EJ in the year 2000, it is likely that economic growth would be affected (see the discussion at the end of section 13.6).

depends on luck, namely on whether commercial quantities of oil are found. These elements of the supply of different fuels are independent and it would therefore be misleading to add an optimistic estimate for oil to optimistic estimates for gas and coal without recognising that the possibility of all three favourable outcomes would be small. Similarly there is some degree of independence amongst policy restrictions on fuel production, and optimistic estimates for different sources and fuels should not be simply added together. The work in this area of uncertainty about energy supply by the authors of this book is still at a preliminary stage, and their estimates given in table 13.4 are therefore both judgemental and provisional. The illustrative projections for world regions given in chapter 14 should similarly be regarded as provisional.

The uncertainty about projections of energy demand has three main origins: economic growth, potential supply, and energy conservation. They are, of course, interdependent: high growth will generate more energy supply and relatively more conservation (through faster replacement of equipment); high conservation will permit more economic growth for a given level of energy supply; limits on energy supply can cause sudden changes in prices and economic disturbances that reduce economic growth but stimulate energy conservation.

Uncertainty in estimating energy conservation has been discussed in chapter 12. For illustration, in table 13.7, if the reduction in the world's energy – output ratio from 56 MJ per dollar in 1975 to 44 in 2030 was attributed entirely to a price effect, it could correspond to a doubling of average world energy prices to the final consumer and a long-run average price elasticity of $-(0.35)$. The result was not derived in this manner but came from more detailed disaggregated calculations; however, there are uncertainties in the latter, just as there are uncertainties about future prices and price-elasticities. Given the median levels for economic growth

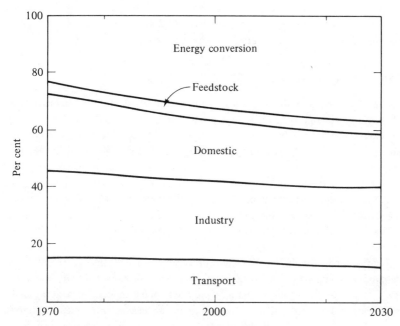

Figure 13.3   World energy shares by major sector 1970–2030.

set out in table 13.5, the authors would certainly accept an uncertainty of plus or minus 10 per cent on the energy demand figure shown in table 13.6 for the year 2000, and plus or minus 20 per cent for the year 2030. The absolute levels of uncertainty are larger than this since no one can reliably forecast the future levels of world economic growth.

The reader will observe in table 13.8 that the median growth scenario gives a world demand for oil in the year 2000 of 173 EJ (or 79 million barrels per day) just outside the upper end of the range for potential supply. At the time of writing (1979) this seems improbably high. However, it does indicate the level of demand that might be expected if there is (on average) steady economic growth not unduly disrupted by oil scarcity. If less oil is available we may expect periods of economic recession caused in part by oil scarcity and sudden changes in price. Our model does not handle this kind of feedback between oil shortages and economic growth but we can readily estimate the average effect if world oil supplies in the year 2000 were 120 EJ instead of 173 EJ; unless there were different levels of achievement in energy conservation or interfuel substitution from those assumed in the median projection, world economic output in the year 2000 would be reduced (in first approximation) by about 10 per cent. This more pessimistic view will be taken into account when illustrative ranges for world regional energy demand are given in chapter 14. The authors, of course, do not exclude the possibility that economic growth may be lower (or higher) than in the median scenario for reasons that are predominantly associated with factors other than energy.

13.7   Chapter summary

Energy forecasting is directed towards the development of energy scenarios that illustrate possible problems that may occur and give guidance on energy planning for governmental and other organisations. Energy models are designed to produce internally consistent scenarios on the basis of specified underlying assumptions, for example about economic growth and about the level of response on energy conservation in the future as compared with the past. Thus energy forecasting does not aim to predict the future, but it seeks to show how a variety of possible futures depend on certain basic assumptions which may include policy variables that are, at least in part, under the control or influence of governments or planners concerned with energy decision making.

Energy models include: (1) simple or complex models that represent energy demand, or components of this demand, in terms of economic activity which may itself be part of the output from a national econometric model; (2) sectoral models concerned with the optimal allocation of particular fuels, for example including the optimal use of the refining and transportation operations for converting a variety of crude oils to meet the estimated demand for different petroleum products; (3) industry market models, for example to evaluate the least cost programme for developing an electric power programme to meet an estimated future demand for electricity; (4) sectoral demand models that aim to project fuel demand in a given economic sector, using a combination of econometric techniques and activity indicators coupled with energy requirements for these activities; (5) energy system models that provide an integrated picture of energy supply and demand for all energy sources.

The second half of the chapter describes in outline how a projection for world energy demand can be developed that takes account of expected ranges for the potential supply of different fuels. The results are illustrated by a median projection based on assumptions about world regional economic growth from 1975 to 2000 and from 2000 to 2030, which are partly influenced by expectations for potential supply.

The chapter concludes with a discussion of some of the uncertainties in projections of energy supply and demand. In particular it is emphasised firstly that it is misleading to combine a series of partly independent optimistic assumptions about energy supply or conservation even though each one may be individually plausible. Secondly it is noted that there are interactions between economic growth, the potential supply of energy, and energy conservation. The manner in which these interactions work out can have a major influence on economic growth and energy demand.

Chapter 13   Further reading

Fried, E. R. and Schultz, C. L., (eds.) (1975) *Higher oil prices and the world economy*, Brookings Institution, Washington, DC.

Hoffman, K. C. and Wood, D. O. (1976) 'Energy system modelling and forecasting' in *Annual Review of Energy*, vol. 1, Annual Reviews Inc.

Hubbert, M. K. (1969) 'Energy resources' in *Resources and man* (National Academy of Sciences), Freeman, San Francisco, Calif.

Hudson, E. A. and Jorgenson, D. W. (1974) 'US energy policy and economic growth 1975–2000', in *Bell Journal of Economics and Management Science*, vol. 5, no. 2, pp. 461–514.

Leach, G. et al. (1979) *A low energy strategy for the UK*, Science Reviews Limited, London.

Mabro, R. (ed.) (1980) *World Energy: issues and policies*, Oxford University Press, London.

OECD (1977) *World energy outlook* (see also later reports with the same title) OECD, Paris.

Pindyck, R. S. (ed.) (1979b) *The production and pricing of energy resources*, vol. 2 of 'Advances in the economics of energy and resources', JAI Press, Greenwich, Connecticut.

Strub, A. (ed.) (1979) *Energy models for the European community*, IPC Science and Technology Press, Guildford, UK, and New York.

UK Department of Energy (1977c) *Report of the working group on energy elasticities*, Energy paper no. 17, HMSO, London.

UK Department of Energy (1978b) *Energy forecasting methodology*, Energy paper no. 29, HMSO, London.

WAES (1977a) *Energy: global prospects 1985–2000*, McGraw-Hill, New York.

WEC (1978b) *World energy resources 1985–2020*, IPC Science and Technology Press, Guildford, UK and New York.

Prospects and strategies for individual fuels, regions and countries

14.1 Scenarios and strategies

The discussion in chapter 13 of the world energy outlook and the studies cited there point to a series of energy problems arising in the first instance from the expectation that world oil production will not match the 'natural' growth in demand during the 1980s and beyond. The problems arising from the inelasticity of world oil supply are compounded by the long lead times and high capital costs for the development of alternative sources of energy and for improving efficiencies through energy conservation. Beyond the year 2000 there may be difficulties in developing total energy supplies to match requirements for high economic growth even if substantial and vigorous efforts are made during the next two decades.

The problems associated with an increasing tightness in international energy supply, especially of oil, will be anticipated, and different countries or groups of countries will develop alternative strategies to deal with them. However, the possible strategies will be constrained and limited by considerations apart from energy, and it is far from certain that difficulties in energy supply will be avoided. In this chapter we will discuss some of the problems, how they might be anticipated, and alternative strategies that may be adopted by different countries or groups of countries.

A potential shortage of oil may be expected as a result of physical scarcity even if all exporting countries allowed their production to increase to near the maximum capacity that could be justified by their reserves. In practice, the onset of such scarcity would be preceded by a rise in prices when it became clear that world oil demand was moving towards the maximum potential supply. However, some producers can be expected to restrain their production below its technical potential for various economic or social reasons that will be discussed later in this chapter, and in chapter 16. High economic growth and/or the failure to develop both conservation and energy sources alternative to oil, coupled with restraints on oil production, would bring closer the onset of an oil shortage.

A rise in the price of oil brought about by scarcity – for whatever reason – would lead to economic problems for importing countries without adequate financial and trade resources, and indirectly through international payment problems it would increase the chances of an economic recession. Indeed, because of the long lead times for developing alternatives to oil it is difficult to identify any quick response that would avoid an oil shortage other than a recession, through which reduced economic growth would lead to reduced growth in the demand for energy. Reduced economic growth would then mask the energy problem and inhibit the potential rise in oil prices, as happened in the period from 1973 to 1977.

In the short- to medium-term future the world energy picture is likely to be dominated by the problems related to a shortage of oil. The onset of serious problems may be soon if there is (initially) high economic growth, or it could be delayed if there is low growth coupled with increased use of alternatives to oil, notably coal, and greater efficiencies in the use of all forms of energy. But low economic growth is not likely to be socially or politically acceptable, either in industrialised countries, where it tends to be associated with unemployment, or in developing countries, where economic targets must be ambitious in order to give a reasonable per capita growth.

If high economic growth is to be a realistic target, the associated strategies would need to include the early and adequate development of alternatives to oil since these will be required to power world economic growth once the supply of oil has reached its expected plateau. If total world energy demand is required to grow at 4 per cent per annum, and oil (which currently provides a half of all energy) stops increasing, the total of other energy sources would need to increase initially at 8 per cent per annum to maintain the same overall growth. In view of the long lead times for many of these alternatives the period of transition may be too short to permit a smooth change. It is therefore necessary to examine not only the strategies for alternatives to oil under steady growth but also the strategies that could develop in 'the years of crisis' that may be unavoidable.

In this chapter, energy strategies will be considered in relation to a time horizon given by the year 2030 and the energy 'prospects' for world regions will be illustrated by ranges of values for demand and supply that are centred around the median projections that correspond to the world picture outlined in chapter 13. It will be recalled from table 13.5 that an annual average of 3.4 per cent was assumed for world economic growth from 1975 to 2000, but the lower figure of 1.9 per cent was assumed for the period 2000 to 2030. The corresponding figures for individual regions would seem unduly pessimistic compared with national plans or expectations, and we emphasise that they are not forecasts but illustrative values chosen to give a consistent world picture. However, to emphasise the uncertainty in relating possible future growth in a region to average world growth we will indicate a range for the average annual growth rates assumed or implied for our energy projections in each world region.

14.2 Energy supply

Oil

Between 1925 and 1975, oil provided 55 per cent of the increment in world energy supply, and natural gas, mostly with access by pipeline to markets, provided another 22 per cent. The average annual growth in oil consumption for this period was about 6.6 per cent, compared with 3.6 per cent for total energy.

Consider first the picture till about 1990. The major proven and probable reserves of oil are in OPEC, with the largest reserves in the Middle East. The production of OPEC oil in 1977 was 31 mbd, which may be compared with a potential capacity at that time of about 35 mbd. The production of OPEC oil in 1990 is likely to be in the range of 25 to 35 mbd. From a purely technical viewpoint it could be higher, and from an economic, political or strategic viewpoint it may be lower. Production of oil from non-OPEC countries in 1977 amounted to 32 mbd of which 13 were from the USSR, East Europe and China (CP – the centrally planned economies). It is unlikely that the CP group will have very significant quantities for export, and the remaining non-OPEC countries are likely to increase production only slightly from 19 mbd in 1977 to the region of 22 mbd in the early 1980s. Thus if the CP group are excluded, the possible supply of oil in 1990 for the rest of the world is likely to lie in the range 47 to 57 mbd (compared to 49 mbd in 1977). Within this range, production will largely depend on OPEC policies and it is clear that we must envisage the possibility that total oil production will remain on average nearly constant during the 1980s, but including periods of growth and decline.

In 1973, the Arab members of OPEC restricted their oil supplies for political and strategic reasons connected with the Arab–Israeli conflict. The restrictions were in effect for only a few months and involved relatively small percentage reductions in total world supplies. However, the resulting marginal scarcity led to very high prices for traded oil outside fixed contracts and encouraged OPEC to increase the posted price of oil five-fold from about $1.80 to $9.00 at 1973/74 prices. Since that period the demand for OPEC oil has remained static due firstly to the recession and some substitution of other fuels and later due to the production of oil in the North Sea and Alaska. With this apparent glut of oil, continued economic uncertainty, and world wide inflation, the real price of oil declined during the period 1974–78 by about 25 per cent, though the increases in 1979–80 brought it about 60 per cent above its previous peak (see figure 10.1).

From the viewpoint of the oil producers it may seem counterproductive to raise oil prices in real terms if there is continued weakness in the world economy and there was also further expected growth in non-OPEC oil production.True, if Saudi Arabia (which produces about 8 mbd) was prepared to absorb, through cuts in its own sales, any reduction in the demand for OPEC oil, as a result both the substitution and the 'income' effects of the price increase – the latter due to the lower world economic growth caused by financial disturbances – then the price rise might not adversely affect the immediate oil revenue of other members of OPEC. But, from a longer-term standpoint, lower world growth would delay the time when any further increase in non-OPEC production was fully absorbed by rising demand, and hence delay the time when demand for OPEC oil itself would begin to rise. As usual, the balance of argument about the virtues of a price rise, from the

OPEC point of view, will be a balance between the present and the future, as in 1978/79. It might be thought in that instance that the 'present' won since oil prices were increased sharply at a time of incipient recession; however, due to temporary, local, or anticipated scarcities, the market also contributed by pushing up spot prices so that, in the absence of an increase either in OPEC production or in OPEC prices, large profits by market traders would have continued to be possible at least for a period. In the event, OPEC chose to increase prices rather than production.

The future behaviour of the price of oil is critical to many aspects of energy strategies, but the uncertainties are compounded further by the existence of large reserves of unconventional oil deposits many of which are economic at current prices (see chapters 4 and 11), and any substantial increase in the real price of conventional oil would provide a major incentive for the development of resources of heavy oil, tar sands and oil shale deposits. The resulting production potential could stabilise or reduce oil prices, particularly if the market weakened due to an economic recession. Although their potential is unlikely to develop fast enough to avoid a substantial requirement for energy from sources other than oil to meet increasing world demand, the threat of their future development does dampen the long-term prospects for the oil price, and hence – through the Hotelling effect – today's prices (these matters are further discussed in chapter 16).

The 1973 oil crisis and subsequent developments provided evidence to the industrialised countries about (1) the pending shortage of oil, (2) the continuing dependence on OPEC for a major fraction of world production, (3) the risk that political and strategic factors may influence future oil supplies, (4) the potential for very large increases in oil or energy prices under conditions of scarcity, (5) the economic and financial strains associated with higher oil prices, (6) the difficulties and long lead times associated with developing measures for energy conservation and for providing higher cost alternatives to oil. Many of these problems affect developing countries particularly severely, since in the early stages of industrialisation the growth in energy demand is often faster than the growth in GNP. Outside OPEC, many developing countries have relatively small indigenous resources of energy and their economic growth will be dependent on their ability to increase exports so as to finance continuing and increasing oil imports.

The central features of all these problems arise from the difficulties of seeking substitution so as to reduce future dependence on oil whilst maintaining economic growth. We will therefore briefly examine the alternatives from a global viewpoint, before discussing possible strategies and responses for individual countries or regions. More detailed discussions of individual fuels will be found in the appropriate chapters elsewhere in the book.

Natural gas
Natural gas provides about 20 per cent of the world energy supply. In 1960 three quarters of world natural gas was consumed in North America, but, with increasing depletion of gas fields in the United States, consumption there has been

declining since the early 1970s and by 1975 was about half the world total. At the same time production and consumption of natural gas has increased rapidly in the USSR, in Western Europe and in some developing countries. The reserves in Western Europe are unlikely to be adequate to maintain current production beyond the end of the century. The estimated 'proven' world reserves of natural gas in 1975 were about half those of oil, but it is possible that substantial further gas resources exist.

Both proven reserves and possible resources of natural gas are located predominantly in the Middle East (28 per cent of proven reserves) and in the centrally planned economies (34 per cent). The development of these reserves and resources over the next few decades will be strongly influenced by transport costs. In the USSR, major pipeline construction would be required to bring gas from Siberia to the existing major markets in western Russia and Europe, or to the Pacific coast for possible export. Some of the Middle East gas potential could be used locally through petrochemicals industries and used for electric power, but most of its development will depend on the economics of liquefaction or conversion and transport as LNG or methanol to the major markets in Western Europe, North America and a potential major market in Japan.

The costs of liquefaction and LNG transport are high, and they include energy losses amounting to about 35 per cent of the primary inputs. Thus LNG sold in Western Europe at the equivalent of (say) $25 (1979 prices) per barrel of oil equivalent (boe) could net the producers less than $10 per boe. However, if the real price of oil was to double there would be a proportionally much greater increase in the net return to producers. This could have a substantial influence on LNG trade but in view of the high capital costs involved it is unlikely to develop rapidly until both the higher prices and the long-term markets are assured.

We must therefore ask how the current natural gas markets in Western Europe and North America will become changed as indigenous supplies begin to decline, and world energy prices rise due to a continuing shortage of oil. The major replacement fuels are likely to be coal and nuclear, with consumer choice lying between the direct use of coal, or synthetic gas, or electricity, or high cost oil. In the longer term, solar energy may be expected to make a significant contribution. The pattern of substitution will clearly be strongly influenced by the large premium markets for domestic gas consumption in Europe and North America and by the lower average costs of coal in North America.

The situation is quite different in developing countries where natural gas is discovered. In general there is no pipeline network for distribution to small users, and in many countries the per capita income would be too low for many householders to finance the domestic use of gas. Thus natural gas is likely to be used principally by major industries and for electricity generation, and its use may be very localised with industrial development brought to the major sources of gas supply.

Coal

In the major industrial regions of the world, coal is used primarily for electricity generation (two thirds of United States coal is used in this way), and almost all of the remainder is used by industry (mostly for iron and steel production). In the United States, coal is on average about half the cost of European coal, but in the past it has been in competition with low cost natural gas so that its relative advantage was not greater than in Europe. Indeed historically the cost of coal to electric utilities in different regions in the United States has varied by factors of at least 3, and the relative costs could differ by a factor of more than 6 with the advent of low cost Western surface coal.

It seems unlikely that prosperous regions like North America and Western Europe will revert to the direct use of coal in the domestic sector, and this may be true also in most parts of the public, commercial and industrial sectors excluding the iron and steel industry. The competition for these sectors would then be between electricity from either coal or nuclear power, natural gas from declining indigenous production, synthetic gas from coal, imported gas largely in the form of LNG but partly by pipeline, and oil products from a petroleum market that would be increasingly moving towards greater emphasis on premium sectors such as transport. The potential for the direct use of coal may be enhanced in the USSR and China by some movement of industry and population towards the major coal producing areas. There may also be some analogous changes in North America, but they are likely to be limited (initially at least) to coal production and energy intensive coal consuming industries.

The expected high cost of oil may limit the economic growth of many developing countries unless they are able to increase their indigenous energy supplies. This requirement may make the use of low grade coal deposits – lignite and brown coal – economically viable, particularly with the use of fluidised bed combustion. Some developing countries, such as Indonesia and countries in southern Africa and possibly South America, may develop a substantial export trade in coal. Unless such a trade is developed, together with increased export from North America, and possibly from the USSR and China, it is unlikely that Western Europe and Japan will have the option of increasing their total consumption of coal to replace their current dependence on oil and gas. Thus the direct or indirect use of coal in Europe and Japan and in many developing countries will depend not only on the identification of assured long-term markets, but it will depend also on the development of transport of coal including the export and import facilities. Key issues on world coal are discussed in the report by Wilson (1980).

Electricity generation

About 25 per cent of the world production of primary energy is used for the generation of electricity, of which half is provided by coal and one quarter by hydro. The cost advantages of nuclear power over coal at high load factors could lead to a rapid growth, and around the end of the century nuclear may be providing about half the electricity generated in many countries. The fraction from hydro-electricity is likely to decline, particularly in Western Europe and in America, and coal fired stations will increasingly replace those using oil.

In many developing countries the potential for hydro-electricity production has only been developed to a small extent, and provided adequate capital is made available hydro-production can be expected to increase very considerably over the next few decades. In many regions there is scope for a ten-fold increase or even more. But developing countries that do not have adequate hydro potential, and do not have indigenous coal or lignite, are likely to require a mix of nuclear power and imported fossil fuel for electricity generation. The former will be limited by the economic size of a single nuclear station and also presents a problem of investment capital comparable with hydro. Fossil fired electricity generation leads to increased energy import charges. Thus electricity requirements will have to be balanced against export potential, and capital requirements for developing export industries may well be in competition with those for electric power to supply energy to those industries.

Nuclear power
The development of nuclear power is likely to become a major feature in world trade. Although much of the cost of building a nuclear power station is indigenous, up to half the total cost may be associated with imports. The greatest potential for production and exports by nuclear electricity industries is in Western Europe, North America and Japan. It is expected that specialised manufacturers will develop so that the production of any single nuclear power station may be associated with components from many different parts of a world wide industry. There are likely to be wide variations in social attitudes to nuclear power which may affect its growth quite significantly in some countries.

Renewable forms of energy
The most important renewable forms of energy at the present time are wood fuel and farm waste, which together account for about 10 per cent of the world's energy supply and meet the minimum needs of more than half the world's population, and hydro-electric power, which (in primary energy terms) provides about 6 per cent of the world's energy. Solar energy has great long-term potential but it is unlikely to contribute more than a few per cent of the world's needs until well into the next century. Expanding demand will therefore be dependent mainly on the growth of supply from fossil fuels and nuclear power.

14.3   Critical years

It has been noted earlier that a potential scarcity of oil will be anticipated and this will result in rising oil prices, increased conservation, substitution of other forms of energy and possibly lower world economic growth resulting in part from the associated economic disturbances. The 1973 crisis initiated the first phase of this response. Oil prices would not have risen dramatically and remained at a high level if there had not been a pending scarcity of oil. Notably, 1973 was the year when North American production of oil and natural gas began to decline.

Theoretically there was no reason why the 1973 oil price rise should have been followed by a world recession, since in principle the oil payments could have been recycled and oil and energy production could have continued to increase. The recession was due in part to the coincidence of problems with oil balances and world wide inflation which was already developing before 1973. Future critical stages could arise in a variety of ways:

(a) If the world economy continues to grow slowly and unsteadily with persistent problems of inflation and unemployment in major industrial countries, the overall growth in the demand for oil will be slow. This could prolong the period when non-OPEC oil production causes a weakness in the demand for OPEC oil, and might delay the time when the OPEC countries were able to achieve further increases in the real price of oil. The consequence for some OPEC countries could be severe in terms of difficulties in meeting their ambitious plans for industrialisation and economic growth. Only Saudi Arabia and the States in the Arabian Peninsula would be free from these difficulties. There would be a strong incentive from most OPEC countries to press for regular real price increases even at the risk of adversely affecting world economic growth. Even after the oil price increases in 1979 it is difficult to see the more needy OPEC countries willingly accepting a real increase of less than 10 per cent per annum for several years. However, a sustained real increase at this level would inevitably accentuate other world economic difficulties and could well trigger, deepen, or extend periods of recession. Under such conditions the longer-run average world economic growth could be very low and the total demand for oil might become nearly constant, declining during recession and rising during recovery. There would be more time available for interfuel substitution and energy conservation measures to take effect. Unless members of OPEC adopted policies to restrict oil supplies so as to maintain conditions of scarcity, oil prices would begin to weaken.

(b) An alternative scenario could arise from political instability or conflict in the Middle East that involved a loss of (say) 15 per cent of world oil for a period of months or longer. It is doubtful whether international arrangements could be strong enough to prevent a scramble for oil similar to that in 1973/74 or 1978/79, with attempts at bilateral agreements and a sharp increase in the real price of oil. If world economic growth was strong at the time, the oil price would probably rise by a larger factor than if growth was weak, and in either case there would be an increased chance of a subsequent recession.

(c) In the period to 1990 there is relatively little scope for an increase in non-oil supplies beyond those already in progress or firmly planned by 1980. If OPEC oil production does not increase beyond 30 mbd the oil crisis is already with us though it may be concealed by a continuing secular recession. If, alternatively, OPEC production increased towards 40 mbd this would both allow continued economic growth and provide an opportunity for developing alternative energy sources and conservation; however, opportunities are not enough, as the wasted years 1973–79 show. It could be argued that unless OPEC production is limited so as to maintain a steady market pressure on oil prices, there will be inadequate reaction by the main oil consuming nations.

In the remainder of this chapter we discuss alternative strategies and prospects for major world regions and for some individual countries.

14.4   OECD regions

North America

The North American region uses annually the equivalent of 2000 million tons of oil or 90 EJ, of which 10 per cent is used by Canada and 90 per cent by the US. This is 30 per cent of total world energy, and annual per capita consumption at more than 8 toe is five times the world average. Up to 1973, this was regarded as an enviable reflection of a vigorous economy and a background of rapidly improving living standards fueled by nearly a century of plentiful cheap energy. Industrial growth was backed by abundant supplies of coal, and by seemingly large resources of oil and natural gas. The abundance of oil in the United States coupled with the economic recession in the 1930s led to limits on oil production through the Texas railroad commission, and to restrictions on the volume of imports of cheap oil from the Middle East and North Africa.

Oil production in the United States reached its peak in 1970 at about 11 million barrels a day (including natural gas liquids), and is currently in the region of 10 mbd, but consumption has continued to increase so that oil imports have risen from 3½ mbd in 1970 to about 10 mbd in the late 1970s. The increase in world oil prices in 1973/74 and again in 1978/79 has made the United States both vulnerable to changes in the world energy situation and more influential in determining the world energy outlook. The economic and political implications of an increasing dependence on oil imports was clearly perceived by some groups in the United States (for example see Akins (1973), and the Ford Energy Policy Project report (1974)) and led to President Ford's Project Independence, ambitiously seeking to reduce demand through energy conservation and by stimulating production so as to achieve independence from energy imports by the second half of the 1980s. The plans and projections were unrealistic from the beginning, but they were further limited by the refusal of Congress to allow the increases in energy prices that many see as an essential part of an energy conservation programme, and needed to stimulate new production. President Carter treated his energy programme as a crusade aimed primarily to reduce demand, but also including a relaxation of price controls that should eventually assist to increase production. His Energy Bill proposed grants for energy saving equipment (including solar energy devices), put a tax on large cars, allowed increases on gas and electricity prices to the consumer, and required large industrial energy consumers and utilities to use coal in their new plants and to convert existing plants by 1990. Earlier legislation had introduced the requirement for phased improvements in the average fuel efficiencies of car fleets sold by major manufacturers in the United States that has already led to substantial energy savings and moderated the continuing increase in energy for transport.

In contrast to these measures, Congress resisted a wellhead tax on domestic oil, taxes on industrial users, and an additional tax on petrol, and environmental legislation has increased the amount of energy required (for transport and coal conversion, for example) and raised potential new obstacles and delays in expanding the production of energy. The campaign for energy conservation, aided by the powerful stimulus of gasoline queues during the 1979 oil shortages, has, it is true, caused a significant increase in the sales of smaller cars, and notable improvements in private home insulation. At the same time, however, the vigorous lobby against nuclear power received a boost from the accident at the Three Mile Island power station near Harrisburg.

The complexity of the energy problems in the United States is rivalled only by the naivety of the miracle solutions to these problems that have been put forward, ranging from the technical fix to radical changes in lifestyle. Admittedly, the uncertain outcome of measures to stimulate conservation or production of energy is not unique to the United States – it is common to all world regions, and will be considered further in chapters 16 to 18.

The additional complexity in the case of the United States arises in part from the form of government and the strength of its democratic institutions, but is also due to the belief that there is apparently a wider range of energy options than in most world regions. The range of options is undoubtedly wide from the viewpoint of resources and technology, but it is likely to be reduced substantially by the different interests that influence the energy market and policy decisions.

Proven reserves of coal in the US amount to about 450 thousand million tons of which one third are accessible to surface mining. The coal resource base is estimated to be about five times as large. Thus coal production could increase from its current annual level of about 600 million tons, eventually (next century perhaps) to 3000 million tons (86 EJ) or possibly more if this proved to be necessary and environmental difficulties could be overcome. Although proven oil reserves are only nine times production, forecasts generally expect production to be maintained for a number of decades near to current levels through improved recovery, extensions of existing fields and further discoveries of conventional oil deposits. There are also extensive resources of oil shale, possibly as high as 1100 thousand million barrels (see Table 4.7) or 300 times current US oil production.

Many forecasts for natural gas show production declining slowly, so that there would be need for both synthetic gas from coal and LNG or pipeline imports, together providing for about 30 per cent of total gas consumption by the year 2000. The potential for nuclear power production is high and uranium resources in the US allow decisions on breeder reactors to be taken more slowly than elsewhere in the OECD; however, the actual levels of nuclear power will be influenced strongly by opposition due to social, political and environmental difficulties. Solar energy and conservation are warmly supported by most groups, but solar energy is likely to be limited initially to the provision of warm water from solar panels and it is unlikely to contribute more than a few per cent to the US energy needs in the year 2000.

The idea of energy conservation is popular and there could be a major public response in some areas such as automobile transport and the insulation of houses, but support for conservation becomes muted when such specifics as higher energy prices or taxes are discussed, and it becomes evident that the silent majority is not without influence.

Finally, the US economy is sufficiently strong that a high level of oil imports could be maintained over a long period – though this would be at the expense of the rest of the world through increasing the chances of higher prices and repeated periods of scarcity. However, such periods of scarcity carry their own risks, not only through the international problems that they cause, but also through actual scarcity in the US. For example, a partial failure of oil supplies in winter could lead to a sudden increase in the demand for electricity for heating that could in turn lead to brown-outs or failures in the electricity supply. Such difficulties may lead to a change in the political outlook on environmental protection and could be followed in the long run by accelerated programmes for coal and nuclear production, but this could not cure a short-term scarcity of energy.

The range of uncertainty in the energy outlook for North America is illustrated in table 14.1, in which Canada accounts for about 10 per cent of both supply and demand. It is likely that Canada will remain nearly self sufficient in energy, with contributions from all major fuels, including a steady increase in production from the large deposits of oil in the Athabasca and other tar sands. The upper limits of the range of energy production from the North American region are attainable and exports would be possible if resources and technology were the determining factors. However, the conflict of the interests and beliefs of different groups in the United States will lead to compromise decisions and it is therefore quite likely that the region will remain a net energy importer of some decades. During this period energy conservation should have a major impact, though it would be unrealistic to suppose that per capita energy consumption in North America will fall to European or Japanese levels. It seems quite possible that net energy demand (by the final consumer) could become constant near the end of the century, but the increased need for energy conversion (coal to synthetic gas or oil, coal or nuclear to

Table 14.1. *North America: possible energy balances 1975–2030.*

North America	Average annual percentage growth	
	1975–2000	2000–30
Population growth	0.7	0.2
Economic growth	2.5–3.5	1.0–2.0
Energy demand growth	1.2–2.4	0.0–1.0

	Year		
	1975	2000	2030
Energy demand (EJ)	83	112–150	130–175^a
Potential production (EJ)	72	100–130	120–170
Possible net (exports) or imports	11	10–30	(20)–30

^{a}The energy demand range for the year 2030 is obtained by extrapolating the low and high values for 2000 at the same median growth rate.
Source: Authors' estimates.

electricity) could still lead to a small annual increase in the total primary energy input. In brief, the authors of this book see the United States at the turn of the century with nearly constant energy demand associated with higher real prices for all forms of energy; oil imports will continue but at a lower level and possibly restricted so as to protect high cost production from shale or conversion from coal; imports of natural gas will have increased and indigenous production will be supplemented by synthetic gas made from coal; the nuclear power programme will have recovered from its current recession though the argument about breeder reactors may continue to flourish; western coal production will be substantial and there may be quite large coal exports from both western and eastern coal production partially (perhaps wholly) offsetting oil imports; solar energy will contribute a few per cent of total energy. Environmental problems will not go away but some of the more extreme requirements may be moderated; accidents will continue in all forms of energy supply including solar energy, and those accidents that are conspicuous will influence procedures and raise costs so as to help reduce them in future. No doubt miracle solutions will still be put forward, but complexity and compromise will in general dominate the decision-making process.

Western Europe
Western Europe has fewer energy options than North America. Large indigenous coal deposits exist in both West Germany and the UK, but they mostly require deep mining. Their costs are much higher than those in North America, expansion of production is likely to take longer, and there may be difficulty in maintaining

existing production levels in Western Europe as a whole, though significant increases are possible for the UK. Oil and gas production from the North Sea is likely to be near peak levels during the 1980s and may decline quite rapidly before the end of the century. Indigenous supplies of uranium are not large and imported supplies are essential for even a low nuclear programme.

Western Europe will therefore continue to be heavily dependent on oil imports in an increasingly difficult world market. Natural gas may also be imported as LNG at costs at least equal to those of oil. Coal production will be important in West Germany and the UK, and coal imports to the region could become important, whether for synthetic gas or oil production, or for direct use, or for electricity production.

There is no way to achieve a plausible world energy balance without introducing a substantial component of nuclear power in Western Europe, unless economic growth is much lower in the future than in the past. Western Europe does not have enough indigenous uranium to proceed for long on a nuclear programme without the use of breeder reactors; in view of the dominance of the 'self-sufficiency aim' in most national policies (see chapter 17), it seems likely that European nuclear power development will be dependent on the acceptability of major development of breeder reactors.

European energy costs have been relatively high during the past 30 years and the potential for conservation is probably less than that in North America. However, conservation is likely to be given a high priority in view of the potential difficulties over future energy supplies.

In contrast to the UK, France has small fossil fuel reserves and has embarked on a vigorous programme for nuclear power which includes provision for breeder reactors and the conversion of hydro-power to pumped storage. The nuclear programme implies an increased use of electricity in the longer term and a high level of energy conservation. Solar energy will make only a small contribution in the next two decades but technological advances may increase its contribution later. During this period France will continue to import oil at a high level but may also increase its coal and gas imports.

Amongst the other countries in Western Europe, Italy is expected to follow an energy policy similar to that in France though at a less ambitious level. West Germany will maintain coal production, if necessary by subsidies as an insurance against over-dependence on imports, but its main expansion of energy production will be from nuclear power, though at a slightly lower level than in France. Continued strength in the West German economy will permit a high level for oil and gas imports, though, as in the United States, conservation will be encouraged so as to obtain an eventual reduction in the need for imported oil. The Scandinavian countries will continue to set high standards for energy conservation, and in these countries as elsewhere the nuclear debate will be influenced by the harsh realities that flow from the expected limits on world oil production.

Table 14.2. *Western Europe: possible energy balances 1975–2030.*

Western Europe	Average annual percentage growth	
	1975–2000	2000–30
Population growth	0.4	0.2
Economic growth	2.3–3.3	1.0–2.0
Energy demand growth	1.4–2.6	0.0–1.0
	Year		
	1975	2000	2030
Energy demand (EJ)	50	71–95	82–110
Potential production (EJ)	23	45–55	50–90
Possible net (exports) or imports (EJ)	27	25–40	20–40

Source: Authors' estimate.

Illustrative projections showing the ranges for possible future energy demand in Western Europe and potential supply are given in table 14.2.

Japan, Australia and New Zealand

Japan accounts for more than 80 per cent of the energy demand in this world region but has almost no indigenous energy resources. Apart from imports of coal for iron and steel production Japan is currently dependent for most of its energy supplies on imported oil. The high technology available in Japan coupled with economic strength will permit a shift towards less energy intensive but high value-added industries, thus moderating the growth of industrial energy demand whilst maintaining a strong export position that will enable a high level of energy imports to be maintained. These imports will continue to be dominated by oil but imports of steam coal and natural gas will increase substantially. It is expected that the nuclear power programme will be maintained at its present fairly high level and it should provide more than half the electricity generated by the end of the century.

The authors' projections for the region are shown in table 14.3. The Australian energy scene is complementary to that in Japan in that extensive reserves of low cost coal provide a major export potential and make a nuclear programme unnecessary for the next decade or two. Australian coal production is expected to expand considerably to provide exports to Western Europe, Japan and East Asia, though it is doubtful whether the full potential implied by the production range in table 14.3 will be realised. Major coal producers may be expected to limit production to conserve resources for the long-term future in the same way as oil producers but at a later period.

Table 14.3.   *Japan, Australia, New Zealand: possible energy balances 1975–2030.*

Japan, Australia, New Zealand	Average annual percentage growth	
	1975–2000	2000–30
Population growth	0.8	0.3
Economic growth	4.6	2.0
Energy demand growth	3.0–4.2	0.0–1.0
	Year		
	1975	2000	2030
Energy demand (EJ)	17	34–48	40–56
Potential production (EJ)	5	15–25	20–40
Possible net imports (EJ)	12	10–25	0–20

Source: Authors' estimates.

14.5   Centrally planned economies

USSR and East Europe

The USSR has very large reserves of coal and has large probable or possible reserves of oil and natural gas. Energy demand and supply are likely to be managed so that they remain nearly in balance for the Comecon region as a whole. If economic growth continues at anywhere near the historical levels of around 5 per cent per annum there will need to be a similar growth in energy production. The major difficulties to be overcome arise from the harsh environment for developing energy resources, and from the large distances from the resource areas to the main centres of demand. These difficulties may act as a brake on planned economic growth in the USSR. It is likely that Eastern Europe will increase export trade and could therefore be in a position to compete for world oil supplies outside Comecon. Both the USSR and Eastern Europe are expected to develop substantial nuclear programmes.

Illustrative ranges for possible future energy balances for the USSR and Eastern Europe are summarised in table 14.4. The high figures for potential demand and production in the years 2000 and 2030 may seem improbably large. However, they should be compared on a per capita basis with those in North America at the present time. The latter amount to about 8 tons of oil equivalent per person. The ranges in table 14.4 correspond to about 5 to just over 7 toe in the year 2000, and to 5.5 to about 8.5 toe in the year 2030. These compare with about 3.5 toe per capita at present in the USSR and Eastern Europe and about half this value in 1960. The estimated energy resources certainly permit the production levels given in table 14.4. Coal resources are estimated at above 5000 gigatonnes (WEC 1978a) and

Table 14.4. *USSR and Eastern Europe: possible energy balances 1975–2030.*

USSR and East Europe	Average annual percentage growth	
	1975–2000	2000–30
Population growth	0.6	0.3
Economic growth	3.0–4.0	1.2–2.4
Energy demand growth	2.1–3.2	0.6–1.4
	Year		
	1975	2000	2030
Energy demand (EJ)	60	100–140	135–190
Potential production (EJ)	60	100–140	120–200
Possible net (exports) or imports (EJ)	—	(10)–10	(20)–20

Source: Authors' estimates.

proven reserves at over 100 gigatonnes, so production levels of 3 gigatonnes annually (75 EJ) are not impossible for the year 2030, provided sufficient priority could be given to production facilities, including infrastructure and transport. Nuclear power could provide an equal amount of primary energy (75 EJ or 1200 GW(e)) with the remaining 40 EJ coming mainly from hydro-power, natural gas and oil. It is not expected that there will be very large net energy imports (or exports) to the Soviet group of countries though this expectation may change if there are new political alignments amongst the major oil producers in the Middle East so that one or more becomes part of the trading group associated with the USSR.

China and centrally planned Asia
The Peoples' Republic of China has a low per capita energy consumption, less than 20 GJ per annum, but has very large coal resources and has significant (perhaps substantial) oil resources. There is therefore great potential for growth and recent diplomatic moves suggest that China is prepared to depart, to a limited extent, from a policy of self reliance and import Western technology in order to accelerate growth in coal mining and in oilfield development. Statistical information is not made generally available by the government of China, but it is estimated that coal production has increased at about 5 per cent per annum since 1961 after a sharp fall (perhaps by as much as 50 per cent) during the period 1958–60 of the 'great leap forward'. Coal resources are thought to exceed 1000 gigatonnes, so there could be major industrial expansion over the next century based mainly on energy from coal. For example, if industrial development in China proceeded at a rate comparable with that achieved by the USSR over the past 50 years, coal

production could increase from its present value of about 350 million tonnes per annum to 3.5 gigatonnes per annum by the year 2030, equivalent to 90 EJ per annum.

There is great uncertainty about the possible oil resources in China, and there has been much speculation arising from the new oilfields announced since 1960. Foreign estimates of possible oil resources from conventional sources range from 2 or 3 gigatonnes up to 70 gigatonnes (including possible offshore fields). Oil production was about 1 million tonnes in the mid 1950s and had probably reached 50 times this figure by the mid 1970s. Japanese estimates suggest that more than 150 million tonnes may be produced annually early in the 1980s. Future growth is expected to be at much slower rates, particularly since a substantial part of new developments may be offshore. Demand for oil products has been low in China and there may be a period during the 1980s when oil will be exported in quantities (perhaps 50 million tonnes per annum) that would be large in relation to China's foreign trade but not very significant in comparison with world requirements for oil. In the longer term, if planned growth continues, the future demand for oil in China is likely to prevent further growth in oil exports, and there may be a switch from oil exports to coal exports.

There are substantial oil shale deposits in China that were producing about 2 million tonnes of oil in 1970 and could be further developed if the growth in conventional oil production is not maintained. Hydro-electric power production in primary energy terms is currently about 12 million tonnes of oil equivalent (0.5 EJ) annually. The hydro potential would permit this to expand at 5 per cent annually for 40 years or more.

Centrally planned Asia, in addition to China, includes North Korea and Vietnam. Either or both of these countries could develop rapidly, with economic growth based on world trade as in other countries in East Asia. The resulting demand for energy would, in part, compensate for the potential (near term) surplus of oil production in the People's Republic of China.

Illustrative ranges for possible future energy balances for the region of China and centrally planned Asia are summarised in table 14.5.

14.6   Developing regions

OPEC developing countries

About half of the OPEC production of oil comes from countries such as Saudi Arabia and the United Arab Emirates, where populations are small in relation to oil resources, and annual energy demand is likely to remain well below the annual production of oil and natural gas. The other half of OPEC production comes from countries such as Iran that prior to 1979 was increasing its own demand by industrialising rapidly, and Nigeria or Indonesia where their own demand is likely

Table 14.5.   *China and centrally planned Asia: possible energy balances 1975–2030.*

China and centrally planned Asia	Average annual percentage growth	
	1975–2000	2000–30
Population growth	1.1	0.7
Economic growth	3.0–5.5	2.0–4.0
Energy demand growth	3.0–5.0	2.0–3.0
	Year		
	1975	2000	2030
Energy demand (EJ)	17[a]	35–57	70–120
Potential production (EJ)	17	35–57	70–120
Possible net (exports) or imports (EJ)	—	(5)–5	(10)–10

[a]Excluding wood fuel. Future years include incremental use of wood.
Source: Authors' estimates.

to increase rapidly due to their large and growing populations as well as to urban and industrial development.

Energy demand for the OPEC group as a whole is illustrated in table 14.6. Now only 10 per cent of the group's production, it could reach 30 per cent by the end of the century and 50 per cent or more 30 years later. These prospects and further increases in the world price of oil may be expected to encourage both resource conservation of conventional oil and the development of unconventional oil such as the large resources of heavy oil in Venezuela.

The large natural gas reserves in the Middle East, together with gas associated with oil, are already leading to a substantial petrochemicals industry. In addition, the increasing scarcity of indigenous natural gas in the major markets of North America and Europe will encourage the development of a major trade in natural gas from the Middle East through pipelines and LNG and methanol shipments.

Indonesia has very large reserves of low grade coal that in the longer term might lead to substantial exports, possibly after upgrading by conversion to synthetic oil. This coal could also provide for local use and industrial expansion, so as to free oil production for export.

The three major uncertainties that affect OPEC oil production are: political stability, policy on production levels and exports, and the price of oil in relation to national economic development. Any radical change of policy by one of the major OPEC producers on one of these issues could have a serious effect on world oil supplies and on world economic growth. It must be expected that on a number of occasions over the next few decades such radical and sudden changes will take place.

Table 14.6.   *OPEC developing countries: possible energy balances 1975–2030.*

OPEC developing countries	Average annual percentage growth	
	1975–2000	2000–2030
Population growth	2.7	1.6
Economic growth	4.0–6.0	2.0–4.0
Energy demand	4.0–6.0	2.0–4.0
	Year		
	1975	2000	2030
Energy demand (EJ)	6	16–26	39–63
Potential production (all fuels) (EJ)	70	70–120	70–140
Possible net (exports) or imports (EJ)	(64)	(55)–(85)	(30)–(60)

Source: Authors' estimates.

Non-OPEC developing countries

Non-OPEC oil importing developing countries include about 40 per cent of the world's population but consume only about 10 per cent of the commercial energy. Following the five-fold increase in world oil prices in 1973–74, because of the short-term inelasticity of demand, these countries had either to increase their borrowing to pay for oil imports or reduce their rates of economic growth. The change in oil prices also led many of these countries to renew or extend their exploration for oil and gas, and (to a lesser extent) to look for potential sources of coal production.

Of the group of non-OPEC developing countries, 13 are net exporters of oil: Angola, Bahrain, Bolivia, Brunei, Congo, Egypt, Malaysia, Mexico, Oman, Syria, Trinidad and Tobago, Tunisia, and Zaire. These countries produce about 80 per cent of the total production in the group. Before 1973, about 10 of the oil importing developing countries produced oil in commercial quantities, and since then further commercial finds of oil and gas have been reported in many of these, and in about 10 further countries. Total oil production of non-OPEC developing countries in 1978 was about 220 million tonnes (9.7 EJ), and gas production was equivalent to nearly 60 million tonnes of oil. Production of oil is expected to double by the late 1980s and gas production could treble. Most of these developments will come from small- or medium-sized oil and gas fields and there appears to be little likelihood of very many large oilfields being discovered. Since 73 per cent of the world's proven oil reserves are found in only 240 very large fields (over 500 million barrels), it is unlikely that discoveries in non–OPEC developing countries will decisively change the world's oil picture. The largest potential oil production in the non-OPEC developing group is in Mexico where new discoveries have led to very high estimates for the resource base. Ultimately reserves may be as high as 100×10^9 barrels, but even at this level it is likely that Mexico would adopt a cautious production policy determined primarily by the economic requirements of its own development plans; this might lead to production levels of between 4 and 6 million barrels a day (compared with 0.5 in 1970 and just over 1 in 1978).

Energy consumption in non-OPEC developing countries grew at a rate of 6.1 per cent from 1960 to 1975, while oil consumption increased at about 7 per cent per annum. This level of growth is unlikely to be maintained in the face of a future potential world scarcity of oil and further price increases for traded oil. Even at a lower level of growth there would be a substantial investment need for energy exploration and development, not only for oil and gas, but also for coal and for hydro-electricity.

Illustrative ranges for possible future energy balances for non-OPEC developing countries are summarised in table 14.7. The upper ends of the ranges for potential production of energy may err on the side of optimism. They certainly depend on luck in new discoveries of oil and gas, and on the development of extensive coal deposits, particularly in Africa, India and Latin America and including low grade coal of qualities not at present used. They would also depend on continued major investments in hydro-electricity and, later on, in nuclear power. Whether or not these optimistic levels are achieved, there will be a need for government or commercial development of solar energy, mainly through afforestation and forest maintenance, but also including new developments in biomass, conversion to alcohol, and solar heating and cooling.

The levels of achievement implied by table 14.7 are very considerable, but they are not high in comparison with planned levels of growth, or with actual achievements in per capita growth in the OECD countries in past decades. There will be political and moral pressure for the richer countries of OECD and OPEC to assist the development of the non-OPEC group. One of the key issues is whether conservation and production from alternative energy sources in OECD will release enough of the world's oil supply for increased use by the developing countries at prices they can afford. It is unlikely that their development plans can succeed unless they obtain increased supplies of oil both through their own discoveries and production and through taking a larger share from the world oil market. The prospects for individual regions within the developing group of countries will be briefly discussed in chapter 15.

14.7 Chapter summary

This chapter is concerned with the alternative options or energy strategies that need to be considered in the light of alternative scenarios, such as those developed by the methods described in chapter 13. The central short- to medium-term problem is the pending scarcity of oil, coupled with the long lead times for

Table 14.7. *Non-OPEC developing countries: possible energy balances 1975–2030.*

Non-OPEC developing countries	Average annual percentage growth	
	1975–2000	2000–30
Population growth	2.3	1.3
Economic growth	4.0–5.0	2.0–4.0
Energy demand growth	4.0–5.0	2.0–3.0
	Year		
	1975	2000	2030
Energy demand (EJ)	24[a]	64–81	135–170
Potential production (EJ)	17	35–70	40–100
Possible net (exports) or imports (EJ)	7	15–30	20–50

[a]Excluding wood fuel. Future years include incremental use of wood.
Source: Authors' estimates.

providing energy supplies from other sources requiring more expensive development. The onset of problems arising from an anticipated scarcity of oil is already
evident, but its full impact could be delayed if there is low growth coupled with the
increased use of alternatives to oil, or if OPEC oil production is allowed to increase
nearer to its technical limit. The future is uncertain and an energy policy based
entirely on a single scenario would be courting disaster. Individual policy makers
will have different objectives and constraints, and different criteria for the
assessment of risk avoidance. Thus energy demand management will tend to
emphasise the need for conservation and may use optimistic scenarios to set targets,
whereas the supply industries may be less optimistic since they wish to avoid the
risk of a supply shortfall and the unpopularity that it would produce.

The special problems associated with the supply of individual fuels are discussed,
including, for example, the constraints on oil supplies that developed in 1973 and
which may develop again in the future. The price of oil is expected to be influenced
by OPEC against the background of a world market that fluctuates with world
economic growth patterns but in the medium term the world price of oil can be
expected to increase. This will lead to increasingly rapid awareness of the need for
alternative fuels, notably coal, natural gas (traded as pipeline gas or LNG), and
nuclear energy. It is unlikely that renewable energy sources such as solar energy
can make a contribution of more than a few per cent of total energy before the year
2000.

The chapter concludes with some comments on the options available to major
world regions, beginning with the OECD regions, North America, Western Europe
and Japan, Australia and New Zealand. This is followed by a discussion of the

centrally planned regions, the USSR and East Europe, and China and centrally planned Asia. Finally there is a brief discussion of the developing group, OPEC and the non-OPEC developing countries, which are also considered further in chapter 15.

Chapter 14   Further reading

Also see reading list for chapter 13.

Attiga, A. 1978, 'The impact of energy transition on OPEC oil resources: some problems and prospects' in *OPEC Review*, vol. 2, no. 5, December 1978.

Daedelus, Journal of the American Academy of Arts and Sciences (1975, Fall issue) *The oil crisis in perspective,* American Academy of Arts and Sciences, Washington DC.

International Energy Agency (IEA) (1977b) *Energy policies and programmes for IEA countries (1977 review), OECD, Paris.*

Mangone, G. J. (ed.) (1977) *Energy policies of the world (vol. 1, 1976, vol. 2, 1977), Elsevier, New York.*

Noreng, O. (1978) *Oil politics in the 1980s,* McGraw-Hill, New York.

Schurr, S. H. et al. (1979) *Energy in America's future,* Resources for the Future, Washington, DC.

Willrich, M. et al. (1975) *Energy and world politics,* The Free Press, New York.

WAES (1976) *Energy demand studies: major consuming countries,* MIT Press, Cambridge, Mass.

WAES (1977b) *Energy supply to the year 2000,* MIT Press, Cambridge, Mass.

WAES (1977c) *Energy supply – demand integrations to the year 2000,* MIT Press, Cambridge, Mass.

World Bank (1979) *World development report, 1979* (see also later reports with the same title) World Bank, Washington, DC.

World Energy Conference (WEC) (1978a) *World energy: looking ahead to 2020,* IPC Science and Technology Press, Guildford, UK, and New York.

Yager, J. A. and Steinberg, E. B. (eds.) (1974) *Energy and US foreign policy,* Ballinger, Cambridge, Mass.

Energy and developing countries

15.1 The Problems

The developing countries group includes over 100 nations, mostly located in tropical or sub-tropical climates but including a great variety of peoples and cultures. With China and centrally planned Asia, their total population was some 3000 million in 1977 and is expected to reach about 4500 million by the end of the century. Although they have 75 per cent of the world's population, their shares of the gross world production (GWP) and of the total commercial energy consumption are little more than 20 per cent. For the industrialised world the energy crisis is a problem of adjustment. For many people in the developing world it is a problem of survival, and for all the crisis will affect the pace and pattern of development. In the short term the burden of payments for imported oil will continue to inhibit economic growth, and in the longer term development will need to be based increasingly on sources of energy other than oil.

Energy problems will tend to enhance, rather than reduce, the great diversity amongst developing countries. Some are richly endowed with oil resources that will last for many decades, though the possibly distant prospect of desert sands reclaiming the land on which oil cities have been built causes unease. Other countries are desperately poor and with few indigenous resources beyond those of their people for whom development may depend critically on aid from richer and more developed nations. Some countries, for example China, have large coal reserves which could provide a bridge through the development period until high technology or new concepts for a low energy society provide a stable energy regime. Some countries in the middle income group, particularly in East Asia and in Latin America, who began to achieve rapid economic growth in the 1970s, may lead the developing world in making increasing demands on world oil supplies.

Oil and its products provide the major part of commercial energy supplies to most developing countries – its share of the total amounts to more than 60 per cent if China is excluded. Coal provides a major component of energy supply in a few developing countries, notably China, India, Korea and South Africa. However this may change considerably in the next few decades, partly due to the prospect of increased world trade in coal, but also because it is likely that coal resources, some of rather poor quality, can be found in a large number of developing countries.

Wood fuel and farm waste meet an important part of the fuel requirements,

352

particularly for domestic or household use, in many developing countries. These fuels are conventionally called 'non-commercial' forms of energy, though they are often bought and sold, since transactions in them are rarely recorded in the commercial energy statistics. In addition, the rural sectors of developing countries often depend on human and animal labour, and to a limited extent on wind and water power, and of course on solar energy, for crop drying and other functions. In some regions, particularly those near the deserts of Africa and in densely populated parts of Asia, but also in parts of Latin America, there is a growing scarcity of wood that can be used as a fuel. Under the pressures from increasing populations the potential scarcity of wood fuel presents a threat that for many people is more serious than the expected scarcity of oil, though the problems of wood fuel and oil are complementary since one scarcity will reinforce the other.

Energy prospects for developing countries cannot be considered in isolation from their economic growth and prospects for development, and their relation to other groups of countries. Their exports depend largely on markets in industrialised countries, and the prices of their imports are usually determined by forces outside their control, such as the competition amongst richer and more developed countries.

Capital inflows depend on the economic health of the industrialised countries as well as the needs and credit rating of each developing country. Since the 1973 oil crisis a number of countries, for example Brazil and Turkey, have maintained their economic growth partly through deficit financing, to the extent that debt servicing has become a large commitment. High economic growth in developing countries – at least for the next decade or two – will depend therefore on whether the industrialised countries achieve a satisfactory level of growth. Such growth would put increasing pressure on world oil supplies, and, coupled with declared policies in OPEC to limit production, further increases in the real price of oil must be expected. This would lead to difficulties for those developing countries whose growth depends on oil imports, and serious problems for those poorer countries that cannot afford such imports and may themselves be encountering problems in the supply of non-commercial forms of energy, particularly wood. In the longer term, if the industrialised countries, through conservation and interfuel substitution, succeed in holding their total oil demand constant or even achieving a gradual decline in demand, the pressure on world oil supplies will depend largely on the rate of economic growth in developing countries and on whether they can follow development paths that are less dependent on oil than has been the case in recent decades.

15.2   Energy and development

The ten countries listed in table 15.1 account for two thirds of the total commercial energy consumption in the developing world, namely Africa, Asia (including

Table 15.1.   *Commercial energy used in major developing countries in 1976* (listed in order of energy per capita).

	Total commercial energy consumption (1976) EJ	Commercial energy used per capita (1976) GJ/capita
India	3.9	6
China, People's Republic of	17.2	21
Brazil	2.3	21
Turkey	0.9	22
Korea, Republic of	1.1	30
Mexico	2.2	36
Iran	1.5	44
China, Republic of (Taiwan)	0.9	52
Argentina	1.4	53
Venezuela	1.0	83
Total 10 countries	32.4	20
Total all developing	50.0	17
Total world energy	280	60

Source: World Bank (1979); Author's estimates.

centrally planned Asia) and Latin America. The energy used per capita gives some indication of the levels of development or industrialisation in these countries, and ranges from an average of 6 GJ per capita in India to 83 GJ per capita in Venezuela.

The relation between economic development and energy consumption is illustrated further in table 15.2, which lists the same ten countries but shows their energy consumption per (1976) dollar of GNP for the two years 1960 and 1976. Except for the case of the People's Republic of China in 1960 (when economic activity was disturbed by the 'great leap forward'), the figures in table 15.2 illustrate the general features, mentioned in chapter 2, that the development process usually leads to increased commercial energy consumption per unit of output, arising partly from the substitution of commercial forms of energy for wood fuel and farm waste in domestic fuel use, and partly from the growth of energy intensive industries in the early stages of industrialisation.

In many developing countries the use of wood fuel and farm waste provides an important component of energy consumption, particularly for household use. In India, wood fuel, cow dung and other farm waste provides some 80 per cent of the energy used for cooking and other domestic purposes. In China the figure is probably similar, though statistical evidence is not available, and straw is a very important component of the fuel used for domestic heating and cooking in rural areas though coal is used in towns. The pattern of commercial energy consumption in different economic sectors is compared in table 15.3 with the pattern of use when non-commercial fuels are also included.

Table 15.2. *Energy consumption per (1976) dollar of GDP in major developing countries 1960 and 1976* (listed in order of energy per capita).

Country	Commercial energy per (1976) dollar of GNP (MJ per dollar)	
	1960	1976
India	37	45
China, People's Republic of	98[a]	56
Brazil	16	16
Turkey	13	21
Korea, Republic of	30	43
Mexico	31	34
Iran	11	21
China, Republic of (Taiwan)	39	50
Argentina	30	33
Venezuela	30	33

[a]data for China are rather uncertain, particularly around 1960.
Source: World Bank (1978 and 1979).

Table 15.3. *Percentage shares by sector of energy consumption in 1976 (a) with commercial energy only and (b) with wood fuel, etc. included.*

	Percentage shares commercial energy only			Percentage shares commercial energy plus wood, etc.	
	USA	Brazil	India	Brazil	India
Transport	25	22	32	14	21
Industry	40	35	30	26	20
Domestic and others	35	43	38	60	59
Total	100	100	100	100	100

Source: Goldemberg (1978).

The changing economic structure in developing countries affects energy demand and is an important factor in assessing future demand. Examples of such changes include urbanisation, industrial growth and modernisation, and the increasing use of commercial energy in both urban and rural areas. As income grows, present luxuries such as home lighting, gas cooking, air cooling, refrigerators, radios and televisions are increasingly used by households in cities and towns. The use of animals for transport diminishes as public transport, bicycles and private automobiles increase in use. Similarly, in rural areas, even though horses, donkeys and cattle still represent the dominant transport system, they are gradually disappearing with the wider use of public transport.

The historical evidence presented in chapter 2 suggests that the development process begins with a period when commercial energy consumption grows faster than economic output and is followed by a period of gradual reduction in the growth of energy relative to economic activity. Most of the developing countries are at early stages of this process and commercial energy demand can be expected to grow rapidly over the next decade or more even though higher energy prices may moderate its rate of growth relative to that for GDP in many countries. But where there is continued substitution of fossil fuels and electricity for non-commercial energy, commercial energy demand will continue to increase faster than total energy demand and perhaps faster than GDP. For example, such substitution had a major effect in Brazil between 1940 and 1975, where the share of non-commercial energy fell steadily from about three quarters to one quarter of the total. Continued urbanisation also tends to enhance both the convenience and the cost advantages of commercial over non-commercial energy for domestic use and hence encourage substitution. However, the major factors affecting growth in energy demand are industrialisation and increasing incomes, and if developing countries move towards the industrial structure and transport pattern of the developed countries there will be increased demand for fossil fuels, particularly for electricity, oil and gas, for which the investment costs to the consumer are often lower than for coal, though in the longer term both indigenous coal and imported coal are expected to be more important.

15.3   Commercial energy resources

The reserves and resources of oil and gas in different world regions have been discussed in chapter 4. Proven oil reserves are dominated by those in OPEC, which holds 70 per cent of world reserves, or 80 per cent of those in the non-communist world. Estimates of ultimately recoverable world resources of oil are more uncertain, but OPEC may hold somewhat more than 40 per cent of these. However, with the exception of Venezuela, member countries of OPEC are poorly endowed with unconventional oil resources, such as tar sands, heavy oils and oil shales. In Venezuela it is possible that the recoverable resources of heavy oil may be comparable in magnitude with the currently proven reserves of conventional oil in Saudi Arabia, or about 150 thousand million barrels.

About 40 per cent of the world's proven reserves of natural gas are located in OPEC, half of these being found in one member country – Iran. Although they are not as large as those for oil, the natural gas reserves in most OPEC countries are substantial, and very large compared with their current consumption. Since much of the natural gas production is associated with oil production, it has led to the flaring of gas in large quantities. For example, in 1977 alone, about one half of the total natural gas production in OPEC was flared, and represented a loss equivalent to 2.6 million barrels of oil per day, or more than the total consumption of commercial energy in India. It is only fair to observe that the practice of flaring gas was initiated by the operating companies at a time when the price of oil was so low that it would have been quite uneconomic to gather the gas or transport it to other locations. The higher prices of oil that have applied since 1973 have encouraged the construction of networks of gas gathering pipelines in producer countries, and, accompanied by increased indigenous production and the development of an export trade, this should reduce the wasteful practice of flaring.

Proven reserves of oil and gas in non-OPEC developing countries are small compared with their needs for development. In 1978 about 8 per cent of the world's oil production came from this group, who hold a slightly smaller percentage of the world's proven reserves. They have about 5 per cent of the proven reserves of natural gas, but owing to the lack of developed markets their share of consumption is much smaller. Thirteen countries in the group are net oil exporters, but these include some relatively large countries such as Egypt, Malaysia, Mexico, Syria and Tunisia, which will need rapidly increasing shares of their production for domestic consumption. Their high absorptive capacity will encourage them to seek earnings from the sale of their oil, but their relatively low reserves are likely to lead to careful policies to preserve their production base, either by restricting production or through a vigorous exploration programme.

The oil importing developing countries comprise the large majority of the population of the third world. Excluding the People's Republic of China, their combined energy consumption in 1978 was about 10 million barrels a day of oil equivalent (mbdoe), or about 10 per cent of total world consumption. Just over half of this was met by oil, and three quarters of the oil consumed was imported. The group includes such large relatively industrialised countries as Argentina, Brazil, India, South Korea and Taiwan, which together take about half of the oil imported by the developing countries.

The study by the World Energy Conference (WEC, 1978b) of ultimately recoverable world resources of oil and gas, described in chapter 4, suggests that there may be quite substantial resources yet to be discovered in the non-OPEC countries of the developing world. Ultimate oil resources in Africa, Latin America, and South and East Asia, may be 5 to 10 times their currently proven reserves. However, with a few exceptions (notably Mexico) it is doubtful whether these countries can increase their oil production very substantially over the next decade or two. A vigorous exploration programme could possibly bring the resources into use at an earlier date, but this would require confidence between the host countries and the foreign companies whose help would be necessary for rapid exploration, discovery and development.

China produced 2 million barrels of oil per day in 1978, and it is thought that production may increase so that by the early 1980s as much as 1 mbd may be available for export. Due to the lack of both pipeline facilities and local industry, much of the natural gas produced in association with oil is currently flared. It is thought that there may be a considerable amount of oil and gas yet to be discovered in China, though it is unlikely that this could be on the scale of the super-giant fields of the Middle East. But if anything like the planned growth in the Chinese economy is achieved, it is to be expected that domestic demand for oil and gas will rapidly catch up with the available production. There are very large reserves and resources of coal in China and provided the necessary infrastructure can be developed these could lead to production in excess of a thousand million tonnes a year around the end of the century compared to about 300 million in 1978.

Excluding China and South Africa, the main production of coal in the developing world is in India, the Republic of Korea, Turkey and Vietnam. Although exploration for coal in developing countries has been on rather a modest scale, they are estimated to have nearly 15 per cent of the world's proven reserves, half of this being in India. As exploration programmes develop, there are likely to be substantial discoveries of coal though much of it may be low grade. About 20 developing countries have already found coal but have not yet begun production (World Bank, 1979). In contrast with petroleum it would be difficult for a developing country to start new coal production on the basis of an export trade, and nearly impossible if their coal is of low quality. New coal production is therefore likely to be slow to develop and will be dependent on the ability of local industry or electric power production to take a substantial share of its use. It may also be held up by lack of investment funds, lack of transport facilities, inadequate technical knowledge, and uncertainties with regard to future demand.

Hydro-power provides over 40 per cent of the electrical generation in the group of non-OPEC non-communist developing countries, but this is thought to represent little more than 4 per cent of their estimated hydro-power potential (WAES, 1977a; WEC, 1978b). Very large hydro resources are potentially available in Africa, Asia, and Latin America, but their development may be held back by its high capital cost, conflicting uses for water resources and land, and by disagreements amongst states over mutually controlled water resources.

A few countries, including Argentina, Taiwan (Republic of China), South Korea, India and Pakistan, already have nuclear power, while others, such as Brazil, Mexico and the Philippines are expected to have commercial production in the near future. The minimum size of nuclear power plants currently available is about 600 MW(e), and, coupled with the demanding requirements of technical and managerial expertise, this will tend to limit the use of nuclear power to middle income and large developing countries.

There is substantial potential for conserving energy in developing countries, particularly in the industrial and transport sectors, which account for 70 to 90 per cent of final consumption of commercial energy. In this context energy conservation means the more efficient use of energy, and the need and possibility of greater efficiency is not in conflict with the need to develop industry, transport and agriculture in ways that will introduce new energy requirements. In order to achieve greater efficiencies, developing countries will have to face the issue of the correct pricing of energy, both in relation to costs and in relation to world market prices. Energy pricing is a complex and difficult issue, since it involves competition between different objectives. For example, kerosene is frequently subsidised to benefit poor consumers, or, in some instances, to prevent the harmful depletion of forests required to produce wood fuel and for other purposes. Energy for industry is often priced below costs in order to encourage industrialisation. In oil producing developing countries, domestic energy prices are often well below international levels because it is politically difficult to raise prices in line with increases on the international market, particularly during periods of inflation. A failure to develop proper pricing systems for energy will not only discourage a proper level of energy efficiency appropriate to a scarce resource, but it will also lead to difficulties over finance for the development of new energy resources, whether these involve electricity from hydro-power or coal, or ethanol from sugar cane, or forests to provide wood fuel.

15.4   Rural areas and non-commercial energy

In most developing countries a large (often major) proportion of the population live in rural areas and any improvements of living standards will depend upon development in the rural sector. Pressing problems in rural areas include the need to provide employment and adequate income, to improve agricultural yields, to increase food supply and to improve sanitation and health care. The provision of adequate energy services will be an important part of rural development but must be considered in the context of related problems of rural life.

Wood, charcoal, plant and animal wastes, human and animal power, solar, wind and water supply the energy needs of 2½ billion of the world's population. Although bought and sold, many of these are called non-commercial energy while some, such as solar, wind and water, are called non-conventional. We shall use the term non-commercial to refer to both types of energy sources. Even though they meet only about 5 per cent of the world energy consumption, these non-commercial sources represent about half the energy production in the non-OPEC developing countries and in some of these countries supply upwards of 90 per cent of the energy needs of the rural areas. These sources are used for agricultural production, fertilisers, cottage industries and domestic cooking, heating and lighting. Half the world's population cook with non-commercial energy (World Bank, 1979).

A serious difficulty in studying energy use in developing countries is that reliable data on either commercial or non-commercial energy is scarce. The data shortage combined with problems of accuracy, definitions, accounting conventions and conversion factors complicate discussions on commercial energy use. Even now, the national and international institutions have not given enough attention to the non-commercial sources and technologies for using them. For example, on the supply side, information on forest cover is rough and only a few countries carry out actual inventories. Similarly, there are no detailed accurate figures for mini-hydro potential, or the availability of crop residues, animal draught power or animal wastes. The data for consumption are in a similar state. Estimates are rarely based on field studies but more commonly on guesses, and on inferences about one country based on imperfect information about another. Even when studies are carried out, there is no consistency as to whether human energy is included or whether efficiency in use is considered. Perhaps most important of all is that there is not yet a good understanding of how subsistence, rural development and energy are related so as to give some guidance as to how energy needs in rural areas might develop, especially in the matter of energy flows in the non-market economy. Many of these issues are only now being addressed. Given the drive to improve the standard of living in the rural areas, it is important to begin to come to terms with the more complicated data issues in developing countries. However, the problems are so important that policies must be initiated on the basis of existing information.

Energy is only one of many requirements for rural life and is needed not for itself but for the uses to which it can be put. The quantity of energy needed can very with climate and season, with social organisation and with methods for producing goods and services. The principal energy needs in these areas may be grouped into the following (Palmedo et al., 1978; Makhijani, 1976):

> *Agriculture.* The principal agricultural needs are for soil preparation, planting, irrigating, harvesting, threshing, grinding and preserving, and for fertiliser, whether from animal and vegetable wastes or from chemicals.
>
> *Cooking.*
>
> *Drinking water.* This is provided by public or private wells, public town pipes, or nearby streams. Pumps for wells are either operated by hand or diesel driven. Town pipes are usually gravity fed or operated with diesel pumps.
>
> *Space heating.* This is not required in all rural areas, but where it is needed it is provided directly by wood fires, charcoal heaters and oil heaters.
>
> *Water heating.* In many areas warm water is a luxury rarely available, and clothes are often washed by beating them against rocks in streams, which may mean they will wear out faster than if they were washed in warm water.
>
> *Lighting.* Where electric lighting is available, either in homes, public places or factories, it is most commonly generated by diesel or hydro-power. Other sources for lighting are kerosene lamps, straw, flashlights, pitch pine, and light from cooking fires.
>
> *Goods transport.* The main commercial demands for transport are

hauling crops to and from fields, moving materials to their place of use, importing and exporting goods from villages and carrying wood. These needs are met by carts pulled by oxen, donkey, camel or man, porters carrying goods on back or head, diesel or gasoline trucks, buses and trains (coal or diesel).

Personal travel. The principal modes of travel are foot, bicycle, motor-bicycles, buses, trains, and animals.

Fishing boats.

Home construction. This is done almost exclusively by hand, except for the movement of goods as noted above.

Community services. These range from electric street lights, operation of public community centres, to water pipelines, town wells, maintenance of schools and hospitals, and public transport. The various needs for energy can be grouped as: lighting, space heating, cooking, water heating, and transport.

Obviously, some of these needs are of higher priority than others and the extent to which they are currently being met varies between countries. Although there is considerable variety in energy sources used in the rural areas, the information in the list illustrates the primary reliance on non-commercial energy sources. Moreover, where machines replace animal and human energy and other fuels replace wood, the principal commercial energy source is petroleum.

Several studies undertaken to examine the structure of energy use in rural areas and to quantify the amounts of energy used to meet the various needs confirm the reliance on non-commercial energy. One of these analysed the energy budgets in six rural areas of the developing world (Makhijani and Poole, 1975). This study found that annual per capita commercial energy use is only 1 to 15 GJ, whereas if the non-commercial sources are counted the per capita energy use is in the range of 20 to 80 GJ per year. Domestic and agricultural needs account for well over three quarters of total energy use per capita in these areas.

Because energy requirements in rural areas are expected to increase with the growing population and with the provision of more services, the importance of domestic uses, particularly cooking, highlights the difficulties in maintaining subsistence levels as supply tightens. Domestic cooking demand is basically inelastic and a decrease in domestic use is not practical. Since the principal fuel for cooking is wood, the pressure of population growth threatens wood supplies as nearby forests, woodlots and shrublands are depleted. To some extent this has led to a very slow adoption of technologies fuelled by commercial sources, primarily kerosene. But, for most, substitution is difficult and expensive; for example, kerosene is expensive and requires new equipment. More commonly, wood must be collected from increasing distances, or dung and vegetable wastes are burned in place of wood instead of being used as fertilisers. Charcoal poses the same problem with supplies as wood. In either case, villages are forced by scarcity to use higher cost fuels – commercial fuels with high market prices or non-commercial fuels with high implicit labour costs, e.g. wood gathered from more distant forests.

Wood fuel shortages are critical in many areas and have been called 'the other energy crisis'. Depleted forests lead to denuded hillsides and erosion, which reduces the fertility and water retention of the soil. Deforestation is a serious problem in Nepal, El Salvador, Haiti, the Sahel (the savannah region to the south of the Sahara) and the Sudan. In at least 12 other countries it is estimated that wood fuel is being used faster than the forests can sustain (World Bank, 1979). Many others suffer from localised wood fuel shortages. Deforestation and increasing wood fuel use, combined with the increasing use of substitutes such as dung and other wastes, pose serious problems for soil fertility, soil erosion, water retention, crop yields and the availability of livestock feed. In the long term the wood fuel problem will need to be tackled by the creation of new and additional resources through afforestation and reforestation programmes. In the meantime, other programmes, such as the substitution of other fuels, using wood fuels more efficiently, and elimination of unnecessary uses of wood fuel (for example cooking animal feed) will need to be considered to reduce the severity of the problem (Arnold, 1979).

A major factor contributing to the energy problem is that the amount of useful heat that the poor in rural areas obtain from the energy they use is quite small. The efficiency of fuel use in cooking is only of the order of 5 to 10 per cent. The annual fuel use for cooking with typical open slow-burning fires is 5 to 7 GJ per capita (1 kilogram of dry wood per capita per day), whereas the per capita use for cooking in the US is about 3 GJ (primary) with electric stoves and about 1 GJ for gas stoves (Makhijani, 1976). Thus, one way to meet some of the pressing energy needs involves introducing new and more energy-efficient equipment, for example improved wood stoves, or the use of more charcoal made in better designed kilns, which can double charcoal yields from a given amount of wood.

One of the major energy requirements in agriculture is draught energy for soil preparation, ploughing, cultivating and transportation. Traditionally, draught energy has been provided by animals, but agricultural activities are highly seasonal whereas animals must be kept and fed for the whole year (Pathak and Singh, 1978). Investment in irrigation is one of the activities where greater energy input and mechanisation can substantially improve yields, especially in years with poor rainfall. Fertilisers and manures are also important as their application can increase yields dramatically. Chemically manufactured fertilisers are energy intensive and expensive; however, locally available manures are not. Energy requirements for irrigation and fertilisers are in the range of 5 to 30 GJ per hectare per crop depending on methods used (Makhijani, 1976). Making agriculture more productive involves other related problems, such as water conservation, soil erosion, inadequate storage, that inhibit agricultural development in many developing countries.

At present there is little industry in rural areas, but a number of developing countries are actively encouraging industry to move away from established centres to rural areas. Future energy demand in rural areas will depend upon the form and extent of development that takes place, while at the same time availability of energy supplies will shape and constrain that development.

15.5 Finance

The rise in international energy prices and the growth of commercial energy consumption, particularly imported oil, has required an increased proportion of export earnings to pay for energy imports in the developing countries. The dollar value of energy imports as a percentage of total merchandise export earnings for 1960 and 1976 is illustrated in table 15.4 for 7 of the 10 countries listed in tables 15.1 and 15.2. This percentage in 1976, which in table 15.4 ranges from 58 per cent in Turkey and 43 per cent in Brazil to 14 per cent in Argentina, compared to the corresponding 1960 figures of 16, 21 and 14 respectively, gives some indication of the increasing financial burden of energy imports.

The aggregate indebtedness of the developing countries nearly doubled between 1973 and 1977. However, the outstanding debt of these countries had also doubled in the 1969–73 period, and from 1973 to 1977 debt service as a percentage of exports did not increase significantly: the levels of indebtedness remained acceptable. This is because most of the debt is owed by a few countries – Argentina, Brazil, Korea, Mexico, Peru and the Philippines account for three quarters of the borrowing on the Euro-currency markets and control nearly one half of non-OPEC financial reserves (World Bank, 1979). Even though these countries' borrowings have resulted in higher indebtedness and debt service ratios, until recently (late 1979) they had not encountered any liquidity problems nor any problems of investment security as their growth prospects are thought to be good. The problems of indebtedness were however looming again by early 1980. For example, in late 1979 two thirds of Brazil's export earnings were required to service its international debt ($52 billion in late 1979).

The rise in energy prices is an increased incentive for developing countries to develop their known energy reserves and to explore for further resources. However, the main obstacle to the development and exploration of indigenous reserves is the scarcity of risk capital. Indigenous energy production requires an increased proportion of national investment and an increased reliance on external capital that, along with the increased burdens of financing other investment projects and present energy use through imports, will heighten the concern about the developing countries' debt problem.

The estimated aggregate investment requirements for the non-OPEC developing countries to develop sufficient indigenous commercial energy supplies to approach

Table 15.4.   *Energy imports as a percentage of merchandise export earnings in developing countries in 1960 and 1976* (listed in order of energy per capita).

Country	Energy imports as a percentage of merchandise export earnings	
	1960	1976
India	11	26
China, People's Republic of	n.a.	n.a.
Brazil	21	43
Turkey	16	58
Korea, Republic of	70	23
Mexico	3	10
Iran	n.a.	n.a.
China, Republic of (Taiwan)	n.a.	n.a.
Argentina	14	14
Venezuela	1	n.a.

Source: World Bank (1979).

self-sufficiency as a group by the year 2000 is about $125 billion (1976 US dollars) (Palmedo et al., 1978). This would require energy investment levels to increase to an average of $6 billion (1976 US dollars) annually in real terms from the 1976 level of $4.2 billion. Moreover, according to this estimate, based on mean projections of future demand and supply and current energy investment policies, over one third of expenditure would be for primary electric power development which will account for only 5 per cent of additional energy supplies by 2000. Oil would account for 40 per cent of the investment funds, gas for 20 per cent and coal for 3 per cent.

The present uneven access by the non-OPEC developing countries to investment capital, if continued, would aggravate the position of the lower income developing countries. As mentioned, six non-OPEC developing countries – Argentina, Brazil, Korea, Mexico, Peru and the Philippines control nearly one half of all non-OPEC financial reserves, which leaves more than 70 countries sharing the remaining half in attempting to develop their potential commercial energy resources of hydro, gas and coal. These countries not only have a small share of known economically recoverable energy resources, but might continue to be energy-poor as a result of financial policies and constraints which may limit further exploration. They will need assistance in obtaining external capital. Expansion in flows of development capital from international institutions and official export agencies would improve overall capital flows. Efforts such as that announced in early 1979 by the World Bank to increase lending by an additional $500 million in 1980 and $1 billion in

1983 for oil and gas development in these countries, which will effectively double the World Bank investment effort in the energy sector, are important. But still further international cooperation and assistance are required.

If capital were available, the development of energy resources might still be constrained by the availability of skilled construction and operating manpower, lack of institutions and personnel to deal with the international energy companies, other infrastructure bottlenecks, such as transport capacity, and legislation inhibiting international cooperation. These constraints must be addressed simultaneously with the financial issues to improve the energy position of the non-OPEC developing countries.

15.6   The future of developing countries as energy consumers

One of the difficulties in predicting future energy consumption of non-OPEC developing countries is that their use of energy is highly dependent on their economic growth and the structure of that growth. Although in the short term major reductions in the use of commercial energy, particularly oil, through conservation or improved technologies or by substitution to other fuels are unlikely, in the long term there can be expected to be more flexibility in the relationship between energy use and economic growth and in the use of other fuels, including the non-commercial fuels, and the use of technologies that are more efficient in energy terms. Since a large part of the world's population have to rely upon non-commercial energy, it is sensible for most developing countries to try to improve the availability and efficiency of use of the non-commercial and non-conventional fuels. For example, rather than trying to supply all rural households with electricity, it might prove more practical to improve the supply and use of locally available fuels.

But the choice of a particular energy system is neither straightforward nor simple and depends on suitability and on the costs involved. The perceived costs and benefits of a form of supply may differ between different consumers and decision makers. Thus, a government in a non-OPEC developing country may be trying to discourage the use of oil because of the pressure oil imports impose on foreign exchange resources, while many consumers within the country continue to find oil attractive in relation to the costs they incur. Social costs are difficult to estimate and can lead to unexpected rejection of new technology and supply systems. A solar cooker which needs to be used outside and in the daytime might be unsuccessful in a country where most cooking is done privately in the evenings. Or, as a result of strengthening women's role in small scale dairy and other activities in Africa or Asia, less time will be available to collect firewood and with cash in hand a switch might be made from wood to kerosene.

The forces which decide which energy processes dominate in the future are the cost of energy production and transportation along with the overall economic and technical structure and social outlook. Energy strategies, and thus technological and economic strategies, may either promote local autonomy, increase productive use of the labour force and employment, and encourage self reliance at the community level, or may lead to centralised and capital intensive technology, possibly lower employment in the energy sector, and centralised organisation at the national level. In the short run the labour intensive strategies may be less expensive and more beneficial to rural development, but in the long run the centralised, capital intensive, interconnected systems may be more efficient and reliable. The different energy strategies require different technologies. Since technological change and economic change are closely related, the consideration of energy options will have systematically to take into account energy needs and resources, cultural values, social organisation, settlement patterns and economic structure.

In rural areas of developing countries some appropriate small scale technologies and energy systems for domestic and agricultural uses, such as improved cookers, village woodlots or biogas units, are attractive because of low investment requirements and simple maintenance and construction. Others, such as solar or wind power, when based on developed-country designs, have high capital costs. Regardless of cost, these technologies and energy systems tend to favour village autonomy and improve village and rural life. Furthermore they lead to improved agricultural yields, reduce food imports, reduce localised problems of food production and hunger and increase employment opportunities in the rural areas.

However, the development of industry in rural areas, as in the urban centres, often depends upon mechanical motion, high temperature heat, and light, requiring a more reliable and higher quality energy supply than present local technologies can offer. Centrally generated electricity may be more suitable although transmission costs to villages will be high. Large scale centralised technologies do not lead directly to increased employment in rural areas, although rural industrial development dependent on these energy systems may do so. However, these technologies present problems of technical specialisation and expert maintenance, and difficulties in providing and financing the basic appliances to use higher grade energy in rural areas.

In rural areas with low density of energy use, small scale energy systems such as solar or wind can be cheaper due to lower transport costs, but the capital costs of currently available technology are uncertain. Other systems like diesel generators, although uncompetitive in high density areas with centralised technologies, can provide relatively inexpensive electricity to rural areas. The capital costs are low, but the fuel and maintenance costs are high, which may inhibit the development of rural light industry, whereas rural areas with an indigenous hydro resource base may obtain lower cost energy.

In the long term, the opportunities for the development of all fuels, commercial, non-commercial plus non-conventional, and improvement in technologies, are considerable. Some countries will be able to make greater use of indigenous resources, and others will be able to introduce more efficient end-use technologies.

This would include development of high- and low-grade coal as substitutes for oil in electricity generation, for railway transport, and for domestic uses. Reforestation programmes, biogas generation and small hydro schemes could contribute to rural energy supplies and if properly designed could be integrated into rural development projects. In industry, the use of modern energy-efficient equipment and the substitution of labour for energy in production methods would reduce energy demand. The domestic sector would benefit from the introduction of improved cooking devices and biogas generation. In transport, the alternatives involve switching back to coal fired railway engines, or using engines powered by non-oil based electricity. Alcohol fermented from agricultural products may be used as an additive or substitute for gasoline; for example Brazil has an ambitious programme to modify auto engines to use ethyl alcohol in place of gasoline. Electric cars may in the distant future provide a solution to transport problems. Increased agricultural yields require greater use of irrigation, fertilisers and tractors and thus more energy, mainly oil. By using methanol or ethyl alcohol for tractors, obtaining fertilisers from biogas generators, and irrigation by wind, there are opportunities in the future to reduce demand for commercial energy in agriculture. In buildings, the adoption of less energy intensive materials combined with clustering and designs for natural solar heating and cooling offer some possibility for lower energy demands.

However, a number of these energy system solutions involve changes in social and economic development. For example, clustering of buildings to optimise for natural heating or cooling or to optimise for transport system efficiency may involve shifts in settlement patterns neither necessarily acceptable nor quick to introduce. Technological, social and economic issues are closely linked, and any consideration of energy options has to take a wide range of needs and effects into account. A developing country with limited capital considering regional and development policy must assess competing needs for capital such as imports of food and other goods, energy provision and improvements in education, health and transport. Even more difficult are changes in the structural path of development traditionally associated with progress, and the accompanying increased energy use, for example increased centralisation and urbanisation and concentration on energy intensive manufacturing. Energy needs will depend on the way development is improved or changed.

15.7 Chapter summary

A substantial part of the energy needs in the group of developing countries is met from non-commercial energy sources – wood, wind, water, sun, animal wastes, vegetable wastes, man and animals, and in many countries these predominate for household uses. Most developing countries have started mechanisation of industry and agriculture, leading to major social changes – urban migration and more energy use in households and for transport, a shift from non-commercial to commercial energy, a change in the fuel mix – which all bring about an increase in commercial energy consumption.

The peak in world oil production is expected to be little more than the present level (1980) and it is doubtful whether many developing countries will for long be able to base their growth on increased use of oil. Some will have indigenous supplies of gas and others can develop and possibly export coal. But, for many developing countries an increased demand for energy in the medium term will need to be met by continued imports of oil, coal and possibly gas, and by hydro-power and solar energy (wood fuel, farm waste, biomass, wind). Nuclear energy will be feasible only where there are extensive electricity systems. Hydro-power projects are capital intensive and this may inhibit their development. This then suggests for the long term that the development and use of all forms of non-commercial and solar energy will be important to meet future demand in the non-OPEC developing countries. Non-commercial energy (biomass) is likely to be used with increasing sophistication in more developed countries in suitable tropical zones.

Nearly two thirds of the world's population live in rural areas and rely upon wood, animal wastes, vegetable wastes and animal and human power for their basic needs. Most of these energy needs are required for food production and domestic uses, primarily cooking. The efficiencies in the use of these non-commercial sources is a fraction (perhaps only one quarter) of that obtained from commercial sources used for similar tasks. Some of the future energy needs could be met through improving these efficiencies, and traditional energy supplies such as wood fuel may be extended through better resource management.

Developing countries need access to energy sources but also to other resources such as capital to finance energy investments. The exploration and development of energy resources also requires resources such as skilled manpower, transport systems, and social and economic organisation to establish and manage energy systems. These technological, social and economic issues are interconnected and must be addressed simultaneously, to improve the energy position of developing countries and to provide improvements in standards of living.

In the short and medium term the future of developing countries as energy consumers is a continuation of the 1970s – dependence on oil, the problem of meeting the basic needs of the urban and rural poor, and the need to obtain alternative energy supplies and to improve the supply and use of non-commercial energy. The long-term future depends upon structural changes in the economy, changes and improvements in non-commercial energy supply systems and technologies, improvements in end-use efficiencies, and the possibilities for less energy-intensive organisation of production.

Chapter 15   Further reading

Brown, N. L. (ed.) (1978) *Renewable energy resources and rural applications in the developing world,* Westview Press, Boulder, Colorado.

Chenery, H. and Syrquin, M. (1975) *Patterns of development 1950–1970*, Oxford University Press, London.

Earl, D. E. (1975) *Forest energy and economic development*, Clarendon Press, London.

Eckholm, E. P. (1975) *The other energy crisis: firewood*, Worldwatch Institute, Washington, DC.

Griffin, K. (1978) *International inequality and national poverty*, Macmillan, London.

Helleiner, G. K. (ed.) (1975) *A world divided: less developed countries in the international economy*, Cambridge University Press, Cambridge, UK.

Henderson, P. D. (1975) *The energy situation in India: World Bank Report*, Oxford University Press, London.

ILO (1977) *Employment, growth and basic needs: a one world problem*, Praeger, New York.

Makhijani, A. and Poole, A. (1975) *Energy and agriculture in the Third World*, Ballinger, Cambridge, Mass.

Palmedo, P. *et al.* (1978) *Energy needs, uses and resources in developing countries*, a report for the US Agency for International Development, Washington, DC.

Parikh, J. K. (1978) *Energy and development*, report PUN 43 to the World Bank, World Bank, Washington, DC.

Ridker, R. (ed.) (1976) *Changing resource problems of the Fourth World*, Johns Hopkins University Press, Baltimore.

World Bank (1979) *World Bank Development Report 1979*, World Bank, Washington, DC.

CHAPTER 16

Markets and prices

16.1 Introduction

Economists have a deep and justified suspicion of the doctrine that this or that raw material may become chronically 'in short supply'. Markets exist to clear the opposing forces of supply and demand, and ex ante gaps between the two are wiped out by suitable movements in the price level. Admittedly, the smaller are the elasticities of demand and supply – the steeper are the curves – the greater will be the movement in price that is required to clear the market after an initial disturbance. Shortages which develop unexpectedly in the supply of materials which are both of great weight in total consumption and difficult to replace by substitutes might cause major disturbances not just in micro markets but in the macro economy generally. The disturbance to world trade and payments, and indeed to economic activity generally, after the oil price rise of 1973 is a well known example of this phenomenon. The sharp rise in the oil price led to an increase in the real income of the OPEC countries which not all of them could usefully spend: the 'low absorbers' amongst the OPEC countries were therefore at one time accumulating surpluses – excess savings in Keynesian terms – at a rate of more than $60 billion a year, or around three per cent of the GDP of the OECD world. Allowing for a reasonable multiplier effect – the amplification of the initial disturbance through its effect on other economic activity, which on a priori grounds should be quite large for an exogenous shock of this sort – this phenomenon could in principle explain the whole of the recession in the OECD world in the late 1970s, although most observers believe that there were other powerful contractionary forces at work as well.

Those economists who are not attached to this traditional Keynesian approach can arrive at very similar conclusions by another route. The oil price rise itself, considering its direct effect only, probably raised the OECD price level by more than two per cent in 1974; and, as is normal, resistance of income receivers of all sorts to this significant cut in their own real spending power – a phenomenon called by economists 'real wage resistance' – led indirectly (through pressure on wages) to a multiplication of this price increase by a factor of two or three. Once again, the oil price rise, and its necessary aftermath, can explain a large part of the acceleration of inflation in the OECD world, and the natural reaction of both government and private sector spenders to such disarray in their financial environment brought about that fall in real spending levels which in turn caused the recession in real economic activity. (See, for a discussion of these events, the McCracken Report, 1977).

Thus economists of all persuasions recognise that price instability in raw material markets can have serious economic effects, and it should be noted that these effects can work just as dramatically in the contractionary or deflationary direction as in the more familiar inflationary way. Indeed, a sound analytical case can be put forward for believing that any sharp price movement is contractionary of real economic activity, although the effect on the general price level of all goods depends on the original direction of the movement in the particular price.

Nevertheless, many economists persist in believing that these dangers and worries are short term in nature, and macroeconomic in content, and that the suggestion that there might be long-run 'shortages' stems from a failure to take account of adjustments along the supply and demand curves brought about, respectively, by changes in price and changed availability of substitutes.

It is important to stress that the disbelief of economists in 'Club of Rome' type projections of ultimate shortages (Meadows et al., 1972) is not based merely on scepticism about the extrapolation of linear or logarithmic trends through time, nor upon some innate optimism about the generosity of nature. Economists recognise as well as anyone that individual materials may well run out, or become extremely expensive to obtain. The more specific the material, the more likely it is that genuine physical scarcity will emerge. However, and this is the essence of the point, a highly specific material source may well be produced under conditions of extremely inelastic supply, but is likely to be consumed under conditions of extremely elastic demand. For example, coal from a given seam is strictly finite in quantity, and will soon be exhausted; but the users of coal are in general almost completely indifferent as to the source of what they burn. On the other hand, there is admittedly a very low price elasticity of demand for fuel in general, but this is matched by the presumption that the elasticity of supply will be relatively great.

This argument, that the supply of energy is elastic, is increased in strength the longer is the allowed period of adjustment. It is a fact of technology, not of economics, that the system takes time to adjust to changes in relative prices. The length of time of adjustment depends on, among other things, the degree of certainty with which decision makers approach a particular price change. If today's spot price is regarded as a reliable indicator of tomorrow's price – if the forward premium is zero or the elasticity of expectations is unity (that is, if a 1% price change today lead's to a 1% change in the expected future price) – then the distinction between the present and the future collapses apart from its purely technological content – the length of time taken, at technical minimum, to change existing equipment and practices. But the more the expected future price is independent of price changes taking place today, the more that technological lag is increased by economic uncertainty. A market which believed that everything that happens today is merely 'noise' will be a market which systematically fails to adjust in the way that economists would expect. This is a matter to which we return below.

16.2   Price setting in practice – the case of oil

Economic theory has a well worked out doctrine – due in its essence to Hotelling (1931), but added to since then – to explain the link between present and future, and between prices and quantities sold, when considering the depletion of natural resources. The essence of the proposition is extremely simple. Any owner of a natural resource who has access to a perfect capital market can compare two critical magnitudes: the rate of expected appreciation in the price of the natural resource $\dot p$, and the rate of interest at which he can borrow or lend money on the capital market π. Each unit of raw material taken out of the ground today can be sold at today's price and the proceeds lent in the capital market, after which it will grow at the rate of π per cent per year. Each unit of resource left in the ground will increase its own value at the rate of $\dot p$ per year. Then the condition necessary for the owner of the resource to be willing to deplete it at the maximum rate that is technologically feasible will be:

$$\pi \geqslant \dot p \tag{16.1}$$

This inequality, when combined with knowledge about the conditions of demand 'today' and assumptions about the state of demand 'tomorrow', determines simultaneously today's prices, the rate of increase of prices through time, and the time profile of depletion. The mechanism works as follows. Decision makers start with a view about the price level in the future, P_f (perhaps determined by the expected cost of a competing but more expensive resource), and the spot price which happens to be ruling today, P_t. The relation between these two of course determines $\dot p$, and this value is read into the inequality (16.1). If the inequality holds – if the expected rate of return to be obtained by selling oil today and investing proceeds in a stock market is greater than the expected rate of appreciation of the oil when held in the ground – then depletion will reach its maximum technical rate; but if the value of $\dot p$ determined by the interrelationship of P_f and P_t is too great, the depletion rate will be cut, in principle to zero: it is more profitable to hold the oil in the ground, waiting for its price to increase, than to sell it now and invest the proceeds.

But a slowing down of depletion today will necessarily, given the conditions of demand, raise the value of P_t; and this, on the basis of any given assumption about P_f, will reduce the size of $\dot p$. There will thus always be *some* rise in P_t which, when fed back into the basic inequality, (16.1), will lead to an increase in today's depletion rate. This simple mechanism is therefore the device which links the present to the future, and keeps the markets in equilibrium.

Now, of course, in the real world the value of P_f is systematically uncertain, the value of π will differ from individual to individual. There will, therefore, be a spread of opinion and depletion decisions through the market, and at any point in time some individuals will find themselves 'at the margin', ready to change their rate of extraction in response to small price changes, and other individuals will find themselves further from the margin. The degree of stability or volatility of the market will depend on this dispersion, and will be influenced also by the effect, if any, of changes in today's spot price on people's expectation of the future.

Another way in which the mechanism can work is to transmit back, into the present, the public's changed assessments of the likely balance between supply and demand in the future. For instance, suppose that, as a result of reading this book, a sizeable batch of decision makers conclude that the future of energy supplies will be easier than they had previously presumed – perhaps because of the plethora of possible alternatives or the possibilities of conservation. This will lower P_f, and for any given value of P_t, will lower also p; and this in turn, when fed into the inequality (16.1), will lead some decision makers to discern an advantage in accelerated depletion, which in turn will lead to extra supply today, hence lowering P_t and tending to restore p to its previous value.

A natural consequence of this mechanism is that 'the system' depletes without conscious thought for tomorrow, and yet the invisible hand of the market brings fears of future shortage back into the present.

These simple mechanisms become in practice far more complex. Among the more useful or important complications are:

1. The relevant 'price' is not known with any certainty, nor are the patterns of future returns in the capital market. The rule needs to take account not only of mathematically expected outcomes, but also of all the usual elements of risk analysis.
2. The relevant 'price' is not the selling price, but the excess of that selling price over the unavoidable costs of production – what economists call the quasi-rent.
3. Costs may be related not only to the number of units produced, but also to the rate of production per unit of time. This fact, recently stressed by Houthakker (1980), acts as a brake on depletion rates.
4. The capital market is of course not perfect, and rates of return may differ widely between the borrower and lender, and between one market and another. For instance, in the case of the low absorbing OPEC countries, monies invested from the proceeds of accelerated exploitation of their oil reserves tend to be placed in the Euro-Dollar market or in Wall Street equities, on both of which the observed return over the five years after 1973 was less than the rate of inflation. On the other hand, in high absorbing countries, such as Iran before the fall of the Shah or in Nigeria or Indonesia, the relevant rate of return may have been the profit on industrial investment at home or the chances of survival of the existing regime – a 'return' normally thought of, in subjective terms, as high and positive. (These considerations merely complicate the story, and do not bias it in any one direction.)

The picture of the market mechanism painted so far in this chapter exaggerates its strength and understates many difficulties. In fact, many observers still believe that the dominant forces at present operating in the market are not the competitive pressures of economic text books, but instead the untidy and unstable struggles between OPEC, the disintegrating monoliths of the international oil companies, and the emerging national oil companies, all locked together in a battle resembling the struggles between pre-historic monsters of Hollywood horror movies. The fact that the outcome of these struggles has been, in the period since 1973, consistent with the behaviour of a market in face of a suddenly revealed expectation of future 'shortage' may seem to leave the choice between these two alternative hypotheses about the causes of oil price rises somewhat indeterminate. Either the price has risen because the market has been rigged, as a result of a sudden shift in the complex balance of power between different groups; or it is the sudden revelation of future energy shortage which, working through the basic inequality of the Hotelling mechanism, has brought back into the present the shadow of events to come. Both elements may well have been operating, but it is illuminating to explore their apparent rivalry further.

The scientific approach to this choice of hypotheses is to attempt, by reasoning, to identify the points at which the two explanations offer different predictions about questions of fact, and to devise investigations which would discover which prediction fits the known facts better. Unfortunately, but not untypically, both sets of predictions can be readily validated, suggesting that both doctrines could be true or, even more distressingly, that the system is in technical terms 'over-determined'.

It is certainly true, for instance, that the informed press, professional writings, and the public consciousness generally are, at the beginning of the 1980s, far more familiar with the propositions about the ultimate exhaustibility of cheap oil supplies than they were in the late 1960s: to this extent, it seems plausible that the cause of the shift in P_t has been a marked change in P_f. But equally, it is a matter of common journalistic observation that the trigger for the price rises of 1973, and for the proportionately smaller but in absolute terms larger price rises of 1979–80, have been political and military events of one sort or another in the Middle East, involving the deliberate flexing of market power muscles by individual companies or countries. It is probably mistaken to regard OPEC as such as a 'cartel' in formal economic terms, but the world market in traded oil has certainly not been perfect in the last decade! True, the political and military events of 1973 preceded the general public consciousness of 'future energy shortage'. But this is not conclusive evidence for the power struggle hypothesis – it is perfectly consistent with the doctrine of those who stress the importance of long-run considerations of ultimate shortages to suggest that the *trigger* of the events of 1973 were political, military, or even collusive market action (involving conceivably both oil companies and Middle Eastern potentates), while the *ultimate cause* was the limited generosity of nature.

To push scepticism to its limits, it may in fact *never* prove possible to disentangle the story sufficiently to make a choice between the alternative hypotheses. For instance, suppose that it were 'really' true that the big oil price rises were the result of political or collusive events. But suppose that it became widely believed in consuming countries that these events were likely to dominate traded energy prices until the end of the century and beyond. It would then be rational for consuming governments, and free economic agents in consuming countries, themselves to make decisions about the production of alternative energy sources or investment designed to minimise energy consumption, at cost levels which would only yield profitable sales if Middle East prices remained at least at their 1979 real levels. Many producers and consumers, and much productive capital, would become 'locked in' to these high cost, high price, energy sources, and a *possible* result might well be collusion between consuming governments at the turn of the century in order to protect their home market, and the profitability of home capital investment, from any low price traded oil which might then be available internationally.

Looking back on events, from the standpoint of the turn of the century, an economic historian would find it extremely difficult to answer the conundrum: 'What was the cause of the energy price rise?'. In terms of temporal priority, it might well be that the Middle Eastern war of 1973 was 'the cause'. In terms of economic forces, it could conceivably be said that it was the strong flow of investment into alternative energy sources which we are hypothesising for the 1980s and 1990s that led to the high prices around the turn of the century. In terms of the underlying psychology of all these events, weight should perhaps be given to the strength and degree of acceptability which the doctrines of the environmentalist lobby have attained.

But this whole line of reasoning may be said to press scepticism too far. The Hotelling mechanism – indeed Hotelling's own original statement of it – has both a competitive and monopolistic form. A cartelised or monopolised market usually has higher prices, and a lower volume of transactions, than does a free market at a given point of time; in other words the trajectory of prices through time in a cartelised market is higher than in a free market. The leaders of the OPEC countries may have restricted output in 1973–80 because they expected shortages to develop later in the century; but they also anticipated (no doubt correctly) their own continued power to control the market in the future. On this argument, what happened in 1973 was that the OPEC producers moved from a relatively gentle competitive Hotelling price trajectory onto the far higher – and perhaps steeper – cartelised trajectory.

Balance in this controversy is hard to achieve, and readers should be warned that informed commentators hold, in all honesty, differing views. The view of the present authors is that the future price of oil P_f, in a hypothetically free market at the end of the century, is likely to be sufficiently high relative to the spot price (P_t) of the late 1970s for $\dot{p}$ to be plausibly similar in magnitude to π – both around 5 per cent. It is therefore unnecessary, we would argue, to suggest that the general level of prices in the late 1970s was monopolistically determined. But of course the particular events of 1979–80, the doubling of prices in a 6 month period, were political in character, and could not have occurred in a free market. So the picture we paint is of underlying trends that require little in the way of collusion or market rigging to explain them, but of year to year changes which are heavily political and cartelised.

16.3   Supply responses

In the energy markets the response of supply is at least as important as the response on the demand side to an increase in price. The essence of the investment decision in projects which take a long time to mature and have a long expected life span is the expectation of a price level at which the output from the new enterprise might be sold. The relevant price is the forward or future quotation, not the spot price. The higher the rate of discount, the less important this effect need be. A simple explanation of this point is as follows: If the rate of discount is zero (a dollar tomorrow is worth as much as a dollar today) then the 'mid-point' of a 30 year project is in fifteen years time, and we can say that an investor may well concentrate on the expected price in fifteen years from now. Any value of the discount rate greater than zero will bring this 'mean point' nearer today, hence reducing the importance of future events. Nevertheless, investment in an oil shale project or a breeder reactor, which have gestation periods of upwards of a decade and a life expectancy of upwards of 30 years, depends upon expected energy prices at the turn of the century. Prices today are of importance only in so far as they offer indicators of what prices will be when today's students are about to become grandparents.

Now the Hotelling mechanism brings the expectation of future events back into the present, and the path of those events itself depends on today's prices. Both these links need to work if anything like an optimal path of investment in alternative energy sources is to be followed. If the response, through the Hotelling mechanism, to expectations of shortages tomorrow is too weak, it will appear uneconomic to leave resources in the ground, depletion will be too rapid, prices today will be too low, and our grandchildren will be in trouble to an extent greater than 'optimal'. If it is too strong, then prices today will be too high, depletion will be too slow, and the amount of investment stimulated by today's excessively high prices will be too great.

Conversely, on the supply side, if the elasticity of expectations is too small (a rise of one per cent in today's price raises the expectation of tomorrow's price by, say, only one tenth of one per cent) then the shortages in the future will be excessive, because investment will not take place on a scale sufficient to meet the excess demand which today's rate of depletion is implicitly predicting.

Economists distinguish usefully between two types of uncertainty – primary uncertainty, which is, given the state of science in all its branches, essentially irreducible; and secondary uncertainty, which could in principle be removed if human institutions allowed it. It is often said that 'planning' is a way of removing secondary uncertainty, by ensuring that each economic agent knows the likely moves of his suppliers, customers, or competitors. In other economic philosophies, the same desired end – the removal of unnecessary uncertainty – can, it is claimed, be achieved by making the working of the market 'transparent', and in particular by reducing collusion and spreading information.

In the energy market, major sources of secondary uncertainty are ignorance of the costs of future technologies, and ignorance also of the possibilities of conservation. Indeed, it might be said that the purpose of this book is to provide diligent readers with information that reduces secondary uncertainty. The more that uncertainty is reduced, the greater will be the link between the present and the future, brought about by the interaction between the Hotelling mechanism and the elasticity of expectations, by the two-way mechanism through which today's expectation of future shortages influences today's prices, today's investment decisions, and tomorrow's supplies.

A sizeable dose of secondary uncertainty, a low elasticity of expectations, and a sizeable dose of market rigging of one sort or another, will make the economists' perfect mechanism for bringing the prospects of future events back into the present very ineffective indeed. A world which has had reasonable experiences of market events of the sorts here described – sudden recognition of future possibility of shortages, political interferences, very sharp price rises, sudden revision of expectations – would be able to cope with the events since 1973 in the energy market with reasonable calm. But although there have been previous periods of alarm about energy supplies – for instance the famous account by Jevons in the third quarter of the nineteenth century of the prospect of running out of coal (Jevons, 1866) – they have been far less all-pervasive than the course of expectations since 1973. Again, the cycles of fashion in economists' predictions about the terms of trade of primary producers generally – roughly a five year cycle of optimism and pessimism in the three decades since 1950 – have been about modest trends of four or five per cent a year in primary product prices, not the very large discontinuities of recent years in energy prices.

We have, therefore, a set of unprecedented events, and an unprecedented penumbra of secondary uncertainty has gathered around the known facts, making prediction and analysis difficult. It is these circumstances that have led to the call for 'leadership' from political figures or from business potentates. Hosts of individual decision makers do not know what to think, and the normal mechanisms of the market cannot come to their aid. Because of the time lags involved, they have to look forward to future prices, and they do not know how much of the signals they are receiving today are mere noise.

16.4 Optimal strategies by producers, consumers, and world economic leaders

Suppose first that those economists who characterise the present world energy scene as one dominated by a cartel or oligopoly were correct. What would be the best strategy for the managers of that cartel, or the oligopolistic price leaders, to adopt? Some economists, considering the optimal market strategies that might be followed by such a group, have had no hesitation in concluding that 'a bumpy ride' would be deemed the best thing to force upon the world. A high price in 1974/75 would extract a large temporary 'rent'; a dip in the (real) price in the second half of the seventies would discourage conservation and raise the hopes of those who were ready to believe that the cartel would break; another sharp rise at the end of the 1970s would extract some more rent; and doubtless another sharp dip would occur in the early 1980s, as the recession in the OECD world cuts back the demand for traded fuels. Such a succession of bumps, operating in the market where decision makers were already unsteady and finding difficulty in distinguishing between noise and signals, would be bound to add to the confusion and perpetuate the period during which the OPEC producers had a strong hold over energy supplies.

The authors of this book do not believe that the effective decision makers of the oil exporting countries had any such aim in mind in the late 1970s, although they doubtless read the analyses which might lead to such a prescription. The events of energy history, perhaps like those of all history, are 'one damned thing after another'. There is no conspiratorial hand guiding the course of events. Nevertheless, because of the likelihood of a succession of uncoordinated and sequentially uncorrelated political or military changes in the oil-producing countries, a series of bumpy ups and downs in prices of traded fuels is extremely likely. The bumpy ride will be provided by the uncoordinated play of events, but its consequences will be, perhaps, very much the same as those which would be brought about by deliberate malevolent action.

In face of this possibility, what sort of strategy should be adopted by the governments of consuming countries or by the strategic directors, if they exist, of the OECD world? It was of course possible that the 'energy shortage' would turn out to be a chimera. Perhaps, as Professor Milton Friedman and many other economists suggested in the immediate aftermath of 1973, the price of oil might have eventually subsided to the $2 or so per barrel which, at the price level of the mid 1970s, represented the marginal cost of production for large tranches of Middle East oil. This was one possible outcome. At the other extreme was the possibility that the price of crude oil, by the turn of the century, might rise another two or three times, in real terms, to a level between $50 and $70 per barrel at 1979 prices.

Faced with this very wide range, the only analytical device open to OECD governments was the apparatus of risk analysis and strategic choice. One simple instrument of policy analysis is to ask 'what is the strategy that I can adopt, in face of this uncertainty and possible different states of nature, in order to minimise the maximum losses which my country, and its heirs and successors, might suffer?'

If such a 'minimax loss' strategy were followed, there is little doubt that an OECD government would choose to make very substantial investment in alternative energy supplies and in energy conservation: the loss, through wasted capital investment, would be smaller than the loss that would arise, at the opposite end of the distribution, if the worst possible fears about future energy prices were to come true, and if the investment had not been made. Only a true gambler – a person choosing to 'maximise the minimum gain on the game' – would choose to place his bets on a low energy price outcome for the close of the century.

There are of course more complex and subtle strategies which could be pursued. One attractive line of policy would be to set out to prove the various alternative sources of fuel – solar, nuclear, coal conversion, even windmills or tidal power – in order to leave decision making in the early 1980s free of secondary uncertainty about these technologies. The trouble with such a dilatory approach to policy making is that it is likely to leave unchanged the degree of uncertainty about the determination of the consuming countries to pursue their own aims, which we diagnose as the most powerful cause of upward price pressure in the market for traded oil in the early 1980s.

The only serious way to cut out the Hotelling loop in the decision–making process – to convince the owners of depletable resources today that today's prices are a reasonable level at which to sell – is to ensure the *commitment* of OECD resources to alternative forms of energy production, or to energy conservation on a large and *irreversible* scale, *forthwith*. It is such a commitment, and only such a commitment, which will take the heat out of the market. In terms of the tired analogies of military deterrence it is no good *pretending* to commit your reserves – you must actually put them to work digging the trenches.

16.5 Domestic distribution effects

The rise in energy prices in the period since 1973 has not been uniformly applied between countries, nor between different fuels, nor between different customers. The extent to which the energy market is 'one market' has already been explored in chapter 10, and here we need remark only that thermal equivalence in energy pricing is neither necessary nor optimal. For instance, some fuels are more efficient than others in transferring heat; some methods of fuel conversion involve heavy fixed costs (for instance electricity generation) and hence off-peak supplies can be provided cheaply; and for some fuels, the time profile of production differs systematically from that of consumption (for instance natural gas), which again justifies cheap offers for final sales of special time profile characteristics. Nevertheless, in a broad sense, we would expect prices of different fuels to tend towards thermal equivalent levels.

Again, although it might be possible for some producing countries to stand out against world prices, and subsidise their own domestic users by providing marginal supplies at less than world prices, such behaviour is bound to attract international objection in so far as the supplies are directed towards industrial customers –

'cheap petro-chemicals' from the Middle East are likely to attract anti-dumping duties in most world markets.

The only form of discrimination which has proved systematically attractive on a widespread scale is the protection of individual favoured household consumers or the customers for some traditional fuels (gasoline in the United States, kerosene in the Far East, domestic electricity in the United Kingdom). For a producing country, discriminatory behaviour of this sort is not necessarily silly. The marginal cost of extra North Sea oil to the United Kingdom, in periods of excess world demand, is the foregone possibility of selling extra oil at some future date, not today's world market valuation, and unless very strong and positive views are held about future prices, along the lines of the Hotelling relationship, this cost may be low.

Be that as it may, the main incentive for specially cheap sales to citizens is not normally careful calculation of this sort, but instead a wish to temper the wind to domestic groups whose political power is great. President Carter's failure in 1979 to raise the gasoline price was a recognition of this sort of pressure.

Mr Tony Benn, the Energy Minister in the British Labour administration which left office in the summer of 1979, exalted such practices into a political doctrine. For him, energy users – particularly the poor ones – who were locked into a particular source of fuel had a right to be protected from sharp price increases: the usual example was that of tenants in public housing whose homes were equipped with 'all-electric underfloor heating'. One way to defend protected pricing for such customers is to argue that wage inflation was thereby held at bay; but the real reason was the normal distributional one that the price mechanism has an influence on relative real incomes as well as on resource allocation, and that the distributional effect is more important than the allocation effect.

From the present point of view, this argument is mainly important as an explanation of the slowness of adjustment in some key markets, particularly the United States; it explains to some extent the sluggishness of the market and the sharpness of the price adjustments in those segments of the system where they were allowed free rein.

16.6   Quick or slow adjustment to energy price increases?

It is sometimes suggested that a rational system should damp the fluctuations, random or regular, in the market mechanism. For instance, in the late 1970s it was standard practice in Eastern Europe for arrangements between the Soviet Union (a large energy exporter) and the other members of the East European Trading Block to take the form of adjusting the energy price to a five year moving average of market prices in the capitalist world. In the period 1973–79, during which the oil price dipped in real dollar terms, returning in mid summer 1979 to somewhere near its peak level of 1974, this mechanism may have worked rather well. The East

European customers moved steadily towards a higher energy price during the whole period, while the OECD countries suffered to some extent from the 'bumpy ride' described above.

But like any other commodity stabilisation scheme, a system of slow adjustment risks leaving the protected price high and dry as the tide goes out. A slow adjustment principle may make change more difficult to achieve, as the home system gets further and further away from the world market. On the other hand, to allow erratic price increases to dominate may do nothing more to decision makers than introduce experimental neurosis.

The error of policy in the 1970s seems, with hindsight, to lie more with those who have restricted the process of price change than with those who have welcomed it. The price mechanism is not, as we shall discuss in the next chapter, by any means a perfect device for achieving rational resource allocation, but deliberate interference with it, in ways or for motives unconnected with market mechanisms, seems to have made things worse, not better.

16.7   Chapter summary

Shortages do occur, and do push up prices, but normally this process is limited by the availability to the consumer of substitutes (demand elasticity) or the availability of alternative supplies (supply elasticity). In the case of energy these two escape routes are weak, and complicated by long time lags and political complexities arising largely from the geographical concentration of oil supplies. How much of the events of 1973 and 1979 were caused by 'collusion' and how much by 'the market' is systematically unknowable.

Depletion policy, today's price, and tomorrow's expected price may all be linked together by simple relationships involving all these terms and an appropriate rate of interest or discount. Of course the real world is far more complex than this analysis suggests, and political factors loom large (see chapters 17 and 18), but the essential pull at today's prices is the fear of future shortages.

Fears of a bumpy ride – of prices responding unevenly to the pull of events – lead to a consideration of the optimal strategy in the fact of uncertainty. One objective is to reduce uncertainty, to increase knowledge, to speed up response times. Another might be to 'prove' all possible alternative techniques for energy production or transformation.

The question of speeding up response by consumers is in part a question of how quickly market prices respond to spot shortages, and in part how quickly economic agents react to price signals in the various energy markets. It appears that markets have been sluggish, and price and quantity response – in key sectors, such as the USA – too slow. Preoccupation with domestic distribution effects – big profits for producers, big increases in costs for locked-in consumers – has had the consequence of delaying necessary changes in the allocation of resources.

Chapter 16   Further reading

Dasgupta, P. and Heal, G. M. (1977) *The use of resources* (Cambridge Economic Handbook Series), Cambridge University Press, Cambridge, UK.

Doran, C. F. (1977) *Oil, myth and politics*, The Free Press, New York.

Griffin, J. M. (1979) *Energy conservation in the OECD 1980–2000*, Ballinger, Cambridge, Mass.

Hotelling, H. (1931) 'The economics of exhaustible resources', in *Journal of Political Economy*, vol. 39, April, pp. 137–75.

Houthakker, H. A. (1975) *The price of world oil*, American Enterprise Institute of Public Policy, Washington, DC.

Noreng, O. (1978) *Oil politics in the 1980s*, McGraw-Hill, New York and London.

OAPEC (1978) *Petroleum and Arab economic development*, Organisation of Arab Petroleum Exporting Countries, Kuwait.

Odell, P. and Rosing, K. E. (1976) *Optimal development of the North Sea's oil fields*, Kogan Page, London.

Pearce, D. W. and Rose, J. (eds.) (1975) *The economics of natural resource depletion*, Macmillan, London.

Pindyck, R. S. (ed.) (1979a) *The structure of energy markets*, vol. 1 of 'Advances in the economics of energy and resources', Jai Press, Greenwich, Connecticut.

Quiros-Corradi, A. (1979) 'Energy and the exercise of power' in *Foreign Affairs*, vol. 57, no. 5, pp. 1144–66.

Policies and Instruments

17.1 Introduction

In the previous chapter we sketched the outline of a possible strategy for a 'consuming' government in the face of an uncertain prospect of a rise in price of energy over the next three decades. We stressed uncertainty, and the possibilities that what economists call 'different objective functions' might lead rationally to the adoption of different strategies.

This is fairly well-worked territory, and has no particular special features when applied to the energy problem, nor does it tell us much about the economics of energy which is not easily accessible to other processes of reasoning.

What is important is the inter-relationship between aims (or objective functions), policies designed to make the attainment of those aims possible, and the instruments available to policy makers.

The discussion of chapter 16 concentrated uniquely on 'cost minimisation' in its various guises: profit maximisation is merely the mirror image of cost minimisation. But, in real life, policy makers have many other preoccupations, of which the security of supply, continuity of supply, and spreading of risk are the traditional components. The balance between domestic and imported sources of fuel, the balance between different types of technological uncertainty, and between cost and security considerations, are the main political inputs to the formation of strategy. We should expect systematic divergence between the strategic choices made by politicians of different views, between countries with different objective conditions, and between the view of one set of politicians at one time and the same set of politicians at another time.

Chapter 16 gave proper weight to the mechanism of the market as an instrument for inducing an appropriate allocation of resources both between fuels and across time. The implied prescription of much of the discussion was 'leave it to the market'. But the present chapter cannot start from that conclusion, because the very possibility of 'policy' by national or international governmental organisation implies actions to supplement, contradict, or at the very least amplify market forces. Admittedly, if one starts from a position in which market forces have been denied their role – for instance the United States in 1979 – a policy decision can take the form of 'allowing the market to operate more fully'; but an act of policy always requires an explicit decision either to leave things as they are, or to encourage them to change in a specified direction.

The instruments of policy – the tools available to government – vary widely, reflecting differences in both political regimes and economic institutions. In much of Western Europe and the Third World, energy investment is a matter for the state, or state-financed monopolies. In North America, a very similar role is played by 'public utilities', but both for financial and managerial purposes these are independent of central government, and often beyond their influence save through indirect means. In virtually every country of the world a central government exercises firm controls over the safety of operations and the financing of technological developments – this is an irreducible role of government in the most liberal of regimes. Because of both the high level of technology and the rapid changes of technology in energy production, this power alone gives to the state an essential role in energy decision making. Less convincingly, it has been claimed that the size and lumpiness of the investment funds required in the energy sector makes the provision of state finance absolutely necessary. While it is undoubtedly true that the requirements for funds are greater than can conceivably be provided from ploughed-back resources of existing energy companies, the banking system of most advanced capitalist countries, and their associated capital markets could, if it were politically acceptable, raise sufficient funds. The role of the state in energy investment is an act of political choice or an implication of past political history, not a necessity of economic or technological fact.

Where governments do not operate directly through the channelling of funds or the authorisation of technological developments, they act indirectly through the finance of research, price regulations, interference in the transport sector, and, of overwhelming importance in most of Western Europe, tax policy. For instance, in formal accounting terms, about 50 per cent of the price of gasoline paid by the UK consumer in the summer of 1979 went as tax to the British Government.

This three-fold division of aims, policies, and instruments provides a framework for discussing the policy options of the 1980s in the OECD world.

17.2   Aims, objective functions, strategies

To the Anglo-Saxon observer, it sometimes appears that the French authorities have a more clear-headed vision of their national purpose, and a more single-minded determination to pursue it, than do some other Western governments. In the energy field, the keynote of French policy both before 1973 and much more sharply since, has been to seek to minimise national dependence on imported fuel, and to insulate the economy as far as possible from international political disturbances by concluding robust treaties with other, oil-rich, countries.

The same theme, to varying extents, has characterised the stream of policy discussions in other OECD countries. Table 17.1 shows the proportionate depen-

Table 17.1.   *Dependence on energy and oil imports.*

	Energy imports as a percentage of total energy demand		Net oil imports as a percentage of world oil trade	
	1973	1977	1973	1977
United Kingdom	50	25	5.7	3.0
United States	16	23	14.5	24.0
Italy	81	81	5.0	5.2
West Germany	54	57	7.3	7.8
France	89	89	6.3	6.6
Japan	91	89	13.4	15.1

Note: The figures for France for energy imports as a percentage of total energy demand relate to 1973 and 1976. (*Source:* OECD, Energy balances of OECD countries, 1976 and 1978.)
Sources: IEA (1979a); British Petroleum (1978a); United Nations (1978).

dence on imported energy supplies of selected OECD countries in 1973 and 1977, and it shows also the net oil imports of those countries, as a proportion of world trade in oil at the same dates. Trade dependence is not too severe a problem for the small country whose purchases are a small component of world trade, and which is accustomed to a considerable dependence on international trade for the rest of its economic activity. For example, not only would a change in Belgium's oil imports have a small impact on the world oil market, but an increased price of oil might require only a modest increase in Belgian exports if the trade balance were to remain unchanged. On the other hand, assuming unchanged policies, the consensus projection seems to suggest that towards the end of the 1980s the United States might still be importing around 8 or 9 million barrels a day of oil, or about 20 per cent of its total energy supplies, and dependence on this scale would threaten problems of quite a different magnitude. Instead of causing only minor changes from today's oil prices, United States oil imports at this level would form so large a component of total US imports, and so large a fraction of world oil needs, that the consequences for the world price of oil and the effect on the balance of trade would be serious. Successive administrations in the United States, and successive occupants of the post of Energy Secretary in Washington, have recognised the dangers implied by such a future, but it was not until late in 1979 that they began to convince Congress that the particular policy mix which the administration recommended was better than inaction.

Be that as it may, the common currency of policy discussion was the scale and rigour of steps to be taken to reduce trade dependence. Was this approach justified? Interdependence, in the modern world economy, is a fact of life increasingly recognised and accepted in many different lines of activity – employment policies, monetary policies, trade policies, and even taxation policies (for instance the European Common Market's 'fiscal harmonisation'). What is there that is so special about fuel interdependence? First, the all-pervasive nature of fuel as an input – it is 'basic' to most industrial processes, in the sense that the matrix of transactions between industries show a significantly positive entry for all cells in the fuel column. Moreover, it is a *necessary* input – no fuel, no output.

Secondly, the generosity of nature is not randomly distributed across the world – hydrocarbons, particularly liquid or gaseous ones, are distributed rather narrowly to a few chosen nations. It is important to be clear what bearing this geo-political fact has on the likely course of events. Put bluntly, a refusal by the OPEC suppliers to offer the United States the oil it needs might *conceivably* lead to a world military disaster, but it is unlikely to bring the United States to its knees – if the rulers of any OPEC country tried to take out an insurance policy with Lloyds of London on the stability of their regime in the face of a serious oil embargo by them against the United States, they would find few takers. In this sense, the anti-OPEC hawks in the United States Congress have some truth on their side. A really determined and aggressive United States foreign policy might run grave risks of war with the Soviet Union, but could conceivably break the will of the more extreme restrictionists amongst the oil producers. However, this type of military-political speculation is not only distasteful in varying degrees to most observers, but also is of limited practical importance. While some bellicose noises may be heard in the US Congress as the price of oil rises, military action on these grounds alone is unlikely even if prices reach double the 1979 level in real terms. A country's national interest may in the limit provoke the use of force to ensure energy supplies, but not to protect against price changes on the scale of the movements in 1979. Hence the OPEC powers do have great scope for price increases, due simply to their geo-political dominance.

The specially irksome nature of the energy problem may have its own safety valve at real prices which are around double the 1979 levels, because of the sharp macro-economic recession such a price rise would provoke, but up to that figure the geographical concentration of the supplies of traded fuels does in fact make the energy problem an order of magnitude more worrying to governments than is the potential shortage of any other material. Not only do the limitations of physical resources offer a threat, but the geo-political concentration of those resources amplifies and augments that threat: the threat is of sharp price rises and their consequences rather than of physical shortage, but it is nonetheless real.

Hence the securing of domestic sources of supply, and the insulation of one's own country as far as possible from the ebb and flow of world trade, is a major continuing policy consideration. Far more than any other matter, it dominates the thinking of policy makers throughout the OECD world.

The other 'non-cost' element in planning is the complex of environmental arguments. As chapter 9 shows, the lessons to be drawn from environmental considerations are far from simple and far from clear. Environmental and social issues range from the ecological disturbance caused by an oil spill, tidal barrage or open cast coal mine to the possible modification of the climate, on a global scale, as a result of the CO_2 produced by burning fossil fuels. They cover health risks from sulphur dioxide (mainly from coal), from inhalation of coal dust by miners, and from radioactivity released as a result of the use of nuclear energy. Account must be taken of the risk of accidents in coal mining, in nuclear power stations, and in the transport and use of natural gas. Social issues, such as the stability of mining communities and the need to discourage the spread of nuclear weapons, will affect the appraisal of different energy sources, as will aesthetic issues such as the visual impact of windmills, oil refineries or coal mines.

Nevertheless, according to the different weighting of different environmental considerations, any government at a point of time has an implied preference pattern for some forms of energy production over others, and probably most governments have an *environmental* preference for energy conservation over energy production. However, both the balance of the environmental preferences on production techniques and the general presumption in favour of conservation need to be weighed against cost considerations.

Summarising all this, the objective function to be minimised or at least set at a satisfactorily low level can be thought of as having three elements: first, a cost minimisation risk assessment, along the lines sketched in chapter 16; secondly, the security of supply or minimisation of import dependence; and, thirdly, an environmental term, which contains predictable bias in favour of conservation, but whose impact on the general pattern of choice is impossible to predict *a priori*.

17.3   Policies

The simplest definition of an energy policy assumes a target energy balance table for some set of future years, either single-valued or, in more sophisticated analysis, with a statistical distribution to take account of risk and uncertainty. Policy is then defined as the set of actions necessary to bring about this outcome. In practice, policies have to be maintained for many years if particular outcomes are to be in any way assured. At least three systematic classes of problems are encountered. First, the initial conditions which policy is designed to correct may themselves change or the appreciation of those conditions by policy makers may vary. For instance, the conditions of what we called in chapter 16 the 'bumpy ride' of energy prices may induce fluctuations in the intensity with which policy makers are attached to particular paths, and the normal economic trade cycle may intensify the bumps.

Secondly, energy policy may conflict with other policy targets, and the priority given to energy will vary from time to time according to the relative ranking of energy and other issues. Thirdly, the aims or strategies of energy policy themselves may change as governments change, the views of electorates as perceived by governments change, or consciousness of the constraints under which policy must operate becomes more widespread.

Thus, in the United States after 1973, policy started by emphasising the possibility of 'breaking the cartel' – or wishing the problem would go away. Then emphasis was put on finding oil – or substitute liquid hydrocarbons – from other sources: more indigenous production, more from other foreign sources, more from shale or through coal conversion. Emphasis then shifted to the possibility of nuclear energy, but the limitations of the use of electricity and the safety difficulties of nuclear power plants made that option lose much ground in the late 1970s. By the time of President Carter's 1979 message, the 'renewable' energy sources had become the fashion, with major emphasis on solar sources.

For the outside observer, the dog that consistently failed to bark in American energy policy making was conservation, particularly conservation forced by higher prices. The paradox that the home of capitalist enterprise was the one OECD nation where the price mechanism was *not* in use to induce rational energy saving was much remarked on, but the remarks provoked little response within the United States until 1979–80.

These American examples of changing fashion, or changing perception of the range of possible alternatives, can be paralleled, although in more muted form, elsewhere in the OECD region. The continuing keynote of UK policy, for instance, at least since 1972, has been the determination to maintain indigenous coal production at a level amounting to about one third of the UK's energy needs. But the enthusiasm with which this aim has been pursued has fluctuated, not only in tune with the political complexion of the government of the day (the UK Labour Ministers being traditionally rather warmer towards the coal-mining interest than are the Conservatives), but also according to national perceptions of the strength of the energy problem at an international level. In periods in which the national priorities have been more a matter of containing inflation than of dealing with potential energy shortage in the 1990s, support for coal mining has waned; and as the prospects for the North Sea have tended to become rosier, so the attractiveness of national coal production has seemed less.

But the fixity of UK national purpose about coal seems remarkable by contrast with changing assessments of the nuclear option. Ever since the early 1960s, a strong battle has raged about the attractiveness of a uniquely 'British' nuclear reactor. After the very successful first generation magnox plant of the 1950s, British fashion swung towards the advanced gas cooled reactors (AGRs) and, for a short time in the mid 1970s, to the steam generating heavy water reactor (SGHWR). At times of great anxiety about energy matters, establishment opinion has tended to favour the 'American' alternative of pressurised water reactors, on the grounds that investment in these devices, while perhaps damaging for British technological interests, would be good energy economics; but at times when straightforward energy problems have seemed less important, the advantages to be gained from backing UK technology have seemed greater, despite fundamental questions about the performance of the AGRs or the potentialities of the SGHWR.

At the end of the 1970s, in the wake of the relatively good performance of at least some of the British AGRs, and the nuclear doubts in the United States after the Three Mile Island accident, it seemed possible to combine nuclear enthusiasm generally with devotion to British technology; but on the basis of past experience systematic schizophrenia on the British nuclear front seems likely to return in the 1980s.

A strictly ironic note is offered by the attitude of the UK to energy conservation. As in most other countries, the fall in the real oil price in the years 1975–78 had diminished fears and pressures somewhat, particularly in the household sector, and official pressure towards energy conservation had been, though consistent, far from strong. The sharp upwards movement in oil prices in the winter of 1978/79 had its primary economic effect in increased estimates of the likely wealth from the North Sea, and the likely consequential strength of sterling in the medium run. It would have been understandable if Britain's position as an oil producer had lessened the pressures for energy conservation. But instead, much of British official comment, even at Ministerial level, began to resemble the speeches of OPEC leaders: 'our oil' was an asset which should not be wasted, but should be conserved above all at home. There seemed if anything a keener sense of the advantages of energy conservation in late 1979, with oil self-sufficiency virtually achieved, than there had been four years earlier, when the benefit from North Sea production was merely a promise. This episode well illustrates the suggestion that energy policy often owes its direction and impetus as much to other elements of political and economic life as to the perceived exigencies of the energy sector itself.

17.4   Instruments of policy

In the previous chapter we examine the traditional economist's proposition that the aim of government policy should be to remove obstacles to competition and act in such a way that market pressures could be smoothly, efficiently, and clearly transmitted to all relevant economic actors. The strategy was to allow consumer preferences to determine choices in the light of technological possibilities; the policy was to act in accord with that strategy; and the instrument was to allow the market to operate. No country, no regime, appears to believe so vehemently in this doctrine as to follow it without detours, and we have already encountered many of the practical reasons which make such single minded determination impossible. But the doctrine nevertheless has an expositional attraction – it is possible to analyse governmental actions in terms of their degree of obedience to market imperatives, and to classify the extent and direction of deviations from market solutions.

An analogy can be struck between the alternative attitudes of economists to international exchange rate variation and their alternative attitudes to variations in the market price of energy. On the one hand, some economists welcomed upwards or downwards movements in the exchange rate after the desertion of the fixed peg system in the late 1960s and early 1970s as a sign that the willingness and ability of governments to interfere with market processes had sharply diminished. The discomfiture of the public authorities in the face of 'speculation' was almost a Kantian good-in-itself, because it symbolised the process of decontrol. On the other hand, some economists merely welcomed, for instance, the downward movement of the United States dollar as a belated step towards the 'equilibrium rate' for the dollar which the computers of most economic model builders had required. The policy prescription of both sets of economists in these circumstances was very similar – let the rate float down. But the ideal which they were envisaging – in the one case a market solution, in the other case an exchange rate more consistent with the other aims of policy and the constraints facing policy makers – were very different indeed.

In exactly the same way, sharp upwards movements in the price of energy in the early 1970s and again in the later part of the decade were welcomed by some economist observers as signs that 'the market was beginning to dominate' and that attempts by governments – particularly in North America – to constrain or limit those market forces were about to break down. Other economists, less enthusiastic in their fervour for market solutions, or less credulous towards the doctrine that it was a free market mechanism rather than the OPEC cartel which was forcing prices upwards, preferred to see the change as a very desirable movement towards a scarcity price. For them, the price rise was desirable because of the adjustment in behaviour, both on the demand and supply side, which their analysis would lead them to expect.

The distinction between the two schools of thought is not perfect, and can be made to diminish if we recognise that Governments may manipulate prices to help achieve their perceived policy aims. Nevertheless, a policy of 'leaving the market to its own devices' is likely, in practical terms, to have very different results indeed from a policy that strives at least to influence economic decisions in a way consistent with the strategy of the economic planners. The European governments who, intellectually, were most attracted to 'free price mechanism' philosophies in the 1970s were in practice as embarrassed as were the American authorities in face of the question of what to do about gasoline prices after the 1979 crude oil price rises. The simple 'pass through' of a fifty per cent increase in the price of crude f.o.b. from the Persian Gulf would have made a price difference of no more than ten per cent in the price of gasoline at the pumps – the burden of downstream costs, and far more important, of consumer government taxes, acts as a powerful damper between the prices of crude and prices in the final market. Was it right for a government dedicated to 'conformity to market forces' to amplify the gasoline price rise or just to let it go through in a rather unexciting way? Almost all governments decided that not only would they continue with an ad valorem tax on gasoline (transforming the ten per cent 'natural' increase into a twenty per cent increase) but also that they would make specific and deliberate increases in tax rates, so as to bring gasoline prices up by thirty or forty per cent in total. Their action certainly showed a devotion to the use of the price mechanism as an *instrument of policy*, and even in the case of the US government (which was by far the most laggardly of the pack in this regard) their action did not amount to an abdication by government in favour of the impersonal forces of the market – it was not an act of surrender of policy intent, nor an *abandonment* of the deliberate use of policy instruments.

So manipulation of prices is one of the possible instruments of policy. Amongst the others, the following loom large in almost all countries:

1. The control of investment in state-owned energy utilities and mining companies.
2. The subsidy of energy-producing activities in privately owned companies (or their taxation).
3. The licensing of technological developments on the grounds of safety, environmental interest, national security, and so on.
4. The control of transport systems to encourage energy savings.
5. Building regulations (influencing the degree of insulation and therefore space heating fuel use), and building practices in state-owned buildings.
6. State-financed information services, persuasive propaganda, and so on – 'conservation programmes'.
7. Research and development expenditure, financed either directly or indirectly by the taxpayer, designed to generate new capacity for energy production or conversion.
8. Finally, governments can impose rationing or other non-price methods of allocating fuel supplies – for the most part, in western style governments, this seems more likely to be a mechanism to deal with a short run temporary shortage than for longer run policy purposes, but fashions may change.

In terms of the paradigm of market behaviour, most of the preceding forms of intervention can be defended on the grounds that, each of them may help to remedy particular failings of the market mechanism. Thus, propaganda about the virtues of 'saving energy' can help to spread information, and make more transparent the workings of the market; discriminatory subsidy of research and development expenditure in the energy field may be justified because governments are more able to see their way through the mists of 'secondary uncertainty' than are private sector decision makers; government decisions on the safety or security aspects of nuclear energy are to be justified on the traditional, liberal, grounds that it is the irreducible role of the state to guard against the negative externalities of hazards like poisoned water or unhealthy air. Even the seemingly hopeless-to-justify rationing, the very antithesis of a price mechanism device, can readily be explained if one assumes that the energy shortage which the rationing scheme purports to avoid is a purely temporary affair, and if one makes the additional assumption that the domestic price and wage system generally is very fragile, in the sense that a once for all shock will push it permanently to a higher rate of inflationary expectations. The shock, and any price signals about future resource costs of energy that might also be erroneously transmitted, can be avoided by taking the strain on quantity adjustment through rationing rather than through price.

Philosophic taste and political opinion, rather than economic principles, decide whether this type of 'justification' for the use of non-price policy tools is attractive. Together they form an armoury of policy weapons which can be very powerful, provided that they are used jointly with appropriate price mechanism weapons. The whole history of planning intervention in socialist economies as well as capitalist ones has been bedevilled by attempts, deliberate or accidental, of governments to run a mutually inconsistent system of controls and settings for their policy instruments. That way lies disaster. For instance, in the circumstances of the late 1970s, it was just no use for President Carter to tell firms in the private sector that he was prepared to use subsidised federal funds to support various schemes for making crude oil synthetically from coal and other hydrocarbons. Any business-man worth his salt, particularly in the competitive environment of North America, would realise that the important element that he had to face was not the cost of research, or development, or capital installation, but the availability of a market in the future at an appropriately high price. The best information today's business-man has about tomorrow's real prices is in fact the price level ruling today. For President Carter to hold back on gasoline prices while subsidising syncrude was, in the classic American motoring metaphor, to drive simultaneously on the accelera-tor and the brake.

So the basic rule is – have a *policy* – even if it is not a crude tableau economique or its equivalent in energy economics, 'an energy balance table', and make sure that all the policy instruments which you decide to use point in the direction from the present towards the future that you wish to follow. It remains to be asked, however, what is the *balance* between the different policy instruments – is there an 'optimum mix' of policy instruments which can be chosen? The appropriate analogy here is with the analysis of regional policy instruments which were designed, for instance, to equalise regional unemployment rates or incomes per head. In many countries, and within the European economic community as a whole, it is conventional to use the whole array of policy instruments for this end: payroll subsidies (and symmetri-cal taxes in congested areas); capital investment subsidies; subsidies for infrastruc-ture investment in roadways or public utilities in regionally deprived areas; special government development corporations (like that for the south of Italy or for the highlands, and islands of Scotland) which will make capital funds available to private business at favourable rates; and many other measures. It is easy to state, in formal and abstract terms, the appropriate test to apply for judging the optimality of the mix of these measures – would it be possible to attain a higher value for the objective function by marginally readjusting the balance between any pair of measures? But because the objective function is rarely specified in sufficiently precise terms, and because the effect of additional doses of any particular policy instrument is systematically uncertain, in practice the broad distribution of the weight of policy amongst the different instruments is more a matter of political fashion than of economic analysis.

In much the same way, it is sometimes suggested that an absolutely clear-headed and cool-minded public authority in the United Kingdom would abandon much of the present support for the coal industry, on the grounds that it is possible now and will also be possible in the future to import large quantities of coal at a marginal cost well below that of coal from the generally poor and deep seams of the British coal fields. But, as we have seen, cost minimisation is only one of the arguments of the objective function, and some (usually unspecified) weight needs to be given to a degree of 'self-sufficiency'; the extent and availability of imports of coal at a period after the turn of the century is extremely difficult to estimate; if a run-down in coal production were attempted, it is not known how smoothly or rapidly it could be achieved; and any rational government, with an eye to the past swings of fashion, would be cautious about throwing all its eggs into one basket. Hence the only policy restriction one can impose on the choice of an appropriate mix of instruments is 'try to keep a diversity of instruments available and in working order, and from time to time ask seriously and open mindedly whether the dosage of any particular policy instrument is roughly of the right scale'.

17.5 Policy considerations under uncertainty

A distinction between lay and professional prescriptions for 'solutions' to energy problems is highlighted by the tendency of some lay groups (including some industry specialists) to put all their eggs in one basket. If there is one form of fuel supply or conservation action which seems at the present time to be more desirable than its competitors with account being taken of present and future costs, environmental factors, reliability, efficiency in use and so on, it may appear to those not directly involved in overall energy policy that the whole or most of the available effort and finance should be devoted to that particular activity. The experienced professional, however, will hedge his bets, preferring to ensure that a proper balance be kept between alternative methods of fuel production or energy conservation.

One reason for this pluralistic approach by the professional is of course his experience of uncertainty; anyone who has ever signed a report recommending the adoption of alternative X because calculations suggested that X was 5 per cent cheaper than Y, will know to his cost that on many occasions Y has turned out to be at least 5 per cent cheaper than X! Uncertainty, particularly in the field of project evaluation, is endemic to the human situation, but where there are n alternatives any piece of new information about the relative advantage of alternative i or j will not shift the optimum balance very much after the new information has been properly discounted for uncertainty. Indeed, one criterion for choosing strategy A rather than strategy B is that A may be more robust to new information than is B – there is positive merit in choosing a strategy which cannot be blown hither and thither by every newspaper headline. In formal terms, we are asserting that one element of the objective function is stability or durability – what might be called the gyroscope criterion. The execution of any energy strategy will involve long lead times and one merit of stability is that wasteful cancellation of projects and changes in specifications are avoided as far as possible.

But there is much more to the distinction between lay and professional opinion than mere experience of past waves of fashion. The essential features of most questions of choice of technique in economics and applied sciences are the twin characteristics of 'diminishing marginal attractiveness' and 'the dynamic nature of technological change'. The former means that the use of a particular type of fuel is appropriate only *up to a certain limit*. For example, it may well be that a balanced set of fuel conversion activities by the end of the century will include a substantial element of synthetic crude oils, where it is worth while to pay the high prices involved, e.g. for some forms of transport. It may also be true that in many districts of the southern United States or the Mediterranean basin the pay-off from solar energy may be considerable, at least for low grade purposes such as horticulture, heated swimming pools, and some industrial process work. And in a similar way it seems plausible that there may be a role for windmills, etc. However, it would not make economic sense to use enough energy from windmills, or solar energy, to drive motor cars, neither should synthetic oil be used in circumstances where wind power is more attractive. Thus 'diminishing marginal attractiveness' means that diversity of fuels is required.

Similar conclusions are suggested when one considers the dynamic nature of energy demand and supply. The fact that it may be impossibly expensive in a hundred years time to use oil for central heating, or to drive what the Americans call 'full size cars' to the golf course, *does not* mean that we have to abandon these activities today. The continuing use of oil forms a part of current strategies in the short term but dynamical change may well either produce, or require, alternatives in the longer run. The fact that one technique is pretty clearly superior to its alternatives today *does not* mean that we must commit ourselves ineluctably to its use for all future time.

The essence of cool, professional energy planning is therefore to ask of each new possibility not 'is the news here so good that we should abandon all our other work?', but instead 'how great a commitment to this particular promising technique is sensible, given all the other things we are doing and the trend of novelty generally in this field?'

There *are* times when an all or nothing choice can be justified or when discontinuous change seems to call for what non-scientists call a quantum leap in policies, but once a basic adjustment has been made in the light of the news that cheap oil will not be with us forever, the occasion for these feats of imagination and vision is probably past. It is time for modest, sober, and painstaking devotion to the building of a portfolio of activities which is robust to the swings of fashion. The problem for the energy planner is to select the optimum amount of diversity to suit the particular circumstances which he faces.

17.6   Chapter summary

Energy policy is concerned with aims (or objective functions), with policies, and with instruments. As to aims, these comprise not only the cost minimisation term discussed in chapter 16, which is itself subject to risk and uncertainty; but also security of supply and environmental considerations.

Security of supply is in part a matter of minimising import dependence; in part also it concerns the avoidance of the military and political threats to world stability which excessive import dependence by major powers bring in their train. Environmental considerations introduce a systematic bias towards conservation rather than energy production by methods alternative to those at present used – this is a theme that recurs in chapter 18.

Policies have often seemed to Governments a matter of 'going for broke' on a particular option – nuclear energy, more coal, renewable, conservation – with little notion of relating these policies to underlying aims. Governments have asked 'how can problems be solved?' rather than how underlying aims can be achieved. Different policies have been stressed more in response to changed conditions in the rest of the policy field than to changes in energy circumstances.

Choice of instruments for the implementation of policies range from that 'reliance on the market' which was the theme of chapter 16, but has never been properly accepted by *any* Government, towards various forms and degrees of intervention. The armoury of instruments is in fact very strong, ranging from the mere amplification of price signals (through *ad valorem* taxing) to Government investment in production or conservation. Regulation of use, without accompanying price signals, is ineffective, and the basic rule is to have a policy and to ensure that all policy instruments assume settings that point broadly in the direction which policy prescribes.

The balance – or optimum mix – of policy instruments is not a matter for scientific precision; but it seems sensible to keep most instruments of the armoury in working order, and to be watchful about the dangers of using any one instrument to excess.

As to the fundamental question – what aims, what policies? – spread your eggs)etween baskets, and do not assume that the technologies of science fiction will be with us very soon!

Chapter 17   Further reading

Brannon, G. M. (1974) *Energy taxes and subsidies*, Ballinger, Cambridge, Mass.

Cook, P. L. and Surrey, A. J. (1977) *Energy policy, strategies for uncertainty*, Martin Robertson, London.

Freeman, D. S. *et al.* (1979) *A time to choose: America's energy future*, report by the Energy Policy Project of the Ford Foundation, Ballinger, Cambridge, Mass.

Gray, J. E. (1975) *Energy policy: industry perspectives*, Ballinger, Cambridge, Mass.

Griffin, J. M. (1979) *Energy conservation in the OECD 1980–2000*, Ballinger, Cambridge, Mass.

Landsberg, H. H. *et al.* (1979) *Energy: the next twenty years*, a report sponsored by the Ford Foundation, Ballinger, Cambridge, Mass.

Mabro, R. (ed.) (1980) *World energy: policies and issues*, Oxford University Press, London.

MacKay, D. I. and MacKay, G. A. (1975) *The political economy of North Sea Oil*, Martin Robertson, London.

Mangone, G. J. (ed.) (1977) *Energy policies of the world* (vol. 1, 1976, and vol. 2, 1977), Elsevier, New York.

Mendershausen, H. (1976) *Coping with the oil crisis*, Johns Hopkins Unviversity Press, Baltimore and London.

Noreng, O. (1978) *Oil politics in the 1980s*, McGraw-Hill, New York and London.

OAPEC (1978) *Petroleum and Arab economic development*, Organisation of Arab Petroleum Exporting Countries, Kuwait.

Posner, M. V. (1973) *Fuel policy – a study in applied economics*, Macmillan, London.

Regens, J. L. (ed.) (1979) *Energy issues and options*, University of Georgia, Athens, Georgia.

Sonenblum, S. (1978) *The energy connections: between energy and the economy*, Ballinger, Cambridge, Mass.

Stobaugh, R. and Yergin, D. (eds.) (1979) *Energy future*, Random House, New York.

UK Department of Energy (1977f) *Energy policy review*, Energy Paper no. 22, HMSO, London.

Yager, J. A. and Steinberg, E. B. (eds.) (1974) *Energy and US foreign policy*, Ballinger, Cambridge, Mass.

CHAPTER 18

Options and uncertainties

18.1 Energy problems revisited

Energy problems are liable to change their character or even fade away for a time like the Cheshire cat so that when only the smile remains one regrets that the creature was not captured and caged whilst its state was more substantial. These problems have a physical basis in the changing availability of energy resources but they are magnified by anticipation or delay and changed by social responses so that they become more serious than would have been expected from the underlying resource situation alone. They are none the less real, since social attitudes determine economic behaviour and modify the options that may be available. The early fears of an energy crisis expressed by Jevons (1866) in the nineteenth century, in the United States in the 1920s, and more generally in the early 1950s were resolved by new discoveries of cheap sources of energy – coal and oil overseas in the nineteenth century, the East Texas oilfields in the 1930s, and the vast Saudi Arabian oilfields in the 1950s. It has sometimes been suggested (Adelman, 1972, Odell 1974) that more recent fears about shortages of oil may be similarly resolved. However, when the oil crisis in the winter of 1973/74 had given way to an apparent surplus of oil and a weak oil market only two years later, this was due not so much to new discoveries as to the economic recession, caused in part by the oil price rise itself. Much the same developments, on a smaller scale, stemmed from the return in 1978/79 of the OPEC prices to the real levels attained in 1974.

These two episodes to some extent illustrate the 'limits to growth syndrome' (Meadows *et al.*, 1972), and raise the possibility that future scarcity of energy may, in combination with other influences, lead more dramatically and permanently to reduced economic growth, or in some regions to a real decline in living standards. In previous chapters on the energy outlook we have taken a less pessimistic standpoint and indicated a range of possibilities for the development of energy supply and conservation, in which economic growth is maintained in all world regions though at a slower rate than in recent decades. At the optimistic end of this range, new energy resources would continue to be developed almost as fast as the technological constraints and lead times permitted, but political constraints and the objective fears of long-run excess demand for oil would continue to limit oil production from the major resource areas. At the more pessimistic end of the range, rather more extreme policy constraints, an uncertain economic climate, and continued opposition to the development of some energy sources would restrain energy supplies and increase the chance of energy scarcity, with consequent feed-back to lower economic growth.

There is no way to predict the consequences of energy scarcity, or of repeated energy crises. They may be salutory, leading to a turn-round on attitudes to energy supply and a vigorous development of the energy sector, which would itself stimulate economic growth. Alternatively they could lead to greater disturbance in world trade or to more serious conflicts in some areas, so that world economic growth was for substantial periods well below the ranges suggested in chapter 14.

In the face of these uncertainties we need to consider how governments and peoples may respond and how policies may change with regard to energy conservation and supply. It is essential to bear in mind that policies and attitudes will be dispersed – different groups and counties will have different objectives and different constraints, and even when similar policies are adopted some will prove more successful than others in achieving objectives.

We have seen in chapters 4, 13 and 14, that world oil production is unlikely to increase much above its present level due to a combination of resource limitations and policy constraints. It has been argued that alternative energy supplies involve higher costs and long technological lead times and/or they are likely to be limited by policy constraints or social and political obstacles. The key question therefore is whether in response to higher prices or conservation policies it is possible for growth in energy demand to be limited in ways that do not disrupt economic growth. If this appears unlikely then the consequent penalties to economic growth must be weighed against the benefits of social or political constraints on energy supply to see whether changes in policies may be desirable. We must not suppose that these competing factors can be assessed with certainty; it is the function of the policy analysts to examine the risks involved and identify the insurance options and the premiums that our fellow citizens might be willing to pay if they were fully aware of the relevant facts and probabilities.

18.2   Perceptions of supply

Three approaches to energy forecasting are commonly observed. The first assumes the world will in future be the same as in the very recent past, the second assumes it will be strikingly different, and the third provides a miracle solution. The first approach, for example, if developed during the depression of 1975 would be likely to assume that future economic growth will be low, but if it were developed in 1979 might suppose that energy crises will remain part of the daily scene. In contrast, the second approach assumes that the future will be quite different from the present: for example, it might be suggested that shortages of oil are a temporary phenomenon that will go away because the world will swiftly adjust to the scarcity and use alternative fuels, or people will develop new propensities for energy conservation that are unobservable at present, or that the resumption in economic activity following a recession heralds a false dawn, or that the well documented relation between economic activity and energy demand discussed in chapter 2 will painlessly change, assisted perhaps by benevolent government intervention. The third approach to energy forecasting is based on the miracle solution. The focus of the miracle may be nuclear power and no windmills, or windmills and no nuclear power, or it may be conservation and solar energy, or coal conversion, or global changes in lifestyle. The common feature of all miracle solutions is the speed with which they are expected to arrive.

There is, of course, a measure of truth in each of these seemingly orthogonal approaches to energy forecasting. In many respects the future can reasonably be expected to be the same as the present or recent past. The world supply of oil will not suddenly cease, and at or not far below current levels it could continue for fifty years or more, so motor transport is likely to be based mainly on petroleum products for many decades. However, if the total world supply of oil stops increasing, oil prices will be high, interfuel substitution will change direction, and alternative energy supplies will be developed accompanied by energy conservation or increased efficiencies in the use of energy. Thus the energy future will be different from the past, but the rate of change and its character will be limited by technological lead times and social attitudes. The nature and influence of these attitudes will be affected by shocks or surprises in the world energy system, whether due to civil disturbance in a major oil producing country, a nuclear accident anywhere in the world, or persistent electricity shortages in major consuming areas.

Similarly, miracle solutions cannot be ignored even though they may seem to be beyond the bounds of plausible expectation. In some respects they provide valuable targets or objectives, through scenarios that show what might be done by a resolute government in a country with a docile population, or what might be achieved through widespread public and popular response to a clearly perceived national or world problem. If these scenarios are well constructed, for example assuming technically feasible and economically reasonable measures for energy conservation, they can make an important contribution in moving public opinion and persuading governments at least partly towards the projected solution. Again, they cannot be ignored, even if they are misconceived and advocate technologically impossible, economically absurd, or socially unacceptable solutions, since they may be believed by a sufficient part of the population of a country to delay more realistic measures.

Both in the long-term future and in the short- to medium-term the interaction between the concepts implied by these alternative approaches is of crucial importance. In the long term the interaction provides a degree of stability – the future will be different from the present, but changes, apart from some short-term shocks, will be gradual. The energy problem will not go away but it will be partly transformed into problems of economic growth and world trade, of agreement or competition between the industrialised nations and the developing world, and social problems of adjustment to change with uneven distribution of benefits or disbenefits.

In the short- to medium-term future, with which we are concerned here, the interaction between different aspects of the energy problem is as likely to produce instability as stability. The anticipation of future problems may lead to actions that create new difficulties or exacerbate present problems. Although there is clearly an interdependence amongst nations and a common interest in resolving energy problems, it is equally clear that important parts of their interests and policies are different, not only between energy producers and consumers, because of obvious potential conflicts, but also because within each group national energy policies are constrained by differing economic policies or social structures.

The picture we have presented in this book is essentially one where oil and natural gas supplies reach a plateau, probably with oil production not significantly above the present level of output, but containing unexpected dips and gullies. Having reached that plateau, exploration and improved technical methods of recovery made possible through higher prices, together with oil production from heavy oil deposits, tar sands and shale, may enable the plateau to be maintained for fifty years or more. However, much of the new oil is likely to be more expensive than the presently available high cost oil from difficult off-shore reservoirs, and, coupled with policy constraints arising from increased awareness of a dwindling resource, this could lead to a long-term decline in available supplies. It may well be possible to top up oil supplies with synthetic crude derived from coal, and this may help to maintain the plateau of oil production or provide a modest increase for a period.

Within the time scale normally considered by economists, where a century or two is a very long time, the vast global resources of coal might suggest that coal supplies can be regarded as freely available at costs not very far above present costs of extraction in real terms. We believe this conclusion to be false. The issue with coal, as with other potential energy sources, is not so much concerned with global energy resources as with the location of known proven reserves and whether their extraction and supply will be limited by social and political constraints, as was discussed in chapters 5, 9, 10 and 11. By far the largest reserves of coal in the non-communist world are found in the United States and it is unrealistic to suppose that these will be freely available to the rest of the world – or even within the United States. We would anticipate restrictions that, on a longer time scale, are the counterpart of the limits now imposed by oil producers. In Europe, in addition to the environmental problems of producing and burning coal, there are likely to be increasing social and political difficulties in providing the labour required for deep mining operations.

These difficulties mean that coal cannot by itself provide an easy or probable solution to increased energy supplies as an alternative to oil. It does, however, provide an important component and an element of stability in the energy future for an industrial society.

This book has not 'taken sides' on the nuclear controversy, but it is a clear implication of chapters 5, 6 and 7 that, if the nuclear option is politically and environmentally acceptable, it will provide a form of electric generation for the next fifty or a hundred years that may be significantly cheaper than coal, and in the absence of which the pressure on coal production and trade might be beyond the bounds of the technically feasible.

The contribution from the renewables foreseen in chapters 8 and 14 – mainly solar power – may within fifty or a hundred years become significant, but we cannot see it making a substantial dent in the call on coal, hydrocarbons and nuclear energy.

We take very seriously the prospects for energy conservation – indeed we prefer to see 'conservation' as a potential source of energy, with costs, investment needs, and payoffs to be analysed in the same way as in the case of any other source of fuel. We distinguish between the technical potential for conservation – a sort of 'resource base' for energy – and the potential from those conservation measures that are economically viable, since only the latter represents an 'energy reserve' in the strict sense that is applied to other energy options. Improvements in technology may move conservation possibilities from the category of resources to the category of reserves or they may make particular reserves more attractive economically than some other sources of energy.

A major change that we expect is that the *increment* of energy demand from now onwards will be met, not from liquid hydrocarbons, but from one of the other sources; and the pressure of fuel substitution, which since the Second World War has been towards oil and natural gas, will now be away from those two fuels. The consequences and costs of this switch, and the degree to which it can be smoothly made, together constitute the 'energy problem' as we see it. It is not a question of 'running out of oil' but rather a matter of ceasing to look to oil as the main source of future increases in energy supply.

18.3   Balance between different energy sources

The essence of the case against a 'technical fix' that seeks to solve the energy problem by massive development of a single preferred fuel (or energy conservation) is that any given fuel is produced under conditions of increasing cost, and, although some fraction of each fuel is likely to be available fairly cheaply, single-minded dependence on any one of them will push demand on to marginal, high cost sources of supply, and therefore, at the margin, make the 'chosen fuel' less attractive than its competitors. In some cases, this simple mechanism will work through the cost of production, as less attractive sources are exploited (oil or coal). In the case of nuclear energy, greater dependence will probably mean more elaborate exploitation of the fuel cycle, designed to economise on natural uranium, because of the increasing cost of supply of that raw material. In other cases (nuclear energy again, or solar energy) 'higher costs' will appear as the chosen source is used for more and more inappropriate purposes – nuclear power stations used to supply the shoulder or even the peak of the electricity load curve; solar energy used, through elaborate heat pump devices, to produce high grade heat; coal used to supply combined heat and power involving expensive long-distance heat transmission.

This consideration on its own will force the world, whether today or in the time of our great grandchildren, to operate with a mix of different fuels. This mix will vary as technology varies, but while 'all additional joules of useful heat' may be traded at much the same price in any one region or neighbourhood, in the world as a whole fuels of high and low cost will co-exist at any one time. The principle of equi-marginal costs does not imply equi-average costs.

Engineers are sometimes tempted to establish a hierarchy of different possible uses of a particular fuel. For instance, the discussion in chapter 3 indicated that the 'premium user' of natural gas is the housewife for her domestic cooker, or the process industry which needs a clean, controllable and reliable heat source. The premium user of liquid hydrocarbons is air transport, and after that the American motor car.

But there is another potential hierarchy – that of wealth and power. At the moment it seems likely that the North American consumer will pre-empt a large proportion of world traded oil well into the next century, because of the depth of his pocket book and the strength of American geopolitical influence in the Middle East and elsewhere. In a sense uncongenial to North American readers of this book, but very familiar to those from other regions of the world, the Americans will be forcing British workers into deep mined collieries under the city of Oxford in the next century, or the French government into elaborate and expensive tidal barrages, because the voters of Pennsylvania are reluctant to incur for their grandchildren the genetic risk that might arise from another Harrisburg accident. So interfuel substitution is not a matter of engineering, but also one of the relative power and wealth of different countries and social groups, and the way that power is exercised. The pressure to self-sufficiency, or at least to security of supply, (imports of uranium are stockable in a sense in which imports of hydrocarbons, liquid or solid, are not), itself implies diversity of different sources of fuel, as explained in chapter 17. And basic uncertainty about the technology of the future, the extent to which as yet untested methods of fuel conversion might work, and doubts about world trading arrangements, will also drive any rational government away from putting its eggs into one basket.

But complete flexibility between different types of fuel is not possible, and it might sometimes be necessary to 'go nap' on a particular option. The formal solution is that 'all or nothing' decisions should be taken only if the present level of the net expected benefits from the decision are great enough to outweigh the present value of the benefits from flexibility. For instance, an electric utility, or a Ministry of Energy, in a particular country, however large or rich, must inevitably decide that a large variety of different models of nuclear power plant will not in practice be producible at any one time, and a choice will have to be made amongst the various techniques available. Again, a decision *not* to go ahead with developing a fast breeder reactor in the next decade will imply a ceiling on the contribution from nuclear energy by the end of the first quarter of the next century, and, therefore, on at least some plausible assumptions, such a negative decision will inevitably force subsequent commitment on a large scale to some other source of energy. And a decision to refuse permission for strip mining on a large scale in the Western United States will force either extremely expensive substitutes for coal, or the use of manpower in deep mining on the eastern seaboard.

All these examples are cases where a decision to shut the door on a particular option has irreversible consequences elsewhere. This at least suggests the conclusion that an appropriate rule for policy makers should be to leave all doors open, and be prepared to spend significant sums to ensure that they are left open (what might be called the 'proving of alternatives' or 'investment in knowledge'). But that conclusion although correct is not all that the argument suggests. The notion that a well judged portfolio of energy sources should be the desideratum of policy captures the sense of 'portfolio theory' more completely; although originally developed as that branch of economics which helps investment managers decide which shares to acquire for their clients' portfolios, it has been extended to deal with the general question of management of risks and choice of assets. There seems no doubt that this is the appropriate language in which to discuss some aspects of energy policy.

It is of course mistaken to believe that any combination of policies can reduce the risk to zero. To start with, risks of technological failure or serious accidents exist for all types of fuel, so that this single dimension of risk cannot be eliminated. More important, risk, and the pattern of disutilities to which the risk applies, contains much more than one single dimension. Thus, for example, there is a risk in the under-supply of a necessary input to industrial processes (here the risk is that shortages of a crucial raw material would lead to multiple losses in output), but over-provision would also cause losses (unnecessary electricity generating capacity, for instance, when the growth in electricity demand has been slower than the electricity planners assumed).

There are of course formal solutions to all these trade-offs, provided the analyst is prepared to offer appropriate weights to the disutilities involved. In practice, the formal solutions are rarely of importance – what is difficult to convey to even the informed public is the concept of choosing a middle path between Scylla and Charybdis.

Technological devices for the reduction of some elements of risk can be purchased, sometimes at quite low cost. For instance, the dual firing of individual power stations (or of individual domestic heating appliances) is one, not very expensive, way of ensuring against shortages of individual fuels. But the system as a whole can find less expensive solutions. An integrated electricity supply system may have power units turned by different sources of heat, and shortages of one particular fuel can be met by increasing the average load factor of generating sets using the other fuels.

But the general problem of energy over the next fifty years as we see it is the problem of arranging a reasonably smooth substitution of one form of fuel for another – including here conservation as, conceptually, a fuel source. The difficulty is that the timing of the substitution, and its precise direction, cannot be predicted in advance. That the incremental demand for energy will not be met over the next few decades in anything like the same way as it has been met in the last few decades is quite certain, and the low place of oil in meeting incremental demand is quite apparent. But the speed with which other sources will need to come on tap, and the mix between them, are both systematically uncertain.

Chapter 9 showed the differing patterns of environmental risks associated with different fuels. It would be quite easy to devise a utility function for policy makers which would lead them to choose to concentrate on one or two particular fuels to the exclusion of competitors. For instance, the chance of a single large accident killing more than 1000 citizens (not workers productively engaged in supplying the fuel in question) is probably greater for hydro-electric schemes than for any other source: a suitably high weight put on the disutility of such an accident will counter-balance the very low probability that would be assigned to it, and therefore deflect policy makers from that line of activity. Again, the notion that permanent genetic damage can be caused by radioactivity could lead to avoidance of nuclear energy as a source (although it appears that the small quantities of uranium in most coal sources might lead to equivalent risks of radiation damage in normal operation from a system which was entirely coal burning as from a system which was entirely nuclear).

But these 'fixes' are of curiosity value only, for analytical purposes to amuse students, or for employment by impassioned enthusiasts for one fuel rather than another. The ordinary citizen and the ordinary policy maker is as foxed as the rest of us in estimating the relative disutility of a small risk of a large accident and the large risk of a small accident; and the comparison between future damage to the biosystem is hard to weigh against the present daily drain of lives caused by work in coal mines or road accidents associated with the transport of liquid-hydrocarbons. It is good fun, and controversial practice, to compute tables showing that by one particular criteria the girl you favour is more beautiful than all her competitors but everybody knows that there is more than one scale of beauty and more than one way of adding them together.

We do not recommend, however, rushing to the opposite extreme, and disregarding all environmental considerations. They are a necessary and often crucial ingredient of the decision making process. It is right that effort should be spent in elucidating and enumerating the various sources of damage, so that the informed public may weigh alternative courses of action with some knowledge of the possible implications. The system of public enquiries of one sort or another into large energy projects is, in the final analysis, a political process, but it does also require an available input of reasonably hard factual evidence which, where possible, can be agreed between the different sides in the controversy before the real political argument starts. It is never possible to relegate all components of the argument to 'resolution by experts', but it is always possible to push some components out of the political arena, leaving the ground a bit clearer and making ultimate compromise a little easier to reach. That is the true function of the technician in environmental controversy – not to resolve the controversy, but to remove unnecessary confusion and argument where this can be done in an agreed way.

The study of the methods that can be used for conducting political argument via 'public enquiries' into energy or other large scale projects has been much furthered in recent years. A recent useful survey of the particular case of the United Kingdom enquiry into the Windscale uranium processing plant (Pearce *et al.* 1979) contains many of the arguments and considerations that are relevant.

18.4   Energy conservation

Technical potential can provide an estimate of the resource base for energy conservation – and as with other resources some estimates are reasonable and some are ridiculous, but only those conservation options that are economically viable represent an energy 'reserve'. Such possibilities do not represent realistic opportunities for energy conservation unless they become associated with sufficient *motivation* for them to be developed and widely adopted. Improvements in technology may move conservation possibilities from the category of resources to the category of reserves, or they may make the reserves more attractive economically. However, there is *uncertainty* about the rate and extent of the adoption of energy conservation, additional motivation is required to bring reserves into production – they have to be needed, and normally they would be developed in sequence beginning with those having lower cost or better pay-back. As more conservation opportunities are developed and adopted, they may therefore become increasingly costly and it may be necessary to run hard in order to maintain the rate of improvement in energy saving. We therefore need to ask about energy conservation *policies*.

Fossil fuels, particularly oil and gas, are an exhaustible resource. This idea is easy for the public to grasp and is of obvious importance politically and socially, and it leads to the view that energy conservation is desirable on ethical grounds in order to save fossil fuel resources for future generations. In economic terms this view would suggest that a low discount rate should be used for judging investment in energy conservation – lower than that used for other decisions. We return to this vexed question below. From the viewpoint of the government of an energy importing country, the exhaustible resource view means that energy conservation has popular support in general terms – though the support may dwindle when particular measures such as increasing fuel prices or taxes are considered. The consumer government will be influenced by other factors, such as:

1. Oil import costs and balance of payments problems; these become especially disturbing if the world price of oil is unstable and liable to sudden and unexpected increases.
2. Avoidance of risks such as the interruption of oil imports; even a partial interruption causing local shortages in a consumer country can have a serious political impact, and the risks of excessive dependence on oil imports may also inhibit foreign policies or have strategic implications for defence policies. This is what we called in chapter 17 'the security of supply' aspect.
3. Vigorous and effective energy conservation policies in oil importing countries will not only help to stabilise longer term expectations about world oil prices but will provide evidence – we may call it a threat instead, but it is really a normal economic response – that excessive increases in the world price of oil will be counter-productive, not only through causing or contributing to recessions and consequent reductions in the world oil demand but also through stimulating more rapid substitution and conservation.

Governments in oil producing countries, like the public in consuming countries, are in favour of world energy conservation in general terms – 'oil is too valuable to burn', 'oil is our most valuable resource and depletion rates must be limited so that it is available for future generations'. Oil exporters are insistent on the need for energy conservation in consumer countries so that world demand is compatible with their own objectives to conserve oil in the ground, but taxes on oil products in consumer countries – perhaps the most effective way to encourage conservation – are regarded as unfriendly if not hostile, as if the consumer government is taking from OPEC countries some of the taxes, royalties, rent or profit, that they might otherwise receive. This is a misunderstanding. The limits on OPEC oil prices are set by the users' ability to provide more exports to pay for oil imports and by their effect on world trade and economic growth; the reason why the US could raise consumer taxes but not pay OPEC more is amply provided by the US balance of payments problems.

The needs of developing countries (as presented in chapter 15), comprising three quarters of the world population, provide the most convincing argument for moderation by OPEC and for energy conservation, especially conservation of oil, in the developed countries, which use nearly 90 per cent of oil supplies outside the communist countries. Concern about exhaustible resources points to the needs of future generations, but the developing countries can point to the present needs of generations already born. Developed countries, it is said, can use their wealth and high technology to achieve a high level of energy conservation and to introduce energy technologies alternative to oil, whereas developing countries are dependent for growth on technologies of medium complexity that require the increased use of oil.

This argument does not absolve developing countries from encouraging energy conservation. This is particularly true of OPEC developing countries where oil products are often sold at prices that bear little relation either to the world need for conservation or to the long-term interests of those countries. In the poorer regions of the developing world where fuel is becoming an increasingly scarce resource it may become necessary to change from traditional methods of burning wood to simple but more effective alternatives. In these regions the world price of oil will be sufficient incentive for governments to seek ways of reducing the rate of growth in oil demand whilst maintaining economic growth. However, there is little doubt that if the developing world is to achieve reasonable levels of growth relative to their increasing populations they will need a greater share of the world's oil. We therefore return to the need for energy conservation in the more developed countries, and to the potential for reducing oil demand in OECD countries.

This need for conservation is recognised by most governments, but there are at least three major classes of obstacles to changing these good intentions into actual achievements. Firstly, the governments themselves have other priorities besides conservation, for example: the control of inflation, reduction in unemployment, investment, and their balance of payments. Higher energy prices, or high taxes on oil products, may stimulate inflationary wage demands; investment in energy alternatives to imported oil may themselves be energy intensive and lead to higher imports in the short to medium term; the encouragement of more economical cars through higher gasoline taxes could worsen a country's balance of payments position through increasing the imports of smaller cars or cars with diesel engines.

The second major obstacle to the implementation of energy conservation is that governments do not themselves use much energy. Energy consumption and hence decisions on energy conservation are widely dispersed through the community so governments must rely on persuasion and possibly compulsion based on a variety of policy instruments, involving fiscal measures, regulations, publicity, and support for research and development. The difficulty here is that there is considerable uncertainty about the results that can be expected from any such measures. If the pay-back is uncertain, the arguments for government intervention are weakened.

The third obstacle to conservation comes from the priorities of the many individual decision makers. The private householder considering retrofit of insulation or double glazing will note that he expects to move house within a few years and such conservation measures may not observably influence the sale price of his house. The same point may be made by the housebuilder, though he might alternatively decide to use high insulation as an advertising aid. The purchaser of a new car may rate prestige, size, speed, comfort, or reliability as highly as he rates economy, particularly if the car is to be used for business purposes. The industrial manager is generally more experienced at assessing the value of other investments than those for energy conservation, and in any case he is likely to have higher priorities such as maintaining the cash flow or the working capital, urgent replacements to keep production lines running, expansion of the business, or the more efficient use of labour.

The most popular option for energy conservation is the *technical fix*. In its more extreme form it provides a miracle solution to the energy problem in which no sacrifices are required – you can have your cake and eat it. In assessing the potential of energy conservation through technical change it is essential to look first at past improvements in technology, partly because they give an idea about what may be possible for rates of change and better energy efficiencies, but also because past changes are built into historical trends and past relations between energy consumption and economic activity. The central theme of the technical fix philosophy is that we can do better in the future than in the past – maybe we can, prices and costs of energy will be higher, but we must be cautious about double counting. Double counting is especially likely in estimating industrial energy conservation potential, where technological change is identified and then estimated on the basis of an instant change giving (say) a potential reduction of 30 per cent in energy demand. It is then said that such a reduction could perhaps be achieved over a 20 year period. However, many industries have historically achieved a 1½ per cent annual improvement in their energy–output ratio, so a 30 per cent reduction over 20 years is no more than the trend which would be obtained by econometric analysis. For example, in the period 1950 to 1976 the energy–output ratio (measured in physical units) for iron and steel production in the UK fell by nearly 30 per cent. This trend can be continued but it would be unrealistic to suppose it can be greatly improved on. Electricity generation in the UK has improved the average conversion efficiency from fossil fuels to electricity from about 8 per cent in 1920 to about 22 per cent by 1940 (unchanged to 1950), then to 31 per cent today. This trend is unlikely to continue since further general improvements are limited by a combination of thermodynamics and requirements for reliability. In special circumstances combined heat and power is economic and gives higher efficiencies, but in the UK it is unlikely to have a large effect on the system average.

The second option for conservation is to allow *market forces* to achieve an energy supply – demand balance. In a sense our discussion in this book is part of the market response – we are anticipating higher energy prices and asking whether action on conservation can help to limit any increase. A key problem is the time required for conservation measures to be adopted by users and for new options to be developed. If energy-conserving action takes place only in response to price rises, the slow market response may greatly limit the ability of such actions to reduce demand so as to hold down further increases in energy prices.

The third option on energy conservation is *government intervention*. This is almost as popular as the technical fix option and is often associated with it, but it is really much wider and its popularity begins to wane when such specifics as price increases, energy taxes or emergency energy rationing are mentioned. Questions about intervention concern policy options, to which we turn below, but here we should note some of the essential uncertainties in government action on conservation. There are several levels of uncertainty here: firstly, we need to know what actions governments might take, then which options will be chosen and the level (for example of regulations on thermal insulation, or taxes or subsidies) and timing of decisions or legislation that may be required. Finally, and this is often ignored, we need to estimate how much would be achieved. For example: housing regulations that require better thermal insulation may have little effect on the large fraction of new dwellings that have traditionally been constructed above the minimum standard: houses designed to have low energy requirements may involve the occupiers in such low energy bills that they become increasingly casual about leaving windows open, particularly if their incomes rise in real terms, and energy costs (or each individual fuel costs, since they are perceived separately) remain a relatively small fraction of total expenditure; alternatively energy saved through living in a low energy house may release funds for more travel, either by car or by air, and hence *more* energy use.

Government policies on energy conservation provide a good example of some of the problems that arise generally. Decisions on the use of energy are so widely dispersed through the community that one might ask whether a government can make much difference – should we not examine policies of other institutions or even individuals? The economist's answer would be that the latter are part of the market, each person optimising, or perhaps failing to optimise, in his own way. We therefore need to consider how the government can influence the market, and the criteria that affect their choice of options. We begin by discussing fiscal measures and conclude with regulations and standards.

The broad categories of *fiscal options* that are available to governments include energy pricing, taxation, and subsidies. It has become fashionable in Western economies for governments to regulate energy prices. In the United States, the large indigenous supplies of oil and gas permit an averaging of energy prices so that the consumer does not normally meet the full impact of an increase in the world price of oil. It is argued that the application of world oil prices to the home production of oil would bring undeserved profits to the oil producers, though there would seem to be no fundamental problem in applying a special tax to reduce windfall profits or direct them towards alternative energy supplies or conservation investment. It is interesting to speculate on the global costs of the failure in the United States to allow oil prices to rise to world levels. If oil prices had been 50 per cent higher on average over the past five years and we assume an oil price elasticity of − (0.4), the oil demand in the US could have been 15 per cent or about 3 million barrels a day below current demand. Under those conditions there need not have been a world shortage of oil during the revolution in Iran, and world oil prices might well have been 30 per cent below current levels. This would have meant that the US oil import bill would have been approximately halved. Of course a lower world price for oil would not have pleased the members of OPEC, and the absence of this year's energy crisis would have weakened enthusiasm for conservation in consumer countries. The moral for consumer governments is clear, conservation is an essential part of the adjustment towards zero growth in oil demand but it needs to be maintained even if the world oil price falls in real terms. There is also a message for OPEC, namely many conservation measures have a considerable degree of permanence and their adoption by consumer countries can be greatly stimulated by sudden increases in the price of oil. Even the United States is moving towards decontrol of oil prices.

There is no single or simple regime for the prices of oil products. Gasoline is taxed in most countries. In 1979 an imperial gallon cost about 1 dollar in the United States, compared with between 2 and 3 dollars in most European countries, equivalent to about $35 per barrel in the US and between $70 and $105 in Europe. In the short term this is probably the most inelastic part of the market for oil products. Motor cars cannot readily be converted to burn coal, so we must wait for technological developments for greater vehicle efficiency and for long-term changes in consumer choice towards smaller and more economical cars.

In practice, taxation of oil products will not provide a miracle solution any more than other simple recipes. Government actions are limited by constraints which vary from one country to another and may change with time in an alarming manner. If gasoline had become expensive in the United States five years ago, this would have been too early for mass production of small cars by the US automobile industry and the level of car imports could have changed so rapidly as to cause other economic problems. But taxation and decontrol of prices for oil products can make a useful contribution towards conservation of oil and the transition to other energy sources. Those countries that have moved some distance along this road can legitimately complain that, through allowing low prices for oil products used by their own nationals, neither the United States nor most OPEC countries are making their proper contribution to this global problem.

Subsidies form the other side of fiscal measures. But as with other options for energy conservation they should be chosen so as to reinforce the market, not to oppose it. For example, price controls below the relevant costs of energy are a form of subsidy to one section of the community, which, when coupled with exhortations to energy conservation, may be unfavourably compared to driving a car with brakes and accelerator applied simultaneously.

Subsidies could make their greatest impact if they were used to stimulate the development and growth of new measures that would become fully economic as soon as they were more widely adopted. They can provide demonstrations that a particular conservation measure is economic. Equally they can show that a measure is not economic, and it is not good publicity to provide 10 cents of warm water by installing a solar system costing 20 thousand dollars. One of the most valuable forms of subsidy that government can provide is support for research, development and demonstration (R, D and D). These activities often involve high (financial) risk and, if successful, a high return, but the return from energy conservation measures will rarely come primarily to the entrepreneur who developed them, but will be shared by many consumers.

There is difficulty about putting too much emphasis on R, D and D for energy conservation, since it may distract attention from actually getting on with the job. Many measures that can save energy are well known – better insulation, heat recovery, instrumentation, better design and better use of materials. The real problem is getting them implemented.

Energy conservation is not a single simple miracle solution to the energy problem. The potential for energy conservation is large but, due to the complexity of values and choices by decision makers, only part of the potential will be realised. Whilst emphasising the importance of energy conservation, its realisation is not aided by exaggerated claims that underestimate the difficulties and complexities involved in converting ideas into widespread achievements. A wide range of actions are required, by institutions and individuals, and by governments; some will prove more successful than others. Each of us has a contribution to make, whether we come from an energy exporting or an energy importing country. Some of us can raise the price of oil, some can take to riding bicycles, others can draft regulations or impose standards for energy efficiencies, most of us can simply use less energy or use it better.

18.5   The present and the future

Oil

Perceptions of the energy problem change and with these changes the problem itself alters. Following the 1973 oil crisis and the associated increase in world oil prices it was believed in many OPEC countries that this new wealth would enable them to accelerate the development process so that they could move swiftly to achieve standards of living comparable with those of the advanced industrial countries. By 1978, from the OPEC viewpoint much of the earlier oil price rise had been eroded by a three-fold inflation in the cost of their imports, and even when measured against inflation in the consuming countries the real price of oil after the 1979 increases was not far above the levels of 1974. More seriously, many major oil producing countries found that they were unable to utilise their revenue in a properly productive manner. Their spending often involved waste and their investment in productive assets at home suffered from a lack of complementary resources. At the same time it had become apparent that the technical skills and higher education necessary to maintain standards in a society based on advanced technology could not become established within the span of a single generation, and excessive haste in development could bring with it risks of social unrest and disturbance such as those experienced in Iran.

Awareness of these problems has increased in oil producing countries, and public opinion now provides an important influence on governments towards conservation of oil to provide revenue for future generations. It is no longer safe to assume that OPEC oil supplies will continue to increase, and even those countries, such as Saudi Arabia, who have used their output levels to maintain a degree of stability in the world oil market are unlikely to retain much flexibility in the future. In a period of inflexible oil supply, and before alternatives have been adequately developed, it must be expected that there will be energy crises. The energy economy will encounter difficulties during the 1980s, and it is not so much a question of avoiding crises as of how to handle them when they come. If these difficulties are indeed widely expected, they should influence the present through the mechanism of the discount rate and so raise current prices (by a larger amount if our fellow citizens have great aversion to risk), or alternatively through the considerable penalties from lower incomes or unemployment if loss of economic growth is allowed to resolve energy scarcity through lack of more positive initiatives.

Trading off the present against the future: the discount rate
Chapter 16 presented the standard economist's argument about discounting the future, and arrived at the standard rules about the depletion of natural resources: depletion is pressed to the limit where the expected rise in the price of the marginal barrel left in the ground is equal to the rate of discount or interest.

But a little earlier in this chapter we did ask explicitly what rate of discount would be appropriate for the conservation decision, and the general economist's presumption that all discount rates at any point of time should be equal is questioned furiously by lobbyists not only for conservation, but for nuclear energy, for investment in research, for devotees of hydro-electric power, and so on.

It is not part of our purpose in this book to resolve long standing economic squabbles of this sort. In practice, discount rates used, implicitly, by different corporations and different governments are *not* all identical. Decisions made about depletion of natural resources tend to be swayed by all sorts of considerations which, although they may in a formal sense be translated into discount rate considerations, are in truth very differently generated and solved. In general, the only safe universal message to give is that sums should not be done and answers should not be given unless the discount rate implications are thoroughly explored and understood.

There is, however, one conceptual point on which we are inclined to insist. This is the proposition that there is a necessary and powerful relationship between expectations about tomorrow's balance of supply and demand for fuels, and experience today of whatever shortages and difficulties do arise. A system which has low energy prices today – in the sense that there seems to be no pressure for conservation or for investment in new sources of supply – is just not consistent with the expectation that tomorrow energy prices will be very high. Either consistency will be established (by raising today's price or by a reduction in our expectation of tomorrow's price rise), or there will inevitable be some abrupt discontinuity between 'today' and 'tomorrow' when the facts and expectations are brought more or less brutally into accord with each other. Of course, in any practical market, consistency (in the formal sense used by the economists) does not obtain: there are always key prices and key quantities that are out of line with each other. The dynamics of markets is in fact the process by which disequilibria are removed or progressively re-created, and it is a familiar exercise for first year research students to devise market systems which oscillate or explode instead of proceeding asymptotically to an equilibrium resting place. Our discussions on Chapter 16 of the 'bumpy ride' that would characterize the energy future was in fact an informal way of engaging in the same sort of analysis.

What should be done?

It is far easier to lay down analytical principles than to make policy recommendations. And it is not the object of this book to give detailed advice to individual world governments or to international organisations. Nevertheless, certain strands of policy implications reappear again and again and can here be drawn together.

First, there is no way in which this set of issues can be neglected by policy makers. Although it is possible to envisage a perfect world where all relevant facts about the present and expectations about the future have been properly assessed and taken account of, that world does not exist: in every country there are obstacles of one sort or another to optimal resource allocation, and degrees of ignorance, greater or lesser, about the underlying facts. Systematic uncertainty, both primary and secondary, fogs our understanding, and the only real advice a 'market economist' can give on the energy problem is the unhelpful suggestion that if you wanted to get there you shouldn't have started from here.

Secondly, there is no 'solution' or technical fix which can be chosen and stuck to by policy makers to the exclusion of all other options. Repeated examples have been offered of cases in which it has proved appropriate to back several horses simultaneously and to seek diverse and complementary methods of balancing supply and demand.

Thirdly, policy decisions in different countries are interdependent. The energy system is global in important respects. Restrictions on supplies of one form of energy or inadequate energy conservation in one part of the world may have serious effects on energy supplies and economic development elsewhere. Sometimes these difficulties may be avoided by discussions and agreements, more commonly constraints and incompatible objectives will prevent a satisfactory solution, but always an awareness of this interdependence should increase the chances of action in the right direction.

Fourthly, the time element is of crucial importance. Most forms of energy alternatives to oil require high capital investment and have long lead times, either for production, transport, conversion or conservation. This imposes on governments and institutions a need for long-term planning and investment to a degree unusual amongst political decisions in general. Conversely, the long-term interests of oil producers will not be served by restrictions on supply that force the price of oil so high that alternatives are prematurely and excessively developed, or economic growth so adversely affected that social and political instability become widespread.

Fifthly, once the strategy has been identified, the policy paths chosen, the question of instruments to be adopted still remains. On the supply side, the options available to governments increasingly involve direct or indirect decisions on energy investments and inter-country agreements on energy trade. Other instruments available for governments to influence both supply and conservation include taxes, subsidies, controls, education, and support for research and development. Governments may also have a major impact on energy supply – positively or negatively – through their approach to environmental issues.

Finally, we observe that energy difficulties are not going to be resolved by governments alone, no matter how well chosen their policies may be. Decisions on energy are widely dispersed amongst institutions and – particularly on conservation – amongst individuals. Governments will need to use all available policy instruments and all sorts of complementary packages, but at the end of the day many of the crucial decisions will be made by others. Education and awareness of our interdependence can be an important factor, but the objectives and time horizons of decision makers vary widely and it would be naive to suppose that any ideal policy exists. Energy problems are embedded in wider economic and social issues and there will always be compromises and trade-offs. There is no single energy problem, there is no ideal strategy, there is no easy way out.

Chapter 18   Further reading

American Institute of Physics (1975) *Efficient use of energy (a physics perspective)*, Conference Proceedings No. 25, American Institute of Physics, New York.

Attiga, A. (1978) 'The impact of energy transition on OPEC oil resources: some problems and prospects' in *OPEC Review*, vol. 2, no. 5, Dec. 1978.

Chenery, H. and Syrquin, M. (1975) *Patterns of development 1950–1970*, Oxford University Press, London.

Commoner, B. (1979) *The politics of energy*, Knopf, New York.

Cook, P. L. and Surrey, A. J. (1977) *Energy policy, strategies for uncertainty*, Martin Robertson, London.

Darmstadter, J., Dunkerley, J. and Alterman, J. (1977) *How industrial societies use energy*, Johns Hopkins University Press, Baltimore and London.

Gordon, R. L. (1978) *Coal in the US energy market*, Heath, Lexington, Mass.

ILO (1977) *Employment, growth, and basic needs: a one world problem*, Praeger, New York.

Inglis, D. R. (1973) *Nuclear energy: its physics and social challenge*, Addison-Wesley, Reading, Mass.

Inhaber, H. (1978) *Risk of energy production,* Report AECB 1119, Atomic Energy Control Board, Canada.

Landsberg, H. H. *et al.* (1979) *Energy: the next twenty years,* a report sponsored by the Ford Foundation, Ballinger, Cambridge, Mass.

Leach, G. *et al.* (1979) *A low energy strategy for the UK,* Science Reviews Ltd, London.

Makhijani, A. and Poole, A. (1975) *Energy and agriculture in the third world,* Ballinger, Cambridge, Mass.

Noreng, O. (1978) *Oil politics in the 1980s,* McGraw-Hill, New York and London.

OAPEC (1978) *Petroleum and Arab economic development,* Organisation of Arab Petroleum Exporting Countries, Kuwait.

Parker, the Hon. Mr Justice (1978) *The Windscale Inquiry,* vol. I, HMSO, London.

Pearce, D., Edwards, L. and Beuret, G. (1979) *Decision making for energy futures,* a report to the UK Social Science Research Council, Macmillan, London.

Pearce, D. W. and Rose, J. (eds.) (1975) *The economics of natural resource depletion,* Macmillan, London.

Penner, S. S. and Icerman, L. (1975) *Energy, volume II: non-nuclear energy technologies,* Addison-Wesley, Reading, Mass.

Pindyck, R. S. (ed.) (1979a) *The structure of energy markets* (vol. 1 of Advances in the economics of energy and resources), JAI Press, Greenwich, Connecticut.

Pindyck, R. S. (ed.) (1979b) *The production and pricing of energy resources* (vol. 2 of Advances in the economics of energy and resources), JAI Press, Greenwich, Connecticut.

Stobaugh, R. and Yergin, D. (eds.) (1979) *Energy future,* Random House, New York.

Turvey, R. and Anderson, D. (1977) *Electricity economics – essays and case studies,* Johns Hopkins University Press, Baltimore and London.

UK Department of Energy (1977f) *Energy policy review, Energy paper no. 22,* HMSO, London

World Energy Conference (WEC) (1978a) *World energy: looking ahead to 2020,* (Report by the Conservation Commission), IPC Science and Technology Press, Guildford, UK, and New York.

Units and conversion factors

(i) The international system of units (SI units)
SI units have been agreed internationally but are slow in coming into use in the area of energy statistics. The unit of energy is a joule, abbreviated J, and the unit of power is a watt, W, equal to one joule per second. Multiples of these units are denoted by the prefixes shown in table A1.

(ii) Conversion to other units
One kilowatt-hour (kWh) is 3.6 million watt-seconds, or 3.6 million joules, or 3.6 MJ. Conversion factors between energy units are illustrated in table A2.
Other energy units in less common use include:

$$1 \text{ therm} = 10^5 \text{ Btu} = 1.055 \times 10^8 \text{ J}$$
$$1 \text{ calorie} = 4.186 \text{ J}$$
$$1 \text{ horse power hour} = 2.685 \times 10^6 \text{ J}$$
$$1 \text{ electron-volt (eV)} = 1.6 \times 10^{-19} \text{ J}$$

Power is defined as the rate of doing work. Conversion factors between units of power are illustrated in table A3.

(iii) Approximate thermal equivalents
In energy economics there are a wide variety of units in use based on approximate thermal equivalents. Thus a tonne of coal equivalent (tce) is used as a standard in United Nations energy statistics, where it is *defined* to mean 7000 million calories, 29.3 GJ approximately. However, this choice is not a standard convention and the meaning of TCE varies from one source to another, for example in UK energy statistics one TCE corresponds to about 26.4 GJ. Similarly the widely used toe (tonne of oil equivalent) varies between sources and reports, sometimes meaning lower and sometimes higher calorific value, and sometimes undefined. One toe may mean anything from less than 42 GJ to more than 45 GJ. These ambiguities are so widespread that the energy economist must learn to live with them, though he should also help to speed on the day when SI units become widely used.

The actual values for the specific thermal content of fuels, as determined by measurements using a 'bomb calorimeter', depend on the nature and quality of the fuel. Typical values are illustrated in table A4.

Table A1. *Prefixes used with SI units.*

Prefix	Symbol	Power	Examples
Exa	E	10^{18}	EJ (Exajoules)
Peta	P	10^{15}	PJ (Petajoules)
Tera	T	10^{12}	TJ (Terajoules)
Giga	G	10^{9}	GJ (Gigajoules)
Mega	M	10^{6}	MW (Megawatt)
Kilo	k	10^{3}	kW (kilowatt)

Table A2. *Energy conversion factors.*

From \ To	joules J	kilowatt-hours kWh	British thermal units Btu
1 J =	1	0.278×10^{-6}	0.948×10^{-3}
1 kWh	3.6×10^{6}	1	3.412×10^{3}
1 Btu	1.055×10^{3}	0.293×10^{-3}	1

Table A3. *Power conversion factors.*

From \ To	watts W	horse-power hp	Btu per hour
1 W =	1	1.341×10^{-3}	3.41
1 hp =	0.746×10^{3}	1	2.54×10^{3}
1 Btu per hour =	0.293	0.393×10^{-3}	1

Table A4. *Approximate thermal equivalents.*

Coal	1 tonne coal	= 29.3 GJ (UN convention)
	1 tonne coal	= 26.4 GJ (UK convention)
	1 tonne lignite	= 16 GJ
Oil	1 tonne crude oil	= 44 GJ
		= 7.3 barrels crude oil
	1 barrel crude oil	= 6 GJ
	1 mbdoe	= 1 million barrels per day oil equivalent
		= 50 million tonne oil per year
Natural gas	1000 cubic metres	= 38.2 GJ
	1000 cubic feet	= 1.08 GJ

Table A4 (*continued*)

Uranium	1 tonne natural uranium at 2% theoretical burnup yields 1.6 million GJ of heat, equivalent to 55,000 tonnes coal equivalent
Electricity	1 tonne natural uranium at 80% theoretical burnup yields 63 million GJ or 2.2 million tce 1 kilowatt hour (kWh) = 3.6 MJ

Notes: (1) These are based on higher calorific values (i.e. including the heat content of water vapour produced in combustion). For gas the lower calorific value is about 10% less, for oil about 5% less, for coal about 1% less.

(iv) Power and energy

Table A.5   *Energy for power production.*

(a) The conversion efficiency from thermal input to electricity output on a modern fossil-fired power station is about 0.35 (35 per cent). Thus 1 J thermal input yields 0.35 J electricity output, or 10 MJ thermal input yields about 1 kWh electricity output.

(b) A power station of 1 GW(e) at 70 per cent load factor gives 6136 GWh or 22 PJ of electrical energy output in one year. At a conversion efficiency of 0.35 this requires a thermal input of 63 PJ,

   = 2.2 million tce per year
   = 1.4 million toe per year

(c) 1 EJ (Exajoule) per year = 10^{18} J/yr = 32 GW
   = 34 million tce per year
   = 23 million toe per year
   = 0.45 million barrels oil per day

Notes on thermodynamics

These notes are intended as an 'aide memoire' to those who once knew but have forgotten basic thermodynamics, and who are interested in the derivations of efficiencies noted in chapter 1 and 3. Those who desire to be instructed in the physics of thermodynamics or the engineering principles of heat engines will need to turn elsewhere, for example to Crawford (1963), Hatsopoulos and Keenan (1965), Lee and Sears (1962) or Zemanksy (1968).

Heat engines: the Carnot cycle

A heat engine is any device that is able to absorb heat, convert some of it into useful work, and repeat this performance indefinitely. It was noted in chapter 1 that it has been found that a heat engine cannot do external work unless it can both draw heat from an external *source* and reject heat to an external *sink;* that statement is a form of the *Second Law of Thermodynamics.* Another form of this law, with which we are concerned here, states that:

'*Given a reversible heat engine operating between two fixed temperatures, then no other heat engine operating between these same two temperatures can have an efficiency greater than that of the reversible engine.*'

A reversible heat engine has an idealised cycle in which no frictional losses occur, and in which thermodynamic variables such as temperature, pressure, volume, are defined at each stage of the cycle. A reversible engine involving only two fixed temperatures is called a *Carnot engine.*

One possible realisation of the Carnot engine, which takes a quantity of ideal gas through four stages, is described as a *Carnot cycle* and is illustrated in figure B.1. The four stages can be pictured in terms of a cylinder of gas, whose volume may be varied by moving a tightly fitting piston, and into which heat may be injected at a high temperature T_1 or extracted at a low temperature T_2. The four stages of the Carnot cycle, shown in figure B.1, are:

$1 \rightarrow 2$ Isothermal (constant temperature) absorption of heat Q_1 at temperature T_1.

$2 \rightarrow 3$ Adiabatic (no heat exchanged) expansion from 2 to 3, cooling the gas.

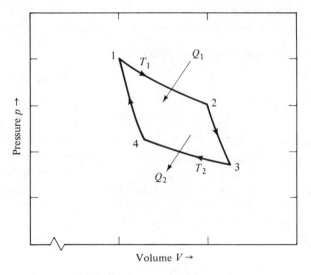

Volume $V \rightarrow$

Figure B.1   The Carnot cycle pV diagram.

3 → 4   Isothermal rejection of heat Q_2 at temperature T_2.
4 → 1   Adiabatic compression from 4 to 1, heating the gas back to T_1.

The *thermal efficiency* η of a heat engine is defined:

$$\eta = \left[\frac{\text{net output of useful work}}{\text{heat input}}\right] = \frac{W}{Q}.$$ (B.1)

For the Carnot engine, by the First Law (see chapter 1),

$$W = Q_1 - Q_2.$$ (B.2)

Hence,

$$\eta = \frac{Q_1 - Q_2}{Q_1} = 1 - \frac{Q_2}{Q_1}.$$ (B.3)

The heat absorbed in the first stage 1 → 2 of the cycle (illustrated in fig. B.1) is related to pressure p and volume V using the First Law:

$$Q_1 = \int_1^2 dU + \int_1^2 p\,dV = \int_1^2 p\,dV$$ (B.4)

since the internal energy U is constant along an isotherm. For an ideal gas, pressure and volume are related by

$$pV = RT.$$ (B.5)

Substituting into (B.4), this gives

$$Q_1 = \int_1^2 \frac{RT_1}{V}\,dV = RT_1 \ln\left(\frac{V_2}{V_1}\right).$$ (B.6)

Similarly, by considering the stage 3 → 4 of the cycle,

$$Q_2 = RT_2 \ln\left(\frac{V_3}{V_4}\right).$$ (B.7)

On the adiabatic stages of the cycle ($2 \rightarrow 3$ and $4 \rightarrow 1$),

$$pV^\gamma = K \quad \text{and} \quad pV = RT. \tag{B.8}$$

Hence

$$T_1 V_1^{\gamma-1} = K' = T_2 V_4^{\gamma-1}, \tag{B.9}$$
$$T_1 V_2^{\gamma-1} = K'' = T_2 V_3^{\gamma-1}. \tag{B.10}$$

Thus for the Carnot Cycle, from eq. B.6, B.7, B.9, and B.10,

$$\frac{Q_1}{Q_2} = \frac{T_1}{T_2}. \tag{B.11}$$

Using eq. B.3 and B.11 we see that the efficiency η of a Carnot engine is given by

$$\text{Efficiency } \eta = 1 - \frac{T_2}{T_1} \tag{B.12}$$

where the temperature T is measured on the Kelvin scale ($0°$ C $= 273$ K).

Carnot's Principle states that the efficiency η given by the formula B.12 is the greatest that can be achieved from any heat engine using two reservoirs or sources.

This derivation of eq. B.12 completes the proof of the Carnot efficiency noted in chapter 1 eq. 1.8. This efficiency is called the *thermal efficiency*, and is a particular case of the *first law efficiency* defined in chapter 1 eq. 1.9 as the ratio of the energy transfer of a desired kind divided by the energy input to a device (e.g. a heat engine).

Heat pumps

The first law efficiency of a heat engine is always less than unity. This is in accordance with the second law since a heat engine takes disorganised energy in the form of heat (involving random motion of molecules of a gas) and converts some of it into highly organised energy in the form of work or mechanical movement. However, if we consider the reverse process, for example going round the Carnot cycle, figure B.1, in the direction 14321, there can be an input of work W to the Carnot engine which now becomes a *heat pump*, and which transfers heat ($Q_1 - Q_2$) from the cool reservoir at temperature T_2 to the hot reservoir at T_1. If the objective is to transfer as much heat Q_1 as possible to the hot reservoir, then Q_1 is the useful energy output and W is the energy input, so the first law efficiency η is Q_1/W. But $W = Q_1 - Q_2$ and hence, for a *heat pump*, the first law efficiency will be

$$\eta = \frac{Q_1}{W} = \frac{Q_1}{Q_1 - Q_2} = \frac{1}{1 - (Q_2/Q_1)} = \frac{1}{1 - (T_1/T_2)} \tag{B.13}$$

In deriving eq. B.13 we have used the fact that the Carnot cycle is reversible so eq. B.11 remains valid also for a heat pump. It will be observed that the first law efficiency (B.13) of a heat pump is greater than unity; this is consistent with the second law since the input of work is highly organised energy in the form of work, whereas the output is disorganised in the form of heat.

Second law efficiencies

The second law efficiency of a device or machine for converting energy is defined so that it is always less than unity, and is designed to indicate how close the conversion device comes to the best possible method that is consistent with the laws of thermodynamics. The second law efficiency ϵ of a device is given by:

$$\epsilon = \frac{A(\text{useful})}{\text{Max } A(\text{useful})} \tag{B.14}$$

where, $A(\text{useful})$ is the heat or work usefully transferred by a *given device* or system, and Max $A(\text{useful})$ is the maximum possible heat or work usefully transferable for the same function or purpose by *any device* or system using the same energy input as the given device or system.

The numerator in eq. B.14 is the same as that used for the first law efficiency eq. B.11, but the denominator is a major change. Note that the maximum in the denominator involves a *task* maximum, not the maximum for a given device. For example, to maximise the heat delivered to a house a furnace would be replaced by an ideal fuel cell and an ideal heat pump.

Second law efficiencies are discussed in the AIP report (American Institute of Physics, 1975). Thus, for example, for a device having work in and work out (e.g. an electric motor) the first and second law efficiencies are equal. For a heat engine or a heat pump involving only two heat reservoirs (a source and a sink) the second law efficiency is the ratio of the actual first law efficiency to the first law efficiency of the Carnot engine or Carnot heat pump. Thus the second law efficiency of such a heat pump is always less than unity since the Carnot cycle corresponds to the maximum attainable efficiency.

Bibliography

Adelman, M. A. (1972) *The world petroleum market,* Johns Hopkins University Press, Baltimore and London.

Akins, J. (1973) 'The oil crisis: this time the wolf is here', in *Foreign Affairs,* vol. 51, no. 3, pp. 462–90.

Allen, R. G. D. (1968) *Macro-economic theory,* Macmillan, New York.

American Institute of Physics (1975) *Efficient use of energy (a physics perspective),* Conference Proceedings No. 25, American Institute of Physics, New York.

American Petroleum Institute (1975) *Basic petroleum data book,* American Petroleum Institute, Washington, DC.

Anderson, D. (1972) 'Models for determining least cost investments in the electricity supply industry', in *Bell Journal of Economics and Management Science,* vol. 3, no. 1, pp. 267–99.

Anderson, K. P. and De Haven, J. C. (1975) *The long run marginal costs of energy,* Report to the US National Science Foundation, Rand, Santa Monica, Calif.

Angrist, S. W. (1976) *Direct energy conversion,* Allyn and Bacon, Boston, Mass.

Armstead, H. C. H. (1978) *Geothermal energy,* Wiley, New York.

Armstrong, E. L. (1978) 'Hydraulic resources' in *Renewable energy resources,* Full report to the Conservation Commission of the World Energy Conference, IPC Science and Technology Press, Guildford, UK.

Arnold, J. E. M. (1979) 'Wood energy and rural communities', in *Natural Resources Forum,* vol. 3, no. 3, pp. 229–52.

Arrow, K. J. and Kurz, M. (1970) *Public Investment, the Rate of Return, and Optimal Fiscal Policy,* Johns Hopkins University Press, Baltimore and London.

Arrow, K. J. and Lind, R. C. (1970) 'Uncertainty and the evaluation of public investment decisions', *American Economic Review,* vol. 60.

Attiga, A. (1978) 'The impact of energy transition on OPEC oil resources: some problems and prospects' in *OPEC Review,* vol. 2, no. 5, Dec. 1978.

Auer, P. *et al.* (1978) 'Unconventional energy resources' in *Renewable energy resources,* Full report to the Conservation Commission of the World Energy Conference, IPC Science and Technology Press, Guildford, UK.

Barrager, S. M., Judd, B. R. and North, D. W. (1976) *The economic and social costs of coal and nuclear electricity generation,* Report for the US National Science Foundation, National Science Foundation, Washington, DC.

Baumol, W. J. and Bradford, D. F. (1970) 'Optimal departures from marginal cost pricing' in *American Economic Review,* pp. 265–83.

Bechtel (1976) *Manpower, materials and capital costs for energy related facilities,* Report for US Brookhaven National Laboratory, Bechtel Corp., San Francisco, Calif.

Beckmann, P. (1976) *The health hazards of not going nuclear,* Golem Press, Boulder, Colorado.

Berkovitch, I. (1977) *Coal on the switchback,* Allen and Unwin, London.

Berlin, E., Acchetti, C. and Gillon, W. (1974) *Perspective on power,* Ballinger, Cambridge, Mass.

Berry, R. S. and Fels, M. F. (1973) 'The energy costs of automobiles' in *Bulletin of Atomic Scientists,* vol. 29, pp. 11–19.

Blackmore, D. R. and Thomas, A. (eds.) (1977) *Fuel economy of the gasoline engine,* Macmillan, London.

Bossanyi, E., Ceriani, B. and Stanislaw, J. (1980) 'An international comparison of energy use in industry: United Kingdom, West Germany, Italy' in *Energy,* vol. 5, no. 1, pp. 13–28.

Brannon, G. M. (1974) *Energy taxes and subsidies,* Ballinger, Cambridge, Mass.

British Petroleum (1978a) *BP statistical review of the world oil industry 1977,* British Petroleum Company Ltd, London.

(1978b) *BP statistical review of the world oil industry 1978,* British Petroleum Company Ltd, London.

Brown, N. L. (ed.) (1978) *Renewable energy resources and rural applications in the developing world,* Westview Press, Boulder, Colorado.

Bullard, C. W. and Herendeen, R. A. (1975) 'The energy costs of goods and services' in *Energy Policy,* vol. 3, no. 4, pp. 268–78.

Central Electricity Generating Board (1971) *Modern power station practice* (8 vols), Pergamon Press, Oxford.

(1974) *Annual report and accounts 1973/74,* CEGB, London.

(1975) *Electricity and heat production: energy efficiency versus cost efficiency,* CEGB, London.

(1976) *The potential of natural energy sources,* CEGB, London.

Chase Manhattan Bank (1979) 'World oil price outlook' in *The petroleum situation,* vol. 3, no. 9, p. 2.

Chem Systems International Ltd., (1976) *Reducing pollution from selected energy transformation sources,* Graham and Trotman, London.

Chenery, H. B. and Clark. P. G. (1959) *Interindustry economics,* Wiley, New York.

Chenery, H. and Syrquin, M. (1975) *Patterns of development 1950–1970,* Oxford University Press, London.

Cheremisinoff, P. N. and Regino, T. C. (1978) *Principles and applications of solar energy,* Ann Arbor Science Publishers, Ann Arbor, Mich.

Commoner, B. (1979) *The politics of energy,* Knopf, New York.

Connolly, T. J. (1978) *Foundations of nuclear engineering,* Wiley, New York.

Conservation Commission of the World Energy Conference (1978) *World energy: looking ahead to 2020,* IPC Science and Technology Press, Guildford, UK, and New York.

Cook, P. L. and Surrey, A. J. (1977) *Energy policy, strategies for uncertainty,* Martin Robertson, London.

Craft, B. C. and Hawkins, M. F. (1959) *Applied petroleum reservoir engineering,* Prentice-Hall, Englewood Cliffs, New Jersey.

Crawford, F. H. (1963) *Heat, thermodynamics and statistical physics,* Hart, Davies and Harcourt, London and New York.

Daedelus, Journal of the American Academy of Arts and Sciences (1975, Fall issue) *The oil crisis in perspective,* American Academy of Arts and Sciences, Washington, DC.

Darmstadter, J., Dunkerley, J. and Alterman, J. (1977) *How industrial societies use energy,* Johns Hopkins University Press, Baltimore and London.

Darmstadter, J., Teitelbaum, P. D. and Polach, J. G. (1971) *Energy in the world economy,* Johns Hopkins University Press, Baltimore and London.

Dasgupta, P. and Heal, G. M. (1977) *The use of resources* (Cambridge Economic Handbook Series), Cambridge University Press, Cambridge, UK.

Deam, R. J. *et al.* (1974) 'World energy modelling' in *Energy modelling*, special issue of Energy Policy journal, IPC Science and Technology Press, Guildford, UK.

Deane, P. and Cole, W. A. (1969) *British economic growth, 1688–1959*, Cambridge University Press, Cambridge, UK.

Desprairies, P. (1977) 'Worldwide petroleum supply limits' in *World energy resources, 1985–2020* (World Energy Conference, 1978), IPC Science and Technology Press, Guildford, UK, and New York.

Dewey, D. (1965) *Modern capital theory*, Columbia University Press, New York.

Doran, C. F. (1977) *Oil, myth and politics*, The Free Press, New York.

Drèze, J. (1964) 'Some postwar contributions of French economists to theory and public policy' in *American Economic Review*, pp. 1–64.

Dryden, I. G. C. (ed.) (1975) *The efficient use of energy*, IPC Science and Technology Press, Guildford, UK.

Dunkerley, J. (ed.) (1978) *International comparisons of energy use*, Proceedings of the workshop on international comparisons of energy use, sponsored by Resources for the Future and the Electric Power Research Institute, Washington, DC.

Dunkerley, J., Alterman, J. and Schanz, J. J. (1979) 'Analysis of dynamic aspects of international energy relationships' draft report prepared for Resources for the Future, delivered at the International Association of Energy Economists Conference on International Energy Issues, Washington, DC.

Dupree, W. G. and West, J. A. (1972) *United States energy through the year 2000*, Bureau of Mines, US Department of the Interior, Washington, DC (See also US Department of the Interior, 1976).

Duret, M. F. *et al.* (1978a) *Nuclear resources*, full report to the Conservation Commission of the World Energy Conference, IPC Science and Technology Press, Guildford, UK.
(1978b) 'The contribution of nuclear power to world energy supply' in *World energy resources 1985–2020*, World Energy Conference and IPC Science and Technology Press, Guildford, UK and New York.

Earl, D. E. (1975) *Forest energy and economic development*, Clarendon Press, London.

Eckholm, E. P. (1975) *The other energy crisis: firewood*, Worldwatch Institute, Washington, DC.

Economist, The (1978) *The world in figures*, Economist Newspaper Ltd, London.

Eden, R. J. (1967) *High energy collisions of elementary particles*, Cambridge University Press, Cambridge, UK.
(1974) *Energy conservation in the United Kingdom*, Report for the National Economic Development Office (NEDO), HMSO, London.
(1978) 'World energy demand to 2020' in *World energy resources 1985–2020*, World Energy Conference report, IPC Science and Technology Press, Guildford, UK, and New York.

Eden R. J. *et al.* (1966) *The analytic S-matrix*, Cambridge University Press, Cambridge, UK.

Electrical World (1976) 'Annual statistical report', *Electrical World*, New York.

Electricity Council (1976) Handbook of electricity supply statistics, Electricity Council, London.

Energy and Buildings (Journal) (1978) vol. 1, no. 3, April 1978 (Princeton issue) Elsevier Sequoia, Lausanne, Switzerland.

Ezzatti, A. (1978) *World energy markets and OPEC stability*, Lexington Books, Lexington, Mass.

Federal Republic of Brazil (1978) *National energy balance*, Ministry of Mines and Energy, Brasilia.

Flowers, Sir B. (1976) *Royal Commission on Environmental Pollution – sixth report: Nuclear power and the environment*, HMSO, London.

Ford Foundation Energy Policy Project (1974) *A time to choose: America's energy future*, Ballinger, Cambridge, Mass.

Foster, J. *et al.* (1978) *Nuclear resources*, Full report to the Conservation Commission of the World Energy Conference, IPC Science and Technology Press, Guildford, UK.

Frankel, P. H. (1946) *Essentials of petroleum: a key to oil economics*, Chapman and Hall, London.

Freeman, D. S. *et al.* (1979) *A time to choose: America's energy future*, report by the Energy Policy Project of the Ford Foundation, Ballinger, Cambridge, Mass.

Fried, E. R. and Schultz, C. L. (eds.) (1975) *Higher oil prices and the world economy*, Brookings Institution, Washington, DC.

Glasstone, S. (1967) *Sourcebook on atomic energy*, Van Nostrand Reinhold, New York and London.

Goldemberg, J. (1978) *Energy strategies for developed and developing countries*, Final report to the US Overseas Development Council, Washington, DC.

Gordon, R. L. (1978) *Coal in the US energy market*, Heath, Lexington, Mass.

Gordon, R. L. (ed.) (1975) *Economic analysis of coal supply*, Report for Electric Power Research Institute, National Technical Information Service, US Department of Commerce, Washington, DC.

Gordon, R. R. (1971) 'Solid mineral fuels' in *Materials and Technology*, vol. II, ed. van Thoor, T. J. W., Longman, London.

Gray, J. E. (1975) *Energy policy: industry perspectives*, Ballinger, Cambridge, Mass.

Griffin, J. M. (1979) *Energy conservation in the OECD 1980–2000*, Ballinger, Cambridge, Mass.

Griffin, K. (1978) *International inequality and national poverty*, Macmillan, London.

Hamilton, L. D. and Manne, A. S. (1978) 'Health and economic costs of alternative energy sources' in *International Atomic Energy Agency Bulletin*, vol. 20, no. 4. IAEA, Vienna.

Hartshorn, J. E. (1967) *Oil companies and governments*, Faber and Faber, London.

Hatsopoulos, G. N. and Keenan, J. H. (1965) *Principles of general thermodynamics*, Wiley, New York.

Health and Safety Commission (1978) *The hazards of conventional sources of energy*, HMSO, London.

Helleiner, G. K. (ed.) (1975) *A world divided: less developed countries in the international economy*, Cambridge University Press, Cambridge, UK.

Henderson, P. D. (1975) *The energy situation in India: World Bank report*, Oxford University Press, London.

Herendeen, R. A. (1974) 'Use of input-output analysis to determine the energy cost of goods and services' in *Energy: demand, conservation and institutional problems*, ed. Macrakis, M. S., MIT Press, Cambridge, Mass.

Herendeen, R. and Tanaka, J. (1976) 'Energy cost of living' in *Energy*, vol. 1, no. 2, pp. 165–78.

Hirshleifer, J. (1970) *Investment, interest and capital*, Prentice-Hall, London.

Hobson, G. D. and Tiratsoo, E. N. (1975) *Introduction to petroleum geology*, Scientific Press, Beaconsfield, UK.

Hoffman, K. C. (1974) article in *Energy Modelling* (special issue of Energy Policy), IPC Science and Technology Press, Guildford, UK.

Hoffman, K. C. and Cherniavsky, E. A. (1974) *Brookhaven energy system optimisation model*, (BNL 19569), Brookhaven National Laboratory Associated Universities Inc. Upton, NY.

Hoffman, K. C. and Palmedo, P. F. (1972) *Reference energy systems and resources data for use in the assessment of energy technologies,* report no. AET8, Associated Universities Inc. Upton, NY.

Hoffman, K. C. and Wood, D. O. (1976) 'Energy system modelling and forecasting' in *Annual Review of Energy,* vol. 1, Annual Reviews Inc.

Hotelling, H. (1931) 'The economics of exhaustible resources' in *Journal of Political Economy,* vol. 39, April, pp. 137–75.

Hottel, H. C. and Howard, J. B. (1971) *New energy technology – some facts and assessments,* MIT Press, Cambridge, Mass.

Houthakker, H. A. (1975) *The price of world oil,* American Enterprise Institute of Public Policy, Washington, DC.

(1980) To be published. Brookings Institution.

Hubbert, M. K. (1969) 'Energy resources' in *Resources and man* (National Academy of Sciences), Freeman, San Francisco, Calif.

Hudson, E. A. and Jorgenson, D. W. (1974) 'US energy policy and economic growth 1975–2000', in *Bell Journal of Economics and Management Science,* vol. 5, no. 2, pp. 461–514.

Humphrey, W. and Stanislaw, J. (1979) 'Economic growth and energy consumption in the UK, 1700–1975', in *Energy Policy,* vol. 7, no. 1, pp. 29–42.

IEA (1977a) *Energy conservation in the International Energy Agency,* OECD, Paris.

(1977b) *Energy policies and programmes for IEA countries (1977 review)* OECD, Paris.

(1978a) *Energy balances of OECD countries, 1974/76,* OECD, Paris.

(1978b) *Steam coal – prospects to 2000,* OECD, Paris.

(1978c) *The electricity supply industry in OECD countries,* OECD, Paris.

(1979a) *Energy policies and programmes of IEA countries – 1978 review,* IEA/OECD, Paris.

(1979b) *IEA workshop on energy data of developing countries,* IEA, Paris.

ILO (1977) *Employment, growth and basic needs: a one world problem,* Praeger, New York.

Inglis, D. R. (1973) *Nuclear energy: its physics and social challenge,* Addison-Wesley, Reading, Mass.

Inhaber, H. (1978) *Risk of energy production,* report AECB 1119, Atomic Energy Control Board, Canada.

International Energy Agency (see under IEA).

International Solar Energy Society (1976) *Solar energy – a UK assessment,* UK-ISES, London.

Jevons, W. S. (1866) *The coal question,* Macmillan, London.

Johnston, J. (1972) *Econometric Methods,* 2nd Edition, McGraw-Hill Kogakusha, Tokyo.

Keeny, S. M. *et al.* (1977) *Nuclear power: issues and choices,* Ballinger, Cambridge, Mass.

Landsberg, H. H. *et al.* (1979) *Energy: the next twenty years,* a report sponsored by the Ford Foundation, Ballinger, Cambridge, Mass.

Lapedes, D. N. (ed.) (1976) *Encyclopedia of Energy,* McGraw-Hill, New York and London.

Leach, G. *et al.* (1979) *A low energy strategy for the UK,* Science Reviews Ltd. London.

League of Nations (1927) *International statistical yearbook,* League of Nations, Geneva.

(1931) *International statistical yearbook,* League of Nations, Geneva.

(1941) *International statistical yearbook,* League of Nations, Geneva.

Lee, J. F. and Sears, F. W. (1962) *Thermodynamics* (2nd edition 1969), Addison-Wesley, Reading, Mass.

Long, T. V. II (1975) *Technology assessment and energy analysis,* prepared for the International Federation of Institutes for Advanced Study Workshop on Energy Analysis and Economics, Stockholm, Sweden.

Lyle, O. (1947) *The efficient use of steam,* HMSO, London.

Mabro, R. (ed.) (1980) *World energy: policies and issues*, Oxford University Press, London.
McCormick, W. T. *et al.* (1978) 'The future for world natural gas supply' in *World energy resources 1985–2020*, (1978) World Energy Conference, IPC Science and Technology Press, Guildford, UK and New York.
McCracken, P. *et al.* (1977) *Towards full employment and price stability*, a report for the OECD, OECD, Paris.
MacKay, D. I. and MacKay, G. A. (1975) *The political economy of North Sea oil*, Martin Robertson, London.
McMullan, J. T., Morgan, R. and Murray, R. B. (1976) *Energy resources and supply*, Wiley, New York and London.
Macrakis, M. S. (ed.) (1974) *Energy: demand, conservation and institutional problems*, MIT Press, Cambridge, Mass.
Maddala, G. S. (1977) *Econometrics*, McGraw-Hill, London.
Maidique, M. A. (1979) 'Solar America' in *Energy Future*, pp. 183–215, ed. Stobaugh, R. and Yergin, D., Random House, New York.
Makhijani, A. (1976) *Energy policy for the rural third world*, International Institute for Environment and Development, London.
Makhijani, A. and Poole, A. (1975) *Energy and agriculture in the third world*, Ballinger, Cambridge, Mass.
Mangone, G. J. (ed.) (1977) *Energy policies of the world* (vol. 1, 1976, vol. 2, 1977), Elsevier, New York.
Manne, A. S. (1976) 'ETA – A model for energy technology assessment' in *Bell Journal of Economics and Management Science* vol. 7, no. 2 Autumn 1976, American Telephone and Telegraph Company, New York.
Markon, G. (1979) 'A special feature article' in *Coal International*, vol. 1, no. 3, pp. 17–29.
Meadows, D. *et al.*(1972) *The limits to growth*, Earth Island, London.
Meinel, A. B. and Meinel, M. P. (1976) *Applied solar energy – an introduction*, Addison-Wesley, Reading, Mass.
Mendershausen, H. (1976) *Coping with the oil crisis*, Johns Hopkins University Press, Baltimore and London.
Miller, S. (1976) *The economics of nuclear and coal power*, Praeger, New York.
National Engineering Laboratory (1976) *The development of wave power – a techno-economic study*, NEL, Glasgow, UK.
National Petroleum Council (1973) *US energy outlook: nuclear energy availability*, US National Petroleum Council.
NATO (1973) *Technology of efficient energy utilisation*, NATO, Brussels.
NCB Medical Service (1977) *Annual Report 1976/7*, National Coal Board, London.
NEDO (1974) *Energy conservation in the United Kingdom*, report prepared by Dr R. J. Eden for the National Economic Development Office, HMSO, London.
Nef, J. U. (1932) *The rise of the British coal industry* (2 vols.), Routledge, London.
Newman, D. K. and Day, D. (1975) *The American energy consumer*, Ballinger, Cambridge, Mass.
Nordhaus, W. D. (1976) 'The demand for energy: an international perspective' in *Proceedings of the Workshop on Energy Demand*, International Institute of Applied Systems Analysis, Laxenburg, Austria.
Noreng, O. (1978) *Oil politics in the 1980s*, McGraw-Hill, New York and London.
Nuclear Energy Policy Study Group (NEPSG) (1977) *Nuclear power issues and choices*, Ballinger, Cambridge, Mass.
Nuclear Engineering International, 1979, July supplement: power reactors.
Nuclear Regulatory Commission (1975) *Reactor safety study*, WASH 1400 (known as the Rasmussen Report), Nuclear Regulatory Commission.
    (1976) *Final generic environmental statement on the use of recycled plutonium in mixed*

oxide fuel in light water cooled reactors, NUREG – 0002 (known as the GESMO report), Nuclear Regulatory Commission.

OAPEC (1978) *Petroleum and Arab economic development,* Organisation of Arab Petroleum Exporting Countries, Kuwait.

Odell, P. (1974) *Oil and world power; background to the oil crisis,* Penguin, Harmondsworth, Middx.

Odell, P. and Rosing, K. E. (1976) *Optimal development of the North Sea's oil fields,* Kogan Page, London.

OECD *Statistics of energy,* (annual) OECD, Paris.

(1976) *Energy balances of OECD countries 1960/1974,* OECD, Paris.

(1977) *World energy outlook* (see also later reports with the same title) OECD, Paris.

(1978) *Energy balances of OECD countries 1974/76,* IEA, Paris.

OECD Nuclear Energy Agency, International Atomic Energy Agency (1977) *Uranium: resources, production and demand,* OECD, Paris.

OECD Nuclear Energy Agency (1978) *Nuclear fuel cycle requirements,* OECD, Paris.

Oil and Gas Journal (1978) *Annual worldwide issue,* vol. 76, no. 52, 25 Dec 1978, Petroleum Publishing Company, Tulsa, Oklahoma.

(1979) *Forecast/review issue,* vol. 77, no. 5, 29 Jan 1979, Petroleum Publishing Company, Tulsa, Oklahoma.

O'Neill, P. G. (1975) *The income-elasticity of demand for primary energy,* report prepared for the UK Department of Environment, London.

Palmedo, P. *et al.* (1978) *Energy needs, uses and resources in developing countries,* a report for the US Agency for International Development, Washington, DC.

Parikh, J. K. (1978) *Energy and development,* report PUN 43 to the World Bank, World Bank, Washington, DC.

Parker, The Hon. Mr Justice (1978) *The Windscale Inquiry,* vol. 1, HMSO, London.

Pathak, B. S. and Singh, D. (1978) 'Energy returns in agriculture' in *Energy,* vol. 3, no. 2, pp. 119–126.

Patterson, W. C. (1976) *Nuclear power,* Penguin, Harmondsworth, Middx, and New York.

Pearce, D., Edwards, L. and Beuret, G. (1979) *Decision making for energy futures,* a report to the UK Social Science Research Council, Macmillan, London.

Pearce, D. W. and Rose, J. (eds.) (1975) *The economics of natural resource depletion,* Macmillan, London.

Pelley, W. C., Constable, J. C. and Krupp, H. W. (1976) 'The energy industry and the capital market' in *Annual Review of Energy,* vol. 1, 1976, pp. 369–90.

Penner, S. S. and Icerman, L. (1975) *Energy, volume II: non-nuclear energy technologies,* Addison-Wesley, Reading, Mass.

Penrose, E. (1968) *The large international firm in developing countries: the international petroleum industry,* Allen and Unwin, London.

Peters, W. and Schilling, H.-D. (1978) *An appraisal of world coal resources and their future availability,* World Energy Conference and IPC Science and Technology Press, Guildford, UK and New York.

Petroleum Publishing Company (1976) *International petroleum encyclopedia,* Petroleum Publishing Company, Tulsa, Oklahoma.

Phillips, A. (1970) 'Structure, conduct and performance – and performance, conduct and structure' in *Industrial organisation and economic development,* pp. 26–37, eds. Markham, J. and Paperek, G., Houghton Mifflin, Boston, Mass.

Phlips, L. (1974) *Applied consumption analysis,* North-Holland, Amsterdam.

Pindyck, R. S. (ed.) (1979a) *The structure of energy markets,* vol. 1 of 'Advances in the economics of energy and resources', JAI Press, Greenwich, Connecticut.

(1979b) *The production and pricing of energy resources,* vol. 2 of 'Advances in the economics of energy and resources', JAI Press, Greenwich, Connecticut.

Pindyck, R. S. (1979c) *The structure of world energy demand*, MIT Press, Cambridge, Mass.

Pochin, E. E. (1976) *Estimated population exposure from nuclear power production and other radiation sources*, OECD, Paris.

Porter, A. *et al.* (1978) *Our energy options – seven important aspects of electric power planning examined by well-known authorities*, Government of Ontario.

Posner, M. V. (1973) *Fuel policy – a study in applied economics*, Macmillan, London.

Pullin, D. J. (1977) *Approaches to the structuring of energy systems*, unpublished PhD thesis, Cambridge University, UK.

Quiros-Corradi, A. (1979) 'Energy and the exercise of power' in *Foreign Affairs* vol. 57, no. 5, pp. 1144–66.

Ray, G. F. (1979) 'Energy economics – a random walk in history' *Energy Economics*, vol. 1, no. 3, July 1979, IPC Science and Technology Press, Guildford, UK, and New York.

Regens, J. L. (ed.) (1979) *Energy issues and options*, University of Georgia, Athens, Ga.

Ridker, R. (ed.) (1976) *Changing resource problems of the Fourth World*, Johns Hopkins University Press, Baltimore.

Rose, J. W. and Cooper, J. R. (1977) *Technical data on fuel*, World Energy Conference, and Scottish Academic Press, Edinburgh.

Rosenbaum, W. (1978) *Coal and crisis: the political dilemmas of energy management*, Praeger, New York.

Rotblat, J. (1977) *Nuclear reactors – to breed or not to breed*, Taylor and Francis, London.

Rothschild, Lord (1978) 'Risk: the Richard Dimbleby Lecture' in *The Listener*, 30 November 1978.

Sampson, A. (1975) *The seven sisters – the great oil companies and the world they made*, Hodder and Stoughton, London.

Schurr, S. H. and Netschert, B. C. (1975) *Energy in the American economy 1850–1975*, Johns Hopkins University Press, Baltimore and London.

Schurr, S. H. and Netschert, R. (1960) *Energy in the American economy*, Johns Hopkins University Press, Baltimore and London.

Schurr, S. H. *et al.* (1979) *Energy in America's future*, Resources for the Future, Washington, DC.

Scientific American (1971) *Energy and power*, Freeman, San Francisco, Calif.

Semat, H. and Albright, J. R. (1972) *Introduction to atomic and nuclear physics* (5th edition), Chapman and Hall, London.

Shell International (1978) *Information Handbook 1978–79*, Shell International Petroleum Company Limited, London.

(1979) *Energy efficiency* (report by A. Beijdorff), Group Planning, Shell International, London.

Slesser, M. (ed.) (1974) *Energy analysis*, IFIAS Workshop report No. 6, International Federation of Institutes for Advanced Study, Stockholm.

Socolow, R. H. (1977) 'The coming age of conservation' *Annual Review of Energy* vol. 2, pp. 239–89.

Sonenblum S. (1978) *The energy connections: between energy and the economy*, Ballinger, Cambridge, Mass.

Stanford Research Institute (1977) *The energy network*, Stanford Research Institute, Palo Alto, Calif.

Starr, C. (1971) 'Energy and power' in *Energy and power*, a Scientific American book, Freeman, San Francisco, Calif.

Stobaugh, R. and Yergin, D. (eds.) (1979) *Energy future*, Random House, New York.

Strub, A. (ed.) (1979) *Energy models for the European community*, IPC Science and Technology Press, Guildford, UK, and New York.

Study of Critical Environmental Problems (1970) *Man's impact on the global environment – assessment and recommendations for action*, MIT Press, Cambridge, Mass.

Summers, C. M. (1971) 'The conversion of energy' in *Energy and power*, a Scientific American book, Freeman, San Francisco, Calif.

Tanner, J. C. (1977) *Car ownership trends and forecasts*, Report TRRL 799, UK Transport and Road Research Laboratory, Crowthorne, Berks, UK.

Theil, H. (1971) *Principles of econometrics*, North-Holland, Amsterdam.

Turvey, R. (1974) 'How to judge when price changes will improve resource allocation' in *Economic Journal*, vol. 84, no. 336, December 1974.

Turvey, R. and Anderson, D. (1977) *Electricity economics – essays and case studies*, Johns Hopkins University Press, Baltimore and London.

UK Building Research Establishment (1975) *Energy conservation: a study of energy consumption in buildings and possible means of energy saving in housing* (CP56/75), Building Research Establishment, Garston, Watford, UK.

UK Central Statistical Office, *Annual abstract of Statistics*, HMSO, London.

UK Department of Energy (1972, 1976) *Digest of energy statistics* (annual).

(1976) *North Sea costs escalation study, Energy paper no. 7*, HMSO, London.

(1977a) *Development of the oil and gas resources of the United Kingdom*, (known as the 1977 Brown Book), HMSO, London.

(1977b) *Energy balances – some further problems and recent developments, Energy paper no. 19*, HMSO, London.

(1977c) *Report of the working group on energy elasticities, Energy paper no. 17*, HMSO, London.

(1977d) *District heating combined with electricity generation in the United Kingdom, Energy paper no. 20*, HMSO, London.

(1977e) *The prospects for the generation of electricity from wind energy in the United Kingdom, Energy paper no. 21*, HMSO, London.

(1977f) *Energy policy review, Energy paper, no. 22*, HMSO, London.

(1978a) *Digest of United Kingdom Energy Statistics, 1978*, HMSO, London.

(1978b) *Energy forecasting methodology, Energy paper no. 29*, HMSO, London,

(1979a) *Combined heat and electrical power generation in the United Kingdom, Energy paper no. 35*, HMSO, London.

(1979b) *Energy technologies for the United Kingdom*, (vol. I and vol. II), *Energy paper no. 39*, HMSO, London.

(1979c) *Report by the Advisory Council on Energy Conservation, Energy paper no. 40*, (this also lists earlier UK reports on energy conservation), HMSO, London.

UK Department of Industry (1977–79) *Energy Audit Series*, 1. Iron casting industry, 2. Building brick industry, 3. Dairy industry, 4. Bulk refractories industry, 5. Glass industry, 6. Aluminium industry.

(1978–79) *Industrial Energy Thrift Series* (reports on energy use in industry), Department of Industry, London.

UK Department of the Environment (1961; 1966; 1976) *Transport Statistics of Great Britain* (annual), HMSO, London.

United Nations *Statistical yearbook* (annual), United Nations, New York.

Yearbook of international trade statistics (annual), United Nations, New York.

Yearbook of national accounts statistics (annual), United Nations, New York.

(1975) *Single-year population estimates and projections for major areas, regions and countries of the world, 1950–2000*, prepared by the Population Division, Department of Economic and Social Affairs, United Nations, New York.

(1976) *World energy supplies 1950–1974*, Statistical papers series J no. 19, United Nations, New York.

(1977) *World energy supplies 1971–1975*, Statistical papers series J, no. 20, United Nations, New York.

(1978) *World energy supplies 1972–1976*, Statistical papers series J, no. 21, United Nations, New York.

US Department of Energy (1979) *Monthly Energy Review*, April 1979 Report No. DOE/EIA – 0035/4(79) US Department of Energy, Washington DC

US Department of the Interior (1976) *Energy perspectives 2*, US Government Printing Office, Washington DC.

US National Academy of Engineering (1978) *US energy prospects (an engineering viewpoint)*, National Academy of Sciences, Washington DC.

US National Coal Association (1977) *Implications of investments in the coal industry by firms from other energy industries*, National Coal Association, Washington, DC.

Van Krevelen, D. W. (1961) *Coal: typology, chemistry, physics, constitution*, Elsevier, Amsterdam.

WAES (1976) *Energy demand studies: major consuming countries*, MIT Press, Cambridge, Mass.

(1977a) *Energy: global prospects 1985–2000*, McGraw-Hill, New York and London.

(1977b) *Energy supply to the year 2000*, MIT Press, Cambridge, Mass.

(1977c) *Energy supply-demand integrations to the year 2000*, MIT Press, Cambridge, Mass.

Watt Committee on Energy (1978) *The rational use of energy*, Watt Committee, 1 Birdcage Walk, London.

WEC (1978a) *World energy: looking ahead to 2020* (report by the Conservation Commission), IPC Science and Technology Press, Guildford, UK, and New York.

(1978b) *World energy resources 1985–2020*, IPC Science and Technology Press, Guildford, UK and New York.

Williams, J. R. (1974) *Solar energy – technology and applications*, Ann Arbor Science Publishers, Ann Arbor, Mich.

Williams, R. H. (ed.) (1975) *The energy conservation papers*, Ballinger, Cambridge, Mass.

Willrich, M. *et al.* (1975) *Energy and world politics*, The Free Press, New York.

Wilson, C. L. (ed.)(1980) *Coal - bridge to the future*, Report of the World Coal Study (WOCOL), Ballinger, Cambridge, Mass.

Wilson, R. and Jones, W. J. (1974) *Energy, ecology and the environment*, Academic Press, New York and London.

Workshop on Alternative Energy Strategies see WAES.

World Bank (1974) *1974 World Bank atlas*, The World Bank, Washington, DC.

(1975) *1975 World Bank atlas*, The World Bank, Washington, DC.

(1978) *1978 World Bank atlas*, The World Bank, Washington, DC.

(1979) *World development report, 1979* (see also later reports with the same title) World Bank, Washington, DC.

Wright J. P. (1974) *The vital spark*, Heinemann, London.

Wyant, F. R. (1977) 'The role of multinational oil companies in world energy trade' in *Annual review of Energy*, vol. 2, pp. 125–51.

Yager, J. A. and Steinberg, E. B. (eds.) (1974) *Energy and US foreign policy*, Ballinger, Cambridge, Mass.

Zemansky, M. W. (1968) *Heat and thermodynamics* (5th edition) McGraw-Hill, New York and London.

Index

440   Index